Lecture Notes in Computer Science 8005

Commenced Publication in 1973
Founding and Former Series Editors:
Gerhard Goos, Juris Hartmanis, and Jan van Leeuwen

Masaaki Kurosu (Ed.)

Human-Computer Interaction

Applications and Services

15th International Conference, HCI International 2013
Las Vegas, NV, USA, July 21-26, 2013
Proceedings, Part II

 Springer

Volume Editor

Masaaki Kurosu
The Open University of Japan
2-11 Wakaba, Mihama-ku, Chiba-shi 261-8586, Japan
E-mail: masaakikurosu@spa.nifty.com

ISSN 0302-9743   e-ISSN 1611-3349
ISBN 978-3-642-39261-0   e-ISBN 978-3-642-39262-7
DOI 10.1007/978-3-642-39262-7
Springer Heidelberg Dordrecht London New York

Library of Congress Control Number: 2013941394

CR Subject Classification (1998): H.5, J.3, K.8.0, K.3, K.4, H.4, H.3, D.2, I.2.7

LNCS Sublibrary: SL 3 – Information Systems and Application, incl. Internet/Web
and HCI

Typesetting: Camera-ready by author, data conversion by Scientific Publishing Services, Chennai, India

Printed on acid-free paper

Springer is part of Springer Science+Business Media (www.springer.com)

Foreword

The 15th International Conference on Human–Computer Interaction, HCI International 2013, was held in Las Vegas, Nevada, USA, 21–26 July 2013, incorporating 12 conferences / thematic areas:

Thematic areas:

- Human–Computer Interaction
- Human Interface and the Management of Information

Affiliated conferences:

- 10th International Conference on Engineering Psychology and Cognitive Ergonomics
- 7th International Conference on Universal Access in Human–Computer Interaction
- 5th International Conference on Virtual, Augmented and Mixed Reality
- 5th International Conference on Cross-Cultural Design
- 5th International Conference on Online Communities and Social Computing
- 7th International Conference on Augmented Cognition
- 4th International Conference on Digital Human Modeling and Applications in Health, Safety, Ergonomics and Risk Management
- 2nd International Conference on Design, User Experience and Usability
- 1st International Conference on Distributed, Ambient and Pervasive Interactions
- 1st International Conference on Human Aspects of Information Security, Privacy and Trust

A total of 5210 individuals from academia, research institutes, industry and governmental agencies from 70 countries submitted contributions, and 1666 papers and 303 posters were included in the program. These papers address the latest research and development efforts and highlight the human aspects of design and use of computing systems. The papers accepted for presentation thoroughly cover the entire field of Human–Computer Interaction, addressing major advances in knowledge and effective use of computers in a variety of application areas.

This volume, edited by Masaaki Kurosu, contains papers focusing on the thematic area of Human–Computer Interaction, and addressing the following major topics:

- HCI in Healthcare
- Games and Gamification
- HCI in Learning and Education
- In-Vehicle Interaction

The remaining volumes of the HCI International 2013 proceedings are:

- Volume 1, LNCS 8004, Human–Computer Interaction: Human-Centred Design Approaches, Methods, Tools and Environments (Part I), edited by Masaaki Kurosu
- Volume 3, LNCS 8006, Human–Computer Interaction: Users and Contexts of Use (Part III), edited by Masaaki Kurosu
- Volume 4, LNCS 8007, Human–Computer Interaction: Interaction Modalities and Techniques (Part IV), edited by Masaaki Kurosu
- Volume 5, LNCS 8008, Human–Computer Interaction: Towards Intelligent and Implicit Interaction (Part V), edited by Masaaki Kurosu
- Volume 6, LNCS 8009, Universal Access in Human–Computer Interaction: Design Methods, Tools and Interaction Techniques for eInclusion (Part I), edited by Constantine Stephanidis and Margherita Antona
- Volume 7, LNCS 8010, Universal Access in Human–Computer Interaction: User and Context Diversity (Part II), edited by Constantine Stephanidis and Margherita Antona
- Volume 8, LNCS 8011, Universal Access in Human–Computer Interaction: Applications and Services for Quality of Life (Part III), edited by Constantine Stephanidis and Margherita Antona
- Volume 9, LNCS 8012, Design, User Experience, and Usability: Design Philosophy, Methods and Tools (Part I), edited by Aaron Marcus
- Volume 10, LNCS 8013, Design, User Experience, and Usability: Health, Learning, Playing, Cultural, and Cross-Cultural User Experience (Part II), edited by Aaron Marcus
- Volume 11, LNCS 8014, Design, User Experience, and Usability: User Experience in Novel Technological Environments (Part III), edited by Aaron Marcus
- Volume 12, LNCS 8015, Design, User Experience, and Usability: Web, Mobile and Product Design (Part IV), edited by Aaron Marcus
- Volume 13, LNCS 8016, Human Interface and the Management of Information: Information and Interaction Design (Part I), edited by Sakae Yamamoto
- Volume 14, LNCS 8017, Human Interface and the Management of Information: Information and Interaction for Health, Safety, Mobility and Complex Environments (Part II), edited by Sakae Yamamoto
- Volume 15, LNCS 8018, Human Interface and the Management of Information: Information and Interaction for Learning, Culture, Collaboration and Business (Part III), edited by Sakae Yamamoto
- Volume 16, LNAI 8019, Engineering Psychology and Cognitive Ergonomics: Understanding Human Cognition (Part I), edited by Don Harris
- Volume 17, LNAI 8020, Engineering Psychology and Cognitive Ergonomics: Applications and Services (Part II), edited by Don Harris
- Volume 18, LNCS 8021, Virtual, Augmented and Mixed Reality: Designing and Developing Augmented and Virtual Environments (Part I), edited by Randall Shumaker
- Volume 19, LNCS 8022, Virtual, Augmented and Mixed Reality: Systems and Applications (Part II), edited by Randall Shumaker

- Volume 20, LNCS 8023, Cross-Cultural Design: Methods, Practice and Case Studies (Part I), edited by P.L. Patrick Rau
- Volume 21, LNCS 8024, Cross-Cultural Design: Cultural Differences in Everyday Life (Part II), edited by P.L. Patrick Rau
- Volume 22, LNCS 8025, Digital Human Modeling and Applications in Health, Safety, Ergonomics and Risk Management: Healthcare and Safety of the Environment and Transport (Part I), edited by Vincent G. Duffy
- Volume 23, LNCS 8026, Digital Human Modeling and Applications in Health, Safety, Ergonomics and Risk Management: Human Body Modeling and Ergonomics (Part II), edited by Vincent G. Duffy
- Volume 24, LNAI 8027, Foundations of Augmented Cognition, edited by Dylan D. Schmorrow and Cali M. Fidopiastis
- Volume 25, LNCS 8028, Distributed, Ambient and Pervasive Interactions, edited by Norbert Streitz and Constantine Stephanidis
- Volume 26, LNCS 8029, Online Communities and Social Computing, edited by A. Ant Ozok and Panayiotis Zaphiris
- Volume 27, LNCS 8030, Human Aspects of Information Security, Privacy and Trust, edited by Louis Marinos and Ioannis Askoxylakis
- Volume 28, CCIS 373, HCI International 2013 Posters Proceedings (Part I), edited by Constantine Stephanidis
- Volume 29, CCIS 374, HCI International 2013 Posters Proceedings (Part II), edited by Constantine Stephanidis

I would like to thank the Program Chairs and the members of the Program Boards of all affiliated conferences and thematic areas, listed below, for their contribution to the highest scientific quality and the overall success of the HCI International 2013 conference.

This conference could not have been possible without the continuous support and advice of the Founding Chair and Conference Scientific Advisor, Prof. Gavriel Salvendy, as well as the dedicated work and outstanding efforts of the Communications Chair and Editor of HCI International News, Abbas Moallem.

I would also like to thank for their contribution towards the smooth organization of the HCI International 2013 Conference the members of the Human–Computer Interaction Laboratory of ICS-FORTH, and in particular George Paparoulis, Maria Pitsoulaki, Stavroula Ntoa, Maria Bouhli and George Kapnas.

May 2013   Constantine Stephanidis
                                          General Chair, HCI International 2013

Organization

Human–Computer Interaction

Program Chair: Masaaki Kurosu, Japan

Jose Abdelnour-Nocera, UK
Sebastiano Bagnara, Italy
Simone Barbosa, Brazil
Tomas Berns, Sweden
Nigel Bevan, UK
Simone Borsci, UK
Apala Lahiri Chavan, India
Sherry Chen, Taiwan
Kevin Clark, USA
Torkil Clemmensen, Denmark
Xiaowen Fang, USA
Shin'ichi Fukuzumi, Japan
Vicki Hanson, UK
Ayako Hashizume, Japan
Anzai Hiroyuki, Italy
Sheue-Ling Hwang, Taiwan
Wonil Hwang, South Korea
Minna Isomursu, Finland
Yong Gu Ji, South Korea
Esther Jun, USA
Mitsuhiko Karashima, Japan

Kyungdoh Kim, South Korea
Heidi Krömker, Germany
Chen Ling, USA
Yan Liu, USA
Zhengjie Liu, P.R. China
Loïc Martínez Normand, Spain
Chang S. Nam, USA
Naoko Okuizumi, Japan
Noriko Osaka, Japan
Philippe Palanque, France
Hans Persson, Sweden
Ling Rothrock, USA
Naoki Sakakibara, Japan
Dominique Scapin, France
Guangfeng Song, USA
Sanjay Tripathi, India
Chui Yin Wong, Malaysia
Toshiki Yamaoka, Japan
Kazuhiko Yamazaki, Japan
Ryoji Yoshitake, Japan
Silvia Zimmermann, Switzerland

Human Interface and the Management of Information

Program Chair: Sakae Yamamoto, Japan

Hans-Jorg Bullinger, Germany
Alan Chan, Hong Kong
Gilsoo Cho, South Korea
Jon R. Gunderson, USA
Shin'ichi Fukuzumi, Japan
Michitaka Hirose, Japan
Jhilmil Jain, USA
Yasufumi Kume, Japan

Mark Lehto, USA
Hiroyuki Miki, Japan
Hirohiko Mori, Japan
Fiona Fui-Hoon Nah, USA
Shogo Nishida, Japan
Robert Proctor, USA
Youngho Rhee, South Korea
Katsunori Shimohara, Japan

Michale Smith, USA
Tsutomu Tabe, Japan
Hiroshi Tsuji, Japan

Kim-Phuong Vu, USA
Tomio Watanabe, Japan
Hidekazu Yoshikawa, Japan

Engineering Psychology and Cognitive Ergonomics

Program Chair: Don Harris, UK

Guy Andre Boy, USA
Joakim Dahlman, Sweden
Trevor Dobbins, UK
Mike Feary, USA
Shan Fu, P.R. China
Michaela Heese, Austria
Hung-Sying Jing, Taiwan
Wen-Chin Li, Taiwan
Mark A. Neerincx, The Netherlands
Jan M. Noyes, UK
Taezoon Park, Singapore

Paul Salmon, Australia
Axel Schulte, Germany
Siraj Shaikh, UK
Sarah C. Sharples, UK
Anthony Smoker, UK
Neville A. Stanton, UK
Alex Stedmon, UK
Xianghong Sun, P.R. China
Andrew Thatcher, South Africa
Matthew J.W. Thomas, Australia
Rolf Zon, The Netherlands

Universal Access in Human–Computer Interaction

Program Chairs: Constantine Stephanidis, Greece, and Margherita Antona, Greece

Julio Abascal, Spain
Ray Adams, UK
Gisela Susanne Bahr, USA
Margit Betke, USA
Christian Bühler, Germany
Stefan Carmien, Spain
Jerzy Charytonowicz, Poland
Carlos Duarte, Portugal
Pier Luigi Emiliani, Italy
Qin Gao, P.R. China
Andrina Granić, Croatia
Andreas Holzinger, Austria
Josette Jones, USA
Simeon Keates, UK

Georgios Kouroupetroglou, Greece
Patrick Langdon, UK
Seongil Lee, Korea
Ana Isabel B.B. Paraguay, Brazil
Helen Petrie, UK
Michael Pieper, Germany
Enrico Pontelli, USA
Jaime Sanchez, Chile
Anthony Savidis, Greece
Christian Stary, Austria
Hirotada Ueda, Japan
Gerhard Weber, Germany
Harald Weber, Germany

Virtual, Augmented and Mixed Reality

Program Chair: Randall Shumaker, USA

Waymon Armstrong, USA
Juan Cendan, USA
Rudy Darken, USA
Cali M. Fidopiastis, USA
Charles Hughes, USA
David Kaber, USA
Hirokazu Kato, Japan
Denis Laurendeau, Canada
Fotis Liarokapis, UK

Mark Livingston, USA
Michael Macedonia, USA
Gordon Mair, UK
Jose San Martin, Spain
Jacquelyn Morie, USA
Albert "Skip" Rizzo, USA
Kay Stanney, USA
Christopher Stapleton, USA
Gregory Welch, USA

Cross-Cultural Design

Program Chair: P.L. Patrick Rau, P.R. China

Pilsung Choe, P.R. China
Henry Been-Lirn Duh, Singapore
Vanessa Evers, The Netherlands
Paul Fu, USA
Zhiyong Fu, P.R. China
Fu Guo, P.R. China
Sung H. Han, Korea
Toshikazu Kato, Japan
Dyi-Yih Michael Lin, Taiwan
Rungtai Lin, Taiwan

Sheau-Farn Max Liang, Taiwan
Liang Ma, P.R. China
Alexander Mädche, Germany
Katsuhiko Ogawa, Japan
Tom Plocher, USA
Kerstin Röse, Germany
Supriya Singh, Australia
Hsiu-Ping Yueh, Taiwan
Liang (Leon) Zeng, USA
Chen Zhao, USA

Online Communities and Social Computing

Program Chairs: A. Ant Ozok, USA, and Panayiotis Zaphiris, Cyprus

Areej Al-Wabil, Saudi Arabia
Leonelo Almeida, Brazil
Bjørn Andersen, Norway
Chee Siang Ang, UK
Aneesha Bakharia, Australia
Ania Bobrowicz, UK
Paul Cairns, UK
Farzin Deravi, UK
Andri Ioannou, Cyprus
Slava Kisilevich, Germany

Niki Lambropoulos, Greece
Effie Law, Switzerland
Soo Ling Lim, UK
Fernando Loizides, Cyprus
Gabriele Meiselwitz, USA
Anthony Norcio, USA
Elaine Raybourn, USA
Panote Siriaraya, UK
David Stuart, UK
June Wei, USA

Augmented Cognition

Program Chairs: Dylan D. Schmorrow, USA, and Cali M. Fidopiastis, USA

Robert Arrabito, Canada
Richard Backs, USA
Chris Berka, USA
Joseph Cohn, USA
Martha E. Crosby, USA
Julie Drexler, USA
Ivy Estabrooke, USA
Chris Forsythe, USA
Wai Tat Fu, USA
Rodolphe Gentili, USA
Marc Grootjen, The Netherlands
Jefferson Grubb, USA
Ming Hou, Canada

Santosh Mathan, USA
Rob Matthews, Australia
Dennis McBride, USA
Jeff Morrison, USA
Mark A. Neerincx, The Netherlands
Denise Nicholson, USA
Banu Onaral, USA
Lee Sciarini, USA
Kay Stanney, USA
Roy Stripling, USA
Rob Taylor, UK
Karl van Orden, USA

Digital Human Modeling and Applications in Health, Safety, Ergonomics and Risk Management

Program Chair: Vincent G. Duffy, USA and Russia

Karim Abdel-Malek, USA
Giuseppe Andreoni, Italy
Daniel Carruth, USA
Eliza Yingzi Du, USA
Enda Fallon, Ireland
Afzal Godil, USA
Ravindra Goonetilleke, Hong Kong
Bo Hoege, Germany
Waldemar Karwowski, USA
Zhizhong Li, P.R. China

Kang Li, USA
Tim Marler, USA
Michelle Robertson, USA
Matthias Rötting, Germany
Peter Vink, The Netherlands
Mao-Jiun Wang, Taiwan
Xuguang Wang, France
Jingzhou (James) Yang, USA
Xiugan Yuan, P.R. China
Gülcin Yücel Hoge, Germany

Design, User Experience, and Usability

Program Chair: Aaron Marcus, USA

Sisira Adikari, Australia
Ronald Baecker, Canada
Arne Berger, Germany
Jamie Blustein, Canada

Ana Boa-Ventura, USA
Jan Brejcha, Czech Republic
Lorenzo Cantoni, Switzerland
Maximilian Eibl, Germany

Anthony Faiola, USA
Emilie Gould, USA
Zelda Harrison, USA
Rüdiger Heimgärtner, Germany
Brigitte Herrmann, Germany
Steffen Hess, Germany
Kaleem Khan, Canada

Jennifer McGinn, USA
Francisco Rebelo, Portugal
Michael Renner, Switzerland
Kerem Rızvanoğlu, Turkey
Marcelo Soares, Brazil
Christian Sturm, Germany
Michele Visciola, Italy

Distributed, Ambient and Pervasive Interactions

Program Chairs: Norbert Streitz, Germany, and Constantine Stephanidis, Greece

Emile Aarts, The Netherlands
Adnan Abu-Dayya, Qatar
Juan Carlos Augusto, UK
Boris de Ruyter, The Netherlands
Anind Dey, USA
Dimitris Grammenos, Greece
Nuno M. Guimaraes, Portugal
Shin'ichi Konomi, Japan
Carsten Magerkurth, Switzerland

Christian Müller-Tomfelde, Australia
Fabio Paternó, Italy
Gilles Privat, France
Harald Reiterer, Germany
Carsten Röcker, Germany
Reiner Wichert, Germany
Woontack Woo, South Korea
Xenophon Zabulis, Greece

Human Aspects of Information Security, Privacy and Trust

Program Chairs: Louis Marinos, ENISA EU, and Ioannis Askoxylakis, Greece

Claudio Agostino Ardagna, Italy
Zinaida Benenson, Germany
Daniele Catteddu, Italy
Raoul Chiesa, Italy
Bryan Cline, USA
Sadie Creese, UK
Jorge Cuellar, Germany
Marc Dacier, USA
Dieter Gollmann, Germany
Kirstie Hawkey, Canada
Jaap-Henk Hoepman, The Netherlands
Cagatay Karabat, Turkey
Angelos Keromytis, USA
Ayako Komatsu, Japan

Ronald Leenes, The Netherlands
Javier Lopez, Spain
Steve Marsh, Canada
Gregorio Martinez, Spain
Emilio Mordini, Italy
Yuko Murayama, Japan
Masakatsu Nishigaki, Japan
Aljosa Pasic, Spain
Milan Petković, The Netherlands
Joachim Posegga, Germany
Jean-Jacques Quisquater, Belgium
Damien Sauveron, France
George Spanoudakis, UK
Kerry-Lynn Thomson, South Africa

Julien Touzeau, France
Theo Tryfonas, UK
João Vilela, Portugal

Claire Vishik, UK
Melanie Volkamer, Germany

External Reviewers

Maysoon Abulkhair, Saudi Arabia
Ilia Adami, Greece
Vishal Barot, UK
Stephan Böhm, Germany
Vassilis Charissis, UK
Francisco Cipolla-Ficarra, Spain
Maria De Marsico, Italy
Marc Fabri, UK
David Fonseca, Spain
Linda Harley, USA
Yasushi Ikei, Japan
Wei Ji, USA
Nouf Khashman, Canada
John Killilea, USA
Iosif Klironomos, Greece
Ute Klotz, Switzerland
Maria Korozi, Greece
Kentaro Kotani, Japan

Vassilis Kouroumalis, Greece
Stephanie Lackey, USA
Janelle LaMarche, USA
Asterios Leonidis, Greece
Nickolas Macchiarella, USA
George Margetis, Greece
Matthew Marraffino, USA
Joseph Mercado, USA
Claudia Mont'Alvão, Brazil
Yoichi Motomura, Japan
Karsten Nebe, Germany
Stavroula Ntoa, Greece
Martin Osen, Austria
Stephen Prior, UK
Farid Shirazi, Canada
Jan Stelovsky, USA
Sarah Swierenga, USA

HCI International 2014

The 16th International Conference on Human–Computer Interaction, HCI International 2014, will be held jointly with the affiliated conferences in the summer of 2014. It will cover a broad spectrum of themes related to Human–Computer Interaction, including theoretical issues, methods, tools, processes and case studies in HCI design, as well as novel interaction techniques, interfaces and applications. The proceedings will be published by Springer. More information about the topics, as well as the venue and dates of the conference, will be announced through the HCI International Conference series website: http://www.hci-international.org/

General Chair
Professor Constantine Stephanidis
University of Crete and ICS-FORTH
Heraklion, Crete, Greece
Email: cs@ics.forth.gr

Table of Contents – Part II

HCI in Healthcare

Games and Gamification

HCI in Learning and Education

In-Vehicle Interaction

Part I
HCI in Healthcare

Software Engineering in Telehealth, an Extension of Sana Mobile Applied to the Process of a Routine Hospital*

Alfredo Veiga de Carvalho, Carlos José Pereira de Lucena, Elder José Reioli Cirilo,
Paulo Henrique Cardoso Alves, Pedro Augusto da Silva e Souza Miranda,
Gustavo Robichez de Carvalho, Fábio Rodrigo Lopes de Araújo,
and Gabriel Vial Correa Lima

Department of Informatics - Software Engineering Lab – LES
Pontifical Catholic University of Rio de Janeiro - PUC-Rio
{alfredo,guga}@les.inf.puc-rio.br,
lucena@inf.puc-rio.br, ph.alves@live.com,
{ereioli,pedroampuc,fabiorodrigo.puc,gvclima}@gmail.com

Abstract. The patient's medical record, containing the reasons for hospitalization, clinical evolution, laboratory tests, prescription drugs and other relevant
information is of utmost importance to medical management care. Information
technology plays a key role in communicating and disseminating the patient's
clinical data [1]. The Sana Mobile, originally developed by MIT (the Massachusetts Institute of Technology) for mobile platform, consists of an open
source electronic medical record. It has revolutionized the delivery of healthcare services in remote areas in a clear and objective way [2]. The mobile device stores Sana medical data, text files, audio and video containing patient's
clinical information while transmitting data over the mobile platform to a web
server, the Open Medical Record System – OpenMRS. This system gathers information about medications, diagnoses, and others crucial data from a patient,
making them available to consultations by many medical experts.

Our tests with Sana Mobile - OpenMRS focus on the development of an experimental extension of this mobile platform and its use in supporting education
and training of medical students encompassing routine free ambulatory care and
multidisciplinary research project. Participating in this study are researches and
students of Software Engineering, Medicine and Design, respectively Software
Engineering Lab - LES of the Department of Informatics of the Pontifical Catholic University of Rio de Janeiro - PUC-Rio, the School of Medicine and Surgery of the State University of Rio de Janeiro - UNIRIO which includes Gaffrée
and Guinle University Hospital - HUGG, Laboratory of Ergonomics and Usability - LEUI of the Department of Arts and Design at PUC-Rio, under the
coordination of LES.

Keywords: Software Engineering, Multidisciplinarity, Telemedicine, Learning, Mobility, Usability, Collaboration.

---

* This work has been sponsored by the Ministério de Ciência e Tecnologia da Presidência da
República Federativa do Brasil by the Conselho Nacional de Desenvolvimento Científico e
Tecnológico – CNPq, process number 560110/2010-3.

M. Kurosu (Ed.): Human-Computer Interaction, Part II, HCII 2013, LNCS 8005, pp. 3–12, 2013.

1   Introduction

This document presents the results of this research, the product of human-computer interactions among these three groups with different characteristics and experiences to improve the education and training of medical students in ambulatory care, in this case, patients of Gaffrée and Guinle Hospital - HUGG, with the support of this mobile platform extended to achieve this purpose.

2   Survey

This work is part of a three year project [3], started in January of 2011. The context of Software Engineering tells its evolution to the present day, with the conception and development of the Sana Mobile's extension and respective applicability in experiments performed in a hospital routine.

The starting point was the interaction between the project coordinators LES, UNIRIO and LEUI in the area of health, the possible scenarios for applicability of the research considering particularly the target corresponding characteristics, constraints, opportunities and difficulties in light of the achievement of the project. Between the various analyzed scenarios, the experiments considered the most important are: **Indigenous Populations, Health Care Workers, Nursing Staff and Medical Teams**.

The main points considered presented below led to the choice of Medical Teams, which does not prevent new scenarios to be incorporated.

- **Indigenous Populations**: Difficulties in ranging and restrictions on usability that require additional time to search for participants and adequate training.
- **Health Care Workers**: Dispersion of the target audience and its particular interest in the location of the population served led to a massive use of voice communication that alone does not characterize research activity.
- **Nursing Staff**: Needs of the population for laboratorial attendance considering statistical data, include the use of equipment already established for data collection, not relevant to the goals of this project.
- **Medical Teams**: With teams of doctors and students of medicine, it was easier to concentrate different target groups in this region. Another favorable aspect, relevant to the applicability of this scenario, is its alignment with the goals of the research currently carried out in the Lab. of Software Engineering - LES PUC – Rio.

In parallel, other important interactions of the coordinating group were made, considering besides the LES visits to the Center for Telemedicine UNIRIO and also to the Department of Arts and Design at PUC-Rio, the surveys of:

- Equipment requirements for specific infrastructures;
- Human resources for students to be engaged, experiments needed to develop the project;
- Mobile devices to be acquired for the various types of experiments.

About the last item and its use in multiple medical settings, several references were raised and made available for further research studies conducted by multidisciplinary group of participants [4, 5, 6, 7, 8, 9, 10].

3 Studies

As a result of the previous phase, equipments for the infrastructure and various mobile devices were purchased as well as the completion of a multidisciplinary team with the incorporation of students in three areas linked to the LES, UNIRIO and LEUI. These actions will potentialize the subsequent studies and research.

Considering the scenario of Medical Teams chosen to lead the experiments, software systems that contemplated all or part of the following segments of the medical field were studied: **Monitoring**, **eHealth** and **Electronic Medical Record**.

The following examples illustrate but do not exhaust the possibilities of use.

- **Monitoring**: Patient connects Bluetooth device attached to its home mHealth device that receives and sends the results to other doctors mHealth from its social network of telemedicine system that can visualize and analyze the results graphically, instructing the patient.
- **eHealth**: The patient arrives at a hospital with a serious injury caused by trauma. The emergency medical team does not have much experience in this case, but immediate surgery is required. The alternative is a high-level monitoring surgical distance by experts on call who would be "biped" to connect their devices mHealth to the sound, images and electrocardiographic parameters, pulse oximetry, heart rate produced by telemedicine system that would guide Local team.
- **Electronic Medical Record**: Built from the monitoring that sends to the patient profile in its network of telemedicine system data files, graphics, photos and videos and exam reports, informing in real time to authorized physicians about the exam which in turn can make diagnoses and prescriptions that are sent to the patient profile that immediately can start the new treatment.

  The patient records "how are you doing" and includes ancient laboratory tests in its electronic medical record system in telemedicine.

  The largest laboratories (three or four) of clinic and image of the city would make an agreement with the telemedicine system and send the results (diagnoses, photos and videos) in standardized formats, from the patient's request, to the cloud of social network making them available immediately to the patient, referring physician and all other doctors already authorized to receive them in their respective mHealth's and so they could interact soon after in order to obtain the optimal collaborative diagnosis.

In these studies, besides Sana Mobile - OpenMRS, Open Source Platform for Patient Monitoring Medical distance, developed at MIT, two additional significant platforms were available:

- **D2L - Capture**: A Cloud platform for creating, recording, editing and publishing Web presentations live or on demand, with perfect synchronization between media, audio and video, developed by the Canadian company Desire2Learn Innovative Learning Technology - D2L [11].
- **Nokia Data Gathering - NDG:** Open Source platform that enables the creation and sharing of forms (for Patients, for example) for quick use at a distance, developed by Nokia [12].

We must remember that, while Sana Mobile Platform - OpenMRS is crucial for experiments and project development, Capture has a significant role in the project documentation as a whole. The NDG assisted in the preparation of the initial draft of the forms of new records. For the operation of Sana Mobile - OpenMRS, we performed a set of installations:

- In mobile devices, Sana Mobile on the Android operating system;
- On the server, the OpenMRS.

After configuring the Android mobile devices purchased for the research, we installed the Sana Mobile in each one, and then we tested some of its native functionality through query simulations. The collection of data in text format and image occurs from a procedure materialized by a succession of screens on the device where the user of the Medical Staff selects the options according to the evaluation of the patient, like a normal consultation. Upon completion of data collection, you can try to connect the device to the Internet to send data to OpenMRS. If there is no connectivity at the moment, the data is queued and sent when the device restores Internet access. The next step was the installation of OpenMRS server to establish the connection to Sana mobile devices. With this goal, we use the operating system Ubuntu 10.04 server and follow the step-by-step installation of OpenMRS documentation MIT, which covers the installation of System Management Databases - DBMS MySQL and Tomcat webserver 6 for its proper operation. Finally we see how the receiving of the OpenMRS data collected is done by the devices and how they can be manipulated by the medical staff on the server. The Sana Mobile, installed on an Android mobile device, works in conjunction with the OpenMRS server as follows:

- A user of the Medical Staff enters the medical records of a patient through Sana;
- These records are sent to the server via an Internet connection;
- Another member of the staff receives data through the OpenMRS interface;
- The health care provider performs the necessary steps so that the patient has the appropriate care.

Upon completion of this phase, this Sana Mobile - OpenMRS Platform original MIT was made available for initial tests by the group of researchers and medical students of the UNIRIO, the set of people that shapes the scenario of the Medical Staff of the project.

4   Tests

The results of the experiments follow the different phases of the evolution of the project and the multidisciplinary group interactions. The first refers to those obtained by initial tests with the original MIT Platform. The second, the presentation of the definition of Sana Mobile Extension. The following, the new tests conducted after the development and installation of the extension. The subsequent, the presentation of changes in extension with the adjustments recommended by the application of the previous tests. The final results, obtained after installation of updates in Extension, are the subject of the next item - Results that leverage new experiments to be conducted until the end of the project.

4.1   Initial Tests

The Sana original MIT was used extensively by the medical staff, particularly by medical students of the Gaffrée and Guinle University Hospital - HUGG through mobile devices of the project (Android tablets and smartphones), to understand its methodology and usability in collecting data and at the same time, see this data transmitted via the Internet server platform, the OpenMRS. We studied the various models of pre-ready medical records of Sana, covering different topics such as oral and cervical cancer, patient care with TB and HIV, ophthalmological and dermatological screening, Image exams and Prenatal. It was found that for the creation of a new patient form you must fill in the fields with the patient's first and last name, its registration number in the clinic and its date of birth. With these data, you can enter the patient's clinical case since this is already established in the system. Each model of clinical medical records follows its own pattern in recording information, indicating for example the main complaint, the onset of the disease, signs and symptoms relevant to that disease, the patient's medical history, family history, co-morbidities, request and laboratory test results, medications and diagnosis. You must take a picture of the patient through the mobile device associated with the file being created. With all this data filled in, you can save the file on the device and later send it (upload) to the server where it is stored in OpenMRS database platform and can be viewed by the medical staff at any time.

The use of Sana in this first phase of testing has brought new experiences to the multidisciplinary group, but there were difficulties concerning data collection and usability of the models pre-ready medical records of Sana Platform, as described below.

Regarding this last item, the problem of initial use of Sana Platform - OpenMRS was caused by storing dates in the original system MIT (U.S. format "mm/dd/yyyy"), which led to inconsistency in DataBase Management System - DBMS, with the dates of birth of patients (Brazilian format: "dd/mm/yyyy"). This was solved by students of software engineering project with the collaboration by exchanging messages with the Sana MIT team, particularly Erick Winkler.

Experiments using the Sana made by medical students at this early stage were performed by compiling data from patients already registered with HUGG paper forms.

The difficulties of data collection were caused by organizational problems, such as missing documents and exams that should be attached to the form of the patient, as well as filling in the paper forms with errors of language (Portuguese) and illegible orthography. Moreover, it was found that the models pre-ready Sana did not cover most of the needs of data collection for patient care at HUGG, given the scope and variety of medical topics, restricting its usability, signaling the importance of defining an Extension of Sana and their development in the project.

4.2   Sana Extension

The experience gained in the previous phase was the starting point for the definition by the Medical Team, particularly the group of medical students from the HUGG, of a new model medical record that encompassed the needs of registering patients in ambulatory and infirmary of the HUGG and could print their records soon after registering through OpenMRS. Through the Nokia Data Gathering - NDG, quoted above, the group of students from UNIRIO created the model of two medical records, called First Step, which covers initial care, and Second Step, for subsequent registration. The records contain the following information about a patient:

- **First Step**: Identifier (Patient registration), First Name, Last Name, Date of Birth, Sex, Photo of the patient (may be more than one), the main complaint, other complaints, comorbidities, other comorbidities, Blood Pressure, Body Temperature, direction, Other Exams and Observations.
- **Second Step**: Identifier (Patient registration), First Name, Last Name, Date of Birth, Sex, Photo of the patient (may be more than one), Provenance, Prescription Drugs in use, Blood Pressure, FR IRMP, Situation, Other complaints, Red blood cells and Creatinine.

The LES team, particularly the group of software engineering students, design software from these medical records created in NDG by medical students of HUGG – UNIRIO, implemented the corresponding medical records in Sana Mobile. The development of this Sana Extension includes new elements called Concepts in OpenMRS server. Each Sana medical records item is associated with a given Concept in OpenMRS. For example, to create a new field - Heart Rate in the medical record on the mobile device with Sana, this concept needs to be inserted before in OpenMRS for the data about Heart Rate can be stored in the mobile device Android with Sana installed, and later, after its transmission via Internet at the Database of the Platform in OpenMRS server. The eXtensible Markup Language - XML was used as the primary tool in the process of building this extension.

4.3   Tests with the New Version

The group of medical students from UNIRIO used extensively the initial Sana Mobile Extension to test the whole before putting it into practice in patient care at the Ambulatory and Infirmary of HUGG, which, as planned in the project, will happen only after the development phase and installation of the Extension Settings.

The group HUGG – UNIRIO found two types of problems with the massive use of the Sana Extension: **Operational** and **Usability**, as reported:

- **Operational**: At this stage, the interactions between UNIRIO students (users of Sana) and of LES (the developers) resolved the following problems:

— "Upload unsuccessfully", i.e. the records generated in Sana were not sent to the OpenMRS: Solution with the explanation that the new version of Sana was accompanied by a new server.

— "Reload Database": This option must be executed only at the very beginning of loading the new version and not all the time causing the loss of data transmitted from Sana to OpenMRS.

— The Portuguese orthography caused errors in the data. This is corrected by the current configuration using Portuguese words in English orthography.

— Topics in OpenMRS were out of order which hindered the clinical thought. This was solved by explaining the use of commands in OpenMRS server.

— Delay in data transmission from Sana mobile devices to OpenMRS server, which was caused by low speed connection to the Internet that HUGG had at the time.

- **Usability**: The following problems reported in detail by medical students of UNIRIO, users of the platform, served as input for the next phase of adjustments in the Extension. They are:

— **New version of Sana**: The extension Sana, containing only the records created for the first and second attendances (called First and Second Stage, respectively), both have limitations in their use in the Ambulatory and Infirmary. Relating to First Stage was found the need to insert a field that could detail the aspects related to the patient's pain near the field of the same name present in this medical records regarding to the use in the Ambulatory. In Infirmary, an adaptation should be made, since it is not a first attendance. It is to replace the main complaint of the first call for the motivation of hospitalization because very often the patient already has a diagnostic exam and brings it. Therefore, not all the information found in the patient of the Infirmary can be placed in the medical record first attendance developed in Sana. The second attendance record of these patients was adapted for use as the latest clinical performance made in the patient. The data from their medical records, such as test results, vital signs and medications during hospitalization complete the registration.

— **Form of the Second Stage**: In this medical record, in a determined topic the setup is geared for entering only numbers and not letters, which prevents the addition of other relevant exams, with their names and results. In another, the patient's condition should be added to the existing options of improvement, deterioration, new complaints and healing.

— **Medical records of the original Sana**: The records of the original Sana were discarded in this new version. However, in despite of having limitations, they are useful in the patient record of the Infirmary. The addition of some of these original records of the MIT model is complementary to the current model of Sana.

4.4   Adjustments in the Extension

Every phase of this project, as the previous and the following, were accompanied and developed in an integrated manner between the teams of LES, UNIRIO and LEUI. The group LEUI interacted more strongly in the phase of adjustments of the Extension. Effective communication among project participants was done through various interactions via the Internet (including teams of discussion groups – Google Groups and sharing of data and information - Dropbox), and meetings both at PUC-Rio (in LES and LEUI) and at the Gafrée and Guinle Hospital - HUGG (UNIRIO).

From the above interactions, adjustments were performed by students of LES, developing topic images for exams, adding and altering records to other topics of the First and Second Step, and incorporating the medical records of HIV, Tuberculosis, Prenatal, Dermatology, Radiological Exams of the original Sana, according to the requests Medical Staff - UNIRIO.

With the adjustments developed, the LES team delivered the final version of the Sana Extension for use by Medical Staff UNIRIO with patients at the Ambulatory and Infirmary of the HUGG Hospital. The results obtained with this are presented in the following section.

5   Results

Along four months, data from 136 patients of the Ambulatory of HUGG were collected by medical students. It was observed that the time spent in completing a medical record using the Extension Sana on mobile device gradually narrowed, because medical students have gained experience with the weekly practice using the system installed in tablets and smartphones, developing assertiveness and also security approach for patients. It was concluded that Sana Extension works as a true facilitator in collecting patient information, optimizing this process, and had contributed greatly to the academic development of the students.

After this period, the multidisciplinary group focused on interactions between UNIRIO and LEUI with the intermediation of LES related to tests using the new platform by medical students of HUGG - UNIRIO. As a result, students test participants showed great familiarity and usability of mobile devices in Sana Extension (as detected in the previous phase above), but not so much with the OpenMRS that until now had not been properly tested, solely for storage purposes of records registered by Sana Extension in its database.

Therefore, the proposal of the new usability test was covering OpenMRS basic functions, such as searching for medical records of patients, organization and editing. We used as parameters the guidelines of students in software engineering of the LES that intermediated the contact of students LEUI and UNIRIO. They were created by LEUI students testing scenarios in OpenMRS with pre-set tasks for students of medicine HUGG - UNIRIO.

During testing, the medical students showed unexpected agility with OpenMRS, because once warned of the test on the system, they studied and learned many of their functions. Therefore, these tasks were performed with reasonable ease. The comments and behavior of the participants during testing the scenarios showed that the domain about the system is more concerning due a sequence of memorized actions than intuition and understanding of an interface.

It was concluded that the OpenMRS offers valuable resources for physicians, but its interface is not yet able to serve this audience. With a language and mechanics facing to software developers and not for doctors, it shows itself unnecessarily complicated and inhibits the insertion of this tool on a doctor's everyday, which does not occur with the interface Extension Sana Mobile.

We should remember that the primary purpose of using Sana Mobile by medical students of UNIRIO, with its extension developed by the project, was experiencing Platform as a fixation method of learning, especially for:

- Practice what was learned in lectures;
- Develop security of medical student towards the patient and
- Evaluate the preparation of the students coursing the first year at HUGG hospital.

All this set has been fully satisfied, understanding that these results will lead to a positive conclusion of the project, signaling the incorporation of new facilities from the continuity of ongoing experiments, as described below.

6   Conclusions

The Extension Sana brought a great contribution to the academic development of medical students engaged in the project. They tested their knowledge acquired in the classroom making medical records and collecting data of patients, through a little anamnesis and basic physical examination such as measuring blood pressure, measuring respiratory frequency and cardiac, capillary glucose and axillary temperature. With this practice, security in managing patients had increased, bringing other good results, including more quickness and efficiency in dealing with them.

Regarding the latter point, it seems that the experimental platform developed besides responding positively to the objective of this part of the project within the context of fixation method of learning for medical students, brought the light of the results, the viability of its incorporation in the process of the daily routine of patient care, particularly in ambulatory care, bringing gains already described as well as the preservation of the patient's history for future visits and possible interactions with other health professionals through the Platform, for example, to share patient data.

For the end of this project, which finishes late this year of 2013, we intend to include also the extension options using GPS, filming and sound recording, existing in original Sana. In addition, a new challenge: incorporating to the platform Sana - OpenMRS the Medical Records Builder which would include the role now performed in a non-integrated mode with the NDG system, as was previously used to define the forms of the extension, as well as the automatic generation of new Concepts in the Platform. This facilitates the definition provided by the construction of new medical records, for example, they can track additional data obtained in the diagnostic investigation of unsolved cases by stages (first and second) established by the project so far, as they were loaded and the use of them in mobile devices with this new Sana installed.

Simultaneously, we intend to survey the computational resources of OpenMRS, through interactions of groups of LES and UNIRIO defining Use Cases that the medical staff would like to use in OpenMRS. With this result and new interactions between these groups together with the LEUI, a software layer interface on OpenMRS will be built by the team of LES with the design of LEUI for the Medical Staff of UNIRIO can use the cases previously chosen.

With this interdisciplinary research project and their interactions, we intend to contribute effectively for the education and training of students in medicine and facilitate the routine care in hospitals, particularly the poor people without costs, integrating health, usability, mobility and collaboration.

References

1. Cirilo, E., Nunes, I., Carvalho, D., Carvalho, G., Veiga, A., Lucena, C.J.P.: Engenharia de software em Telessaúde: aplicações e desafios. In: Gold Book, 50th Scientific Congress of HUPE, Rio de Janeiro, pp. 371–404 (2012)
2. Sana Care Anywhere. MIT, http://sana.mit.edu
3. Lucena, C.J.P.: Modelos Computacionaispara Apoioa Avaliaçãodo Ergodesignde Interfacespara Telemedicina: Usabilidadeem Sistemasde Informação Móvel - Edital MCT/CNPq N º 09/2010 – PDI, Rio de Janeiro, PUC-Rio, Departamento de Informática, 54 p. (2010)
4. IBM Institute of Business Value. The future of connected health devices. IBM Corporation, 17 p. (2011),
   http://public.dhe.ibm.com/common/ssi/ecm/en/gbe03398usen/GBE03398USEN.PDF
5. World Health Organization. mHealth New horizons for health through mobile technologies, 112 p. (2011),
   http://www.who.int/goe/publications/goe_mhealth_web.pdf
6. University of Cambridge. Mobile Communications for Medical Care, 120 p. (April 21, 2011), http://www.csap.cam.ac.uk/media/uploads/files/1/mobile-communications-for-medical-care.pdf
7. Medgle - On-Demand Clinical Case Analysis for Patients and Providers, http://www.medgle.com
8. iNurse - Advanced Health and Care, http://www.advancedcomputersoftware.com/ahc/products/inurse.php
9. Indivo X - Developer Community, http://indivohealth.org/developer-community
10. Collaborhythm - Redefining health care delivery - Mit Media Lab, http://newmed.media.mit.edu/collaborhythm
11. Desire2Learn Capture, http://desire2learncapture.com/products/capture-software
12. Nokia Developer. Nokia Data Gathering, https://projects.developer.nokia.com/ndg

Cross Cultural Design Considerations in HealthCare

Joyram Chakraborty

Towson University
7800 York Road, Towson Maryland 21252
jchakraborty@towson.edu

Abstract. Increasing number of health care providers are leveraging the power of technology to provide access to medical practitioners and patients on a global scale. However, there is limited research in the area of cross cultural design of the tools being used. This paper presents a work-in-progress in the area of cross cultural design of health care tools. The main interest is to outline some of the cross cultural challenges of designing and implementing healthcare tools on a global scale and some possible solutions.

Keywords: Healthcare, Cross-Cultural, User Experience, Usability.

1 Introduction

The use of technology in the administration of healthcare is increasing at an explosive rate. However, usability research in this field is lacking. Too often healthcare providers and patients alike are faced with using tools that they are unaccustomed to within their local culture [1-3]. These tools are often forced into usage by market forces rather than local user needs. As a consequence, medical providers often spend more time dealing with the intricacies of the new tools and less time with patients [1-3].

In many developing countries, the modern day health care provider is not bound by an office. In many instances the care provider will travel to the site of the patient to gauge the extent of the illness and provide necessary care. Armed with new technologies such as diagnostic tools and decision support systems, the new breed of care providers can: take better readings; make more accurate diagnosis; and offer more effective treatments. These new tools have changed the nature of the relationships between healthcare providers and patients in rural settings. However, there are significant cultural ramifications of this new status quo. In many environments, there is a degree of distrust with the new tools that recommend alternate treatments. These new treatments often come with smaller prescriptions than what the patients are accustomed. In some instances the direct questions asked in the data gathering process using the new tools can be deemed offensive and lead to resistance in the sharing of vital personal information. This can lead to inaccurate assessments of the health condition and subsequent treatment. Often, the misunderstandings can be attributed to the poorly designed interfaces of the respective tools being used in the healthcare. Since these tools are typically developed in countries other than where they are used, there

M. Kurosu (Ed.): Human-Computer Interaction, Part II, HCII 2013, LNCS 8005, pp. 13–19, 2013.

is usually a gap between the end user and the developer. This may lead to cross cultural misunderstandings. This paper describes some of these cross cultural challenges.

The remainder of the paper is organized as follows. Section 2 proposes a working definition of culture and the internationalization and localization process. Section 3 introduces the SLICK model and describes its various components. Section 4 describes the experiment design and what will be carried out and section 5 draws conclusion that can be expected out of the findings.

2   Background

2.1   Culture

Culture is hard to define. Various researchers have developed their own definitions. Ting-Toomey defines culture as "a complex frame of reference that consists of patterns of traditions, beliefs, values, norms, symbols, and meanings that are shared to varying degrees by interacting members of a community"[4]. A signification amount of Human Computer Interaction (HCI) research applies Hofstede's findings towards the understanding of culture and its significance to their product [5]. Hofstede carried out perhaps the largest study of culture by surveying over 120,000 IBM employees worldwide about people's behavior's in large organizations. Using this survey he discovered significant differences in people's behaviors using which he developed national rankings. However, critics of this cultural model cite the lack of correlation between Hofstede's anthropological findings and cultural attitudes towards information technology[6].

2.2   Internationalization and Localization

The literature is filled with examples of product acceptance failures due to cross cultural misunderstandings. A product designed for an international audience must be carefully designed to gain acceptance within the local community[7]. Internationalization refers to the process of isolating the culturally specific elements from a product; for example the isolation of French text from a program development in France. Internationalization occurs in the country where the product is originally developed. It is not uncommon for development groups to focus only on elements related to text, numbers and dates [7].

Localization refers to the process of infusing a specific cultural context onto a previously internationalized product [8]; for instance, translating French text and message files into Spanish for Spanish users. Like internationalization, localization is usually limited to translating the text, date and number formats. But creating a product that functions in another culture involves more than this. Properly localized software applications, just like properly localized automobiles, toasters, beverages, and magazines, reflect the values, ethics, morals and language (or languages) of the nation in question [8]. In localizing a product, in addition to idiomatic language translation, such details as time zones, currency, local color sensitivities, product or service names, gender roles, and geographic examples must all be considered. A successfully localized service or product is one that appears to have been developed within the local culture [9].

3 The SLICK Model

Any healthcare tool that is localized carefully has a greater chance of acceptance. Research findings indicate that mobile health and electronic health product launches in several countries have met with varying degrees of acceptance from the local community. The objective of this paper is to propose a new methodology for testing the design of the product using the SLICK model [10]. The SLICK model was developed as a result of a meta search of the most widely used cultural variables – *symbolism, local variables, individualism, color and knowledge gathering patterns.* Culturally specific examples of each variable could easily be identified in the literature and tested with the specific product.

3.1 Symbolism

Russo and Boor [7] claim that "Images are the visual language of culture that does not always translate – just like words." Images or symbols that may reflect one meaning in one culture may not map the equivalent meaning in another. Del Galdo [11] and Marcus and Gould [12] point out the use of symbolic representations from a culture in user interface design will increase the preference and acceptance of the application.

3.2 Local Variables

One of the first steps in the preparation of entering a product into an international market is the issue of translation of all interface text into the local language. This can be a very complicated task as the translation must make accommodations for issues such as computer-human interaction [13]. The list of local variables that can be tested for the internationalization of user interfaces can be extensive. The list includes: Translation, Jargon, words that don't exist, product names, text flow, character sets, number date time formats, phone numbers, people's names, masculinity, religious practices and holidays.

3.3 Individualism

Triandis defines Individualism "as a social pattern that consists of loosely linked individuals who view themselves as independent of collectives; are primarily motivated by their own preferences, needs, rights, and the contracts they have established with others; give priority to their personal goals over the goals of others; and emphasize the rational analysis of the advantages and disadvantages to associating with others"[14]. Triandis defines Collectivism as "a social pattern consisting of closely linked individuals who see themselves as parts of one or more collectives (family, co-worker, tribe, nation); are primarily motivated by the norms of, and duties imposed by, those collectives; are willing to give priority to the goals of these collectives over their personal goals; and emphasize their connectedness to the members of these collectives." Triandis explains that as these terms are used by many people in different parts of the world and are given various meanings, they can be difficult to measure [14].

3.4 Color

What color represents and how it is interpreted varies greatly across cultures [15]. Findings from Courtney [16] and Russo and Boor [7] suggest that color can impact the acceptance of a user interface design.

Culture	Red	Blue	Green	Yellow	White
United States	Danger	Masculinity	Safety	Cowardice	Purity
France	Aristocracy	Freedom Peace	Criminality	Temporary	Neutrality
Egypt	Death	Virtue Faith Truth	Fertility Strength	Happiness Prosperity	Joy
India	Life Creativity		Prosperity Fertility	Success	Death Purity
Japan	Anger Danger	Villainy	Future Youth Energy	Grace Nobility	Death
China	Happiness	Heavens Clouds	Ming Dynasty Heavens Clouds	Birth Wealth Power	Death Purity

Fig. 1. The meaning of color in different cultures (Russo and Boor, 1993)

3.5 Knowledge Gathering Patterns

Kaplan [17] indicated that cultures have different thought patterns. Kaplan's work has highlighted the correlations between language and thought pattern. Kaplan's study reports several types of thinking patterns namely linear, parallel, and circular or indirection (random). Kaplan attributed the differences in these language styles to cultural variations.

English   Semitic   Oriental   Romance   Russian

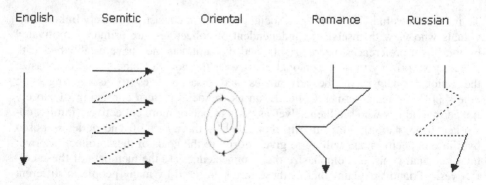

Fig. 2. Kaplan's Cultural Thought Patterns (Kaplan, 1966)

4   Experiment Design

The SLICK model can be applied in the design of culturally sensitive healthcare tools for an international setting. To test the effectiveness of the model, data about user preference of healthcare tools will be collected from an existing framework where eHealth tools are currently being used. A partnership with a healthcare provider in rural Uganda is currently being developed for this study. It is envisioned that for this study, data will be gathered from eHealth providers and recipients in a two-step process after IRB approval.

In the first stage, user satisfaction data will be collected from 10 randomly selected adult users of eHealth tools. This will include both providers and recipients of the service. This data collection will be carried out using a closed questionnaire that will be administered by personnel in Uganda. The responses from the questionnaire will be used to measure the levels of satisfaction with the cultural sensitivity of the user interfaces of the eHealth tools.

Based on the findings of the data collection, a modified prototype of the user interface of the same eHealth tool will be developed by applying the SLICK model. Through the SLICK model, we can assume the following information about the Ugandan culture:

Symbolism: From the literature, we know that the Ugandan culture has certain symbols that are unique to the country. For example, the waste basket symbol used in the West should be modified to resemble a closed trash can for Uganda. The use of any symbols in the user interface of the eHealth tool should be carefully selected not to cause offense.

Local Variable: From the literature, we know that British English is the primary language of Uganda. Therefore, all translation should employ British English standards. We also know there are certain customs that are indigenous to the *Ugandan culture*. For example, Uganda has a high degree of masculinity and the user interface of the eHealth tool should be aware of this fact.

Individualism: From the literature, we know that Uganda is a collectivistic country where the greater good of many outweighs the good of one. An example of the possible implications of this cultural factor could apply to the sharing of sensitive medical information. In the Western cultures, medical information is highly sensitive and is not shared with anyone else but the patient. However, in collectivistic countries, medical information will be readily shared with members of the local community.

Color: From the literature, we know that certain colors have different meanings in different parts of the world. While color in Uganda is not as sensitive, there are still color preferences within the culture. For example, Green, Red and Black are the national colors of Uganda and are more commonly used in the culture.

Knowledge Gathering Pattern: From the literature, we know that Ugandan culture has an Oriental language pattern. An implication of this could be that direct questions might be deemed offensive. For example, information about medical history should be sought out using indirect questioning techniques.

Once the modified prototype of the interface is developed, it will be shown to 10 adult users of eHealth tools. User satisfaction data will then collected from these end users using the same questionnaire used in step one of the data collection process. The two data sets will then be statistically compared to determine if the cultural modifications made using the SLICK model resulted in any improvements with the end user satisfaction with eHealth tool. The resulting outcome of the study would be shared with the eHealth tool developer to incorporate in any future versions.

5   Conclusions

The goal of this research paper is to outline some of the cross cultural challenges of designing and implementing healthcare tools on a global scale. The results of the experiment described in the paper will shed light on some of the cultural factors that affect user satisfaction and a possible solution. The paper also highlights the need for more user experience research to better understand the international end user. User experience research would assist software developers to develop cross culturally sensitive products that would be well received within the local community. The results from this study will further research in this field. The findings of the study can be further strengthened by replicating the study in another environment and also by using a different eHealth tool. The findings from such a comparative study would extend our understanding of the field of cross cultural interface design.

References

1. McCurdie, T., Taneva, S., Casselman, M., Yeung, M., McDaniel, C., Ho, W., Cafazzo, J.: The Case for User-Centered Design. Horizons (2012)
2. Walsh, T., Vainio, T.: Cross-Cultural Design for mHealth Applications. Extended Abstracts of the Third International Workshop on Smart Healthcare Applications
3. Anderson, L.M., et al.: Culturally competent healthcare systems. American Journal of Preventive Medicine 24(3), 68–79 (2003)
4. Ting-Toomey, S.: Communicating across cultures. Guilford Press (1999)
5. Hofstede, G.: Cultures and Organizations: Software of the Mind. McGraw-Hill, New York (1991)
6. Holden, N.: Why marketers need a new concept of culture for the global knowledge economy. International Marketing Review 6, 563–572 (2004)
7. Russo, P., Boor, S.: How fluent is your interface?: designing for international users. In: Conference on Human Factors in Computing Systems (CHI), Amsterdam, Netherlands (1993)
8. Taylor, D.: Global Software. Springer, New York (1992)
9. Stengers, H., De Troyer, O., Baetens, M., Boers, F., Mushtaha, A.N.: Localization of Web Sites: Is there still a need for it. In: International Workshop on Web Engineering. McGraw-Hill, Munich (2004)
10. Chakraborty, J.: A Cross Cultural Usability Study on the Internationalization of User Interfaces Based on an Empirical Five Factor Model. In: Department of Information Systems 2009, University of Maryland, p. 215. ProQuest LLC, Baltimore County (2009)

11. Del Galdo, E.: Internationalization and Translation: Some Guidelines for the Design of Human-Computer Interfaces. In: Nielsen, J. (ed.) Designing User Interfaces for International User. Elsevier, New York (1990)
12. Marcus, A.: Cross-cultural web user-interface design. In: Human Computer Interface International (HCII), New Orleans, Louisiana, pp. 502–505 (2001)
13. Evers, V., Kukulska-Hulme, A., Jones, A.: Cross-cultural understanding of interface design: A cross-cultural analysis of icon recognition. In: International Workshop on Internationalisation of Products and Systems (IWIPS), Rochester, NY (1999)
14. Triandis, H.C., Bontempo, R., Villareal: Individualism and collectivism: Cross-cultural perspectives on self-Ingroup relationships. Journal of Personality and Social Psychology 2, 323–338 (1988)
15. Thorell, L.G., Smith, W.J.: Using computer color effectively: an illustrated reference. Prentice-Hall, Inc. (1990)
16. Courtney, A.J.: Chinese Population Stereotypes: Color Association. Human Factors 1 (1986)
17. Kaplan, R.B.: Cultural thought patterns in inter-cultural education. Language Learning 1 (1966)

Designing Copresent Cycling Experience

Yun-Maw Cheng[1,2], Wei-Ju Chen[2], Tong-Ying Wu[2], Frode Eika Sandnes[3],
Chris Johnson[4], and Chao-Yang Yang[5]

[1] Institute of Design Science, Tatung University, Taipei, Taiwan
[2] Department of Computer Science and Engineering, Tatung University, Taipei, Taiwan
[3] Institite of Information Technology,
Oslo and Akershus University College of Applied Science, Oslo, Norway
[4] School of Computing Science, University of Glasgow, UK
[5] Department of Industrial Design, Chang Gung University, Tao-Yuan, Taiwan
kevin@ttu.edu.tw, g10006005@ms.ttu.edu.tw, wutony211@gmail.com,
Frode-Eika-Sandnes@hioa.no, christopher.johnson@glasgow.ac.uk,
dillon.yang@mail.cgu.edu.tw

Abstract. There has been much UbiComp research into motivating people to live more active and healthy lifestyle with sports. The idea behind these approaches is centered on social and peer effects in enhancing exercise adherence. While research of this kind has been prolific, there has very little work been done to identify factors that embody comfortable and informed accompanied exercise experience. This paper takes an increasingly attractive cycling theme as a testbed and proposes an unobtrusive and intuitive interface arrangement based on light. It can create a sense of being together with each other for distant apart cyclists. The initial results yield a good level of comprehension and motivation towards the use of the interface. The hope is that the elicited recommendations can guide the design of UbiComp technologies for social motivational physical exercises.

1 Introduction

The increment in habitual physical inactivity has brought multidisciplinary domain experts together including behavioral, social, mechanical, and computer scientists to confront this via their consensus of motivating people to discard sedentary lifestyle [1][2][3][4][5][6][7]. Specifically, this paper looks for answering the question: How we should take steps to encourage personal exercise through technology.

Nowadays, mechanical and computer technologies have jointly shown their popularity to provide people with variety of controlled exercises within stationary settings. Jogging on a treadmill and riding on an exercise bike are the most common forms of synergy between the two. The measurement and support of attuned exercises can simply be done by the relevant sensing and reasoning technologies. The estimated level of fitness is then delivered, perceived, and experienced mainly through the computerized console. There are also liberal research attempts on the advantages of social-enhanced applications for physical exercises [8][9][10]. The implementations

M. Kurosu (Ed.): Human-Computer Interaction, Part II, HCII 2013, LNCS 8005, pp. 20–25, 2013.
© Springer-Verlag Berlin Heidelberg 2013

mostly focus on the techniques of tracing and sharing progress of physical activities. However, guided directions to the embodiment of how the motivation is set up in terms of the interface design are surprisingly limited.

This paper aims to elicit the design recommendations for interfaces that can create a sense of mutual awareness for distant physical exercisers. Specifically, this research investigates the possibilities of using light to peripherally convey workout information, which notifies personal and partner's physical status, while doing exercises in the real scene. Although a number of exercises could act as a potential testbed to better understand the insight on designing interface of this kind, cycling is selected not only due to its nature to health and environment but the appreciation and its increasing popularity as a means of exercise [11][12][13][14]. In order to look into the implications of designing the interface in context, a prototype for case study has been developed based on the concept of user-centered design. The focus is on discovering the parameters, which the interface is made of, along with the manner of how a medium for communication within exercise settings is chosen and positioned.

The following pages expand this by presenting the design and implementation of the prototype. The second half of the paper describes the user studies in an attempt to identify the perception, comprehension, and experience of the interface usage. The closing sections then focuses on eliciting recommendations for the design of the interface for social motivational physical exercises.

2   Design of the Prototype

The aim of this design is to create a sense of cycling together via bridging the physical distance between cyclists without explicitly demanding much of their attention. The target scenario in this paper is a two-person cycling activity. This specific case was selected in an attempt to echo the atmosphere of busy lives these days. Hard to find mutually convenient time and place to do exercise with partner is the common cause that hinders turning exercise into habit. The initiative herein is to identify what information can be tracked and how it is shared to form the sense of cycling with a companion. As can be seen from most of the recent exercise bikes in the market, the information they provide is about level of personal activity, which comprises speed, distance, heart rate, calories burned, and etc. Also, as noted by social comparison theory, humans have an instinct to gauge the self through contrasting themselves with those contextually relevant others [15][16]. It is, therefore, synchronously sharing the activity information between cyclists could create a sense of copresence and motivate them to be more active towards the exercise [17].

The progress in mobility with a range of sensors and actuators has provided the possibility to move from immobile to ubiquitous exercise experiences. However, the challenge facing is how technology should act to enhance which sensory abilities in order to implicitly restore a sense of copresence as in locomotion and exercise. The emphasis at this stage is on the selection of an appropriate medium to convey the

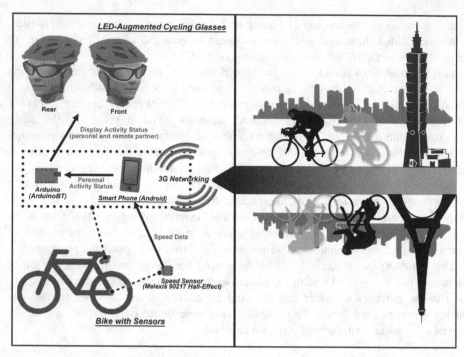

Fig. 1. Prototype schematic diagram

activity information via augmented existing sport equipments. Ishii et al. argued that a more engaged personal experience could be realized by virtue of allying the metaphor of artifacts with the way they prompt human senses [18][19][20]. Cycling helmet and glasses are the most common wearable accessories for safety purposes. They share the metaphor of cover and protection. The glasses, however, has yet another symbolic meaning of assistive viewing. Colored and prescription lenses allow cyclists with different level of eyesight to adopt to see properly in various weather and lighting condition. To elaborate the metaphor further, the glasses could have lenses, which can allow seeing and feeling the remote cycling partner in an ambient manner. It is, therefore, use of light as the stimulus to increase the expressiveness of a cycling glasses has its inherent nature of sensory mapping.

The prototype utilizes variables of light, such as color, intensity, and frequency of flashing to deliver a general overview of the personal activity and the progress of the distant cycling partner. More importantly, the prototype intends to act and present in the light of intuitive and unobtrusive fashion, thus keeping the augmentation of the glasses as simple as possible is the key to this approach [21][22]. To go along with the idea of simplicity, there is a need to filter out the least data from the personal activity information. Speed is conceivably the core among the information. The rest of the data can be implicitly derived from it based on the idea that the higher the speed and time, the greater the heart rate and calories burned [23].

The mapping between the data and the light is as follows: The speed data corresponds to the intensity of light while the difference in riding distance determines to the color of light. When the cyclist exerts more effort into their speed, the brighter is the light [24]. Green and red indicate the relative position, in front or behind, to each other. In addition, the flash of light notifies approaching of the distance in between. To keep pace staying or placing a light competition with their partner, in either case, correlates to the aim of the design. The prototype is made of a Hall-effect wheel speed sensor, an ArduinoBT microcontroller[1], a cycling glasses with two LED built-in temples, and an Android-based mobile phone. The placement of each part is shown in figure 1.

3   Testing

A two-phase, in-lab and in-field, user study with 12 participants (postgraduates and undergraduates in both phases, 6 females, 6 males, M = 22.75 years, SD = 1.48) was conducted to see whether the design of the interface can be accurately and unobtrusively perceived. Three among the participants exercise regularly at least four times per week. The rest all expressed positively to the idea of exercise as a health behavior and go with it on friends-invitation basis. Prior to beginning of the in-lab study, a brief instruction regarding the information coding was given. The result indicates 92% of the participants can accurately identify the personal and remote partner's activity level. However, one female participant argued that the change in frequency of flash has more apparent implications on speed.

In the second phase, the participants were randomly paired. They all geared up as shown in figure 1 and took a 5km test ride in a riverside park on different bikeways. After completing the ride, all participants gathered and rested up in a cafe and were asked to verbally express their perceived level of personal activity. During the discussion, they all reported the increase in their activity level and considered that it is mainly due to the more aware of their personal activity as well as the comparison with remote partner's provided by the interface. Also, none of them felt distracted while riding. One pair of participants, a relatively active in doing exercise and a mild one, said that it started like a subtle competition, then in a matter of about ten minutes, it became more like a group ride. The more exercise-experienced peer naturally took the lead in terms of riding speed and so as distance. The other peer, at first, attempted to attack off the front and later figure out the different physical ability in between, then slow down to their moderate pace. At this point, the experienced peer also lowered their speed in order for the other peer to catch up.

4   Recommendations and Conclusion

This paper contributes towards a better comprehension of the copresence interface design for cycling. The hope is that the recommendations presented could help designers who are interested in this trend have a guided experience of placing technologies to create a motivational illusion for physical exercises. The

---

[1] ArduinoBT: http://arduino.cc/en/Guide/ArduinoBT

recommendations are as follows: (1) identifying personal physical activity information and the way it is delivered; (2) selecting and augmenting already-in-use accessories with relevant display media; (3) applying intuitive information encoding semantics. Hence, applications with an interface designed following the recommendations can be more assistive in motivating their users to exercise.

This research is in its early stages. The initial results that have raised a host of further questions:

- Will increased feelings of presence increase motivation in the long term so that the health and fitness goals will be achieved?
- Can the feedback be used to sustain the sense of presence in the longer term and will users find ways to appropriate the feedback mechanisms in ways that the designers never intended?
- Will the use of these complementary feedback mechanisms increase the feeling of presence without increasing the risks through distraction and ideally reducing the risks of cycling in large groups on busy roads?

The next stage will involve thorough usability evaluation of the prototype base on the above questions to see the influence on the cycling experience.

References

1. Barkhuus, L.: Designing ubiquitous computing technologies to motivate fitness and health. In: Grace Hopper Celebration of Women in Computing (2006)
2. Froehlich, J., Dillahunt, T., Klasnja, P., Mankoff, J., Consolvo, S., Harrison, B., Landay, J.A.: UbiGreen: investigating a mobile tool for tracking and supporting green transportation habits. In: Proceedings of the 27th International Conference on Human Factors in Computing Systems, pp. 1043–1052. ACM (2009)
3. Purpura, S., Schwanda, V., Williams, K., Stubler, W., Sengers, P.: Fit4life: the design of a persuasive technology promoting healthy behavior and ideal weight. In: Proceedings of the SIGCHI Conference on Human Factors in Computing Systems, pp. 423–432. ACM, Vancouver (2011)
4. Abowd, G.D.: What next, ubicomp?: celebrating an intellectual disappearing act. In: Proceedings of the 2012 ACM Conference on Ubiquitous Computing, pp. 31–40. ACM, Pittsburgh (2012)
5. Boks, C.: Design for Sustainable Behaviour Research Challenges. In: Matsumoto, M., Umeda, Y., Masui, K., Fukushige, S. (eds.) Design for Innovative Value Towards a Sustainable Society, pp. 328–333. Springer, Netherlands (2012)
6. Chang, T.-R., Kaasinen, E., Kaipainen, K.: What influences users' decisions to take apps into use?: a framework for evaluating persuasive and engaging design in mobile Apps for well-being. In: Proceedings of the 11th International Conference on Mobile and Ubiquitous Multimedia, pp. 1–10. ACM, Ulm (2012)
7. Consolvo, S., Everitt, K., Smith, I., Landay, J.A.: Design requirements for technologies that encourage physical activity. In: Proceedings of the SIGCHI Conference on Human Factors in Computing Systems, pp. 457–466. ACM, Montréal (2006)
8. O'Brien, S., Mueller, F.F.: Jogging the distance. In: Proceedings of the SIGCHI Conference on Human Factors in Computing Systems, pp. 523–526. ACM, San Jose (2007)

9. Priedhorsky, R., Jordan, B., Terveen, L.: How a personalized geowiki can help bicyclists share information more effectively. In: Proceedings of the 2007 International Symposium on Wikis, pp. 93–98. ACM (2007)
10. Babu, S., Grechkin, T., Chihak, B., Ziemer, C., Kearney, J., Cremer, J., Plumert, J.: A Virtual Peer for Investigating Social Influences on Children's Bicycling. In: Virtual Reality Conference, VR 2009, pp. 91–98. IEEE (2009)
11. Eisenman, S.B., Miluzzo, E., Lane, N.D., Peterson, R.A., Ahn, G.-S., Campbell, A.T.: BikeNet: A mobile sensing system for cyclist experience mapping. ACM Transactions on Sensor Networks (TOSN) 6, 6 (2009)
12. Rowland, D., Flintham, M., Oppermann, L., Marshall, J., Chamberlain, A., Koleva, B., Benford, S., Perez, C.: Ubikequitous computing: designing interactive experiences for cyclists. In: Proceedings of the 11th International Conference on Human-Computer Interaction with Mobile Devices and Services, pp. 1–11. ACM, Bonn (2009)
13. Outram, C., Ratti, C., Biderman, A.: The Copenhagen Wheel: An innovative electric bicycle system that harnesses the power of real-time information and crowd sourcing. In: EVER Monaco International Exhibition & Conference on Ecologic Vehicles & Renewable Energies (2010)
14. Reddy, S., Shilton, K., Denisov, G., Cenizal, C., Estrin, D., Srivastava, M.: Biketastic: sensing and mapping for better biking. In: Proceedings of the 28th International Conference on Human Factors in Computing Systems, pp. 1817–1820. ACM (2010)
15. Yasuda, S., Ozaki, F., Sakasai, H., Morita, S., Okude, N.: Bikeware: have a match with networked bicycle in urban space. In: ACM SIGGRAPH 2008 Talks, p. 41. ACM (2008)
16. Plante, T.G., Madden, M., Mann, S., Lee, G., Hardesty, A., Gable, N., Terry, A., Kaplow, G.: Effects of Perceived Fitness Level of Exercise Partner on Intensity of Exertion. Journal of Social Sciences 6, 50–54 (2010)
17. Zhao, S.: Toward a Taxonomy of Copresence. Presence: Teleoperators and Virtual Environments 12, 445–455 (2003)
18. Chang, A., Ishii, H.: Sensorial interfaces. In: Proceedings of the 6th Conference on Designing Interactive Systems, pp. 50–59. ACM, University Park (2006)
19. Antle, A.N., Corness, G., Droumeva, M.: What the body knows: Exploring the benefits of embodied metaphors in hybrid physical digital environments. Interact. Comput. 21, 66–75 (2009)
20. Jelle, S., Miguel Bruns, A., Stephan, W., Stoffel, K.: How to design for transformation of behavior through interactive materiality. In: Proceedings of the 7th Nordic Conference on Human-Computer Interaction: Making Sense Through Design, pp. 21–30. ACM, Copenhagen (2012)
21. Kalnikaite, V., Rogers, Y., Bird, J., Villar, N., Bachour, K., Payne, S., Todd, P.M., Schöning, J., Krüger, A., Kreitmayer, S.: How to nudge in Situ: designing lambent devices to deliver salient information in supermarkets. In: Proceedings of the 13th International Conference on Ubiquitous Computing, pp. 11–20. ACM, Beijing (2011)
22. Lund, A., Wiberg, M.: Ambient displays beyond conventions. In: British HCI Group Annual Conference (2007)
23. Lee, C.-L., Lee, D., Cheng, Y.-M., Chen, L.-C., Chen, W.-C., Sandnes, F.E.: On the implications of sense of control over bicycling: design of a physical stamina-aware bike. In: Proceedings of the 22nd Conference of the Computer-Human Interaction Special Interest Group of Australia on Computer-Human Interaction, pp. 13–16. ACM (2010)
24. Djajadiningrat, T., Geurts, L., Munniksma, P.R., Christiaansen, G., de Bont, J.: Rationalizer: an emotion mirror for online traders. In: Proceedings of DeSForM, Taipei, pp. 39–48 (2009)

Achieving Electronic Health Record Access from the Cloud

Brian Coats and Subrata Acharya

Department of Computer and Information Sciences, Towson University,
Maryland, United States
bscoats@umaryland.edu, sacharya@towson.edu

Abstract. There is an impending requirement for healthcare providers to enable widespread access to their electronic health record systems for the patients they serve. Programs such as the Department of Health and Human Services' Meaningful Use are providing monetary incentives to providers for offering this type of access but affording virtually no guidance as to how it could be accomplished. This research proposes a solution to this challenge by creating a flexible, proven framework that sets the stage for ubiquitous patient access to electronic health records, while preserving security and privacy. Using technologies such as OpenID and federated authentication, this research establishes a standardized approach for healthcare providers to follow to bridge their EHR systems to the Cloud and offer the type of pervasive electronic access the connected world demands.

Keywords: Healthcare Information Security, Identity Assurance, OpenID, Portable Identity, Identity Management, Federated Authentication.

1 Introduction

Healthcare providers are faced with mounting pressure to provide their patients easy and immediate access to their health information. The federal government has insttuted numerous programs and initiatives that account for much of this pressure. While these programs have mandates to provide access, virtually no stipulations have been given for usability or guidance for how this should be accomplished, merely that access provisions must exist. As such providers are left with the daunting task of making the process of electronic patient access simple and straightforward, while ensuring privacy and security. This research addresses the looming requirement of widespread electronic access to electronic health record (EHR) systems by patients.

The healthcare industry, like most industries, entered the digital age with each provider creating its own silos of data stores and corresponding security frameworks to access that data. The traditional model for authentication for all electronic systems, including EHR systems, is credentials used to validate identity are stored within the application being accessed, as depicted in Figure 1. This model involves users - practitioner and patient alike - being issued a credential such as a username and password, within their particular healthcare provider's EHR system. When the user

M. Kurosu (Ed.): Human-Computer Interaction, Part II, HCII 2013, LNCS 8005, pp. 26–35, 2013.

attempts to access the EHR system, they must enter the credential associated with that system to validate their identity. Therefore, if an individual interacts with multiple healthcare providers, thereby needing access to multiple EHR systems, they are required to have provider-specific credentials for each system. The establishment, issuance, and maintenance of digital identities and corresponding credentials creates a usability barrier for patients and similarly an efficiency barrier for healthcare providers. Now, many healthcare providers are finding themselves poorly positioned to enable the types of distributed access that EHR systems are supposed to facilitate. One of the most visible forces driving electronic patient access is the Department of Health and Human Services' (HHS) Meaningful Use programs. These programs authorize incentive payments to healthcare providers that use EHR technology to accomplish specific objectives in care delivery. Amongst the Meaningful Use objectives are requirements to provide patients timely access to their health records[1]. The recently released Stage 2 objectives, that start in 2014, require hospitals to grant patients access to view, download, and transmit their health information online within 36 hours of discharge; Eligible Professionals (EP) must provide this access within 4 business days[2]. These same regulations and programs that are driving EHR adoption provide almost zero guidance on how to address these enormous usability issues and efficiency challenges.

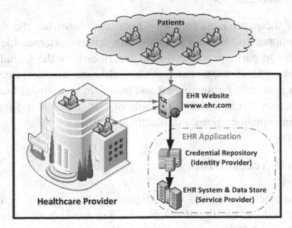

Fig. 1. Traditional EHR Access Model

In addition to the regulatory and financial pressures created by HHS, the White House is now creating yet another impetus. In April 2011 the White House released its final draft of the National Strategy for Trusted Identities in Cyberspace (NSTIC). NSTIC is singularly tasked with creating an "Identity Ecosystem" of interoperable technology standards and policies to be used across all sectors to provide increased security and privacy, but most importantly ease of use for individuals[3]. This strategy will force the healthcare industry to structure their identity access approaches to use a distributed model. All federal government agencies, including the HHS, are intimately involved in the development of NSTIC so it is imperative that healthcare providers ensure they are strategically aligned for participation.

This research proposes a solution to this challenge with a framework for healthcare providers to allow access of their EHR systems by their patients from the Cloud. The framework involves creating identity assurance profiles that follow National Institute of Standards and Technology (NIST) e-Authentication specifications. By conforming to the NIST standards, the profiles will introduce varying degrees of trust and assurance for the different identities the providers manage or interact with. Healthcare providers can then establish trust relationships based on these profiles with external authentication systems or Identity Providers. This would enable patient access to their EHR system using the patients' familiar Cloud credentials. These trust arrangements work within the HIPAA compliance guidelines to meet the Meaningful Use objectives while preparing providers to become engaged in cross-industry initiatives such as NSTIC. Specifically, the key contributions of this research to the healthcare information technology industry are:

- A comprehensive framework for healthcare providers to follow to enable external authentication systems to be used for patient access;
- A set of identity assurance profiles for Identity Providers to follow to ensure their practices conform to industry standards and meet HIPAA guidelines;
- Enhanced patient access for a national healthcare provider that assisted in the qualification for Meaningful Use Stage 1.

The remainder of the paper is as follows: Section 2 describes the federated access model and its components; Section 3 details the criteria external Identity Providers must meet in order to participate; Section 4 describes how the Cloud is specifically incorporated as an authentication source for a healthcare provider; Section 5 explains how this research is already being applied and benefiting a national healthcare organization; finally Section 6 summarizes the goals of this research and its importance to the landscape of information security in healthcare.

2   Federated Access Model

When it comes to electronic access to applications, there are 3 core questions to be addressed: 1) who does the digital identity belong to, 2) how does the individual prove their identity, and 3) what should the user be allowed to access or carry out in the application? Within the digital identity space, these questions are known as identity management (IdM), authentication, and authorization respectively. The IdM aspect of access consists of the systems that establish and track who an individual is and allows other systems to relate a digital identity to an physical human. The majority of individuals have any number of identifiers that make up their digital identity and it is the IdM system that correlates that information. Authentication and authorization are often confused and mistakenly used interchangeably, but it is important to understand their distinct purposes. The authentication step is how users assert their identity to an application whereas authorization deals with what that user can do within that application such as read, write, or modify data. It is important to understand this differentiation as this research is specifically aimed at the authentication portion of the access equation. The authentication event itself can be broken down into 3 key pieces: the user, known as the Subject, with possession of some set of credentials; an authentication system that can validate credentials, known as the Identity Provider (IdP); and the application to which identity is attempting to gain entry, known as the Service Provider (SP). As Figure 1 shows, traditional systems have the credential repository or IdP built into the application itself. This model creates a dependency that in order to access the application the corresponding, internal credential must be used. A primary objective of this research is to eliminate this dependency. While authorization decisions must inherently be made with the application itself, the authentication decisions can almost always be externalized. The premise of this research contends that all EHR systems should allow the authentication process to be externalized from the rest of the EHR application. Fundamentally, EHR applications need to be able to use other identity stores to validate credentials, beyond those stored in the local EHR database. Luckily, this basic functionality is supported by all the major commercial EHR offerings in some fashion and the real effort lies in getting these EHR systems to play by the same basic rules.

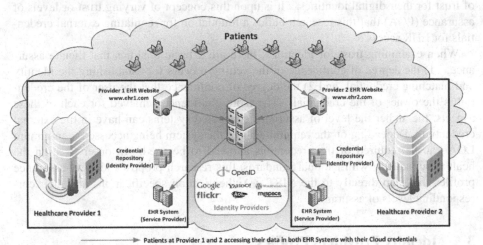

Fig. 2. Federated EHR Access Model using the Cloud

By leveraging the ability to separate the authentication process from the EHR application, this research proposes a framework by which multiple authentication systems can be used by a single EHR system, as shown in Figure 2. As long as the authentication is performed by a trusted Identity Provider, the EHR system can be assured the user has adequately verified their digital identity. The true value of this model is realized in healthcare providers effectively outsourcing the entire patient credentialing effort to other entities that have already made significant investments in that arena. The central function of an IdP is to be an authoritative source for establishing and maintaining identities and corresponding credentials. As such, potential IdPs could be commercial vendors like Verizon, Comcast, or AT&T that have existing business relationships with individuals. These companies already have processes in place for validating the identity of their customers and providing them credentials. Likewise, an IdP could be an entity such as Google, Yahoo!, Microsoft, or MySpace, that may have a different type of business relationship but nonetheless tracks relevant identity information and credentials.

It is essential to recognize that while the federated access model moves the authentication of users to an external system, the healthcare provider must have an internal identity management system to map the external IdP's identifiers to EHR users. It is extremely unlikely that the healthcare provider and the external IdPs all have the same key identifier. For many of the free IdPs, this identifier is an email address, whereas most EHR systems will likely use something entirely different such as a Social Security number, Patient code, or some other such identifier. Once these different identification schemes are reconciled, a healthcare provider's IdM system can translate an external identifier into the internal identifier. Beyond the identifiers of a digital identity, it is imperative to analyze the security requirements and practices of each Identity Providers for establishing their identities and credentials. Depending on how these practices are carried out, IdPs should effectively be extended a proportionate amount of trust for their digital identities. It is upon this concept of varying trust or levels of assurance (LOA) that this research builds a foundation for regulating external credentials for EHR access.

When examining trust for identities, there are 2 basic qualities that dictate assurance: 1) the degree of confidence in the vetting process for establishing the identity and matching credential, and 2) the degree of confidence that the user of the credential is the owner of the credential. The more confidence achieved for each of these aspects, the higher the level of assurance connected systems can have in the external credential. Depending on the requirements of the system being accessed, a minimum LOA can be required of the credentials allowed to be used. In order to align the healthcare industry with national standards, this research proposes identity assurance profiles that map directly to the NIST e-Authentication specifications and their corresponding levels of assurance.

3   Identity Providers Profiles

In 2003, NIST was mandated by the Office of Management and Budget (OMB) to establish technical standards to support 4 key levels of assurance. As a result, NIST published the Electronic Authentication Guideline[4] which still serves as the regulatory standard for all electronic authentication of federal agencies. The four levels are:

- Level 1: Little or no confidence in the asserted identity's validity.
- Level 2: Some confidence in the asserted identity's validity.
- Level 3: High confidence in the asserted identity's validity.
- Level 4: Very high confidence in the asserted identity's validity.

In response to the NIST standards, the Centers for Medicare & Medicaid Services (CMS) issued detailed requirements for e-authentication and levels of assurance when accessing electronic protected health information (ePHI) covered by the Health

Insurance Portability and Accountability Act (HIPAA)[5].   CMS requires the equivalent of NIST LOA 2 identity assurance for accessing your own health information and LOA 3 for accessing someone else's.   Therefore potential IdPs for EHR systems must be able to achieve the appropriate identity assurance equivalence depending on the activity.   This research provides detailed identity assurance profiles for IdPs to follow to achieve NIST Levels 1-3, enabling them to reliably guarantee the LOA their digital identities assert.   For the purposes of EHR access, the LOA 1 profile is out scope, although it does have a number of other useful applications.   While many of the criteria are the same for all the profiles, key difference is the higher the LOA of the identity being asserted, the higher the standard for how the identity was established, how the credentials issued, how the user asserts their identity, and the general integrity of the business practices of the IdP.   A summary of the criteria for each profile is provided in Table 1.

Table 1. Criteria for Identity Provider LOA Profiles

Category	Criteria	LOA 1	LOA 2	LOA 3
A. Organizational Requirements	1. Certification	♦	♦	♦
	2. Legal Status	♦	♦	♦
	3. Liability Provisions	♦	♦	♦
	4. Policies and Practices	♦	♦	♦
B. Infrastructure Guidelines	1. Software Security		♦	♦
	2. Physical Security		♦	♦
	3. Network Security		♦	♦
C. Identity Creation and Proofing	1. Identity Establishment		♦	♦
	2. Identity Proofing		♦	♦
	Existing Relationship		♦	♦
	In-Person Proofing		♦	♦
	Remote Proofing		♦	♦
	3. Record Retention		♦	♦
D. Identity Management Practices	1. LOA Classification per Identity	♦	♦	♦
	2. Consistent Data Definitions	♦	♦	♦
	3. Informed Consent	♦	♦	♦
E. Credential Management	1. Subject Interactions		♦	♦
	2. Revocation		♦	♦
	3. Reissuance		♦	♦
	4. Record Retention		♦	♦
F. Authentication Guidelines	1. Unique Identifier	♦	♦	♦
	2. Minimum Entropy of Authentication Secret	14 bits	20 bits	64 bits
	3. Protection of Authentication Secrets	♦	♦	♦
	4. Assertion Security	♦	♦	♦
	5. Multi-Factor Authentication			♦
G. Risk Mitigation	1. Acceptable Use Policies	♦	♦	♦
	2. Business Continuity	♦	♦	♦
	3. Attack Resistant	♦	♦	♦
	4. Single Sign-on (SSO)	♦	♦	♦
	5. Credential Sharing Resistant	♦	♦	♦

The Organizational Requirements category details the basic guidelines for each IdP to obtain certification for each level of assurance.   IdPs must demonstrate they are a legitimate entity and qualify to be recognized as an authoritative source of identity for other organizations. IdPs must also establish they can provide appropriate levels of liability for their actions. Finally, IdPs must guarantee they possess documented policies and procedures and their actual practices are consistent with those documents.

The Infrastructure Guidelines section provides guidelines the Identity Provider's IT environment must follow. All software used for: transactions of identities, credentials, and assertions; the authentication process; credential issuance and maintenance; and identity data storage must be kept up to date and patched to ensure appropriate security. Similarly, IdPs must have adequate physical and network security at the locations where their identity data is stored.

The Identity Creation and Proofing category covers how identities are created, vetted, and proofed. While LOA 1 provides no true confidence that the identity being asserted matches an actual person, LOA 2 and 3 must verify the identity data collected is based on public records or government-issued IDs. Following identity registration, the identity must be proofed to ensure the information collected represents an actual person, that the information can uniquely distinguish a single individual within the IdP's system, and that the person requesting the registration matches the identity being registered. There are 3 basic methods that can be used to perform the identity proofing: the person is already known through an existing relationship; the person can be proofed in-person; or the person can be proofed remotely using additional verification checks against established accounts at financial institutions or utility companies. This category also includes requirements for record retention.

The Identity Management category describes how each Identity Provider defines, asserts, and releases identity information. IdPs must assign their digital identity to a specific LOA and address the possibility of accidental LOA elevation. This section lays out a standard set of data definitions for identity data for all IdPs to utilize to ensure interoperability with EHR systems. Finally, IdPs must incorporate informed consent capabilities into their transactions such that users are presented the specific data being released about them and have the ability to consent or deny its release.

The Credential Management section covers how credentials are to be used in transactions. IdPs must ensure users reassert their identity for each transaction in some reliable fashion. IdPs will also guarantee that credentials will be revoked immediately if they are no longer valid for any reason. Additionally, if credentials are ever reissued, users must provide information from prior transactions like pre-registered questions and responses before the identity is reinstated. Lastly, IdPs are required to maintain a record of all credential management activities including issuance, revocation, expiration, and reissuance for a period of at least 180 days. This amount of documentation is vital for IdPs to satisfactorily establish non-repudiation for the user's transactions.

The Authentication Guidelines category covers the requirements of the authentication process for the different levels of assurance. This includes IdPs ensuring all issued credentials are universally unique to a single individual. The authentication secret portion of the credential - often a password - must meet a minimum entropy or resistance to guessing, depending on the LOA. Entropy can be impacted by a variety of methods such as the length of the password, complexity requirements of characters included in the password, and expiration period and reuse of the password. For LOA 2 and 3, the CMS-approved LOA for ePHI access, a minimum entropy for the authentication secret is 20 bits and 64 bits respectively. This means LOA 2 secrets must have no fewer than a 1 in 1,048,576 or 2^{20} chance of being guessed and LOA 3 resistance is 2^{64}. Additionally, IdPs that assert LOA 3 identities need to employ multi-factor authentication when validating the user. All levels require that IdPs use industry-standard encryption algorithms to provide ample protection to their identity data both while at rest and during all transmissions.

Risk Mitigation is described in the last section of the profile. Every IdP must possess acceptable use policies and record their users' periodic agreement to said policies. IdPs must also make efforts to minimize the chance of system failures to ensure normal business continuity. Further, if a failure does occur, the IdP must make certain the failure wouldn't compromise the security of their system or allow an inaccurate identity assertion to be sent to an EHR system. Additionally, IdPs are required to show their authentication systems are resistant to various attacks including replay and eavesdropping. For IdPs that utilize any type of single sign-on (SSO) technologies, industry-standard techniques and encryption must be employed to guarantee the integrity of the identity assertions. Lastly, each IdP is responsible for enacting safeguards to resist credential sharing, either accidental or intentional.

4   Integrating the Cloud

The identity assurance profiles provide all participating entities a known set of technical and functional rules in which to operate. Before an actual implementation can begin, it is vital for the participants to standardize on a specific technology to facilitate the actual sharing and exchanging of identity information. There are actually quite a number of organizations and foundations currently working in the identity space related to portable digital identities and a handful of mature standards have emerged. The prominent standards that have emerged are: 1) Security Assertion Markup Language (SAML), 2) OAuth, 3) WS-Trust, and 4) OpenID. While all these technologies can potentially offer a similar solution, this research proposes that OpenID is the most suitable identity standard currently available. As many organizations decide to adopt one standard or the other, significant work is being done in parallel to erect bridges between the technologies to expand the possibilities of interoperability even farther. Therefore it is arguable that the specific standard decision is as critical as the commitment to adopt a standard and then move quickly and surely to make the necessary organizational and technical choices.

There is a clear advantage to choosing a standard that has wide adoption already as it lowers the barriers for entry. OpenID consists of the most common Identity Providers in the Cloud including Google, Yahoo!, Flickr, MySpace, and AOL. Its corporate members include such companies as Microsoft, PayPal, Symantec, and Verizon, which combine to form an organization with momentous market share in the digital identity space. Over a billion OpenID enabled accounts exist already and are in use by more than 50,000 websites today[6]. The federal government legitimized

OpenID as a key integration technology by certifying an OpenID profile for LOA 1 and expansion to include LOA 2 and LOA 3 is currently underway. This only further signifies the wide adoption of this technology by the public and private sectors. OpenID is a seasoned, established standard and has been incorporated into this proposed framework to be the underpinning for identity and credential creation.

While the OpenID standard accommodates the authentication event, it is critical providers have a mechanism by which a user's OpenID identity can be correlated to the organization's record of that identity. This mapping process can happen any number of ways, either with end-user involvement or not. A simplistic approach offered by this research is a user-driven registration process. This process involves the patient going to a registration site, hosted by the healthcare provider, and entering key pieces of personally identifiable information to establish their identity with the provider. Next, the patient would choose an OpenID IdP and enter the corresponding credentials. After the credentials are validated by the OpenID IdP the correlation is complete and the user then can use their Cloud credentials to access the healthcare provider's systems. This straightforward approach is used extensively within the Cloud today by many merchants and web resources, presenting options such as 'Register with Google'. Healthcare providers can easily emulate this process by letting their patients attach a Cloud credential to their identity in the provider's EHR.

5   Pilot Implementations

To demonstrate the feasibility of this research, a partnership was formed with a large national hospital to host a series of pilots and proof-of-concept activities. The partner hospital has over 800 licensed beds and more than 300,000 patient admissions every year. As such, this hospital wanted to leverage industry standards and technologies, without taking on additional overhead, to solve their patient access issues. Using this research's framework, the hospital was able to integrate with Cloud IdPs as well as act as an IdP itself for some federal government resources. By acting as an IdP, the hospital was able to provide their practitioners access to 11 National Institutes of Health (NIH) resources using their hospital credentials, most notably PubMed, the Clinical Translational Sciences Award (CTSA) Management System, the Flow Cytometry Experiment and Reagent Management System (FERMS), and the Address Lookup Tool (ALT) for National Children's Study. The hospital also implemented an OpenID pilot project for a variety of scheduling applications including the radiology and diagnostic testing. These integrations allowed their patients to schedule, modify, and view appointments using their Cloud credentials and then viewing results following their visits. These pilots have noticeably improved the usability of these systems for patients, while reducing the associated support costs of the hospital. Reducing user support overhead is a key benefit of the Cloud access model. With only a very modest time investment, healthcare providers can effectively outsource patient account support to the Cloud and get out of the business of supporting an internal system that issues, maintains, and revokes identities and credentials for all their patients. The projects and pilots at the partner hospital have demonstrated this research offers practical solutions to the dilemma of providing widespread patient access to a health-care provider's resources. The hospital is evaluating how this model can be extended to other and e-Prescription applications based on the success thus far.

6   Conclusion

There is significant work being done in the digital identity space across all industries. It is not surprising all this work is moving in the same relative direction resulting with all industries and technologies converging to form a larger interoperable community. Ubiquitous access is rapidly becoming both a reality and expectation of our connected society. The Meaningful Use programs are just a piece of this larger evolution and force healthcare providers to enable patients greater and easier access to their health information. Concurrently, NSTIC is building a solid foundation for cross-industry collaboration of user access to a multitude of electronic resources within both the private and public sectors. With healthcare providers contemplating when not if, it is imperative that they adopt scalable and interoperable solutions to not only satisfy the immediate needs but be poised for the future. This research combines and builds on many of the lessons learned by other industries to provide a practical solution to a potentially overwhelming issue. Even with the early success being realized by the adoption of this initial research, there is much work left to complete to further broaden its application. The next stage of this research involves examining how the different federating technologies and standards can work together. The next permutation of the proposed access model is to become technology-agnostic to only expand the horizon of possible integrations even further. This framework, with OpenID at the core, will bridge the gap from the healthcare industry to the commercial/social identity space and ensure interoperability with all other industries into the future.

References

1. United States. Department of HHS. CMS. CMS EHR Meaningful Use Overview,
   http://www.webcitation.org/6E1KQGZLj (last accessed June 2012)
2. United States. Department of HHS. CMS. Stage 2 Overview Tipsheet,
   http://www.webcitation.org/6E1LmvS1B (retrieved December 2012)
3. United States. Department of Commerce. NIST. About NSTIC,
   http://www.nist.gov/nstic/about-nstic.html (last accessed November 2012)
4. United States. Department of Commerce. NIST. Electronic Authentication Guide (rev 1),
   http://csrc.nist.gov/publications/nistpubs/800-63-1/
   SP-800-63-1.pdf (retrieved December 2011)
5. United States. Department of HHS. CMS. CMS System Security and e-Authentication Assurance Levels by Information Type,
   http://www.webcitation.org/6E1MqJfeW (retrieved November 2012)
6. OpenID Foundation. What is OpenID?
   http://openid.net/get-an-openid/what-is-openid/ (retrieved November 2012)

User Requirements for the Development of Smartphone Self-reporting Applications in Healthcare

Michael P. Craven[1], Kirusnapillai Selvarajah[1], Robert Miles[2], Holger Schnädelbach[2], Adam Massey[3], Kavita Vedhara[3], Nicholas Raine-Fenning[4], and John Crowe[1]

[1] The University of Nottingham, Electrical Systems & Optics Research Division, Faculty of Engineering, University Park, Nottingham NG7 2RD, United Kingdom
{michael.craven,kirusnapillai.selvarajah,
john.crowe}@nottingham.ac.uk
[2] The University of Nottingham, School of Computer Science and Information Technology, Jubilee Campus, Nottingham, NG8 1BB, United Kingdom
{psxrsm,holger.schnadelbach}@nottingham.ac.uk
[3] The University of Nottingham, School of Community Health Sciences, University Park, Nottingham NG7 2RD, United Kingdom
{mjxajm,kavita.vedhara}@nottingham.ac.uk
[4] The University of Nottingham, Division of Obstetrics & Gynaecology, School of Clinical Sciences, Queen's Medical Centre (QMC), Nottingham, NG7 2UH, United Kingdom
nick.raine-fenning@nottingham.ac.uk

Abstract. Two case studies of the development of Smartphone self-reporting mHealth applications are described: a wellness diary for asthma management combined with Bluetooth pulse oximeter and manual peak flow measurements; and a questionnaire for ecological assessment of distress during fertility treatment. Results are presented of user experiences with the self-reporting application and the capture of physiological measurements in the case of the asthma diary project and the findings from a phone audit at an early stage of design in the case of the in vitro fertilisation (IVF) study. Issues raised by ethics committees are also discussed. It is concluded that the optimal adoption of Smartphone self-reporting applications will require a good appreciation of user and ethics panel requirements at an early stage in their development, so that the correct design choices can be made.

Keywords: mHealth, Self-monitoring, Adherence, User experience, Consumer and User, Ecological interfaces, Evaluation methods and techniques, Human Centered Design and User Centered Design, Human Factors Engineering Approach, Meaningfulness and Satisfaction, New Technology and its Usefulness.

1   Background

Mobile health (mHealth) applications based on cellular phones, Smartphones and tablet computers are a rapidly growing trend in healthcare. The World Health Organization recently surveyed fourteen categories of mHealth services: health call centres,

M. Kurosu (Ed.): Human-Computer Interaction, Part II, HCII 2013, LNCS 8005, pp. 36–45, 2013.
© Springer-Verlag Berlin Heidelberg 2013

emergency toll-free telephone services, managing emergencies and disasters, mobile telemedicine, appointment reminders, community mobilization and health promotion, treatment compliance, mobile patient records, information access, patient monitoring, health surveys and data collection, surveillance, health awareness raising, and decision support systems [1].

In the area of patient monitoring, the recording or self-reporting of patient health state or well-being has the potential to become ubiquitous through the use of Smartphone Apps. Furthermore, connection of Smartphones to sensors capable of physiological measurement (carried or wearable on/in the body or clothes, or present in the near environment) and storing or transmitting the data, promises to expand the established uses of medical 'remote' and 'ambulatory' monitoring based on conventional medical devices. These innovations should enable individuals to better monitor their own health, keep carers informed, or aid healthcare professionals in giving advice or informing treatments. Examples of applications in existence include self-reporting of physical health states or mood, behaviours (such as alcohol use) and those recording regular or continuous readings from devices (e.g. weight, level of exercise, blood glucose levels), entered either manually or through wireless connections. Another example of self-reporting that could transfer well to Smartphone technology is ecological momentary assessment, a methodology which highlights the benefits of repeated sampling in real time in subjects' natural environments [2].

With Smartphone technologies the distinction between health service remote monitoring and patient self-monitoring is becoming blurred. For instance the involvement of clinicians in presenting or interpreting results for the patient may be reduced with users either expected to, or wishing to, do more for themselves.

Whilst the usability of Apps and mobile devices is a natural area of study for HCI researchers [3] and context of use has been studied for medical devices from a human factors systems perspective, including adherence to self-monitoring [4], the contextual user requirements of mHealth have been little explored. McCurdie et al. have noted that mHealth interventions are often designed from the healthcare system perspective rather than with a user-centred approach [5]. Whilst Smartphones (and tablets) are becoming ubiquitous, potential users of mHealth applications will also have different existent practices for communication and receiving reminders, e.g. text messages on non-internet mobile phones, and different prior experiences in their use of the Internet, e.g. on a Desktop or Laptop PC, or none at all.

2   Case Studies

2.1   First Case Study: Mild Asthma Self-reporting with and without Physiological Measurement

The first case study concerns persons with mild asthma. This condition presents a measurable lowering of blood oxygenation levels both leading into and during an exacerbation, such that sufferers are often given oxygen following an attack [6]. Furthermore asthma can be directly or indirectly related to psychological states such as anxiety, panic or depression [7] which may be manifest in other physiological measurements, e.g. heart rate. Severity of asthma can also be measured by lung function, one measure of which is Peak Expiratory Flow (PEF). This project was a pilot study of self-reporting by means of a daily Smartphone questionnaire with or without regular additional physiological measurements, to study user requirements and interactions between self-reporting and measurement tasks. Eleven volunteers self-reported their wellness once a day for two weeks using a Smartphone web App, with physiological measurements taken in the second week only. Participants were males of age 18+ who reported having mild asthma, recruited by emails to university mailing lists and poster advertising. Ethical approval was obtained from the University of Nottingham Computer Science ethics committee and participants received a cash inconvenience allowance of £25 each week of the two week study. Volunteers were scheduled to visit the university to begin their participation, where they were provided with a Participant Information Sheet and given an opportunity to ask questions and ensure that they fully understood the information before signing a consent form.

The ethics committee initially expressed a concern for data security which was fulfilled by using an HTTPS connection with password protection. For analysis, the data was downloaded over a secure connection to university computers, with the usual safeguards restricting access to named personnel. Smartphones were lent to the users by the project researchers and no user identification was collected or stored on the phone. In addition, participants were able to set a passcode to lock the phone, preventing unauthorised access.

Each participant first completed a questionnaire devised by Juniper et al. [8] which involves choosing up to five activities in which the individual feels limited by their asthma and answering a series of questions about their health over the last two weeks. The questions included the extent to which the person was limited in their activities, the frequency of specific symptoms and emotions (e.g., breathlessness, interference with sleep, fear of not having medication available) and degree of discomfort or distress experienced (e.g., from coughing). The responses were then used to pre-populate an electronic version of the questionnaire (Fig. 1) that was closely based on Juniper et al. but modified in our study to ask only about the current day and prefaced with an additional yes/no question, 'Have you had a severe exacerbation of your asthma today?'. The daily questionnaire was hosted as an online form, to be accessed through the Smartphone web browser.

For the additional physiological measurements (collected in the second week only) the study used off-the-shelf technologies (Fig. 2): an Android phone running the SimpleEye Live Pulse Oximeter App [10] in association with a Nonin 9560 Onyx II Bluetooth-enabled fingertip pulse oximeter which is able to record heart rate and blood oxygen saturation (SpO_2) data with a one second sampling period. In addition, peak expiratory flow was measured using a Mini-Wright Standard Range peak flow meter, using the EU scale in accordance with ISO 23747.

The details of the self-monitoring task were as follows:

— **First week**
  • *Each weekday evening*
    ■ Complete the questionnaire on the Smartphone.
— **Second week**
  • *Each weekday morning*
    ■ Take 3 peak expiratory flow measurements and enter on the Smartphone.
    ■ Record 5 minutes of pulse oximeter data using the App.

- *Each weekday evening*
  - Take 3 peak expiratory flow measurements and enter on the Smartphone.
  - Record 5 minutes of pulse oximeter data using the App.
  - Complete the questionnaire, as done in the first week.

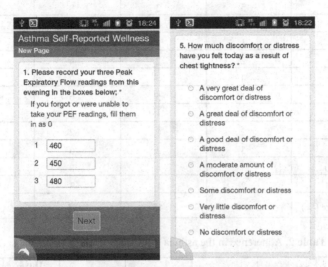

Fig. 1. Screenshots from the Asthma Self-Reporting Wellness mHealth web App

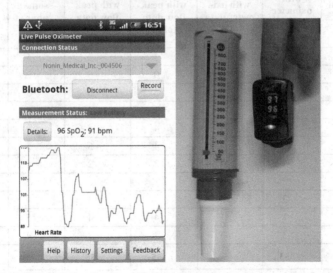

Fig. 2. SimpleEye Live Pulse Oximeter App, pulse oximeter and peak expiratory flow meter (screenshot and photograph by authors)

Table 1. Adherence in the asthma pilot study: Diary data

Participant	Days with diary entries, week 1 (of 5)	Days with diary entries, week 2 (of 5)	Days with diary entries, total (of 10)	Days with full diary data (of 10)
1	5	3	8	6
2	3	0	3	3
3	1	1	2	2
4	2	2	4	3
5	4	5	9	8
6	1	5	6	4
7	4	1	5	4
8	2	0	2	2
9	3	3	6	4
10	4	4	8	4
11	2	1	3	3
Average (%)	56	45	51	39

Table 2. Adherence in the asthma pilot study: Physiological data

Participant	Mornings with oximeter data (of 5)	Afternoons with oximeter data (of 5)	Mornings with peak flow data (of 5)	Afternoons with peak flow data (of 5)	Days with some phys. data (of 5)	Days with full phys. data (of 5)
1	4	4	3	3	5	1
2	0	0	0	0	0	0
3	2	2	5	5	5	2
4	3	4	1	2	4	1
5	4	5	4	5	5	4
6	3	4	4	5	5	3
7	4	3	2	2	5	0
8	2	2	1	0	2	0
9	3	3	3	3	4	1
10	1	1	4	4	5	0
11	3	3	3	1	4	1
Average (%)	53	56	55	55	80	24

The time of each data collection episode was recorded in order to analyse user adherence to the self-monitoring. A short semi-structured interview was conducted at the end of the two week session to ask participants questions about: 'Using the technology'; 'Effect on Lifestyle'; 'Effect on Condition'; 'Thinking about Condition';

'Difference between the two weeks'. Statistical analysis of the data in SPSS using the Wilcoxon Signed Ranks Test was also performed to compare the questionnaire answers between the two weeks (although no significant correlations were subsequently found, which may be due there being no difference or because of the small sample size).

It can be seen from Table 1 that, on average, participants completed the diary on around half of the intended number of days, with a maximum of 5 days in both weeks and a minimum of 1 day in week one and 0 days in week two. On average, the second week with the additional physiological readings resulted in a smaller number of diary days being completed (although this difference was not statistically significant in a Wilcoxon Signed Ranks Test). No participant fully completed the diary every day for the full ten days. Users fully answered the questionnaire on an average of four out of the ten days (with at least one answer omitted on the other days). In the second week adherence to (or ability to perform) physiological data collection was a little over half of the maximum number of days with little difference between morning and afternoon, however the proportion of days with full physiological data was only one quarter overall (Table 2).

From summarising the post-study interview transcripts it was found that:

- 5/11 participants said they found the technology 'nice' or easy to use. Two found it 'interesting'. Six experienced some (mostly minor) technical problem either with internet/Wi-Fi, Bluetooth or battery. One was not confident about data upload having succeeded. One said it was 'sometimes a bit of a hassle ... overkill for mild asthma'.
- 5/11 participants said that taking part had had little to no effect on their lifestyle or that they had 'got used to it'. One said he had been more cautious about remembering his inhaler. One reported the need to plan when going out. One reported interference with daily activities. Two reported difficulty or annoyance scheduling the recordings correctly. One mentioned the inconvenience of having to sit down to take measurements.
- 11/11 participants said that taking part in the study had no effect on their condition itself, although one had experienced a worsening during the study.
- 7/11 participants said that they were thinking more about, or were more aware of, their condition whilst taking part. Two qualified this by saying it was a 'good thing'. One expressed the opinion that 'thinking about a cough exacerbates it'.
- 8/11 commented on differences between the two weeks. Two commented on the quantitative nature of the recordings and its relation to how they were feeling. Three said the second week with the physiological recording was 'less convenient' or 'took a bit more time'. One said it was 'a lot more difficult'. One reported 'no inconvenience'.

2.2   Second Case Study: IVF Treatment Stress Diary

The second project concerned women undergoing in-vitro fertilisation (IVF) treatment. It is known that IVF is a 'multidimensional stressor' and the treatment itself is most likely to evoke anxiety [10]. Ecological momentary assessment during IVF treatment may shed light on the dynamics of distress, using a technique that is already considered to be highly promising for mood disorder research, see [11] for example. 76 women attending a fertility clinic completed a questionnaire about mobile phone usage in order to inform the App design in a forthcoming study to examine distress during IVF treatment. The new App would be run on patients' own phones, allowing them to complete entries in a stress diary in a secure manner [12]. First, information was obtained regarding phone usage and preferred modes of communication amongst the user group (since this was an audit it did not require ethical approval). Audit questions were posed as follows:

1. What type/model of mobile phone do you have?
2. Is your mobile phone a smart phone?
3. Which air time provider are you with?
4. Is the phone on pay as you go or on contract?
5. Do you use email or internet access on your phone?
6. Is internet coverage included in your contract?
7. Do you use an alarm clock function?
8. Are you familiar with the use of 'Apps' on your phone?
9. How regularly do you use an 'App' on your phone?
10. If you were to be asked to report your distress levels throughout your treatment which of the following methods would you prefer?

Table 3. Results of phone audit (a) Phones & functions   (b) Frequency of App use (c) Communication preference

(a) Phones & functions	Yes %
Is your mobile phone a smart phone?	75
Do you use email or internet access on your phone?	80
Is internet coverage included in your contract?	82
Do you use an alarm clock function?	92
Are you familiar with the use of 'Apps' on your phone?	80

(b) Frequency of App use	%
Not at all	26
Everyday	53
Weekly	17
Monthly	4

(c) Communication preference	%
App	58
Text Message	30
Telephone conversation	8
Questionnaire	1
Other	3

From the survey, in which all participants had access to some kind of mobile device, it was found that 75% of users owned what they considered to be a Smartphone. The majority (74% of all phone users) had either Apple iPhones or ones that were Android based. Minority phones included Blackberry devices or Nokia handsets (mostly without internet access). App use was found to be prevalent amongst 74% of all phone users (and almost all Smartphone owners). In addition, 90% of all phone users were on a contract with the rest on Pay-As-You-Go (across a wide variety of networks). Communication preferences are given in Table 3 that also contains details of responses to the other audit questions. These results show a majority preference for an App but also include preferences for other modes of communication (SMS text, voice, paper questionnaire). Email was mentioned in the 'Other' category. Furthermore, there was a high usage of an alarm clock function.

The subsequent ethics committee submission to an NHS panel raised some interesting points. In particular, the panel thought that text messaging could potentially compromise confidentiality and security of the data if the phone was lost. In contrast an advantage of using an App would be that data would be recorded on a secure server with password protection. Also for this particular project, the potential use of telephone conversations as a method of prompting/signalling users to carry out the ecological assessment was considered to be an unacceptable burden because this would entail ringing the patients every two days; it would also have been a burden to the researcher.

The panel did not specifically comment on the use of email as a means of communication, although there are similar issues to that of texting with respect to confidentiality. However, the main issue with email from a study point of view is that signalling the patient and their response by email would be subject to delays, dependent upon how their inbox is updated. A benefit of developing an App with immediate prompting is that the signal to the patient and their response are expected to be as close in time as possible, which is fundamental to the method of ecological momentary assessment.

3   Conclusions

The results of the two case studies highlight some important user considerations when using Smartphones for patient self-reporting of wellness. In a patient population, even one where all users have experience with some kind of mobile device, there will be a spectrum of phone capabilities and different existent preferences for modes of communication. This is a shifting landscape which will continue to change as newer mobile devices become more prevalent (e.g., iPads/tablets) and older ones become obsolete. Furthermore, some communication preferences will not be easily supported by a single stand-alone App, especially if the implementation is not a native App that is able to access all of the functions of the phone (e.g. the alarm clock).

If patients/users are using their own phones there are additional ethical concerns with respect to confidentiality compared with a study where phones are supplied by researchers. Modes of communication that are ethically acceptable are dependent on the security of the data handling and their burden on the user. Security concerns may limit the use of SMS texting or email as alternative modes of communication in contrast with more secure server-based methods that can be used via an App. Texting and voice calling to signal a patient may place an unacceptable burden on them if a high frequency of self-reporting is required. Ethics experts may therefore need to be included as stakeholders in the App development process before committing to particular aspects of technology or study design. Regulators are also clearly aware of the potential risks of Apps, especially those that are associated with medical devices.

A self-reporting task inevitably interacts with a user's lifestyle, which whilst it may not be a problem to some can cause difficulty, inconvenience or annoyance to others. Even if the self-monitoring task does not detrimentally affect their condition, as we found in our small asthma study, some users may become more aware of it and find this intrusive. However, this could be viewed as a positive effect that could result in better adherence to medication (as referred to by the user who was reminded to take his inhaler out more often during the study). Alternatively, users may believe that thinking about a symptom (e.g., a cough) can act to exacerbate it, although this effect was not reported.

Obtaining self-reported data on only half of all possible days in the asthma diary study was not entirely unexpected, since treatment adherence is known to be low for chronic conditions, but this clearly has implications for study designers who wish to ensure consistent data collection and achieve a statistically significant sample size. Adherence to self-reporting can also be affected by the intensity of the task. It is seen in the asthma diary case study that in the second week with more intensive testing (with the addition of physiological measurements), self-monitoring was found to be more inconvenient to some users and this is also possibly borne out by the smaller number of days of self-reporting, on average, compared to the first week (although this difference was not statistically significant). An intensity effect has also been noted in patient self-monitoring of blood glucose, where adherence was lower for more intensive self-monitoring during a research trial [13]. Such effects should be noted when introducing multiple measurements or more frequent sampling with a self-monitoring App, or if the App is used in parallel with other forms of data collection.

Acknowledgements. MC, KS and JC acknowledge support of this work through the MATCH Programme (EPSRC Grant EP/F063822/1) although the views expressed are entirely their own. MC was involved with both case studies, KS and JC with the IVF case study. HS and RM acknowledge support of a Xerox Research Centre Europe (Grenoble) donation for the support of studentships in Ubiquitous Computing within the Mixed Reality Laboratory at the University of Nottingham, for the asthma diary project. The IVF project and involvement of NRF, KV and AM was supported by Nurture Fertility.

References

1. World Health Organization: mHealth: New horizons for health through mobile technologies: second global survey on eHealth (2011),
   http://www.who.int/publications/goe_mhealth_web.pdf (accessed December 17, 2012)

2. Preece, J., Rogers, Y., Sharp, H.: Interaction Design: beyond human-computer interaction, 3rd edn., p. 191. Wiley (2011)
3. Sharples, S., Martin, J., Lang, A., Craven, M., O'Neill, S., Barnett, J.: Medical device design in context: A model of user-device interaction and consequences. Displays 33(4-5), 221–232 (2012)
4. McCurdie, T., Taneva, S., Casselman, M., Yeung, M., McDaniel, C., Ho, W., Cafazzo, J.: mHealth Consumer Apps: The Case for User-Centered Design, pp. 49–56, AAMI Horizons (Fall 2012)
5. Shiffman, S., Stone, A.A., Hufford, M.R.: Ecological Momentary Assessment. Annual Review of Clinical Psychology 4, 1–32 (2007)
6. Inwald, D., Roland, M., Kuitert, L., McKenzie, S.A., Petros, A.: Oxygen treatment for acute severe asthma. BMJ 323(7304), 98–100 (2001)
7. Cooper, C., Parry, G., Saul, C., Morice, A., Hutchcroft, B., Moore, J., Esmonde, L.: Anxiety and panic fear in adults with asthma: prevalence in primary care. BMC Family Practice 8(1), 62 (2007)
8. Juniper, E., Guyatt, G., Epstein, R., Ferrie, P., Jaeschke, R., Hiller, T.: Evaluation of impairment of health related quality of life in asthma: development of a questionnaire for use in clinical trials. Thorax 47(2), 76 (1992)
9. SimpleEye Live Pulse Oximeter App., http://simpleeye.com/platforms/android/live-pulse-oximeter/ (accessed October 10, 2012)
10. Verhaak, C.M., Smeenk, J.M.J., Evers, A.W.M., Kremer, J.A.M., Kraaimaat, F.W., Braat, D.D.M.: Women's emotional adjustment to IVF: a systematic review of 25 years of research. Hum. Reprod. Update 13(1), 27–36 (2007)
11. Wenze, S.J., Miller, I.W.: Use of ecological momentary assessment in mood disorders research. Clinical Psychology Review 30, 794–804 (2010)
12. Selvarajah, K., Craven, M., Massey, A., Crowe, J., Vedhara, K., Raine-Fenning, N.: Native Apps Versus Web Apps: Which is best for healthcare applications? In: Proc. HCI International 2013 (in press, 2013)
13. Farmer, A., Wade, A., Goyder, E., Yudkin, P., French, D., Craven, A., Holman, R., Kinmonth, A.-L., Neil, A.: Impact of self monitoring of blood glucose in the management of patients with noninsulin treated diabetes: open parallel group randomised trial. BMJ 335(7611), 132 (2007)

Electronic Health Records: A Case Study of an Implementation

Guillaume Cusseau, Jon Grinsell, Christopher Wenzel, and Fan Zhao

Florida Gulf Coast University, Florida, USA
fzhao@fgcu.ed

Abstract. Since healthcare institutions have to manage efficiently many tera-bytes of data on their patients, they need tools that allow them to have an easy access to their data and that enable them to share their data with every specialist involved in the treatment of a patient. That's why they increasingly adopt EMR and EHR systems. As they are quite recent systems, healthcare institutions usually lack of experience to implement these systems. The purpose of this paper is to do a case study on the implementation of an EHR system in a local healthcare institution, and then to analyze this case study to give directions so as to avoid some arising issues.

Keywords: EHR, EMR, Implementation, Case Study.

1   Introduction

Health services play a crucial role in society. By curing people adequately, they participate to the increase in their lifetime. According to the *Bureau of Labor Statistics* [1], there were about 661,400 physicians and surgeons in the US in 2008, which means that for a population of about 310 million, each one has about 470 patients. When we consider this number, we think that the doctors should be very well organized to collect and analyze information on their patients, in order to deliver an adapted treatment. That's why information systems are very useful to help healthcare institutions to manage large quantities of data on their patients. There are mainly two types of information systems dedicated to the healthcare industry: the Electronic Medical Record (EMR) and the Electronic Health Record (EHR).

"An Electronic Medical Record (EMR) is a computerized medical record created in an organization that delivers care, such as a hospital or physician's office." (Wikipedia). EMR is the legal record created by healthcare providers. Essentially, it is just an electronic version of the same paper form doctors have used for decades. EMR allows physicians to get rid of large quantities of stored paper files on their patients, and enables them to have easily access to structured information. In the electronic form, the information is allowed to be shared and viewed much more quickly by those who need the information. The main limitation to this technology is that it is cannot easily be sent out from the original location to other doctors or caregivers. In this way, they are similar to paper records in that many times they must be printed out and sent physically to other locations for processing.

M. Kurosu (Ed.): Human-Computer Interaction, Part II, HCII 2013, LNCS 8005, pp. 46–55, 2013.
© Springer-Verlag Berlin Heidelberg 2013

The term EHR can briefly be defined as the concept of a longitudinal and cross-institutional record of a patient's health and healthcare. [2]

Tatum states, "Electronic health records are copies of an individual's medical history that is stored as electronic data" [3]. According to Walker, Bieber, and Richards [4], EHR improves communication of clinical data that facilitates doctors and concerned health professionals carry out their duties effectively and efficiently. EHR is one of the most important aspects of any healthcare company or organization because it helps doctors and employees manage all administrative and professional activities using the information stored in the EHR system by the authorized employees.

Carter states, "EHR systems designed for physicians' offices represent the simplest architecture consisting of three basic components: the database management system, user interface, and external interfaces" [5]. An EHR system is not only used for collection of patient related data but also it is used to process, analyze, and disseminate the collected information or data in order to carry out different activities related to provision of healthcare to the patients. "The medical records can cover a wide range of aspects of the patient's health while stored in a format that is easily transferable between health providers" [3].

It is necessary to understand the difference between Electronic Medical Record (EMR) and Electronic Health Record (EHR). Often these terms are used interchangeably however these terms are certainly different.

The main difference between EHR and EMR is the ease of transmission. EHR is designed to allow the patient records to be sent and received by those who need the information. The information moves with the patient wherever they go. Whether it is a specialist or simply a laboratory which is conducting blood analysis, the information can be shared quickly with EHR. Additional EHR functionality is that it may allow the patient to review and look at their own medical records. By being able to look at a timeline of blood tests the patient may be able to ask his or her doctor more informed questions. Patients may also be more motivated to make lifestyle improvements if they are able to view their progressively worsening health. This is done much more quickly via electronic means. EHR possesses this capacity and are thus the direction the health industry is moving towards.

As EHR is better adapted to the current needs of healthcare institutions, and as EHR is a quite recent trend in the industry, we focus our study on the implementation of EHR in a local healthcare institution.

Many vendors now offer EHR systems. But as this type of systems is quite recent, their functions may not be well adapted to physicians' needs yet. Moreover, the experience in the implementation of EHR is not very extensive. However, any error in the information on the patient may make the doctor interpret wrongly symptoms and deliver an inadequate treatment, which may lead to devastating consequences for the patient.

This study investigates the problems that a typical physician may encounter while implementing and then using EHR systems. Through an investigation in a local healthcare institution, which has recently adopted EHR, we look for the common problems that any physician can encounter while implementing EHR systems, and then we analyze them to give directions on how to solve them. This study is aimed at helping healthcare institutions to manage the implementation of their EHR.

2   Literature Review of Success Factors in Implementing EHR

The success of a healthcare company without implementation of an EHR system is impossible in the today's world. It is because there is a lot of competition between companies these days and only those companies can get competitive advantage which keep up to date information about different issues related to diagnostic methods and treatments. An EHR system provides companies with various benefits related to the information management. A health company can make use of an EHR system to ensure quick processing of data needed to provide quick treatment to the patients.

The benefits and efficiency of using EHR system can be evaluated by comparing the past and present organizational performances. EHR systems definitely improve the performance of any healthcare organization by providing them with many considerable benefits, such as, documentation of patient-doctor interactions, retrieving medical histories quickly, making referrals, increased storage capacity, and customized view of relevant information. "An EHR also represents a huge potential for cost savings and decreasing workplace inefficiencies" [12]. Considering these advantages, a well-structured EHR system is definitely productive for any healthcare organization.

The implementation of electronic medical records (EMR) decreases patient sufferance, which often occur because of medical errors [13]. Quick collection of information and provision of accurate information to the healthcare providers are two of the most significant aspects related to the EMR systems. As we know that doctors often write in illegible style, which leads to inaccurate data entry into files by a second or third party. "With EMR this problem will mostly become a thing of the past" [14].

"Electronic health records reduce the chances for medical errors because they contain all information necessary, which in turn creates more accurate and clearer reports" [15]. Data security is another key aspect of EHR because the computerized data prevents unauthorized people from accessing the data. An efficient EHR system not only improves data security but also provides benefits to the health consumers. Moreover, the data is not lost in case of any hazard because it can be saved at more than one place. EHR also helps health professionals in the analysis of information by providing them with accurate and up to date information about the patients. Complete medical histories of the patients can be stored in their respective folders, which can help health professionals retrieve that data easily and quickly when needed. Quick retrieval of accurate information also helps doctors provide instant medical care to the patients, which is a considerable benefit for the health consumers.

ERP systems also facilitate healthcare companies in managing their business processes through providing them with efficient mechanism in the form of electronic health record system to manage information. Oz states, "Information is the lifeblood of any organization" [16]. An Electronic Health Record system means management of all medical information, which is required to administer different business activities.

An EHR system is a part of internal business control system that manages company's documents, people, procedures, and information technology. Stahl found that information systems promote efficiency and optimal control of business processes [17]. Today, a health services providing company can never be successful without implementation of an EHR system because such systems keep proper record of all information that is needed to run the business activities effectively.

There are a number of factors, which make a healthcare company implement an electronic health record system. Let us discuss some of those factors in some detail in order to get a better understanding of how those factors influence the working of the healthcare companies.

One of the main challenges in the implementation of this system in a healthcare setting is the ability of the employees to use such system. Management of the healthcare organization where such system is to be used, should first provide proper training to all concerned employees regarding use of this system and then they should go to implement it. The management should consider all technical and social issues while training the employees. The employees should be made aware of the importance of information security or privacy of the patients' information so that they should not disclose any patient's information to any unconcerned person. Young found that some other problems in the implementation of electronic health record system are organizational and human issues, such as, untrained medical professionals and rise in unemployment due to automated systems that need to be resolved in order to implement for an electronic documentation record system in the healthcare companies [19]. Although money is saved by using electronic medical records, such as, reduced cost of papers and labor, but the concerns arising due to these factors should not be ignored.

Next important element of an EHR system is its consistency and reliability. Only authorized employees are allowed to collect the data. The EHR system processes the data in a consistent manner. It is because if the data will be processed consistently, the users of the EHR system will not have any difficulty in using the information generated by the system. The management of any healthcare company needs to apply such mechanisms that should be able to bring necessary changes to the system when required. Data consistency acts as the foundation for an efficient EHR system. If the data will not be processed and compiled in a consistent manner, it will be very difficult for the users of the EHR system to run the business operations of any organization efficiently.

Accuracy is another key element of an EHR system. It means that information provided to the users of the system should be precise and accurate in all aspects. All departments of an organization make use of reports generated by the system, so it is essential for an EHR system to generate accurate and properly checked information in the reports. Accuracy of internal controls is of extreme importance for the proper functioning of the system.

Another important element of an EHR system is relevance, which means providing relevant information to the concerned departments. The EHR system provides relevant information to the concerned professionals. Irrelevant or unrelated information is of no use and it leads to time wastage and ineffective decision-making. An efficient EHR system is one that provides relevant and desired information to the users.

Completeness is also one of the key elements of an EHR system, which means to provide users with complete information regarding any matter. However, completeness does not mean that the report should have a huge detail about any specific matter as it creates information overload, rather only relevant and pertinent information should be provided to the concerned departments.

3   Research Method

Data was primarily collected for the case study using semi-structured interviews with doctors, transcriptionists and the resident EMR specialist at the Cape Coral office location.   Qualitative and quantitative data was collected including certain e-mails regarding the implementation of the system.

4   Analysis and Discussion

Southwest Florida Neurosurgical Associates (SWFNA) is a full service medical practice which treats patients showing symptoms of back, spine or brain injury.   The company employs six different doctors which are spread throughout the three locations.   SWFNA offices are located in Fort Myers, Cape Coral and Punta Gorda.   The practice was begun with only three neurosurgeons in 1990.   At this time they only provided surgical care.   The organization now includes six neurosurgeons, two physical therapy divisions, an onsite spinal decompression unit, five physiatrists and a therapy suite which includes onsite MRI capabilities.

The practice is board certified to treat such symptoms as neck/lower back pain, herniated disks, arthritis of the spine and degenerative disc disease.   SWFNA regularly prescribes over 100 prescriptions per month to their patients.   Due to the nature of their field, many times these prescriptions are for pain medication to be taken after surgery.   The abuse of pain medication by certain individuals has made it necessary for any EMR platform to track and monitor all prescriptions for such drugs.

After gaining an understanding of why EHR is superior to EMR it is easy to see why healthcare providers may wish to make the switch.   This was the case with Southwest Florida Neurosurgical Associates.   SWFNA had employed EMR in the form of Misys, a popular platform used by many healthcare providers.   This system had been in place for some time and the employees were able to become adjusted to the system.   The system was well liked by the staff and performed all functions which were deemed necessary.

Although the system was functioning properly and there were few complains, the management team was compelled to change to EMR.   Management feared that soon EHR would be mandated.   In addition to this the government was offering subsidies to medical practices which would make an early switch to EMR.   Motivated by this favorable environment, management decided to make the financial decision to adopt the new EHR system at this opportune time.   The decisions about switching to a new system fell into the hands of the chief financial officer.   This individual acts as the CEO of the organization.   Research was done primarily online and through speaking to salespeople.   Finally the CFO decided on Allscripts EHR solution.

The timeline for implementation was somewhat rushed due to time constraints involving the government subsidy to migrate to EMR. As a result, employees were only alerted to the fact that the switch would be taking place approximately one month before the go live date. Due to the small size of the organization, SWFNA did not employ a CIO or even any in house technical staff. The practice outsources all of its IT needs. Many of the decisions that were made prior to the implementation were made solely on the information provided by the proposed EHR provider.

SWFNA elected to use Allscripts EHR solution. Again, due to the size of the organization SWFNA would rely on Allscripts to implement the EHR themselves and provide any technical support needed. Allscripts informed the practice that their employees would need twenty hours of training each prior to the implementation. This training was scheduled to take place online at the leisure of the employees. Allscripts has a website called AllscriptsAcademy. At this website trainees are allowed to log in through a portal and access a sample of Allscripts EHR. The employees however had their own ideas. They were paid for an eight hour work day. These eight hours were filled with medical related tasks that fit their job description. The employees would be required to use their own free time if they were to receive training on the system.

Obviously this did not create great motivation on the employees end to go out of their way to receive the needed training. The staff communicated to management that if they were not being compensated, they would not be willing to receive this extra treatment. Management was then faced with a decision to either stop their business processes for a period of time to allow training or alter their plans. Understandably, the revenue generating business processes were given priority and the training was reduced to a single training session on 9/12/2011 which did not include hands on experience for the trainees. One employee however in each office received extensive training with the system. In interviews, the employees admitted that they viewed the training session as unneeded and did a very poor job of paying attention.

For the implementation Allscripts sent down three EHR specialists from North Carolina to oversee the process and troubleshoot any issues for the first three days of implementation. One specialist was stationed at each office. A big bang approach was used as all offices went live on the same day. The system first went live on 4/18/2011. Employees of the company described this day as a day of chaos.

On the day the system went live, employees hated the new system. They had not received training and were not able to use the Allscripts platform. Employees hated the new platform and expressed that they liked the old system. The new Allscripts system was not used on this day by the employees. Employees would instead hand write prescriptions for patients. They also had no access to patient information. In a very embarrassing situation, each patient had to be asked about their medical history as it could not be retrieved from the system by the untrained staff. The staff hated the new platform. The first day of implementation was extremely embarrassing and unproductive for the employees.

In each office there was one employee (usually a transcriptionist) that received extensive training with the system. On the second day of implementation this employee took the time to show the rest of the staff how to use the basic functions that were needed to treat patients. If an employee had a problem they would call the extensively trained individual over for help. Over time, the employees learned the new system and can now appreciate its benefits. Although the lack of training disallowed the system to support the staff initially, the system in itself performed exactly as it should and no major technical glitches were observed during the implementation.

There was little to no modification of the Allscripts EHR. SWFNA employed a small R implementation strategy. Minor changes in business processes however did occur. These small changes mostly included learning the new steps to complete the same task as well as adjusting to the process of sending and receiving EHR information. The system does not match the business process requirements of SWFNA exactly. In some instances which are detailed later employees are forced to perform certain tasks manually or without the help of the Allscripts EHR. The practice however lacks the ability and motivation to change the Allscripts EHR to better fit the needs of the employees and patients and simply makes do with what they were given.

In interviews with employees it was learned that overall the Allscripts EHR works very well. The main resistance with the program stems from the initial learning process employees had to undergo to learn the program. The biggest complaint about the system is the amount of information the employees are required to enter into the system. Every small piece of information must be entered in the system whether it may be a new allergy or test results. This however is more a matter of medical bureaucracy and thoroughness of care and has little to do with the Allscripts platform. Employees are required to keep extremely detailed records regardless of EMR or EHR platforms.

The Misys EMR which was used prior to Allscripts is still used in one regard. SWFNA employees were not impressed with the Allscripts appointment system so they retained the Misys version. There is no single individual responsible for the EHR system. At each of the three offices there is one person assigned to look over the system. These individuals receive very little training and typically get in touch with Allscripts support to fix any problems. In addition to this minimal training these individuals are also in charge of medical coding at the office. Their time is divided and mostly spent on the medical coding portion of their job.

Each employee at the practice has their own computer station. So that they can access the needed information the employees use a remote desktop application. In this way employees can access the EHR when they are on call and at home without ever walking into the office or hospital. The system typically updates every few weeks and users are asked to be logged off at that time to avoid any issues. Allscripts provides any support the SWFNA employees require. There is no on site EHR specialist.

The employees of SWFNA like that Allscripts allows them to easily look up patient history such as allergies. Another major advantage of Allscripts is that employees are able place and view flags on certain patients. These flags are useful for those patients who are often no-shows or have a history of abusing pain medication. Employees also value the ability to see what other doctors have dictated during their visits with a patient. The sharing of this information makes it much easier when conducting a second opinion or reviewing past visits. Overall the system does exactly what it is meant to.

SWFNA employees however do not like the system Allscripts uses to identify when patients in the waiting room are ready to see a doctor. Often times patients are filling out paperwork and the physician's assistant is not able to discern if they have finished yet to know when to call them back. Also the system does not display what room a patient is in for the appointment. This can lead to the doctor seeing patients out of order and long wait times for some patients. Another con to this system is that it takes so long to chart the patients vitals in the Allscripts system that the employees often do not have time to enter them into the system. These valuable records are often lost due to time constraints.

Another major problem employees had with the system was a malfunction which appeared after an update of the system. Allscripts performed an update which was incompatible with the firm's appointment system. This incompatible update caused roughly half the appointments to not shown in the Misys appointment system. The next Monday patients were coming in without the staff knowing they were going to come in. One of the doctors had even left the office under the false impression he had no patient appointments. Allscripts was contacted and found a solution within three days. For those three days all patient appointments had to be entered and tracked manually to ensure accuracy.

SWFNA employees also complained about the patient message system. When a patient has a question for the doctors the phone number of the patient and the question are entered into the Allscripts EHR so that the employees can call this patient back. The Allscripts solution does not allow employees to identify if the patient has been responded to by another employee. This leads to confusion and often times repeat calls to the patient increasing the work load of the staff. The last complaint of the staff is that the EHR does not differentiate which doctor the patient belongs to. The staff must then sometimes spend time to figure out which doctor the patient is seeing. These redundant tasks take away from the efficiency of the practice.

5   Conclusions

The SWFNA implementation of Allscripts yields some valuable information about small business EHR implementation. In particular one of the main lessons learned was that it is extremely difficult to get employees to actually receive training. Employees have long workdays and must even be called in to perform emergency surgeries. The last thing an employee wants to do when he or she gets home is begin EHR training.

It is suggested that another firm undertaking a similar implementation should pay their employees to learn the system before the go live date. Employee resistance should be expected as any change will require additional work on their part. The employees will lack motivation to learn new systems if they are not forced to do so. One critical factor in the implementation that prevented training to occur was the lack of a project champion. The CFO of the company was the driver for change. This individual knows very little about EMR software implementation. He simply relied on the information given to him from Allscripts.   He did not realize the problems the lack of training would induce.

Management should also make a point of notifying their employees of the EMR change more than a month prior to implementation, as was the case in this example. Employees must be well informed and not surprised by any changes to the system.

The decision to have one Allscripts EHR staff member at each location seemed to work very well.   These employees were sorely needed to teach the staff how to use the EHR and deal with any glitches the implementation may have ran into. Staying for three days appears to be a reasonable amount of time to train employees.

The strategy of extensively training one employee at each office location seems to have worked very well.   SWFNA made it one specific person's job to learn the EHR program extensively.   This person was a transcriptionist meaning they use the program very often and never see patients.   This allows them to always be available for any questions other employees may have.   This is a very economical solution to not having any in house IT staff.   By blending jobs they kill two birds with one stone.

Overall SWFNA performed admirably in implementing Allscripts EHR.   Other than some minor glitches the system works very well.   None of the employees have any technical experience with any EMR software yet they were still able to identify a suitable EHR solution and implement it on budget and on time.   Such an accomplishment is not easy for a small business which does not have a CIO or any IT staff of its own.

References

[1]   Bureau of Labor Statistics, Occupational Outlook Handbook, 2010-2011 Edition, http://www.bls.gov/oco/ocos074.htm#emply
[2]   Burns, F.: Information for Health: An information strategy for the modern NHS 1998-2005. A national strategy for local implementation (2006)
[3]   Tatum, M.: What are Electronic Health Records? Wisegeek.com, n.d. Web, http://www.wisegeek.com/what-are-electronic-health-records.htm (November 21, 2011)
[4]   Walker, J., Bieber, E., Richards, F.: Implementing an Electronic Health Record System. Springer, London (2005)
[5]   Carter, J.: Electronic Health Records: A Guide for Clinicians and Administrators, 2nd edn. American College of Physicians, U.S.A. (2008)
[6]   Hoerbst, A., Ammenwerth, E.: A Structural Model for Quality Requirements regarding Electronic Health Records – State of the art and first concepts
[7]   Blacharski, D.: What is ERP (Enterprise Resource Planning)? Wisegeek.com. Web (September 22, 2011), http://www.wisegeek.com/what-is-enterprise-resource-planning.htm (November 21, 2011)
[8]   Chester, K.: Benefits of Enterprise Resource Planning (ERP) Systems. Ezinearticles.com. Web (February 04, 2011), http://ezinearticles.com/?Benefits-Of-Enterprise-Resource-Planning-(ERP)-Systems&id=5855906 (November 21, 2011)
[9]   Ge, X., Paige, R.F., McDermid, J.A.: Domain analysis on an Electronic Health Records System

[10] Hristidis, V., Clarke, P.J., Prabakar, N., Deng, Y., White, J.A., Burke, R.P.: A Flexible Approach for Electronic Medical Records Exchange

[11] Torrey, T.: The Benefits of Electronic Medical Records (EMRs). About.com. Web (April 11, 2011),
http://patients.about.com/od/electronicpatientrecords/a/EMR benefits.htm (November 21, 2011)

[12] Gurley, L.: Advantages and Disadvantages of the Electronic Medical Record. Aameda.org. Web (2004),
http://www.aameda.org/MemberServices/Exec/Articles/spg04/ Gurley%20article.pdf (November 21, 2011)

[13] Chimezie, O.: Electronic Health Record. Articlebase.com. Web (April 11, 2011),
http://www.articlesbase.com/health-articles/electronic-health-record-4581106.html (November 21, 2011)

[14] Artio, C.: Advantages of Electronic Health Record System. Ezinearticles.com. Web (August 06, 2009),
http://ezinearticles.com/?Advantages-of-Electronic-Health-Record-System&id=2720601 (November 21, 2011)

[15] Pounders, A.: What Are Electronic Health Records? Ezinearticles.com. Web (October 01, 2011),
http://ezinearticles.com/?What-Are-Electronic-Health-Records?&id=6598849 (November 21, 2011)

[16] Oz, E.: Management Information Systems, 5th edn. Thomson Learning, Canada (2009)

[17] Stahl, B.: Information Systems: Critical Perspectives, 6th edn. Routledge, Oxon (2008)

[18] Kuziemsky, C.E., Williams, J.B.: Towards Electronic Health Record Support for Collaborative Processes

[19] Young, K.: Informatics for Healthcare Professionals. F.A. Davis, Philadelphia (2000)

[20] Frankk, D.: Enterprise Resource Planning - An Introduction. Ezinearticles.com. Web (August 01, 2011), http://ezinearticles.com/?Enterprise-Resource-Planning—An-Introduction&id=6464120 (November 21, 2011)

[21] Sartipi, K., Yarmand, M.H., Down, D.G.: Mined-knowledge and Decision Support Services in Electronic Health

[22] Tang, C., Carpendale, S.: Evaluating the Deployment of a Mobile Technology in a Hospital Ward

[23] Ebadollahi, S., Tanenblatt, M.A., Coden, A.R., Chang, S.-F., Syeda-Mahmood, T., Amir, A.: Concept-Based Electronic Health Records: Opportunities and Challenges

Healthcare Interoperability: CDA Documents Consolidation Using Transport Record Summary (TRS) Construction

Philip DePalo, Kyung Eun Park, and Yeong-Tae Song

Dept. of Computer & Information Sciences, Towson University, Towson, MD, USA
pdepal1@students.towson.edu, {kpark,ysong}@towson.edu

Abstract. Thanks to recent medical record standards and distributed technology, the exchange of medical documents has become readily available. Healthcare institutions are able to share documents with other providers; however, patients who require medical transport are still subject to rudimentary exchange of information through verbal reports and outdated hand written medical notes. An ongoing exchange of medical documents between patient transport units and the facilities they serve would help reduce medical errors. Our approach searches for available documents that are relevant to the patients' current conditions based on medical coding within these documents, clinical document architecture (CDA) documents, using HL7 message exchange mechanism in SOAP envelopes. These CDA documents are then consolidated into a single transport record summary (TRS) document to filter out redundancies and provide destination medical service provider with the most pertinent information that is readily accessible to both human and machine. In a time critical environment, access to multiple documents from difference sources is not likely feasible. For this reason, we proposes a CDA document consolidation tool, the TRS Constructor, which creates a TRS by querying and analyzing patient's multiple CDA documents. The new TRS will be registered into the Health Information Exchange (HIE) environment for cross-reference across healthcare facilities and other providers.

Keywords: Enterprise architecture, electronic health records (EHR), electronic health record, hospital IT management, health information technology, interoperability, clinical document architecture (CDA), Health Level Seven (HL7), Transport Record Summary (TRS).

1 Introduction

Sharing a single medical record among medical facilities is the goal of the US Government defined meaningful use directive. It is not only the adoption of the electronic health record (EHR), but the ability to use it in multiple specific ways. Blumenthal [1] objectifies the need to exchange key clinical information electronically between providers. Our proposed method addressed this objective in a patient population that is transported annually by critical care transport teams. Johns Hopkins [2]

M. Kurosu (Ed.): Human-Computer Interaction, Part II, HCII 2013, LNCS 8005, pp. 56–65, 2013.
© Springer-Verlag Berlin Heidelberg 2013

estimates 27,500 patients are transported by the Johns Hopkins Lifeline Critical Care Transport team. This accounts for only one hospital in one state. Currently transport medicine clinicians do not have access to patients' electronic health records. Boockvar [3] hypothesized transitions of care without an EHR would lead to increased adverse drug events. EHR absences can also lead to unrecognized medical drug allergies, incomplete medical histories and poor access to previous care provided. Our methods provide access to a health information exchange (HIE) to retrieve current medical documents on a patient requiring transport, reducing errors and improving patient outcomes through more directed cares and accurate medical histories.

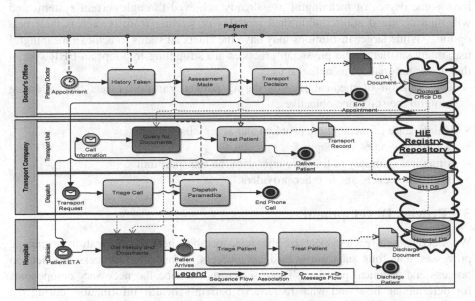

Fig. 1. Proposed Medical Transport Business Process Model

We propose new methods to querying medical documents during patient transport and consolidating them into a single XML compilation based on relevant information for the specific problem. This query uses the local HIE and the eHealth Exchange, formerly the Nationwide Health Information Network [4]. Through these two step processes, we form a machine readable XML-based CDA document that provides up-to-date information of the patient.

In section 2 we review meaningful use and explain its objectives and how our methods meet some of these objectives and provide benefits to providers. In section 3, we show our analysis methods used to develop our proposal through various enterprise architecture scenarios affecting health IT. Section 4 details our plan for medical record consolidation and proposes a tool for the construction. Section 5 and 6 wrap up our findings along with our plan to implement the proposed tool.

2   Meaningful Use

In the American Recovery and Reinvestment Act the US government details a staged approach to standardizing electronic health records. Only the first two stages have been released to date with the second only recently released. We concentrate on stage one for our proposal. There are 15 specific criteria for Meaningful Use [6] stage one. Among these basic criteria includes computerized medication order entry, drug-drug and drug-allergy check lists, generate and transmit electronic prescriptions, and maintaining medication, problem and allergy list. Many larger institutions will have some degree of meaningful use already achieved through current systems and will then decide if adding additional modules or starting from scratch is their best option. While larger institutions may have the financial status to achieve meaningful use, many smaller single physician practices are struggling to adopt an EHR system that meets the goals of meaningful use.

Consolidation of medical records during patient transport meets the following meaningful use stage one objectives:

- Maintenance of medication, problem and allergy lists.
- Documentation of vital signs
- A medical summary of the encounter with the transport unit
- Information exchange to other providers.

3   Process Development

We decomposed each aspect of the interoperable health information exchange processes into four subgroups: business process, information process, application process and technical process. These scenarios describe the necessary components for determining how and what to retrieve patient's health information during the transport.

3.1   Business Scenario

Fig 1. shows the proposed business process model. The darker colored sections indicate where changes have been made to the current process. The doctor creates a medical summary document based on the current visit and stores it in his office on their local data store that participates in the state HIE. A transport request is made by the doctor to 911. The transport clinicians are now able to query the HIE for any relevant documents about this patient. The transport unit creates a transport record and stores it in their local data store which also participates in the HIE. The transport unit also updates the destination hospital with estimated time of arrival (ETA). Upon notification the hospital team can query for records that include both the doctor's office visit medical summary and the Transport Record Summary (TRS) [8] which we previously developed. They are then able to begin to treat and determine the appropriate care plan for this patient upon arrival, which may include an additional medical transport to a higher level of care.

3.2   Information Scenario

Information during the patient visit is compiled into a medical summary XML document. When the document is stored, the type of document and patient identifiers are updated in the HIE registry. Steel's ontology describes messaging resources using on call type and location to dispatch a transport unit using EDXL Sharp [9]. The transport unit queries the HIE for information.

During this process relevant information about the patient is gathered. The goal is to provide pertinent medical history that can assist with the current problem. A semantic search will produce these results based on current factors and additional medical coding available in all documents. It is formatted into a single XML document that eliminates redundancies, but highlights areas of concerns based on current patient conditions and past medical histories. The transport unit also interacts with the patient and updates the local data store with a TRS document. The receiving hospital is electronically notified about the incoming patient. This notification allows the hospital to access all available documents.

3.3   Application Scenario

The doctor's office can view the Personal Health Record for updated information through their EHR system. This system also allows creation of continuity of care documents. Two applications are in use during the medical transport: Computer Aided Dispatch (CAD) and an EHR. The calls are triaged by dispatch by entering details gathered during the phone call as well as the location information which can be acquired through the Enhanced 911 (E911), permitting emergency response personnel to pinpoint the location of a cellular telephone caller anywhere in the United States following the events of "9/11" [10]. The CAD determines the closest and appropriate level of transport unit.

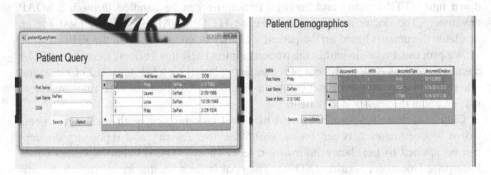

Fig. 2. Transport Application Interface Screenshots

The transport unit has an EHR system which will access the HIE and produce a single document, by consolidating CDA documents, comprising of all relevant information based on a semantic search. An example of such a system is shown in Fig 2. This EHR will also update the HIE with a new TRS document based on the care provided.

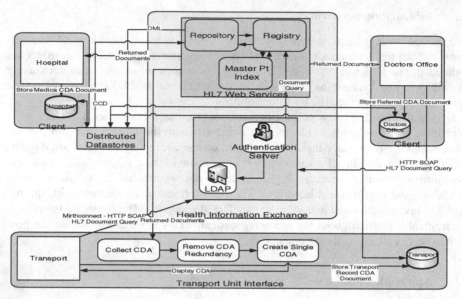

Fig. 3. Interoperable Transport Architecture

3.4   Technical Scenario

Fig 3. shows the applicable software architecture along with the messages to post and retrieve documents. The client application interface is used to interact with the HIE. There are multiple ways Health Level Seven (HL7) messages can be specified. The transport interface has the ability to use client or server side connections such as HTTP [11] and mirthconnect [12] as an interface engine. The HTTP can be broken down into HTTP headers and bodies. Packaging can be handled through a SOAP envelope. The doctor's office can make an HTTP SOAP message request for an available documents based on the patient's history or update made in the PHR [13].

We propose a module within the transport units EHR that collects the queried CDA documents, strips each document of redundancy, based on XML tags, ICD Codes, and other recognized standards, and creates a single CDA document with relevant information about the transported patient.

Chiu [14] describes standards used in global e-commerce, with trade agreements stored as documents between business entities; this registry and repository concept can be applied to healthcare information technology. The standard is called Cross Enterprise Document Sharing (XDS). The goal is for a healthcare institution or entity to be able to provide and register an HL7 continuity of care document set [15]. The clinical documents are organized into three levels: the narrative documents, section level content and entries for unique coding and semantics [16]. The documents are provided to the repository and then the repository is asked to register them with the registry. This request must contain the metadata describing the documents, at least one object per document, a link to the new documents and references to existing documents. If the request does not complete, the repository will send an error.

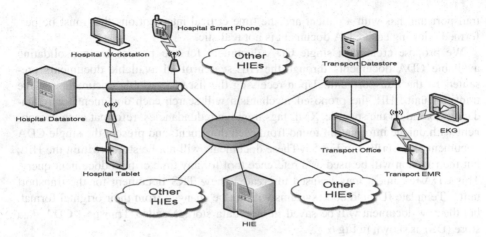

Fig. 4. Network Model

Fig 4. shows that collection starts at the personal medical environment of patient monitoring devices such as an Electrocardiography or EKG. These can be connected via USB or Bluetooth methods and even low powered local area networks such as ZigBee Health [17]. Aside from the connection of local monitoring devices, the transport unit would use Wide Area Networks technologies such as Cellular GPRS, EDGE, 3G/4G and WiFi. Wired networks such as Ethernet or DSL are more unlikely given the mobile environment of the service.

Databases can consist of MSSQL servers and messages between these doctor/hospital systems are handled through Message Oriented Middleware (MOM). MOM allows applications to talk over different systems and network protocols which would be encountered when moving between systems. Applications would typically run on computer equipment designed for a rough environment. These devices are manufactured to withstand the rugged environment of 911 and interfacility transport providing waterproof, impact proof and drop proof systems.

4 CDA Document Consolidation

A CDA document is an XML-based clinical document standard to be exchanged across health care community [15], [18], [19]. The HL7 CDA is a document markup standard that specifies the structure and semantics of a clinical document (such as a discharge summary, progress note or procedure report) for the purpose of exchange [15]. The CDA scheme provides the healthcare interoperability by presenting syntactic standard of clinical documents. Accordingly, the adoption of the CDA document results in enhancing the healthcare information sharing and decreasing interface burdens across the related parties.

Generally, CDA documents are too complex and huge for emergency medical workers to check all the scattered medical information from multiple documents while transporting a patient in emergency situation. Given the limited amount of time a transport unit has with a patient and the time critical interventions that must be performed, viewing each CDA document is not realistic.

We propose creating a single CDA document for the patient by consolidating available CDA documents through the HIE search of all available documents presented to the transport unit. Upon receiving the list of available documents on the transport unit EHR, the proposed mechanism will search each document for redundancies based on the specific XML tags, remove redundancies, reformat each component with unique information found from each document, and present the single CDA document as described in Fig 5. These documents will not be stored within the HIE, but the function will be used as a reference tool for any time critical document query. This CDA document may be used to create a new TRS document for the transport unit. Template IDs and code systems will not be changed from their original format, but the new document will be saved in new data storage called Transport CDA data store (DS) as shown in Fig 6.

4.1   TRS Constructor

The TRS constructor module is composed of patient query manager, CDA XML processor, transport CDA consolidator, and CDA document optimizer. A TRS constructor module is installed within a transport unit and generates a TRS document by searching for patient's CDA documents and analyzing and optimizing the documents in order to create a pertinent TRS document.

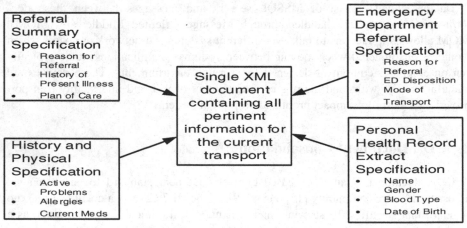

Fig. 5. CDA Document Consolidation

The TRS constructor module provides a transport unit interface which includes a user authentication procedure which identifies a patient by patient identifier and additional recognizable information such as birth date, address, race, etc. In addition, CDA filtering function of patient query manager provides extended search options like symptom and keyword-based search and semantic-based extended search.

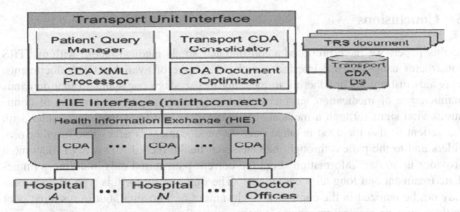

Fig. 6. TRS Constructor with CDA Consolidation

XML-based CDA documents are decomposed by CDA XML parser. Decomposed patient's health records are analyzed to extract appropriate patient records by CDA semantic analyzer within CDA XML processor. The extracted records are filtered to remove redundant information by CDA document optimizer. The suggested optimization presents two options for generating both preliminary CDA document based on the associated symptom and keyword analysis and extended CDA based on semantic analysis. Transport CDA consolidator organizes a new TRS document and provides the transport staff with the consolidated document through the transport unit interface. The TRS documents are stored in the transport CDA data store.

The TRS constructor searches for available CDA documents through HIE interface which provides HIE connection and is implemented by applying mirthconnect [12], an open source HL7 healthcare integration engine.

4.2   CDA TRS Document

The following example shows a consolidated TRS CDA document written in XML:

```
<ClinicalDocument xmlns='urn:hl7-org:v3'>
  <typeId extension="POCD_HD000040"
    root="2.16.840.1.113883.1.3"/>
<templateId root='1.3.6.1.4.1.19376.1.5.3.1.1.1'/>
<templateId root='1.3.6.1.4.1.19376.1.5.3.1.1.2'/>
  <id root=' ' extension=' '/>
  <code code=' ' displayName=' '
    codeSystem='2.16.840.1.113883.6.1'
    codeSystemName='LOINC'/>
<title>Medical Summary</title>
  <effectiveTime value='20081004012005'/>
<confidentialityCode code='N' displayName='Normal'
    codeSystem='2.16.840.1.113883.5.25'
    codeSystemName='Confidentiality' />
```

5   Conclusions

In this paper, we have proposed a consolidated single medical record with our TRS constructor using an HL7 interface for the exchange of available CDA documents. This aids institutions in adhering to meaningful use stage one standard that demands maintenance of medication, problem and allergy lists. Creating a report of continuous vital signs through a medical summary of the transport unit's encounter with the patient is also included in stage one. Our document is accessible to other providers and to the patient through their personal health record. This XML document provides up to date information about the current patient and aids in defining immediate treatment and long term care plans. The opportunity for this type of document may not be realized in the controlled environment of a hospital, but in resource poor settings such as medical transports, ease of immediate access to relevant information is paramount.

6   Future Work

Our future direction will be on using semantic queries with the TRS Constructor to build our CDA document. Our ontology based approach will first utilize existing medical protocols to determine differential diagnosis based on a group of symptoms; utilize a combination of measurements through a framework approach that is repeatable, reliable, consistent, complete and optimized. We will then retrieve the available data in the HIE and consolidate it using the TRS constructor based on the patient's particular symptoms.

References

1. Blumenthal, D., Tavenner, M.: The "Meaningful Use" Regulation for Electronic Health Records. Massachusetts: The New England Journal of Medicine 363(6) (2010)
2. Hospital, Johns Hopkins. Lifeline: Program Description. Johns Hopkins Hospital, http://www.hopkinsmedicine.org/lifeline/about/description.html (cited: December 12, 2012)
3. Boockvar, K.: Electronic health records and adverse drug events after patient transfer. Quality and Safety in Healthcare (2010)
4. Coordinator, Office of the National. HealtheWay, http://healthewayinc.org/ (cited: December 12, 2012)
5. CMS. Meaningful Use. Center for Medicare Service. US Government, http://www.cms.gov/Regulations-and-Guidance/Legislation/EHRIncentivePrograms/Meaningful_Use.html (cited: January 13, 2013)
6. Jha, A.K.: Meaningful Use of Electronic Health Records - The Road Ahead. Journal of the American Medical Association 304(15) (2010)
7. Marcotte, L., et al.: Achieving Meaningful Use of Health Information Technology: A Guide for Physicians to the EHR Incentive Programs. Arch. Intern. Med. 172(9) (2012)

8. DePalo, P., Song, Y.-T.: Implementing Interoperability using an IHE Profile for Interfacility Transport. ACIS, Jeju Island (2011)
9. Steel, J., Iannella, R., Lam, H.-P.: Using Ontologies for Decision Support in Resource Messaging. In: ISCRAM, Washington DC (2008)
10. Futch, A., Soares, C.: Enhanced 911 Technology and Privacy Concerns: How Has the Balance Changed Since September 11? Duke Law & Technology Review (2001)
11. Heidemann, J., Obraczka, K., Touch, J.: Modeling the Performance of HTTP Over Several Transport Protocols. IEEE/ACM Transactions on Networking 5(5) (1997)
12. Mirth Connect, The Leading Open Source HL7 Interface Engine. Mirth Corporation, http://www.mirthcorp.com/products/mirth-connect (cited: January 6, 2013)
13. Namli, T., Aluc, G., Dogac, A.: An Interoperability Test Framework for HL7-Based Systems. IEEE Transactions on Information Technology in Biomedicine 13(3) (2009), 10.1109/TITB.2009.2016086
14. Chiu, E.: ebXML Simplified: A Guide to the New Standard for Global E-Commerce. John Wiley & Sons Inc., New York (2002) ISBN 0-471-20475-7
15. Dolin, R., et al.: HL7 Clinical Document Architecgture. Journal of American Medical Informatics 13 (2006), doi:10.1197/jamia.M1888
16. Eichelberg, M., Aden, T., Riesmeier, J.: A Survey and Analysis of Electronic Healthcare Record Standards. ACM Computing Surveys 37(4) (2005), ACM 0360-0300/05/1200-0277
17. ZigBee Healthcare Standard Overview. ZigBee Alliance, http://www.zigbee.org/Standards/ZigBeeHealthCare/Overview.aspx (cited: December 26, 2012)
18. Dolin, B.: HL7 Clinical Document Architecture. Health Level Seven International (2009), http://www.hl7.org/documentcenter/public_temp_A84802EC-1C23-BA17-0CADAA4BB170D9BA/calendarofevents/himss/2010/presentations/HIMSS2010%20cda.pdf (cited: January 13, 2013)
19. Hui, J., Knoop, S., Schwarz, P.: HIWAS: Enabling Technology for Analysis of Clinical Data in XML Documents. In: Proceedings of the VLDB Endowment at the 37th International Conference, vol. 4. s.n., Seattle (2011)
20. Dogac, A., et al.: Exploiting ebXML Registry Semantic Constructs for Handling Archetype Metadata in Healthcare Informatics. International Journal of Metadata, Semantics, and Ontologies (2002), ACM 1581134975
21. Valdes, I., et al.: Open Source, Open Standards, and Health Care Information Systems. Journal of Medical Internet Research 13(1) (2011)
22. IHE. Integrating the Healthcare Enterprise - Technical Frameworks. Integrating the Healthcare Enterprise, http://ihe.net/Technical_Framework/upload/IHE_ITI_TF_Vol3.pdf (cited: January 13, 2013)

Designing, Implementing and Testing a Mobile Application to Assist with Pediatric-to-Adult Health Care Transition

Jeremy Dixon[1], Josh Dehlinger[1], and Shannan DeLany Dixon[2]

[1] Department of Computer and Information Sciences, Towson University, Towson, MD, USA
jdixon6@students.towson.edu,
jdehlinger@towson.edu
[2] Department of Pediatrics, University of Maryland - School of Medicine, Baltimore, MD, USA
smdixon@som.umaryland.edu

Abstract. As development of mobile applications continues to expand, accessibility and utility for users who are differently-abled will become essential. One aspect that impacts a large portion of the differently-abled population is the process of medical transition. Medical transition for patients with chronic diseases from pediatric-based care to adult-based care is one that has been studied, developed and implemented for a number of years; recently, it has become a top priority in healthcare. Due to the complexities of the transition process, a well-designed, intuitive mobile application may improve the standardization and ease of care for these patients. This paper proposes and analyzes the design for a mobile transition navigator application (MTNA) while taking into account some of the most common considerations when working with differently-abled users. Specifically, three aspects of mobile application design are examined: (1) mobile user interfaces are different than traditional interfaces; 2. a variety of mobile platforms exist; and, 3. mobile platforms generate benefits and concerns such as the wide variety of screen sizes and resolutions.

Keywords: mobile applications, differently-abled technologies, human-computer interaction, accessibility.

1 Introduction

As mobile applications become ubiquitous in our everyday lives, accessibility and utility for users who are differently-abled becomes essential [1]. Both Google and Apple have spent considerable resources including new accessibility tools into their most recent versions of their mobile operating systems in order to help support the differently-abled populations [2][3]. One important topic that impacts a large portion of the differently-abled population is the process of medical transition. The period of transition is when an individual is required to move from one healthcare team to another. In the medical field, transitions commonly occur when a young adult transitions from pediatric care to adult care, typically between the ages of 18 and 21

M. Kurosu (Ed.): Human-Computer Interaction, Part II, HCII 2013, LNCS 8005, pp. 66–75, 2013.
© Springer-Verlag Berlin Heidelberg 2013

[4]. If the transition fails or is incomplete, it may cause physical and/or mental health issues for adolescents with chronic conditions [5]. Medical transition for patients with chronic diseases from pediatric-based care to adult-based care is one that has been studied, developed and implemented for a number of years; recently, it has become a top priority in healthcare [4]. Due to the complexities of the transition process, a well-designed, intuitive mobile application should improve the standardization and ease of care for these patients. The significance of this applied research is to bring needed attention to the evaluation and necessity of a mobile application that assists with pediatric-to-adult transition which is considered to be a critical issue in healthcare today.

Helping children and young adults with chronic conditions (e.g., people with inborn errors of metabolism, such as phenylketonuria or individuals who have Down syndrome) transition from their pediatric care team to an adult care team is a much more common occurrence than it was just thirty years ago [6]. For children without known chronic medical issues (including physical, emotional, or behavioral issues), transition to adult medical care is typically not a task that is noteworthy or challenging. Specifically, most typically functioning individuals would be expected to identify and meet with a new primary care physician, typically an internal medicine specialist, without much thought or planning [6].

A mobile application is being developed and will be tested on a small pilot study group after the application has been implemented. This paper provides a design framework for an application to be used on a tablet computer to help with the medical transition for young adults with a chronic disease. The work presented in this paper is a part of a larger effort to enable a smooth transition for children with chronic diseases to adult care through a comprehensive, usable mobile application.

The remainder of the paper is organized as follows. Section II provides the background of the pediatric-to-adult care transition process. Section III discusses the Mobile Transition Navigator Application (MTNA) and the related software engineering considerations. Section IV introduces additional considerations such as mobile user interfaces, the different mobile platforms, and hardware differences. Section V examines the pilot study and the expected outcomes. Section VI provides some concluding remarks and thoughts. Finally, the resources appear in Section VII.

2   Transition

The primary period of transition in medicine occurs when an adolescent transfers from pediatric to adult care between the ages of 18 and 21 [4]. A transition that provides uninterrupted, high-quality care is an important goal, yet it can be inconsistent. According to the American Academy of Pediatrics, "The goal of a planned health care transition is to maximize lifelong functioning and well-being for all youth, including those who have special health care needs and those who do not" [4]. For people with chronic medical conditions, this transition process is both complex and critically important [6] [7]. Transition most commonly involves the following key topics:

1. Transferring care between large health care teams which may include multiple physicians, allied health professionals, nurses, and counselors [4].
2. Changing insurance coverage and practices.
3. Learning to discuss the disease, medications, and self-promotion.
4. Helping to ensure that all aspects of the transition are completed via checklists.

Orchestrating the transition from a pediatric team to an adult care team requires significant planning and execution. In order to help minimize obstacles and maximize independence required to successfully implement and monitor this transition, a mobile application will be designed for users who may be differently-abled.

As the number of children with chronic medical conditions who are surviving into adulthood increases, it is becoming essential to create and maintain an efficient transition process that is patient driven. Adolescents with a wide variety of chronic conditions make up almost one-fifth of children (18%) in the United States [8]. Transition plans are often complex because they need to integrate patients, caregivers, and health care professionals. As the child transitions to adult care, health care providers who frequently have a different philosophy and approach to medicine than their pediatric counterparts often assume responsibility for the now adult patient [8]. These adult medicine health care providers may not be familiar with the nuances of the patient's particular condition as well as current treatment and management regimens. This can make the transition challenging for both the patient and the medical care team.

Many chronic conditions require a team of health care providers to meet the unique needs of all of the prospective issues that may arise. The loss of a pediatrician and pediatric subspecialists can be a traumatic experience for the adolescent because the pediatric provider is likely to have had a long-standing relationship with the patient and family. In some cases, specialists (or subspecialists) may act as the primary care physician due to the complexities of the condition which may complicate the coordination of the transition. Also, finding an adult facility that has all of the required specialties and subspecialties may be difficult, especially in more remote areas [9].

A failed transition process can have severe effects on the physical and mental health of adolescents with chronic conditions. Many adolescents with a chronic health care condition have established a long-term relationship with their pediatrician and other health care providers [5]. Research suggests that most pediatricians and internal medicine doctors do not feel comfortable providing primary care for young adults with chronic illnesses of childhood origin. For example, only 15% of internists stated that they would feel comfortable providing primary care for a patient with cystic fibrosis compared to 38% of pediatricians. Similarly, 32% of internists thought they would feel comfortable providing primary care to an adult with sickle cell disease compared to 35% of pediatricians [10].

As many parents become comfortable with their child's health care providers over time, it becomes more difficult to try and motivate individuals to transfer care from their current pediatric care team for a variety of reasons. First, people are resistant to change especially when it involves their children who have chronic medical conditions. Second, the transition process is complex as it involves changing doctors, locations of care sites, reeducation, and changes to insurance coverage. Transition is sometimes initiated by the change in insurance that occurs when the patient reaches the ages of 18-21, which is when many children are no longer eligible to receive coverage under a parental policy [9]. This motivation for transition may be changed by the Patient Protection and Affordable Care Act that was signed into law on March 23, 2010; this law increases the dependent age limit to 26 [11]. Lastly, patients may not feel pressured to complete transition by the pediatric team and so lack motivation to undergo the complex transition process.

3   Mobile Transition Navigator Application

The proposed mobile application will be called the Mobile Transition Navigator Application (MTNA). It is being designed to help children and young adults facilitate the transition process. Children and young adults with chronic conditions may also have a wide variety of visual, hearing and motor impairments. Thorough evaluation of the accessibility of the MTNA during the design process will improve ease of use for the intended users. Similar accessibility considerations that affect web design may also affect mobile application design because of the user diversity.

1.	Strive for consistency
2.	Cater to universal usability
3.	Offer informative feedback
4.	Design dialogs to yield closure
5.	Prevent errors
6.	Permit easy reversal of actions
7.	Support internal locus of control
8.	Reduce short-term memory load

Fig. 1. Schneiderman's Eight Golden Rules [12]

As technology within tablet computing advances, a primary challenge is to identify novel research within the human-computer interaction subspecialty. Additionally, as this young field continues to evolve, additional resources will be identified and assessed for interface design and utility. A significant piece of interface design research, not specific to tablet computing, has been reported by Shneiderman and colleagues at the University of Maryland. The research identified Eight Golden Rules of Interface Design (Figure 1) [12] that one must adhere to for a well-designed interface. These rules should be considered during the design of the MTNA.

As discussed in Schneiderman's Eight Golden Rules, designing a consistent display can increase the usability of the application [12]. There are several aspects relating to the organization of the display that need to be taken into consideration. As the MTNA will be required to gather data from the users based on responses to the transition plan, it is important that the display is well organized. Smith and Mosier identified several aspects of data display to be taken into consideration. Most importantly, data displayed needs to be consistent. That is, each aspect of the interface should use the same vocabulary, abbreviations, form design, colors, and navigation [13].

Designing an appropriate user interface that is usable has additional complications as the size of tablet devices vary in size from ~5" to ~10". Importantly, because the user interface will be accessed using a multi-touch interface, the menu system needs to take into consideration the size of the user's forefinger as well as gross and fine motor skills. Research by Chen et al. suggests that for users without disability, a button size of 0.78" is optimal while users with a disability's performance continued to improve as button size increased [14]. Specifically, the menu system should provide an icon or click point to on the interface which is easily accessible by people with a variety of finger sizes and mobility. Tablet devices have the ability to be used in either a portrait or a landscape orientation. There is a significant difference whether the screen is 9.5" x 7.5" or 7.5" x 9.5" regarding the amount of text that is available on the screen. By taking advantage of some of the larger screens greater than 10", some of the accessibility considerations may be improved as the screen will be larger.

The MTNA will use a 2D menu structure using a broad hierarchy. This will allow the full height of the screen to be maximized so that scrolling will be reduced. The primary, and most commonly used parts of the tool, will be emphasized [15].

Data entry will be done by either tapping a virtual keyboard or by using Swype technology [16]. Swype technology allows users to drag their fingers across a virtual keyboard rather than having to lift their fingers up between characters. As an add-on to the virtual keyboard that is common on mobile devices, Swype does not interfere with more traditional tapping [16].

From an accessibility standpoint, children and young adults with chronic conditions may have a wide variety of visual, hearing and motor impairments. Because so many prospective users may have accessibility requirements, evaluating accessibility considerations during the design improves the available population of testers. Some of the same accessibility considerations that affect web design may also affect mobile application design because of the user diversity. In this section, some of the more common accessibility considerations are discussed for a mobile application.

The web content accessibility guidelines (WCAG 2.0) describe a variety of recommendations for making web content more accessible [17]. While these are intended for use on a web site, many of the same accessibility concerns may affect mobile application. For applications that use any non-text content (e.g., images, graphs, or figures), it is important to provide a means with which to translate that content into a form more usable by users. Users with visual impairment may require the text or text alternatives to be in large print or Braille. Other users may require text-to-speech or symbols. Creating a clearly distinguished foreground and background can also help make the screen more easily viewed. It is important to choose a color scheme that is easily readable for users who may have partial or full color blindness. For visually impaired users, providing a mechanism for resizing the text will be worthwhile consideration. Some users who have chronic conditions may have an increased risk of seizures. Thus, the applications designed for this population should not have content that can increase the likelihood of seizures. Specifically, applications should not flash more than three times in a one second period [17]. Additionally, a small study conducted by the University of Washington suggests that screen readers, voice input, large buttons, screen magnification, improved contrast, and optical character recognition may considered for designing an application for differently-abled [18].

The MTNA will aid with transition by helping the patient answer some of the critical key questions. Based on recommendations from the American Academy of Pediatrics, the application will help guide a patient through four main components of transition. First, the application will illustrate key questions to help decide if a patient is ready to initiate the transition process. If the patient is not ready to start the transition process, the application will provide guidance as to what tasks need to be established prior to starting the transition. Second, the application will help a patient plan the transition process. It will provide suggestions for goals along with realistic timelines. The main goal of this phase is to help educate a patient as to what is involved in a successful transition. Third, the application will help initiate patient transition. The primary goal of the implementation phase is to educate all involved parties as to the situation. In many cases, this will require the patient, caregivers, family members and the healthcare team to be educated as to a patient's condition, the expectations of care, and the timeline for completion. The application will provide a list of resources, and talking points to help with the implementation phase but will not provide any disease-specific resources. Finally, the application will help document important aspects of the transition process, such as important insurance information, contact information for the healthcare team, and checklists to help ensure that nothing is missed [4].

4   Additional Considerations

The widespread availability of mobile devices introduced a number of challenges to traditional software engineering, including: 1. mobile user interfaces are different than traditional interfaces; 2. a variety of mobile platforms exist; and, 3. mobile platforms generate benefits and concerns such as the variety of screen sizes and resolutions [1].

There are a wide variety of mobile devices that could be used with many differently-abled users. By using a mobile device, it is expected that users will increase their efficiency by having increased access to the computing device [19]. Further, many mobile devices have a variety of features to help the differently-abled interact with a mobile device. Specifically, many mobile devices have the ability to use text-to-speech, haptic feedback, alternative input devices (trackballs and D-pads) and audio feedback.

Most table devices today have a multi-touch interface that would be compatible with a wide variety of application designs. In order to meet the needs of all of the transitional aspects of the MTNA, the devices will have to have at least a 9" multi-touch screen with WiFi. In order to keep the maintenance and services costs of the pilot study at a minimum, as well as maximizing connectivity, the devices will not be required to be 3G or 4G cell enabled. Based on current advances in the mobile device chip technology, tablet speed is not expected to be a consideration for this application.

One of the initial considerations for developing for mobile devices is that there are two distinct options: native and web [20]. Native applications are programs that use the programming language most commonly associated with the operating system

(OS) of the device. For these native applications, the device supports embedded software development kits (SDK). The most prominent are Android SDK, iOS SDK and BlackBerry Java SDK. For the most part, native applications are different for each of the operating systems. Specifically, an application developed for the Android OS has to be recoded for a device running iOS. Native applications are often installed directly onto the mobile application by way of an App Store (i.e., Google Play or iTunes). A mobile web application, however, is designed to run from a web browser. Web based applications can be installed directly on the device or accessed from a remote server. In many cases, these web applications can run across devices and operating systems with minimal additional code but without the ability to use some of the native rich functionality.

Recently, software reusability options for mobile application development have improved because of technologies such as PhoneGap and Sencha Touch [21]. In the early days of iOS, Android, and Blackberry, application development was difficult because each application needs to be developed for each platform. PhoneGap, Sencha and other similar cross-compilation technologies allow the developer to code an application once that is then usable across platforms.

Sencha Touch uses a Model-View-Controller (MVC) architecture that is a design pattern that separates data from an application, the user interface, and the logic of business in three components. The origin of the MVC architecture or paradigm goes back to 1979 but the concepts introduced then are valid in modern mobile device software development. The three primary objects to the MVC each provide a specialized task. The visual representation (view) provides feedback to the user is the first task. The view would display the images and textual output. The second task connects the user input from a mouse, a keyboard, or a touchscreen to the model and the view [22]. Of the third task, the model, Burbeck states, "Finally, the model manages the behavior and data of the application domain, responds to requests for information about its state (usually from the view), and responds to instructions to change state (usually from the controller)" [22].

Fig. 2. Screenshots of the MTNA on both Android (left) and iOS (right)

Figure 2 shows the prototype MTNA on an Android-based phone and an Apple-based phone as developed using Sencha Touch 2. The application can run on all HTML 5 enabled phones, tablets and personal computers.

Ultimately, Sencha Touch allows developers to create HTML5 based mobile apps that work on Android, iOS and Blackberry devices. While the application was not developed specifically for the device specific OS, in some cases it can take advantage of native functionality. Since Sencha Touch can be used to create an application that is cross-platform compatible while leveraging the MVC architecture, it will be used to create the MTNA application.

5   Pilot Study

The application will be tested using a small cohort of young adult patients, between the ages of 14-25 years old. While the users are new to the MNTA application, they are expected to have some familiarity with touch screens as most individuals in this demographic have access to or experiences with this technology. Successful implementation of the MTNA will be determined by the following criteria:

- Users will successfully complete their transition in less than 6 months.
- Users will have no lapses in medical care during the transition process and for the six months after the transition has been completed.
- The MTNA will receive generally positive reviews from both the patients and care givers.

The data collected from the pilot study will be analyzed using a mixed methodology. 1. survey data will evaluate the ease and success of the transition process when using the MTNA; and, 2. semi-structured interviews will collect comments, suggestions, and future features for the MTNA and will undergo thematic analysis. This combination of data will help drive future direction of the MTNA.

The survey will generate data assessing overall ease of usability and frequency of application use for the participants. Additionally, it will assess perceived helpfulness of the application and motivation to use the application based on physical access to a tablet computer. Participants will be asked to report the frequency of use of the transition timelines and self-assessment check lists as well as degree of helpfulness of discussion question prompts. Lastly, participants will be asked to propose additions to the application as well as features that should be considered for elimination from the application.

While survey data is collected, participants will be asked to participate in semi structured interviews. For those that agree, interviews will be used to explore and expand themes identified in the survey as well as allow for participants to further qualify feedback regarding the application so as not to be limited to only those choices provided in survey responses. The interview structure will also allow for participants to propose additional concepts that should be considered in development of the application. Lastly, the interviews will provide feedback regarding the benefits and limitations of medical transition using a phone or tablet based application.

In addition to the pilot study, data will be collected during a more traditional usability study. The usability study will be used on a variety of adolescents both typically functioning and differently abled. Tasks and/or interviews evaluating efficiency, accuracy, recall, and emotional response will be conducted prior to the pilot study. Additional data such as demographics will be included as part of the usability study.

6   Conclusion

The best transition experiences are those where the care is uninterrupted and high quality. The design, implementation and testing of a mobile application may significantly help with the transition process. By leveraging modern cross-compilation tools, the MTNA application can be implemented on multiple mobile operating systems. This will lead to a variety of users, including those who may be differently-abled, to have a more fluid transition to their new health care providers.

Providing high quality healthcare to a person going through the transition from pediatric care to adult care can be a complex and time consuming effort. The best transition experiences are those where the care is uninterrupted and high quality. Currently, there are a variety of checklists and tools available to help people who are going through the transition period to complete the process but with varying results.

Advances in medical knowledge and skills are helping children and young adults with chronic conditions live much longer than in previous generations. Due to this, the population of people going through the transition process is increasing. By designing a mobile application framework that helps with the transition process, the efforts required to successfully complete this may be improved. Once the application is developed and validated, the application may be distributed to a broader patient base throughout the medical system to determine effectiveness to a global patient population.

Acknowledgements. We would like to acknowledge New York Mid Atlantic Consortium for Genetics and Newborn Screening Services (NYMAC) for their support and funding of this project.

References

1. Dehlinger, J., Dixon, J.: Mobile Application Software Engineering: Challenges and Research Directions. In: MobiCase 2011 - Mobile Software Engineering Workshop, Santa Monica (2011)
2. Apple Inc. iOS Accessibility (2013),
   https://developer.apple.com/technologies/ios/accessibility.html
3. Google Inc. Android 4.2, Jelly Bean - Accessibility (2013),
   http://www.android.com/about/jelly-bean/
4. American Academic of Pediatrics, Supporting the Transition from Adolescence to Adulthood in the Medical Home. Pediatrics, 182–200 (2011)
5. Binks, J.A., Barden, W.S., Burke, T.A., Young, N.L.: What Do We Really Know About the Transition to Adult-Centered Health Care? A Focus on Cerebral Palsy and Spina Bifida. Archives of Physical Medicine Rehabilitation 88, 1064–1073 (2007)
6. Peter, N., Forke, C., Ginsburg, K., Schwarz, D.: Transition From Pediatric to Adult Care: Internists' Perspectives. Pediatrics, 417–423 (2009)
7. Lotstein, D.S., McPherson, M., Strickland, B., Newacheck, P.W.: Transition Planning for Youth With Special Health Care Needs: Results from the National Survey of Children With Special Health Care Needs. Pediatrics 115(6), 1562–1568 (2005)

8. Callahan, S.T., Feinstein Winitzer, R., Kennan, P.: Transition from Pediatric to Adult Oriented Health Care: A Challenge for Patients with Chronic Disease. Current Opinions in Pediatrics 13, 310–316 (2001)
9. American Academy of Pediatrics, Transition of Care Provided for Adolescents with Special Health Care Needs. Pediatrics, 1203–1206 (1996)
10. Okumura, M., et al.: Comfort of General Internists and General Pediatricians in Providing Care for Young Adults with Chronic Illnesses of Childhood. Journal of General Internal Medicine 23(10), 1621–1627 (2008)
11. U.S. Department of Health & Human Services. Young Adults and the Affordable Care Act (August 2011), http://www.healthcare.gov/news/factsheets/2011/08/young-adults.html
12. Shneiderman, B., Plaisant, C.: Designing the User Interface, 5th edn. Addison Wesley, Boston (2010)
13. Smith, S., Mosier, J.: Guidelines for Designing User Interface Software, Bedford, Massachusetts, USA (1986)
14. Chen, K., Savage, A., Chourasia, A., Wiegmann, D., Sesto, M.: Touch Screen Performance by Individuals With and Without Motor Control Disabilities. Applied Ergonomics 44, 297–302 (2013)
15. Kim, K., Jacko, J., Salvendy, G.: Menu Design for Computers and Cell Phones: Review and Reappraisal. International Journal of Human-Computer Interaction, 383–404 (2011)
16. King, I.: Spreading: Swype's Touchscreen Keyboard Technology, Businessweek.com (2010)
17. Caldwell, B., Cooper, M., Reid, L.G., Vanderheiden, G.: Web Content Accessibility Guidelines (WCAG) 2.0 (December 2008), http://www.w3.org/TR/WCAG20/
18. Kane, S., Jayant, S., Wobbrock, J., Ladner, R.: Freedom to roam: a study of mobile device adoption and accessibility for people with visual and motor disabilities. ACM, Pittsburgh (2009)
19. Martins, H., Jones, M.: Relevance of Mobile Computing in the Field of Medicine. In: Mobile Computing: Concepts, Methodologies, Tools, and Application, pp. 1429–1441 (2009)
20. Sutter, B.: HTML5 for the Java Web Developer (2012), http://vimeo.com/29403374
21. Christ, A.: Bridging the Mobile App Gap, pp. 27–32. Inside the Digial Ecosystem, Sigma (2011)
22. Burbeck, S.: Applications Programming in Smalltalk-80: How to use Model-View-Controller (MVC) (1987), http://st-www.cs.illinois.edu/users/smarch/st-docs/mvc.html

Study on Relationship between Foot Pressure Pattern and Hallux Valgus (HV) Progression

Saba Eshraghi[1], Ibrahim Esat[1], Pooyan Rahmanivahid[1], Mahshid Yazdifar[1],
Mona Eshraghi[3], Amir Mohagheghi[2], and Sara Horne[2]

[1] School of Engineering and Design, Brunel University West London, Uxbridge, UK
[2] School of Sport Science, Brunel University West London, Uxbridge, UK
[3] School of Engineering, University of Twente, Netherlands
Saba.Eshraghi@brunel.ac.uk

Abstract. Hallux valgus is one of the most common foot deformities. Plantar pressure technologies are used widely for determination of biomechanical changes in foot during walking. There are already published claims relating to the pressure distribution of HV condition. However some of these claims are disputed and challenged. Although, disputed or otherwise, association *of* HV to sole pressure widely presented as a means of identifying such condition. Or knowing that HV exist, establishing what kind of pressure variation is expected may lead to better foot wear design for HV patients. Despite of extensive work on sole pressure patterns of patients, there has been no reported work found on conditions which leads to HV. Considering the fact that 23% of adults develop such condition during their life time, understanding HV is badly needed.

To have better understanding of how plantar pressure patterns can be linked to the deformity progression or existence, extracting some patterns out of force and pressure measurements can be beneficial in recognising the patients with and without deformity during their gait cycle. We examined the dynamic changes of the forces that applied to the whole sole of the feet in control group and in the patients group when they walked at different speeds.

It was observed for those with HV condition having higher forces on 2nd and 3rd metatarsal heads, and less force on the 1st metatarsal head compared to those without the condition. Although this finding was previously reported in the literature what was new was the fact that, speed of walking shown to have a significant influences on plantar force distribution. This finding in itself is significant as no sole pressure distribution given in conjunction with walking speed in the past.

It was observed that there was significant variability of pressure distribution of the same individual from one trial to another indicating that getting consistent pressure pattern is an important hurdle to overcome. After many trials individuals' walking regulated giving consistent readings. After achieving this, it was further discovered that pressure pattern very much depended on walking speed. Considering the fact that inconsistency of pressure of unregulated (casual) walking and variability of due to speed raises doubts of validity of previously published work on HV which ignored such factors. Having said that, in our studies too, raised loading is observed on Metatarsal 2 and, 3 although it was not possible to give statistical significance to these finding. Although the

M. Kurosu (Ed.): Human-Computer Interaction, Part II, HCII 2013, LNCS 8005, pp. 76–83, 2013.
© Springer-Verlag Berlin Heidelberg 2013

loading on metatarsal 2 and 3 may indicate existence of HV, in authors' opinion, there is little chance of using pressure pattern as a predictive tool as no
such pressure increase observed on those appeared to be at the start of HV condition or any individual with normal feet.

Keywords: Hallux Valgus, Force pressure pattern.

1   Introduction

Hallux Valgus (HV) is an angulation of the big toe of more than fifteen degrees [3].
23% percent of people develop this disease during their lives. It is postulated that HV
causes abnormal pressure distribution on the fore- and mid-foot especially at the joint
next to the HV zone. HV is associated with pain, poor balance, inflammation, reduction in motion and risk of falling [1, 2]. Furthermore, it is accompanied by collapse of
the forefoot transverse arch during standing, metatarsal pain and callus formation.[10]

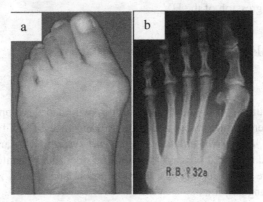

Fig. 1. (a) A foot with Hallux Valgus deformity [4]; (b) typical X-ray image of a HV foot before and after operation [5]

Severity of HV and intervention are determined by several factors such as age, gait
deviation, pain location and duration [10].

For redistributing the pressure evenly over the sole of the foot in patients with HV,
Gait analyses are widely used to determine how anatomical variations and disorders
of the foot affect walking patterns [11].

This paper investigates the differences between foot plantar pressure pattern in foot
with and without HV in order to evaluate the possible effects of various gait patterns
on the progression of HV.

Recent studies have shown that women are more predisposed to HV than men by a
ratio of 2 to 1 [6]. There is genetical predisposition to HV, but it could be the case that
the footwear aggravates the condition.

Wearing narrow toe box and high-heels shoes have direct effect on reconstruction
of the bones. Studies on the early humans show that once they started wearing foot

support mechanical factors over their feet changed, and as a consequence foot deformities appeared [7].

A direct relationship claimed by many between changes in distribution of pressure underneath the foot and changes in the shape of the first metatarsal bone.

In the foot with HV the pressure from the first metatarsal head is transferred to the 2nd and 3rd metatarsophalangeal joints [8].

The first quantitative study of plantar pressure in HV has been done and found significantly lower peak force under the great and second toes and higher peak force under the third to fifth metatarsals. However, other studies found decreased peak pressure under the fourth and fifth metatarsals and increased pressure under the first to third metatarsals [10]. In hallux valgus feet the medial plantar peak and mean pressures are higher under the first, second and third metatarsal heads [12].

Plank conducted the study on plantar pressure and patients with Hallux valgus observed to have the highest pressure on the third, second, first, fourth and fifth [9].

HV can be treated using surgical methods by cutting the first metatarsal bone and relocating the bone to a new position, but designing suitable shoes and shoe support can reduce the progression of the HV.

2   Methodology

2.1   Subjects

10 volunteers recruited, six without HV and four who had developed HV. The forces to the foot in different anatomical zones at walking race of 0.5 Hz stride frequency have been studied. *Foot-scan advanced & hi-end system* (RSscan International NV, Belgium) was used to record pressure distribution over the 10 anatomical zones under the feet to evaluate the differences between different speeds and zones, especially in the metatarsophalangeal joints.

HV diagnosis was based on the first metatarsal angel relative to the first proximal phalanx for more than 15 degrees.

There were eight females and two males participated in the study with the mean age of 39.25 years old, and mean weight of 68.75 kg.

Informed consent was obtained from each participant before data collection and the experimental procedures were approved by the ethical committee of the Brunel University.

2.2   Data Collection

The plantar measuring system [RsScan Inc.] was used to measure the plantar force distributed over the right foot of each volunteer. The pressure plate was 578 mm*418 mm*12 mm in dimensions. And the active sensor area was about 488 mm *325 mm. The pressure range is between $0 - 200$ N/cm^2.

Initial results proved to be inconsistent; the same individual found to produce widely varying pressure distributions from one walk to another, in some cases as much as 20% on the maximum pressure values. In order to regulate the results to achieve consistency the influence of various parameters were studies. The most important element found to be the speed of walking. It was observed that at certain speed, individuals appeared to be walking steadier giving more repeatable pressure distributions. To achieve this start and end points of the walking was defined for volunteers. They were asked to walk between those points to be familiarising with the process of the experiment. They were asked to have 4.6 second speed when they past the mat. The tenth of a second accuracy seems to be too precise but soon found to be achievable and individuals managed to remain within +/- 0.1 second of 4.6s. Anybody failing to achieve this was asked to repeat the walk. Each individual performed 10 successful trials. Ten valid trials were collected for each subject. A valid trial means that individual's foot is completely within the pressure mat and that individual does not change his walking speed or gait in order to step in the mat. In other word the walking style should not change as he or she steps on the mat.

2.3   Data Analysis

The software, "foot scan", divides each foot to the 10 anatomical zones; the relative force related to each region of the foot was data logged and saved in excel sheets. There are options for data logging, either force or pressure. In this case force option is chosen because pressure depends on the size of the region as well as the actual force value, whereas force value is the total force carried by each region which seems to be more meaningful. The force values recorded are normalised against the body weight. For each region the time axis was also normalised. Then Mean, standard deviation and the cross correlation of regions has been calculated.

3   Results and Discussion

A typical result is shown in Figure 2. Here 10 trials of normal walking force pattern for metatarsal 2 is plotted. It is important to see such large variation despite of great care taken in running the experiment. Two of the graphs appear to be smaller than the others, 3 of the graphs are in the mid-range and the rest are very much together. It is shown that keeping repeatable pattern depended very much on the individuals. It is also found that at faster walking speed consistency appeared to increase, as it will be discussed later. Furthermore consistency is influenced if individuals taken up walking as regular exercises. Those "walkers" presented more regular walking patterns at slow or fast walking speeds.

Starting the experiments, the very first thing was done is to ensure that the results were reliable and for that any weight and speed influences were eliminated, the force readings were normalised with respect to the weight of individuals. Furthermore time axis was normalised. The second thing was done is to ensure that the results were repeatable and for that any fluctuations in the mean value and standard deviations were studied. The Figures 3 shows normalised mean weight plotted against standard deviation for 2nd metatarsal as an example of all the experiments carried out. Repeatability and consistency of results were equally good in individuals with or without HV condition. It can be seen from the graph that both the mean and the SD fluctuates no more than +/-3%.

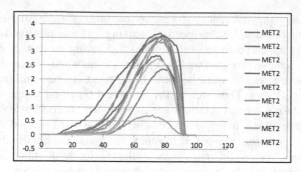

Fig. 2. The sample of the force graph in the 2nd metatarsal

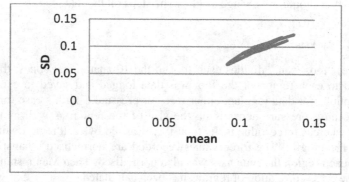

Fig. 3. Mean against standard deviation for 2nd metatarsal

3.1   Correlation

Although it was reported by previous researchers that the load during walking shifts to 2nd and 3rd metatarsal heads, studying load patterns shows that there is some difficulties with this kind of conclusion. In some cases although the maximum load may shift from one metatarsal to another, the actual values of load remain very close and if one plots the maximum pressure line, as shown in Figure 4, screen dump from foot-scan software, in some cases load almost equally distributed among several metatarsals.

It is probably much more reliable to study correlation of load distribution among metatarsals. With the correlation, the time element is removed but similarities of patterns are compared, thus how similar the loading on each metatarsal is investigated. This approach removes the uncertainty of attributing the maximum load to specific metatarsal and identify if they are similarly loaded (although not necessarily at the same moment in time).

A typical (a normal walking individual) correlation results are shown in Table 1(a) among all 5 metatarsal. The best correlation is between 1 and 2, 2 and 3 metatarsals. Furthermore, all neighbouring metatarsals show good correlation (1 and 2, 2 and 3, 3 and 4 etc). Table 1(b) shows the same individual walking a faster speed Table 1(a). These results give a strong indication that correlation results are unaffected by walking speeds.

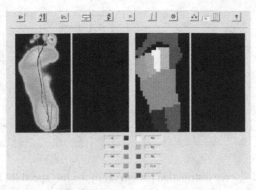

Fig. 4. Force distribution under the foot

Table 1. (a) Presents the correlations between metatarsals at normal speed. (b) Presents the correlation between metatarsals at fast speed.

(a)	MET1	MET2	MET3	MET4	MET5
MET1	1				
MET2	0.987665	1			
MET3	0.89879	0.948886	1		
MET4	0.628394	0.725185	0.899859	1	
MET5	0.22128	0.353986	0.584925	0.852624	1

(b)	MET 1	MET2	MET3	MET4	MET5
MET1	1				
MET2	0.997054	1			
MET3	0.951535	0.968637	1		
MET4	0.710258	0.749726	0.876622	1	
MET5	0.255242	0.305956	0.467135	0.815737	1

3.2 Speed of Walking

Speed of walking from the correlation appears to have a little influence on the force pattern of each region. However it was observed that consistency of pattern was very much speed dependent. The correlation appears to be inconsistent with observed fluctuation of pressure patterns not only among individuals but among samples of the same individuals. This can be observed in the results below, the first graph(a) shows normal walking and graph (b) shows faster walking with improved repeatability.

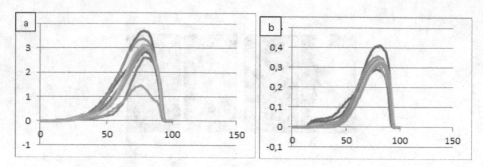

Fig. 5. Metatarsal 2nd force distribution pattern (a) in the fast speed (b) in the normal speed

3.3   Loading on 2nd and 3rd Metatarsals

It is reported by many that load increases on the 2nd and 3rd metatarsal.   In this report this is also investigated.Figure6 (a), shows force loading of a person without HV and one with HV condition. It is shown that such increase may be observed, Figure 5, although what we observed also support the generally accepted finding, combining this finding with the difficulty of measuring reliable force patterns raises serious questions. It is therefore in the opinion of the authors that results are reliable only when studied together with the influence of walking speed.

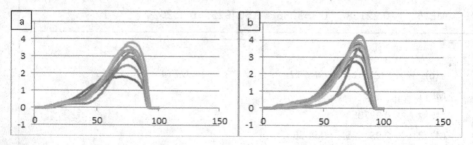

Fig. 6. Metatarsal force distribution in normal speed (a) in the normal foot (b) foot with HV condition

4   Conclusion

It is shown that there is variability of force distribution under the sole when measured on the same individual. Getting consistent patterns proved to be challenging. This finding raises questions of reliability of previously reported results. A great deal of work has gone into achieving consistent results. Variability of due to walking style and variability of possible effect of HV condition is roughly the same order of magnitude which put doubt on the pressure mat measurements.

Furthermore it was discovered that the speed of walking also had a significant effect on the force distribution.

Although many investigations have been done in previously published works on HV, many of them neglected the importance of speed and the style of walking.

In this study, higher force on 2nd and the 3rd metatarsals for foot with HV condition, in comparison with the normal foot is observed. It is difficult to make a conclusive remark that this is a firm indication of the condition given that other variations reported in this report. Even if such results were taken to be a conclusive indicators of the condition as claimed by many previously, it is worth stressing that our investigation showed no such pressure increase within the population considered to be vulnerable to the condition.

References

1. Drake, L., Vogle, R., Mitchell, A.W.M.: Gray's anatomy for students. Elsevier Inc. Ian Dick and Antbits Illustration Ltd., USA (2005)
2. Rao, S., Song, J., Kraszewski, A., Backus, S., Ellis, S.J., Deland, M.J.T., Hillstrom, H.J.: The effect of foot structure on 1st metatarsophalangeal joint flexibility and hallucal loading. Gait and Posture 34, 131–137 (2011)
3. Milner, S.: Common disorders of the foot and ankle. Orthopaedic Surgery, 514–517 (2010)
4. http://www.rucosm.com/operations/hallux.php (accessed at May 20, 2012)
5. Trnka, H.J., Zembsch, A., Easley, M.E., Salzer, M., Ritschl, P., Myerson, M.S.: The Chevron Osteotomy for Correction of Hallux Valgus: Comparison of Findings After Two and Five Years of Follow-up. The Journal of Bone & Joint Surgery 82, 1373–1373 (2000)
6. Nguyen, U.S.D.T., Hillstorm, H.J., Li, W., Dufouri, A.B., Kiel, D.P., ProcterGray, E., Gagnon, M.M., Hannan, M.T.: Factors Associated with Hallux Valgus in a Population-Based Study of Older Women and Men: the MOBILIZE Boston Study. Osteoarthritis and Cartilage 18, 41–46 (2010)
7. Trinkaus, E., Shang, H.: Anatomical evidence for the antiquity of human footwear: Tianyuan and Sunghir. Journal of Archaeological Science 35, 1928–1933 (2008)
8. Mickle, K.J., Munro, B.J., Lord, S.R., Menz, H.B., Steele, J.R.: Gait, balance and plantar pressures in older people with toe deformities. Gait & Posture 34, 347–351 (2011)
9. Plank, M.J.: The pattern of forefoot pressure distribution in hallux valgus. The Foot 5, 8–14 (1995)
10. Wen, J., Ding, Q., Yu, Z., Weidong Sun, W., Wang, Q., Wei, K.: Adaptive changes of foot pressure in hallux valgus patients. Gait & Posture (2012)
11. Rosenbaum, D., Hautmann, S., Gold, M., Claes, L.: Effects of walking speed on plantar pressure patterns and hindfoot angular motion. Gait & Posture 2, 191–107 (1994)
12. Bryant, A., Tinley, P., Singer, K.: Radiographic measurements and plantar pressure distribution in normal, hallux valgus and hallux limitus feet. The Foot 10, 18–22 (2000)

A Server-Based System Supporting Motor Learning through Real-Time and Reflective Learning Activities

Naka Gotoda[1], Yoshihisa Sakurai[1], Kenji Matsuura[2], Koji Nakagawa[1], and Chikara Miyaji[1]

[1] Japan Institute of Sports Sciences, Japan Sport Council, Japan
{naka.gotoda,yoshihisa.sakurai,koji.nakagawa,
chikara.miyaji}@jpnsport.go.jp
[2] Center for Administration of Information Technology, The University of Tokushima, Japan
ma2@tokushima-u.ac.jp

Abstract. This paper describes a design of training-diary system intended for motor learning regarding daily outdoor activities including sports. As for motor skill, both monitoring and advising based on the key points which are hard to obtain, are significant factors for improving such motor skills. The points comprise the timing of advice and content. Therefore, we propose a system which automatically generates coaching materials based on real-time monitoring data. It aims to become helpful in finding out such points. During training, the server provides learners and the coaches with an annotation on timeline messages of a mobile-device application by adjustable biomechanical/physiological threshold parameters while receiving the data via the mobile device with wireless sensors. After training, s/he can reflect the reconstructed annotations as diary for next training. Thus, the learners can discuss the key points with the coaches through a trial and error process concerning the threshold adjustment.

Keywords: Bio-feedback, remote coaching, wireless sensor, annotation, content management system.

1 Introduction

Physical training in our daily life is recognized as one of requisite human activity in order to promote our health. Some people tend to try to begin the easy training by themselves anytime and everywhere. Those people face dropout problems because of less motivation based on lack of training knowledge through communication with others who take roles like physical educator [1]. To learn the knowledge and acquire the fundamental skill is called as "motor learning" in sense of basic learning in relation to physical activities. Additionally the skill is called as "motor skill" [2]. When a learner is new to a specific task of physical training, s/he needs to acquire appropriate strategies as such knowledge.

On the other hand, in the field of sports athletes require effective methods to improve their performance. Especially it depends on methodologies of monitoring and advising by coaches. The advice from monitoring corresponds to feedback based on

M. Kurosu (Ed.): Human-Computer Interaction, Part II, HCII 2013, LNCS 8005, pp. 84–93, 2013.

finding out key points. Motor learning literatures reports that feedback combined with practice is one of significant factors for affecting motor learning [2-3]. Therefore, an appropriate feedback derives remarkable promotion regarding performance and motivation as a result. Thus, in physical training including sports, educational environment which offers such a feedback through coaching, is essential regardless of athlete or non-athlete.

Generally the key points are hard to obtain because of difficulties in the analysis and detection. In many cases, the process frequently takes much time compared with actual training time. Therefore, such complex procedures are conducted after training. However, the key point comprises the appropriate timing of advice in addition to the content. The timing often means a certain point which appears bad habit concerning posture, movement and so on. Thus, real-time feedback is desirable from the viewpoint of practice reflecting the timing. Moreover, after training, reflective learning which promotes comprehension in real-time learning should be considered because learner generally discuss problems with coaches for next training and makes a note in the training diary.

Meanwhile, current bio-feedback technologies which support by computer-based system with sensors can facilitate improvements of the above mentioned requirement. Feedback system assists learners by monitoring their training and providing relevant specific information during training for the purpose of achieving better performance [4-6]. Therefore, in daily training, a feedback system which consistently can support aforementioned real-time and reflective learning activities has potential to promote motor learning more efficiently. In particular, it contributes daily outdoor activities which coaches do not stay on-site because of need from remote coaching.

Thus, this paper describes a design of training-diary system intended for motor learning regarding daily outdoor activities including sports. We propose a server-based system which automatically generates coaching materials based on real-time monitoring data. It aims to become helpful in finding out such points. During training, the server provides a learner and the coach with an annotation on timeline messages of a mobile-device application by adjustable biomechanical/physiological threshold parameters while receiving the data via the mobile device with wireless sensors. After training, s/he can reflect the reconstructed annotations as her/his diary for next training. Thus, the learners can discuss the key points with the coaches through a trial and error process concerning the threshold adjustment.

2   Motor Skill in Dynamic Environment

2.1   Engineering Approach for Motor Learning

Researches on motor skill were conducted with a central focus on scientific field. That is to say, principal results of this domain to the present were based on analytically-based efforts. For instance, potential technics of Olympic gold medalists or other excellent athletes are ideal topics for such projects. In contrast, a process of understanding simple actions on early childhood learning environment is typical target too. When desirable or not desirable performance appears as a result of actions, researchers analyze features by sensors, video, interviews, and so forth to clarify reasons which making a difference in results. Many studies thus far are conducted quantitatively and qualitatively in different cases. However, as for professional skill in such a technique like passing the ball of soccer game, some reasons in a certain cases would be not effective to recommend a way of improvement for the next training. It is because either environmental or physical conditions of trials would be different from those in the past. In the same way, as for fundamental skill limited to the specified environment without any outside influences like a vertical jump test of kindergarten children, some reasons would be inapplicable to more complex conditions such as jumping rope.

Therefore, these describes that the scientific approach has a certain limitation to define reasons. The main concern of this study is not the scientific approach but the engineering for learning with sensor/feedback devices and server-based system.

2.2   Skills in Daily Outdoor Activities

Regarding types of skills, Poulton defined skills displayed by performance in a consistent, typically as stationary environment as closed skills [7]. On the contrary, open skills is in a moving and dynamic environment. Allard and Starkes claimed the difference between open skills and closed skills in two respects [8]. The first difference point is the environment in which the skill is displayed. Most open skills are trained in a dynamic environment. For closed skills, the environment is a stable situation in addition to exercise in predictable conditions.

The second difference between open and closed skills involves the role of a particular motor pattern. Closed skills assume that motor patterns are the skills; it is critical that the learner is able to reproduce consistently/reliably a defined/standard movement pattern. In other words, once a learner developed the skill, s/he can do it again in the same situation. On the other hand, for open skills, it is effectiveness of a motor pattern in producing a particular environmental outcome that constitutes the skill. Concretely speaking, a learner tries something in facing different conditions at every trial time. Since most daily outdoor activities mainly requires open skills.

In respect to physical training, it is a type of gross motor skill that interlocks whole body with coherent movements. Gross motor ability shares connections with other physical functions. In the case of road cycling as an example, repetitive actions itself, combined with pedaling is regarded as closed skills. However, from another viewpoint discussed previously, the outdoor activity is considered as open skills because outdoor cyclist always meets different physical conditions, course conditions, competitor and so forth.

According to a retrospective discussion, regarding training of open skills, it is necessary for learners and the coaches to discuss the key points through a trial and error process because of updated conditions each time. Additionally, remote-coaching environments are required as real-time coaching and reflective learning. Because there are many outdoor activities like road cycling in sports. Therefore, from the viewpoint of engineer approach, we discuss a methodology of real-time and reflective learning for open skills of training in daily outdoor activities which are dynamic environments.

3   Support Scenario of Coaching/Training Environment

Fig. 1 compares a general feedback scenario and our proposal feedback scenario. In the case of the former, basically the coaching is based on the result of analysis regarding the last monitoring data as it was mentioned in Chapter 1 because generally it takes much time for coaches to analyze the data. However, from the viewpoint of open skills, real-time feedback is desirable from the discussion of previous chapter. For this reason, in our proposal, both monitoring and coaching are conducted on parallel under supports from our system. The supports are provided by coaching materials generated automatically through analysis of monitoring data for the purpose of avoiding excessive fatigue of the analysis procedure. During training, the server provides learners and the coaches with an annotation on timeline messages of a mobile-device application by adjustable biomechanical/physiological threshold parameters while receiving the data via the mobile device with wireless sensors.

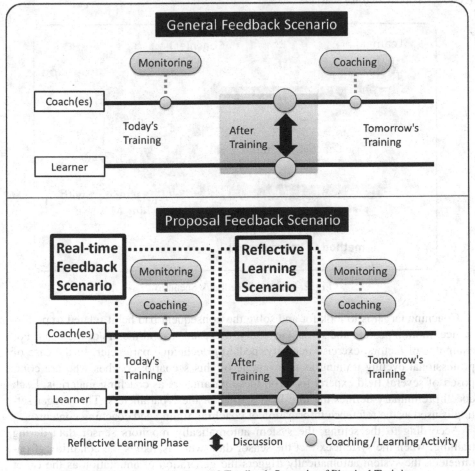

Fig. 1. Comparison with General Feedback Scenario of Physical Training

Furthermore, after training, the other scenario enables deep discussion between coaches and learners. Because after training, s/he can reflect the reconstructed annotations as her/his diary for next training. Following subsections explain to these scenarios.

3.1 Real-Time Feedback Scenario

Fig. 2 shows the real-time feedback scenario during training. We propose a simple decision-making process in order to an achievement of both real-time monitoring and coaching without excessive fatigue. At first step, in monitoring streaming data which includes sensor and video information about training, the system provides an automatic generation of coaching materials. Coaching materials in this real-time scenario mean the information that is help to coaches' judgment in order to provision of an appropriate advice. At second, the system contributes to swift discussion with such coaching materials for feedback. At last simple advice of method to improvement as feedback is provided for learners.

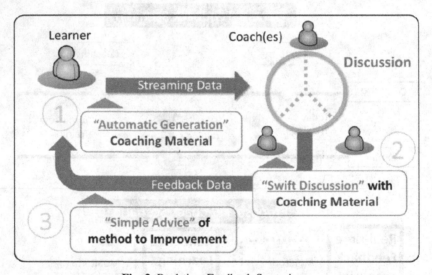

Fig. 2. Real-time Feedback Scenario

Coaching target is to look for and solve the consequent bad habit related to performance, motion posture and so on. Generally, there are several factors of the habit. For examples of factors, exercise intensity, pedaling technique parameter. In the case of professional cycling training as an example of this scenario, coaches who are composed of several field experts focus on these parameters as coaching materials. Each coach preliminary defines the threshold setting of these parameters. This trigger setting is used as the reference information of coaching timing and coaching content.

According to the setting, the system automatically monitors sensor data during training, when the system extract the sensor data which satisfies the condition of parameters, the system automatically triggers the generation of annotation as the tweet message on social service like the left side of Fig. 3.

At the step of swift discussion, while individual coaches monitor video and sensor stream within their area of specialty deeply, coaches share the triggers and the evidence of expertise each other for judgments of simple advice. For example of this discussion in Fig. 3, when the system detects a low rotation of pedaling rate, a coach of biomechanical expert recommends lower gear than current gear. Additionally, another coach of physiological expert indicates the possibility of fatigue because of high intensity compared with training objectives. Consequently the other coach who takes a leading role in coaching integrates with these experts' opinions and instructs learner to "Shift down". Of course, the basic style of coaching is trial by trial. The scenario like this example achieves the improvement of bad habit repeatedly. Regarding concrete real-time feedback, coach pushes the advice buttons among several candidates like the interface of advanced research [4], after that, while the system generates message on twitter timeline, advice is transmitted to learner as the feedback by smartphone application. On the basis of this flow, the real-time feedback is conducted during training.

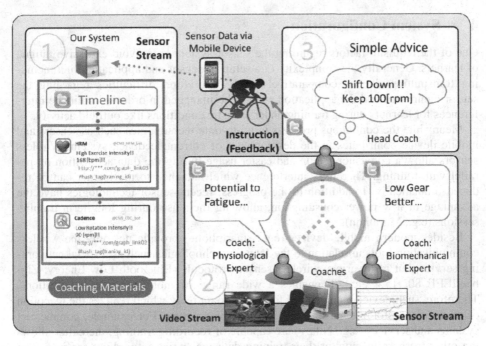

Fig. 3. Real-time feedback based on Timeline message

3.2 Reflective Learning Scenario

On the last stage, reflective learning as an asynchronous task is conducted on the web site of training-diary CMS. Though coaches provide learners with appropriate feedbacks, in fact, learners cannot be always successful in improvement of problems which are revealed in training. The quality and quantity of information which leaner can get and understand them in training are limited because learners have to concentrate on exercise while receiving feedbacks. Much the same is true on coaching of coaches. Therefore, this stage helps learners and coaches to deepen their consideration of awareness from feedbacks in order to enhancement of upcoming training for both learners and coaches. From the viewpoint of effective feedback and reflect, it is significant for both learner and coaches to improve communication which they understand the intention behind sensor data and feedback. For instance, coach's intention is equivalent to indication contained in feedback. Moreover, learner's intention appears as change action according to feedback.

Training-diary CMS gives them a web interface which they can replay streaming video linked feedback triggers during the entire training on a time-series plots in addition to sensor data. By showing such a synchronous video archive with the traces of feedbacks and the chart of sensor data concurrently, the system facilitate the reflective leaning that learner and coach can remember the situation (e.g., biomechanical conditions) when feedback triggered. For this reason, they can check each other's intention surrounded by several conditions. Thus, this stage contributes to the improvement regarding quality and quantity regarding feedback and reflection.

4   System Configuration

One of the requisite factors regarding the sensor system is to avoid excessive fatigue of learners. Generally the complexity of a setup of sensor and application link including transmitting data is comparatively high. Therefore, difficulties regarding the sensor equipment and the application need to be managed in order to minimize interferences for learners during training under realistic conditions like outfield activity.

Meanwhile the continuous progress in up-to-date technologies such as sensors and mobile device contributes to the development of current feedback system. Wireless sensors allow a convenient setup and easier usage during the data acquisition on parallel with training. Therefore, interference which attached to the learner can be reduced dramatically. In addition to the progress, recent sensor technologies have the advantage of low power consumption, allowing their use during long-term training sessions (e.g., Marathon).

Besides modern mobile devices (e.g., smartphone) provide not only the wireless communication tools in relation to the Internet technologies such as a social networking service, but also various wireless sensor protocols (Bluetooth Low Energy, Zigbee/IEEE 802.15.4 etc.). It enables a wide range of mobile training-applications. Therefore, such devices can be used for mobile data relay which realizes the reception of sensor data, storage and transmission to a web server. For example, commercial systems and services (e.g., Nike+) are capable of recording training, thereafter allowing other learners to monitor their training data via social networking services. The mobile system integrated with such wireless sensor could create the potential for the feasible remote coaching environment which prevents excessive fatigue.

Furthermore, live video streaming service (e.g., Ustream) which can now improve the utilization of broadcast because of a simple method and convenient equipment with only a few devices. Moreover, in the case of broadcast regarding training scene, it means that at least one of coaches can monitor learner's training data at individual remote places. Monitoring sensor data synchronized with streaming video of training can enhance coaches' analysis towards feedback.

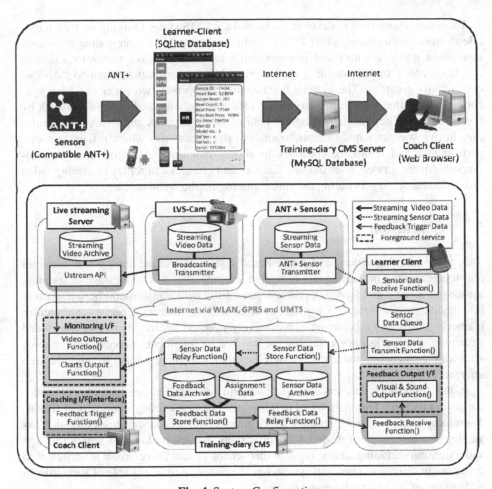

Fig. 4. System Configuration

Fig. 4 shows a system configuration based on the requirements. On the stage of training, bidirectional data flow based on sensor monitoring and feedback is constructed from data transmission between a mobile device and the server via wireless network and the Internet. Coaches can monitor learner's situation by browsing consecutively-updated sensor chart and live video streaming. Feedbacks during training are invoked by judgment of coach. On the stage after training, coaches and learners can reflect their coaching/training through a time-series plots of the web interface.

In this framework, learners are equipped with wireless sensors using ANT+ protocol during training. Our main focus in this paper is set on cycling, running and fitness. Therefore, we chose HRM, speed/distance monitors and cadence sensors as such examples of wireless sensor device. Of course, there are several kinds of sensor function and extension including analog input in this sensor series. Therefore, it is sufficient to cover many activities. Thus, our system has the potential to be capable of supporting a wide range of skill acquisition and so on under educational environment with coaching.

Thus, our objective is to develop training-diary CMS system linking up with a mobile devices (smartphone, tablet PC etc.) which are capable of integrating the aforementioned wireless sensor and live streaming technologies. We tackle to a remote coaching which makes use of a high compatible sensor platform named "ANT+" connectivity solution. The system functionality comprises two services. As a synchronous/real time service, the server provides coaches with analysis and feedback by remote access. They take advantage of data of ANT+ sensors and live video streaming. In this way, coaches are able to analyze the parameters which reflect learners' performance and return the feedback in almost real time. Also for an asynchronous/subsequent service, after training learners and coaches can replay streaming video linked feedback triggers during the entire training on the web interface.

5   Conclusion

This paper describes a design of server-based system of training diary which provides real-time coaching in training and reflective learning after it. On the stage of training, sensor monitoring and feedback is constructed from data transmission between a mobile device and the server via wireless network and the Internet. Coaches can monitor learner's situation by browsing consecutively-updated sensor chart and live video streaming. Feedbacks during training are invoked by judgment of coach. On the stage after training, coaches and learners can reflect their coaching/training through the web interface.

In this framework, learners are equipped with wireless sensors using ANT+ protocol during training. Our main focus in this paper is set on cycling, running and fitness. Therefore, we chose HRM, speed/distance monitors and cadence sensors as such examples of wireless sensor device. Of course, there are several kinds of sensor function and extension including analog input in this sensor series. Therefore, it is sufficient to cover many activities. Thus, our system has the potential to be capable of supporting a wide range of skill acquisition and so on.

Our future work concentrates on the implementation and experimentation. For implementation, we have a plan to develop the system, in particular software on mobile device, in several major platforms of mobile devices in order to meet practical demands. Moreover, for experimentation regarding improvement skill, we will obtain knowledge for knowledge-based and expert systems for the automatic generation of feedback [5]. Therefore, we aim to investigate the identification of movement patterns from the viewpoint of coaching by experts [9].

Acknowledgements. This work was partially supported by Nakajima Foundation.

References

1. Power, T., Bindler, R., Goetz, S., Daratha, K.: Obesity Prevention in Early Adolescence: Student, Parent, and Teacher Views. J. Sch. Health 80, 13–19 (2010)
2. Schmidt, R.A., Lee, T.D.: Motor Control and Learning: A Behavioral Emphasis, 4th edn. Human Kinetics, Champaign (2005)

3. Feltz, D.L., Landers, D.M.: The effects of mental practice on motor skill learning and performance: a meta-analysis. Journal of Sport & Exercise Psychology 5(1), 25–57 (1983)
4. Gotoda, N., Matsuura, K., Otsuka, S., Tanaka, T., Yano, Y.: Remote Coaching System for Runner's Form with Wearable Wireless Sensor. IJMLO 5(3-4), 282–298 (2011)
5. Gotoda, N., Matsuura, T., Hirano, S., Tanaka, T., Yano, Y.: Supporting Real-time Awareness for the Community of Runners. IJKWI 1(3-4), 289–303 (2010)
6. Gotoda, N., Sakurai, Y., Matsuura, K., Nakagawa, K., Miyaji, C.: A Coaching CMS with Wireless Sensors using ANT+ Connectivity Solution. In: Workshop Proceedings of ICCE 2012, pp. 508–515 (2012)
7. Poulton, E.C.: On prediction in skilled movements. Psychological Bulletin 54(6), 467–478 (1957)
8. Allard, F., Starkes, J.L.: Motor-skill experts in sports, dance, and other domains. In: Ericsson, K.A., Smith, J. (eds.) Toward a General Theory of Expertise, pp. 126–150. Cambridge University Press (1991)
9. Marsland, F., Lyons, K., Anson, J., Waddington, G., Macintosh, C., Chapman, D.: Identification of cross-country skiing movement patterns using micro-sensors. Sensors 12, 5047–5066 (2012)

Usability Evaluation of a Voluntary Patient Safety Reporting System: Understanding the Difference between Predicted and Observed Time Values by Retrospective Think-Aloud Protocols

Lei Hua[1,2] and Yang Gong[2]

[1] Informatics Institute, University of Missouri, Columbia, MO, USA
[2] School of Biomedical Informatics, University of Texas Health Science Center, Houston, TX, USA
lh5cc@mail.missouri.edu, Yang.Gong@uth.tmc.edu

Abstract. The study evaluated the usability of a voluntary patient safety reporting system using two established methods of cognitive task analysis and retrospective think-aloud protocols. Two usability experts and ten end users were employed in two separated experiments, and predicted and observed task execution times were obtained for comparison purpose. According to the results, mental operations contributed to the major effort in reporting. The significant time differences were identified that pointed out the difficulty in human cognition as users interacted with the system. At last, the data collected by retrospective think-aloud technique, e.g. the response consistency on structured questions and the user's attitudes, revealed the frequent usability problems impeding completion of a quality report.

Keywords: patient safety, voluntary reporting, cognitive task analysis, retrospective think-aloud.

1 Introduction

The Institute of Medicine called for nationwide reporting systems to collect medical incidents for patient safety improvement in 1999, the year when "To Err is Human" report was released [1]. It is believed that the reporting systems would be a data source to learn from the lessons, if safety events were collected in a properly structured format for the detection of case patterns, discovery of underlying factors, and generation of solutions. Since 2008, 26 States had implemented hospital medical error and incident reporting systems [2]. However, there are gaps between the status quo and the potential of the reporting systems, because of the challenges in user engagement [3] and data quality[4, 5]. As a critical contributing factor, usability has received little attention in dealing with the challenges.

In this study, we employed two usability methods of cognitive task analysis and retrospective think-aloud protocols to evaluate a patient safety reporting system. The difference between predicted and observed time from two experiments drew attention to the sites where the user's performance was significantly affected. The analysis of task responses and think-aloud protocols helped identify usability problems and their underlying factors at the sites.

M. Kurosu (Ed.): Human-Computer Interaction, Part II, HCII 2013, LNCS 8005, pp. 94–100, 2013.
© Springer-Verlag Berlin Heidelberg 2013

2   Methods

2.1   The Study System

The development of the tested system was based on the navigational structures of an implemented reporting system in a local health organization [6]. It implemented the Common Formats (CFs) for collecting case details. Developed by the Agency for Healthcare Research and Quality (AHRQ), the CFs aim to diminish the disparity of categorizing and describing patient safety events among the existing patient safety organizations and reporting systems. For each event category, CFs offer a standardized list of multiple-choice questions (MCQs) to promote case reporting.

2.2   Cognitive Task Analysis, GOMS and KLM

Cognitive task analysis (CTA) is a widely used usability evaluation method to describe the tactics and knowledge that underlay task performance. The method employs usability experts and GOMS (Goals, Operators, Methods, and Selection rules) model to examine the user's physical and cognitive steps and barriers in the task execution. For the measures of execution time and mental-physical ratio, Keystroke Level Model (KLM) was used to estimate mental and physical operations in seconds. It refers to seven operators with estimated execution time on each.

- K – Keystroke : 0.28 Sec
- T (n) - Type a single chuck of n characters in a sequence on a keyboard : n*K Sec
- P - Point with mouse to a target on the display : 1.1 Sec
- B - Press or release mouse button : 0.1 Sec
- BB - Click mouse button : 0.2 Sec
- H - Home hands to keyboard or mouse : 0.4 Sec
- M - Mental act of routine thinking or perception : 1.2 Sec

Differing from the peers under the GOMS family [7], GOMS-KLM considers the individual operations in a linear sequence and sum them up for predicted execution time as shown in Table 1. In the study, the predicted time served as a baseline of reporter's performance, to pinpoint the observed data that significantly varied from the prediction.

Table 1. "Entering occurrence time of an event" subtask using GOMS with KLM technique

| | GOMS | | KLM | |
| | | | KLM | |
Step #	Step description	Distributed cognition Physical/Mental operator	Operators	Time (s)
Step 1	Locate the field for date entry	Mental	M	1.2
Step 2	Point the mouse to the field	Physical	P	1.1
Step 3	Click to put the cursor into the field	Physical	B	0.1
Step 4	Verify the date field that obtains the focus	Mental	M	1.2
Step 5	Hand keyboard	Physical	H	0.4
Step 6	Retrieve the date	Mental	M	1.2
Step 7	Interpret the date value into required format	Mental	M	1.2
Step 8	Type the formatted date	Physical	T(10)\	2.8
Step 9	Verify the date and its format are correct	Mental	M	1.2
Step 10	Home hand to mouse	Physical	H	0.4
			Total	10.8

2.3   Retrospective Think-Aloud Protocols

We applied the retrospective think-aloud (RTA) to measuring user's performance in aspects of execution time, data quality and user's attitudes. The method asked participants to verbalize their thoughts after the reporting session activity, instead of during the session. The method avoids obtrusive task disturbances that were usually introduced by concurrent think-aloud technique to the performance.

2.4   Participants

Two usability experts and ten end users were recruited for the CTA and RTA experiments separately. In RTA, the invitation letter and screening form were emailed to the School of Nursing and the School of Medicine at the University of Missouri for qualified participants. The qualified respondents were those who had reported patient falls at least once and were interested in online patient safety reporting systems. The first ten available candidates became the testing participants. Every study participant was required to sign on an informed consent form, according to the approval of the Institutional Review Board in the university.

2.5   Task Scenarios and Testing Steps

The task was to report three patient fall events in the system. Three fall cases in a written format were selected from a library of 346 fall reports. The cases were reviewed by domain experts to ensure quality and readability. Fall event cases were chosen for the test because the fall reporting form in the CFs is simple and structurally representative, and falls are typical in hospitals at all levels. An example of a fall event scenario selected from the library is shown in the following excerpt:

> ... the patient indicated need to be toileted. He stood with a walker and walked to the bathroom. He noted less steady than yesterday, dragging right leg. He turned while in the bathroom toward the sink ...

Table 2. Time performance and material accessibility by subtask

Subtask	Task name	Time (s)	Access to written materials
#1	Answer initial questions	18.3	Yes
#2	Rate a harm score	28.1	No
#3	Enter patient related info	100.8	Yes
#4	Answer structured MCQs	102.2	No
#5	Document further comments	34.5	No
	Total	283.9	

In both experiments to fulfill a reporting task, the participants needed to complete five subtasks sequentially as shown in Table 2. In practice, the reporters at the work site documented case-specific information upon memory. Thus, in a simulated setting as it was in the RTA test, the participants were not allowed to review the written materials for completing case-specific subtasks #2, #4 and #5, once did the reporting start.

In CTA, GOMS was performed on the set of five tasks to identify common task steps. Two evaluators (LH and RG) independently conducted GOMS on each of the five tasks. Inter-rater reliability was calculated to determine the extent to which two evaluators agree with each other on dividing task steps and assigning physical/mental operators.

In RTA, the ten participants were assigned separate time sessions for the test. They were trained by a video demonstrating how to manipulate the system for completing a report. Each session was audio and video recorded using Camtasia Studio® 7. Ten participant's task performance and verbalization were collected for data analysis.

2.6   Processing of the Data

For the purpose of comparison, we focused on time performance in the two experiments. Predicted and observed execution times were collected from the two experiments and then contrasted by tasks and subtasks. The time performance in CTA consists of two parts. The sum of six physical operators' time on the task represents user's physical execution time, and the amount of mental operators involved determines user's mental execution time. These predicted time values were served as a benchmark to contrast with counterparts observed through RTA, in which the observed execution time was split into two parts based on the collection of physical operators and execution times by the session review. The difference between the predicted and observed time served as an indicator of the system usability problems that users encountered in RTA.

Since the usability problems might have negative effects on the quality of reports and user's attitudes, related data were collected for the evaluation. The response consistency on structured questions was calculated by generalized Kappa[8], to account for the kind of easiness that users were able to reach a consensus. A low consistency inferred the existence of usability issues on the question. In addition, the participants' think-aloud verbalizations were transcribed and coded by a scheme developed by Zhang et al[9]. The coding scheme comprised 14 usability heuristics assisted in classifying usability problems that influenced participant's performance in the test. Any disagreement in classification was resolved in discussions among research team members until a full agreement was reached.

3   Results

In CTA, the mean counts of task steps was 225 that consisted of 93 physical and 132 mental operations. In total, a report took 266.6 seconds averagely for a report and 108.2 seconds and 158.4 seconds respectively. The ratio of mental/physical operators was 58.67% as shown in Table 3.

In RTA, the mean of reporting completion times is 277.9 seconds. 102 physical operators were involved for each report and accounted for 96.5 seconds. The difference between total and physical times of 181.4 Sec is construed as the mean of actual mental times on a report. All above results are listed in Table 4.

Table 3. Time performance and material accessibility by subtask

Task #	Task name	Total steps	Operators Mental	Physical	% Mental	Est. time (s) Mental	Physical	Time in total (s)	Kappa
1	Answer initial questions	22	11	11	50.00%	13.2	6.9	20.1	0.937
2	Rate a harm score	14	10	4	71.43%	12.0	2.4	14.4	0.606
3	Enter patient information	103	56	47	54.37%	67.2	32.4	99.6	0.888
4	Answer structured MCQs	72	49	23	68.06%	58.8	34.2	93.0	0.802
5	Document further comments	14	6	8	42.86%	7.2	32.3	39.5	0.651
	Total	225	132	93	58.67%	158.4	108.2	266.6	

Table 4. User Testing with KLM and think-aloud technique

Task #	Task name	Total Time(s)	Observed Physical Operators	Time(s)	Mental time (s) Obs.	Pred. in Table 3	Diff.
1	Answer initial questions	18.3	11	11	11.4	13.2	-13.64%
2	Rate a harm score	22.1	10	4	19.7	12	64.17%
3	Enter patient information	100.8	56	47	65.5	67.2	-2.53%
4	Answer structured MCQs	102.2	49	23	76.9	58.8	30.85%
5	Document further comments	34.5	6	8	7.9	7.2	9.72%
	Total	277.9	132	93	181.4	158.4	14.52%

Considering CTA results as a benchmark, the majority of observed execution times from RTA were within the error limit of +-21% suggested by GOMS-KLM[10]. Task #2 and #4 were exceptional as shown in Table 4. We thus looked into them at the single question level as subtasks as shown in Table 5. Half of the subtasks (6 out of 12) were beyond the limit that took either much less or more time than the prediction. The agreement of the choice selection on each of the subtasks was calculated and attached except for subtask #4.9 that allows checking multiple choices for the answer.

Table 5. Comparison of estimated and actual mental time on subtasks of task #2 and #4 (multi-choice questions), with agreement rate of 10 subjects' choice selection

Subtask #	Subtask name	# of choices	Mental time (s) Obs.	Pred.	Diff.	Generalized Kappa
2.1	Rate a harm score	6	19.7	12	64.17%	0.385
4.1	Q(1) Assisted fall or not	3	3.57	3.6	-0.93%	0.748
4.2	Q(2) Observed fall or not	3	1.97	3.6	-45.37%	0.867
4.3	Q(3) Observed by who	2	2.68	3.6	-25.51%	0.719
4.4	Q(4) Patient Injured or not	3	3.23	3.6	-10.19%	0.933
4.5	Q(5)* Type of injury	5	9.00	4.8	87.58%	1.000
4.6	Q(6)* Prior doing ahead of falling	11	12.45	4.8	159.31%	0.304
4.7	Q(7) Fall risk assessed or not	3	7.41	3.6	105.74%	0.363
4.8	Q(8) Patient at risk or not	3	3.95	3.6	9.72%	0.833
4.9	Q(9)*~ preventive protocols	16	24.76	20.4	21.37%	N/A
4.10	Q(10) Med increased risk or not	3	4.06	3.6	12.78%	0.630
4.11	Q(11) Med contributed to fall or not	3	3.87	3.6	7.41%	0.696
			76.9	58.8	30.85%	

In the think-aloud protocols, fifty-seven comments were coded into nine categories of usability problems reflecting user attitudes. Some comments that referred to multiple categories were categorized into the best fit. The most frequently identified problem was the language problem – 15 comments (26.3%) and every subject had at least one comment on CFs questions. The common issues were match (22.8%), memory (15.8%), visibility (12.3%) and feedback (8.8%). Most of the coded problems in the top five categories were commenting on cognitive difficulties that subjects encountered in the task completion process.

4   Discussion

In two experiments using different usability techniques, three types of data were collected with respect to the reporting time, consistency and user's attitudes. Supposing the time variables from CTA as a benchmark, the comparison identified several significant differences between the prediction and observation. The data regarding the response consistency and user's attitudes from RTA accounted for the underlying factors that might lead to the differences.

Overall, the predicted and observed execution times for a report completion were very close. All time differences regarding physical and mental operations were under the error limit regulated in KLM for time prediction. It indicated that the unknown disturbances, if the RTA had, did not influence the execution times in the observation significantly in comparison of the predicted values.

To complete a report, 93 physical operators were predicted comparing 102 operators in the observation. Not in an ideal circumstance as the testers in CTA that had no hassles on unpredictable redo and typo, the ten participants in RTA might need extra keystrokes or mouse clicks in the real context.

On the other hand, the differences of mental execution times between the two experiments exceeded the error limit on task #2, #4 and some corresponding subtasks as shown in Table 5. For example, the percent variations were 159.31% and 105.74% on the subtask #4.6 and #4.7. Meanwhile, the low responding consistency (considering 0.600 as a dividing threshold [11]) might occur accordingly. It indicated in a few of subtasks reporting case details, extra mental operators and user errors were introduced for unpredicted problems in human cognition. According to the coded comments, usability problems of language, information mismatch, visibility and feedback dominated the cognitive issues that burdened the participants and lowered the participant's performance.

5   Limitation

The findings were based on a specific domain and obtrusive study techniques that might limit the generalizability of identified problems and user's performance in a natural context. To make a comparison of mental execution times between two experiments, we subtracted estimated time of physical operators from the total to obtain the mental time values based on an arguable assumption. It assumed the estimated execution times of physical operators by GOMS-KLM were accurate and physical and mental operations in RTA could be treated in a linear sequence of execution.

6   Conclusion

The study showed that mental operation accounted for the majority of effort in a report using the system. The mental effort could be affected by usability problems as a reporter interacted with the system interface that slowed the process and undermined the quality of reporting. Cognitive task analysis and think-aloud user testing was helpful to identify these problems and pave the way towards the system usability enhancement.

References

1. Rosenthal, J., Takach, M.: 2007 guide to state adverse event reporting systems. National Academy for State Health Policy (2007)
2. Levinson, D.R.: Adverse events in hospitals: state reporting systems. US Department of Health and Human Services, Office of the Inspector General Washington, DC (2008)
3. Kim, J., Bates, D.W.: Results of a survey on medical error reporting systems in Korean hospitals. Int. J. Med. Inform. 75(2), 148–155 (2006)
4. Gong, Y.: Data consistency in a voluntary medical incident reporting system. J. Med. Syst. 35(4), 609–615 (2009)
5. Gong, Y.: Terminology in a voluntary medical incident reporting system: a human-centered perspective. In: Proceedings of the 1st ACM International Health Informatics Symposium, pp. 2–7. ACM, Arlington (2010)
6. Kivlahan, C., et al.: Developing a comprehensive electronic adverse event reporting system in an academic health center. Jt. Comm. J. Qual. Improv. 28(11), 583–594 (2002)
7. John, B.E., Kieras, D.E.: The GOMS family of user interface analysis techniques: comparison and contrast. ACM Trans. Comput.-Hum. Interact. 3(4), 320–351 (1996)
8. Fleiss, J.L.: Measuring nominal scale agreement among many raters. Psychological Bulletin 76(5), 378–382 (1971)
9. Zhang, J., et al.: Using usability heuristics to evaluate patient safety of medical devices. J. Biomed. Inform. 36(1-2), 23–30 (2003)
10. Card, S.K., Moran, T.P., Newell, A.: The psychology of human-computer interaction (1983), http://books.google.com/books?id=JeFQAAAAMAAJ
11. Devore, J.L.: Probability and statistics for engineering and the sciences. Brooks/Cole Pub. Co., Monterey (1982)

Usability in RFP's: The Current Practice and Outline for the Future

Timo Jokela, Juha Laine, and Marko Nieminen

Aalto University, Department of Computer Science and Engineering/SoberIT,
P.O. Box 15400, FI-00076 Aalto, Finland
{timo.jokela,juha.laine,marko.nieminen}@aalto.fi

Abstract. Studies show that healthcare and other government systems suffer from poor usability. In this research, we aim to understand the reasons and propose solutions to this problem. We conclude so far that (1) the critical phase where to address usability in government system development contracting is request for proposals (RFP), (2) the appropriate place for usability in a RFP is requirements rather than selection criteria and (3) usability requirements should based on user performance, rather than on design principles, usability guidelines, process requirements, or such. We find that defining user performance based usability requirements is a challenging task and a most relevant subject for further research.

Keywords: Usability; government systems; RFP, request for proposals; usability requirements; performance requirements; process requirements; design requirements; usability measures.

1 Introduction

Government organizations widely suffer from poor usability. Studies show that doctors find the healthcare systems difficult to use [14]. A widely used travel management system is another example of what kind of consequences the usability problems lead to. Users report that making a single travel expense report may take three hours, and requires contacting user support every time.

Why do these kinds of usability problems exist? Obviously, this should not a matter of the application area: commonly used office software (word processing, spreadsheets, etc.) represents at least reasonable good usability. It should be quite feasible to develop usable travel management systems - the web is full of easy-to-use travel services.

We find that it is reasonable to examine the specific context of how government systems are developed. European Union legislation requires that the development of government systems has to be open for free and fair competition. Any interested contractor should be in a position to submit a proposal. Therefore, government authorities must issue a public *request for proposal (RFP)* for the development of a new system.

A RFP is includes two main elements: (1) the requirements for the system to be developed, and (2) selection criteria. The system contractor has to meet – or promise

M. Kurosu (Ed.): Human-Computer Interaction, Part II, HCII 2013, LNCS 8005, pp. 101–106, 2013.
© Springer-Verlag Berlin Heidelberg 2013

to meet – the requirements; otherwise it will be excluded from the competition. From those contractors that (promise to) meet the requirements, the one is selected as the contractor who gets the highest points based on the selection criteria.

One selection criterion is always price; in addition there may be quality criteria. The selection criteria are defined so that maximum total is 100 points. The weight for price could be, for example, 60 points, and the weight of quality factors could be 40 points. It is the choice of the purchaser to define what are the selection criteria and their the weights. The selected contractor is then committed deliver what is stated in the requirements in the RFP.

Related Research. Usability in government system acquisition has not been a big topic in literature. A late contribution is a recent book on usability of government systems [2], including one chapter on usability in contracts [7], co-authored by one of the authors of this paper. He also has done earlier research where RFP's issue by Finnish public authorities were examined [10]; and a RFP case study is presented [8].

Lauesen [9] addressed earlier the issue. He proposes usability requirements in performance style and process style) metrics and target values. He, however, does not report practical experience.

Some authors have studied software contracting [1], [11], [4] but their focus has been usability after the system developer is selected.

The aim of our research is to understand how this kind of competitive system acquisition setting explains the poor usability of government systems; and what would be the solutions for improve the acquisition process.

2   Description of the Work So Far

We have achieved the following outcomes so far:

- We conclude that request for proposals (RFP) is the critical phase where usability should be addressed in government system acquisition
- We conclude that the appropriate place for usability in a RFP is requirements, rather than selection criteria.
- We argue that usability requirements should based on user performance, rather than on design principles, usability guidelines, process requirements, or such.

The Criticality of Request for Proposals (RFP) in Government System Development. The system procurement process starts when the government authority launches a RPF. The selection of the contractor is a formal process, with two main steps:

1. Exclude those contractors that to not meet – nor do not promise to meet - the requirements defined in the RFP.
2. Select to contractor that get the highest score based on the selection criteria.

What does this selection process mean from the contractors perspective? Any 'wise' contractor would make a proposal that (1) exactly fulfills the requirements with minimal costs and (2) gets high points in terms of the selection criteria with lowest cost.

As a consequence, it is natural that a wise contractor allocates resources for usability activities in their proposals only to the extent to which usability is among the requirements and selection criteria. If usability is not among the requirements or selection criteria, it is not wise to assign resources to usability, because it would make the proposal less competitive.

As a conclusion, request for proposal (RFP) is a most critical phase in government system development. The contractors consider usability only to the extent that usability is required in the RFP.

What is the Right Place for Usability in a RFP? Usability may be included in the requirements, the selection criteria, or both of them in a RFP.

What would be the right choice? Our conclusion is that *the right place for usability is requirements.*

The reasoning is quite simple: only requirements guarantee that usability is truly considered in the development. Usability of the system must meet the requirements (to the extent that stated in a verifiable way).

If usability is among selection criteria, good usability naturally contributes to the total points of the proposal. But it is always possible that a contractor with low – even zero - points in usability will be selected. A contractor that gets low points from usability but high points from other criteria may be selected if the total sum of points is higher than with competitors.

How Should One Define Usability in Requirements in RFP's? We have concluded that usability must be in requirements of a RFP. To have impact, usability requirements should be such that their satisfaction truly results to a usable system.

What makes such requirements? The requirements should be verifiable, valid, and comprehensive:

- Verifiable: It is possible objectively determine whether a requirement is satisfied or not. Actually, if a 'requirement' is not verifiable, it is not a true requirement at all.
- Valid: The content of the requirement is correct, so that its satisfaction means that the system is appropriately usable.
- Comprehensive: The requirements cover the system substantially enough.

In an earlier study on government issued RFP's [10], it was found that usability was included in requirements with four main types of approaches:

- General usability requirements
- Usability process requirements
- Usability design requirements
- User performance requirements

Which types of requirements are verifiable, valid, and comprehensive?

General Usability Requirements. An example of a general usability requirement is "The system must be easy to use".

These kinds of general 'requirements' are, simply, not requirements at all because they are not verifiable. These kinds of statements do not have any impact on system development. A contractor does not need to pay any attention to this kind of 'requirement'.

Process Requirements. Examples of process requirement are that a contractor "must do three cycles of prototype – usability testing"; or "the contractor must present a proof, declaring that the system was usability inspected".

These kinds of process requirements have a problem: there is a risk that the contractor cannot provide a satisfactory design by "three iterative cycles". The reason is simple: if the original design is poor, even a large number of usability tests do not guarantee good usability.

Another problem with process requirements is that processes as such do not ensure quality. The CUE studies [12] have shown that the quality of even the very basic activity, usability testing, may greatly diverse.

Design Requirements. Design requirements are about requiring to follow general design guidelines, such as 9241-110 [6]; examples:

- "The format of input and output should be appropriate to the task."
- "The steps required by the dialogue should be appropriate to the completion of the task."

We find these kinds of guidelines most relevant to the system. We conclude, however, that these kinds of requirements are problematic.

First, we could not think any other way of referring a guideline in a measurable way, but the number of design solutions that violate the guidelines. And the only target value that we could think of was 'zero': no violations against the guidelines accepted. And this is obviously not realistic.

Another problem is that most of the guidelines are not verifiable; e.g. the examples above.

User Performance Requirements. Our conclusion is that the only valid way of defining usability requirements is through user performance. In other words, one should state in the requirements how well users should perform – carry out their tasks and achieve the desired accomplishments – with the system to be developed.

If one can define valid and comprehensive enough performance requirements in a verifiable way, they form a solid basis for truly achieving usability.

3   Future Work

Our research has indicated the need for developing a pragmatic method for defining user performance based usability requirements.

We find this a challenging task because usability is always context sensitive:

- The method should guide for determining appropriate measures. Which should one measure: effectiveness, efficiency or satisfaction?
- The method should also guide to defining the target level: how good usability one should aim at?

- It is essential to define the right user accomplishments; this is also a challenging task if one wishes to cover the users' world comprehensively.

There are other interesting research questions, too. So far, earlier research has examined RFP's issued in Finland [10]. It would be interesting to do similar studies in other countries. Especially, do practices in other European countries differ the ones in Finland?

It also would be interesting to learn where the current – and inappropriate – practices of RFP's stem from?

Recommendations for Practice. Our two basic pieces of advice for practitioners – i.e. to the government authorities, who prepare RFP's - are:

1. Include usability in the requirements, rather than in selection criteria
2. Base usability requirements on user performance; do NOT use general requirements, design guidelines nor process requirements

The challenge is that how define such user performance based requirements in a valid, verifiable and comprehensive way. As said, this is a challenging task that we find a new research agenda. Therefor, we can give another, a bit provocative advice: Unless you know how to define proper user performance based usability requirements – do NOT include any usability requirements or criteria in a RFP at all! This way you at least avoid self-delusion: thinking that *some* usability requirements would lead to usability. (As the history shows, this is simply not true).

Impact on HCI Community. Usability requirements has not been a major research topic recently. The main papers are from 1980's, such as [3][16][5][13], and[15].

Our conclusions indicate that usability requirements should be considered in practitioners' work – especially among government authorities – and in the research focus again. There is a need for methods for defining valid, verifiable and comprehensive usability requirements. It just seems that such requirements are critically needed to ensure the usability of government systems.

References

1. Artman, H., Zällh, S.: Finding a way to usability: procurement of a taxi dispatch system (2005)
2. Buie, E., Murray, D. (eds.): Usability in Government Systems: User Experience Design for Citizens and Public Servants. Morgan Kaufmann (2012)
3. Good, M., Spine, T.M., Whiteside, J., George, P.: User-derived impact analysis as a tool for usability engineering. In: Conference Proceedings on Human Factors in Computing Systems, pp. 241–246 (1986)
4. Gulliksen, J., Göransson, B., Boivie, I., Blomqvist, S., Persson, J., Cajander, Å.: Key Principles of User-Centred Systems Design. Behaviour & Information Technology 22(6), 397–409 (2003)

5. Hix, D., Hartson, H.R.: Developing User Interfaces: Ensuring Usability Through Product & Process. John Wiley & Sons, New York (1993)
6. ISO/IEC. 9241-110 Ergonomics of human-system interaction – Part 110: Dialogue principles (2006)
7. Jokela, T., Buie, E., Getting UX into the Contract. In: Buie, E., Murray, D. (eds.) Usability in Government Systems: User Experience Design for Citizens and Public Servants. Morgan Kaufmann (2012)
8. Jokela, T.: Determining Usability Requirements into a Call-for- Tenders. A Case Study on the Development of a Healthcare System. In: NordiCHI 2010, pp. 256–265 (2010)
9. Lauesen, S.: Usability requirements in a tender process. In: OZCHI 1998 (1998)
10. Lehtonen, T., Kumpulainen, J., Jokela, T., Liukkonen, T.: How Much Usability Truly Matters? A Study on Usability Requirements in Call-for-Tenders of Software Systems, Issued by Public Authorities. In: NordiCHI 2010 (2010)
11. Markensten, E., Artman, H.: Procuring a Usable System Using Unemployed Personas. In: NordiCHI 2004 (2004)
12. Molich, R., Ede, M.R., Kaasgaard, K., Karyukind, B.: Comparative Usability Evaluation. Behaviour & Information Technology 23(1), 65–74 (2004)
13. Nielsen, J.: Usability Engineering. Academic Press, Inc., San Diego (1993)
14. Viitanen, J., Hyppönen, H., Lääveri, T., Vänskä, J., Reponen, J., Winblad, I.: National questionnaire study on clinical ICT systems proofs: Physicians suffer from poor usability. International Journal of Medical Informatics 80(10), 708–725 (2011)
15. Whiteside, J., Bennett, J., Holtzblatt, K.: Usability Engineering: Our Experience and Evolution. In: Helander, M. (ed.) Handbook of Human-Computer Interaction, pp. 791–817. North-Holland, Amsterdam (1988)
16. Wixon, D., Wilson, C.: The Usability Engineering Framework for Product Design and Evaluation. In: Helander, M., Landauer, T., Prabhu, P. (eds.) Handbook of Human-Computer Interaction, pp. 653–688. Elsevier Science B.V., Amsterdam (1997)

Design and Interface Considerations for Web-Enabled Data Management in Civil Infrastructure Health Monitoring

David E. Kosnik[1] and Lawrence J. Henschen[2]

[1] Infrastructure Technology Institute, Northwestern University, Evanston, IL 60208
[2] Dept. of Electrical Engineering & Computer Science, Northwestern University, Evanston IL 60208

Abstract. We present principles and techniques for design of Web-enabled data aggregation, storage, and visualization software for structural health monitoring of civil infrastructure: the process of collecting and analyzing sensor data related to the condition or behavior of constructed facilities (e.g., bridges, dams, tunnels) to promote safe and efficient service at a reasonable cost. Due to widely variable user requirements and the vast range of data types and display methods required, good human-computer interfaces for engineering applications are still difficult to design and implement, and continue to be constructed in more-or-less ad hoc manners. We approach human-computer interaction in the civil engineering domain through common HCI methods, such as user interviews, use case design and analysis, representation in UML, and so on. However, this paper is focused on two special techniques that are not commonly found in HCI development: (1) a rigorous analysis of the nature of the data and how it will be used, and (2) a general method for sending data into functions for display on the user interface. The addition of two techniques like the above adds new tools to the engineering HCI toolkit and increases HCI designers' ability to meet the needs of engineers who examine large volumes of engineering data.

1   Introduction and Application Domain

Good human-computer interfaces for engineering applications are still difficult to design and implement, and continue to be constructed in more-or-less ad hoc manners. The widely varying needs of users of such systems and the vast range of data types and display methods makes development of a small number of techniques to cover all such interface design problems difficult. Therefore, it is important to see examples of such interfaces. This paper illustrates useful design principles and considerations for design of an engineering software interface. The application is structural health monitoring (SHM) in the civil engineering domain: the process of collecting and analyzing data related to the condition or behavior of constructed facilities (e.g., bridges, dams, tunnels) to promote safe and efficient service at a reasonable cost. In addition to steps common to most human-computer interaction (HCI) applications — user interviews, use

M. Kurosu (Ed.): Human-Computer Interaction, Part II, HCII 2013, LNCS 8005, pp. 107–116, 2013.

case design and analysis, Unified Modeling Language (UML) representation, and so forth — we developed two special techniques that are not commonly found in HCI development: (1) rigorous analysis of the nature of the data and how it will be used, and (2) a general method for sending data into functions for display on the user interface.

Several factors guide development of SHM software and data requirements. First, data required for SHM can come from a large variety of sources, including, among others, sensors in the structure, data entered by hand by engineers or other stakeholders, and live data streams such as meteorological and hydrological data feeds from government agencies. All these data must be piped to a single point from which useful SHM information can be distilled and displayed. Second, various representations and scales of time play a crucial, but difficult, role in SHM analysis and interpretation. Third, special care is required in SHM of constructed facilities due to system uniqueness — unlike factory-manufactured systems such as airplanes, each bridge, tunnel, or building is unique in terms of design, loading, and field conditions [1]. Consequently, many measurements (in space and time) may be required to characterize structure behavior and inform mechanical or stochastic models of structure behavior. A well-planned data management scheme supports human engineers' interpretation of structure behavior to identify (1) normal or baseline behavior and (2) deviations from that behavior. Such deviations can be interpreted as various changes in the system, whether from changes in loading or the onset of damage, which may be characterized in a variety of ways [2].

A Web application service, dubbed RAMSES-CI (Remote Autonomous Monitoring Software Environment Service for Civil Infrastructure) provides a convenient mechanism for displaying SHM data to a variety of stakeholders. As an application service, it operates independently of the information technology architecture of the agencies that own the monitored infrastructure. The RAMSES-CI system was developed as part of long-term structural health monitoring deployments at 27 real-world sites in ten states and the District of Columbia, 12 of which are active at this writing.

2   Taxonomy of SHM Data

Classification of data and analysis of how each type is used and how different types of data relate to each other were crucial first steps in HCI design for engineering SHM. Specifically, recognizing that civil infrastructure SHM data may be obtained or derived from a wide variety of sources and may take a number of conceptual forms, it is useful to define a taxonomy of data for analysis. Types of data range from time series data (e.g., read a sensor every minute) to burst data (e.g. when an event occurs, wake up and record at millisecond intervals until the event is over) to single point entries (e.g., the weight of a truck crossing over a bridge) to mixtures of these.

2.1   Time Scales and Granularity

Classification of SHM data is determined in large part by varying time scales and representations found in civil infrastructure and related engineering domains; such time-related data require careful treatment in storage, visualization, and analysis [3]. Unfortunately, fundamental assumptions and concepts relating to time may be suppressed or simplified away when stored electronically [4]. The rate at which data will vary depends upon the quantity being measured and the physical behavior of the structure to be investigated. If one is interested in quasi-static phenomena, it is sufficient to keep time in familiar human-readable year-month-day, hour-minute-second format. However, if one is interested in short-term dynamic phenomena (quantities varying quickly over a few seconds or minutes) — particularly those which occur randomly without a priori notification, such as a triggered burst of dynamic time history data as a truck crosses a bridge — two distinct time scales describing the event must be considered: (1) the year-month-day, hour-minute-second timestamp at which the event began, which establishes the time of the event in context of long-term measurements, and (2) the sub-second resolution elapsed time since the beginning of the event, which establishes the time base for analysis of structural dynamics.

2.2   SHM Data Types

We adapt an information visualization taxonomy from the literature to fit SHM data. In a type-by-task taxonomy of information visualizations, Shneiderman defined seven key data types: one-dimensional, two-dimensional, three-dimensional, temporal, multi-dimensional, tree, and network [5]. The tree and network types, which describe collections of and relationships among items, are outside the scope of this analysis; however, the other types are readily adapted to the domain of civil infrastructure monitoring. Following Shneiderman's classification scheme, we propose the following basic types for structural health monitoring data, with the corresponding type from Shneiderman [5] in brackets:

1. **continuous time histories** — measurements made more or less continuously at regular intervals, e.g., hourly measurements of the response of a structure to changes in ambient temperature [temporal data]
2. **burst time histories** — measurements made at high frequency for a short period of time, e.g., recorded at 100 Hz for five seconds when a trigger condition is met [temporal data], as is the case for structure response recording as a heavy truck crosses a bridge. Many burst time histories may be recorded over the course of a project.
3. **discrete and continuous external events** — measurements with various degrees of time granularity [temporal data]. For example, a truck crossing a bridge is a discrete event with granularity on the order of seconds, while changes in river stage are continuous external events with granularity of hours or days. Examples of continuously-varying, discrete, and mixed continuous/discrete events are shown on the external event spectrum in Fig. 1.

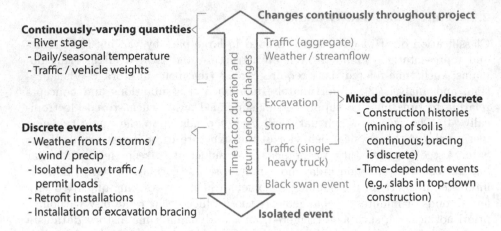

Fig. 1. Spectrum of external events

4. **measurements distributed in one dimension** — for example, lateral movements along a borehole [1-D data]
5. **measurements distributed in two or three dimensions** — for example, readings from a field of instruments around a construction site [2-D data]
6. **heterogeneous data** — data containing comparisons between two arbitrary measurements [multi-dimensional data]. Other heterogeneous data include still photographs or video clips associated with trucks crossing a bridge or other events. These data are not "plotted" per se, but are included in SHM reports in other ways.

3   Principles and Techniques for SHM Data Aggregation

The RAMSES-CI data management system is designed to aggregate SHM and related data from various sources, store it in a central database, and process queries against the database to support engineering analysis. This is accomplished by

1. converting data from the various formats associated with different data loggers, sensor networks, and external data streams into standardized abstracted formats
2. storing the abstracted data in a relational database, where the database tables fit stereotypes designed for each of the SHM data types described in Sect. 2.2 above
3. serving user requests by executing queries against the database and reporting the data in a graphical Web report

Data are sent to the central point in many forms and formats. However, each display function requires data in a particular format. We propose a general methodology based on four steps that allows easy specification of how raw data can be reformatted and reformulated into a database from which each display function can extract what it needs:

1. **Convert datalogger output to a plain text intermediate format**, if it is in a binary format, using a preprocessor module developed for each data stream. While the numerical data will eventually be stored as integers, floating-point numbers, or packed decimal numbers in database tables, it is convenient to use plain text files as a common intermediate format to encourage modularity and reuse of existing tools; furthermore, plain text is readable by humans and machines alike, promoting easier development and debugging.

2. **Establish a common time base** and, for each data mode, an appropriate time concept, as noted in Sect. 2.1. For quasi-static measurements, a calendar date and time with minute or second accuracy is sufficient. However, for burst data, the datalogger clock may not have sufficient resolution to uniquely identify each measurement within the burst (particularly in cases where dataloggers store elapsed time as a floating point number which loses precision as the magnitude of the number increases). In such cases, the two-part timestamp system introduced in Sect. 2.1 is employed.

3. **Write preprocessed output to temporary text files**. The text preprocessor creates a delimited text output file for each data mode extracted from the input file generated by the polling computer.

4. **Import the preprocessed data into a database table** for final processing and storage. Factors to convert from datalogger voltages to engineering units are applied if necessary. The final storage table includes the entire history for a particular data type over the course of the project.

Four agents take part in this preprocessing and import procedure:

Polling Computer. The polling computer obtains raw data from the field sites, and, if necessary, converts the raw data to plain text for subsequent processing. Typically, the polling computer is a dedicated machine (or virtual machine), such that the Web server is insulated from problems that might arise during the polling and text conversion process, such as crashes of datalogger interface software.

Conversion Script. The conversion script invokes a text preprocessor to create importable temporary text files for each data mode and initiates import of the temporary files to appropriate database tables. The conversion script is also responsible for notifying an administrator by e-mail if part of the conversion process fails.

Text Preprocessor. The text preprocessor reads files from the polling computer and establishes the time base for each data mode. The text preprocessor may be a component of the conversion script or a stand-alone program invoked by the conversion script. The text processor outputs a delimited text file for each data mode which can then be imported into the appropriate database tables.

Database Engine. An off-the-shelf SQL database provides data storage and search capability.

4   Software Model

To promote modular design and extensibility, the implementation follows Model-View-Controller principles [6], separating the code that stores and updates object data (the Model) from the code that displays results to the user (the View) and the logic that makes calculations and executes queries against the data (the Controller).

4.1   Site/System Descriptor Classes

The proposed model includes classes to describe metadata for the monitored facility, the SHM system, and the quantities being measured: Site, DataSource, and Channel, respectively. A UML class diagram showing the properties of and relationships between Site, DataSource, and Channel is presented in Fig. 2.

Fig. 2. UML class diagram illustrating properties of and relationships between the Site, DataSource, and Channel objects

Site: A top-level Site object represents a monitoring field site, e.g. a bridge or tunnel under continuous SHM. The Site object encapsulates metadata for the monitored facility, such as its name, identification number, location, and notes; more importantly, Site is a container for data sources associated with the monitoring program, such as autonomous data acquisition systems, external data streams, or manual readings; these are represented by the DataSource object.

DataSource: Sources of monitoring data — autonomous data acquisition systems or manual readings on the monitored facility, nearby weigh stations, or government weather or stream flow data, to name a few — are encapsulated by the DataSource object. As indicated in Fig. 2, each DataSource belongs to exactly one Site and contains zero or more Channel objects, each of which represents a given sensor or instrument.

Channel: The Channel object encapsulates an individual sensor or observation.

4.2   View Classes

The user's interface to the data is represented by instances of the Report class, which serves as a container for individual report elements — instances of the

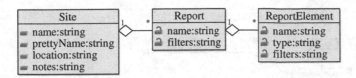

Fig. 3. UML class diagram illustrating properties of and relationships between the Site, Report, and ReportElement objects

ReportElement class — which may be graphs, tables, text fields, or other items. Associated with each ReportElement subclass and each display platform is a function which displays the data in the selected format on the selected platform. A UML class diagram showing the properties of and relationships between Site, Report, and ReportElement is presented in Fig. 3.

Report. The Report class encapsulates a generic view of some set of data from the Site with which it is associated. Each Report is associated with exactly one Site, though in the future it may be useful to share Report templates among Sites with similar properties. Report is a container for zero or more ReportElements, which actually provide a graph, table, or other means of displaying data.

ReportElement. The abstract ReportElement class represents any component that may be included in a Report, such as graphs, tables, listings, or external documents. The properties of ReportElement include the element name and element type (i.e., the name of the concrete subclass of a given ReportElement instance).

Any concrete subclass of ReportElement may be included in a Report. Thus, configuring the RAMSES-CI software to display certain data in a particular manner is a matter of creating instances of the appropriate ReportElement subclass. New report elements may be created with a small amount of coding. Some of the currently available report elements include TimeSeriesGraph, to plot one or more Channels against time with day, hour, or minute granularity (SHM Data Type 1); BurstGraph to plot short bursts of data from Channels against time with second or millisecond granularity (SHM Data Type 2); and SimpleEventListing to provide a tabular listing of the start times of dynamic events, wherein each start time is shown as a link to a particular Report showing the event.

4.3   UML Model Summary

The complete UML model for data organization and display is summarized in Fig. 4. As shown in the figure, a given Site may have zero or more DataSources and Reports associated with it. Each DataSource has zero or more Channels. Each Report acts as a container for zero or more ReportElements, which may be instances of Graph or Listing, or other elements that might be created in

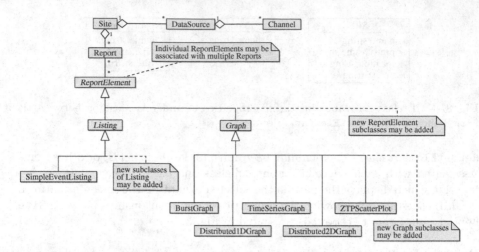

Fig. 4. UML class diagram summarizing relationships and multiplicities among RAMSES-CI data display abstractions

the future. A given `ReportElement` may appear in multiple `Reports`. A given concrete subclass of `Graph` will typically draw data from one or more of the established `Channels`; a single `Graph` instance may include data from `Channels` associated with different `DataSources`. This removes an artificial barrier between analysis of data from different sources.

5   Use Cases

The proposed model and implementation are designed to promote easy transitions from identification of use cases to new data views. Administrators and users may develop and customize `Reports` to support each use case. No programming skills are needed, as instances of `Report` are created through an administration Web interface. Three use case stereotypes were identified from user interviews:

On-line monitoring: an engineer interprets SHM data as part of a daily decision to keep a structure or facility open. If the data remain within normal limits, the engineer's confidence to keep the facility in service is increased. If data exceed normal limits, the engineer may close the facility or order additional investigation.

Periodic reporting for asset management: an engineer interprets the SHM data at regular (e.g., monthly, quarterly) intervals to identify trends and investigate outliers that may be relevant to ongoing management of the monitored infrastructure facility, including scheduling of maintenance and rehabilitation interventions.

Post-hoc reporting: a researcher investigating a specific phenomenon or behavior identifies trends and outliers to draw conclusions directly or import data into analytical or numerical models.

6   Lessons Learned

Different Users Interact Differently. Individual users of the data management system — e.g., engineers, technicians, researchers, government officials — interact with the data management system and computing resources in general in varied and sometimes unanticipated ways. Thus it is important for the system to be extensible and adaptable to meet various user expectations with a minimum of additional effort. One way of examining user expectations, and therefore software requirements, is through identification of user attitudes and habits. While it may be reasonably assumed that nearly all engineers possess at least a modest level of experience with computing in general and Web sites in particular, the speed and enthusiasm with which users adopt new technology is based upon users' knowledge, experience, and attitudes, and varies considerably. Three user types identified in HCI literature [7] are particularly descriptive. *Anxious* users are afraid of somehow "breaking" the system, while *Enthusiast* users enjoy experimentation with new technology for its own sake; *Efficient* users want to use new technology only insofar as it adds immediate value to their work. If it is to be useful at an organizational level, an SHM data management system must be sufficiently (1) robust to assuage the Anxious user's fear of breaking something, (2) flexible to enable the Enthusiast user to customize the system for specialized investigations, and (3) streamlined to allow the Efficient user to accomplish a well-defined task quickly without experimentation. While these requirements may seem mutually exclusive, a balance may be struck by classifying users such that each is granted permissions according to personal needs and skill level. For example, *Basic users* may only view Reports; they may not create nor edit them, and thus fears of breaking the system are relieved. Meanwhile, *Advanced users* may view, create, and edit Reports and ReportElements and may grant read-only access to their Reports to basic users. *Power users* may view, create, and edit Reports, ReportElements, Sites, DataSources, and Channels; *Administrators* have all the privileges as power users as well as control over the underlying database and Web server software.

Screen — Print — Mobile. One key aspect of user interaction with SHM data (and data in general) is the user's preferred method of viewing a report; that is, some users prefer to look at reports on a desktop or laptop computer screen, while others prefer hard copy. Mobile devices such as smart phones and tablets are an emerging and increasingly popular display method, particularly among engineers who are frequently in the field and thus away from the office. Nevertheless, we have found that some users are comfortable only with hard copy reports. There are a variety of possible reasons for this: ability to mark the report with a pencil for easier interpretation; ability to bring the report to a meeting in which a computer is unavailable or would be considered disruptive; or eye discomfort from computer displays. This preference became apparent during an urban tunnel monitoring project, wherein a city official printed the tunnel data Web page daily to bring to his morning construction meeting. Even with proliferation of mobile devices, the importance of hard-copy output must be considered when designing SHM data management reports.

7 Conclusion

We have presented a theory, taxonomy, and model of SHM data. The theory and taxonomy were built upon ideas from the literature. The SHM data taxonomy informed development of procedures for processing and storing data from a variety of sources in a relational database. A set of data storage and display abstractions were then developed and implemented in software.

The generic view model and implementations associated with ReportElements enable civil engineers to design sophisticated SHM interfaces without the need for programming. Furthermore, systems such as RAMSES-CI could easily be adapted to other engineering fields where data monitoring is a key factor, such as monitoring of manufacturing processes, chemical plant processes, and so on.

References

1. Aktan, E., Chase, S., Inman, D., Pines, D.: Monitoring and managing the health of infrastructure systems. In: Proc. 2001 SPIE Conference on Health Monitoring of Highway Transportation Infrastructure, Irvine, California. SPIE (2001)
2. Farrar, C.R., Worden, K.: An introduction to structural health monitoring. Phil. Trans. of the Royal Society A 365(1851), 303–315 (1851)
3. Keim, D., Mansmann, F., Schneidewind, J., Ziegler, H.: Challenges in visual data analysis. In: Proc. 10th Int'l Conf. on Information Visualisation (IV 2006), pp. 9–16. IEEE (2006)
4. Frank, A.U.: Different types of 'times' in GIS. In: Egenhofer, M.J., Golledge, R.G. (eds.) Spatial and Temporal Reasoning in Geographic Information Systems, pp. 40–62. Oxford University Press (1998)
5. Shneiderman, B.: The eyes have it: a task by data type taxonomy for information visualizations. In: Proceedings 1996 IEEE Symposium on Visual Languages, pp. 336–343. IEEE Computer Society (1996)
6. Jacobson, I.: Object-Oriented Software Engineering: A Use Case Driven Approach. Addison-Wesley, Reading (1992)
7. Hermann, F., Niedermann, I., Peissner, M., Henke, K., Naumann, A.: Users interact differently: Towards a usability- oriented user taxonomy. In: Jacko, J.A. (ed.) HCI 2007, Part I. LNCS, vol. 4550, pp. 812–817. Springer, Heidelberg (2007)

Empowering Young Adolescents to Choose the Healthy Lifestyle: A Persuasive Intervention Using Mobile Phones

Lies Kroes[1] and Suleman Shahid[2]

[1] Department of Communication and Information Science,
Tilburg University, The Netherlands
lieskroes@hotmail.com
[2] Tilburg Center for Cognition and Communication, Department of Communication and
Information Science, Tilburg University, The Netherlands
s.shahid@uvt.nl

Abstract. Overweight is one of the major health problems in the Netherlands. Young adolescents with a lower socioeconomic background are especially vulnerable to overweight. This study examines the potential of mobile applications to influence the unhealthy behaviour of young adolescents. A mobile application is proposed to assist in the prevention of overweight using persuasive technology. The application encourages young adolescents to increase fruit consumption and decrease snack consumption. Results of the evaluation show that participants perceive the app as easy to use and useful. Overall, participants showed a more positive attitude and self-efficacy regarding the consumption of fruit, and a more negative attitude towards snacks, which is subsequently expected to influence their behaviour in the long term. According to participants, social influences generated by the app further contribute to this change in attitude and behaviour.

Keywords: Persuasive technology, overweight, behaviour change, attitude - social influence - efficacy model, Fogg's behaviour model, theory of change.

1 Introduction

Overweight and obesity are considered to be one of the worldwide risk factors that are associated with increased mortality and morbidity [1]. Several diseases may result from overweight and obesity, such as cardiovascular diseases, diabetes, several types of cancer, and non-fatal diseases such as arthritis. According to the National Institute for Public Health and the Environment (RIVM), 40 to 50% of the Dutch population has overweight, and approximately 10% is obese [2]. They either fail to achieve the standard of physical exercise or, moreover, do not meet the required daily intake of fruit and vegetables. Although behaviour of exercising and healthy consumption has not worsened for several years, more than half the Dutch do not meet the standards for healthy nutrition. This indicates that a change in healthy lifestyle is required.

According to both the World Health Organization (WHO) and RIVM, people with a lower socioeconomic position are especially at risk to become overweight and

M. Kurosu (Ed.): Human-Computer Interaction, Part II, HCII 2013, LNCS 8005, pp. 117–126, 2013.

obese. In a study by Pigeot et al. [3], worldwide statistics regarding overweight were combined from several large organizations such as the WHO. Their results show that overweight is also a worldwide problem for adolescents, as an increasing number of children between the age of 2 and 20 weight too much.

1.1   Target Group and Target Behaviour

The present study focuses on encouraging changing the behaviour of young adolescents. One of the major problems contributing to overweight in the Netherlands is the unhealthy consumption of adolescents [4]. Their unhealthy lifestyle generally entails low fruit consumption, skipping breakfast and the consumption of many high-fat snacks. The habits of adolescents are still weak at this age and can be influenced more easily than those of older people. Improving nutritional habits of this target group can prevent diseases in later stages of their lives. Adolescents with moderate overweight are especially relevant in this regard as their health problems do not yet require medical intervention, and problematic overweight (i.e. obesity) can still be prevented.

As overweight is predominantly a problem for people with a low socioeconomic background, we focus on pupils of VMBO (preparatory secondary vocational education) which is the lowest regular high-school education in the Dutch school system. This results in the following research question: *How can VMBO adolescents between the age of 12 and 15 with moderate overweight be persuaded to eat healthier, using mobile technology?* The main purpose of this study is to examine the motives for fruit and snack consumption of adolescents, and to develop a mobile persuasive interface that targets these motives. This paper also presents the results of an early evaluation of this interface.

The Health council of the Netherlands advices young adolescents to eat at least two pieces of fruit each day, and reduce the consumption of saturated fat (snacks) to less than 10% of the total energy intake. Young people often do not meet these guidelines [5]. Meeting the guidelines of the Health council of the Netherlands will thus be the ultimate goal of the proposed intervention.

2   Persuasive Mobile Healthcare and Previous Work

This study aims at changing the inapt eating behaviour of adolescents using mobile persuasive technology. Previous research has shown that web-based tailored nutrition education is appreciated better and has more impact on the intention to change behaviour than traditional nutrition information [6]. Computer technologies have the ability to reach many people on a daily basis with persistent messages. This strategy is called persuasive technology, and aims at changing people's attitude and behaviour via interactive computing systems [7]. In the past few years, more researchers have started using mobile phones for persuasion because mobile technology provides further benefits such as the possibility of push messages without any time and location constraints, location based intervention, and always availability of a mobile device for relevant intervention.

A large number of mobile applications have already been created to assist people in making healthier food choices. To date, no mobile application could be found that focuses specifically on adolescents of 12 to 15 years old. The majority of the applications aim at young adults, with for instance grocery advice or calorie counters. More importantly, commercial applications that have been developed so far, are rarely evaluated on their effectiveness. This is confirmed in a review article by Tufano and Karras [8], who state that "there are no evaluation studies of these tools currently available in the published literature". Furthermore, research on existing eHealth interventions provides indecisive results. This is in agreement with a review of 23 eHealth interventions by Enwald and Huotari [9], who state that "the evidence of the effectiveness of these interventions was inconclusive".

3   Conceptual Framework

The conceptual framework of this study is primarily based on the ASE model, Fogg's behaviour model and the theory of change. Each of these frameworks is examined during user research and subsequently used in the design and evaluation of the proposed persuasive intervention.

The attitude - social influence - efficacy (ASE) model states that an individual's attitude, self-efficacy and social influences predict the behavioral intention, and that the behavioral intention subsequently determines whether he or she will carry out a given behaviour [10]. Adolescents are at an age where they become responsible for their own nutrition and are prone to social influences (of friends and other external factors such as the media). These influences can be used to change their attitude and efficacy.

According to Fogg's behaviour model (FBM), three elements must simultaneously occur for behaviour to take place, which are motivation, ability and triggers [11]. Both the ability and motivation to perform a given behaviour should be high for that behaviour to occur. Motivation can be established by creating core motivators (e.g. pleasure, hope or social acceptance) and an individual's ability can be enhanced by making the behaviour easier to perform. In addition, a trigger relating to the behaviour that needs to be changed must be present in order for the target behaviour to occur. Nearly 50% of the young adolescents accesses the internet on their mobile phone [12], indicating the potential of reaching adolescents via their smartphones. Triggers can thus be transferred via this medium to enhance motivation and ability.

The theory of change states that people undergo five stages while changing addictive behaviour, which are pre-contemplation, contemplation, preparation, action and maintenance [13]. Adolescents with moderate overweight are generally in the stage of contemplation. They are aware of their problem and want to change the behaviour, but have not committed themselves to do so. They often do now know what 'healthy' precisely entails as they are unaware of the Dutch recommendations [2]. In some cases, adolescents are in the stage of pre-contemplation, which means that they are not aware of their health problems yet. The persuasive intervention should thus create awareness for this group, and create knowledge for the group in the stage of contemplation.

The general objective of the persuasive method is to increase fruit intake and decrease snack intake. The ASE model is used to determine needs and current behaviour of the target group. Fogg's behaviour model is applied to establish triggers that contribute to an improved ability and motivation to eat fruit (and the opposite for snacks). The theory of change helps to determine in which stage adolescents are and which behaviour change is required. The study aims to assist adolescents up until the action stage, when they perform the target behaviour and meet the recommendations of the Health council of the Netherlands.

4   User Research

Seven adolescents participated in a longitudinal user research. All participants were 12 to 15 years of age and studied preparatory secondary vocational education (VMBO). Privacy concerns made it infeasible to recruit more participants with moderate overweight in this age group.

Procedure. A semi-structured interview was used to assess the determinants of fruit and snack consumption. After this interview, participants recorded their fruit and snack consumption for seven consecutive days, which provides insight into the habits and consumption behaviour of adolescents. A post-test interview was used to assess the awareness of habits of participants and their underlying attitudes and beliefs regarding those habits.

Measures. Four major measurements were done to obtain the relevant information, which include i) theory of change (consumption pattern, knowledge and awareness), ii) ASE model (attitude, social influence, self-efficacy), iii) mobile application use and iv) Fogg's behaviour model (motivation, triggers and ability).

Theory of Change. As expected, participants are in between the stage of precontemplation and contemplation. However, they do not know how their snack consumption relates to the Dutch recommendations. Most participants were unaware of their consumption pattern, though a clear pattern was found when the results of the interviews and diaries were compared. Keeping track of their habits assisted in creating this awareness.

ASE Model. Results show that attitude towards snacks overrules the positive attitude towards fruit, causing participants to choose a snack over fruit. The positive attitude towards the ease and availability of snacks should make place for reminders to eat fruit. Participants were predominantly influenced by friends to eat snacks (at school) and by their family members to eat fruit (at home). Furthermore, the number of locations where fruit is consumed should be increased, causing an automatic decrease of snack consumption to reduce hunger.

Fogg's Behaviour Model. Participants are generally not intrinsically motivated to eat fruit, which is why triggers are often not activated. Extrinsic motivational factors have the greatest impact on participant's behaviour, which are the availability and social influences. In general, fruit is not triggered at all, while there are too many triggers for snacks. Participants suggest goal setting, an alarm and a weekly schedule as triggers. With the schedule, they can justify their choice for a snack on a specific day (they will eat more fruit the next day), and overcome habits as they follow a structured consumption pattern. Goal setting and an alarm will create awareness about their aims and produce triggers with immediate call for action. Feedback and daily messages could further motivate them to improve their behaviour.

Mobile Application Use. Most participants possess a smartphone and all of them use it to play games or contact others. The majority accesses social media via their smartphone and uses his or her smartphone for other informative and entertaining purposes (e.g. travel information, news and photo editing). Participants indicate that they do not use an app when it is too complex, although they enjoy games that require active involvement and multiple routes.

5   Design

User research resulted in design requirements, as previously described. The requirements were processed into three design alternatives, of which a final design was chosen. The design consists of a real life kitchen with multiple items that users can click on. These items include all aspects of the design requirements (i.e. an alarm, goals, tips, consumption records, view consequences and friends). The progress of goals is shown with a barometer below the kitchen screen. A major consideration for choosing this design is that the target group becomes engaged in a playful manner. To remove initial errors and assess the first impression of the target group, a paper prototype test was developed (Figure 1).

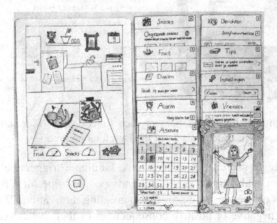

Fig. 1. Paper prototype with the home screen (left) and ten sub screens

Results of the paper prototype test were processed into a final design. The final design (described in figure 2) is based on results of the user research, and provides users with motivation (consumption record, tips, messages, a mirror and friends), triggers (goal setting, alarm and a planner) and ability (alarm and tips). A point system is included to create a point of reference for users and compare their own behaviour to that of others. In the persuasive tool, users are triggered by push messages, either by means of a spark, facilitator or a signal.

| Introduction | Updates from friends | Add fruit | Planner |

Introduction (prior to the home screen) Create a profile and information about the user's BMI

Home Kitchen layout with clickable functionalities in colour. The lower bar shows a user's progress of points.

Alarm Set an alarm or change existing alarms. The alarm sends push messages (default), and the alarm shakes when it rings.

Mirror View the appearance in relation to the consumption; an avatar becomes fatter and gets pimples etc., when eating unhealthy.

Friends Includes: a) Updates from friends, b) Friends overview, c) Profile, and d) Top scores (with one user weekly highlight).

Tips Advice about limiting snack consumption and increasing fruit consumption.

Messages Messages from friends and general messages from the system with feedback about the performance.

Candy jar Enter snack consumption. There is a distinction between unhealthy snacks (minus 2 points) en less unhealthy snacks (minus 1 point).

Fruit bowl Enter fruit consumption. Users receive 3 points for each fruit intake.

Planner Includes: a) Agenda, b) Goals (weekly goals for fruit and snack consumption with advice according to the Dutch recommendations) and c) Results of achievements.

Settings General settings regarding the username, email, sounds, push messages, privacy settings and help.

Fig. 2. Final design including descriptions of each functionality (four sub screens are shown above). *Note.* The app is in Dutch because of the Dutch target group.

A spark is a trigger that creates motivation, a facilitator triggers behaviour by making it easier to perform, and a signal simply reminds people to perform the task [11]. Feedback and progress of friends serve as a spark, creating motivation. The mirror, in which users can see the negative or positive consequences of their behaviour, also serves as a spark. The alarm mainly functions as a signal, as users are reminded of eating fruit by this functionality. The agenda, point system and entering fruit and snack consumption all serve as facilitators. These functionalities make the behaviour easier to perform, as they provide a point of reference and make users aware of their consumption.

The final application was design for an iPhone. The app has been called the Krachtvoer app (in English: Powerfood app), as it connects to an existing offline program (called *Krachtvoer)* with a similar goal and target group. Consequently, the app can be promoted via a multiple channel strategy and the brand name is already familiar among pupils.

6   Evaluation

An evaluation of the mobile application has been performed to provide support for the persuasive power of the Powerfood app. A usability test was performed to detect final usability issues. The design was evaluated by questioning participants about the attractiveness of the application and their perceived ease of use of the system. Finally, the effects on the ASE model were tested with a similar diary study and post interviews. The constructs information quality and openness to influence, adopted from a study by Nass, Fogg and Moon [14], were added to the final interview. Results were analyzed using qualitative data analysis. The interviews were fully transcribed and subsequently translated into a data matrix.

To rule out an interview bias, an additional online questionnaire was performed. The questionnaire was based on the technology acceptance model (TAM) [15]. TAM suggests that users are influenced by their perception of usefulness and ease of use when they are presented a new information system. Although this model originally does not measure behaviour change, the model does measure the intention to use the application and to what degree users perceive the app to be beneficial. A total of seven participants completed all three phases of the evaluation.

6.1   Results

The results showed that some tasks could not be completed properly as the intention of buttons was unclear or clickable items did not stand out enough. An improved version of the app have already been made based on this feedback (as presented in Figure 2). Participants often tried several buttons before reaching their destination. They said they were exploring the app, indicating the app engages them in a playful manner.

Results also indicated that participants expect a positive change in attitude when using the app in the long run. Confrontation with negative consequences and positive social influence especially contribute to this predicted shift in attitude. One participant said that "Attitude will probably change for snacks, because you are confronted by the consequences, especially by the mirror". Two participants were not sure to what degree their attitude will change by the app.

Participants feel that the app makes the behaviour easier to perform because they are reminded by the alarm in the app. One of the participants described this improved efficacy by saying "Normally you don't think about it and this helps reminding to eat fruit, for instance by the alarm". Two other participants stated that many children are constantly busy with their mobile phones, indicating the potential persistency of the app. Majority of the participants thought that social influences would help them to change their unhealthy behaviour. One participant stated that "Because of the point system you know you're not doing well and you can see that others perform better. You do not want to lose". Another participant was unsure if social influences would work, and thinks it would only make a difference when many other people do not approve his behaviour.

Information quality and design were appreciated by participants. According to participants, all information and buttons in the app are relevant and complete. The reminder, goal orientation and monitoring consumption especially contribute to the perceived usefulness of the app. All participants find the appearance attractive and the interface easy to learn and easy to use. Participants indicated it would be beneficial if the app is distributed by school and therefore the connection with *Krachtvoer* is very useful. Finally, participants suggested that social media should be included in the app.

The items of the questionnaire could be answered on a scale from 1 to 5, ranging from strongly disagree (1) to strongly agree (5). Interestingly, all participants indicated they would download the app as soon as it becomes available (mean scale value 4.6). Four scales were two-sided, of which all participants opted for the maximally positive side of the scales (*good*, *wise*, *favourable* and *positive*), suggesting their positive attitude towards the app. Participants find the app easy to use (mean 4.3) and indicate that the app does what they want and they find the design clear. Nonetheless, two participants indicated it costs much mental effort when using it for the first time, which could be solved with a short tutorial for new users. Participants were divided in whether they think their behaviour would permanently change (and eating habit would not go back to the old routine) when using the app on daily basis and in long run (mean 3.6). A possible explanation is that participants cannot fully predict behaviour that would result after the actual use of the app over a longer period of time, which indicates that longitudinal research is necessary for more decisive evidence.

7   Discussion and Conclusion

This paper examines the motives for fruit and snack consumption of adolescents, and proposes a mobile persuasive application that targets these motives. As predicted by the ASE model, one's attitude predicts the intention to carry out a given behaviour. Hence, when an individual's attitude is influenced by the application, the intention and subsequent behaviour could also be influenced. One's perceived control over the behaviour (i.e. self-efficacy) might further influence the intention, as the app makes the behaviour easier to perform by providing a reminder at relevant moments. Finally, users are challenged by other users and thereby encouraged to eat more fruit and less snacks. Results of the evaluation shows that all concepts of the ASE model are targeted with the Powerfood app. Thus, it can be predicted that the mobile application positively influences the attitude and self-efficacy of users, which is further reinforced by social influences in the application.

Currently, users are in between the stages of pre-contemplation and contemplation of the theory of change. The Powerfood app guides users to the preparation phase as it creates awareness, knowledge and subsequently a shift in attitude. One major limitation is that, due to a number of constraints, the mobile application could not be fully developed, which made a it difficult to run an independent comprehensive longitudinal study. Results from this study should only be taken as predictions and trends of a specific behaviour. These results do not fully show the actual change in behaviour. Consequently, the action stage of the theory of change could not be validated with this study. For future research it is recommended to examine whether the application causes an actual increase of fruit intake (to 2 pieces a day) and a decrease of snack intake (to less than 10% of the total energy consumption).

Another limitation regarding the evaluation is that the target group was too small for the questionnaire to obtain statistically significant results. Although, we were able to get quite rich qualitative data, the quantitative analysis requires bigger sample size. For future research we would like to to use a larger sample, or a small sample that can be tested for weeks if not months. Furthermore, the period after use of the application has not been taken into account with this study. It is possible that users relapse into their old habits when they stop using the application. The aim of the Powerfood app is to create new strong habits, and therefore in future research we will examine these effects over time.

The study provides support for several existing frameworks, such as the ASE model, Fogg's behaviour model and the theory of change. Although these models were not fully validated in practice, the evaluation does indicate results that support the models. In addition, the models have been adjusted to frameworks for testing health interventions, which can be used for future research. Only few existing frameworks were found that evaluated health interventions, which is partly because each intervention requires tailor made and different evaluation methods. Nonetheless, future research could make an attempt in creating a general framework for evaluating persuasive mobile healthcare applications.

This study contributes to an increase of insight into the problems associated with the prevention of one of the greatest health problems, namely overweight. It provides handgrips for future research and supports existing research on overweight and health interventions. The application will additionally be of practical use when it is fully developed by the Dutch institution *Krachtvoer* or one of its partners. What the Powerfood app will eventually bring about for young adolescents remains to be proven in practice, but the hereby presented design and analysis create a strong foundation for an operational version of the Powerfood app.

Acknowledgments. We would like to thank the participants for their contribution to the user research and evaluation of this study. Especially their willingness to record their food consumption is highly appreciated. We also thank the organization of *Krachtvoer* for their support.

References

1. World Health Organization: World Health Statistics 2011. WHO press, Geneva (2011)
2. Van der Lucht, F., Polder, J.J.: The Dutch 2010 Public Health Status and Forecasts Report, Bilthoven (2010)
3. Pigeot, I., Buck, C., Herrmann, D., Ahrens, W.: Overweight and obesity in children and adolescents. The Worldwide Situation 53, 653–665 (2010) (in German)
4. Martens, M.K., Assema, P.V., Brug, J.: Why do adolescents eat what they eat? Personal and social environmental predictors of fruit, snack and breakfast consumption among 12 - 14-year-old Dutch students. Public Health Nutrition 8, 1258–1265 (2005)
5. Van den Berg, G., van Dijk, S.: Description worksheet intervention: Powerfood. RIVM, Dutch youth institute, Maastricht (2011) (in Dutch)

6. Oenema, A., Brug, J., Lechner, L.: Web-based tailored nutrition education: results of a randomized controlled trial. Health Education Research 16, 647–660 (2001)
7. Fogg, B.J.: Persuasive Technology: Using computers to change what we think and do. Morgan Kaufmann, San Fransisco (2003)
8. Tufano, J.T., Karras, B.T.: Mobile eHealth Interventions for Obesity: A Timely Opportunity to Leverage Convergence Trends. Journal of Medical Internet Research 7, e58 (2005)
9. Enwald, H.P.K., Huotari, M.A.: Preventing the Obesity Epidemic by Second Generation Tailored Health Communication: An Interdisciplinary Review. J. Med. Internet Research 12, e24 (2010)
10. De Vries, H., Dijkstra, M., Kuhlman, P.: Self-efficacy: the third factor besides attitude and subjective norm as a predictor of behavioural intentions. Health Education Research 3, 273–282 (1988)
11. Fogg, B.: A behavior model for persuasive design. In: Proceedings of the 4th International Conference on Persuasive Technology - Persuasive 2009, article no. 40. ACM Press, New York (2009)
12. Statistics Netherlands (2011),
    http://www.cbs.nl/en-GB/menu/themas/vrije-tijd-cultuur/publicaties/ artikelen/archief/2011/2011-3438-wm.htm?Languageswitch=on
13. Prochaska, J.O., DiClemente, C.C., Norcross, J.C.: In search of how people change. Applications to addictive behaviors. The American Psychologist 47, 1102–1114 (1992), http://www.ncbi.nlm.nih.gov/pubmed/1329589 (retrieved)
14. Nass, C., Fogg, B.J., Moon, Y.: Can computers be teammates? Int. Int. J. Human - Computer Studies 45, 669–678 (1996)
15. Davis, F.D.: A Technology Acceptance Model for Empirically Testing New End-User Information Systems: Theory and Results. Unpublished doctoral dissertation, MIT Sloan School of Management, Cambridge (1986) (retrieved July 2, 2012, from MIT database)

Telemedicine and Design: Relationships that Create Opportunities

Carlos Alberto Pereira de Lucena[1], Claudia Renata Mont'Alvão[1],
Felipe Pierantoni[1], and Leonardo Frajhof[2]

[1] Pontifícia Universidade Católica do Rio de Janeiro, PUC-Rio - Rio de Janeiro, Brasil
[2] Hospital Universitário Gaffrée e Guinle, Núcleo de Telemedicina,
Universidade Federal do Estado do Rio de Janeiro, UNIRIO -Rio de Janeiro, Brasil
beto.lucena@izzui.com, cmontalvao@puc-rio.br,
{felipepiera,leonardo.frajhof}@gmail.com

Abstract. Every Project that involves Design in its process requires the gathering of information related to the current contexto, the technologies involved and concepts to be approached. In this research, the first step after the delimitation of the scope of the project was to develop a profound analysis of the related areas to Design. In accordance to this procedure, it became possible to start understanding the relationship between different areas. Telemedicine being the central issue of this research, it becomes necessary to limit its connections with the other areas, such as Design. To begin with, it is necessary to explain the topics of interest of the researchers: Design, HCI (Human-Computer interaction) and ergonomics. From this point on, it could be added the interest in areas such as collaborative learning and mobility, that could influence the paths of the research. Moving forward, such concepts can be explored.

Keywords: Human Centered Design, Design, Telemedicine, Collaborative Learning, Mobility.

1 Introduction

Azin Raskin, entrepreneur, renowned interface designer and CEO of Massive Health dedicated the theme of his lecture TEDxSF (local version of San Francisco Event TED - Technology, Education and Design) to the relationship between Design and Medicine. Throughout the lecture, Raskin shares the need of the increasing involvement of Design in projects related to medicine so that methods and tools applied in Design can contribute to the efficiency of the interaction between patients and doctors. According to Raskin:

> One in every 5 patients in the U.S. who need to take their antibiotics prescribed by your doctor stops ingesting the drugs before the time stipulated by the physician. How can this happen in an age where we have so many technologies to monitor our treatments? Is this a medical problem? Is

M. Kurosu (Ed.): Human-Computer Interaction, Part II, HCII 2013, LNCS 8005, pp. 127–133, 2013.
© Springer-Verlag Berlin Heidelberg 2013

it a technologycal problem? No... it is a Design problem. (...) If you cannot use the remote control of your VCR, the fault is not yours but the designer's who designed the control. If you do not follow the medical treatment that is prescribed to you, the blame should also rely over the designer of the intervention. If we want the success of Medicine in this country, attacking the deeper problems that we face, we need to use the human constraints to our advantage. We need to bring Design to Medicine. (RASKIN 2012)

The research of Raskin, integrating Design, Medical, Mobility and collaboration brought practical results such as the application The Eatery (https://eatery.massivehealth.com/#/main), for use on mobile devices. This app brings an interesting concept of sharing food habits, based on studies that argue that by sharing your own eating habits with a community, the trend is that these habits become healthier. Today the application already is widespread in the U.S. and used by thousands of users divided into different communities.

Fig. 1. Application picture of The Eatery company Massive Health

The PhD research of Luiza Novaes that took place in the university PUC-Rio (2007), raises issues related to the relationship between Design and Telemedicine. In accordance to this research, there are innumerous possibilities and opportunities for a designer to act in projects related to Telemedicine. Nowadays projects related to Telemedicine are planned and executed by interdisciplinary teams that gather professionals from different fields such as Health, Education, Communication and Technology. Therefore, it becomes necessary the intervention of the designer in this context.

Novaes adds that it exists a strong ongoing context of projects related to Telemedicine in Brazil and in the world, many times supported by important organizations such as the World Health Organization (WHO). Such projects have extreme relevance, especially in countries under development, and count with strong structures of research and development. The designer already participates in projects like this, but still in small proportions, in contexts that prioritize the aspects of the interaction between the user and the solutions developed. Novaes suggests a deeper relation:

> In front of many levels and types of interactions found in the field of Telemedicine, it becomes clear the necessity of prepared Design professionals to face the challenges presented. Designers should participate in the productive chain of health in a more effective way, contributing with creative and original solutions for the field. (NOVAES, 2007)

The designer has the opportunity to participate in such multidisciplinary teams, with the possibility to contribute in different fases of planning and execution of a project. Each phase involving the gathering of data, common practice in the Design area, should be enriched by the perspective of a designer. From this point on, the possibilities become innumerous once the designer can add in aspects such as the elaboration and evaluation of the solutions proposed. This research tries to demonstrate such possibilities.

Telemedicine, therefore, has the objective of using the channel offered by technology in order to exchange relevant information to the medical field between doctors, professionals connected to Health and patients. In accordance to this analysis, Novaes determines Telemedicine:

> Telemedicine is the exercise of Medicine through the use of interactive methodologies of audiovisual and data communication, with the objective of assistance, Education and research in Health. (NOVAES, 2007)

It is possible to identify throughout the world many iniciatives related to Telemedicine. We can observe projects that involve technological resources extremely advanced, in contexts of highly recognized institutions that use advanced laboratories that broadcast surgeries and other interventions. In the US, as an example, the University of Miami's Telemedicine laboratory uses technology to identify cases located in distant locations of the country.

2   Design Presence

High end technology is being developed constantly in order to meet the needs raised by the field of Telemedicine. Companies like American Liberstream (www.librestream.com) dedicates their efforts on designing products that allow specialists to interact in telemedicine projects. An example of a product designed by Liberstream is the camera *Onsight*, that allows the transmission of video and images to equipment located at a distance. The camera allows the user to exchange information in real time with another specialist in possession of a computer so that the product can be presented in operating rooms or in the search field. This solution is focused on mobility concept that includes both the design of interventions product planning and in its communication interface.

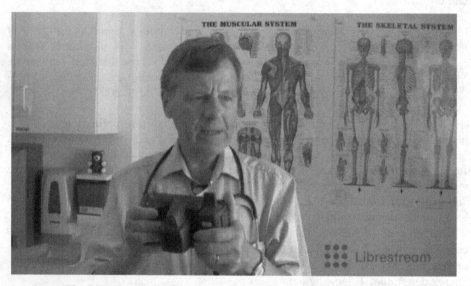

Fig. 2. Illustrative image of a doctor manipulating the Onsight camera

On the other hand, countries that have difficulties in allocating health care professionals in remote locations develop scalable and creative solutions. A group of researchers at the University of California (Berkeley) and the INTEL company, located in Ghana, Africa, use Design methods to gather the required data to develop the solutions needed. In the article entitled "Applying user-centered Design in Telemedicine in Africa" (HO, 2009), the group demonstrates the approach developed for the creation of a system designed for remote consultations, focused on the specific needs of groups located within the country. Acting as Telemedicine solution integrators, the group analyzed the actual contexts of activity of the project, including the locations, resources, technologies, and government support specialists involved. The use of user-centered design methods contributed to the adaptation of the research.

Fig. 3. Images of the sites of the research project

In another initiative, located in India, a country with large population and difficulties with standardization of its health system across the country, we can also identify the need for contextualization of projects related to Telemedicine. The foundation Apollo (http://www.telemedicineindia.com/) has inumerous local projects with the goal of prevention of diseases and medical care for patients across the country. One initiative that calls attention is the "Hospital on Wheels," that enables a bus equipped with medical experts and resources for disadvantaged communities throughout India. With the equipment contained in the bus, the experts can meet local people and communicate directly with teams on duty in hospitals located in large urban centers. Thus diagnosis can be performed instantly, drugs can be ordered quickly and sent to needy regions. According to Professor K. Ganapathy, President and Head of the Foundation in an interview with team communications company Ericsson, the practice of telemedicine can be defined simply as:

"The basic goal of telemedicine is to provide physicians where there aren't any." (GANAPATHY, 2011)

Fig. 4. Illustrative image of buses equipped with technologies dedicated to communications with hospitals in major centers

Another good example is the online community for Physicians: Sermo (www.sermo.com) . This community allows physicians to communicate and to share valuable information about specific topics related to Medicine. The community already counts with over 125 thousand users and can be accessed through computer desktops and mobile devices.

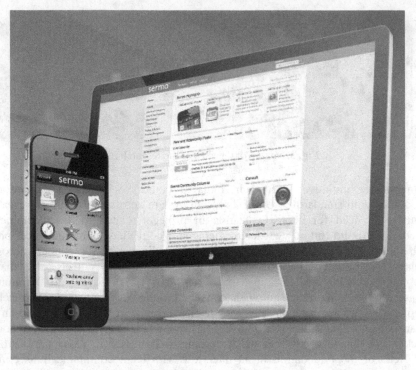

Fig. 5. Illustrative image of the online community Sermo being accessed both by computer desktop and mobile device

3 Conclusion

It is possible to assure that in fact there are many opportunities for design professionals in the field of Telemedicine. Inside and outside Brazil. They are opportunities that go around planning, research, product Design, interface Design, Ergonomics and others.

This research explores such possibilities bringing examples and cases. The main focus of the research is to bring together options for designers to understand the relations of their practice with Telemedicine with the perspective on the use of learning interfaces that can engage learners and teacher during the process of exchanging knowledge.

Acknowledgments. This study have received the financial resource from CNPq – National Council for Scientific and Technological Development.

References

1. O'Reilly, T.: What is Web 2.0: Design Patterns and Business Models for the Next Generation of Software. Communications & Strategies 1, 17 (2007)
2. Pimentel, M., Fuks, H.: Sistemas Colaborativos. Elsevier, Rio de Janeiro (2011)

3. Lucena, C.A.P., Mont'Alvão, C.R., Frajhof, L.: Collaborative learning platform in the field of telemedicine. In: IADIS International Journal on Computer Science and Information Systems, IADIS International Conference e-Health (2012)
4. Chamorro-Koc, M., et al.: Human experience and product usability: Principles to assist the design of user– product interactions. Applied Ergonomics 40, 648–656 (2009)
5. Norman, D.A.: The Design of Everyday Things, 257 p. Currrency Doubleday, New York (1990)
6. Meister, D., Enderwuick, T.P.: Human factors in system design, development and testing, 247 p. Lawrence Erlbaum, London (2001)

A Proposal of the New System Model for Nursing Skill Learning Based on Cognition and Technique

Yukie Majima[1,2], Yasuko Maekawa[2], Masato Soga[3], and Masayuki Sakoda[1]

[1] Graduate School of Engineering, Osaka Prefecture University, Osaka, Japan
[2] College of Sustainable System Sciences, Osaka Prefecture University, Osaka, Japan
{majima,yasuko_m}@kis.osakafu-u.ac.jp
[3] Faculty of Systems Engineering, Wakayama University, Wakayama, Japan
soga@center.wakayama-u.ac.jp

Abstract. It is necessary to acquire not only specialized knowledge but also appropriate nursing skills in nursing education. In this paper, we propose an e-learning system model to support a high level of technique learning, such as "tacit knowledge" and "proficient art" in nursing skills, which have been heretofore learned only from experience. This e-learning system enables self-learning in addition to intellectual learning, thereby enhancing knowledge of procedures and understanding of nursing skills. The results of evaluation experiments showed that each system had learning effects. However, simultaneously, they indicated the importance of the capability of self-training with actual trial-and-error to acquire skills. For that reason, adding "check point learning" to the already developed cognitive learning support system as a new function, we made improvements to provide nursing skills training covering detailed items. Based on this, we propose step-by-step learning after completing learning in the cognitive domain through spiral learning, which is the first step (from intellectual learning support to skill learning support again to intellectual learning support), learners move on to the second step (technique learning support) in a phased manner. We think that other evaluation given by instructors by checking between the first and second steps, as well as checking self-leaning, reduces the sense of loneliness, which is a common pitfall an e-learning, and which provides satisfaction with self-learning outcomes and a motivation for additional learning development.

Keywords: Nursing skill, E-learning, Cognition, Tacit knowledge, Finger motion capture.

1 Introduction

Medical care as it is practiced today is highly sophisticated and specialized, as represented by genetic medicine and transplant medicine. Furthermore, against the backdrop of changes in social structure, the diversity of people's lives and quality of life, and the diversity of patient needs, it is readily apparent that people demand health and medical services that ensure their safety and security. Because of the progress of

M. Kurosu (Ed.): Human-Computer Interaction, Part II, HCII 2013, LNCS 8005, pp. 134–143, 2013.
© Springer-Verlag Berlin Heidelberg 2013

aging society, with fewer children and more numerous elderly people who must be cared for, the importance of nurses is becoming increasingly recognized. In Japan, nursing education is being taught increasingly in universities at a rapid pace: the number of programs offered increased from 11 universities in 1991 to 200 universities in 2011. Because of the lack of nursing teachers, efficiency and quality improvement in nursing education have become daunting challenges.

It is necessary to acquire not only specialized knowledge but also appropriate nursing skills in nursing education. Nursing skills are direct actions with a sense of purpose for security, comfort, and self-help of subjects based on specialized nursing knowledge. They reflect practitioners' views of nursing and levels of skill acquisition [1]. Nursing skills of different types are classifiable into classes such as "skills for living assistance", "skills for assistance associated with medical care", "skills for interpersonal relationships", "skills for developing the nursing process", "skills for hearth assessment", and "skill for education and advice".

Intravenous injection, which draws much attention among all nursing skills, is related to body invasiveness by inserting a needle and infusing medicine into a blood vessel. In recent years, after the change of the new administrative interpretation to "intravenous injection conducted by a nurse is treated as a category of auxiliary action of medical treatment" in Japan (Health, Labour and Welfare Ministry, 2003), it has been noted that education related to intravenous injection must be improved (Japanese Nursing Association, 2003). Consequently, nursing students are now required to master the skills to administer intravenous injection safely.

Nevertheless Hagi et al. [2] reported that "self-learning of intravenous injection" and "technical training in college" are less useful for skill acquisition of intravenous interjection of new nurses, presumably because few students feel that learning at college is useful in a field or because new nurses tend to be passive in skill acquisition. Moreover, "reviewing one's own failure" and "knowing one's own tendency by personal experience" are described as highly valued factors for skill acquisition. Therefore, encouraging a support system to enable a nurse to review personal failures and ascertain personal tendencies is important.

In many cases, the evaluation of nursing by patients tends to base on whether nursing skills are good or bad. For example, we often hear it said: "That nurse is good at injections", or "That nurse is sloppy, so I do not want her/him to wipe my body clean." It is necessary for learning support to make nursing skills understood and to make them familiar. Inaba [3] states: "Embracing both the scientific (knowledge), which skills themselves have, and the humane (mentality) sides, nursing skills are a specific and meditating instrument that actually embodies role functions of nursing." It can be said that nursing skills that people being treated evaluate here incorporate not only the mere accuracy of procedures, but also something like the invisible atmosphere surrounding each nurse, including interpersonal relations skills that produce tender-ness and politeness and an ethical perspective that includes respect for others. Such empirical knowledge and technique that cannot be verbalized are called "tacit knowledge [4]". We can learn more from tacit knowledge than we can learn from what we can verbalize.

In this paper, we propose an e-learning system model to support a high level of technique learning, such as "tacit knowledge" and "proficient art" in nursing skills, which have been heretofore learned only from experience, and also to enable self-learning, in addition to intellectual learning that deepens procedures and understanding of nursing skills.

2   Theoretical Background

In conventional classes designed to teach nursing skills, instructors first explain the purpose, necessity, and procedures of nursing skills in lectures and then demonstrate them in technical seminars. Nursing students gain skill training individually or in a group in a series of learning processes. In skill training, even if the students sometimes teach each other in a group, they often put questions directly to the instructor. However, few teachers can answer their questions adequately on the scene. Therefore, students might be unable to gain nursing skills sufficiently within college classes, given present conditions.

In nursing education, learning using videos is well known to be effective. Libraries of nursing training institutes have numerous nursing skills video materials. Watching corresponding materials is often necessary as a task before the class. For novices, imaging of procedures using videos is effective to make learning go smoothly. Today, because of the development of information and communications technology, including the internet, e-learning and learning support systems incorporating nursing skills videos have been increasingly introduced into the field of nursing education [5]–[9].

The definitions of e-learning vary. The Japanese Ministry of Economy, Trade and Industry (2005) defines it as "independent learning using communications and networks based on information technology; the content is edited according to learning objectives. The interactivity is ensured between learners and content providers (Information Services Industry Division, Commerce and Information Policy Bureau, Ministry of Economy, Trade and Industry)." Majima (2005) defines it as "what is provided in a learning environment using ICT, and a form of learning which can be provided solely by self-learning or collaborative (group) learning or in combination of them [10]." E-learning in the field of nursing skills education often aims to make students learn procedures and grounds of skills. Jacqueline B. et al. report that (computer-assisted learning versus conventional teaching methods on the acquisition and retention of hand washing theory and   skills in pre-qualification nursing students), learning with computers is at least as effective as face-to-face learning [11].As described, studies of learning support using videos to learn procedures have been actively conducted in nursing skills education, but almost no studies exist on learning support systems to learn proficient techniques (art).

Regarding techniques in nursing care and their verbal description, Tanaka [12] argues that "Even if one forcibly verbalizes techniques (techniques that can be transformed into formal knowledge such as manuals) that have already been verbalized, techniques which can be verbalized but have not been verbalized yet and techniques which are impossible to be verbalized (non-verbalizable techniques), by their nature, cannot be used unless each nurse understands the circumstances of each case and the other individual party, namely patients. Put another way, for some knowledge (tacit knowledge), verbalization is apparently completely meaningless." (emphasis added).

To date, we have examined "nursing techniques which can be verbalized but which have not been verbalized yet". We have also begun to analyze characteristics of skilled nurses' techniques in intravenous injection techniques; it has begun with methods and the line-of-sight in practice. Results revealed that line-of-sight flows differed between novices (nursing students) and experts (nursing personnel) and that experts move their lines of sight to the next practice (prior treatment). Many nurses believe that once they have identified a vein, they are able to perform an intravenous injection. They often verbally express the moment when they have done it well as "feeling like entering a blood vessel 'smoothly ('sutto' or 'kukutto' in Japanese)'". Nonetheless, they consider that it is difficult to express exactly how they feel. In contrast, novice nursing students consider that the knack for techniques is to remember procedures. It is therefore important for the process of learning support to compel novices to master procedures before their advancement to sharing the performance characteristics of experts.

Using medical simulators is also effective to acquire skills. There are widely diverse medical simulators available. In recent years, an increasing number of training centers are using dolls to master lifesaving emergency treatment through experience, costing 10 million yen or so per doll [16]. However, such training is not available to all learners, and its cost performance is far from good [17]. This does not also teach items such as tacit knowledge that nursing skills have. To clarify tacit skills and knacks included in nursing skills [18] and support to learn them, we have produced a system with which learners can conduct self-learning for the two sides—the intellectual side [19] [20] [21][22][23] and the technique side [24][25]. Now we are verifying the system [26].

3   System Supporting Cognitive Learning of Nursing Skills

3.1   System Configuration

This learning support system aims to acquire nursing skills through self-evaluation and self-reflection. The system has four learning functions as follows:

(1) Skill procedure study function: Identification of one's own skill's procedures

This function enables nursing students to learn technical procedures. Nursing students understand that the knack of skills should be to conduct the procedures precisely, suggesting that learning methods allowing learners to remember the procedures among others are good for them. Figure 1 below shows that this function is a type by which a user can confirm procedures by checking a radio button.

(2) Skill video comparison function: Comparison of model images with one's own technical images

This is a function by which a user can work with two video images simultaneously or alternately to compare them. If the learners use this function, then they are helped by comparison to experience and consider the difference of time between that required by a skilled nurse and by themselves.

(3) Reflection function: Comparison of each image in one's own practice progressions

With this function, nursing students can enter text while answering questions. Learners can think by themselves through comparison and freely describe what they have found. It helps learners to promote their reflection and think by writing using the system. The questions are set so that learners can make a comparison in every procedure of intravenous injection.

(4) Portfolio function: Output and identification of learning results

With this function, users output the procedures that they have input by themselves or described what they have found. It is also used as a portfolio of the process of skill acquisition, by which the learners can be conscious of their own findings and can thereby advance their own learning.

3.2   Evaluation

Results of two verification experiments using the system are explained in 3.2.1 and 3.2.2.

3.2.1   Evaluation of the Acquisition of Nursing Skill Procedures

We asked that five nursing students use the system to learn intravenous injection skills and examined their usefulness. The skill evaluation was conducted at three times: (1) pre-testing, (2) testing after practicing self-skills training, and (3) testing after practicing the learning support system. Results show that four students became able to insert a needle into a vein correctly at stage (2), but mistakes in the procedures had not been corrected. Results showed that the improved intravenous injection skills, such as performing correct procedures and correctly injecting medicine into a vein, were identified in stage (3) [22].

3.2.2   Acquisition of Tacit Knowledge Included in Nursing Skills

Another evaluation experiment was conducted with another 16 nursing students. Scores for nursing skills increased significantly among the group who performed reflective learning with the system compared to the group (control group) who did not do any learning [23]. When we examined the action of "releasing a tourniquet after selecting a blood vessel and fixing the tourniquet again after wearing gloves and preparing for disinfection", which is not included in procedural manuals (only included in model video images) and sought to reduce the burden on patients, students other than the control group showed great improvement. It was verified that learning with the learning support system was useful to learn tacit knowledge and actions contained in the videos [26]. However, with regard to the "identification of a reverse blood flow (whether or not inserting into a vein)", which is an item to notice, all the control group tried to identify a reverse blood flow in the experiment this time, but only one person was actually able to insert an injection needle and identify a reverse blood flow. The results described in 3.2.1 revealed that a reverse blood flow was identified through self-skills training alone. Therefore, it is readily apparent that the effect of skills training strongly influences the acquisition of techniques to insert an injection needle and identify a reverse blood flow: taking skills training was found to be necessary in technique acquisition, even actually trying and failing [23].

4   System Supporting Technique Learning of Nursing Skills

4.1   System Configuration

Based on the verification results of the system supporting cognitive learning, we developed a system to support technique learning [24] [25].

This system is intended to build a learning-support system using virtual reality by reproducing finger movements used in practicing nursing techniques. Those reproductions can then be used by later generations to show the non-verbalized part of nursing techniques that have heretofore only been learned from experience. We have already developed a prototype system to acquire finger position data when a syringe is grasped. The system was used for practicing blood drawing techniques with a finger motion capture system. Using the acquired data, it reproduces the practicing process of the techniques three-dimensionally.

4.2   Evaluation

We asked seven nursing students to use the system. Their opinions after completing the experiment were positive overall in terms of learning support by the system. However, because it takes 30 min to put on finger sensors, the development of devices to obtain data more easily, including devising a way to repair the sensors, has become a challenging task [24][25].

Subjects participating in the evaluation experiments learned about the cognitive learning support system in advance, in which instructors gave comments individually, with viewing of nursing skills video images in the post-test when they were wearing the finger sensors. The following characteristic comments were made as their opinions after completing the experiment.

"I think that lessons are important as knowledge for processes such as memorizing procedures. However, using a computer helped me review my techniques from different perspectives, such as video images, and helped me to compare them with others. I understood what I had been unable to understand in class."

"For the parts which could not be recognized by the learning support system, I think that it is better to receive advice or instruction from a third party, such as a teacher, to understand the contents well. In some cases, it might be difficult to learn by self-learning alone."

"It is better to have advice from teachers after having looked back and considered matters individually. Without some review, I think that the consciousness (about the lesson) will fade."

These opinions suggest that the order of learning, doing technique learning after reflective learning, and setting up an opportunity to receive guidance from teachers
between the sessions of learning, in addition to self-training, will engender the improvement of learning enthusiasm and the enhancement of learning effects.

5   E-learning System Model Supporting Self-learning from Cognition and Technique Sides in Nursing Skills Acquisition

Although some skills can be learned with knowledge that is prescribed in a manual, it
is difficult to learn nursing skills, which include implicit knowledge, as physical
knowledge, according to a manual. Knowledge acquired from experience or practice
could be called experiential knowledge, or "Deep Knowledge" (meaning the expertise
or special skills which proficient engineers or managers accumulate from their various
experiences). For learners to obtain such knowledge, they must acquire, experience,
and reinforce that knowledge through additional learning including practice, observations, problem resolution, and experiments, especially under the guidance of
instructors [27].

In the field of nursing education, the chances for learners to gain skills through on-
the-job training (OJT) in clinical training are offered. In the field of college education
under the pressures of several instructors or times, however, it is not easy to use OJT
for the learning of various skills. In addition, because nursing students have many
skills to learn, it is difficult for them to take much time to master any one of them.
Consequently, to support them in acquiring nursing skills, we shed light on what is an
effective learning-support method and examine the skill-learning support model.

The acquisition process of nursing skills is said to comprise three phases by which
the improvement can be promoted: "the phase of knowing", "the phase of mastering",
and "the phase of using". New nurses learn practicing intravenous injections through
first "following the instructors' model," "benefiting by their experience," and "repetitive practice". Additionally, in a traditional learning method, at first, it is common that
the nursing student imitates the technique of an expert nurse [29]. In other points of
our previous study [18], we found that linguistic expressions differed among nurses in
terms of the sensation of fingers that nurses recognize at perceiving blood vessels by
touch or inserting a hypodermic needle, which suggests that formal knowledge by
visualization would be better than that by verbalization to share and use know-how of
nursing skills which cannot be verbalized.

The results of our previous evaluation experiments indicated the importance of the
capability of self-training with actual trial-and-error to acquire skills. For that reason,
adding "check point learning", "skill procedure study", "skill video comparison",
"reflection", and "portfolio" functions of the already developed cognitive learning
support system as a new function, we make improvements to provide nursing skills
training covering detailed items (Figure 1). We think that technique acquisition at the
tacit knowledge level can be attained by learning in the following order: 1) doing
cognitive learning of knowledge and procedures of nursing skills; 2) repeating

self-skills training until one becomes capable of practicing correctly; and 3) repeatedly following experts' finger movements using the technique learning support e-learning system.

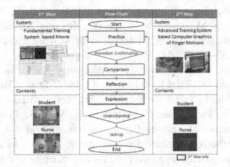

Fig. 1. New System Model for Nursing Skill Learning Based on Cognition and Technique

In other words, the ideal e-learning system model to perform nursing skills self-learning is a model which, after completing learning in the cognitive domain through spiral learning (the first step from intellectual learning support to skill learning support again to intellectual learning support), learners move on to the second step (technique learning support) in a phased manner. Moreover, we think that other-evaluation that is given by instructors by checking between the first and the second steps, as well as checking self-learning, will engender a reduced sense of loneliness, which is a common pitfall of e-learning, and provide satisfaction with self-learning outcomes in addition to motivation for additional development of learning.

6   Conclusions

As described in this paper, we proposed an e-learning system model to support a high level of technique learning, such as "tacit knowledge" and "proficient art" in nursing skills that have been heretofore only learned from experience, and also to enable self-learning, in addition to intellectual learning that deepens procedures and understanding of nursing skills. In the future, we will make improvements to the techniques of the learning support system to facilitate its use.

Acknowledgements. We thank all the people who cooperated with this study. A part of this study was supported by a Grant-in-Aid for Scientific Research (B) from the Ministry of Education, Culture, Sports, Science and Technology, Japan (MEXT; No. 19390548) and a Grant-in-Aid for Challenging Exploratory Research from MEXT (No. 21659500).

References

1. Aso, Y.: Nursing Art, Igaku-Shoin's Medical Dictionary, 2nd edn., p. 504 (2009)
2. Hagi, Y., Ito, F., Nishibori, Y., Toyoshima, Y.: The experience for newly graduated nurses to learn skills of drip infusion to vein. Bulletin Department of Nursing Seirei Christian University 15, 51–59 (2007)

3. Inaba, Y., Hanaoka, M.: A Consideration of the Concepts of Nursing Skills: The changes and development seen from nursing textbooks. Kyojugaku no Tankyu 17, 65–88 (2003)
4. Polanyi, M.: The Tacit Dimension. The University of Chicago Press (1966)
5. Majima, Y., Hosoda, Y.: The nursing skill education by visualization materials. Journal of the Educational Application of Information Technologies 9(1), 31–35 (2006)
6. Nagumo, H., Sugawara, M., Satoh, N., Kurai, Y., Koyama, S., Nakano, M.: Nursing Students' Attitude towards E-Learning Materials with Moving Pictures. Bulletin of Niigata Seiryo University 5, 33–48 (2005)
7. Sakyo, Y., Toyomasu, K., Ttsukamoto, N., Nakayama, K., Ozawa, M., Kaharu, C., Yokoyama, M., Yamazaki, Y.: Trial Introduction of e-learning as a Tool for Reviewing Nursing Skills. Journal of St. Luka's Society for Nursing Research 10(1), 54–60 (2006)
8. Holland, A., Smith, F., McCrossan, G., Adamson, E., Watt, S., Penny, K.: Online video in clinical skills education of oral medication administration for undergraduate student nurses: A mixed methods, prospective cohort study. Nurse Education Today (2012) (in press), journal homepage: http://www.elsevier.com/nedt (February 16, 2012)
9. Cardoso, A.F., Moreli, L., Braga, F.T., Vasques, C.I., Santos, C.B., Carvalho, E.C.: Effect of a video on developing skills in undergraduate nursing students for the management of perfectly implantable central venous access ports. Nurse Education Today 32(6), 709–713 (2012)
10. Majima, Y.: New evolution of nursing education through e-learning. Nursing and Information 12, 58–66 (2005)
11. Jacqueline, B., Julia, R., Alison, W.: The effect of computer-assisted learning versus conventional teaching methods on the acquisition and retention of hand washing theory and skills in pre-qualification nursing students: A randomized controlled trial. International Journal of Nursing Studies 47, 287–294 (2010)
12. Tanaka, M.: Practical Knowledge: Tacit Knowledge: Boundary Knowledge. Official Journal of the International Council of Nurses 2009 32(4), 12 (Summer 2009)
13. Majima, Y., Soga, M., Maekawa, Y.: Development of an E-learning System to Support Reflectional Nursing Skills Training. Japan Journal of Medical Informatics 30(suppl.), 256–259 (2010)
14. Majima, Y., Maekawa, Y.: Converting Tacit Knowledge into Formal Knowledge in Intravenous Injection Skills: Paying attention to nurses' line-of-sight. In: Proceeding of the 29th Academic Conference Japan Academic of Nursing Science, p. 229 (2009)
15. Maekawa, Y., Majima, Y.: Comparison of Consciousness between Expert Nurses and Nursing Students for Knacks (Tacit Knowledge) in Practicing Intravenous Injection Skills: An interview survey. In: Proceeding of the 29th Academic Conference Japan Academic of Nursing Science, p. 315 (2009)
16. Kozu, T.: Medical Education in Japan. Academic Medicine 81(12), 1069–1075 (2006)
17. Trung, Q.T., Albert, S., Jan Van, D., Pamela, E.W.: Teacher-made models: The answer for medical skills training in developing countries? BMC Medical Education 12, 98 (2012)
18. Majima, Y., Maekawa, Y.: Comparative Analysis of Vein Injection Skill Difference Between Skilled Nurses and Nursing Students, Focus to Radial Motion and Skill Procedures. In: Proceedings of the 33rd Annual Conference of Japanese Society for Information and System in Education, pp. 28–29 (2008)
19. Majima, Y., Soga, M., Maekawa, Y.: Development of an E-learning System to Support Self-learning of Nursing Skills. In: Proceedings of the IADIS International Conference, WWW/INTERNET 2010, pp. 400–402 (2010)

20. Sakoda, M., Majima, Y., Soga, M., Yasuko, M.: Skill Learning Model for Nursing Students in Intravenous Injection Training. In: Proceedings of the 35th Annual Conference of Japanese Society for Information and System in Education, pp. 28–29 (2010)
21. Sakoda, M., Majima, Y., Soga, M., Yasuko, M.: Evaluation of Skill Learning Support System for nursing Students. Japan Journal of Medical Informatics 30(suppl.), 252–255 (2010)
22. Majima, Y., Sakoda, M., Maekawa, Y., Soga, M.: Evaluation of an E-learning System to Support Self-Learning of Nursing Skills. In: Proceedings of the 19th International Conference on Computers in Education, pp. 523–530 (2011)
23. Majima, Y., Sakoda, M., Maekawa, Y., Soga, M.: Evaluation of Nursing Skills Acquisition of Reflective e-Learning System for Nursing Students by Different Learning Methods. In: The 20th International Conference on Computers in Education, pp. 460–467 (2012)
24. Majima, Y., Soga, M., Maekawa, Y.: Learning Support System by Hand Motion Reproduction for Nursing Skill Training. JSiSE Research Report 26(1), 51–54 (2011)
25. Majima, Y., Maekawa, Y., Soga, M.: Learning Support System Reproducing Finger Movements in Practicing Nursing Techniques. In: Proceedings of the 2012 11th International Congress on Nursing Informatics, pp. 278–282 (2012)
26. Majima, Y., SakodaM., M.Y., Soga, M.: Self-learning Support System Design for Nursing Student and Analysis of Nursing Skill Acquisition Process. IEICE Technical Report 111(39), 65–70 (2011)
27. Dorothy, L., Walter, S.: Deep Smarts. Harvard Business Review 82(9), 88–97 (2004)
28. Norman, D.A.: Things That MakeUs Smart: Defending Human Attributes in the Age of the Machine. Addison-Wesley (1993)
29. Kikuoka, S., Honjo, K., Sugita, H., Nakagi, T., Kawashima, M., Kawaguchi, T.: Qualitative Analysis of Practicing Intravenous Injection Skills by Graduates of a College of Nursing. Learning despite Difficult Situations. Journal of the Japanese Red Cross College of Nursing 19, 11–19 (2005)

Usability Testing for e-health Application:
A Case Study for Sana/Open MRS

Claudia Renata Mont'Alvão, Felipe Pierantoni, and Carlos Alberto Pereira de Lucena

Ergonomic Laboratory LEUI, Pontifical Catholic University of Rio de Janeiro,
Rua Marquês de São Vicente, n 225, Gávea, Rio de Janeiro/ RJ - Brazil - 22453-900
cmontalvao@puc-rio, felipepiera@gmail.com,
beto.lucena@affero.com.br

Abstract. This paper presents the conduction of a usability test with users of Sana/ Open MRS system. These users are Medicine students that performed four tasks, using distinct scenarios. As part of a bigger research, the objective of this procedure was evaluating user´s opinions and from these results, supports system developers in new interfaces.

Keywords: e-health, usability testing, user´s evaluation.

1   Context

Everyday mobile technologies and its apps are part of our lives. Address books, mobile banking, GPS, and search information at the internet are some examples that describe what is possible to do nowadays with a mobile phone, using 3G or 4G technology.

Human factors/ ergonomic researches can and must play an important role during the development process of these technologies. Together, the appropriate test environment and its tools can lead to a significant data interpretation that will contribute to make these applications safer, more usable, and better accepted by final users.

As Gorlenko & Merrick (2003) mention the concept of mobile interaction is related not only to the device mobility, but also the users' mobility: the equipment must be portable and must allow the users' mobility during the interaction. Ballard (2007) affirms that the word "mobile" refers, fundamentally, to the user and not to the device or application.

Usability concept and usability testing are common terms when talking about to users' interfaces and human factors/ ergonomics interventions.

The starting point of this research is Open MRS system. It´s a collaborative project in open code for software development that focus in care taking in underdeveloped countries. Based on concepts of data liberty and sharing, this system allows access and modifications to its code, besides its use within other systems or products. Open MRS is a web based platform, but can also be implemented in one unique computer or server.

M. Kurosu (Ed.): Human-Computer Interaction, Part II, HCII 2013, LNCS 8005, pp. 144–149, 2013.
© Springer-Verlag Berlin Heidelberg 2013

As shown in Figure 1, Open MRS homepage is simple. After logged in, user can see a navigation bar in the top of the page, which options are: *Home, Find/ Create Patient, Dictionary, Cohort builder, Sana*, and *Administration*.

When used alongside the mobile application Sana, developed by MIT, it works as an electronic health (e-health) recorder, which allows a data collection of health information that can be accessed from a mobile application. This system is the central of this research gathering professionals and students from Design, Engineering and Medicine areas. The main objective of this study is a usability evaluation of this mobile application - Sana - based on Open MRS - taking into account its public, the assistant doctors. In this way, a usability test was carried out with three Medicine students.

Fig. 1. Sana/Open MRS homepage, after log in, where navigation bar can be seen

2   Method

To ensure the development of user-friendly products, it is important to guarantee that needs and limitations of users are taken into account throughout the whole development process (Rubin et al., 2008). According to these authors, "usability testing employs techniques to collect empirical data of the interaction of representative end users with the product by completing representative tasks in a controlled environment". In a usability test, the usability of a product is evaluated by means of user trials, with the aim to analyze or improve the usability of the evaluated product.

A usability test is a good way to identify usability problems in this case. According to Rubin et al. (2008), some test steps must be considered:

- Develop a test plan;
- Choose a testing environment;

- Find and select participants;
- Prepare test materials;
- Conduct the sessions;
- Debrief with participants and observers;
- Analyze data and observations;
- Create findings and recommendations,

Following these steps, and focusing the firsts, research plan consisted of plan a test that, when using mobile app Sana, the user can record individual patients personal data, data related to his/her visit, symptoms and diagnostics. This record is sent to Open MRS, setting a databank - this was the test environment.

When considering the participants, subjects in this field study, albeit being familiarized with Sana app, they don't have a deep knowledge on Open MRS, using it merely as a databank for recorded data.

From this point of view, the main proposal of the usability test was to verify their performance with the system - if they need to use Sana app, they must also be capable to complete simple tasks on Open MRS, as finding a patient record, editing it and organizing it. To do this, some parameters determined by the group of Systems Engineering helped researchers to define the scenarios and tasks to be accomplished. Participants were contacted and tested during August 2012, in the Ergonomics Lab, at PUC-Rio.

The research problems and proposed scenarios used in this test are in Table 1.

Table 1. Research problems and scenarios used in usability test

Research problem	Scenario description
Search for a patient's record	Using Open MRS/ Sana, find the last registered patient
Access and edit a record	You´ve just diagnose a patient and registered him at Open MRS/Sana. At the end of the appointment, the patient told that is also a dizzy feeling. It´s good edit patient´s record, and add this information. To do this, use the term "giddiness" in the item "other complaints".
Search patient record	Your patient John Smith called, once he needs the name of the medication you´ve prescribed. To answer him, you will need to open his register, and check which is the medication that you wrote down. Find John Smith´s record and medications registered in Open MRS/Sana.

Test materials – as scenarios, debriefing formulary and the online system - were prepared before the test began. After arriving, participants did a cooperative evaluation, using four scenarios to perform the tasks. When concluded, subjects answered a post-test questionnaire, and also gave their personal impressions and/or comments about the system, using a debriefing formulary.

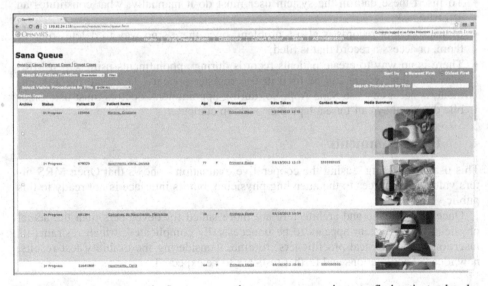

Fig. 2. Patient *Search* page of Sana system, where user can find records of patient already registered or create a new patient

Fig. 3. SANA *Queue* page in Sana system, that users must navigate to find patients already registered and access their data.

3   Some Results

During tests volunteers showed a surprising self-assurance while using the system. They mentioned that a couple of days before test, they logged in the system and tried to understand how it works. So, during test, this familiarity interfered in tests results, once all scenarios were concluded in an easy and fast way.

But besides this, participants referred that what happened during performing the scenarios was that they memorized which was the sequence of actions, once interface wasn´t intuitive, nor easy to understand or navigate.

Testing using scenarios was also important to point out ambiguities in the website, as sections that can be reached using different tags and the lack of integration between the App Sana and Open MRS website. If patient isn´t recorded with his all data in Sana App, data related to the appointment can´t be created in Open MRS website.

Answers after test and debriefing showed some similarities concerning the opinions of all participants. Open MRS isn´t an attractive or stimulating interface to interact, once it´s difficult to be used, and sometimes, too and unnecessarily complex. All of them agreed that a tutorial is needed to learn how to use it and they also believe that learning process is slow. None of them said that fell confident while using the system.

During debriefing phase, participants emphasized general problems in the website, as the need of too many steps to conclude simple tasks, a confusing interface and non-intuitive navigation. But some other points were more specific:

- The need of register medications and illness in a section named "*Dictionary*". Just after each register is inserted in database, these information can be an option to be included in patients records;
- To insert these data in the system user must do it manually, what constitutes an effortful task;
- Manage patient records is also a problem, once there´s no way to delete some of them, or access a record that is filed;
- There is no way to create patients records during appointments using Open MRS website - this system can be used just to register patients. To create the appointment, is necessary use Sana App. So, during appointment, doctors must use a mobile device, they can´t use a laptop or desktop computer.

4   Final Comments

This usability testing - using the cooperative evaluation - shows that Open MRS offers valuable resources to the attending physician, but its interface is not ready to this public yet.

Once its language and architecture are more suited for developers than the actual physicians, this system appears to be unnecessarily complicated, which restrains its insertion in the medical practitioners' routine. Considering the usability test results, new ideas of applications and further tests are to be expected.

5   Next Steps and Future Research

5.1   Survey of Apps that Focus the Communication and Information Sharing between Doctors and Patients

Aiming a better comprehension of available tools that allow information sharing between doctors and patients, the next step of this research is a survey to identify applications (apps) that are focused in m-health.

The objective of this phase is identify, among apps available at *Google Play Store* – that offers apps to Android system – which are the apps that allow patients record their personal data, and if he/she wants, share them with his/her assistant doctor. Apps that are directed to doctors will be also considered, pointing out similarities and differences with Open MRS/Sana. *Google Play Store* was chosen once Android system is the base of the system used in Open MRS/SANA system.

All apps found in this phase will be organized and analyzed, and shared with all members of the research team.

5.2   Future Usability Test of Open MRS/SANA

Once the research team includes developers that are working with technical aspects of Open MRS/Sana system, after putting together all this information, it is desirable carry out another usability test with real users.

This new evaluation has as objective compare and evaluate users opinions suggestions and performance after changes in this system, from users perspective

Acknowledgments. Authors take this opportunity to express our deep regards to National Council for Scientific and Technological Development– CNPq that supported this research.

References

1. Agapie, E., et al.: Seeing Our Signals: Combining location traces and web based models for personal discovery. In: MobileHCI 2008. Proceedings of the 10th International Conference on Human Computer Interaction with Mobile Devices and Services. ACM, Amsterdam (2008)
2. Ballard, B.: Designing the Mobile User Experience, 1st edn, 260 p. (2007)
3. Booth, P.: An Introduction to Human-Computer Interaction, 3ard edn., 268 p. LEA Ltd. (1992)
4. Church, K., Smyth, B.: Understanding the intent behind mobile information needs. In: International Conference on Intelligent User Interfaces. Proceedings of the 13th International Conference on Intelligent user Interfaces, Sanibel Island, Florida, USA, pp. 247–256. ACM, New York (2009) ISBN:978-1-60558-168-2
5. De Sá, M., Carriço, L.: Lessons from Early Stages Design of Mobile Applications. In: MobileHCI 2008. Proceedings of the 10th International Conference on Human Computer Interaction with Mobile Devices and Services. ACM, Amsterdam (2008)
6. De Vries, I.: Mobile telephony: realizing the dream of ideal communication? In: Hamill, Lasen (eds.) Mobile World. Past, Present, Future, 218 pp. 11–28. Springer (2005)
7. Gorlenko, L., Merrick, R.: No wires attached: Usability challenges in the connected mobile world. IBM Systems Journal 42(4), 639–651 (2003)
8. Meister, D., Enderwuick, T.P.: Human factors in system design, development and testing, 247 p. Lawrence Erlbaum, London (2001)
9. Rubin, J., et al.: Handbook of Usability Testing: Howto Plan, Design, and Conduct Effective Tests, 2nd edn., 384 pages. Wiley (2008)

Introducing Emotional Interfaces to Healthcare Systems

Rangarajan Parthasarathy and Xiaowen Fang

School of Computing, College of Computing and Digital Media,
DePaul University, Chicago, Illinois, USA
{rparthasarathy,xfang}@cdm.depaul.edu

Abstract. The use of healthcare websites is gaining importance in the United States. It is conceivable that when using healthcare websites, the users may not be in a happy or euphoric emotional state, and would like to be comforted. In this paper, we argue that using emotional interfaces in healthcare systems will attract users, and motivate them to stay, participate and return. We suggest a possible future state for emotional interfaces in healthcare systems. In this context, we present a review of relevant theories and research studies from Computer Science and Psychology, and a subjective ranking of some well-known healthcare websites in the United States with respect to their hedonic and emotional values. Lastly, we discuss our proposal for developing emotional interfaces for healthcare websites.

Keywords: Healthcare Websites, Hedonic Websites, Emotional Websites, Emotional Interfaces.

1   Introduction

Research on patterns of Internet use has found that people primarily use the Internet for communicating through e-mails, and for searching for information ([31]). This information search includes searching for health, disease, and medical information on healthcare websites.

Internet use in healthcare by way of use of healthcare websites has increased significantly between 2000 and 2013. A study by Pew Internet and American Life Project found that 52 million American adults, or 55% of those with Internet access, have used the Internet to obtain medical or health information ([15]). Health care websites have been created in the past few years at a cost of between $250,000 and $1 million ([20]). It is estimated that more than 145 million people use healthcare websites to get health related information ([30]). Healthcare websites satisfy the need of people to obtain health and disease related information in a quick and efficient manner without having to step out of their homes. Before the Internet revolution, patients were dependent on the doctor and the hospital system to instruct and educate them about diseases, and describe various treatment options ([79]). In the computer and Internet age of today, patients are able to obtain healthcare information from healthcare websites, and are thus knowledgeable. They are in a position to discuss or negotiate with the doctor about their individual situations and treatment options. Clearly,

M. Kurosu (Ed.): Human-Computer Interaction, Part II, HCII 2013, LNCS 8005, pp. 150–162, 2013.
© Springer-Verlag Berlin Heidelberg 2013

access to the Internet and the proliferation of healthcare websites have changed the way patients interact with the doctors and hospitals ([51]).

According to the Kaiser Foundation web site ([36]), 51% of the healthcare expenditure of the United States is accounted for by hospital care and physician/clinical services. Although the spending on health care was about $75 billion (7.2% of GDP) or $356 per United States resident in 1970, it rose to $2.5 trillion (17.6% of GDP) or $8160 per United States resident by 2009. This increase in healthcare spending is commensurate with the increased use of healthcare facilities, hospitals, clinics, and doctor services by the public, which has put a tremendous pressure on the healthcare system. The use of healthcare websites by the public somewhat alleviates this pressure, because it is conceivable that many people who find from the healthcare websites that their symptoms are related to common illnesses, may prefer to buy off-the-shelf medication from a drug store, instead of spending many hours of the day to make an appointment, drive to the hospital, and wait in the waiting room to see a doctor. For this and other pertinent reasons, there has been an increasing push in recent times to encourage the use of healthcare information technology ([8], [39]).

Research literature points to differences between functional websites and hedonic websites. Websites are made up of user interfaces. In this paper, both terms are used interchangeably, because emotional interfaces and emotional websites are one and the same with respect to their impact on user emotions. Hedonic websites are designed to provide fun, emotional experiences, feelings of arousal, pleasurable experiences, and pleasurable outcomes, and are designed with individuals seeking sensations on multi-sensory channels. Functional or utilitarian websites have been associated with business and professional purposes ([72]), and usability goals such as efficiency, effectiveness and learnability ([63]). Functional websites allow the users to accomplish tasks in the most efficient and effective way, and are not developed with ease of use, emotions or aesthetics as important considerations. The outcomes from functional or utilitarian websites are resultant from attentive, rational, and task-oriented actions ([3]). By contrast, hedonic websites are designed to provide fun, emotional experiences, feelings of arousal, pleasurable experiences and pleasurable outcomes, and are primarily designed for individuals seeking sensations on multi-sensory channels ([32], [38], [46], [72]). Emotional websites are thus a subset of hedonic websites and convey the same values as hedonic websites, but with an increased emphasis on the emotional aspect. It should be understandable that some hedonic and emotional websites may not have utilitarian values, and vice-versa.

Laurel ([40]) states that emotions play an important role in social interaction through computers. Users of healthcare websites do so primarily to find health related information when they are sick, find ways to prevent sicknesses, or find health insurance information ([15], [51], [77]). Understandably therefore, when using healthcare websites, they experience a range of emotions, mostly negative. They are likely not in a happy or euphoric emotional state and would like to be comforted. Though researchers have explored hedonic, and emotional interfaces, little research has been done with respect to applying these to healthcare systems. Herein lies the research gap for our current research. We argue in this paper that the use of emotional interfaces in healthcare systems will attract users to healthcare websites, comfort and entertain users, and motivate them to stay, participate and return. This behavior, in turn, may reduce or eliminate the need of face-to-face doctor-patient encounters for information gathering, discussion of treatment options available, and other similar purposes.

2   Hedonic and Emotional Interfaces

Research has shown that both rational and irrational factors play a role in user selection and continued use of websites ([24], [27], [46], and [67]). Rational factors are in tune with the goals of functional or utilitarian websites, and concern themselves with whether the websites facilitate accomplishment of tasks in an effective and efficient manner. By contrast, irrational factors are related to emotions, and therefore are in tune with the goals of hedonic or emotional websites. For example, habit is an example of irrational behavior, whereby the website user will continue to use websites by habit, without subjecting the behavior and the outcomes to detailed analyses ([46]). Van der Heijden ([72]) found determinates of future use intentions concerning hedonic systems. Kim and Hwang ([37]) state that emphasizing the hedonic aspects of mobile Internet applications make them more attractive for younger generations. Schrepp et al. ([63]) found that hedonic qualities have an impact on the attractiveness of interfaces, and the more attractive the interfaces or websites, the higher the user preference for them. Kim and Forsythe ([38]) found that the hedonic aspect of perceived entertainment value was a stronger determinant of attitude toward using product virtualization technologies than perceived usefulness. Fiore et al. ([21]) conducted path-analysis studies and found statistically significant paths between hedonic value and resulting emotional pleasure, and arousal variables, and also statistically significant paths between these three variables and global attitude, willingness to purchase, and willingness to patronize an online store. Hu and Chuang ([34]) found hedonic value to be one of the 'value components' that had a direct and positive effect on customer loyalty intention toward e-retailer websites. Pillai and Mukherji ([58]) found that the playfulness aspect in hedonic social networking websites had a significant impact in the user acceptance of such websites.

Human computer interaction is a social process in which emotions play a significant role ([54], [56], [57]). Research has linked emotions to the consumption of products and services ([3], [4], [32]). Although the term 'consumption' has been primarily associated with consumer behavior with respect to product and service purchases, the same could be extrapolated to apply to the use (consumption) of websites as well. Emotions relating to service provided have been associated with satisfaction and future behavior intentions ([2], [5]). These studies indicate that positive emotions experienced during consumption and service actions greatly influence commitment to the relationship with the providers, and intention to continue the relationship.

Picard ([56], [57]) discusses the importance of building computer systems that respond to user frustrations so as to alleviate them. Isbister ([35]) contemplates the designing of computer interfaces and websites that will translate the movements associated with computer use to "feel good" and pleasurable emotions that will result in less stressful and more healthy human computer interactions. Lim ([45]) found that individuals' sensation seeking behavior and gender influence their emotional responses to visual stimuli during computer mediated slot machining gaming. Lee ([42]) examined the interface-based antecedents of trust in the agent-assisted shopping context, aiming at discovering potential interface strategies as a means to enhance consumer trust in the computer agent. This work examined the effects of certain interface design factors, including face human-likeliness, script social presence, information richness, and price increase associated with upgrade recommendation by the computer agent, for their usefulness in enhancing the affective and cognitive bases for consumer trust. On the basis of this study, the researchers suggested that it is important for computer agents to reduce information overload experienced by many online shoppers. They further suggested that future development of computer interfaces should aim at flexible adaptation of agents to meet the unique individual needs customizing for situational idiosyncrasies, thus providing high performance and enjoyable experiences to consumers. Tuch et al. ([71]) found through their research that the user's affective experience in an online shopping environment impacts the aesthetics-usability relationship, and contributes to altering the paradigm "what is beautiful is useable".

Gugliotta and Paterno ([25]) present a set of design criteria for designing websites that can be adapted to emotion-related aspects. Miranda et al. ([50]) discuss the use of emotional design in the development of low technology products and the addition of emotion causing strategies in such design that can result in a more desirable interface. Hao et al. ([28]) contend that the emotional response of users has become a key factor to be considered in product designs, and discuss how user's emotional responses can be used to develop new automobile outlines. Welzel et al. ([76]) discuss the term "emotional ergonomics" in the light of cognitive interdependency between ergonomics and marketing of products. Yung et al. ([80]) while acknowledging the importance of emotions for human cognition, motivation, learning, decision-making and intelligence, discuss the development of adaptive interfaces, which would support the users with positive emotion eliciting elements. Walter ([75]) stresses the importance of emotional experiences and alludes to their applications in website design, which he states should create an experience for users that makes them feel like there is a person, and not a machine at the other end. Scaglione ([60]) stresses the need to build emotion evoking websites to attract and retain customers for life, since at the core of every human being is the desire to connect and find meaning in the world. Martin et al. ([63]) found emotion based satisfaction to be a better predictor of future behavioral intention than cognitive measures of satisfaction.

It follows from the above discussion that a healthcare web site that can provide comfort in the form of emotional adaptations involving appropriate emotional responses can attract and retain users, and serve its intended functions both, from an information system perspective, and from an emotional interface perspective. Such a website or interface must be able to evoke a positive emotional response from the user, and eventually improve their mood state by causing an emotion shift from negative to positive emotions.

3 Subjective Evaluation of Healthcare Websites for Hedonic and Emotional Values

To evaluate the extent to which hedonic and emotional values are present or absent in the healthcare websites that are in use today, we selected 15 healthcare websites for evaluation, based on rankings by the Consumer and Patient Health Information Society (CAPHIS), a section of the United States Medical Library Association (CAPHIS,

2012). A thorough literature review pertaining to hedonic websites and emotional websites was conducted, with a view to come up with a list of measures that have been used by researchers to evaluate hedonic and emotional values. The preliminary list yielded 70 measures. This list was examined carefully to select measures that would be most appropriate for a subjective evaluation, because the preliminary list contained measures like "emotional arousal" which may be difficult to assess subjectively. The final list of measures, thought to be appropriate for subjective evaluation purposes, yielded 27 measures which are listed in Table 1. Based on these measures, the authors developed a scale comprising questions of a "yes-no" nature, and also questions that needed an evaluation on a scale of 1 to 5 (with 1 being "very much not so" and 5 being "very much so"). Table 2 and Table 3 present a list of these questions (*Tables 2 & 3 could not be included in this submission due to space constraints, and are available from the authors upon request*).

Table 1. Measures Selected For the Subjective Evaluation

Authors	Paper title	Year	Hedonic Web Site Attributes
Fiore, A., Jin, H., and Kim, J.	For fun and profit: Hedonic value from image interactivity and responses toward an online store	2005	Emotional pleasure (happy-unhappy, annoyed-pleased, dissatisfied-satisfied)
Hartmann, J.B. and Samra, Y.M.	Hedonic and utilitarian aspects of web use: an empirical study among United States teenagers	2008	download videos or movies
			meet new people on the web
Hu, F.L., and Chuang, C.C.	A study of the relationship between the value perception ad loyalty intention toward an e-retailer website	2012	This site not only sells products and services, but also entertains me
			I get so involved when I shop on this website that I forget everything
			I enjoy surfing and shopping from this web site
Hung, W.T., Tsang, S.S., and Liu, H.Y.	Website characteristics and the impact of user perceived value on user behavior	2010	Novelty (web attribute that is perceived by web users as comprising novel information and information)
			Flow experience (a state of consciousness that is sometimes experienced by individuals who are deeply involved in an enjoyable activity)
Hur, Y.	Determinants of sports website acceptance: An application and extension of the TAM model	2007	Enjoyable or not enjoyable
			Also perceived enjoyment which consists of following questions:
Kim, D. and Hwang, Y.	A study of mobile internet user's service quality perceptions from a user's utilitarian and hedonic tendency perspectives	2010	chatting
			sports scores or variety
Kim, J. and Forsythe, S.	Hedonistic usage of product virtualization technologies in online apparel shopping	2007	it is fun
			enjoyable
			interesting
Lee, R. and Murphy, J.	The moderating influence of enjoyment on customer loyalty	2008	Enjoyment (and pleasure)
Li, D.C.	Online social network acceptance: a social perspective	2011	perceived enjoyment
Liao, C., To, P., Liu, C., Kuo, P. and Chuang, S.	Factors influencing the intended use of web portals	2010	visual attractiveness (esp. color scheme & overall layout)
			pleasant layout
			aesthetics
Massey, A.P., Khatri, V., and Montoya-Weiss, M.M.	Usability of online services: The role of technology readiness and context	2007	No direct measures, but refers to the following wrt Hedonic websites:
			Self-fulfilling value (interacting with the site is an end in itself)
			Enjoyment
Pillai, A., and Mukherjee, J.	User acceptance of hedonic vs. utilitarian social networking web sites	2011	Perceived ease of use
Yang, K. and Lee, H.	Gender differences in using mobile data services: utilitarian and hedonic value approaches	2010	feel good when using
			enjoyable
			gives pleasure
			makes me want to use
			web page design style
			graphics
			colors
			attractive visual images

The developed scale was used to perform a subjective evaluation of the 15 health-care websites selected. The results of this subjective evaluation are presented in Table 2 and Table 3 (*Tables 2 & 3 could not be included in this submission due to space constraints, and are available from the authors upon request*). From the results of the subjective evaluation, only 1 (Mayo Clinic) of the 15 healthcare websites evaluated (7% of the total healthcare websites evaluated) got an average score of better than 2.5 on scale type 1, and only 2 (Mayo Clinic, WebMD) of the 15 healthcare websites evaluated (14% of the total healthcare websites evaluated) got an average score of less than 1.5 on scale type 2. This means that of the 15 healthcare websites evaluated, at best 2 websites had *some* hedonic and emotional values, but all the other websites did not. These results reflect that there is a tremendous opportunity to improve the exist-ing healthcare websites to make them hedonic and emotional, and to develop new healthcare websites that are hedonic and emotional.

4   Building Emotional Computer Interfaces in Healthcare Systems

Theories from Psychology have guided computer programmers and researchers in Computer Science, by way of helping to understand human behavior and emotions during computer use ([6], [7], [36], [47], and [61]). Emotions are very complex, more pronounced in evolutionarily advanced animals like human beings as compared to primitive animals, and valuable in producing appropriate actions to good and bad situations ([33], [37]). A thorough review of extant research literature in Computer Science and Psychology has revealed that 'appraisal theories' of emotion ([22], [41], [55], [62]) have been favored the most by computer scientists and researchers, for application to hedonic and emotional computer systems. Appraisal theories place the cognitive component at the very onset of an emotional episode, prior to bodily res-ponses, and thus the cognitive component can be invoked as the one that determines which emotion should be produced and how intense it should be ([33]). This is related to the suggestion that an emotional web interface can help with managing the emotion shift of the user from a negative emotional state (Ex. depression, sadness) to a posi-tive emotional state (Ex. hopeful, excited).

We found further, that of all the appraisal theories, the most frequently used theory by researchers in Computer Science is the "Cognitive Structure of Emotions" theory proposed by Ortony, Clore, and Collins ([55]). In this theory, the authors try to stress the holistic nature of emotions, while pointing to the individual emotions evoked by certain conditions. According to this theory, Emotions are "valenced reactions to events, agents or objects, with their particular nature being determined by the way in which the eliciting situation is construed". Ortony et al. ([55]) define an "event" as "people's construals about things about to happen, considered independently of any beliefs they may have about actual or possible causes". When an individual is reacting to events, that individual is reacting to the consequences of the current event, has in mind the consequences of past events, and may either be pleased or displeased with such outcomes. Ortony et al. ([55]) define an "agent" as "things considered in light of their actual or presumed instrumentality or agency in causing or contributing to events". Agents could be human or non-human, "animate beings or inanimate objects or abstractions, such as institutions and even situations, provided they are construed as causally efficacious in the particular context". When an individual is reacting to agents, that individual is reacting to the behavior or actions of the agents, and may either approve or disapprove of such behavior. Ortony et al. ([55]) define "objects" as "objects viewed *qua* objects", with the possibility that objects could be treated as both objects and as agents depending on the situation. They explain this with the following example: a person who buys a new car that is a constant sources of trouble might blame the car for his series of misfortunes, and in doing so treats the car as an agent (hence disapproves of it), and also as an object only (hence dislikes it). The emotion of liking an object could have the following tokens: adoration, affection, attraction, liking, and love. Similarly the emotion of disliking an object could have the following tokens: aversion, disgust, hate, loathing, repulsion, detest and revulsion. When an individual is reacting to objects, that individual is reacting to the aesthetics of the object such as color, shape, form or size, and may either like or dislike such aesthetics. This is just the starting point. Ortony et al. ([55]) then sub-classify this initial set of emotions into further emotional states based on the aforementioned fundamental hierarchy. For instance, the emotional reaction to objects may elicit "attraction emotions" such as hate or love. Figure 1 shows the complete classification of emotions proposed by the model.

We argue that Ortony ([55])'s theory can be applied to build emotional interfaces for healthcare systems by creation of events, agents and objects in the interface. We posit that in the context of emotional interfaces in healthcare systems, the following would be desirable events: having an interesting session with the website that makes one forget everything else during the interaction, having a web session that provides the answers sought by the user along with detailed explanations in one session (high quality of service), animated and voice-based narratives in the web session (as if one were interacting with a human), and a web session that loads and transitions from one page to the next quickly so that the user gets the desired response in a relatively short time (similar to a hospital visit where one can meet the doctors and nurses without any check-in counters or waiting rooms). In practical terms, while some of the above events (for example the first two) may be achieved with the inputs provided by the domain experts (healthcare experts such as doctors and nurses), the others can be achieved purely through the expertise of the programmer. Hu and Chuang ([34]) consider the impact of websites that provide interesting sessions and flow, in enabling users to get very involved with and forget everything else. This is similar to having an experience involving a book of fiction, in which the reader finds it difficult to stop reading the book from cover to cover, because the chapters are so interesting and 'pull' the reader from one chapter to the next. Massey et al. ([81]) discuss the self-fulfilling value offered by a website, whereby interacting with the website is considered a reward in itself. Ltifi ([43]), Carlos ([13]) and Tarafdar ([70]) have explored the role of website quality in user satisfaction. Yeung & Lu ([80]) and Sharples ([64]) studied the impact of animation, graphics and narrative style in website use. Moustakis et al. ([53]), Cao et al. ([12]) and Tarafdar ([70]) investigated the impact of quick response times including loading times in website use.

We posit that in the context of emotional interfaces in healthcare systems, the following would be desirable agents: chat rooms and blogs that enable the website users to meet and interact with people with similar medical issues, play rooms with quizzes relating to medical issues, videos and animated movies about the medical issue under consideration with the ability to be downloaded and viewed offline, human like interactions such as asking whether the user is satisfied with the information obtained so far or needs more information, or asking the user what they would like to see or where they want to go next (similar to a human like interaction with the user during a face-to-face hospital encounter with a doctor or nurse). In practical terms, the agents mentioned above will primarily involve the expertise of the programmer, while the content and context of the object (for example, what animations should be provided or what questions should be asked) are provided by subject matter experts like doctors and psychologists. Curtis ([52]), Pillai et al. ([58]), Mack et al. ([48]), and Burke ([10]) explored the role of playfulness, chat rooms and blog use in website user satisfaction. Hartmann & Samra ([82]), Hahn et al. ([26]) and Yeung & Lu ([80]) researched the presence of downloadable materials in enhancing website use and user satisfaction. Aldiri et al. ([1]), Sicilia et al. ([65]), and Sundar et al. ([68]) investigated the impact of interactivity in website use.

We posit that in the context of emotional interfaces in healthcare systems, the following would be desirable objects: vibrant and pleasing color schema (for the screen in general, the dialog boxes, the animations and for all related aspects), animation (especially two and three dimensional animations involving the human anatomy to explain the medical condition queried by the user), humorous narratives with interactive graphics that lighten emotions and the mental load (especially when explaining the technical details, symptoms or consequences concerning the medical condition queried by the user), clipart (three dimensional in pastel colors), high brightness, and stability of color tones (associated with mood elevation). Wang et al. ([74]), Cook & Finlayson ([18]), and Cutshall ([19]) explored how beauty in a website through the use of color schema (influenced by cultural values) impacted its continued use. Lim ([44]), and Content ([17]) investigated the advantages of using three dimensional animation to enhance website characteristics. Hem ([29]) addresses the use of animations involving body parts to help patients understand what is wrong with them, and understand the healing process. Webb ([78]) describes the use of animation in an ophthalmology practice, which helped to boost the sale of optical products and services. Gao ([23]) and Chung-Hoon & Young-Gul ([14]) studied the effects of humor in e-commerce. Wagner ([73]) and Tao ([69]) studied the mental load involved in web use. Reed et al. ([59]) and Bucy et al. ([9]) explored the use of clipart in the light of website complexity.

The healthcare website user can be presented with the emotional interfaces in two ways, as follows. Picard and his colleagues ([56], [57]) have created new technologies that enable a computer to sense, understand and respond to human signs of confusion, frustration, anger, interest and joy. The computer is then able to respond with the appropriate emotional interface. Other researchers have presented the user with emotional interfaces pre-fabricated to evoke particular emotions. For example, Kim and Moon ([83]) discuss the development of an emotional interface through the manipulation of clipart (form, size and motion manipulations) and color (tone, background, brightness and symmetry manipulations), that will evoke feelings of trustworthiness in users of an online banking interface, The second method seems to be the easiest path for deployment of emotional interfaces in healthcare systems. Since it is likely that healthcare website users are not in a happy or euphoric emotional state and would like to be comforted, emotional interfaces with appropriate events, agents and objects should be able to comfort the user, make him or her feel secure and entertained, and thereby cause a shift in the emotional state from negative to positive. This, in turn will motivate the users to stay, participate and return.

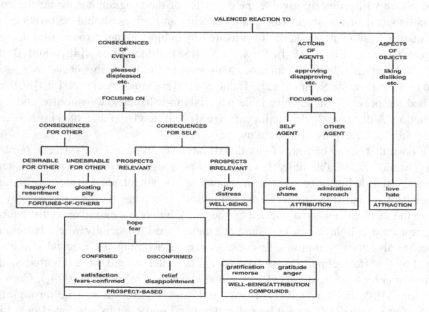

Fig. 1. Cognitive Structure of Emotions Theory*(Source: Ortony et al., 1988)*

5   Conclusion

This paper proposes to use Ortony's ([55]) theory to develop emotional interfaces involving events, agents, and objects that may transform the emotional state of the user from negative to positive. The development of emotional interfaces and websites has much relevance in this day and age of the Internet revolution, in which a larger proportion of the public than ever before, are turning to healthcare websites for information about diseases and treatments. Using emotional websites and interfaces in healthcare systems will permit a better connection with the users and make the user interaction entertaining and informative. This will further encourage the use of healthcare websites, and help to alleviate the pressure on the healthcare system, especially in the United States. Concrete guidelines must be developed in future research concerning how to induce positive emotions in a healthcare website.

References

1. Aldiri, K., Hobbs, D., Qahwaji, R.: Human Face of E-Business: Engendering Consumer Initial Trust Through the Use of Images of Sales Personnel on E-Commerce Web Sites. International Journal of E-Business Research 4(4), 58–78 (2008)
2. Allen, C.T., Machleit, K.A., Kleine, S.S.: A comparison of attitudes and emotions as predictors of behaviour at diverse levels of behavioral Experience. Journal of Consumer Research 18(4), 493–504 (1992)
3. Babin, B.J., Darden, W.R., Babin, L.A.: Negative emotions in marketing research: affect or artifact? Journal of Business Research 42(3), 271–285 (1998)
4. Bagozzi, R.P., Gopinath, M., Nyer, P.U.: The role of emotions in marketing. Journal of the Academy of Marketing Science 27(2), 184–206 (1999)
5. Barsky, J., Nash, L.: Evoking emotion: affective keys to hotel loyalty. Cornell Hotel and Restaurant Administration Quarterly 43 (2002)
6. Bilal, D.: Children's use of the yahooligans! web search engine: Cognitive, physical, and affective behaviors on fact-based search tasks. Journal of the American Society for Information Science 51(7), 646–665 (2000)
7. Bilal, D., Bachir, I.: Children's interaction with cross-cultural and multilingual digital libraries: Information seeking, success, and affective experience. Information Processing and Management: An International Journal 43(1), 65–80 (2007)
8. Birkmeyer, J.D., Birkmeyer, C.M., Wennberg, D.E., Young, M.P.: Leapfrog Safety Standards: The Potential Benefits of Universal Adoption. The Leapfrog Group, Washington, DC (2000)
9. Bucy, E.P., Lang, A., Potter, R.F., Grabe, M.E.: Formal features of cyberspace: Relationships between web page complexity and site traffic. Journal of the American Society for Information Science 50(13), 1246–1256 (1999)
10. Burke, K.: Humanizing the Web. Target Marketing 31(5), 23–24 (2008)
11. Caphis 2012: Consumer and Patient Health Information Society (CAPHIS), a section of the United States Medical Library Association (CAPHIS) (2012), http://Caphis.mlanet.org
12. Cao, M., Zhang, Q., Seydel, J.: B2c e-commerce web site quality: an empirical examination. Industrial Management & Data Systems 105(5/6), 645–661 (2005)
13. Carlos, F., Gurrea, R., Oraos, C.: The effect of product representation mode on the perceived content and continent quality of web sites. Online Information Review 33(6), 1103–1128 (2009)
14. Chung-Hoon, P., Young-Gul, K.: The effect of information satisfaction and relational benefit on consumers' online shopping site commitments. Journal of Electronic Commerce in Organizations 16(5), 20–25 (2006)
15. Chyna: The top 20 healthcare websites and how your patients are using them. Healthcare Executive 16(5), 20–25 (2001)
16. Website of Computers 14(2), 93–118, http://www.sciencedirect.com/science/article/B6V0D-44GF457-1/2/9601b14ed27badfe069784931ea7cc31
17. Content, T.: Preview automation can help businesses set deals. Knight Rider Tribune Business Review (September 27, 2004)
18. Cook, J., Finlayson, M.: The impact of cultural diversity on website design. SAM Advanced Management Journal 70(3), 15–45 (2005)
19. Cutshall, R.C.: An investigation of success metrics for the design of e-commerce websites. Doctoral Dissertation, University of North Texas. Retrieved from ProQuest Dissertations and Theses (2004)

20. Dash, J.: Healthcare moving sites beyond brochureware. Computerworld 34(18), 14–16 (2000)
21. Fiore, A.M., Jin, H.J., Kim, J.: For fun and profit: Hedonic value from image interactivity and responses towards an online store. Psychology and Marketing 22(8), 669–694 (2005)
22. Frijda, N.H.: The place of appraisal in emotion. Cognition and Emotion 7, 357–387 (1993)
23. Gao, Y.: An experimental study of the effects of interactivity and humor in e-commerce. Review of Business Information Systems 15(1), 9–14 (2011)
24. Gefen, D.: TAM or just plain habit?: A look at experienced online shoppers. Journal of Enduser Computing 15(3), 1–13 (2003)
25. Giuditta, G., Fabio, P.: Design of websites adaptable to emotion related aspects. Psychology Journal 10(1), 23–38 (2010)
26. Hahn, R.W., Litan, R.E., Singer, H.J.: The economics of wireless net neutrality. Journal of Competition Law and Economics 3(3), 399–451 (2007)
27. Ha, L.: Crossing offline and online media: a comparison of online advertising on TV websites and online portals. Journal of Interactive Advertising 3(2), 33–48 (2003)
28. Hao, T., Jianghong, Z., Zhengyu, T., Fangzhen, Z., Wei, W.: Building the user emotional genetic model to generate new form in automobile concept design. Automobile Concept Design 3(2), 33–48 (2011)
29. Hem, B.: 3D animation gives patients new understanding of illness. Mcclatchy Tribune Business News (November 08, 2007)
30. Herrick, D.: Web replaces doctors as patients' top health information source. Health Care News (2009), http://healthcare.ncpa.org/commentaries/web-replaces-doctors-as-patients-top-health-information-source
31. Hills, P., Argyle, M.: Uses of the internet and their relationships with individual differences in personality. Computers in Human Behavior 19, 59–70 (2003)
32. Holbrook, M.B., Hirschmann, E.C.: The experiential aspects of consumption: consumer fantasies, feelings, and fun. Journal of Consumer Research 9(2), 132–140 (1982)
33. Houwer, J.D., Hermans, D.: Cognition and emotion. Psychology Press, New York (2010)
34. Hu, F.L., Chuang, C.C.: A study of the relationship between value perception and loyalty intention towards an e-retailer website. Journal of Internet Banking and Commerce 17(1) (2012)
35. Isbister, K.: Emotion and motion: Games as an inspiration for shaping the future of interfaces. Interactions, 24–27 (September-October 2011)
36. Kim, K.-S.: Effects of emotion control and task on web searching behavior. Information Processing and Management: An International Journal 44(1), 373–385 (2008)
37. Kim, D.J., Hwang, Y.: A study of mobile internet users' service quality perceptions from a user's utilitarian and hedonic value tendency perspectives. Information Systems Frontiers 2(3) (2010)
38. Kim, J., Forsythe, S.: Hedonic usage of product virtualization technologies in online apparel shopping. Distribution Management 35(6), 502–514 (2007)
39. Kohn, L.T., Corrigan, J.M., Donaldson, M.S. (eds.): To Err Is Human: A Safer Health Care System. National Academy Press (2000)
40. Laurel, B.: Computers as theatres. Addison-Wesley Publication (1993)
41. Lazarus, R.S.: Thoughts on the relations between emotion and cognition. American Psychologist 37, 1019–1024 (1982)
42. Lee, E.J.: Factors that enhance consumer trust in human computer interaction: An examination of interface factors and moderating influences. Doctoral Dissertation, University of Tennessee-Knoxville. Retrieved from ProQuest Dissertations and Theses (2002)
43. Litifi, M., Gharbi, J.E.: The moderating role of the type of product on the relation between perceived quality and satisfaction towards a commercial website. Romanian Journal of Marketing 2, 37–47 (2012)

44. Lim, H.S.: Three dimensional virtual try-on technologies in the achievement and testing of fit for mass customization. Doctoral Dissertation, North Carolina State University. Retrieved from ProQuest Dissertations and Theses (2009)
45. Lim, C.: Examining the influence of sensation seeking and gender on comsumers' emotional to visual stimuli in computer simulated slot machines. Doctoral Dissertation, University of Maryland-College Park. Retrieved from ProQuest Dissertations and Theses (2007)
46. Liao, C., To, P., Liu, C.C., Kuo, P.Y.: Factors influencing the intended use of web portals. Online Information Review 35(2), 237–254 (2011)
47. Lopatovska, I., Cool, C.: Online search: Uncovering affective characteristics of information retrieval experience. Presented at the 2008 ALISE Annual Conference (2008)
48. Mack, R., Blose, J.E., Pan, B.: Believe it or not- credibility of blogs in tourism. Journal of Vacation Marketing 14(2), 133–144 (2008)
49. Martin, D., O'Neill, M., Hubbard, S., Palmer, A.: The role of emotion in explaining consumer satisfaction and future behavioral intention. Journal of Services Marketing 22(3), 224–236 (2008)
50. Miranda, C.A.S., Mottin, A.C., Ribeiro, D.G.: Emotional design: Assigning attractive values in low technology casting products. Presented at the 17th World Congress on Ergonomics (2012)
51. Misra, R., Mukherjee, A., Peterson, R.: Value creation in virtual communities: The case of a healthcare website. International Journal of Pharmaceutical and Healthcare Marketing 2(4), 321–337 (2008)
52. Mosiah, A.: From monologue to dialogue: Using performative objects to promote collaborative mindfulness in computer mediated group discussions. Doctoral Dissertation, Indiana University. Retrieved from ProQuest Dissertations and Theses (2009)
53. Moustakis, V., Tsironis, L., Litos, C.: A model of website quality assessment. Quality Management Journal 13(2), 22–37 (2006)
54. Nass, C., Reeves, B.: The media equation. Cambridge University Press, Cambridge (1996)
55. Ortony, A., Clore, G.L., Collins, A.: The cognitive structure of emotions. Cambridge University Press, Cambridge (1988)
56. Picard, R.W.: Toward computers that recognize and respond to user emotion. IBM Systems Journal 39(3/4), 705–719 (2000)
57. Picard, R.W., Wexelblat, A. (Moderators): Nass, C.I., Picard, R.W., Warwick, K., Breazeal, C.: Panel Interview at CHI 2002, Minneapolis, Minnesota, USA, April 20-25 (2002)
58. Pillai, A., Mukherjee, J.: User acceptance of hedonic versus utilitarian social websites. Journal of Indian Business Research 3(3), 180–191 (2011)
59. Reed, D.B., Bielamowicz, M.K., Frantz, C.L., Rodriguez, M.F.: Clueless in the mall: A website on calcium for teens. Journal of the American Dietetic Association (Adolescent Nutrition Supplement) 3(2002), 73–76 (2002)
60. Scaglione, J.: Why web designers are choosing the emotional approach to attract more clients. Design (June 2012)
61. Scheirer, J., Fernandez, R., Klein, J., Picard, R.W.: Frustrating the user on purpose: A step towards building an affective computer. Interacting with Computers 14(2002), 93–118 (2002)
62. Scheirer, K.R.: Emotions as episodes of subsystem synchronization driven by a nonlinear appraisal process. In: Lewis, M.D., Granic, I. (eds.) Emotion, Development and Self Organization: Dynamic Systems Approaches to Emotional Development. Cambridge University Press, Cambridge (2000)
63. Schrepp, M., Held, T., Laugwitz, B.: The influence of hedonic quality on the attractiveness of user interfaces in business management software. Interacting with Computers 18, 1055–1069 (2006)

64. Sharples, H.: How animation boosts sales at e-commerce sites. Graphic Arts Monthly 71(6), 116–117 (1999)
65. Sicilia, M., Ruiz, S., Munuera, J.L.: Effects of interactivity in a website. Journal of Advertising 34(3), 31–45 (2005)
66. Smashing Media: Give Your Website Soul With Emotionally Intelligent Interactions. Emotional Design (Published on March 28, 2012), http://www.smashingmagazine.com
67. Smith, P.A.C., Sharma, M.: Rationalizing the promotion of non-rational behaviors in organizations. The Learning Organization 9(5), 197–201 (2002)
68. Sundar, S.S., Kalyanaraman, S., Brown, J.: Explicating web site interactivity: Impression formation effects in political campaign sites. Communications Research 30(1), 30–59 (2003)
69. Tao, C.C.: Cognitive processing during web search: The role of memory load in selective attention and inhibitory control. Doctoral Dissertation, Indiana University. Retrieved from ProQuest Dissertations and Theses (2006)
70. Tarafdar, M., Zhang, J.: Analyzing the influence of website design parameters on website usability. Information Resources Management Journal 18(4), 62–80 (2005)
71. Tuch, A.N., Roth, S.A., Hornback, K., Opwis, K., Bargas-Avila, J.A.: Is beautiful really usable?: Toward understanding the relation between usability, aesthetics and affect in HCI. Computers in Human Behavior 28(2012), 1596–1607 (2012)
72. Van Der Heijden, H.: User acceptance of hedonic information systems. MIS Quarterly 28(4), 695–704 (2004)
73. Wagner, N.M.: The impact of age on website usability. Doctoral Dissertation, McMaster University-Canada. Retrieved from ProQuest Dissertations and Theses (2011)
74. Wang, Y.J., Hong, S., Lou, H.: Beautiful beyond useful?: The role of web aesthetics. Journal of Computer Information Systems 50(3), 121–129 (2010)
75. Walters, A.: Designing for emotion. Stanford Speciality Books (2011)
76. Welzel, B., Michels, J., Hofman, T.: Cognitive interdependency between ergonomics and marketing. Emotional Ergonomics (2011)
77. Weber, D.O.: Websites of tomorrow: How the internet will transform healthcare. Health Forum Journal 42(3), 40–45 (1999)
78. Webb, J.A.: High-tech animation: Worthwhile tool for patient education. Opthalmology Times 31(11), 44–45 (2006)
79. Wilson, A.: Emanicipating the professions. John Wiley and Sons Publishers (1994)
80. Yeung, W.L., Lu, M.T.: Gaining competitive advantage through a functionality grid for website evaluation. Journal of Computer Information Systems 44(4), 67–77 (2004)
81. Zmassey, A.P., Khatri, V., Montoya-Weiss, M.M.: Usability of online services: The role of technology readiness and context. Decision Sciences 38(2), 277–308 (2007)
82. Zhartmann, J.B., Samra, Y.M.: Impact of personal values and innovativeness on hedonic and utilitarian aspects of website use: An empirical study among United States teenagers. International Journal of Management 25(1), 77–94 (2008)
83. Zkim, J., Moon, J.Y.: Emotional usability of customer interfaces: Focusing on cyber banking systems interfaces. Extended Abstracts on Human Factors in Computing Systems (March 1997)

Human Adequate Lighting in Optimal Healing Environments – Measuring Non-visual Light Effects of a LED Light Source According to German Draft Pre-standard DIN SPEC 5031-100:2012

Herbert Plischke[1,2], Christoph Schierz[3], Peyton Paulick[5], and Niko Kohls[1,2,4]

[1] Generation Research GmbH, Prof.-Max-Lange-Platz 11, 83677 Bad Toelz, Germany
[2] Generation Research Program, Human Science Center,
University of Munich, 83677 Bad Toelz, Germany
info@grp.hwz.uni-muenchen.de
[3] Ilmenau University of Technology, 98684 Ilmenau, Germany
[4] Brain, Mind and Healing Program, Samueli Institute, Washington, USA
[5] Department of Biomedical Engineering, University of California Irvine,
2227 Engineering Gateway, Irvine, CA 92697, USA
plischke@generation-research.de,
christoph.schierz@tu-ilmenau.de,
{nkohls,paulickpeyton}@gmail.com

Abstract. Exposing human beings to natural light has many empirically and experimentally corroborated effects on health, well-being and quality of life. One important effect is the entrainment of the human "master clock" to the 24h rhythm of the solar day. In contrast, being surrounded by darkness during the night increases blood levels of melatonin, the brain derived "sleep hormone", and thus signaling other organs aside from the brain. However, in contrast to earlier times, particularly in urban areas distinct periods of the day marked by bright and dark light conditions are scarce, as modern lifestyle has changed and artificial lighting is present in cities on a 24 hour basis. In addition to the merely "visual" effects, light also exhibits non-visual, but biologically relevant (time, spatial, quality and quantity dependent) effects, that are mediated by specialized cells in the eye. These non-visual effects, such as the suppression of melatonin during nighttime may potentially be regarded as a severe risk factor to human health. Due to the discovery of the relationship of light exposure and melatonin suppression, studies have been conducted to evaluate which properties of light are most effective in suppressing melatonin.

In 2009 a first pre-standard for determining the non-visual effects of light mediated through the eye was established by the German Institute of Standardization (DIN). In this paper we describe, according to the standard, one approach to assess melatonin suppressing potential of light sources on the basis of mathematical algorithms that can be utilized as a conceptual platform for planning visual and non-visual effective lighting for optimal healing environments.

Keywords: Natural light, artificial lighting, human eye, melanopsin, retinal ganglion cells, melatonin suppression, sleep, circadian rhythm, Irradiance, Luminance, melanopic sensitivity function, visual angle, DIN V 5031-100:2009.

M. Kurosu (Ed.): Human-Computer Interaction, Part II, HCII 2013, LNCS 8005, pp. 163–172, 2013.
© Springer-Verlag Berlin Heidelberg 2013

1   Introduction and Motivation

Natural light plays an important role in our daily lives. Living organisms have adapted to the 24h rhythm of light and darkness, activity and rest. The individual metabolism of an organism can react and adapt to specific needs of activity- and sleep-cycles, allowing some organisms to be night-active, while others are day-active. Human beings are as a consequence of evolutionary processes specifically adapted to day-active (diurnal) live with resting periods during dark periods. The concomitant metabolic imprint is useful for survival as human beings are not well prepared to remain active in darkness. Since time immemorial human beings have reduced their activity level and hidden away during night, thereby instead using the time for resting and sleeping. Many million years of pertinent evolutionary processes have led to the development of the human organism with its useful metabolic adaptation to fulfill the demand of optimal functioning in interaction with the environment. As organisms are all exposed to night- and daytime, they have developed several types of "inner clocks" that are synchronized and entrained by a "master clock" in the brain. Light exposure, i.e. daylight period entrains this "master clock".

Some 10 years ago, two independent research groups described a new type of photoreceptor in the human eye, a ganglion cell, containing the pigment melanopsin with photosensitive properties. An action spectrum was found for this cell type with a peak of excitation in the visible blue segment (maximum at wavelength 460nm-480nm) of natural and artificial light. These ganglion cells were found to be responsible for the regulation of non-visual effects of light exposure. Specifically, the entrainment of the circadian rhythm is thereby realized by transducing the light signal to the Suprachiasmatic Nucleus (SCN), a small region above the optic chiasm where the "master clock" is situated. Mediated by the SCN over sympathic pathways Melatonin, a "sleep-inducing" hormone is secreted by the pineal gland during the night. Melatonin is proportionally suppressed by exposure to nocturnal monochromatic light [1, 2]. Moreover Melatonin also acts as a free radical scavenger, and therefore, the hormone may also be important for immune functions and cancer protection [3]. Since the industrial revolution at the end of the 19th century, artificial light has become an important factor of our economy. Shiftwork was introduced and nighttime was correspondingly no longer considered to be a resting period. As gradually more efficient light sources were developed, artificial lighting became almost similar to daylight for non-visual effects. As the entrainment function of light was no longer modulated by natural light, but also by artificial light, concomitant altering working conditions such as the introduction of shiftwork has led to chronodisruption. Chronodisruption has been conceptualized as a relevant disturbance of the circadian organization of physiology, which links light and biological rhythms. Some studies have shown that chronodisruption has been linked to the development of certain types of cancers. Particularly shiftwork has been identified as a risk factor for chronodisruption severely impeding health and wellbeing [4].

In modern economies employees spend a considerable amount of time in reduced daylight conditions in buildings, sometimes in workplaces with artificial light over 24 hours. Many of these individuals report to have sleep problems and complain about distress. While different factors may be responsible for sleep problems and distress, a protective factor for a sufficient quantity and quality of sleep during the night is maintaining adequate exposure to daytime light with suitable intensity and biological effectiveness (adequate exposure to blue spectral components), so as to entrain the inner clock. Bright artificial light can also prevent accidents as a consequence of suppressed mid-afternoon sleepiness [5]. Consequently, light leading to melatonin suppression during night time should be avoided, as melatonin is crucial for good sleep. However, the activating effects of light may be used in the evening, but exposure to high amounts of the blue spectral component may lead to delay of melatonin secretion and shifting of circadian rhythms [6]. This paper aims to describe one approach to assess the melatonin suppressing potential of light sources on the basis of mathematical algorithms that can be utilized as a conceptual platform for planning visual and non-visual effective lighting for optimal healing environments. We thereby describe the assessment of non-visual effects of artificial light using radiometric and photometric measurements in a LED-based integration sphere.

2   Material and Methods

The German Institute for Standardization (DIN) has established a committee for the standardization of the non-visual effects of light. In June 2009, the committee published a first pre-standard known as DIN V 5031-100 with the heading: Non-visual effects of ocular light on human beings - Quantities, symbols and action spectra". This pre-standard was intended to act as a conceptual basis for the evaluation of non-visual effects of light, as they are mediated by intrinsic photosensitive retinal ganglion cells (ipRGC) of the human eye. A prototype of a goggle allowing to assess chromatic pupillometry, the physical properties of specific LEDs were measured in an integrating sphere, and the non-visual effects are computed. In a first step, we will define the integrating sphere and the characteristics of the measured solid angle and visual angle of our prototypical measurement instrument.

2.1   The Integrating Sphere

A special application for Lambert's cosine law is the integrating sphere shown in figure 1. A light source (Q) is placed in the middle of a diffuse painted white sphere. Through an observation window (F), which is protected by a screen (S) from direct radiance, the intensity of the radiant can be measured. Although the light source might illuminate the sphere's surface in an inhomogeneous manner, the radiance through the observation window is almost consistent. In our measurement prototype the integrating sphere is a half bowl with red, green and blue LEDs circular placed on the outside of a commercially available safety goggles that is used to indirectly illuminate the mounted sphere. By means of this technological setup, an almost homogenous measurement of the irradiance at the eye level (with a cone shaped visual angle) can be performed.

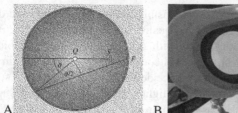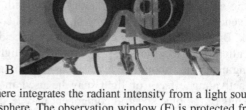

A   B

Fig. 1. A: In principle the integrating sphere integrates the radiant intensity from a light source (Q) over the whole solid angle of a 4π-sphere. The observation window (F) is protected from direct radiance by a baffle (S)[1]. B: In our prototype the integrating sphere is a half bowl with red, green and blue LEDs placed outside the left part of safety goggles and three different LEDs illuminating the sphere indirectly. With this technological setup an almost homogenous radiance distribution in front of the eye (within a cone shaped visual angle) can be achieved.

2.2   Solid Angle and Visual Angle

If we determine the solid angle Ω_s (cone shaped visual angle) we assume that the light source has a homogenous luminance (or radiance). We can determine the solid angle from the measured illuminance E and the mean luminance L_s according to (1) with $\Omega_0 = 1$ sr

$$\Omega_S = \frac{E}{L_s} \cdot \frac{2}{1+\sqrt{1-\dfrac{E}{L_S \cdot \pi \cdot \Omega_0}}} \tag{1}$$

The visual angle at the edge of the cone θ_s is computed with equation (2)

$$\sin(\theta_S) = \sqrt{\frac{E}{L_S \cdot \pi \cdot \Omega_0}} \tag{2}$$

2.3   "Melanopic"[2] Spectral Sensitivity Function

Since the discovery of intrinsic photosensitive Retinal Ganglion Cells (ipRGC), the melanopsin mediated action spectrum associated with suppression of the endogenous melatonin hormone was described by different working groups [1, 7, 8]. However, until now the action spectrum is not exactly defined. In 2011 the term "Melanopic" spectral Efficiency Function was suggested by an European research group [9].

Some years earlier an approximation of the "action spectrum" from Thapan and Brainard was interpolated by Gall [10], and that definition was used to build the

---

[1] D. Meschede. Gerthsen Physik, Volume 24. Springer-Verlag, 2010.
[2] "Melanopic spectral efficiency function", English expression introduced by al Enezi et al, 2011

German pre-standard DIN V 5031-100:2009 [11]. For this paper we will use the agreement in the DIN V 5031-100:2009 with revisions in 2012 (unpublished yet).

$$X_{mel} = K_{mel} \cdot \int_{380nm}^{580nm} X_\lambda(\lambda) \cdot s_{mel}(\lambda) \cdot d\lambda \tag{3}$$

X_{mel}[3] represents a photometric quantity to estimate melatonin suppressing effects of a given spectrum. K_{mel}[4] (is analog to K_m) a maximum equivalent for melanopic effective radiation, whereas K_m[5] is the maximum equivalent for visual effective (photopic) radiation. $X_\lambda(\lambda)$ is the spectral radiometric quantity, representing the given spectrum and $s_{mel}(\lambda)$ is the relative melanopic spectral sensitivity (normalized to "1"). If we compare X_{mel} with the photometric quantity for photopic vision X_v, shown in equation (5), the parameter $a_{mel,v}$[6] can be used as an indicator for the melanopic effectivity compared to the photopic effectivity. X_v is computed accordingly (4).

$$X_v = K_m \cdot \int_{380nm}^{780nm} X_\lambda(\lambda) \cdot V(\lambda) \cdot d\lambda \tag{4}$$

The difference from equation (3) to equation (4) is only K_m and the relative photopic spectral sensitivity for human vision $V(\lambda)$. The advantage of the melanopic factor of luminous radiation $a_{mel,v}$ is the easy computation of melanopic efficiency out of a photopic quantity.

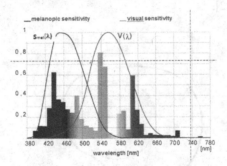

Fig. 2. In a spectrum of a standard fluorescence lamp the melanopic ($s_{mel}(\lambda)$) and photopic ($V(\lambda)$) sensitivity functions (normalized to "1") are depicted. With the given factor $a_{mel,v}$ from the manufacturer the "melatonin suppressing effectivity" (melanopic photometric quantity e.g. in Lux) can easily be computed. (Picture adapted with kind permission of OSRAM).

$$a_{mel,v} = \frac{K_m}{K_{mel}} \frac{X_{mel}}{X_v} \tag{5}$$

---

[3] X_{mel} = melanopic photometric quantity
[4] K_{mel} = melanopic daylight equivalent = 726 lm/W for daylight illuminant D65
[5] K_m = luminous efficacy of radiation = 683 lm/W
[6] $a_{mel,v}$ = melanopic factor of luminous radiation

The melanopic photometric quantity X_{mel} can be computed in accordance with equation (6) without having to use a radiospectrometer, e.g with a "normal" illuminance meter, if a $a_{mel,v}$ is given from the manufacturer of a lamp or luminaire.

$$X_{mel} = \frac{K_{mel}}{K_m} \cdot a_{mel,v} \cdot X_v = 1.0627 \cdot a_{mel,v} \cdot X_v \qquad (6)$$

3   Results

3.1   Visual Angle of the Light Source

With homogenous distribution of luminance in the integrating sphere with light condition "blue" (blue LEDs), E/L_S had a value of 1.35 sr. With equation (1) an equivalent solid angle can be computed to 1.53 sr. With equation (2) we compute an equivalent visual angle θ_s at the edge of the cone shaped visual field with 40.9°. In Fig.3 the equivalent visual angle is marked with a filled circle. The black line represents the polar diagram of the maximum field of vision for the left eye. The upper limit of the visual field is determined by the eyelid; while the limit to the median is represented by the nose. The size of the marked visual angle is approximately the main field of vision of the left eye. Although the relevance of this area for melanopic effects is currently not exactly known, we can assume from the anatomical distribution of ipRGCs that the majority of the melatonin suppressing effects are realized in this illuminated area [12].

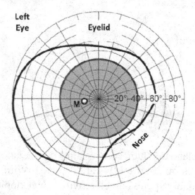

Fig. 3. The black line represents the polar diagram delineating the maximum field of vision for the left eye. The limit of the visual field above is the eyelid; the limit to the median is the nose. Other limitations are due to the functional borders of the retina. M represents the blind spot (passage of the optical nerve). The filled area represents the equivalent visual angle for the light stimulus. The size is approximately the usable field of vision of the left eye[7]. Although the relevance of this area for melanopic effects is currently not exactly known, we can assume from the anatomical distribution of ipRGCs that the majority of the melatonin suppressing effects is realized in this illuminated area.

---

[7] CIE Report 196 (2011): CIE Guide to Increasing Accessibility in Light and Lighting.

3.2 LED Light Source Characteristics

The measurements in this investigation were conducted with a spectroradiometer JETI specbos 1201. This instrument can be used for measurements of irradiance, radiance, illuminance and luminance. In Table 1 the electrical and optical characteristics are shown. In Fig.2 the spectral distribution is displayed for the red, green and blue stimulus.

Table 1. The given characteristics of the LEDs used in the measurement system with the measured characteristic parameters λ_{max} and $E_{e,\lambda\,max}$.

Name	Wavelength λ_{max} (at Maximum)	Fwd. Current	Fwd. Voltage	Maximum Spectral Irradiance $E_{e,\lambda\,max}$
LED-red	655.2 nm	20 mA	1.8 V	33.7 mW m^{-2} nm^{-1}
LED-green	518.0 nm	20 mA	2.2 V	79.9 mW m^{-2} nm^{-1}
LED-blue	472.8 nm	20 mA	3.5 V	46.9 mW m^{-2} nm^{-1}

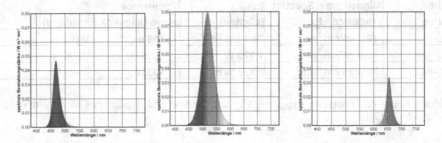

Fig. 4. In this figure the spectral irradiance of the three lighting conditions in the integrating sphere is shown. The maxima of the curves are described by the parameters λ_{max} and $E_{e,\lambda\,max}$.

With the melanopic irradiance $E_{e,mel}$ (measured in W m^{-2}), the "melanopic daylight equivalent illuminance" E_{mel}, (measuring unit lux), at the eye level can be calculated with equation (7)

$$E_{mel}=725{,}82 \text{ lm/W} \cdot E_{e,mel} \tag{7}$$

Table 2. Light source, wavelength, max. spectral irradiance, measured melanopic irradiance $E_{e,mel}$ (W m^{-2}) and "melanopic daylight equivalent illuminance"[8] E_{mel} (lx) at eye level

Light source	Wavelength λ_{max} (at maximum)	Max Spectral Irradiance $E_{e,\lambda\,max}$	$E_{e,mel}$	E_{mel}
LED-red	655.2 nm	33.7 mW m^{-2} nm^{-1}	31.27 µW m^{-2}	0,0227 lx
LED-green	518.0 nm	79.9 mW m^{-2} nm^{-1}	1.773 W m^{-2}	1286 lx
LED-blue	472.8 nm	46.9 mW m^{-2} nm^{-1}	1.249 W m^{-2}	906 lx

---

[8] According to draft DIN SPEC 5031-100:2012.

If we measure the „photopic" illuminance at eye level of the three light qualities, and the factor $a_{mel,v}$ with the spectroradiometer, we can compute the melanopic daylight equivalent illuminance according equation (6) in an alternative way (see table 3).

Table 3. Light source, max. spectral irradiance, measured illuminance E (lx), $a_{mel,v}$ and "melanopic daylight equivalent illuminance" E_{mel} (lx) at eye level

Light source	Max. Spectral Irradiance $E_{e,\lambda\,max}$	Illuminance at eye: E	$a_{mel,v}$	E_{mel}
LED-red	33.7 mW m^{-2} nm^{-1}	58 lx	3.671 10^{-4}	0,0227 lx
LED-green	79.9 mW m^{-2} nm^{-1}	1866 lx	0,649	1286 lx
LED-blue	46.9 mW m^{-2} nm^{-1}	113 lx	7,545	906 lx

Table 4. Light source, aligned maximum irradiance, aligned melanopic irradiance $E_{e,mel}$ (W m^{-2}), aligned illuminance E (lx) and "melanopic daylight equivalent illuminance"[9] E_{mel} (lx) at eye level. Alignment was performed to better compare the melanopic effects of the light sources.

Light source	Aligned max. Spectral Irradiance $E_{e,\lambda\,max}$	$E_{e,mel}$ (aligned)	Illuminance at eye (aligned): E	E_{mel} (aligned)
LED-red	79,9 mW m^{-2} nm^{-1}	74.1 µW m^{-2}	138 lx	0,054 lx
LED-green	79.9 mW m^{-2} nm^{-1}	1,773 W m^{-2}	1866 lx	1286 lx
LED-blue	79,9 mW m^{-2} nm^{-1}	2,128 W m^{-2}	193 lx	1543 lx

For a better comparison of E_{mel} we aligned the spectral irradiances to 79.9 mW m^{-2} nm^{-1} (see Table 4).

4   Discussion

With modern luminaires and light sources, we have not only the possibility to create good visual lighting conditions, but also to execute non-visual effects on the basis of "melanopic" effective lighting. During daytime non-visual effects are important because humans are in need of light for the proper entrainment and synchronization of the inner clocks. Today, the lighting conditions for entrainment are not always sufficiently extant in work places with 24 h artificial lighting and no exposure to natural daylight (e.g. control rooms in ships or power plants). On the other hand human beings are in need of a dark environment during the night, so as to allow them to sleep and recover adequately. In many instances - be it during shift work or in urban areas - due to outside ambient light ("-pollution") darkness is not sufficiently present. However, as light has a distinct ability to suppress melatonin, it is essential to know how much light exposure is needed for entrainment during the daytime. In a similar way, if light exposure is needed during night time, it is also pivotal to know, how much unwanted suppression of melatonin may be created as a consequence of being exposed to the respective light source. The "melanopic daylight equivalent illuminance" E_{mel}

---

[9] According to draft DIN SPEC 5031-100:2012.

provides the necessary information about the melatonin suppressing effects of a given light source. E_{mel} can be easily computed, in accordance with equation (6), on the basis of a measurement with a lux meter at eye level and a given factor $a_{mel,v}$ provided by the manufacturer of the light source. If a spectroradiometer is available, E_{mel} can be estimated by measuring the melanopic irradiance $E_{e,mel}$ (measured in W m^{-2}) and calculated with equation (7). We conducted sample measurements of light conditions with different maximum irradiances at the characteristic wavelength (see table 2 and 3). For a better comparison we aligned the spectral irradiances to 79.9 mW m^{-2} nm^{-1}. We can observe that the red light situation has almost no melanopic effectivity. This result is in accordance with the fact that red light is far out of the relative melanopic spectral sensitivity $s_{mel}(\lambda)$ range. Of interest is the finding that a green light situation with equal irradiance produces an approximately ten times greater measured "photopic" effectivity than red or blue light, while the melanopic effectivity is comparable to the blue light situation. The described procedures in accordance with draft DIN SPEC 5031-100:2012 can be used to estimate the melanopic effects of a light source. However, this pre-standard does not consider the already established effect of a spectral opponency in melatonin suppression [8]. Additionally the melanopic spectral sensitivity function $s_{mel}(\lambda)$ is still not finally confirmed, due to unsatisfying curve fitting of the known measurement points. Nevertheless this method does not allow the exact assessment of melatonin suppression; it is an assessment of the melanopic potential of light and may be considered as an adequate estimate for practitioners.

5   Conclusion

In this paper, we have demonstrated how the melatonin suppressing potential of a light source can be estimated by means of calculations that are in accordance with the German Standard DIN V 5031-100. We consider this to be fundamental knowledge for biomedical engineers, light planners and architects and all individuals interested in designing lighting and luminaires for optimal healing environments. The consideration of melanopic effects of light is not only relevant to promoting and maintaining health and well-being, as it may actually help to avoid accidents, raise vigilance as well as lead to better sleep. Moreover, as individuals may gain more resilience against distress and prevent depressive episodes, human adequate lighting is certainly one pivotal aspect of optimal healing environments.

Acknowledgements. The authors would like to thank DIN FNL 27 for an unrestricted research grant to support this work. Niko Kohls work is made possible through the longstanding support of the Samueli Institute, USA.

References

1. Thapan, K., Arendt, J., Skene, D.J.: An action spectrum for melatonin suppression: evidence for a novel non-rod, non-cone photoreceptor system in humans. J. Physiol. 535(Pt. 1), 261–267 (2001)

2. Brainard, G.C., et al.: Influence of near-ultraviolet radiation on reproductive and immuno-logical development in juvenile male Siberian hamsters. J. Exp. Biol. 204(Pt. 14), 2535–2541 (2001)
3. Carrillo-Vico, A., et al.: A review of the multiple actions of melatonin on the immune system. Endocrine 27(2), 189–200 (2005)
4. Erren, T.C.: Shift work and cancer research: can chronotype predict susceptibility in night-shift and rotating-shift workers? Occup. Environ. Med. (2013)
5. Hayashi, M., Masuda, A., Hori, T.: The alerting effects of caffeine, bright light and face washing after a short daytime nap. Clin. Neurophysiol. 114(12), 2268–2278 (2003)
6. Teixeira, L., et al.: Exposure to bright light during evening class hours increases alertness among working college students. Sleep Med. 14(1), 91–97 (2013)
7. Brainard, G.C., et al.: Action spectrum for melatonin regulation in humans: evidence for a novel circadian photoreceptor. J. Neurosci. 21(16), 6405–6412 (2001)
8. Figueiro, M.G., et al.: Preliminary evidence for spectral opponency in the suppression of melatonin by light in humans. Neuroreport 15(2), 313–316 (2004)
9. Enezi, J., et al.: A "melanopic" spectral efficiency function predicts the sensitivity of me-lanopsin photoreceptors to polychromatic lights. J. Biol. Rhythms 26(4), 314–323 (2011)
10. Gall, D., Bieske, K.: Definition and measurement of circadian radiometric quantities. In: Proceedings of the CIE Symposium 2004 on Light and Health, pp. 129–132 (2004), http://www.db-thueringen.de/servlets/DerivateServlet/Derivate-8659/CIELuH2004_GB.pdf
11. NA 058 Lighting Technology Standards Committee (FNL), http://www.fnl.din.de/projekte/DIN+SPEC+5031-100/en/134406590.html
12. Do, M.T., Yau, K.W.: Intrinsically photosensitive retinal ganglion cells. Physiol. Rev. 90(4), 1547–1581 (2010)

Discussion of Some Challenges Concerning Biomedical Ontologies

Osama Rabie and Anthony F. Norcio

Department of Information Systems, University of Maryland, Baltimore County (UMBC),
1000 Hilltop Circle, Baltimore, MD, USA 21250
{eternal_eternity,norcio}@umbc.edu

Abstract. According to F.P. Brooks, werewolves are the most terrifying of all monsters because they are common people who are transformed into nightmares. Likewise, nothing can be more concerning than having a semantic system that produces inaccurate results due to unidentified problems in the ontology. Inaccurate medical information can have catastrophic consequences. This paper will briefly discuss some issues with existing biomedical ontologies. For instance, the *part-of* and *has-part* dilemma may lead to alternative interpretations and incompatibility among ontologies. Challenges concerning biomedical ontologies can cause inadequate mappings between data elements and contents. Therefore, causing major problems that can corrupt biomedical ontologies for large multiscale and multidomain integration. Moreover, this can result in problems with current methods used to manage biomedical ontology, and ambiguous and inconsistent relation definitions between terms.

Keywords: Meaningfulness and Satisfaction, Service Engineering, Universal Usability, Biomedical Ontology.

1   Introduction

If a person started only eating junk food and began getting sick, would the issue be mainly in the person's digestive system? The probable answer is: no. His digestive system maybe working properly; however, the issue would most likely be the kinds of foods the body is being fed. Arguably, to heal from the symptoms he should 'fix' his diet. Arabs have a saying "stomach is the house of disease and medication". This implies: what enters a body (through the stomach) can make it sick or healthy. The problems may be: not identifying the concerns about junk food and discussing them. The same can be said about biomedical ontology. There can exist the best semantically integrated system that uses different topics of ontologies, but if there is a problem with the ontology itself, the results will not be accurate. Apparently, there are more articles about diet issues than there are on concerns about the challenges of ontology usage.

It is important to mention that data elements are essential to decide the level of accuracy at different stages of data process (Maojo et al. 2011). Semantics enable machines to understand context and the type of data they utilize. Thus making machines

M. Kurosu (Ed.): Human-Computer Interaction, Part II, HCII 2013, LNCS 8005, pp. 173–180, 2013.

more able to understand at the human-level (Gangemi 2003). Semantics are going to enhance the independence of knowledge management by delegating everything to the machines (Cayzer 2004). An ontology is a "domain-specific dictionary", It captures the semantic meaning and relationship of terms which allows for further usage of the term's concept (Maojo et al. 2011). It contains terms along with defined properties that can be executed by a computer. Ontologies are created by domain-experts. It is a formal representation about things that can be "talked about" in a way systems can handle (Simperl 2009). "Ontology is a representation of universals; it describes what is general reality, not what is particular. (Maojo et al. 2011)" Ontology differs from databases because databases represents instances of entities where as ontology represent classes of entities. Ontology provides engineers with the semantics of data which can be used with problem-solving methods along with reasoning services to produce a great system with fewer resources (Schulz et al. 2006).

An ontology represents and shares concepts of a domain in a formal way that can be understood by software agents, which makes ontology an important element in artificial intelligence implementations. Ontology provides information management systems with a way to handle unstructured contents, which may be impossible for computers to handle without ontologies. Ontologies are spread through distribution systems, such as the semantic web. Ontologies are needed for knowledge description, natural language processing, and as a reference for standardizing language modeling. The more varying ontologies that are available, the greater the chance there will be of having more inaccurate ontologies, especially with the absent of more stricter standards on some aspects of ontology creation.

Currently, vast amounts of data require transmission and manipulation, and without sharing it, the data may become useless. Because of the amount of data, people can no longer manually do the necessary transmission, interpretation, and manipulation. The reason for this is related to the semantic web (web 3.0) (Gómez-pérez 2004). On the other hand, using computers to manipulate large amounts of heterogeneous data can cause an integration problem. Ontology can solve this problem by providing computers with an understanding of information, and using it for reasoning without interference from humans. The problem here is that some ontologies are corrupted or unusable, and it may be difficult to find an ontology that is good enough to produce effective and accurate decisions or inferences. Furthermore, it can be a challenge to use such ontologies because ontologies are written in different languages, and these languages are still in the development phase (Gómez-pérez 2004). Another challenge facing ontologies in general is that ontology description is so loose unlike databases (Baader 2002). However, a good ontology should consist of good concepts and specifications, which can be used to make effective and accurate reasoning within in its domain.

A biomedical ontology is an ontology that is developed to serve bioinformatics needs (Maojo et al. 2011). There is the open biomedical ontology (OBO) library which was established in 2001 and, as of Aug 2008, contains 70 ontologies. Biomedical ontology "may ease the integration of heterogeneous clinical data (Sugumaran et al. 2002)." The main goal for using biomedical ontologies is to enhance automatic information exchange between disease classification systems (Domingue et al. 2011).

It is good to mention that computational ontologies can be considered the most successful scientific and practical prospective in the Biomedicine field (Maojo et al. 2011) and biomedical ontologies are the most important and very developed application domain of the semantic web (Domingue et al. 2011). On the other hand, there are many challenges facing biomedical ontologies. For example: the possibility of having different interpretations and incongruity between ontologies (Chen et al. 2005; Schulz et al. 2006); mapping challenges between data elements for multi-scale data (Cook et al. 2009); and poor relations definition between terms (Yu 2006). However, this paper concentrates on the mereological relations such as parthood relations concerns (Schulz et al. 2006).

2   Parthood Relations Concerns

In the world of biomedical ontologies, since semantic web is about machines working together with little or no human interference, a clear formal ontology criteria should be constructed. A standardization of mereological relations in biomedical ontologies is needed (Schulz et al. 2006). Literature suggesting standards for mereological relations are relatively new in biomedical ontologies (Schulz et al. 2006).

Is-a relation shows an inheritance relation from a class, where part-of and its inverse has-part are mereological relations which when used in the biomedical field describes the structure of a biological organism (or its components). According to Schulz, Kumar and Bittner, 2006, part-of and has-part are considered the second relation after is-a (Schulz et al. 2006). Relations, especially foundational ones, should be well defined and characterized to prevent any "human-dependent semantic bias (Schulz et al. 2006)". However, the is-a relation is relatively well-defined and has a formal restriction (Brachman 1983). The definition of part-of and has-part is not well-defined, and has a lack of standardizations, and can be ambiguous (Schulz et al. 2006). For example, part-of (Toe, Foot) doesn't have that much of a difference with part-of (my toe, my foot) (Schulz et al. 2006). In other words, there is no clear distinguished difference between the class-level and the instance-level (Smith et al. 2004). The parthood relations are more complex between classes and goes beyond standardized mereology (Schulz et al. 2006). However, formal mereological relations in biomedical definition needs to be improved to prevent alternative interpretations of relations among ontology engineers especially by mixing has-part and part-of relations or giving them inaccurate definitions since the structure of them is still "implicit" (Schulz et al. 2006). Otherwise, the integration between systems may be broken.

The parthood dilemma has three aspects: time challenge, location wonder, and occurrence doubts (Maojo et al. 2011). The attempts to solve these aspects are relatively recent (Schulz et al. 2006). This paper will focus on the first two aspects. According to Schulz, Kumar and Bittner, 2006, there are "Four mutually disjoint categories for material objects and processes"(Schulz et al. 2006):

1. Parthood between tangible and non-tangible elements.
2. Parthood status over time.
3. Parthood based on the pertaining to space.
4. Parthood based on what is actually occurring or observable.

According to Schulz, Kumar and Bittner, 2006, biomedical ontology has four categories (Schulz et al. 2006), biomedical elements can be classified as a "universal" or a "particular" and either as a "continuant" or an "occurrent". On one hand, "particulars" are actual entities that can be uniquely identified, counted, and pointed to e.g., my hair and a skin cell. On the other hand, "universal" can be properties as well as entities which can be demonstrated by "particulars" e.g., Hair and Cell. "Particulars" can be under two main categories: "continuants" (or "endurants") and "occurrents" (or "perdurants") (Simons 1987). Unlike "occurrents", "continuants" are more constant (or persistence) over time. A "particular" can be "continuants" at a certain period of time. For instance, my skin cell can be a "continuant" of my body the period before it dies. However, "occurrents" don't exist as wholeness at a certain instance (Schulz et al. 2006). "Occurrents" consist of processes among a phase or phases (e.g. phase of thinking of this line and the phase of thinking about the whole paper) (Schulz et al. 2006). Based on the definition, "universals" also have "continuants" and "occurrents". For example, a "continuant universal" would be something like Skin and an "occurrent universal" would be something like Academic Semester. Parthood relations in biomedical ontologies are represented between "universals" and not "particulars" (Schulz et al. 2006). For instance, part-of(Brain, Head) Brain and Head are "universals" and don't represent a "particular" brain or head. However, we say that is usually the case, but not always. For instance, part-of(my brain, my head).

Class-level relations should be distinguished from instance-level. However, the fact is such distinction is ignored in biomedical definitions (Schulz et al. 2006). A reason behind this fact is the focus on concepts definitions rather than working on their way of representation (Schulz et al. 2006; Smith et al. 2004). This can work well for clinical coding purposes, but not as well for automated reasoning (Schulz et al. 2006). Reiteration: automation is the main goal behind having ontology that can produce semantic systems. According to Schulz, Kumar and Bittner, 2006(Schulz et al. 2006), there are four different readings of the class-level part-of:

1. "All instances of A have part-of some instance of B."
2. "All instances of B have part-of some instance of A."
3. 1 and 2.
4. "At least one instance of A which is part-of some instance of B."

A formal definition is needed to clarify the part-of relation between classes and instances (Hahn 2005). This would help eliminate alternative interpretations of the part-of relation.

The original mereology was built upon the instance-level part-of. This can be transitive, antisymmetric, and reflexive (Schulz et al. 2006). This can cause confusion in the interpretation (Schulz et al. 2006). Such confusion can even be found in medical textbooks: is Y a whole structure or a part of X (Schulz et al. 2006)?

Another challenge exist with the domain and range restrictions for the part-of relation when it comes to intangible (Casati et al. 1994), limits, and spots (Varzi 1997). Cavities may not be considered as part of their hosts based on some literature (Donnelly 2004b; Hahn 2001; Smith 2003). The following is a more focused look at the time and location challenge for the parthood relation.

2.1 Time of Parthood

The biggest challenge of the time of part hood is having too many different theories and definitions (Hawley 2004). A discussion is basically about whether or not "continuant" is always a part of an entity overtime (Schulz et al. 2006). One solution is to add more formality and restrictions on the interpretations. A suggested solution for the time challenge is to add a third attribute (Thomson 1983). For example, part-of(Thumb, Hand, Dec 1, 2012 11am) means: Thumb is a part of Hand at a certain time. In other words, the *part-of* relationship may no longer exist after that time. In the same direction, having temporary-part-of(child, female) and permanent-part-of(thumb, hand) (Bittner et al. 2004). The first indicates that thumb may not always be a *part-of* hand for some instance of the hand's life. The second means thumb is a *part-of* hand for the entire life of thumb.

Since many systems that use ontologies are made to accept triples (i.e. relation(x, y)), adding a third attribute can be problematic. On the other hand, having temporary-part-of may not indicate the element's parthood situation based on time. Permanent-part-of(a, b) looks appealing, but what about microorganisms in which *a* can be no longer part of *b* and both would still within their lifecycle. A good suggested solution is to have historic-part-of (thumb, hand) (Schulz et al. 2006). It represents thumb as a temporal *part-of* hand and not permanent. It clearly states: the *part-of* did exist sometime in the past. Therefore, it provided accurate information based on a time period (the past). It may be an assured presentation as human beings tend to know the past more preciously (or at least like to think so). On the other hand, it doesn't consider the current or future parthood situation nor it states the actual time of the relation to be considered true. Our suggestion is to have part-of-at-writing. This will indicate that a non-permanent-part-of elements had the part-of relation at the time the relationship was written-down. It gives a time-based description about the parthood situation and gives a guess it may still be the case in the future. For instance part-of-at-writing(my thumb, my hand) which indicates that my thumb was a part-of my hand at the time the relation was written. It also gives the assumption: it may still be the case while the relation is read and will continue to be the case in the future; however, it may not be the case anymore (after the relation was written). *Part-of-at-writing* indicates the relation is true for more recent time than the *historic-part-of* relation.

2.2 Location Vs. Part-of

Basically, an entity is located in another entity at a certain time only if the first was at the same spatial location as the second (Donnelly 2004a; Donnelly 2005). On the other hand, not every entity that is located at a biological structure at a time is a part of that structure (Schulz et al. 2006). For instance, air in lungs. Another unsolved issue is the location status of biological objects in constant exchange like some cells and protein (Cohn 2001).

If an element is located inside another element, does it mean the first is *part-of* the second? For instance, located-in(Blood, Head) is it equivalent to Part-of(Blood, Head) at a certain time? Few articles indicate *located-in* and *part-of* are the same (Donnelly 2004a; Varzi et al. 2004). The remaining question: is it always the case? and if yes, should we keep using both relations? Such questions can be answered more easily than in some cases where objects are constantly exchanging forms with their surroundings (Schulz et al. 2006). In the same direction, for how long the "lo-cated-in" relationship is considered true?

According to (Schulz et al. 2006), they suggest solving the challenge of the distin-guish between *part-of* and *located-in* by saying: they can be the same relation under three principles. One of them: if an object is permanently-located-in another object then it is permanent-part-of as well. They said it holds true in the case of an object a comes to into existence after object b (part-of(a, b)). This suggestion can be argued via the case of transplanting adult kidneys into infants and children. In such a scena-rio, an adult kidney existed long before it became permanently located in the infant or the child. In other words, a existed before b. Although it satisfies the other two prin-ciples (i.e. kidney is not an artificial object and its functionality is critical for the infant's or child's body), it existed before the host body and it became permanently-located-in and permanently-part-of. Therefore, we think the principle should be mod-ified to include the case of a exiting before b.

3   Conclusion and Future Work

Biomedical ontology is essential in the advancement of both research and communi-cation. It may be the best solution for integrating different biomedical systems. On the other hand, biomedical ontology faces numerous challenges that prevent it from achieving its full potential. Such challenges should be addressed in order to resolve them. A crucial challenge is in the definition of the (arguably) second most important relation (the parthood).

Basically, restriction and definition challenges are open for opinions. The environ-ment of ontology in general and biomedical ontologies especially is indicated to be open for trail-and-error experiments.

Furture work would include encouraging communication between different com-munities involved in biomedical ontology. The lack of communication and discus-sion between different biomedical ontology groups is one of the challenges facing solving the concerns ontology faces (Rubin et al. 2008). We would also try to meas-ure the difference of biomedical ontology usage sufficiency before and after some "recommended" modifications. Finally, having only few articles addressing biomedi-cal ontologies challenges and even fewer discussing solutions is another obstacle in the face of resolving the issue.

Acknowledgements. We would like to thank Linda Hansen for her help and effort editing this paper.

References

Biological Data Mining, 1st ed. Chapman and Hall/CRC

Baader, F.: The description logic handbook: theory, implementation, and applications. Cam-bridge University Press, Cambridge (2002)

Bittner, T., Donnelly, M.: The mereology of stages and persistent entities. In: ECAI 2004, p. 283 (2004)

Brachman, R.J.: What ISA Is and Isn't: An Analysis of Taxonomic Links in Semantic Networks. IEEE Computer 16(10), 30–36 (1983)

Casati, R., Varzi, A.C.: Holes and other superficialities. MIT Press, Cambridge (1994)

Cayzer, S.: Semantic Blogging and Decentralized Knowledge Management. Communications of the ACM 47(12), 47–52 (2004)

Chen, H., Fuller, S.S., Friedman, C., Hersh, W.: Medical informatics: Knowledge management and data mining in biomedicine. Springer (2005)

Cohn, A.G.: Formalising bio-spatial knowledge. In: Proceedings of the International Conference on Formal Ontology in Information Systems, pp. 198–209. ACM (2001)

Cook, D.L., Mejino, J.L.V., Neal, M.L., Gennari, J.H.: Composite annotations: requirements for mapping multiscale data and models to biomedical ontologies. In: Annual International Conference of the IEEE Engineering in Medicine and Biology Society, EMBC 2009, pp. 2791–2794. IEEE (2009)

Domingue, J., Fensel, D., Hendler, J.A.: Handbook of semantic web technologies. Springer (2011)

Donnelly, M.: A formal theory for reasoning about parthood, connection, and location. Artificial Intelligence 160(1), 145–172 (2004a)

Donnelly, M.: On Parts and Holes: The Spatial Structure of the Human Body. International Journal of Medical Informatics (2004b)

Donnelly, M.: Relative places. Applied Ontology 1(1), 55–75 (2005)

Gangemi, V., Benjamins, R., Casanovas, P., Breuker, J., Gangemi, A.: Law and the Semantic Web, an Introduction. In: Benjamins, V.R., Casanovas, P., Breuker, J., Gangemi, A. (eds.) Law and the Semantic Web. LNCS (LNAI), vol. 3369, pp. 1–17. Springer, Heidelberg (2005)

Gómez-pérez, A., Lozano-Tello, T.: ONTOMETRIC: A Method to Choose the Appropriate Ontology. Journal of Database Management 15(2), 1–18 (2004)

Hahn, U., Schulz, S.: Mereotopological reasoning about parts and (w)holes in bio-ontologies. In: International Conference on Formal Ontology in Information Systems, pp. 210–221 (2001)

Hahn, U., Schulz, S.: Part-whole representation and reasoning in formal biomedical ontologies. Artificial Intelligence in Medicine 34(3), 179–200 (2005)

Hawley, K.: Temporal parts. In: The Stanford Encyclopedia of Philosophy, vol. 4 (Winter 2004)

Maojo, V., Crespo, J., Garcia-Remesal, M., De la Iglesia, D., Perez-Rey, D., Kulikowski, C.: Biomedical ontologies: toward scientific debate. Methods of Information in Medicine 50(3), 203 (2011)

Rubin, D.L., Shah, N.H., Noy, N.F.: Biomedical ontologies: a functional perspective. Briefings in Bioinformatics 9(1), 75–90 (2008)

Schulz, S., Kumar, A., Bittner, T.: Biomedical ontologies: What part-of is and isn't. Journal of Biomedical Informatics 39, 350–361 (2006)

Simons, P.: Parts: a study in ontology (1987)

Simperl, E.: Reusing ontologies on the Semantic Web: A feasibility study. Data & Knowledge Engineering 68(10), 905–925 (2009)

Smith, B., Rosse, C.: The role of foundational relations in the alignment of biomedical ontologies. Medinfo 11(Pt. 1), 444–448 (2004)

Smith, B., Donnelly, M.: Layers: A New Approach to Locating Objects in Space. In: Kuhn, W., Worboys, M.F., Timpf, S. (eds.) COSIT 2003. LNCS, vol. 2825, pp. 46–60. Springer, Heidelberg (2003)

Sugumaran, V., Storey, V.C.: Ontologies for conceptual modeling: their creation, use, and management. Data & Knowledge Engineering 42(3), 251 (2002)

Thomson, J.J.: Parthood and identity across time. The Journal of Philosophy, 201–220 (1983)

Varzi, A.C.: Boundaries, Continuity, and Contact. Nous 31(1), 26–58 (1997)

Varzi, A.C., Vieu, L.: Formal ontology in information systems. In: Proceedings of the Third Conference (FOIS 2004). IOS Press, Amsterdam (2004)

Yu, A.C.: Methods in biomedical ontology. Journal of Biomedical Informatics 39(3), 252–266 (2006)

Web Searching for Health Information:
An Observational Study to Explore Users' Emotions

Pallavi Rao Gadahad, Yin-Leng Theng, Joanna Sin Sie Ching, and Natalie Pang

Wee Kim Wee School of Communication & Information, Nanyang Technological University
pallavi1@e.ntu.edu.sg, {tyltheng,joanna.sin,nlspang}@ntu.edu.sg

Abstract. To-date, most of the research concerning online health information search has focused on how users search the Web and how they evaluate health websites. Despite the concerns raised on the impact of online health information on users, there is little research specifically exploring the problems users encounter and emotions they exhibit during the search process. In this paper, we address this gap by conducting an observational study to understand how users search the Web for health information, the problems they encounter and the emotions they express during the search process. Through eye-tracking, think-aloud and interviews, we examined users' search process holistically. Results showed that users exhibited various negative emotions during the search process especially when there are perceived health risks. Highlighting the theoretical and practical implications of this study, this paper makes recommendations for future research to delve deeper into understanding users' emotions during Web searching for health information.

Keywords: Web Search, Online Health Information, Emotion.

1   Introduction

Currently, searching for health information constitutes an important use of the Web. As per the recent Pew Internet & American Life study, healthcare is high among Web searches [1]. This growing trend has triggered new research directions relating to users' Web searching for health information and has provided challenging opportunities for system developers. Building better systems requires a holistic understanding of how users interact with the Web and the content they find on the Web [2].

In spite of many advantages, studies have reported that online health information significantly impacts users' healthcare decisions such as wrong self-diagnosis [3], engaging in treatment strategies inconsistent with professional recommendations [4] and buying over the counter drugs [5]. A few studies have also raised concerns regarding negative emotions such as increased depression [6] and health anxiety [7, 8, 9] after being exposed to online health information.

Most of the research concerning Web searching for health information has focused on how users search the Web and how they evaluate health websites. Despite the concerns raised on the impact of online health information on general public, there is little research specifically exploring the problems users encounter and emotions they exhibit during the search process. Prior studies in healthcare have shown that negative emotions about health are one of the major causes for users' healthcare decisions

M. Kurosu (Ed.): Human-Computer Interaction, Part II, HCII 2013, LNCS 8005, pp. 181–188, 2013.
© Springer-Verlag Berlin Heidelberg 2013

[4, 10]. Thus, it is important to investigate the problems users encounter and the emotions they exhibit during the search process which might have an impact on their healthcare decisions. Hence, the objective of this paper is to understand how users search the Web for health information and to investigate the problems they encounter and the emotions they exhibit during the search process.

2   Observational Study

As a preliminary exploratory study, we conducted an observational study with eight participants (ages 20 to 35; six female and two male) who frequently search the Internet for health information. Mixed methods of data collection, combining observations of participants searching the Web, think-aloud and post-search in-depth interviews were used along with an eye-tracking instrument to capture participants' eye movements while searching for health information. Approval from the Institutional Review Board was taken for conducting the study.

Table 1. Coding themes identified from the transcripts

#	Themes
1	Using Google as search tool
2	Selecting from the results list - Ranking of the results - Description/bold words below the link - Identifying authentic websites
3	Problems encountered - Contradictory results - Information overload - Source not credible - Ranking of the results - Not able to understand medical terminology - Not relevant
4	Emotions expressed - Negative emotions (Anxiety, Worry, Tension, Fear) about health - Positive - Neutral
5	Actions taken (in the past) after searching for online health information - Search repetitively for the problem - Searching for severe illness based on current symptoms - Contact physicians - Go for repetitive tests - Purchase medicine - Wrong self diagnosis

Prior to the observational study, participants were questioned about their perceived health risks if any and their frequently searched health topics. Based on this information, search tasks for each participant were created. During the study, each participant was given a maximum of 10 minutes per task to find an answer that they felt confident about. No specific search engine or method was prescribed. The entire study session for each participant was transcribed individually and coding themes (Table 1) were deductively constructed from the data.

2.1   Theme 1: Using Google as a Search Tool

As mentioned previously, the participants in the current study literally "Googled" the search tasks. Most of the participants claimed that they always select the websites from Google search results list. One of the male participants who began all of his searches at Google stated: *"I always use Google because I am a layman. Don't understand if I go to .gov websites. Of course, if I want more in depth, then I go to health sites."* Another female participant while talking about the general search practice, asserted: *"Google, and type whatever I want."*

When participants landed in health portals filled with too much of text, most of them went back to Google and refined their search terms instead of continuing to read the text from the portals which they were looking at.

2.2   Theme 2: Selecting from the Results List

The second emergent theme concerned with how participants selected from the search results list. Participants most often selected from the first few hits from the first page of Google's search result list. While searching for cure for Alzheimer's disease (search task #3), one of the female participants went to second page in the search result list. When asked about it, she said: *"I normally search from the top links. But in this case, may be because it doesn't have a treatment, the first page talked about how you can prevent it, how to delay it. So I had to go to the second page. Otherwise, I always see the first search results that I find appropriate."*

Most of the participants went through the short description (especially the bold words) provided below each link. From the list, most of the participants selected websites which according to them was authentic. However, perception of authenticity varied between participants.

The gaze plots obtained from the eye-tracking experiment also showed that participants spent time gazing on the first page of the search results, selected from the top links and also they looked at the description given below the link before selecting it.

It was observed that none of the participants selected the advertisements. It was also observed that some of the participants searched further whenever they found something new. For example, throughout the session, a male participant investigated further whenever he came across with a new disease or a new term associated with the search query. When asked about it, he said that he is interested to know more and he finds the information useful.

Overall, participants did not appear to consider any other quality criteria other than the name of the sources before selecting the websites. Even after selecting the websites, most of the participants did not check the date, author or information quality markers provided in the website. During the interview sessions, all of them said that they generally do not check for the date of the article, author or information quality markers. However, some of them said they normally check for the date if it was a news paper article and user ratings in the discussion forums.

2.3   Theme 3: Problems Encountered

The third emergent theme identified was problems encountered by the participants while searching for health information. From the screen recording, think-aloud and interview sessions it was observed that participants encountered some of the problems like contradictory results, information overload, source not credible, ranking of the results, not able to understand the medical terminology and irrelevant results while searching online for health information.

Most of the participants complained about not being able to understand the medical terminology used, either due to the technical language used or due to some of the names of the drugs or treatment procedure. A female participant said: *"I don't understand all the drugs. They don't tell you what they do."*

During the interview session, on asking about problems faced while searching online for health information, a female participant highlighted the problem of irrelevant results by saying: *"The first few results – either they all talk about the same or they all may not have relevant information. It depends on the urgency of the situation."* Most of the participants felt that information overload is a major problem and it is usually frustrating experience as they would not know which one to pick. Participants also worried about the credibility and relevance of the information provided online.

2.4   Theme 4: Emotions Exhibited

The fourth theme was about the emotions exhibited by participants during the study. All except one participant expressed negative emotions (anxiety, worry, tension and fear) either during the search process or during the post search interview session.

Anxiety towards health was one of the major emotions expressed by the participants during the study. Most of the participants felt that they relate to the disease searched for and felt anxious.

Some of the participants also showed some positive emotions during the study. Knowing more about a disease or a drug gave them awareness. However, in all these cases, these participants did not have perceived health risk of the disease they were searching for. Also, these participants showed negative emotions in other search tasks where they or their family members had perceived health risk. Similarly, a male participant who did not show any negative emotions during the entire study session said that he does not feel any kind of negative emotions because he does not see himself in the potentially risk situations. Hence, whatever information he found was useful for him.

Apart from feeling positive and negative, at certain search tasks, some of the participants said that they did not feel anything, neither positive nor negative. These participants either did not perceive any potential health risk or they already knew the information beforehand. Hence, no emotions were associated with it.

2.5   Theme 5: Actions Taken (in the past) After Searching for Online Health Information

The last emergent theme was about the actions taken by the participants in the past after searching for online health information. Participants were asked to narrate about their past experiences about what they did after searching for health information. Except the two male participants, all others reported that they have searched repetitively for the problem and have searched for serious illness based on the Web searches.

Two female participants recalled their past experience where they had searched online for health information on some specific health problem, and they have contacted their physicians and also have gone for tests to cross verify the information they have found online and also to release the tension. One of the female participants informed that she has purchased medicine after searching online for health information. Another female participant while recalling her past experience on checking for a specific disease, narrated: "*I did self-diagnosis. When I inserted my symptoms into some symptom checker, it gave a list. After reading, I felt this is what I have. At that point, I guessed I had that disease. However, doctors don't really consider it as much of a problem like how I do.*" Explaining further, she said that though she take information from both doctors and Internet, in terms of this specific disease (where she did self-diagnosis), she believed the Internet more.

3   Discussion

The observational study has investigated how users search the Web for health information and their search strategies. In addition, this study has attempted to understand the problems associated with searching online for health information and the emotions expressed by users while searching. The results suggest that search engine is a preferred source for getting health information. All the participants in the observational study used "Google" search engine. This shows that search engine is an interface to health information and a shortcut to health websites. The findings showed that participants were heavily influenced by the order in which the results are presented. In a similar study on the students' use of Google [17], the researchers have examined college students' use of Google through an eye-tracking experiment and found that the students had substantial trust in Google's ability to rank results by their true relevance to the search query. The students in their study consistently selected links in the higher positions even though they were less relevant to the search queries. Though it has been reported that the ranking of the search results is not associated with content quality [10], most of the people believe it to be a measure of relevance. In a study on young adults' usage of online sexual information [2], researchers state that by retrieving results more efficiently than websites' internal search engines and by even providing answers in the search results, Google proves itself to be trustworthy. Similarly, participants in the current study went back to Google, when they either found too much information or did not find the required information in the website selected.

It was observed that participants, from the search result list, most likely selected the websites based on the ranking of the search results, the description given below each link and their perceived authenticity of the websites. While most of the participants selected the links from the top and checked the description below the link before selecting them, their opinions varied greatly in terms of what constitutes a reliable website.

The gaze plots obtained from the eye-tracking experiment showed that participants selected the results from the top-down approach and they looked at the description given below the link before selecting the link. Past Web search study by Sherman [21] on evaluating search results on Google showed that users' search pattern mimicked an "F" shape, with eyes scanning the top of the page horizontally and then scanning downwards. Nielsen's Alertbox [15] also reports evidence of a dominant F-shaped pattern for eye movements exhibited while people read Web pages in general. Similarly, the current study also showed that participants viewed first few results. Also, for the links lower on the search results page, the words below the link are critical because they easily caught participants' attention while scanning the page.

The findings also showed that though useful, online health information has certain problems like contradictory results, source not credible, scattered results, ranking of the search results and information overload. This finding compliments past studies [24] on the barriers of online health information.

The important finding of the study is the emotions exhibited by the participants – either during the study or while recalling their past experiences on searching online for health information. Negative emotions like "anxiety", "fear", "tension" and "worry" about health were apparent among participants especially when the information they were looking for was about their perceived health risks. As highlighted by the previous studies [26, 29], such negative emotions about health are one of the major causes for users' healthcare decisions. By showing that the participants' exhibit negative emotions while searching for health information, this study has opened up areas for further research in understanding the factors causing such negative emotions.

3.1   Implications and Future Research

The present study is notable in several aspects. By showing that searching online for health information can trigger negative emotions in users especially when they search for their perceived health risks, this study has added to the extant work in Web searching for health information, which has focused mostly on cognitive factors and has largely neglected the role of emotions that can trigger during searching for health information.

By understanding search engine use for health information, this study has implications for the design and evaluation of search engines. The study respondents selected the health websites based on the ranking of the search results. This shows that search engine designers have a responsibility to improve their ranking algorithms so that the ranking of the search results should be associated with quality of health websites. Another contribution of this study is to the HCI community which says the development of information systems and services must take into account users' emotions. Most of the study respondents exhibited negative emotions during the search process. Efforts should be made to reduce such negative emotions by improved search designs once specific causes of such negative emotions are identified. By showing users elicit emotions during Web searching for health information; this study opens areas for further developments in Web searching for health information to examine how to design a positive search experience for health information seekers.

This paper is a part of ongoing research on investigating users' emotions during Web searching for health information. This study being the first phase of the ongoing research showed that study participants relied heavily on search engines to look for health information and they exhibited negative emotions especially when they were looking for information based on their perceived health risks. Building on these initial results, the factors causing the negative emotions during their Web searching for health information need to be investigated further.

References

1. Baumgartner, S.E., Hartmann, T.: The role of health anxiety in online health information search. Cyber Psychology, Behavior and Social Networking 14(10) (2011)
2. Buhi, E.R., Daley, E.M., Fuhrmann, H.J., Smith, S.A.: An observational study of how young people search for online sexual health information. Journal of American College Health 58(2) (2009)
3. Cline, R.J.W., Hayes, K.M.: Consumer health information seeking on the internet: The state of the art. Health Education Research 16(6), 671–692 (2001)
4. Eysenbach, G., Kohler, C.: How do consumers search for and appraise health information on the world wide web? Qualitative study using focus groups, usability tests, and indepth interviews. British Medical Journal (2002)
5. Fox, S.: The social life of health information (June 2011),
   http://pewinternet.org/Reports/2011/
   Social-Life-of-Health-Info.aspx
6. Fox, S., Jones, S.: The social life of health information: Pew Internet & American life project (August 2011),
   http://www.pewinternet.org/~/media//Files/Reports/2011/
   PIP_Social_Life_of_Health_Info.pdf
7. Freudenheim, M.: Health care is high among Web searches (June 2011),
   http://www.pewinternet.org/Media-Mentions/2011/
   NYT-Health-Care-Is-High-Among-Web-Searches.aspx
8. Gibbs, G.: Analyzing qualitative data. The SAGE Qualitative Research Kit. Sage publications (2008)
9. Gray, N.J., Klein, J.D., Sesselberg, T.S., Cantrill, J.A., Noyce, P.R.: Adolescents' health literacy and the Internet. Journal of Adolescents Health 32(2) (2003)
10. Griffiths, K.M., Christensen, H.: The quality and accessibility of Australian depression sites on the World Wide Web. The Medical Journal of Australia (2002)
11. Hansen, D.L., Derry, H.A., Resnick, P.J., Richardson, C.R.: Adolescents searching for health information on the Internet: An observational study. Journal of Medical Internet Research 5 (2003)
12. Mackert, M., et al.: Designing e-health interventions for low health literate culturally diverse parents: addressing the obesity epidemic. Telemedicine and e-Health 15, 672–677 (2009)

13. McKnight, D.H., Choudhary, V., Kacmar, C.: The impact of initial consumer trust on intentions to transact with a website: a trust building model. Journal of Strategic Information Systems 11, 297–323 (2002)
14. Muse, K., McManus, F., Leung, C.: Cyberchondriasis: Fact or fiction? A preliminary examination of the relationship between health anxiety and searching for health information on the Internet. Journal of Anxiety Disorders (2011)
15. Nielsen, J.: F-Shaped pattern for reading Web content (May 2012),
    http://www.useit.com/alertbox/reading_pattern.html
16. Ogolla, J.A.: Usability evaluation: Tasks susceptible to concurrent think-aloud protocol, in Department of Computer and Information Science (IDA), Linkoping University (2011)
17. Pan, B., Hembrooke, H., Joachims, T., Lorigo, L., Gay, G., Granka, L.: In Google we trust: users' decisions on rank, position, and relevance. Journal of Computer-Mediated Communication 12(3) (2007)
18. Pernice, K., Nielsen, J.: Eyetracking methodology (March 2012),
    http://www.useit.com/eyetracking/methodology
19. Pilowsky, I.: Dimensions of hypochondriasis. The British Journal of Psychiatry, 89–93 (1967)
20. Salkovskis, P.M., Warwick, H.M.C.: Morbid preoccupations, health anxiety and reassurance: a cognitive behavioural approach to hypochondriasis. Behaviour Research and Thereapy 24, 597–602 (1986)
21. Sherman, C.: A new F-word for Google search results (May 2012),
    http://searchenginewatch.com/showPage.html?page=3488076
22. Sillence, E., Briggs, P., Harris, P., Fishwick, L.: Going online for health advice: Changes in usage and trust practices over the last five years. Interacting with Computers 19(3), 397–406 (2007)
23. Singh, S.: The cyberchondriacs; WELL-BEING. Sydney Morning Herald, Australia (2011)
24. Treiman, K., Squiers, L.: The CIS research agenda: Overview of relevant research (2005)
25. Usui, N., Kamiyama, M., Tani, G., Kanagawa, T., Fukuzawa, M.: Use of the medical information on the internet by pregnant patients with a prenatal diagnosis of neonatal disease requiring surgery. Paediatric Surgery International 27, 1289–1293 (2011)
26. Weaver, J.B., Thompson, N.J., Weaver, S.S., Hopkins, G.L.: Healthcare non-adherence decisions and internet health information. Computers in Human Behavior 25, 1373–1380 (2009)
27. White, R.W., Horvitz, E.: Cyberchondria: Studies of the escalation of medical concerns in Web search. ACM Transactions of Information Systems 27(4), 1–37 (2008)
28. Crano, W.D.: Primacy versus recency in retention of information and opinion change. The Journal of Social Psychology 101, 87–96 (1977)
29. Rosner, F.: Patient noncompliance: Causes and solutions. Mount Sinai Journal of Medicine 73, 553–559 (2006)
30. Bessiere, K., Pressman, S., Kiesler, S., Kraut, R.: Effects of Internet use on health and depression: A longitudinal study. Journal of Medical Internet Resarch 12(1) (2010)
31. Mayne, T.J.: Negative affect and health: The importance of being earnest. Cognition and Emotion 13(5), 601–635 (1999)
32. Arora, N.K., Hesse, B.W., Rimer, B.K., Viswanath, K., Clayman, M.L., Croyle, R.T.: Frustrated and confused: the American public rates its cancer-related information seeking experiences. Journal of General Internal Medicine 23(3), 223–228 (2007)

Native Apps versus Web Apps:
Which Is Best for Healthcare Applications?

Kirusnapillai Selvarajah[1], Michael P. Craven[1], Adam Massey[2], John Crowe[1],
Kavita Vedhara[2], and Nicholas Raine-Fenning[3]

[1] The University of Nottingham, Electrical Systems & Optics Research Group,
Faculty of Engineering, University Park, Nottingham NG7 2RD, United Kingdom
{Kirusnapillai.Selvarajah,Michael.Craven,
John.Crowe}@nottingham.ac.uk
[2] The University of Nottingham, School of Community Health Sciences,
University Park, Nottingham NG7 2RD, United Kingdom
{mjxajm,kavita.vedhara}@nottingham.ac.uk
[3] The University of Nottingham, Division of Obstetrics & Gynaecology,
School of Clinical Sciences, Queen's Medical Centre (QMC),
Nottingham, NG7 2UH, United Kingdom
nick.raine-fenning@nottingham.ac.uk

Abstract. Smartphone applications (Apps) provide a new way to deliver
healthcare, illustrated by the fact that healthcare Apps are estimated to make up
over 30% of new Apps currently being developed; with this number seemingly
set to increase as the benefits become more apparent. In this paper, using the
development of an In Vitro Fertilisation (IVF) treatment stress study App as the
exemplar, the alternatives of Native App and Web App design and implementation are considered across several factors that include: user interface, ease of
development, capabilities, performance, cost, and potential problems. Development for iOS and Android platforms and a Web App using JavaScript and
HTML5 are discussed.

Keywords: Web Apps, Native Apps, mHealth, Ecological Momentary Assessment, User Interface, User Experience, JavaScript, HTML5, Android, iOS.

1 Introduction

Smartphones are becoming the central computer and communication device in people's
lives offering multiple means of interaction via many built-in sensor types such as accelerometers, gyroscopes, GPS, cameras and microphone [1]. Most Smartphones are now
integrated with Wi-Fi, Wi-Fi Direct, Bluetooth and NFC networking capabilities which
also enable them to connect to external sensors, devices and various networks. These
capabilities are enabling new applications in, for example, the area of healthcare [2, 3],
transportation [4], retail, banking and environmental monitoring. Healthcare Apps build
upon earlier work in telehealth, mobile computing and pervasive computing in healthcare
settings [5, 6]. Application areas for Smartphones in healthcare include education and

M. Kurosu (Ed.): Human-Computer Interaction, Part II, HCII 2013, LNCS 8005, pp. 189–196, 2013.
© Springer-Verlag Berlin Heidelberg 2013

awareness, remote data collection, communication and training for healthcare workers, disease and epidemic outbreak tracking and diagnostic and treatment support [7].

This paper describes the design and development of a Web App and two Native Apps for use in a prospective observational study whose aim is to examine what psychosocial factors influence distress levels in patients throughout the duration of one cycle of In Vitro Fertilisation (IVF) treatment. The study uses a number of questionnaires which ask patients to report their health status in relation to their infertility and its treatment. The patients need to be signalled to complete the questionnaire at different time points throughout the treatment process. To support this, a Smartphone application (IVF App) has been designed so that, at each selected time point, the patient receives a reminder to complete the set of questionnaires. One of the questionnaires has different questions presented on different days. Each time they complete the questionnaires, response data is sent to a server for analysis.

2   IVF Treatment Stress Study

This study aims to examine what psychosocial factors may predict levels of distress in women who are undergoing a cycle of In Vitro Fertilisation. A methodological weakness of past research within this area relates to the timing and implementation of the distress measures which, to date, have tended to be administered at single time points, often before treatment commences, using conventional paper-based methods [8]. A cycle of IVF treatment generally consists of three stages: down regulation; stimulation; and embryo transfer. Each stage is characterised by different physical and psychological demands upon the patient. For example, the down regulation and stimulation stages routinely entail self-administering drugs via injection, which occurs whilst patients ready themselves for the emotional and physical burdens of undergoing the embryo transfer surgical procedure. As such, each stage of the treatment is considered somewhat separate and indeed it does appear that they differ in the extent to which they lead to patients experiencing distress. Therefore, administering psychosocial measures at a single time point fails to adequately capture the considerable heterogeneity in which patients will respond to different aspects of the treatment process.

The over-reliance on single time point measures within the literature has been based on the premise that it is necessary to reduce the degree of potential burden that successive paper-based questionnaires or diaries may confer. Therefore, it is crucial that novel approaches must be user-friendly so that they optimally capture psychological distress throughout the stages of the IVF process in ways that minimise this burden. Alternatives to paper-based diaries include Personal Digital Assistants (PDA) and more recently Smartphones. The methodology underpinning the use of such methods is commonly referred to as Ecological Momentary Assessment (EMA) [9].

Within this study, patients are signalled every two days at varying time points. The facility to vary the time points of patient signalling confers an advantage in that certain moods may become entrained to particular routines and times of day [10] and thus impact upon the levels of distress that are subsequently reported. A further advantage of a flexible signalling facility over and above the use of paper based methods is that the response delay (i.e. the time it takes to respond to the signal and complete the task) may also provide an indirect measure of response reliability.

A response that is too long after the initial signal is susceptible to retrospective recall bias and thus compromises the central tenet of EMA [9, 11]. Another significant advantage of the method is that data is transferred to a secure server and thus streamlines the data collection and storage.

3   IVF App Design

In order to design the IVF App, it was necessary to consider the different viewpoints of the developers, clinical researchers and users (i.e. patients). First, a small survey was conducted to gather information from the IVF fertility clinic at the Queens Medical Centre in Nottingham. For this a questionnaire was designed to examine smartphone usage in order to gather information for the IVF App design and development. 76 females attending the fertility clinic for IVF treatment completed the questionnaire and the findings are presented in Table 1 below.

Table 1. User phone models survey result

Phone Model	Frequency	Percentage
iOS	31	41
Android	25	33
Symbian	11	14
BlackBerry OS	9	12

As reported in Table 1, the majority of the patients use the iOS and Android smartphone platforms, representing 74% of the total. It was therefore decided that the IVF App should be developed on both platforms to optimise the number of patients included in the study. Furthermore 80% of patients reported familiarity with Smartphone Apps and use of the phone for internet access. This is important because internet access is required for transfer of the patient responses to the secure server. A related question therefore was whether internet coverage was included in the patient's contract to determine if this would result in additional expense to them. 82% of patients reported that their internet coverage was covered by their contract agreement with their air time provider. To inform the use of any signalling mechanism patients were asked whether or not they used an alarm facility on their mobile phones with 92% reporting that they did, so indicating that it could be incorporated into the IVF app design.

The purpose of the IVF App is to measure distress by asking the patients about their current mood and feelings of stress with measures taken every two days. The patients are asked first "How stressed are you feeling right now" and then to indicate whether this stress is related to their fertility issue in general and/or the IVF treatment itself. These questions are designed to measure conscious mood, that is, feelings relating to fertility and the treatment that the patient is aware of. The second task delivered via the IVF App is designed to capture the extent of unconscious stress the patient may be experiencing [8].

One instrument designed to capture unconscious mood is the IPANAT [13] that requires respondents to rate the extent to which a nonsense word represents or sounds like a particular descriptive. The descriptives used within this IVF study were adapted from those used in the original IPANAT so as to represent feelings more closely related to the experience of infertility. Patients are asked to what extent the nonsense words SAFME, VIKES, TUNBA, TALEP, BELINI and SUKOV 'sound like' the descriptives CALM, TENSE, UPSET, RELAXED, CONTENT and WORRIED. Only one nonsense word from the list of six (SAFME, VIKES, TUNBA, TALEP, BELINI and SUKOV) was presented to the patients every two days. This was to avoid presenting the full IPANAT which it was considered would have been a burden to the patient. Presenting one word at each time point also allows for changes in mood to be assessed over time.

3.1   IVF Web App Implementation

Web Apps are application programs that can be accessed over the internet through a Smartphone's web browser. Web Apps enable information processing functions to be initiated remotely on the server. A Typical Web App consists of: a client layer; application layer (on a server); and database layer. Based on the survey, patients used different smartphone platforms such as iOS, Android, Symbian and BlackBerry OS. Therefore we initially decided to investigate the possibility of building a Web App to support all phones with a web browser which would also reduce development time.

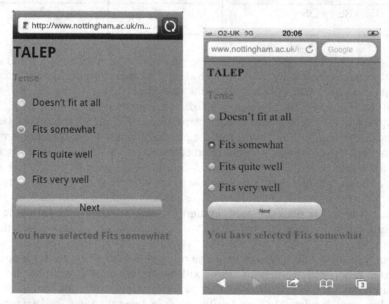

Fig. 1. Screenshots of IVF Web App implementation on Android and iPhone

Screenshots of the Web App implementation (with Android and iPhone displays) are shown in Fig 1. The basic questionnaire of the IVF treatment stress study was implemented using HTML5, JavaScript and jQuery Mobile but it was not possible to implement a sensible continuous signalling mechanism for different time points, because Smartphone notifications and persistent data storage features are not normally accessible through web technologies (i.e. HTML5, JavaScript). Another possible way of providing signalling is via SMS from a server although control over the response timing is lost. Furthermore, a Web App cannot work offline and mobile internet connections (GPRS, GSM, EDGE, HSPA etc.) are often unreliable inside buildings or in the urban canyon environment and Wi-Fi is not always available or accessible. One of the main requirements for the IVF App is that it should provide signals (alerts) to the patient in a predefined time irrespective of the mobile network coverage. Furthermore, there was a concern from the NHS ethics committee about the usage of SMS text messaging due to data confidentiality. However, since some kind of signalling is still required to prompt the completion of the questionnaires it was considered better to use to an integrated signalling mechanism inside the Native App rather than a separate signalling mechanism with a Web App. Consequently the Web App implementation of the IVF study was abandoned.

3.2 IVF Native App Implementation

Native Apps only work on the proprietary smartphone operating system for which they are developed (e.g. iOS, Android, Windows Mobile) and each smartphone platform has its own development process (e.g., Xcode, Eclipse, Windows Mobile Development Tool) and uses a different programming language (e.g. Objective C for iPhone, Java for Android Phones and C# for Windows Mobile). Native Apps can be stand-alone applications without any need server interaction. The following sections briefly discuss IVF Native App implementations for Android and iOS.

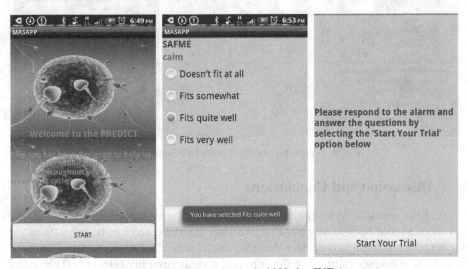

Fig. 2. Screenshot of the Android Native IVF App

Android Native App Implementation

The Android IVF Native App was developed using the Eclipse Android Development Tool (ADT) plugin with Java programming language. The common user interface elements (*Buttons, TextView, Radio Buttons, Message Notification (Toast)* and *Activity*) were used from the Android Library [14]. Android *AlarmManager* functionalities were used to provide signalling at specified time points. At each time point the user responses (with timestamps) are transferred to the secure server when a connection becomes available, or if there is no internet connection, the data can be recorded in the phone's memory.

iOS Native App Implementation

The iPhone IVF native App was developed using Xcode with the Objective-C programming language with user interface elements (*Buttons, Labels, TextFields, Local Notification* and *View Controller*) from the iOS Cocoa Touch library [15]. As no Radio Button objects are provided with Cocoa Touch, standard Button Objects were customised to produce a 'Radio button' object. The Local notification mechanism provided by the iOS (UILocalNotification) was used to provide a continuous signalling mechanism for different time points. Similar to the Android IVF Native App, at each time point the user responses (with timestamps) are transferred to the secure server and are also recorded in the phone's memory. Screenshots are presented in Fig. 3 from the first version of the iOS IVF Native App implementation on an iPhone (hence further tests may result in a slightly different output).

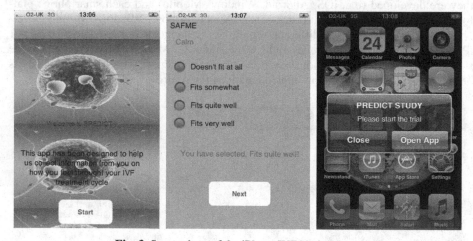

Fig. 3. Screenshots of the iPhone IVF Native App

4   Discussion and Conclusions

Native Apps are able to leverage elements of their native operating system so that they have a more responsive and attractive User Interface and can be run offline. If an internet connection is necessary then they can resume the necessary action with the server (e.g. file uploading) when the connection is successfully restored. The rest of the time, the App can run stand-alone.

Native Apps can more effectively use phone hardware such as accelerometers, gyroscopes, GPS, cameras and microphones as well as phone software applications such as contacts and calendar. The IVF Native App implementations used *AlarmManager* functionalities, *Local Notification* features and *File Storage* access which are not normally possible in the case of a Web App implementation using JavaScript and HTML5. Also, importantly, some healthcare Apps need a high rate of sampling of the sensor reading which can be achieved using Native processing (e.g. Java Native Interface in Android) whilst others may need to interface with external sensors with wireless communication technologies where access to the native networking related native APIs (Application Programming Interface) is necessary.

However, since they only work on the platform they were designed for, porting a Native App across different platforms takes up more resources for code development and testing time. In some instances there may need to be a complete re-redesign of the App since different host systems provide different restrictions to the access of hardware and software functions.

Web Apps can run on any mobile web browser and can be developed using JavaScript, HTML5 and CSS3 so that device-specific customisation can often be achieved easily. Because of this, the cost of developing a Web App for use across different platforms is significantly lower than developing multiple Native Apps. This is particularly relevant as hardware fragmentation increases and more platforms must be supported. However, Web Apps cannot have direct access to the hardware features and functionalities of the native operating system of the host platform. They can achieve access to some functions via abstraction using JavaScript and HTML, but generally not all, and this access is platform-dependent. Web Apps are generally less secure than Native Apps as they require constant connection with the server where private information could potentially be compromised.

In the IVF App development, it was decided that a Web App would be less able to deliver a complete and reliable solution for a stress study using EMA compared to that achievable via a Native App.

However, the decision to build either Native Apps or a Web Apps depends not only on technical requirements and functional requirements but budget, resource constraints and time. In some cases, a Web App will be technically possible and so provide the most cost-effective solution. In other cases it will be necessary to expend the extra cost and effort of producing Native Apps.

It should be noted that Hybrid Apps are beginning to emerge that provide cross platform solutions with abstraction via use of the same Native APIs so that developers can write Apps only using JavaScript and HTML5. However, hybrid Apps may not currently provide adequate performance compared to Native Apps due to the overhead introduced by abstraction and HTML rendering in addition to the time to execute the native code, although this may be overcome in the future.

Acknowledgements. MC, KS and JC acknowledge support of this work through the MATCH Programme (EPSRC Grant EP/F063822/1) although the views expressed are entirely their own. The IVF project and involvement of AM, KV and NRF was supported by Nurture Fertility.

References

1. Lane, N.D., Miluzzo, E., Lu, H., Peebles, D., Choudhury, T., Campbell, A.T.: A Survey of Mobile Phone Sensing. IEEE Communication Magazine 48(9), 140–150 (2010)
2. Boulos, M.N.K., Wheeler, S., Tavares, C., Jones, R.: How the smartphones are changing the face of the mobile and participatory healthcare: an overview with example from eCAALYX. BioMedical Engineering Online 10(24) (2011)
3. Emerging mHealth: Paths for growth (2013),
   http://www.pwc.com/en_GX/gx/healthcare/mhealth/assets/
   pwc-emerging-mhealth-full.pdf (last accessed on February 28, 2013)
4. UC Berkeley/Nokia/NAVTEQ, Mobile Millennium (2011),
   http://traffic.berkeley.edu/ (last accessed on February 28, 2013)
5. Kumar, S., Nilsen, W., Pavel, M., Srivastava, M.: Mobile Health: Revolutionizing Healthcare Through Transdisciplinary Research. IEEE Computer Magazine 46(1), 25–38 (2013)
6. Bardram, J.E., Mihailidis, A., Wan, D. (eds.): Pervasive Computing in Healthcare. CRC Press, Taylor & Francis Group (November 2006)
7. World Health Organization: mHealth: New horizons for health through mobile technologies: second global survey on eHealth (2011),
   http://www.who.int/publications/goe_mhealth_web.pdf (last accessed February 27, 2013)
8. Matthiesen, S.M.S., Frederiksen, Y., Ingerslev, H.J., Zachariae, R.: Stress, distress and outcome of assisted reproductive technology (ART); A meta analysis. Human Reproduction 26, 2763–2776 (2011)
9. Smyth, J.A., Stone, A.: Ecological momentary assesement in behavioural medicine. Journal of Happiness Studies 4, 35–52 (2002)
10. Smyth, J., Ockenfels, M., Porter, L., Kirschbaum, C., Hellhammer, D., Stone, A.: The association between daily stressors, mood and salivary cortisol secretion. Psychoneuroendocrinology 23, 353–370 (1998)
11. Schwartz, N., Sudman, S.: Autobiographical Memory and the Validity of Retrospective Reports. Springer, New York (1994)
12. Brosschot, J.F., Pieper, S., Thayer, J.F.: Expanding stress theory: Prolonged activiation and perseverative cogntiion. Psychoneuroendocrinology 30, 1043–1049 (2005)
13. Quirin, M., Kazan, M., Kuhl, S.: When nonsense sounds happy or helpless: The implicit positive and negative affect test (IPANAT). Journal of Personality and Social Psychology 3, 500–516 (2009)
14. Android Developer Website, http://developer.android.com/index.html (last accessed February 28, 2013)
15. Apple Developer Website,
    https://developer.apple.com/devcenter/ios/index.action (last accessed February 28, 2013)

Experiences with Arthron for Live Surgery Transmission in Brazilian Telemedicine University Network

Tatiana A. Tavares[1,2], Gustavo H.M.B. Motta[1], Guido Souza Filho[1,2], and Erick Mello[1,3]

[1] Informatics Institute, Campus Castelo Branco, s/n,
58059-900 João Pessoa-PB, Brazil
[2] LAVID - Digital Video Applications Lab, Campus Castelo Branco, s/n,
58059-900 João Pessoa-PB, Brazil
[3] IFPB, Campus Campus Guarabira, s/n,
58059-900 Guarabira-PB, Brazil
{tatiana,guido,erick}@lavid.ufpb.br, gustavo@ci.ufpb.br

Abstract. The increasing network bandwidth capacity and the diminishing costs of related services have led to a rising number of applications in the field of Information and Communication Technology. A special case is applications based on video streaming. Telemedicine can be highlighted in some scenarios for applying this technology, such as clinical sessions, second medical opinion, interactive lessons or virtual conferences. These scenarios often imply a dedicated transmission environment. A restriction in such solutions is the inability to handle multiple video streams. Thus, this paper presents a low-cost infrastructure for video collaboration in healthcare and based on open technologies. The proposed infrastructure enables remote management of simultaneous multiple streams. We also discuss results of experiments held in the Lauro Wanderley Academic Hospital, Brazil. One of the results is the contribution for teaching experiences, particularly by allowing students to remotely regard surgical procedures and providing real-time interaction. Finally, we present new prospects for using the developed technology on other applications in Telemedicine and Telepresence.

Keywords: New Technology and its Usefulness, eHealth and Telemedicine Systems.

1   Introduction

The advances in Information and Communication Technologies (ICT) have been going through a notable transformation which is characterized by the global connectivity and the increasing use of multimedia devices. These factors have afforded the development of new transmission networks to handle large volumes of data and increasing power transmission [01], as the Internet2 [02]. High power transmission networks enable the development of applications that require a large bandwidth, as eHealth or Telemedicine applications.

M. Kurosu (Ed.): Human-Computer Interaction, Part II, HCII 2013, LNCS 8005, pp. 197–206, 2013.
© Springer-Verlag Berlin Heidelberg 2013

Telemedicine can be defined as the usage of information technologies and tele-communication systems to provide health support and medical attention when the distance separates the participants [03].

Telemedicine promotes the exchange of valid information for diagnosis, treatment of diseases and the continuous education of health professionals [04]. One scenario of telemedicine is videoconference, which allows real time integration between geo-graphically distant sites by receiving and sending high quality audio and video. Tele-medicine often involves transmission of sensible data, such as personal data, so that it is necessary to use security mechanisms that ensure the secure data transmission [05].

Actions directed to Telemedicine and eHealth is growing around the world at an accelerated pace. Large technology companies like Polycom [06], Tandberg [07] and Cisco [08] are investing heavily in these areas. Cisco, for example, presented in 2010, the Cisco HealthPresence, at the Healthcare Information and Management Systems Society (HIMSS) Conference. Cisco HealthPresence is a new technology in advanced Telemedicine that enables remote medical appointments, with features and technolo-gies never used before. All of this combining high-definition video and high quality audio, as well as enabling medical data transmission, which gives the patient the feeling of being in a face-to-face appointment. According to Lima [09], among the several forms of Telemedicine there are videoconferences, which allow real-time integration, by sending and receiving high-quality video and audio along geographi-cally distant points. Thus it is essential to ensure a secure data transmission.

In the surgical field, RUTE network can be used to mitigate the problems due to inequality in skilled health workforce distribution in Brazil [10] by implementing telementoring/teleconsultation programs for general surgery. However, to keep dedi-cated videoconferencing equipment into OR is not economically feasible, due it high cost. In addition, the standard equipment used by RUTE has only one video input with high definition (1,280×720) and two inputs with standard definition (720×480). In this sense, we present an infrastructure capable to manage and transmit live surgery multi-stream video in full high definition (1,920×1,080) that was developed to be used in the Brazilian telemedicine university network.

The management tasks are performed via web, as a service in the cloud, and the overall solution has a low cost. The software components of the infrastructure have open source licenses and the hardware components are based on standard PC (running Linux) and on off-the-shelf video capture devices and cameras. This infrastructure is an evolution of Arthron [11], [12], a tool designed to manage and transmit live media of distributed artistic performances.

In an effort to develop solutions to supporting Telemedicine activitites, many projects are underway. In this paper we discuss our experiences with Arthron for live surgery transmission in Brazilian Telemedicine University Network (RUTE). For three years we have been using Arthron for Telemedicine activities and testing the software solution and several formats of interaction, as discussed bellow.

2   Brazilian Telemedicine Network

The Brazilian Telehealth initiatives achieved their federal ministerial integration stage to establish a Telemedicine University Network called RUTE (in portuguese: *Rede*

Universitária de Telemedicina) [13]. This network is based on the implementation of telecommunication infra-structure in the University Hospitals, starting in January 2006 as is shown in Fig.01. After providing telecommunication infrastructure, The National Education and Research Network (RNP) [14], a Brazilian organization that promotes the development of technologies in the field of networks and innovative applications, is looking to build user communities to integrate Brazilian eHealth researh groups through RUTE network.

At this way, the "Video Collaboration in Health" Workgroup or GTAVCS (in portuguese: *Grupo de Trabalho Ambiente de Video Colaboração em Saúde*) is one initiative supported by RNP. GTAVCS [15] proposes an infrastructure based on hardware and software with remote management for capturing and securely distributing multiple simultaneous streams in order to provide support for several scenarios of video collaboration in health. As an obtained result of GTAVCS we also have Arthron [16], a software solution for media streaming management during telemedicine sessions. Arthron combines different software technologies to improve a virtual environment where Health professionals can share multimedia experiences, as surgery transmissions.

Fig. 1. Brazilian Telemedice University Network (RUTE). This shows a figure consisting of different types of RUTE memberships. Academical hospital, universities, presence points and telemedicine rooms. Currently RUTE connects 68 University Hospitals, will connect 80 across all federal states until 2015.

3   Arthron for Telemedicine

Initially Arthron was developed to address telematic dance perfomances requirements [01,17]. Since GTAVCS began in 2011, we are working hard to adapt Arthron to Telemedicine requirements [16,18]. So, Arthron has been applied effectively in the telemedicine domain. For example, currently it implements also a strategy of asymmetric/symmetric key cryptography methods to guarantee the confidentiality of the transmitted media. Despite this improvement, there were performance issues when applying data encryption in transmissions of multiple streams with different codifications. For solving that problem, a strategy of Video Reflectors was created. A reflector, as explained in [19], is an entity that receives a copy of a stream and then forwards multiple copies to other destinies (e.g. reflectors or streaming servers); in other words, the responsible for the video stream distribution is the network of the machine running the reflector.

The software architecture illustrated in Fig 2 shows the main Arthron software components: articulator, decoder, encoder, reflector, videoserver, videoroom and webservice. It also shows the possibilities for transmission rates: high quality (HD, SD) and low quality (mainly directed to the Web).

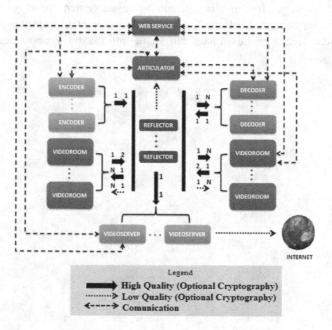

Fig. 2. Architecture overview. This shows a figure consisting of different types of lines. Elements of the figure described in the caption should be set in italics, in parentheses, as shown in this sample caption.

The **encoder** is responsible for making the media source encoding, which can be either a capture device or files stored in the hard disk – AVI, WMV or TS files. It is also responsible for streaming and sending the captured media to a reflector that will distribute the stream to the targets set by the articulator.

The **decoder** has the main feature of capturing a single media stream and decoding it in order to display the media on an appropriate device. The capture of the stream is done via a UDP port, which is automatically combined in advance with the articulator.

The **videoserver** has the core functionality of streaming low resolution video to the Web in various formats, specifically popular file formats used nowadays, such as FLV, OGG and H.264, allowing a wider range of options for users viewing the video streamed to the Internet. But to broadcast the media in different formats, it is required a robust machine that can perform the original audiovisual content transcoding.

The **videoroom** encloses the functionalities of encoder and decoder components, which makes easier the simultaneous communication with multiple clients. The development of this component had the main goal to meet an easier configuration of capture and display devices in a surgery room. Spaces such as surgery rooms are usually limited. Moreover, considering infectious disease control issues in a surgical environment it is advisable to concentrate on a single device the functions of capturing and displaying media.

The **webservice** main features are (a) create/update session, (b) create/update user, (c) insert or remove user from a session, (d) finalize a session. Sessions are composed of encoders, decoders and/or videorooms. In each session, you can isolate a specific configuration of components so that you can forbid access for unauthorized users to a particular audiovisual content. Thus, a single articulator is capable of manage various audiovisual sessions. This component meets requirement of easily manage multiple independent surgeries within the same hospital, for example. Thus, the content of each session (i.e. each surgery) is restricted to authorized users, who may be Medicine students, residents or doctors within the surgery room.

The **reflector** optimizes the distribution of media streams over the network. This component works in two different scenarios: one is the direct send of stream to a decoder or a videoroom, at the same rate it received; the other scenario is characterized by transcoding the media into a lower rate, in order to send it to the articulator.

The **articulator** is the principal and most complex component. It is responsible for remote managing all others components, enclosing much of the functionality offered by the tool. One of its main features is the scheduling of video streams, with which you can program the hour when media streams are sent from encoders to decoders.

4   Experiences of Using Arthron for Telemedicine

The development of Arthron for telemedicine used a multidisciplinary approach. The development team worked together with Health professionals to bring together the goals of each view. The first development cycle began using Arthron (v 1.0) for surgery transmission inside the Lauro Wanderley Academical Hospital of Federal University of Paraiba (UFPB). Using Arthron in practices, we could observe things that worked well and things that should be done. The use experience was very important to check requirements and to introduce new ones. We also have used Arthron for transmitting surgeries to other academic hospitals of RUTE as: São Paulo Academic Hospital, Center for Telemedicine and Telehealth of Federal University of Tocantins and   Academic Hospital of the Federal University of Maranhão.

The surgeries transmission by Arthron had tested several setups according with technology and medical assets. By the way, it is one of the main advantages of Arthron comparing with another videoconference systems. Arthron deals with a variable number of media sources and offering a unique interface to manage them. This feature enables Arthron to cover several telemedicine scenarios as presented in what follows.

Scenario A is the most common scenario that we work in UFPB. This telemedicine scenario setup includes the surgery and the telemedicine rooms. Inside the surgery room we have the capture nodes (the cameras and microphones). Usually we work with two cameras: a mobile and an environmental one. But, we also can connect an endocamera used for laparoscopy procedures.

In this experiment, streams (audio and video) were transmitted between the surgery room, where the clinical procedure was performed, and the telemedicine room, where students and professors could interact and follow the procedure in real time. The procedure transmitted was an inguinal hernia surgery using laparoscopy. While a surgeon performed the surgery another doctor (the professor) followed the procedure with their students in the telemedicine room. The rooms were always connected by the surgeon and professor audios.

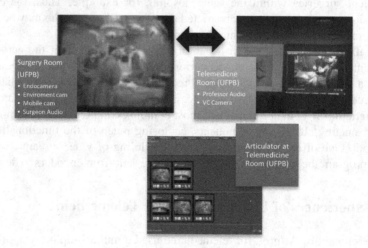

Fig. 3. Telemedicine **Scenario A**. Inside the Surgery Room, located in UFPB, we have the capture nodes. The Telemedicine Room used a VC cam to connected to Arthron. The both rooms were interacting by audio using Arthron. The Articulator illustrates a screenshot of Arthron for managing the multiple streams remotely.

Scenario B illustrates the distributed possibilities of using Arthron for telemedicine. The connected nodes could interact via audio or video when appropriate. In this experience we had four nodes. The main node was held in João Pessoa at the academical hospital Lauro Wanderley. Two cameras were used during the surgery transmission: the endocamera (internal view) and another mobile camera responsible to capture the external view. The surgery room and the UFPB telemedicine room sent and received streams, which allowed interaction among participants of the two rooms.

We also have remote participants using Tandberg VC Systems located in Tocantins and Sao Paulo. Multimedia streams were captured in the telemedicine rooms and displayed in the surgery room. These streams were switched according with participants' needs allowing to follow the surgery from different views.

Fig. 4. Telemedicine **Scenario B**. The Surgery Room (UFPB) was the source node. The telemedicine room (UFPB) was the control node where we can observe and manage all the other nodes activities. The National Library (DF) and the two telemedicine rooms (TO and SP) used VC systems and also were integrated to Arthron as output nodes.

Fig.05 brings the scenario C that illustrates the adoption of innovative user interfaces for enriching the user experience using Arthron. An innovation of Arthron is to provide the possibility to manipulate 3D objects, especially human anatomical structures, while viewing other streams, such as video. The addition of these 3D models is especially useful as a didactic resource focused to distance training and learning. Through this feature the physician-teacher can show students in an integrated manner to live video, models that demonstrate the normal functioning of organs, tissues or structures of the human body. Furthermore, a user interace using Kinect was introduced. This feature makes easier the manipulation of the 3D models while viewing other streams managed by Arthron. In advance, not using hands to manipulate the computer during a telemedicine session prevent infection. Also, it enables the doctor inside the surgery room to manage some Arthron functions, as change a video stream or choose a 3D model to be presented.

In this work we use the natural interaction as a way to access the main control functions used for 3D manipulation [20]. For do that, we have to use tracking information defined by user hands, the primary and secondary hands. First it is necessary that the user use the mouse to choose the 3D model. After the user will see the initial screen where the user can choose a hand to begin waving to the Kinect, getting the tracking of both hands. The first hand tracked is responsible for handling the option chosen by the second hand. That is, if the user chooses with his second hand the "Zoom" button what will define how the object will approach or move away from the screen are the movements of approach or departure from first hand tracked, in relation to the Kinect.

Fig. 5. Telemedicine **Scenario C**. This figure shows a illustration of the user interface of Arthron Web used to managed the streams. In the telemedice room we can see the students view of Arthron with the use of a cideo wall. We also can see a 3D model in detail, manipulated by natural interaction improved by Kinect.

In Fig.05 we also can observe other innovation for user experience: the video wall. The video wall is a set 42'' monitors used simultaneos to show the multiple streams transmitted by Arthron. So each video stream could be exhibited while the surgery is running. The students have also the whole views of the surgery in the same time and can choose which of them will be their focus.

5   Discussion

The most common solutions for telemedicine activities in Brazil are concerned in closed platforms [06,07,08]. In this work we presented a software based solution that included experiences for evaluating the effectiveness and acceptability of different technologies for providing telemedicne services. The predominant theme of these experiences is the use of digital technology to support live surgery transmissions. Live surgery transmission can be very useful as a teaching instrument, but also, as a research way to investigating new clinical procedures.

The review demonstrates that Brazilian Health iniciatives have been concerned with technologies platform and right now applications are the main goal. The sustainability of telemedicine projects has been also been a problem.

The implementation of telemedicine services could have a major impact on the organisation if Health professionals work together with the development team at the beginning. In this experience we have always the participation of Health professionals. There is thus a clear need for more well done telemedicine experiences.

Our experiences have demonstrated the feasibility of establishing systems using telecommunications technologies for live surgery transmissions. When considering the use of digital technologies, Health professionals must recognise that the use of telemedicine technologies may require some specific efforts as the use of communications functions and different modes of interaction. These issues need more telemedicine research study, mainly, multidisciplinary studies.

Acknowledgments. The current work has been made possible thanks to the financial support provided by CAPES, under the RH-TVD Program for human resources training in Digital TV. We also thank RNP (National Network for Education and Research) for funding the workgroups cited on this work, specially, GTMDA and GTAVCS. Finally, we thank the Lauro Wanderley Academic Hospital for the indispensable partnership to the conclusion of this project.

References

1. Melo, E.A.G., et al.: Arte e tecnologia: Lições aprendidas com a realização de performances artísticas baseadas na distribuição de conteúdo multimídia. In: Conferência Latino Americana de Informática, Pelotas, RS, Brasil, 8 p. (2009)
2. Carvalho, M.S.: A trajetória da Internet no brasil: do surgimento das redes de computadores à instituição dos mecanismos de governança. Dissertação de Mestrado, Rio de Janeiro (2006)
3. National Research Council 1996, Telemedicine: A Guide to Assessing Telecommunications for Health Care, 1 - Introduction and Background, pp. 16–33. The National Academies Press (1996)
4. Bashshur, L.: Telemedicine and health care. Telemedicine Journal and eHealth (2002)
5. Lima, C.M.A.O., Monteiro, A.M.V., Ribeiro, E.B., Portugal, S.M., Silva, L.S.X., Junior, M.J.: Videoconferências. Sistematização e experiências em telemedicina. In: Radiol Bras (2007)
6. POLYCOM. Polycom Healthcare Solutions,
   http://www.polycom.com/solutions/industry/healthcare.html
   (acessado em Fev - 2010)
7. TANDBERG. TelePresence Conferencing Infrastructure,
   http://www.tandberg.com/video-conferencing-multipoint-control.jsp (acessado em Fev - 2010)
8. CISCO. Cisco lança HealthPresence Tecnologia inovadora para Telemedicina,
   http://www.cisco.com/web/PT/press/articles/100412.html (acessado em Fev - 2010)
9. Lima, C.M.O., et al.: Videoconferências: sistematização e experiências em telemedicina. Radiol Bras 40(5) (2007),
   http://www.scielo.br/scielo.php?script=sci_arttext&pid=S0100-39842007000500012&lng=pt&nrm=iso

10. Sousa, A., Poz, M.R.D., Carvalho, C.L.: Monitoring inequalities in the health workforce: the case study of Brazil 1991-2005. PLoS One 7, e33399 (2012)
11. Vieira, E.S.F., et al.: EstratégiadeSegurançaparaTransmissãode Fluxos de Mídia em Alta Definição. In: WebMedia, Florianópolis, Santa Catarina, Brasil (de Outubro 3-6, 2011)
12. Vieira, E.S.F., et al.: Uma Ferramenta para Gerenciamento e Transmissão de Fluxos de Vídeo em Alta Definição para Telemedicina. In: SBRC – Simpósio Brasileiro de Redes de Computadores, Ouro Preto, Minas Gerais, Brasil, April 30-May 04 (2012)
13. RUTE - Telemedicine University Network, http://rute.rnp.br/
14. RNP - National Education and Research Network, http://www.rnp.br/
15. GTAVCS – Grupo de Trabalho em Ambiente de Vídeocolaboração em Saúde, http://www.lavid.ufpb.br/gtavcs
16. Tavares, T.A., Ferreira, A., Vieira, E., Silva, J.C.F., Melo, E.A., Motta, G.H.M.B.: A Tool for Video Collaboration in Health. In: Proceedings of IADIS WWW/Internet 2011, Rio de Janeiro. Proceedings of IADIS WWW/Internet (2011)
17. Melo, E.A., Pinto, A.A., Silva, J.C.F., Toscano, R.N., Tavares, T.A., de Souza Filho, G.L.: ARTHRON 1.0: Uma Ferramenta para transmissão e gerenciamento remoto de fluxos de mídia. In: Salão de Ferramentas do SBRC, Gramado. Anais do Salão de Ferramentas do SBRC, vol. 1 (2010)
18. Silva, J.C.F., Ferreira, A., Vieira, E., Passos, M., Melo, E.A., Tavares, T.A., Motta, G.H.M.B., de Souza Filho, G.L.: A Multi-Stream Tool to Support Transmission in Surgery Applied to Telemedicine. In: International Workshop on Health and Social Care Information Systems and Technologies - HCIST 2011, Algarve, Portugal. Proceedings of HCIST 2011 (2011)
19. Vieira, E., Silva, G., Oliveira, H., Ferreira, A., Melo, E.A., Tavares, T.A., de Souza Filho, G.L., Motta, G.H.M.B.: A Strategy of Multimedia Reflectors to Encryption and Codification in Real Time. In: IEEE International Symposium on Multimedia Proceedings, Irvine-CA. IEEE International Symposium on Multimedia Proceedings (2012)
20. Medeiros, A., Castro, R., Tavares, T.A.: Natural Interaction for 3D Manipulation in Telemedicine: A Study Case developed for Arthron Video Collaboration Tool. In: Workshop de Realidade Virtual e Aumentada, Paranavaí. Anais do WRVA, vol. 1 (2012)

User Experience in Public Information Service Design for Smart Life

Qiong Wu[1], Guanshang Wu[2], and Xin Tong[3]

[1] Academy of Arts and Design, Tsinghua University, Beijing, 100084, China
[2] College of Engineering & Information Technology, Graduate University of the Chinese Academy of Sciences, Beijing, 100049, China
[3] School of Electronic Engineering, Beijing University of Posts and Telecommunications, Beijing, 100876, China
qiong-wu@tsinghua.edu.cn, {gogobird.wu,txmaylnjz}@gmail.com

Abstract. In the context of accelerated development of information technology and knowledge--based economy, smart life comes near to us. In this paper, we would talk about the design of intelligent public information service. We take the project "Beijing Electronic Health Records" as cases to analyze the problems encountered in our life, and we will analyze digitized resources and the application in the city and clarify public information needs from the user's perspective. On this basis, this paper will also include an in-depth study of urban public information service design principles and methods, and conduct cross-disciplinary research in information science, social sciences and design. Finally, we conclude three main perspectives to design and evaluate the smart public information service system: interfaces of technology-mediated mobile terminals, process of information based on advanced technology such as Mobile Cloud Computing, and a feedback mechanism to strengthen human interaction accessibility in public information service system. Not only do the three points maintain system performance, but also they play a significant part in enhancing User Experience (UX) in public information service system.

Keywords: Public Information Service, Interaction Design, User Experience.

1 Introduction

Interaction Design (IxD) is "about shaping digital things for people's use", alternately defined as "the practice of designing interactive digital products, environments, systems, and services." IxD concerns the intersection of people and technology. With the development of technology, more and more intelligent products have been around us, a convenient, smart life comes true. At the same time, a series of problems brought about by the rapid development of the city disturbed people's life, people were swamped by information flood, Designers need to think more about how to use information technology to make people's lives better place from a full-scale perspective. In fact, a word "smart city" has already been a hot topic on many fields. The concept of "smart city" is defined as "can take full advantage of all the

M. Kurosu (Ed.): Human-Computer Interaction, Part II, HCII 2013, LNCS 8005, pp. 207–215, 2013.

interconnected information available today, in order to better understand and control urban operations, and optimize the use of the limited resources of the city." Moreover, smart city is heavily focused on satisfying the needs and desires of the people, bringing them pleasure to live in such environment.

Along with the development of information technology and the information network, many products have been extra multi-functionalities and full of various kinds of contents. With the "intelligence", products become complexity, and the users often have to work hard to blend them into daily life. Obviously, the user experience hasn't been thought carefully, or it hasn't been enhanced or has a corresponding improvement in this information explosion environment. The fact shows sufficiently that public information service design should consider more from the perspective of users to improve the quality of information service.

In this paper, we will discuss what kind of features should be considered highly for public information system, and our practice on developing for both the mobile terminals and data processing terminals, we also analyze the current state of smart city research and study users needs on public information service, then giving crucial design principles and direction of future development. Finally, based on experiences and cases study, we distill a set of design recommendations and describe how they will bring an intelligent life to ordinary people.

2   Related Research

There is no doubt that the smart city should have efficient and convenient public information service system.

2.1   The Connotation of UX in Public Information Service System for Smart Life

User Engagement

Public information service system is an interface between smart services and ordinary users. It should provide user-targeted service, which could be easily understood by users. In the context, we should have an accurate understanding of users' real demand. Nowadays, The Internet provides a convenient access to information, and support the interaction between users, system, contents and other users. Moreover, more useful information in Internet motivates users' participation and impel them interact with the information service system.

Dynamic Experience

"User" in "user experience" is an abstract concept of groups, and it varies in specific environment with different users, for instance, the skilled users and non-skills have very different needs on the functions of the software. Even to the same user, different environment fuels different aspire. Public service should not only think highly of users' instantaneous experience but also pay more attention to a long, lasting development experience. Only in this way, could the information service system build a lasting learning relationship with users, use the Internet to lead user demand and improve the service system.

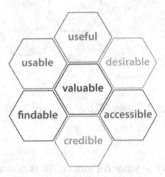

Fig. 1. Peter Morville Model

Technology Integration

Advanced information technology is the foundation of smart life. Information technology has penetrated to the information service system in every side. Many people thought that the intelligent quality depends on the extent of the intelligent. However, it is really not that the success of product is the technology. From the point of the users, how to choose and use technology needs more thoughtfully consideration.

2.2   Public Information Service System Model Viewed from the Design and Engineering

Design Procedure

The UX target is to experience public interactive information service from user view while not to evaluate the effectiveness of this system for the design procedure. Peter Morville brought up a beehive model UX target model (picture 1).

On the basis of Peter Morville, James Melzer made complement of his model on two aspects (picture 2). First amendment is to change the position of the accessible and credible information, which leads to the second amendment --- change the outsides into two groups: utility and affordance.

Utility answers whether the information satisfy users' demands and expectations; affordance tells us whether users could be able to seek out and use public information service, or the communication between users and system. If applied to the public information service system design, user requirements such as information access, quality and value could be reflected from the two sides.

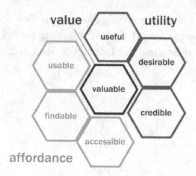

Fig. 2. James Melzer Beehive Model

Engineering Procedure

The public information service system for smart life is actually a system in which users could fulfill his/her demands and complete communication with machines or other users. Core elements included in public information service for smart life are personal interfaces, processing background, and a feedback mechanism connected background and personal interfaces together. In this paper we introduce the process of interaction about input interfaces, background data process method and connection mechanism for engineering procedure.

Intelligent Interface (Interactive Device)

Interactive device is the media to finish the interaction between user and public information service. Traditional interactive devices, such as mouse, keyboard, have poor operability and understandability during the interaction with public information service system. Novel interfaces that consider more about human factors, like tangible desktop, virtual keyboard, and electronic devices become popular and they can also control and communicate with background terminal.

Processing Background (Web Information)

The combination of UX and web information, on one hand, optimize UX from aspects like content organization, structure design, support for complicated interaction, which lead to an excellent performance to achieve user target, psychological satisfaction and emotional dependence; on the other hand, through the network information or web-based applications, data and some user information could be uploaded to the background to start a cloud computing and then got feedbacks from the web server. In this method, the dynamic interaction happens as a positive communication between users and the public information service system. Background design based on network and web information considers an overall UX, takes interactive process, function design and users' feelings as a whole in order to improve the system usability, intelligibility, and aesthetic value.

Feedback Mechanism (Communication Platform)

Interactive feedback mechanism to the user interface model provides a variety of feedback data with the web information through interactive process. Feedback mechanism is a communication platform for users, mainly including correlation data feedback and user feedback information. The indirect correlation data feedback is an interactive process of recessive user behavior tracking from the public information service system. It discovers and captures the users' actual intention and behavior patterns. Meanwhile, the direct user feedback data is an independent feedback entrance to the system for users to submit various problems and relevant evaluation, which could be viewed as separate interactive channel for both the designers and users and also a direct access towards the users' thoughts. The interactive feedback module supplies many kinds of relevant feedback data and user information to the background.

3   Case Studies

Here we would like to present the case of Electronic Health Records in Beijing to discuss more deeply. These information service systems involve different levels of user activity: intelligent interfaces, computing terminals and evaluation feedback mechanism.

Electronic Health (E-health) Records in Beijing

E-health is defined as the cost-effective and secure use of information and communications technologies in support of health and the related fields, including health-care related services, surveillance, literature, education, knowledge, and research, both at the local site and at a distance. And e-health is definitely a necessary part in public information service system. It will make personalized medicine possible and affordable in the near future. The adoption of e-Health technologies in medical fields creates huge opportunities yet lots of challenges still need to be resolved to build reliable, secure, and efficient networks or platforms with great flexibility.

In this case, we would analyze the e-health records (EHR) built up recent years in Beijing. EHR is directly emerged from health related activities and saved for future reference value. It takes health as a center point and chooses life as a main line, which achieves an accumulation record for the user from his/her birth to death. Recorded the development of change of health and death, health information service becomes a continuous, comprehensive, individualized health record information database. At present, the whole country is promoting the community medical service model of this EHR transformation and user-oriented residents EHR becomes the key point.

Here in the case, this public information service background is web-based and strongly organized. It allows the public e-health system to provide data for medical treatment, prevention, health care, rehabilitation, health education and family technical health guidance. The establishment and application of EHR information service system turns into the most concerned research topics and it proves to be a significant symbol of regional health information. The network and data processing procedure accomplish a large health file, a useful tool for the community doctors to provide a complete data of residents' health and help doctors to master residents' health status. Furthermore, this background database and information network makes the community medical treatment, prevention and health care develop towards a scientific management orbit of systematization and institutionalization so as to monitor disease, dynamic changes. Still, it permits the transfer among different systems so that the EHR could be updated continuously and used secondly to future medical quality control, epidemic situation analysis and database for infectious diseases.

Moreover, the feedback mechanism is set up for users to be aware of their health status. Users could check out the electronic records periodically in order to be aware of their health status. In this feedback mechanism, correlation data feedback gives an overall comprehension of their current health situation and relevant health recommendations. And user feedback information provides information to doctors and information service organization for them to maintain residents' digital records of their diagnosis and treatment activities.

However, a convenient and dynamic user interfaces are needed like the wearable devices in order to manage users a dynamic communication with information service system. With the dynamic interfaces, the community health service agencies are able to keep tracking a continuous data or physiological indexes. And these files will become foundation for the establishment for children EPI (Expanded Program on Immunization) file, maternal health records, and students' health files. The interfaces should be designed to make users' life more convenient and promote users' communication with information service system regardless of interface forms. For instance, the Georgia Institute of Technology developed a home medical nursing robot which could fetch items like medicine bottle, open and close doors, chat with users and then deal with their problems by becoming users' life and emotional assistant. If robots could send users' information and data back to the service system, the information service would be more flexible to provide desirable information services. However, in public information service system, this field is still in a stage developing and designing a single sensor, such as the non-contact infrared thermometer, pulse sensor and blood pressure measuring instrument. And in the respects of network interfaces, portability and wearable resistance much left to be improved. Along with the development of information service and interaction technology in medical care and EHR, we believe that the e-health records and information service will develop rapidly.

Using ubiquitous computing technology, e-health information service can get the physiological information parameter thus detecting the abnormal diagnosis and enhancing the reliability of the information service system. Consequently, EHR is considered to reduce the avoidable hospitalization in nursing homes and community hospital for a short-term or long-term treatment. From the structure and construction of EHR information service system, it could be concluded that the doctor-centered information system is transforming into a user-centered information system which could be applied to scenes outside hospitals.

Further researches and efforts should be paid into body sensor networks and wearable sensor systems, clinical bio-feedback, decision support systems, e-health information and network infrastructure, and e-health for public health (including

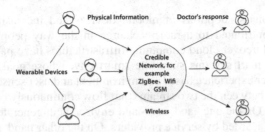

Fig. 3. An information Service Model with Feedback Module

disease prevention, emergency preparedness, epidemiologic interventions) when designing improvement information service system. E-Health for ageing (to support quality of life for older adults, aging in place and independence) is also emerging novel e-health applications with functions of health monitoring and the technology of health grid and health cloud.

When establishing public information service system, as concluded from cases, are harmony interfaces settings, strong communication through web information platform and a feedback mechanism that can make continuously self-improvement and self-maintenance.

4   The Interaction Design

As above, there are three main dimensions in the interaction design of public information service: technology for individuals' information engagement, accessible interfaces of technology-mediated mobile terminals, and a feedback mechanism to adapt to human accessibility.

4.1   Harmony Interfaces of Technology-Mediated Mobile Terminals

Nowadays, more Internet services are becoming ubiquitous. With the growing capabilities of the network and the rising penetration of broadband services into our life, users are experiencing a new model of human-computer interaction in which information processing has been thoroughly integrated into everyday objects and activities. Some cutting edge HCI interfaces are increasing, such as Remote Phone, Virtual Keyboard, Smart Desktop and so forth. During the development of user experiences, the accessibility and usability of the interfaces become essential.

Nowadays, wearable computing is thought to be a good choice. Google Glass or TTP Glass sees the world through users' eyes and makes them aware of location, Internet fresh news, or even presenting images when calling. Strata Watch can be linked to cell-phone and other terminals to upload applications and monitor devices, replacing the traditional mobile phone and producing a fantasy user experience. Heads-up displays, such as Vuzix Displays could be set up around the city corner so that you touch news on the screen commodiously.

The pervasive model in which we have many processing units for users is well suited for smart city design. Wearable Computing interfaces could be a personal device that opens the gates for ubiquitous computing to the smart city entertainment.

4.2   Process of Information Based on Mobile Cloud Computing

In recent years the mass adoptions of mobile devices and increasingly ubiquitous connectivity have contributed to a radical change in the way people interact with computer systems. Moreover cloud computing infrastructures have paved the way for the development of smart systems such like smart city, whose goal is to provide a service to enhance user experience based on environment and user sensed data. There is a clear disconnection between the two streams that flow continuously between user and cloud-based systems. On the one hand, user- and environment generated data is being, for the most part, disregarded by service providers. On the other hand, services offered do not address users' specific needs and preferences. In addition, service discovery is a cognitive demanding process and it may have detrimental consequences in user experience. Hence, we propose user-centric frameworks. The framework facilitates the design and development of smart city systems. It aims at leveraging existing technology, such as environment sensors and personal devices, to aggregate localized user-related data - defined as a bubble - into the cloud.

This aggregation later supports the delivery of personalized services, contextually relevant to users. Above all, we could handle data sent back from individual more accuracy, and then present a pinpoint service for users. Meanwhile, smart city construction direction can be determined by specified information visualization. The delivery of services with such characteristics has the potential to enhance quality of experience and influence user behavior.

4.3   An Efficient Feedback Mechanism to Strengthen Human Accessibility

Traditional HCI interfaces scarcely have a feedback mechanism. However, by utilizing the cloud computing technique to collect, analyze and transfer information, controller terminal can be more intelligent that they could be self-control and self-adjusting to a more accurate level. That is to say, intelligent and adaptive interfaces and data processing allow service to follow up easily changed human needs.

5   Limitations and Expectations for UX Desing Model

5.1   UX Design Model

Emphasizing on UX connotation and strengthening interaction have important significance in designing a public information service system for users to leading a smart life. The information service should supply a targeted and personalized service in order to obtain a pleasant UX.

5.2   Limitations

Technology has been providing a good service for human beings. And the best interfaces in public information service system should be disappeared when not in use and appears again naturally for users when needed in the process towards an intelligent and comfort life. However, technique cannot go that far at present considered the limitations of software, hardware or network. And the storage and analysis of dynamic large scale information in daily life also put barriers to public information service development.

5.3 Expectations

Human-computer symbiosis is the highest level of human computer interaction in the public information service design. A design of the close integration between human brains and computer information will make it possible for computers to figure out huMAN THOUGHTS AND DEAL WITH DATA from a novel perspective. Thus, this means helps people realize what their real demands are and fulfill those needs. However, public relationship and society moral problems should also be taken into deep considerations when achieving such expectations.

6   Conclusion

Technology is developed to serve human being. Smart City creates a better environment for citizens to enjoy their life. These smart computing technologies or cutting edge interface devices should be emerged when in need and disappeared if not necessary. In other words, they need to be invisible into daily life. The way we spend our lives and deal with information will be distinguished a lot. Harmony interfaces, computing technology in the information network processing procedure and a feedback mechanism established the public information service design basis for smart life. Based on the three factors as mentioned in this paper, the traditional single design thinking would be changed and a whole system thinking would be the main considerations for user experience.

Acknowledgments. This research was part of Interaction Design Research Project, and was supported by Tsinghua University Research Funding 2011wkyb005.

References

1. Endsley: Design and evaluation for Situation Awareness enhancement. In: Proceedings of the Human Factors Society 32nd Annual Meeting, vol. (1), pp. 97–101 (1988)
2. Christiansen, E., Kanstrup, A.M.: A mobile design lab for user-driven innovation – history and concept,
   http://old.ell.aau.dk/fileadmin/user_upload/documents/staff/
   Ellen/DHRS07ChristiansenKanstrup.pdf
3. Herczeg, M.: The Smart, the Intelligent and the Wise: Roles and Values of Interactive Technologies. In: IITM 2010, pp. 28–30 (2010)
4. Giordano, C., Modeo, S., Bernardi, G., Ricchiuti, F.: Using Mobile Phones as Remote Control for Ubiquitous Video-recording. In: MUM 2007, pp. 12–14 (2007)
5. Nam, T., Pardo, T.A.: Conceptualizing Smart City with Dimensions of Technology, People, and Institutions. In: Proceedings of the 12th Annual International Conference on Digital Government Research, pp. 282–291 (2011)

The Proposal of the Remote Consultation Service System Using the Outline Function for Consultation

Hiroshi Yajima and Takuto Gotoh

Tokyo Denki University, 5 Senjyu Asahi-cho Adachi-ku,Tokyo, Japan
yajima@im.dendai.ac.jp

Abstract. Remote welfare services for caregivers have recently been offered in response to the recent increase in demand for care that has accompanied the aging of society. However, due to the often extended periods of caregiving involved, care consultations can sometimes lack cohesion unless information about the early stages of care are available. In order to address this issue, the whole history of communication between care experts and family members should be structured and visualized when remote welfare services are provided. We propose a form of remote consultation where care experts can offer coherent and efficient consultations using all available information, such as up-to-date information from "lifelogs" and past processes of care consultations obtained from the use of all historically available information.

Keywords: remote consultation, care, computer-mediated communication, care assistance.

1 Introduction

With the aging of the Japan's population in recent years, the number of elderly people requiring care (hereinafter, care recipients) is increasing. With that, the number of care-related consultations from care recipients or family members providing care at home (hereafter caregiver) is fast increasing. The condition of the care recipient, being particular to each person, requires a detailed response after the individual circumstances have been ascertained. Although care workers or care professionals provide a portion of the care based on the care plan created by the care manager, the reality is that the main portion is left to the caregiver. As Japan's care system [6] itself has yet to reach a high level of sophistication, caregivers face the problem that in dealing with the care recipient's daily changing condition, they cannot obtain expert care advice when it is needed [1] from care workers or care professionals who are present at only specific times. Remote consultations with care experts by telephone, for example, therefore occur often. Such consultations, however, have the following issues.

1. Because caregivers are often novices in the field of care, they find it difficult to explain the condition they are faced with in a systematic manner. Therefore several

M. Kurosu (Ed.): Human-Computer Interaction, Part II, HCII 2013, LNCS 8005, pp. 216–225, 2013.

issues often emerge mixed up with one another during consultation without having been arranged in an orderly manner. This then makes it difficult for the expert to distinguish between high- and low-priority issues.
2. Care often stretches over many years. Generally, consultations about care with experts therefore take place many times. It is inefficient for the expert to retrace and inquire after the care recipient's history during the consultation. From the caregiver's viewpoint the consultation will not proceed smoothly if the expert is not aware of the care recipient's progress and treatment. Also, there might arise situations in which the effectiveness of the advice is not understood because the caregiver does not understand the fundamental ideas and the numerical reasoning provided by experts from their professional points of view.

We have proposed and tested a system that enables effective consultation by enabling experts to deal with multiple caregivers simultaneously in remote consultations [4], but have yet to address the issues described above. Moreover, although there are handover mechanisms such as providing handwritten notes on site about the care recipient's condition as assessed by care workers or care professionals, because the time spent on site by care workers or care professionals is short they cannot form an accurate understanding of the care recipient's overall condition. Also, because the structures for collaboration are insufficient, there is no framework for the effective use of information. Meanwhile, development of sensor technology and systems technology has begun for monitoring care recipients' daily living conditions based on information such as biological and positional information, imaging information and environmental information [3, 5, 8, 13], but these technologies are not yet being sufficiently utilized.

To deal with the issues outlined above, in this report we propose a care consultation system that enables smooth and effective care consultation, where experts systemize and visualize the consultation process and share it with caregivers, and where experts in their consultations show the caregivers, together with past consultation processes which have been accumulated chronologically, the lifelogs [14, 2] containing the general living conditions of the care recipient.

This system's characteristic feature is to enable the expert to engage in deeper consultation with the caregiver through providing a function for systemizing and visualizing the consultation process, as well as a function for displaying consultation points that are mutually agreed upon between the expert and the caregiver, past consultation processes and daily living conditions (lifelogs). We evaluated the characteristics of remote consultation in care consultation using this system, and we found that the use of this system increased users' level of satisfaction with the consultation content.

2   Conventional Remote Consultation Technologies and Their Issues

Remote consultation is a format whereby a caregiver can consult with a care expert at a remote location. The scope of remote consultation has broadened in recent years to include, for instance, technical support for PC users, consultation on financial products, and consultation on clinical issues [9, 11]. At the same time tools have been introduced for this consultation format that use video communication or that support asynchronous consultation via bulletin board system [7].

In conventional remote consultation, the expert often, upon clarifying the caregiver's issues, proceeds with the consultation following a standard procedure (e.g. formats where flowcharts or templates are filled out), which then results in an answer to the issue under consultation. This is done to raise experts' time efficiency [12] by standardizing the consultation process, as experts often spend unnecessarily long times on consultations due to the inexperience of the average user with the consultation process.

In the field of care [10], however, the following issues arise with the conventional remote consultation methods.

1. Because various individual factors in a care recipient's condition, including medical history and past interventions, are often intricately entwined, it is difficult to proceed with a consultation following a standard procedure. Caregivers also find it difficult to explain these factors separately. The factors therefore often come up in a mixed up manner during a consultation, without past conditions or overlapping issues having been arranged in order. It is for this reason also difficult for the expert to distinguish between the high- and low-priority issues.
2. Because of this characteristic, experts are forced to deal with the caregiver's multiple issues on a case-by-case basis. At that point, the caregiver often loses the ability to understand the relationships between the proposed measures. In other words, forming an overall image of the eventual measures to be taken is difficult. As a result, caregivers are often left without having gained a clear understanding sufficient to dispel any anxiety regarding the condition of concern or an unknown condition, and left wondering as to whether all issues really have been resolved.

3   Proposed Method

3.1   Concept

In this study, we constructed a consultation outline system, thus enabling the visualization of the overall consultation content and confirmation by the expert of past consultations, in order to deal with and increase caregivers' levels of satisfaction with the results of consultation using computer-mediated communication, while dealing with the issues outlined above. At the same time we propose a system that, by providing a means for the expert to further monitor the care recipient's condition since past consultations via a lifelog, enables the expert to conduct a deeper consultation upon forming a more detailed understanding of the changes in the care recipients' situation.

3.2   Consultation Outline

The purpose of the consultation outline is to systematically and chronologically visualize the communication process of current and past consultations, and, with the expert sharing information with the caregiver, to conduct a deeper consultation regarding the care recipient's condition. In the consultation outline, the entire consultation is systemized. We propose the following features and techniques in order to achieve the goal outlined above (Fig. 1).

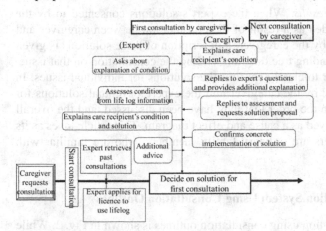

Fig. 1. Visualization structure of consultation process

1. *Visualization of the consultation process.* The conversation between the caregiver and the expert regarding a specific issue raised by the caregiver is displayed as a tree diagram. At that time, the expert creates a tree diagram with the issue raised by the caregiver as the top-level event. The tree diagram displays the caregiver's questions and remarks as well as the expert's opinions about them, following the conversational flow. As the conversational flow can be expressed chronologically in this tree diagram, discrepancies between the perceptions of the caregiver and the expert disappear. In this conversation, the expert expresses his views based on the lifelog [8], and conveys the care recipient's condition based on quantitative criteria to the caregiver. When a solution has been decided, the expert adds a relevant keyword to the top-level event thus making it searchable at a later date.
2. *Systemization of the consultation process.* Because caregivers are unfamiliar with the consultation process, their questions and opinions sometimes shift to other issues. On occasion there is such a plethora of issues to consult on that it is difficult to discuss them. In that case the expert itemizes them and proceeds with the consultation on the particular issues. In other words, when the caregiver's conversation moves from the current topic to a different topic, the expert creates a new top-level event for this different issue, generates a different tree diagram to the one for the conversation up to that point, and engages in a consultation for which the overall structure has been made clear.
3. *Searching similar consultations in the past.* Using the keywords attached to the top-level events in past cause and effect diagrams, the expert can search past consultation histories (top-level events and the associated tree diagrams) for consultations similar to the one currently engaged in. Any applicable items are displayed

and the conversation is facilitated by the caregiver and the expert sharing information relating to solutions for the current issue, using the consultation histories as a reference.

4. *Displaying consultation results.* When the expert's solutions consented to by the caregiver have been decided as a result of the consultation between caregiver and expert on an issue raised by the caregiver, a description of these solutions is given at the end of the corresponding tree diagram, ending the consultation on that issue. This enables the caregiver to clearly confirm the solutions for individual issues. In this way, the issues raised by the caregiver and the expert's eventual solutions for each of them are settled in the order that they have been discussed, and the overall care consultation is displayed as a cause and effect diagram. This article takes as its premise that the caregivers are ordinary family members, who are familiar with using a PC.

3.3   Building a Consultation System Using Consultation Outlines

The system's basic configuration using consultation outlines is shown in Fig. 2. While listening to the caregiver's issues, the expert ascertains the care recipient's daily condition through the lifelog information accumulated through, for example, sensors, and at the same time pulls up outlines for similar past consultations using related keywords and thus forms a deeper understanding of the care recipient's condition. On the basis of this understanding, the expert responds to the caregiver, adds the individual conversations to the "current condition outline" and, by sharing this outline with the caregiver, continues the consultation with both parties in agreement.

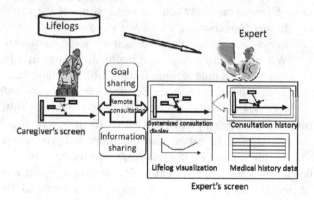

Fig. 2. Overall system configuration for remote care consultation

3.4   Advantages of Consultation Outlines

Advantages for the Expert. The expert can obtain, before the start of the consultation, information on the care recipient's condition through the caregiver's past outlines and through the lifelogs, and can embark on the consultation after having formed a sufficient understanding of aspects such as the caregiver's ideas, preferences and characteristics. By displaying the aim of the current consultation and the conversation content on a screen shared with the caregiver during the consultation, information sharing with the caregiver can be planned. The entered consultation content is saved as the current consultation outline, and can be used as reference information for consultation at a later date. In other words, the expert can extract relevant past consultation outlines as needed and can ensure smooth communication by presenting them to the caregiver. When caregiver's remarks are inconsistent with past remarks, past consultation records can be shown and changes in the care environment or the caregiver's true intention can be checked. Moreover, by having a shared aim with the caregiver, if a conversation veers off topic, this can be made clear and, with the caregiver's assent, the consultation can proceed under the expert's guidance.

Advantages for the Caregiver. For the caregiver, consultations with an expert that extend over a number of days become simpler, and also when unfamiliar with the consultation process consultations that extend over long periods of time become possible. As consultation outlines moreover clarify the expert's advice and views, a more profound understanding can be gained of the consultation content, providing the caregiver with a sense of security and trust in the consultation. At the same time, the mutual trust between caregiver and expert grows through the sharing in the consultation, enabling a more profound consultation. The caregiver can also achieve a sense of security because it is possible to check the consultation histories, which are saved, once the consultation has finished. By starting the next consultation after having checked the previous consultation outline in advance, the caregiver can facilitate a smooth conversation.

4   Consultation Procedure

4.1   Consultation Overview

For this study, we engaged in remote consultation about care using computer-mediated communication (in this case Skype). We performed the consultation while monitoring, using consultation outlines, consultations performed in the past, the flow of the current consultation and the care environment.

4.2   Consultation Procedure

The consultation was performed through the following procedure.

1. Start the consultation.
2. Display one consultation issue.
3. Share content regarding one consultation issue (questions by the expert and answers by the caregiver).

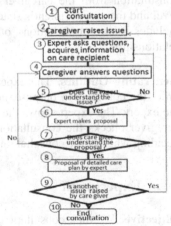

Fig. 3. Procedure for outline building

4. Has the expert understood the issue? If not, return to step 3.

5. Expert obtains care recipient's lifelogs and past related outlines.

6. Expert indicates direction for a solution.

7. Caregiver can ask about the expert's proposed solution.

8. Expert provides concrete explanation of the proposal.

9. Does the caregiver agree with the proposed solution? If not, caregiver provides reasons; return to step 6.

10. Expert gives detailed presentation and explanation of the care plan.

11. If the consultation has finished, go to step 12; if there is another consultation issue, go to step 2.

12. Input the date and the names of the expert and caregiver. Expert attaches keywords to the individual top-level events.

13. End consultation.

Through these steps an outline is created and shared between the expert and the caregiver.

4.3   Important Aspects of the Consultation Procedure

Clarifying the Aim of the Consultation. The caregiver conveys the current issue to the expert. If the consultation is about many issues at the same time, the expert divides them into individual issues, and engages in a consultation on each separate issue. If the caregiver has sought consultation about similar kinds of issues in the past, the expert will communicate while referring to related parts in past consultation outlines. At that time, the expert enters the current consultation content in the allocated box. The caregiver proceeds with the consultation while checking the consultation exchanges displayed on a PC screen.

Information Acquisition on the Care Recipient. Depending on the circumstances, before the consultation the expert acquires the information necessary to the current consultation from the caregiver database, for example, the caregiver's knowledge level and the care recipient's state of health. The information included in the database includes past consultation outlines, lifelogs, and information on personal relationships.

Generating Outlines. The expert systemizes, visualizes and puts in chronological order the consultation purpose, consultation content and the information acquired by the expert. The expert shows the generated consultation outline to the caregiver. The caregiver checks the consultation outline and proceeds with the consultation while deciding whether the consultation content matches the consultation purpose.

5   Experiment

Objective. We took consultation on the creation of a care plan as the subject of the experiment. Through trials with and without the consultation outline, we examined the expert's level of understanding toward the caregiver, the caregiver's level of understanding and satisfaction with regard to the consultation content, and changes in the burden on the expert.

Conditions
Condition 1: For examining the efficacy of the consultation outline, the consultation was performed more than twice. For the consultations following the second one, the previously performed consultation content is confirmed in advance.
Condition 2: Experts and participants are experienced PC users.
Condition 3: Caregivers engage in the consultation in a role play form which follows a scenario.

Participants. The experiment was carried out with one expert and six caregivers. The expert in the experiment was a student with knowledge of care. The caregivers were novices in care, but were students in their 20s who studied care beforehand.

Experimental Environment. We used a PC running Skype, a conversation-sharing system, and PowerPoint.

Experimental Procedure. We carried out the experiment according to the following procedure.

1. The first consultation was performed without using a consultation outline.
2. After the first consultation finished, a consultation outline and a care plan were drawn up and handed to the caregiver.
3. After a period of time, a second consultation was conducted, in one scenario with a consultation outline and in the other with only notes.

Experimental Results. We evaluated results after the experiment had finished through a questionnaire administered to caregivers. The questionnaire asked about the following eight points: level of satisfaction with the overall consultation, level of understanding of the consultation process and content, reliability of the consultation, smoothness of the consultation, level of concentration during the consultation, atmosphere of the consultation process, operability of the consultation processing and readability of the consultation screen. The questionnaire results are shown in Table 1. Ratings were given on a scale of 1 to 5, with 5 representing the highest rating.

The experiment results show that by adding past consultation outlines to the current one and by incorporating lifelogs, good ratings were given for the level of satisfaction with the consultation, and the levels of the understanding, smoothness and reliability of the consultation.

An analysis of variance between conditions showed a clear difference in the level of satisfaction (significance level 10%, F value 3.4). The caregiver's level of understanding of the consultation process was also significantly improved (significance level 10%, F value 2.9). The reliability of the consultation was also improved (significance level 10%, F value 3.5). Through the visual consultation process display, the smoothness of the consultation was also better (significance level 10%, F value 2.8).

5.1   Discussion

In concrete terms, we saw the following benefits and were able to solve the following problems on the caregiver's side.

1. Levels of satisfaction can be taken to have increased based on the following: caregivers and experts were able to have a discussion while confirming, during the consultation, the purpose and the content of the consultation, and caregivers were able to conclude the consultation after having formed a sufficient understanding, which was also based on the consultation history. In concrete terms, we improved the quality of remote consultation from the former level of "dissatisfied" to a level of "mostly satisfied".
2. It becomes possible for caregivers to check, by using the consultation outlines, the sequence through which the care plan has been reached, and thus their level of understanding increases.

Table 1. Questionnaire result (1-5 evaluates five steps altogether)

Item	Without outline	With outline
Degree of conversation partners' satisfaction	2.8	4.1
Degree of conversation partners' understanding	2.8	4.5
Reliability	3.0	4.2
Degree of conversation smoothness	3.0	4.0
Easiness of operation	3.3	3.3
Conspicuousness	2.6	4.0
Relaxed grade of conversation	3.2	3.3
Degree of conversation partners' concentration	3.2	3.8

6   Conclusion

In this paper we introduced consultation outline when engaging in care consultation using computer-mediated communication. We proposed a support system that uses consultation outlines to ensure consistently high level of satisfaction with respect to consultations which extend over long periods of time. We also verified the system's usefulness in an experiment. We can conclude from the experimental results that through remote consultation using consultation outlines caregivers and experts are well supported. Specifically, we can conclude from the experimental results that because the high-priority issues of the care under discussion came to the fore through remote consultation using consultation outlines, both caregivers and expert are provided satisfactory support. We have used a cause and effect diagram as the format for the consultation outline here, but plan to investigate display methods that match the respective characteristics of experts and caregivers. Further research is needed to investigate additional functions for use of the system in actual care environments.

Acknowledgements. We thank Ms. Toyoko Tsunoda of the Yokufukai Social Welfare Corporation for sharing valuable opinions during the course of this study. We also thank all the students who participated in the experiment. This study was supported by a Grant-in-Aid for Scientific Research (Basic Research C).

References

1. Huhanabara, A., Itouh, N.: Content of difficulties of care supporter in care management situation. Seinanjyogakuin Univ. Annual Report 11, 9–21 (2007) (in Japanese)
2. Kato, H., Hiraishi, H., Mizoguchi, F.: Log summarizing agent for web access data using data mining techniques, vol. 5, pp. 2642–2647. IEEE (2001)
3. Takahashi, H., Izumi, Y., Kobayashi, Y., Kinoshita, T., Shiratori, N.: Realization of health support system with gentle watching function. IPSJ SIG Multimedia Communication and Distributed Processing Technical Report, 35–40 (2008) (in Japanese)
4. Yajima, H., Sawamoto, J., Matsuda, K.: Proposal of remote consultation system using hierarchy structured agents. In: IWIN (International Workshop on Infomatics) Cession, vol. 2(6) (2008)
5. Tei, K., Nakagawa, H., Kawamata, Y., Yosioka, N., Hukazawa, R., Hoida, S.: Research trend of Application development method in ubiquitous computing. Computer Software 25(4), 121–132 (2008) (in Japanese)
6. Longterm Care Insurance Law (in Japanese)
7. http://law.e-gov.go.jp/htmldata/H09/H09HO123.html
8. Ministry of Internal Affairs and Communications: Measure to remote medical care
9. http://www.kantei.go.jp/jp/singi/it2/iryoujyouhou/dai9/siryou4_1.pdf
10. Yosioka, N., Hoida, S.: Agent in ubiquitous environment. IPSJ, Journal of Information Processing Society of Japan, 264–270 (2007) (in Japanese)
11. Itoh, S., Ashizaki, T., Kimura, J., Morigaki, T.: Remote consultation system using video communication. IPSJ SIG Multimedia Communication and Distributed Processing Technical Report 9, 85–90 (2006)
12. Social welfare corporation Yokuhukai: Telephone consultation report of social care (2009)
13. Goto, T., Takayama, T., Isiki, M., Ikeda, T.: Remote consultation system for doctor with the patient of an outside domain. IPSJ SIG DataBase System Technical Report 68, 629–636 (2005) (in Japanese)
14. Tanaka, T., Koizumi, Y., Yajima, H.: Proposal of remote consultation support system using asymmetrical communication mode. Journal of Human Interface Sciety 4(3), 167–174 (2002)
15. Yamaguchi, T., Sakano, K., Fujii, R., Andou, H., Kitamura, S.: Remote medical consultation system using super high resolusion display equipment. Journal of IEICE J84-D-II(6), 1203–1212 (2001) (in Japanese)
16. Uesugi, Y., Goto, T., Sakakura, N., Sawamoto, J., Yajima, H.: Development of Remote Consultation System Using Outline Generation Agent. In: Proceedings of the 2010 IEICE General Conference, B-19-12 (2010)

Part II
Games and Gamification

Design Guidelines for Audio Games

Franco Eusébio Garcia and Vânia Paula de Almeida Neris

Federal University of Sao Carlos (UFSCar), Sao Carlos, Brazil
{franco.garcia,vania}@dc.ufscar.br

Abstract. This paper presents guidelines to aid on the design of audio games. Audio games are games on which the user interface and game events use primarily sounds instead of graphics to convey information to the player. Those games can provide an accessible gaming experience to visually impaired players, usually handicapped by conventional games. The presented guidelines resulted of existing literature research on audio games design and implementation, of a case study and of a user observation performed by the authors. The case study analyzed how audio is used to create an accessible game on nine audio games recommended for new players. The user observation consisted of a playtest on which visually impaired users played an audio game, on which some interaction problems were identified. The results of those three studies were analyzed and compiled in 50 design guidelines.

Keywords: audio games, accessibility, visual impairment, design, guidelines.

1   Introduction

The evolution of digital interfaces continually provides simpler, easier and more intuitive ways of interaction. Especially in games, the way a player interacts with the system may affect his/her overall playing experience, immersion and satisfaction. Currently, game interfaces mostly rely on graphics to convey information to the player. Albeit being an effective way to convey information to the average user, graphical interfaces might be partially or even totally inaccessible to the visually impaired. Those users are either unable or have a hard time playing a conventional game, as the graphical content of the user interface is usually essential to the gameplay.

Auditory interfaces [1] provide an alternative way of conveying information for user interfaces and are accessible to visually impaired users. Using an auditory interface, an entire interface can be built upon sounds. Audio games [2–4] present auditory interfaces that can fully represent game elements and gameplay, creating an auditory gaming experience. The graphical interface is not required to play the game: the game might have one (audio-based game) or not (audio-only game). Thus, as the main interface is aural, a well-designed audio game could be played by and be accessible to average and visually impaired users alike.

Although accessible game design and its challenges are discussed in [5–9] and guidelines for accessible games are available in [10, 11], we could not find specific

M. Kurosu (Ed.): Human-Computer Interaction, Part II, HCII 2013, LNCS 8005, pp. 229–238, 2013.

guidelines to designing more accessible audio games for visually impaired players. The available information regarding the design of audio games is mostly papers on the design, implementation or analysis of particular games (c.f. [12–21]). Hence, the starting point for new audio game designers is to learn with previous designs available on the literature and play the games created.

Specific guidelines on accessible audio usage for gaming interaction could further aid new designers on creating more accessible audio games. Hence, this paper presents 50 audio games guidelines containing desirable features and audio usage to aid designers on the creation of more accessible audio games. A more comprehensive list can be found at lifes.dc.ufscar.br. The guidelines combine features described in the literature with the results of a case study and an observation of a playtest performed with visually impaired players.

This paper is organized as follows: Section 2 comments our literature research, by presenting relevant related works. Section 3 describes our research approach. Section 4 presents the case study whilst Section 5 describes the user observation. Section 6 introduces the audio game guidelines. Section 7 presents conclusions and future work.

2   Related Work

In 2004, the International Game Developers Association (IGDA) presented a white paper describing the importance of game accessibility [6]. This paper presented approaches used by games to improve the gaming experience of disabled players and suggested possible methods to improve game accessibility. General guidelines for gaming accessibility are presented in [5]. Guidelines for developing accessible games are presented in [10, 11]. Those are general accessibility guidelines, which can be applied on the development of any kind of game. Universal accessibility in games is discussed in [7, 22]. Those papers present and discuss the design of Universally Accessible Games (UA-Games), games that follow the principles of Design for All [22].

However, we could not find a compilation of specific guidelines to help designers to create audio games. Most of the papers we found focus on decisions and challenges of the design and implementation of particular games. Some parts of these papers emphasize more specific goals with more depth, such as creating auditory interfaces or game entities – like objects and scenario – with audio. The parts we considered the most relevant for our work are succinctly indicated below. They were our starting point and might provide insightful advice for new audio game designers.

The creation of auditory interfaces and auditory objects in audio games is discussed in [4, 12, 14, 18, 23–25]. Navigation and orientation in audio games scenarios or worlds are discussed in [4, 12, 14, 15, 19, 21, 23]. Those could be useful for designing interfaces and entities for the game and how to use them more effectively in the gameplay.

In audio games, sounds have to be used both to convey information to the player as for aesthetics. Different classification of game sounds, their uses and function in games can be found in [13, 14, 25, 26]. Functional and aesthetical uses of sound and their importance in the design of audio games is discussed in [4, 14, 25, 26].

The design of audio games is addressed with more depth in [4, 12, 14, 15, 17, 19, 21, 25], especially regarding audio usage for gameplay. The importance of audio feedback for user inputs is commented in [10, 23, 24]. Ideas on implementation are described in [4, 15, 18, 19, 21]. Input design is commented in [24, 25], whist provide insights on how to use different input devices is provided in [4, 16, 17, 26].

3   Research Approach

We performed a literature research, a case study and a user observation to propose the guidelines. The goal of these three studies was to find how audio is used on audio games and how to help new designers to create audio games. We researched how one could use game audio, such as music, sound effects and speech, to:

- Create and characterize game entities, such as objects, characters and puzzles;
- Create and characterize ambient, scenes and game worlds, how to handle spatial localization and how to navigate in the game's space;
- Control the player's avatar, handle control input and provide input feedback;
- Teach the player how to play or how to give instructions;
- Create game menus and how to navigate on them.

The literature research was described in Section 2. We performed the case study and the user observation to complement and to verify in the practice what we found.

The case study analyzed nine audio games with various genres regarding the audio interfaces, audio usage and interaction. The games choices were based on lists of games recommended to beginner players [3, 27]. Some were also chosen because they had versions in Portuguese, which was necessary for the user observation. The case study is discussed in Section 4. The user observation consisted of two blind users playing an audio game and describing their experience. We also observed how they interacted with the game and how they responded to the game's information and feedback. The user observation is further discussed in Section 5.

We then combined all the information, results and problems gathered to propose some design guidelines for audio games. The guidelines address problems identified on one or more of our studies and were organized in eight categories, as presented in Section 5. Each proposed guideline has the recommendation, the problem(s) it addresses and the rationale. The resulting guidelines feature advice on how to present the audio in an audio game trying to achieving better accessibility, focusing the audio usage on enhancing the gameplay, representing game objects and providing useful information to the player when needed.

4   Case Study on Audio Games

The case study consisted of the researchers playing and checking audio usage in nine audio games, with diverse genres, to verify how the games used audio to create accessible game experiences. The chosen games were: Dark Destroyer [28], an arcade/action game; Deekout [29] an action game; Drive [30], a racing game; Fear of the Dark [31], a maze game; GMA Tank Commander [32], another action game; Lone Wolf [33], a simulation game; Mudsplat [34], an arcade game; Ten Pin Alley [35]; a bowling game and Top Speed 3 [36], another racing game.

The setup of all the games, except [29], used a graphical installer. The installer, although simple to sighted players, might be inaccessible on some screen readers – especially as the install progression was shown using progress bars. Before playing, we noted some games [35, 36] requested the player to disable assistive technologies, such as screen readers, whilst playing. However, they did not remind the player to enable them when he/she finished playing the game.

Despite the different genres, the studied audio games adopted similar strategies to those described in the literature to convey the game with audio. We found most of the sounds, especially speech and sound effects, were used in the games focused primarily on gameplay. The games' sounds were mostly used to convey relevant information to the player (such as game events) and to provide feedback on his/her performance. Music was used mostly for aesthetics. Some games also used music or played simultaneous sounds to enhance the gameplay, such as [30] which used the rhythm to report game status and progress.

All audio games provided feedback for users' inputs. Some provided different feedback for correct and incorrect player inputs. Time constraints in game events were more severe on some game than others – this was expected due to the different genres. However, the games provided enough time for reaction. Spatial sounds were mostly used to describe the games' worlds and objects positions – mostly relative to the player's position. [28, 32, 35] provided a spatial sound test, a useful feature to allow the user to check his audio hardware position and/or configuration.

The presentation of the rules, instructions and goals varied among the audio games tested. Some games provide an in-game help [30, 32–35] or tutorial [30, 32]. The others required the player to read the extern manual to learn how to play, providing little to no information in-game. Some games offered the players additional aids during gameplay, such as sonars [33], radars [32, 33] or void-acted non-playable characters [30, 36].

In menus, all games allowed skipping options without hearing it all. [34] differentiated the first from the last option in a menu - indicating when it started or when it ended – and informed the player to which menu he/she was heading back. [32, 34–36] allowed the repetition of the current option without scrolling back and forth. [32, 35, 36] allowed audio settings to be changed within the game. [28, 32, 34] provided a sound test mode which is especially useful when the sound was created to be used on the game or when the player had never heard the sound before.

5   User Observation with Visually Impaired Players

We wanted to observe how visually impaired users interacted with audio games and how would the users perceive the interface and gaming elements. To perform this observation, we went to Espaço Braille (Braille Space), a place to promote training, leisure and entertainment for visually impaired people, in São Carlos, Brazil. Two blind users played the audio game Top Speed 3. The users played a quick race, trying to figure out how to play, by themselves, after some initial explanation about the study. Albeit we could observe only two users, their interactions with the game fulfilled our observation's goals.

Both players became visually impaired on their adulthoods. One of the players had previous experience playing conventional games; however, he had never played an audio game. The other player had no prior experience on playing games. Both users were learning how to use computers.

The users were free to race without worrying with their performance, as we were interesting in observing the interaction. We provided some basic information to the users on how to play, such as the game's goals, controls and suggested how to interpret the sound feedback. Figure 2 illustrates the users playing the game. Both users managed to navigate the game's interfaces and play the race without problems.

It was noticed that, similarly to conventional games, the comprehension of the interface facilitates the game. The user observation suggested the importance of the feedback and the controls used on an audio game in helping the user to play. The players' control on the car rose the more they understood the game and its interface, by hearing the audio cues and adjusting their inputs accordingly. In Top Speed 3, spatial sound is used to position the car in the road - the balance of the stereo sound informs the player whether the car is centralized on the road or leaning away from the center. If the car is distant from the center, it collides with a wall and the game plays a sound effect to warn the player. If the player keeps colliding with a wall, the game provides further feedback, such as an explosion sound.

Top Speed 3 features a NPC who helps the players to navigate on the track, announcing curves and allowing the users to know what was ahead of them by prerecorded speech. This feature was noted and appreciated by the players. The users also commented it was easier playing with stereo headphones, confirming the literature [15]. The headphones facilitated them to recognize on which side the sound was playing, making it easier to play.

The users' main problem with the audio game was the default keyboard keys used by the game. One of the users reported the game's keys were different from what they were used to use on assistive technologies. This made it difficult for him to reposition their hands on the game keys when his hand wandered off the keyboard. They explained it was hard positioning the hands back to the keyboard as the game's keys were not tactile marked keys – like 'A' and 'F' on a QWERTY keyboard layout. Figure 2 (c) illustrates this problem – the hand of one of the users is hovering the keyboard, but unable to find the arrow keys used by the game.

This suggests that, especially for new users, the buttons or keys used to play the game might hinder the experience if they are not properly chosen. If the game uses a keyboard, for instance, using keys the visual impaired players use regularly or allowing him/her to customize the keys for the commands may increase the accessibility of the game.

Fig. 1. (a), (b) Two blind users playing the audio game Top Speed 3. (c) The user is having trouble to reposition his left hand on the keyboard. The absence of the tactile keyboard marks on the arrow keys made it harder to the player find them after losing.

6   Guidelines for Audio Games

The results from the literature and from Section 4 were compiled and analyzed. Recurring audio games features and problems were identified. We combined the information available on the literature with the results and problems identified on the case study and the user observation to propose some design guidelines for audio games. The resulting guidelines feature advice on how to present the audio in an audio game trying to achieve better accessibility. They combine existing recommendations discussed on the literature with audio usage and features recognized on the case study. Recommendation of solutions to identified problems on the case study and user observation were also included.

The complete list of guidelines is available at lifes.dc.ufscar.br. Thirteen guidelines are present here.

- *Category 1.* Install and Access to the Game.

1.1. Easy to understand and to follow to follow setup, planned in a logical and sequential way. Problem. The setup interface might contain large texts or too many options or details. Rationale. Easy setups should be preferred [5]. The messages should be conveyed as simple as possible to the user, to avoid confusing or overwhelming him/her. As the audio interface is perceived sequentially [24], it is important the setup should also be clear. The options and its consequences should be clearly stated. Many of the studied games used wizards to be installed [28, 29, 31–36] or a single zip-file [30]. Also recommended in [11].

1.2. If the game needs to disable assistive technologies, remember the player to enable assistive technologies when he finishes playing. **Problem.** Some games require or recommends assistive technologies to disabled before playing (for instance, [35, 36]). **Rationale.** The game might be accessible if an assistive technology is disabled; however, the user's operating system might be not. It is important to remember him/her to re-enable it after quitting the game.

- *Category 2.* Interaction Output.

2.1. Use audio for all game events, and provide enough time for player reactions. **Problem.** Some audio games provide low time between events or use complementary outputs, such as haptic or graphical, which might not be perceived the same way as audio. **Rationale.** Sound is perceived by time [4], unlike graphics. Therefore, all game events must be conveyed by sound: the player must know what is happening [23] and what will happen [17] to have enough time to act accordingly; provided the information when needed, at a very good time [24].

2.2. Allow repetition of information. Allow additional information to be requested by the player. **Problem.** Some games don't allow information to be repeated. **Rationale.** The user might not hear or understand the provided information the first time he/she hears it. This might happen especially in long explication or dialogues. It is important to allow the player to request the information to be repeated [5]. It is also interesting to allow the player to request for further information. Also recommended in [11].

- *Category 3.* Interaction Input.

3.1. Allow input controls to be customized by the player. **Problem.** Some games do not allow remapping or configuring the commands in an input device. Players might have difficulties on using some keys or buttons, as they might be hard to access or to be pressed on controllers [17] or keyboards. Our visually impaired players used the home row in a keyboard to locate the keys, and thus had difficulty finding the arrow keys. Only two of the tested audio games allowed customizing the controls [32, 36]. **Rationale.** Allowing customization, the user may choose the keys or buttons more adequate to his/her needs or preferences. This might facilitate the interaction between the user and the game. This is also recommended in [5]. Also recommended in [37].

3.2. Provide immediate sound feedback for player inputs. **Problem.** The user must know the results of his/her input command or even if the game accepted the input. **Rationale.** It is important to provide immediate feedback to the player upon his/her action [11, 14, 24]. This helps the player to know if his/her action was processed by the game. For instance, sound effects, such as footsteps when walking [12], allow the player to know his movement input was successful. Also recommended in [11].

- *Category 4.* Menu Navigation.

4.1. Suspend the menu's label reading when the player changes an option. **Problem.** Hearing the same options many times in a menu can be annoying to the player. **Rationale.** This follows the same rationale of Guideline 2.4. Allowing the user to skip the option also may increase his/her navigation speed in the menu.

4.2. Numerate options in menus. **Problem.** If the user is unsure of what option he/she needs to select in a menu, he/she will either have to count its position or remember where it is. **Rationale.** Numerating the options allows the player to remember the number and might allow him/her to navigate to the chosen option faster. Or after using a menu several times, the user might know the exact position of a desired option, however, may still have to navigate all others [23]. Allowing the number to be a shortcut to the option could be adequate.

- *Category 5*. Ambient, Scenarios and Space Representation.

5.1. Avoid reproducing many sounds at once. **Problem.** Listening to several parallel audio signals simultaneously can be confusing [22] to the user. **Rationale.** Sound is perceived by time [14]. A user listening to many sounds at once might be overloaded with information and have a hard time distinguishing or understanding each sound individually. Too many sounds at once might be detrimental to the experience [13]. When many sounds are played, the vision is used to solve ambiguities [23] – which is not possible in an audio game. If it is necessary to play many sounds, try making them complementary, with planned timing [22] and/or using them spatialized [14].

- *Category 6*. Object Representation.

6.1. Try describing objects with the most accurate and representative sound possible. **Problem.** The user has to recognize an object by hearing its sound. **Rationale.** An object should be described by using it more accurate sound or combination of sounds available [12]. The sound must match the player's mental model to be recognized [19] and should be sounds that are relevant by themselves [24]. As a rule of thumb, if objects are different, they should sound different [23] in the game. If there is no good sound to describe an object, an artificial, created sound can be used; however, it should be described and explained to the user.

6.2. Present an option to describe a new sound to the player. **Problem.** The user might not have heard the sound of an object before. For instance, this could happen if an object was created for the game or the player does not know it. **Rationale.** Sometimes, a sound will be created to describe an object. This sound should be presented to the user in the context of the game. To accomplish this, some of the games featured a sound sample mode, in which the user could listen to all the game's sounds [28, 32, 34].

- *Category 7*. Character Representation.

7.1. Use sounds of to describe the status of objects or characters. **Problem.** Inform the player about the status of objects or characters and their whereabouts in the scenario. **Rationale.** The status of an object or character can be described by using different sounds. This can be done to compensate the lack of visual information [14] in audio games. For example, different sounds can be used to describe if a machine is operating or if it is broken; the pace and tempo of the sound can suggest it activities. This can also be applied to characters, with breathing or walking sounds or exclamations and questions.

- *Category 8*. Miscellaneous.

8.1. Provide an audio tutorial to first time players or enough in-game information to help them to play the game. **Problem.** Help first time users to play the game. **Rationale.** An in game tutorial could help new users to play and get to know the game, as it could be a good idea to teach the basics to user. As the goals and objectives, sounds and controls are game-specific, the tutorial might suggest the player how to interpret the sounds in the game in order to play. This could be especially used if the game used many sounds the user is not familiarized with. Of the case study games, only two [30, 32] offered a tutorial. Also recommended in [11].

7   Conclusions and Future Work

This paper presented some guidelines to help new designers to create audio games, an accessible gaming alternative for visually impaired player. Their goal is to complementing existing game accessibility guidelines, aiding designers on using audio to create more accessible audio games, especially for visually impaired players. They were proposed by the systematization of features, problems and solutions discussed on literature's papers and accessibility guidelines, a case study and a user observation.

As future work, the authors will follow the guidelines to implement some audio games, to improve their applicability. We want to find more effective ways of presenting the game's content, without sacrificing the interactivity or the fun. The authors are also researching ways to create accessible games to other disabilities. We are aiming to provide alternative modal representations to the same content, trying to minimize losses on the absence of one or more modalities. The goal is to allow players play a game with their friends, in a universal approach, regardless of disabilities.

Acknowledgement. We acknowledge the financial aid from CAPES and FAPESP (2012/22539-6) for the realization of this work.

References

1. Mynatt, E.: Auditory Presentation of Graphical User Interfaces, pp. 533–555 (1992)
2. Targett, S., Fernström, M.: Audio Games: Fun for All? All for Fun? In: International Conference on Auditory Display, Boston, p. 4 (2003)
3. AudioGames.net, http://audiogames.net/
4. Röber, N., Masuch, M.: Leaving the Screen: New Perspectives in Audio-only Gaming. In: International Conference on Human Computer Interaction with Mobile Devices and Services, Salzburg, pp. 92–98 (2005)
5. Ossmann, R., Miesenberger, K.: Guidelines for the Development of Accessible Computer Games. In: Miesenberger, K., Klaus, J., Zagler, W.L., Karshmer, A.I. (eds.) ICCHP 2006. LNCS, vol. 4061, pp. 403–406. Springer, Heidelberg (2006)
6. International Game Developers Association: Accessibility in Games: Motivations and Approaches. White Paper (2004)
7. Grammenos, D., Savidis, A., Stephanidis, C.: Designing universally accessible games. Magazine Computers in Entertainment (CIE) - Special Issue: Media Arts and Games 7, 29 (2009)
8. Grammenos, D., Savidis, A., Stephanidis, C.: Unified design of universally accessible games. In: Stephanidis, C. (ed.) HCI 2007. LNCS, vol. 4556, pp. 607–616. Springer, Heidelberg (2007)
9. Yuan, B., Folmer, E., Harris, F.: Game accessibility: a survey. Universal Access in the Information Society 10, 81–100 (2011)
10. UPS Project: Guidelines for the development of entertaining software for people with multiple learning disabilities,
http://www.medialt.no/rapport/entertainment_guidelines/index.htm

11. UPS Project: Guidelines for developing accessible games,
    http://web.archive.org/web/20110724181620/http://gameaccess.
    medialt.no/guide.php
12. Drewes, T.M., Mynatt, E.D., Gandy, M., Mynatt Maribeth, G.E.D.: Sleuth: An Audio Ex-
    perience. In: International Conference on Auditory Display, Atlanta (2000)
13. Parker, J.R., Heerema, J.: Audio Interaction in Computer Mediated Games. International
    Journal of Computer Games Technology 2008, 1–8 (2008)
14. Friberg, J., Gärdenfors, D.: Audio games: New Perspectives on Game Audio. In: Interna-
    tional Conference on Advances in Computer Entertainment Technology, pp. 148–154.
    ACM Press, Singapore (2004)
15. McCrindle, R.J., Symons, D.: Audio space invaders. In: International Conference on Disa-
    bility, Virtual Reality and Associated Technologies, Alghero, pp. 59–65 (2000)
16. Glinert, E., Wyse, L.: AudiOdyssey. In: Conference on Future Play, pp. 251–252. ACM
    Press, Toronto (2007)
17. Yuan, B., Folmer, E.: Blind hero. In: Conference on Computers and Accessibility, pp.
    169–176. ACM Press, Halifax (2008)
18. Miller, D., Parecki, A., Douglas, S.A.: Finger dance. In: International ACM SIGACCESS
    Conference on Computers and Accessibility, pp. 253–254. ACM Press, Tempe (2007)
19. Lyons, K., Gandy, M., Starner, T.: Guided by Voices: An Audio Augmented Reality Sys-
    tem. In: International Conference on Auditory Display, Atlanta (2000)
20. Collins, K., Krapalos, B.: Beyond the Screen: What we can learn about game design from
    audio-based games. In: Annual International Conference on Computer Games, Multimedia
    and Allied Technology (2012)
21. Nordlinder, M.: Lair of Beowulf: a study of 3D positional sound in an audio mostly game
    (2007), http://epubl.ltu.se/1402-1617/2007/059/index-en.html
22. Grammenos, D., Savidis, A., Stephanidis, C.: Unified Design of Universally Accessible
    Games. In: Stephanidis, C. (ed.) HCI 2007. LNCS, vol. 4556, pp. 607–616. Springer, Hei-
    delberg (2007)
23. Andresen, G.: Playing by Ear: Creating Blind-Accessible Games (2002),
    http://www.conceptlab.com/uci/us12b/
    us12b-week9-andresen-playingbyear.pdf
24. Archambault, D., Olivier, D.: How to make games for visually impaired children. In: ACM
    SIGCHI International Conference on Advances in Computer Entertainment Technology,
    pp. 450–453. ACM Press, Valencia (2005)
25. Eriksson, Y., Gärdenfors, D.: Computer games for partially sighted and blind children,
    http://www.tpb.se/barnens_tpb/spel/projekt/report.html#_04
26. Parker, J.R., Heerema, J.: Musical interaction in computer games. In: Future Play 2007,
    Proceedings of the 2007 Conference on Future Play, p. 217. ACM Press, Toronto (2007)
27. Game Accessibility, http://www.game-accessibility.com/
28. Dark Destroyer. PB-Games (2004)
29. Deekout. BSC Games (2002)
30. Drive. AudioGames.net (2003)
31. Van Hooren, M.: Fear of the Dark
32. GMA Tank Commander. GMA Games (2002)
33. Lone Wolf. GMA Games (2000)
34. Mudsplat. TiM Games (2005)
35. Ten Pin Alley. Draconis Entertainment (2003)
36. Top Speed 3. Playing in the Dark
37. IGDA: Curriculum Framework,
    http://www.igda.org/curriculum-framework

SWord: A Concept Application
for Mitigating Internet Terminology Anxiety

Santosh Kumar Kalwar, Kari Heikkinen, and Jari Porras

Department of Software Engineering and Information Management,
Lappeenranta University of Technology, Lappeenranta, Finland
{santosh.kalwar,kari.heikkinen,jari.porras}@lut.fi

Abstract. The Internet is a dynamic, democratic, and multicultural platform where a wide range of users access sites daily. We cannot presume users on the Internet will understand every single word/term used on any given site. This paper presents a concept for assessing users' anxiety regarding commonly used words on the Internet, particularly words related to technology and computer science. The concept is highlighted by an application, called SWord, which enables users to collaborate, share, play, and mitigate with difficult words on the web.

Keywords: Wellness, human anxiety, Anxiety, Internet, Design, user experience.

1 Introduction

> *"The pen is mightier than the sword"*
> *-Edward Bulwer-Lytton (Richelieu; Or the Conspiracy, 1839)*

As pointed out by English author, Edward Bulwer-Lytton, the power of freedom, opinion, and thoughts is stronger than the power of violence through weapons. This insight suggests words can solve problems more imaginatively than force; i.e., the sword. In the present context, the web, or the Internet, acts as the pen where the ideas and opinions of the public are read, collected, shared, and discussed. But, sometimes the words used on the web can be difficult to understand. For example, while reading an article on a specific site(s), the user might find terms or words difficult to comprehend. Consequently, a novice user on the web might, for instance, either "look up" a difficult word(s) or simply ignore it. What if we place the word power in the hands of the users? The users gain in full control to define, share, and play with the words they find difficult to understand.

SWord is a social mobile application, a word game that will help users online [15] to both define and conceptualize difficult terms in a game-like manner using social networking features. Any founded or defined terms are read, recommended or further commented so that the term might become understandable and thus, measuring and reducing Internet Terminology Anxiety (ITA) [1, 2]. The major contribution in this paper is the conceptualization, design and development of the SWord utility for

M. Kurosu (Ed.): Human-Computer Interaction, Part II, HCII 2013, LNCS 8005, pp. 239–248, 2013.

possible mitigation of ITA. The approach is based use-case, empathy (capability to think, feel, and sense users' emotional needs) [19] and design research. Additionally, the play and learn brainstorming process [9, 10] is used when designing this utility. Thus, the main research question we seek to explore is: *Can the 'Sword 'utility mitigate Internet terminology anxiety (ITA)?*

Our paper is structured as follows. The next section provides the related work of Internet terminology anxiety. Section 3 introduces SWord utility and its elements. Section 4 illustrates the mitigation of ITA. Section 5 describes an end-user evaluation, and Section 6 and 7 discusses on findings and conclusions.

2   Related Work

Internet anxiety (IA) is a recent phenomenon, and not widely studied or explored. Some researchers are, however, actively working to understand this phenomenon [1, 4-5]. Presno defined IA as "a more specific form of computer anxiety" [1]. Thatcher et al. studied and conceptualized Internet anxiety as relating to computer anxiety [5]. Joiner et al. studied gender variables and their impact on Internet experience and behavior [2]. Internet anxiety occurs mainly when dealing with various issues and problems related to general Internet use (e.g. difficulties in understanding terms, Internet connection failure). Many researchers argue that people suffer from the Internet as they would suffer from any real disease [4, 8, 20]. These studies have reported that users on the Internet show signs of frustration, anger, depression and loneliness [21, 22]. A user who has problems with words/terms on the web is considered to possess, "Internet terminology anxiety" (ITA) [1, 6, 8]. This paper presents a study in which a tool/utility for users who have issues understanding words/terms on the web is conceptualized and designed.

2.1   Internet Terminology Anxiety

Accurate use of terminology is clearly central to effective communication but management of terminology often poses challenges for businesses and software developers [15]. Internet terminology is terms used as words or word combinations that provide meaning for specific concepts on the Internet [1, 8]. ITA is defined as "an anxiety caused by Internet terminologies" [9]. More specifically, Internet Terminology Anxiety (ITA) is "feelings of anxiety as they were introduced to a host of new vocabulary words and acronyms. For example, HTML (Hypertext Markup Language), and SLIP (Serial Line Internet Protocol) etc [1, p. 153]." There are several benefits from managing terminology. Namely, it enables users to engage and share knowledge, and learn new vocabulary/words; it reduces technical documentation or translation costs for managing software; it facilitates agreement on cross-cultural differences for terms in the software development life-cycle; and it ensures consistency and coherent use of terms throughout software development processes [15, 17].

3   SWord Utility

The approach of the SWord utility is partly similar to the game *Balderdash,* where the concept is to self-invent definitions of the words and by convincing peers to get points based on deception. The SWord utility is different in that the concept is NOT to self-invent definitions but utilize knowledge and insights to define difficult words that might, eventually, help anxious users and other end-users, thus mitigating their Internet Terminology Anxiety.

As the goals of interaction design [9, 13] (Ixd) are to make the application, system and product more useful for users, the SWord utility (or application) uses exploratory interaction design styles to build the utility. Using this method, various game elements are explored and introduced to users. The utility can enable users to engage in social activities by actively participating and learning. The "terms" used on the web can be interpreted differently by Internet users from different countries and cultures. The design [10] presented can enable users to define the terms (irrespective of their country and culture); collect user defined terms; display user defined meaning for anxiety-inducing terms, share terms (e.g. on Facebook, Twitter and others), play with terms, and get rewarded (e.g. by winning badges or scoring points) for the collected terms. The benefit of SWord can be seen from the conceptual aspects. The conceptual diagram of SWord is shown in Figure 1, where it can be seen that Sword can be used as a plug-in or as a gaming interface utilizing *FeelCalc* [7], i.e. with a set of algorithms.

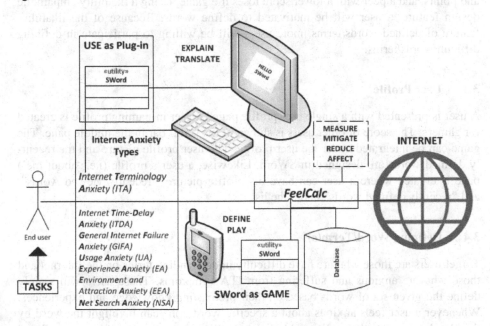

Fig. 1. SWord conceptual diagram

3.1   User Motivation

The goal of the study is to increase users' contributions to 'SWord' and design a reward system to motivate users. To motivate users, the following hypotheses were posited: *would it be fine to visit sites without feeling anxious as the words are becoming less cryptic? And would you like to learn the terms without feeling anxiety?* For example, a reward system is given to the user with reward coupon (e.g. an archetypal user named Matti Mainio has 'word knight' status). In addition, users can challenge friends, build leagues of their own with friends, etc. using social networking capabilities.

3.2   Social Aspect

SWord helps users define difficult terms in a gaming-like manner (utilizing social media functionality). The end-user reads these definitions for terms they do not understand. The social aspect of 'SWord' can run on 'word-of-mouth' and welcoming users with a 'newcomer of the day' concept design could encourage newcomers. The gaming aspect will provide learning opportunities for users, thereby encouraging social participation. The social participation of the game can be based on peer scores for correctly defined word(s). For example, a user can define as many words as he wants but the correct answer is only with one peer. A score is calculated based on numerical values of 1-5. The peer with a highest score wins the game, gaining various badges and points, and a peer with a lower score loses the game. Using a likability empathetic design feature, a user will be motivated to define words. Because of the likability feature of defined words/terms, more users will be willing to participate in defining difficult words/terms.

3.3   User Profile

A user is presented with a single user profile page. A user in-gaming profile is created for gamers. The score of other users is shown in the scroll bar in the middle pane. The game can be integrated under the user profile. The user profile picture and the recently defined words are designed in SWord. Likewise, a user's profile (i.e. 'about me') page is created where a user can have his profile picture, "recently viewed words", and "recently defined words" under the list.

3.4   Defining Word/Term(s)

Target users are those who are have difficulty understanding terms on the Internet and those who are anxious and suffering from ITA symptoms. These users will simply define the given set of words based on their preexisting knowledge and experiences. Whenever a user feels anxious about a specific word (s)he can highlight the word by double clicking and then (s)he right-clicks on the term to "collect," "compete," and "share".

3.5 Gaming Aspect

The in-gaming aspects of 'SWord' are shown in Figure 2. The work of Blashki and Nichole highlights the importance of welcoming newcomers to a game. In their article [16], terminology used among gamers is used, for example, "leet speak or 1337 5p34k," which divides users between expert gamers and newcomers. In SWord, their advice is adopted with the design of a "newcomers of the day" feature. The upper part in Figure 2 shows basic statistics about the user's social virality (e.g. LIKES, number of defined words). A user is given five terms at a time, and his task is to define those terms by typing-in the definitions. The rectangle (on the right side of the screen) shows the user has defined the term and the other empty rectangle shows the term being currently defined. There are two buttons at the end of the interface: "That's Enough" and "Give Me More!" The game can be stopped by clicking on 'That's Enough,' or there is a possibility to get five more terms to play with by pressing 'Give Me More'.

Rules for Playing the Game

Figure 2 illustrates the in-gaming aspect of 'SWord'.

1. The upper part (1, 2, and 3) shows basic statistics about the user's social activity (e.g. what does the user like, number of defined words).
2. A user is given five terms (4) at a time, and his task is to define those terms by typing-in the definitions (5). Upon challenge by an opponent, an automated word cloud (7), and dictionary usage for determining authentic definition for terms can be acquired.
3. The rectangles show the user has successfully defined the term and the white bubble shows the term being defined (5).
4. The rectangles (6) show terms that have not yet been defined. There are only two buttons at the bottom of the interface: "That's Enough" (9) and "Give Me More!" (8)
5. The game can be stopped by clicking on 'That's Enough' or another five terms elicited by pressing 'Give Me More'.

4   Mitigating Internet Terminology Anxiety

Many wellness applications exist that increase users' participation in physical activity [11, 12]. This design utility is built with the objective of mitigating ITA symptoms shown by users on the Internet, focusing and combining interdisciplinary concepts; e.g., medical, psychological, and HCI aspects. In the development stage, a user usage scenario was considered where the SWord utility is used by 1) the user who defines the terms (end user), and by 2) the anxious user. In the SWord utility, an end-user defines the word(s) and the anxious user competes in the in-game interface by defining difficult words from a word cloud.

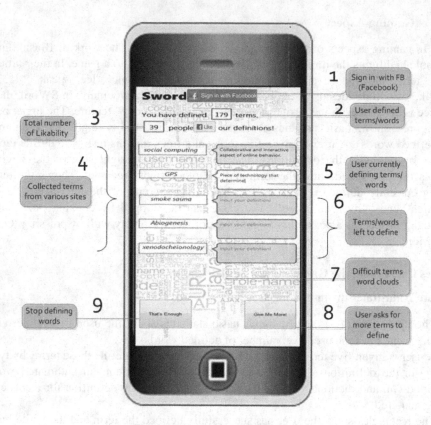

Fig. 2. SWord in-game screenshot

The result of 'SWord' utility can be used by increasing users' motivation to contribute. Users will be more likely to feel committed if they share some form of attachment or bonding (e.g., here most users are feeling anxious about terms/words on sites). To mitigate ITA, the following steps are employed:

1. A user visits any site and starts reading its contents. In Figure 3, the user has visited the ACM home page (i.e. www.acm.org).
2. The SWord prototype is running in the background. This is shown in Figure 3 at the bottom right corner with a SWord utility logo 'S'.
3. The user highlights the word/term and clicks. Figure 3 shows the chosen word/term, i.e., "computing."
4. The user can start defining the difficult word(s). As task were designed with level of difficulty, this task was assumed "*extremely difficult*" since users might possess cognitive load and lack motivation for defining terms. Figure 3 shows the SWord utility panel that enables the user to click for defining words.
5. A user can either collect, compete, share, and play with difficult word(s).

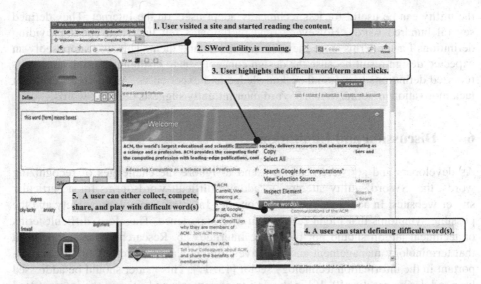

Fig. 3. Screenshot of a user reading an ACM home entry as (s)he comes across a difficult word (e.g. "Computing")

5   End User Evaluation

User evaluation is considered an important aspect of developing the SWord utility. A small number of participants (*n*=7) volunteered to test the effectiveness of the design concept of SWord. Each of the evaluators was provided with the sets of tasks. Following questions related with the tasks, the evaluators reported on the results for the tasks. As the aim of the SWord utility was to mitigate user anxiety for difficult words/terms on the Internet. SWord utility was installed in the *Mozilla Firefox browser* as an add-on/plug-in. The following task was given to the evalutors:

1. Read content on Internet sites, e.g., the ACM home page
2. Whenever you find a difficult word(s)
3. Click on the difficult word(s)
4. A 'SWord' menu should appear
5. Click on "Define word(s)", see Figure 3
6. Click "collect, compete, and share" buttons as appropriate (*Collect* is used to collect user defined difficult terms, *compete* UI will show the gaming interface and *share* UI will allow you to share the word in social networking sites)
7. If you press compete, you will be asked to input your own definitions for difficult words, you may quit the 'SWord' utility by pressing, "That's Enough".

The result of the evaluation gave fruitful insight towards the main research question. In general, there was consensus among participants that the 'SWord' utility can be useful in helping anxious users with a difficult word. Participants reported that the 'SWord' had capability in reducing ITA. More interestingly, participants reported that the utility can be useful for less technically adept users on the Internet. They defined several hundred words. However, some participants felt uncertain about providing definitions for the terms since they did not understand them. This was supposedly an expected design result because the design concept was to challenge participants' self-reported definitions based on their knowledge and experiences. As an end-user might lack motivation to define terms, SWord intermittently suggests defining words.

6   Discussion and Limitations

As developers and software designers tend to ignore the challenges of recognizing words, the 'SWord' utility attempts to address difficult words/terms for a particular site or websites. In addition, one has to consider Internet terminology anxiety and the possible symptoms that might result from user experience. Therefore, difficult terms or technical jargon should not be on the Internet/web. Researchers have concluded that terminology management and effective communication of terminologies are important in the information technology sector [15, 17]. This matter should be addressed by good design practice [9, 10] in the design of contents and sites on the Internet, and by taking into account the knowledge level of targeted end users.

The anxiety symptoms associated with Internet terminology anxiety (ITA) on the Internet are not the result of user action or inaction but result from poor design. This statement is supported by Don Norman's book, "The Design of Everyday Things" [18, p. 131] where he states, "Change the attitude toward errors. Think of an object's user as attempting to do a task, getting there by imperfect approximations. Don't think of the user as making errors; think of the actions as approximations of what is desired." End-users and anxious users are both Internet users and they are not to blame for experiencing Internet terminology anxiety or the symptoms associated with anxiety. In addition, the playful nature of SWord utility might assist an anxious user to learn a difficult word and simultaneously compete/play with new users. The game is not designed as a way to help users to memorize the defined terms because some users might then feel anxious about typing the definitions.

7   Conclusion and Future Work

This concept paper presented initial designs for helping anxious users online. We believe users will be very motivated to play the game with peers and define specific terms. Interestingly, users can play in any device e.g., tablet, phone, PC, because SWord is designed in a multi-device platform. This design approach allows the SWord utility to be used both online and offline, enabling users to be less dependent on Internet access. The design concepts presented in this paper can mitigate ITA symptoms by connecting anxious users with other users in relation to their health problems, activities and goals. Furthermore, a user might gain knowledge and insights about the word(s) on the Internet. The take-home message is that the SWord' utility increases users' know-how, learnability (about Internet terms), understanding and ability to have positive Internet user experience by defining difficult words/terms that result in pleasurable experiences. Future work could comprise the following:

- This paper focuses on Internet terminology and possible mitigation of Internet terminology anxiety via the SWord utility, which is implicitly linked to wellness technologies Other similar application and utilities for different types of Internet anxiety could be designed and created.
- Functional improvements and implementations in the SWord utility could be carried out. However, added functionality does not always lead to better accessibility.
- The user evaluation could be carried out with a larger and more diverse group of participants.

Acknowledgments. This work has been partially supported by ECSE (East Finland Graduate School in Computer Science and Engineering), the Foundation of Nokia Corporation, LUT Foundation grant (Lauri ja Lahja Hotisen rahasto, Väitöskirjan viimeistelyapurahat), and the Finnish Foundation for Technology Promotion (Tekniikan edistämissäätiö). I would like to thank: Tommi Kähkönen, Erno Vanhala and Harri Karhu for active participation in the "Social Computing" course lectured by Dr. Rosta Farzan at ECSE Summer School, Joensuu where we initially worked on this concept.

References

1. Presno, C.: Taking the byte out of internet anxiety: Instructional techniques that reduce computer/internet anxiety in the classroom. Journal of Educational Computing Research 18(2), 147–161 (1998)
2. Joiner, R., Gavin, J., Brosnan, M., Cromby, G., Gregory, H., Guiller, J., Maras, P., Moon, A.: Gender, internet experience, internet identification, and internet anxiety: A ten-year followup. CyberPsychology, Behaviour and Social Networking 15(7) (2012)
3. Amichai-Hamburger, Y., Hayat, Z.: The impact of the Internet on the social lives of users: A representative sample from 13 countries. Computers in Human Behavior 27(1) (2011)
4. Turkle, S.: Alone Together: Why We Expect More from Technology and Less from Each Other, 1st edn. Basic Books (2011)
5. Thatcher, J., Loughry, M., Lim, J.: Internet anxiety: An empirical study of the effects of personality, beliefs, and social support. Information & Management 44(4) (2007)
6. Kalwar, S.K., Heikkinen, K., Porras, J.: Finding a relationship between internet anxiety and human behavior. In: Jacko, J.A. (ed.) Human-Computer Interaction, Part I, HCII 2011. LNCS, vol. 6761, pp. 359–367. Springer, Heidelberg (2011)
7. Kalwar, S., Heikkinen, K., Porras, J.: Measuring user reaction to reduce Internet anxiety. In: IEEE Symposium on Computers & Informatics (ISCI), pp. 738–742. IEEE (2011)
8. Kalwar, S.K., Heikkinen, K.: Study of human anxiety on the Internet. In: Jacko, J.A. (ed.) HCI International 2009, Part I. LNCS, vol. 5610, pp. 69–76. Springer, Heidelberg (2009)
9. Cooper, A., Reimann, R., Cronin, D.: About Face 3: The Essentials of Interaction Design, p. 610. Wiley, Indianapolis (2007) ISBN 978-0-470-08411-3
10. Buxton, B.: Sketching the User Experience. New Riders Press ISBN 978-0-470-08411-3

11. Jarusriboonchai, P., Väänänen-Vainio-Mattila, K.: How Can Technology Bring Families Together: Exploring User Needs and Design Qualities. A Workshop Paper in the Workshop Mobile Family Interaction: How to use Mobile Technology to Bring Trust, Safety and Wellbeing into Families
12. Ahtinen, A., Mattila, E., Väätänen, A., Hynninen, L., Koskinen, E., Salminen, J., Laine, K.: User Experiences of Mobile Wellness Applications in Health Promotion. Pervasive Health (2009)
13. Zimmerman, J., Forlizzi, J. & Evenson, S. Research through design as a method for interaction design research in HCI. In: CHI 2007 (2007)
14. Caplan, S.E.: Preference for online social interaction: A theory of problematic Internet use and psychosocial well-being. Communication Research 30, 625–648 (2003)
15. Muegge, U.: Disciplining words: What you always wanted to know about terminology management. Tcworld (tekom) (3), 17–19 (2007)
16. Blashki, K., Nichol, S.: Game Geek's Goss: Linguistic Creativity in Young Males Within an Online University Forum. Australian Journal of Emerging Technologies and Society 3(2), 77–86 (2005)
17. Schmitz, K.-D.: Indeterminacy of terms and icons in software localization. In: Indeterminacy in LSP and Terminology. Studies in Honour of Heribert Picht, pp. 49–58. John Benjamins, Amsterdam (2007)
18. Norman, D.: The design of everyday things. Basic books (2002)
19. Wright, P., McCarthy, J.: Empathy and experience in HCI. In: Proceedings of the Twenty-Sixth Annual SIGCHI Conference on Human Factors in Computing Systems, pp. 637–646. ACM (2008)
20. Caplan, S.E., High, A.C.: Online Social Interaction, Psychosocial Well-Being, and Problematic Internet Use. In: Young, K.S., de Abreu, C.N. (eds.) Handbook and Guide to Evaluation and Treatment. John Wiley & Sons, Inc., Hoboken (2007)
21. Kraut, R., Kiesler, S., Boneva, B., Cummings, J., Helgeson, V., Crawford, A.: Internet paradox revisited. Journal of Social Issues 58(1), 49–74 (2002)
22. Kalwar, S.: Human behavior on the internet. IEEE Potentials 27(5), 31–33 (2008)

Extreme Motion Based Interaction
for Enhancing Mobile Game Experience

Youngwon Kim, Jong-gil Ahn, and Gerard Jounghyun Kim

Digital Experience Laboratory,
Korea University, Seoul, Korea
{kimforever920,hide989,gjkim}@korea.ac.kr

Abstract. In this paper, we propose to enact interaction by "extreme" motion involving multiple body parts and thereby maximize the whole body experience. By detecting the relative movements among multiple body parts, rather than an extended motion of just a single body part, the extreme motion can be contained within the personal space (not to disturb others around). Such a scheme was tested on a simple mobile game and compared to interfaces that were based on conventional touch interface and absolute motion detection. Experimental results showed that while incorporating extreme "relative" motion resulted in higher level of excitement and user experience by involving more body parts, the control performance significantly suffered (due to the head movements).

Keywords: User Experience, Extreme motion, Whole Body Interaction, Motion Detection.

1 Introduction

Games interfaces are evolving fast to become more experiential. One representative approach is to employ body-based interaction as well demonstrated by the recent successes of the Nintendo Wii [1] and Xbox Kinect [2]. The same trend is slowly spreading to the mobile games as well. While most mobile games still use touch based interfaces (e.g., buttons, flicks), several motion based games are appearing. For example, there are games that make use of the tilt [3] and acceleration sensors [4], however, motion based interaction is inherently problematic because it would typically entail moving of the screen and disturb others around in a public setting. Thus, at best, only limited motion is incorporated into the game interaction and this restricts the full potential of the body based user experience. In this paper, we propose to detect and use the "relative" motion between the upper body and the hand-held device as extreme body motion so that it can enrich the mobile game experience, while containing the interaction within the personal space, and possibly providing minimum visibility for the moving screen (at least to some extent). Figure 1 illustrates our proposal.

M. Kurosu (Ed.): Human-Computer Interaction, Part II, HCII 2013, LNCS 8005, pp. 249–257, 2013.
© Springer-Verlag Berlin Heidelberg 2013

Fig. 1. An example of extreme motion based mobile game playing by moving both the hands and upper body

At the core of our approach lies the estimation of the body movement by tracking the face and optical flow using the camera in relation to that of the mobile device (measured by e.g. the accelerometer, gyro and tilt sensor). This enables users to interact with the mobile device not only through the touch display with buttons and other touch interfaces, but also with their whole (or upper) body. In this paper, we describe the design of such an interface and game interaction, called the EMMI (Extreme Motion based Mobile Interaction). We also validate the overall technique by running a comparative experiment to a non-motion based and conventional "absolute" motion based mobile games.

2   Related Work

Employing whole body interaction is an effective method to enhance the immersive quality of interactive contents [5, 6, 7, 8, 9, 10]. Possible methods of realizing whole body interaction include using body worn sensors (or markers and large scale surround sensing system) and haptic/tactile device (body worn [11, 12, 13] or platform type). While they may be effective, they have the obvious problems of usability and cost.

However, whole body interaction does not necessarily require separate sensing and feedback mechanisms for all the body parts involved. Through clever interaction and interface design, whole body interaction can be induced with minimal sensing. For instance, the arcade game, "Dance Dance Revolution" [14], utilizes a very simple foot switch pad, but the interaction is designed to induce the use of whole body. The situation is similar for the Nintendo Wii (or acceleration sensor) based games [15]. However, when designing interaction for mobile devices, the interaction, whether is purposely designed or induced, must consider the issue of containment within the personal space.

3   Recognizing the Extreme "Relative" Motion

The recognition of the "extreme" motion system is based on detecting the user's face (see Figure 3) and its movement, and comparing it to the motion of the device (using the phone sensors). Several researchers have applied face detection, optical flow, motion flow and sensors for motion based interface in various ways, but rarely in a combined form [16][17]. Figure 2 illustrates the main idea. It also illustrates that the motion based interaction can be contained within the personal space so that it can be used in a social setting as well. The face detection is used in conjunction with optical flow so as to estimate the user distance from the phone and use for zoom in/out action (not just sideway motion). Our implementation on the smart phone is based on the standard face detection and optical flow routines available from OpenCV [18]. Note that when trying to detect the relative movement of the head during when the phone holding hand is also moving in the other direction, the imagery of the head can go beyond the field of view of the phone camera. This limits the extent of how much the head/upper body or the hand/sensor to move with respect to the center of the personal space as well.

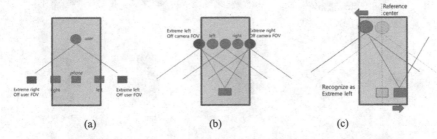

(a)   (b)   (c)

Fig. 2. Detecting motion with (a) phone sensors only, (b) camera only (head movement only), and (c) both sensors (phone/hand) and camera (head/upper body)

Fig. 3. Using face detection from the phone camera to approximate the relative user movement

4   Interaction Design

Figure 4 shows possible interaction design. It is illustrates the richness of motion based interaction possible by including such body gestures. In most cases, the extreme motions are not just motions with large displacements or inertia, but rather carry particular interactional meaning (e.g. zoom-in vs. microscope, move left vs. bumping). This way we believe the mobile interaction can be much enriched and overall experience enhanced.

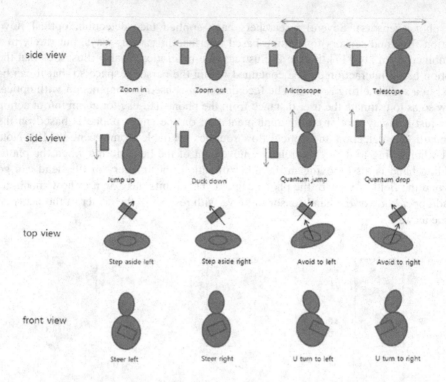

Fig. 4. Enriching motion based interaction with extreme gestures

5   Experimental Evaluation

The proposed technique (EMMI) is validated by carrying out a comparative experiment to conventional mobile interfaces for a simple game. User experience and control performance were measured and compared among four interfaces that employed different ways to enact "extreme" motion/event: (1) touch based, (2) touch + momentary motion (e.g. jerk), (3) absolute motion by hand (phone sensor) only (e.g. by moving distance of the holding hand), (4) relative motion (e.g. by combined moving distances of the holding hand and face/upper body). That is, the experiment is designed as 1x4 (one factor with four levels) within-subject repeated measure, the factor being the type of interface employed for extreme action.

Our hypothesis is that at least the user experience will be improved by the motion based interfaces, and more so with relative motion which involve more body parts. We expect the control performance to suffer due to the difficulty for fine control, unfamiliarity and erratic screen movement.

5.1   Experimental Task and Set Up

The experimental task for the user was to play a simple described as follows. There were 5 vertical lanes through which object fell from the top. The game is played by controlling the basket in the bottom (and move between the lanes) to catch the falling objects. Normally, the objects mostly fall along lanes 2, 3 and 4 but sometimes special objects fall through lanes 1 and 5 in the extreme left and right. Thus the user needs to react to such events e.g. in an "extreme" way to place the basket there and catch the special objects. Figure 5 shows the snap shot of the game being played. The four tested interfaces operated as shown in Table 1.

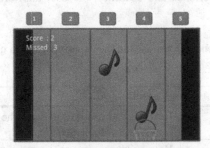

Fig. 5. "Catch the Falling Object" game used in the experiment. The objects fall in five different lanes caught by the user controlled basket. The user need to enact "extreme" action to catch the objects in the far right/left lanes.

Table 1. How the four tested interfaces operated

Interface type	Symbol	Explanation
Touch based	Touch	Touch the respective lane (e.g. lanes 1 and 5) to directly place the basket
Touch + Acceleration	T+M	Use direct touch and motion (detected by an acceleration threshold) simultaneously to move into lanes 1 and 5
Absolute motion by hand	Absolute	Use only hand motion (approximated by an acceleration threshold[1])
Relative motion by hand/head	Relative	Use hand motion (approximated by an acceleration[1] threshold) and head movement (approximated by the face detection / optical flow measurement from the phone camera)

5.2 Detailed Experimental Procedure

Ten paid subjects (9 male and 1 female aged between 25 and 32) participated in the experiment with the mean age of 27.3. After collecting one's basic background information, the subject was briefed about the purpose of the experiment and

---

[1] For now, hand movement distance is only "approximated" by an acceleration threshold per unit time, under the assumption that user moves fast to make extreme and long distanced motion.

instructions for the experimental task. A short training was given for the subject to get familiarized to the interfaces and the task to be completed (about 5~10 minutes).

Each subject tried out the four interfaces in a balanced order and two trials were carried out each for lasting about 2 minutes. That is, the user was asked to catch as many objects as possible during 2 minutes. As for the control performance, the number of missed objects was counted per single session (which is equivalent to the score). As for user experience and usability, the user answered a survey as shown in Table 2.

Table 2. The user experience survey used in the experiment. Each question was answered in 7 Likert scale.

	Category	Question
Q1	Usability	How easy to use did you feel the game/interface to be? (1: difficult ~ 7: easy)
Q2	Usability	How much were you apprehensive about the people around you? (1: not at all ~ 7: very much apprehensive)
Q3	Usability	Rate your preference among the four game/interfaces. (1: not preferred ~ 7: very much preferred)
Q4	Usability	Rate how much fatigue was induced by the given game/interface. (1: very tiring ~ 7: not too tiring)
Q5	UX	How much fun or exciting did you feel the game/interface to be? (1: not at all ~ 7: very much exciting)
Q6	UX	How much immersed or experiential the game/interface to be? (1: not at all ~ 7: very immersive/experiential)

5.3   Experimental Results

Figure 6 shows the results with regards to the usability (first four survey questions). Generally, users found the motion based interfaces (T+M, Absolute, Relative) to be much more difficult to use than the conventional touch. This is somewhat expected given the very short amount of time (5~10 minutes) to get familiarized to the motion based interfaces. The Relative interface was rated the most difficult and most tiring as it involved a coordinated move between the hand and upper body. Also as expected, all interfaces that involved significant body movement (T+A, Absolute and Relative) induced apprehensive behavior around one's personal space. However, the extent of the motion with the Relative interface was contained within the personal space, as explained in the earlier section. The users were apprehensive nevertheless. Despite the difficulty, fatigue and apprehensiveness, users showed strong preference toward the motion based, and particularly, the Relative interface.

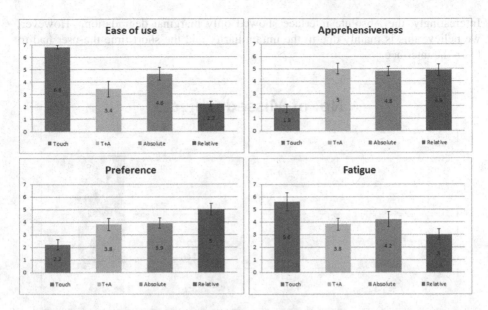

Fig. 6. Responses to the usability questions (Q1~Q4). Subjects generally found the motion based interfaces to be difficult, tiring and causing apprehensiveness. Despite it, they strongly preferred motion based, and particularly, the Relative interface.

Figure 7 shows the results with regards to the user experience (Q5 and Q6). In tune with the preference results, users found the motion based interfaces (T+M, Absolute, Relative) to be more exciting, immersive/experiential to use. The Relative interface induced the highest level of excitement and UX with a statistical significance. This reconfirms the positive effect of whole body interaction to the affective state of the user and ultimately to heightened user experience.

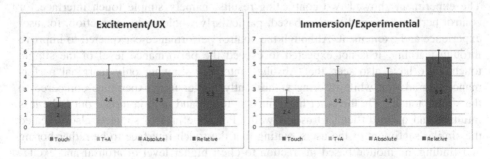

Fig. 7. Responses to the UX questions (Q5 and Q6). Subjects generally found the motion based interfaces, particularly the Relative" to be more exciting and immersive/experiential.

Finally, Figure 8 shows the results with regards to the performance (number of missed objects). Again as expected, due to the difficulty of the interface, the performance was much lower for the motion based interfaces, particularly for the Relative.

Interestingly, the Absolute interface showed only marginal degradation. However, we believe this is mainly due to the unfamiliarity and the short time the user had to learn the interface.

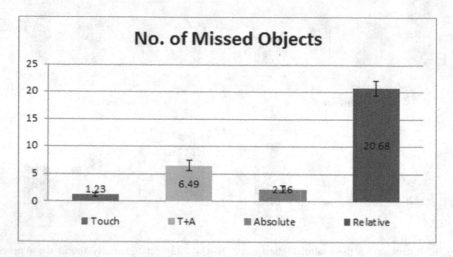

Fig. 8. The number of missed objects for the four tested interfaces. Motion based interfaces, particularly the Relative, show degraded performance. However, this is believed to be due to the unfamiliarity and the limited time for the user to learn the interface.

6   Conclusion

In this paper, we described the design of a motion based interface platform called the EMMI (**E**xtreme **M**otion based **M**obile **I**nteraction). We also presented an example interaction design for mobile games or application and ran a validation experiment. The experiment showed two contrasting results, namely simple touch interface for control performance and motion based, particularly whole body interaction, for user experience and excitement. Although the control performance is expected to improve through learning, it is not expected to exceed the performance level of the simple touch. We have also seen that Absolute interface showing only marginal performance degradation while offering significantly higher user experience compared to the simple touch. On the other hand, mixing touch and motion turned out to be less intuitive and quite difficult to use as well. Post-briefings of subjects also revealed the similar sentiment of the users, stating that the touch interface to be rather boring and finding the motion based interaction to elicit higher level of arousal and excitement. In the case of games, the purpose of the application is often excitement rather than just compiling high score. This would be an important issue to consider in mobile game interface.

There still are several limitations that need to be addressed. For instance, we need to address the use of body gestures in a social context (even though even the extreme motions are somewhat contained in the personal space), and the missing of the display screen due to high speed motion even though the visibility is geometrically possible. In the future, we hope to make use of multimodal interface to compensate for the lowered screen visibility and extend to get leg movements involved in the interaction as well.

Acknowledgements. This work was supported by the National Research Foundation of Korea(NRF) grant funded by the Korea government(MEST) (No 2012-0009232).

References

1. Nintendo Wii, http://www.nintendo.com/wii
2. Kinect-XBox, http://www.xbox.com/en-US/live/default.htm
3. Chang, K.: Review of free Android games that uses your Droid tilt sensors (2012), http://kschang.hubpages.com
4. Ravado, R.: 10 Best Free Accelerometer Apps for iPhone and iPod Touch (2012), http://rikravado.hubpages.com
5. Boulic, R., Maupu, D., Peinado, M., Raunhardt, D.: Spatial Awareness in Full-Body Immersive Interactions: Where Do We Stand? In: Boulic, R., Chrysanthou, Y., Komura, T. (eds.) MIG 2010. LNCS, vol. 6459, pp. 59–69. Springer, Heidelberg (2010)
6. Benyon, D., Smyth, M., Helgason, I. (eds.): Presence for Everyone: A Short Guide to Presence Research. The Centre for Interaction Design Report, Napier University, UK (2009)
7. Peterson, B.: The Influence of Whole-Body Interaction on Wayfinding in Virtual Reality. PhD Thesis, University of Washington (1998)
8. Slater, M., Wilbur, S.: A Framework for Immersive Virtual Environments (FIVE): Speculations on the Role of Presence in Virtual Environments. Presence 6(6), 603–616 (1997)
9. Hwang, J., Jung, J., Kim, G.J.: Hand-held Virtual Reality: A Feasibility Study. In: Proc. of the ACM Virtual Reality Software and Technology (2006)
10. Groenegress, C.: Whole-body Interaction for the Enhancement of Presence in Virtual Environments. PhD Thesis, University of Barcelona (2010)
11. Hanyu, R., Tsuji, T., Abe, S.: A Simplified Whole-body Haptic Sensing System with Multiple Supporting Points. In: IEEE International Workshop on Advanced Motion Control, pp. 691–696 (2010)
12. Noda, T., Miyashita, T., Ishiguro, H., Hagita, N.: Super-Flexible Skin Sensors Embedded on the Whole Body, Self-Organizing Based on Haptic Interactions. In: Proc. of Robotics: Science and Systems IV (2008)
13. Lindeman, R., Page, R., Yanagida, Y., Sibert, J.: Towards Full-body Haptic Feedback: The Design and Deployment of a Spatialized Vibrotactile Feedback System. In: Proc. of the ACM Symposium on Virtual Reality Software and Technology, pp. 146–149 (2004)
14. Dance Dance Revolution, http://www.konami.com/ddr
15. Wii, http://wii.com
16. Hwang, J., Kim, G.J.: Provision and maintenance of presence and immersion in hand-held virtual reality through motion based interaction. Computer Animation and Virtual Worlds (2010)
17. Hrabar, S., Sukhatme, G.: Combined optic-flow and stereo-based navigation of urban canyons for a UAV. Intelligent Robots and Systems, 3309–3316 (2005)

Influence of Gaming Display and Controller on Perceived Characteristics, Perceived Interactivity, Presence, and Discomfort*

Hyunji Lee[1] and Donghun Chung[2,**]

[1] Dept. of Journalism and Communication, Kwangwoon University, Seoul, Korea
hyunjilee.good@gmail.com
[2] School of Communications, Kwangwoon University, Seoul, Korea
donghunc@gmail.com

Abstract. The purpose of this study is to examine gamers' psychological experience according to the display and controller. The research used 2D and 3D as gaming display and joypad and Move as gaming controller. It examined the effects of those variables on perceived characteristics, perceived interactivity, presence, and discomfort. Sixty four participants joined the experiment and the main findings are as follows: First, the interaction effect of the display and controller was not significant for any of the variables. Second, the main effect of the display was significant in the perceived characteristics of clarity and materiality. Finally, the main effect of the controller was significant in the perceived interactivity, spatial involvement, dynamic immersion, and realistic immersion. Although the present research found significant effects of those independent variables, a follow-up study is needed to investigate why the interaction effects are not supported.

Keywords: 3D, controller, discomfort, display, game, perceived characteristics, perceived interactivity, presence.

1   Introduction

Since the success of the movie Avatar and the resultant interest in the format, 3D technology has influenced much visual media and the field is working to expand its area from broadcasting to the gaming industry. In fact, games have already used 3D technology for a long time; for instance, graphics have different depth levels, which are not seen in traditional 2D games. 3D graphics enhance user's perception through a variety of depth levels compared to 2D [1] and for the same reason, 3D displays are assumed to give us a greater perception of 3D than simply 3D graphics on 2D displays. In addition, this will have an effect on enjoyment while playing a game; flow will help the game industry keep their growth on track.

* This work was supported by the National Research Foundation of Korea Grant funded by the Korean Government (NRF-2011-32A-B00297).
** Corresponding author.

M. Kurosu (Ed.): Human-Computer Interaction, Part II, HCII 2013, LNCS 8005, pp. 258–265, 2013.
© Springer-Verlag Berlin Heidelberg 2013

Games also spur 3D display adoption. A good combination of interaction and realism, in other words, a good combination of motion control and 3D stereo display will serve as a new game condition and experience. Although this game condition has never been seen before, there has been little research on the comparative analysis of 2D and 3D displays [2][3], or about controller difference [4]. However, we do not know what would happen when combining the display with the controller. Therefore, the purpose of this study is to examine gamers' psychological feedback, such as perceived characteristics, perceived interactivity, and presence as effects of the combination of the display and controller. Furthermore, discomfort from wearing 3D glasses is often one of the most talked-about topics among media today, so we looked at that as well.

2   Related Work

A great deal of research is being carried out to discover the benefits of stereoscopic 3D since 3D stereo games first came out. Takatalo et al. [5] set three different display disparities (2D, medium stereo, high stereo separation) according to their pilot testing, and found that medium stereo separation offered the best user experience, such as involvement and presence. However, Mahoney et al. [6] showed that games converted to stereoscopic 3D that were basically designed for 2D did not transfer well and caused tiredness in one's eyes. They also said that using 3D stereo in games did not improve the game-play but did improve the visuals.

What matters to game research is not only the display but also the controller. In prior studies, researchers reported that 3D stereo was different from 2D in display [5][6] and that the keyboard was different from the Joystick in regard to the game controller [7]. It is reasonable to infer that game users may have different experiences with different game displays and controllers. Kulshreshth et al. [8] studied user performance benefits of playing video games using a motion controller in a 3D stereoscopic view in relation to 2D and found that a 3D stereo display helped user performance significantly compared to a 2D display. Even though they found that 3D stereo was perceived to be more enjoyable and immersive than 2D, it was only qualitative data.

Unfortunately little research is interested in the combination of display and controllers and there is no guarantee that one study will explain it all. Despite the interest in 3D effects and the introduction of various controllers in the game industry, it is not clear why interaction effects are not focused. It is necessary to evaluate how viewers recognize the features that 3D displays provide because it is a different matter as to whether or not they really perceive 3D stereo [9]. Also, in terms of controller, the same point of view will be applied; for instance, whether a controller that involves the gamer's body using so called state-of-the art technology is better than a traditional controller in any game. Thus, the present research would disclose the effects of display and controllers on various psychological outcomes, such as perceived characteristics, which are how users perceive five levels of characteristics displayed images; perceived interactivity, which is how users perceive three levels of interactivity from the controller; presence, which is a perceptual flow composed of four levels requiring directed attention; and the discomfort which came from wearing 3D glasses.

RQ1. Will the display (2D vs. 3D) interacting with the controller (joypad vs. Move) make a difference in the gamer's perceived characteristics of the display?

RQ2. Will the display (2D vs. 3D) interacting with the controller (joypad vs. Move) make a difference in the gamer's perceived interactivity?

RQ3. Will the display (2D vs. 3D) interacting with the controller (joypad vs. Move) make a difference in the gamer's presence?

RQ4. Will wearing 3D glasses interacting with the controller (joypad vs. Move) make a difference in the gamer's comfort?

3   Method

3.1   Participants

Sixty-four students were recruited from a university in Seoul, Korea. 32 males and 32 females joined this experiment and the age range is from 18 to 28. The mean age is 22.31 (SD=2.44).

3.2   Procedure

Before the participants played the game, they were asked to fill out a questionnaire that asked about their age, gender, previous game experience, and other such information. Then all participants entered a game lab and a researcher explained how to play the tennis game (Top Spin 4) on the PS3. The researcher demonstrated how to play the game ('X', 'O', '□' button of the joypad are a flat shot, topspin and slide, respectively) and they were asked to practice for 2 minutes each as a training session. After confirming that no problems existed, the researcher restarted the game and the participants played for 15 minutes. The game was then stopped and the participants were given a main questionnaire that asked about perceived characteristics, perceived interactivity, presence, and discomfort from wearing 3D glasses.

3.3   Instrument

The questionnaire was mainly composed of four parts: perceived characteristics, perceived interactivity, presence, and discomfort from wearing 3D glasses. Perceived characteristics were composed of four parts: proximity, clarity, materiality, message transmit and tangibility, coined by Chung and Yang [9]. Proximity had six items (e.g., I felt the perspective very well), materiality had four items (ex. I could distinguish the edge of things). Clarity had three items (e.g., I felt it had a sharp picture), message transmit (e.g., I understood very well what message they wanted to deliver) and tangibility (I felt like the picture seemed to leap off the screen). Perceived interactivity was composed of three parts: speed, range and mapping, made by Steuer [10]. Speed had four items (e.g., I could move my character more quickly), range (ex. My character's position changed as I controlled it) and mapping (e.g., The reaction appeared natural as I controlled the character). Presence was composed of four parts: spatial involvement, temporal involvement, dynamic immersion and realistic immersion, revised from Chung and Yang's questionnaire [9]. Spatial involvement had four items (e.g., I felt like I was in the game), and so did temporal involvement (e.g., I lost all track of time as I was playing the game). Dynamic immersion (e.g., I felt I had to move actively) and realistic immersion (e.g., I felt that the image in the game was real) each consisted of three items. Finally, discomfort from wearing 3D glasses had eight items, revised from Knight et al. [11] and Kim et al.'s questionnaire (e.g., I felt awkward wearing 3D glasses) [12]. All the items used a 5-point Likert scale.

Table 1. Variables' mean, SD and reliability

		Items	M	SD	a
perceived characteristics	proximity	6	3.59	.60	.81
	clarity	3	4.05	.75	.91
	materiality	4	3.32	.66	.72
	transmit	3	3.96	.80	.86
	tangibility	3	2.61	.87	.87
perceived interactivity	speed	3	2.68	1.03	.91
	range	3	3.07	.98	.85
	mapping	3	3.01	.95	.86
presence	spatial involvement	4	2.89	1.04	.94
	temporal involvement	4	3.72	.99	.91
	dynamic immersion	3	2.63	.85	.73
	realistic immersion	3	2.73	1.03	.86
3D glasses discomfort		8	1.98	.70	.87

3.4   Gaming System

The PS3 was chosen for this research and the game title is the full 3D sport game, Top Spin 4 by the 2K Sports company. It supports gaming options including whether users can choose 2D or 3D environment and joypad or Move. Users grab the Move stick, which is one of the PS3 controllers, and swing it as though they are really playing tennis.

Fig. 1. Experiment environment

4   Result

To analyze the performance data, a mixed ANOVA was conducted in order to examine the effect of gaming display and controller on the user-perceived psychological experience. The results show that the interaction effect of the display and controller was not significant for every part of perceived characteristics. In contrast, the main effect of the display was significant in clarity $[F(1,62)=4.65, p<.05]$ and materiality $[F(1,62)=4.06, p<.05]$. Concretely, 2D (M=4.23) reported much more clarity than 3D (M=3.86), and 2D (M=3.46) reported much more materiality than 3D (M=3.18).

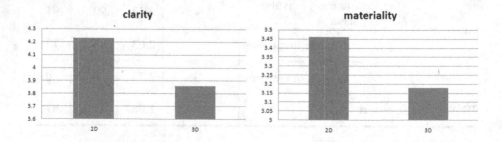

Fig. 2. Clarity and materiality on the gaming display

The results show that the interaction effect of the display and controller was not significant in every part of perceived interactivity. Yet the main effect of the controller was significant in range $[F(1,62)=4.15, p<.05]$, and joypad (M=3.23) reported much more range than Move (M=2.91).

Fig. 3. Range on the gaming controller

The result shows that the interaction effect of the display and controller was not significant for presence. In contrast, the main effect of the controller was significant for spatial involvement $[F(1,62)=17.00, p<.001]$, and the Move (M=3.15) had much more spatial involvement than the joypad (M=2.63). Also, the main effect of the controller was significant in dynamic immersion $[F(1,62)=36.78, p<.001]$ and realistic immersion, too $[F(1,62)=13.87, p<.001]$. Concretely, Move (M=2.96) has much more dynamic immersion than joypad (M=2.92), and Move (M=2.93) has much more realistic immersion than joypad (M=2.52).

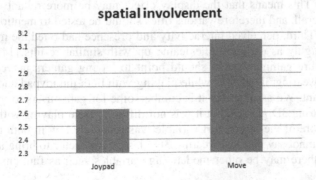

Fig. 4. Spatial involvement on the gaming controller

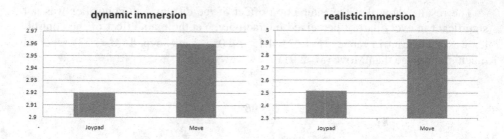

Fig. 5. Dynamic and realistic immersion on the gaming controller

Finally, discomfort from wearing 3D glasses was not significant between joypad and Move $[F(1,30)=1.71, p>.05]$.

5　　Discussion

This study examined the effects of display and controller type on gamers' perceived characteristics, perceived interactivity, presence, and discomfort from wearing 3D glasses. From the data analysis, we could see that the interaction effect between those two independent variables provided no significant perceived psychological experience. The implication of this research can be described in following way. First, the quality of the gaming title may be a factor. In most cases, 2D effect is more positive in this research. For instance, subjects had rated perceived characteristics (clarity and materiality) on 2D higher than 3D which is quite the opposite outcome than that based on common sense. However it is clearer when we understand the characteristics of 3DTV. Active Shutter Glasses have insufficient brightness to reduce image crosstalk and ghosting [13] which leads to problems with viewing comfort. Also, how 3D game titles provides quality may be another issue in 3D gaming which is distinct from the 2D or 3D issue. This means that the display effect may be more reliant on the title itself, not 3D overall, and therefore various titles should be tested to mention a 2D and 3D comparison. Third, perceived interactivity and presence had rated the motion controller (Move) highly as earlier studies came up with similar results [14][15]. This means that a future gaming system should point to having gamers move their own bodies. Finally, wearing 3D glasses while playing with both the joypad and the Move was not significant. We assume that it is cumbersome for game users to move themselves while wearing 3D glasses, but it was not different from playing with a joypad, and the mean score of the discomfort variable was relatively low in both cases. This means that we cannot say that just wearing 3D glasses is a factor to bring a feeling of discomfort, but there may be other moderating variables such as fun, enjoyment, or others.

There may be many reasons why the hypotheses of this research were not supported. It may come from the game title itself, the level of difficulty and entertainment, or some other factor. It is necessary for future research to find out various cause-and-effect psychological variables according to the level of the display and controller.

References

1. Balakrishnan, R., Kurtenbach, G.: Exploring Bimanual Camera Control and Object Manipulation in 3D Graphics Interfaces. In: SIGCHI Conference on Human Factors in Computing Systems, pp. 56–63. ACM, New York (1999)
2. Litwiller, T.: Evaluating the Benefits of 3D Stereo in Modern Video Game. Unpublished master's thesis, Florida (2010)
3. Schild, J., LaViola, J., Masuch, M.: Understanding User Experience in Stereoscopic 3D Games. In: SIGCHI Conference on Human Factors in Computing Systems, pp. 89–98. ACM, New York (2012)
4. Skalski, P., Tamborini, R., Shelton, A., Buncher, M., Lindmark, P.: Mapping the Road to Fun: Natural Video Game Controllers, Presence, and Game Enjoyment. New Media & Society 13, 224–242 (2011)
5. Takatalo, J., Kawai, T., Kaistinen, J., Nyman, G., Hakkinen, J.: User Experience in 3D Stereoscopic Games. Media Psychology 14, 387–414 (2011)
6. Mahoney, N., Oikonomou, A., Wilson, D.: Stereoscopic 3D in Video Games: A Review of Current Design Practices and Challenges. In: 16th International Conference on Computer Games, pp. 148–155. IEEE Press, New York (2011)
7. Wilson, A.D., Agrawala, M.: Text Entry Using a Dual Joystick Game Controller. In: SIGCHI Conference on Human Factors in Computing Systems, pp. 475–478. ACM, New York (2006)
8. Kulshreshth, A., Schild, J., LaViola Jr., J.J.: Evaluating User Performance in 3D Stereo and Motion Enabled Video Games. In: International Conference on the Foundations of Digital Games, pp. 33–40. ACM, New York (2012)
9. Chung, D., Yang, H.: Reliability and Validity Assessment in 3D Video Measurement. JBE 17, 49–59 (2012)
10. Steuer, J.: Defining virtual reality: Dimensions Determining Telepresence. Journal of Communication 42, 73–93 (1992)
11. Knight, J.F., Baber, C., Schwirtz, A., Bristow, H.W.: The comfort Assessment of Wearable Computers. In: 6th International Symposium on Wearable Computers, pp. 65–72. IEEE Press, New York (2002)
12. Kim, H., Lee, K., Mah, K., Chung, S., Oh, H.: A Study on the Complaints of Spectacle Wearers. Korean J. Vis. Sci. 2, 197–203 (2000)
13. Jung, K., Kang, M., Kim, D., Sohn, K.: 3D Video Quality Improvement for 3D TV using Color Compensation. JBE 15, 757–767 (2010)
14. Wong, E.L., Yuen, W.Y.E., Choy, C.S.T.: Designing Wii controler: A Powerful Musical Instrument in an Interactive Music Performance System. In: 6th International Conference on Advances in Mobile Computing and Multimedia, pp. 82–87. ACM, New York (2008)
15. McGloin, R., Farrar, K.M., Krcmar, M.: The Impact of Controller Naturalness on Spatial Presence, Gamer Enjoyment, and Perceived Realism in a Tennis Simulation Video Game. Presence: Teleoperators & Virtual Environments 20, 309–324 (2011)

A Cross-Cultural Study of Playing Simple Economic Games Online with Humans and Virtual Humans

Elnaz Nouri and David Traum

{nouri,traum}@ict.usc.edu

Abstract. We compare the simple online economic interactions between a human and a multimodal communication agent (virtual human) to the findings of similar simple interactions with other humans and those that were run in the laboratory. We developed protocols and dialogue capabilities to support the multi modal agent in playing two well-studied economic games (Ultimatum Game, Dictator Game). We analyze the interactions based on the outcome and self-reported values of possible factors involved in the decision making. We compare these parameters across two games, and the two cultures of US and India. Our results show that humans' interaction with a virtual human is similar to when they are playing with another human and the majority of the people choose to allocate about half of the stakes to the virtual human, just as they would with another human. There are, however, some significant differences between offer distributions and value reports for different conditions (game, opponent, and culture of participant).

Keywords: Culture, Values, Decision Making, Virtual Human, Economic Games, Communicative Agents.

1 Introduction

In this paper we present a cross-cultural study of online negotiation in simple economic games, where participants play opposite either a virtual human or someone from their own culture. Economic models of rational behavior typically assume that people try to maximize their own profit in such games[15]. However, in social settings, including these games, previous research has found that people from most cultures take other factors into account as well, such as relative gain (cast as competition or fairness), gain of the other, and joint gain[17]. Online interaction represents an intermediate point between normal social interaction, and individual performance[6]. The participants are alone, acting on a computer interface, however, the situation is still posed as a social interaction: playing with either another person from their culture, or with a virtual human: an animated character who engages in spoken dialogue and non-verbal communicative behavior. We are interested in whether people playing under these conditions act similarly to those playing face in laboratory settings and with other humans. We are looking at both the game play and participants' self-report of what values they are concerned with when making moves.

M. Kurosu (Ed.): Human-Computer Interaction, Part II, HCII 2013, LNCS 8005, pp. 266–275, 2013.
© Springer-Verlag Berlin Heidelberg 2013

We attempt to address the following questions. How different are players from the United States from Players in India? What impact does the type of game have on players' decisions and values? How similar or different do participants feel and act when playing a virtual human versus another person?

In the next section, we review related work in this area. In section 3, we describe our experimental conditions, and independent and dependent variables. We present the results in Section 4, and conclude in Section 5.

2   Background and Related Work

Two well-studied examples of economic games are the Dictator Game and Ultimatum Game. Both games involve allocation of a certain amount of money between two people. In both games, players are asked to split a sum between themselves and the other party. In the dictator game, one player decides on a partition of the sum. In the single shot ultimatum game[9], the first player proposes a partition. If the other player accepts the proposal, then the sum is partitioned to the players according to the proposal but if the other player rejects, then both players receive nothing.

Previous studies have extensively investigated human behavior in these games and some show that social factors affect the giving behavior in these games. For example even minimal social cues such as three dots in the watching eyes configuration in the dictator game affect the giving behavior in a positive way [20]. We expect that virtual humans would have a similar effect on humans and prompt participants to show giving behavior toward the agents. We are also interested to see whether the results obtained online are comparable to laboratory conditions when people are recruited and compensated for their time according to the amount of time they put in participation. However few studies have looked into what happens in these games when played online. One would suspect that online strangers playing with each other might not be influenced by social constraints but some recent studies have reestablished the classical findings such as the effect of framing and priming on Mechanical Turk[18] [2]. Experiments investigating the reliability of self-reported demographics on Mechanical Turk show that above 97% of these tasks are reliable [12][23]. [1] has also shown that running economic games experiments on Mechanical Turk are comparable to those run in laboratory setting even when using very low stakes for payment. The effect of adding stakes and the average behavior in the stakes conditions is also similar to what has been observed in the laboratory setting. These experiments alleviate concerns about the validity of economic games experiments run online versus ones in the laboratory.

Previous research shows that in the Dictator Game the subjects were more generous when there were no stakes involved compared to when high stakes or low stakes were involved [5] [8]. In the Ultimatum game increasing the stakes size does not increase the average proposals but increases the variance observed in them [8]. The responder behavior didn't change in [8] but decreased significantly in [4].

In the virtual agent community, researchers have investigated whether expression of emotions by virtual humans has the same effect of human emotion expression on humans. Such effects have been mostly investigated in the context of the Prisoner's dilemma [13][7].

Prior research (e.g. [3][10]) has documented the influence of social and cultural factors on the decision making process. In the most general case, a human decider does not consider only the impact on his own utility, but also the impact on others, including individuals, groups and society as a whole. There are also differences in how individuals value the options in a decision-space as well as broad similarities in outlook between similar individuals. Culture also plays a role [3][10].

In our own previous work [16,17], we have attempted to model differences in game play as a result of differences in values. In [17], we considered four type of values and set weights on each of these depending on the social setting of the players (in-group/out-group, status differences) and intuitions based on Hofstede's culture model[16]. In [14], we learned weights using inverse reinforcement learning. While this work showed that learned values were better able to predict the behavior of the culture they were learned from than other culture, it was not conclusive about the actual values that the players had.

3   Experiments

3.1   Method

In our experiments participants played single shot versions of either the dictator game or the ultimatum game. Each game was played to split a sum of 100 points. In the ultimatum game the responder's policy was to accept any offer more than 40 points in both human and virtual human conditions.

Participants filled out a demographic questionnaire before starting the experiment. They received a $0.5 show up fee for participating in the task and were told that they will be playing over points and will earn another $0.05 for each additional 10 points that they accumulate in the game.

Participants were given a description of the game (ultimatum or dictator), and then asked for their move as proposer in the game. Once the participants in the experiment made their decisions in the games, they were asked to report how much they cared about each of the values in table 1, on a scale from -5 to 5 (-5 meaning that they were strongly against, 0 meaning that they didn't care at all, and 5 meaning that they cared a lot about achieving the goal). After this survey, they were given the results of the game (which was determined by their offer for the dictator game).

3.2   Opponents

There were two opponent conditions. In the first case, players were told that they were playing against another person from their country (US or India). In the second case they played against a virtual human. In the second case, the pre-game survey and the values questionnaire was administered by the virtual human as well, while in the human condition, they filled out a purely textual form.

Table 1. Values survey

Value	Description Given to participant
V_{self}	Getting a lot of points
V_{other}	The other player getting a lot of points
$V_{compete}$	Getting more points than the other player
V_{equal}	Having the same number of points as the other player
V_{joint}	Making sure that added together we got as many points as possible
V_{rawls}	The player with fewest points gets as many as possible[19]
$V_{lower bound}$	Making sure to get some points (even if not as many as possible)
V_{chance}	The chance to get a lot of points (even if there's also a chance not to get any points)

Our virtual human was developed using the SimCoach virtual human authoring platform, called Roundtable (described in [22]). The platform is built upon a broad set of virtual human technologies developed at USC-ICT that make it easier to create, test and deploy conversational virtual characters on the web. Characters can be developed to understand natural language textual input as well as fixed-choice menu options[21]. The Flores Dialogue manager [14] selects character actions based on the authored policy and the developing context. Finally, the textual form of character responses are explicitly authored and are bound to dialogue acts specified in the policy. Actions can be realized as speech performances, references to web resources or purely nonverbal reactions. The character was launched on the web and once provided the link to the server the participants were able to interact with the virtual character that can interact through audio and text. The character is shown in Figure 1.

3.3   Participants

Six hundred participants total, were recruited using Amazon Mechanical Turk. Roughly ½ were from the United States, while the other ½ was from India.

Table 2. Number of participants from the two countries playing two games

	US	India
Dictator Game Human	107	107
Dictator Game Virtual Human	46	38
Ultimatum Game Human	101	101
Ultimatum Game Virtual Human	53	47

Participants were assigned to one of the eight conditions, based on culture (US or India), game (Ultimatum or Dictator) and opponent (human or virtual human). Human studies were conducted one month earlier, with about 100 participants per condition, while virtual human conditions had about 45 participants per condition. The exact number of participants per condition is shown in table 2.

Fig. 1. Screen shot of the Simcoach character Ellie

4   Results

In this section we report the results of the experiments and possible explanations for the observed behavior. Figures 2 and 3 show offer distributions for the two games, contrasting cultures and opponents. Our results are broadly consistent with what has been shown in the literature for laboratory play[11][3]. Figures 4 and 5 show the differences in reported values in different conditions. The upcoming parts in this section examine the effect of culture, game and opponent in detail.

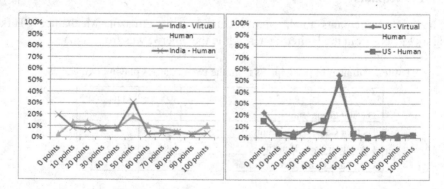

Fig. 2. Offer distribution in dictator game

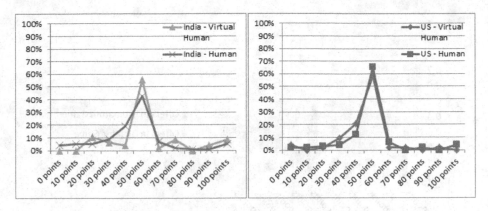

Fig. 3. Offer distribution in ultimatum game

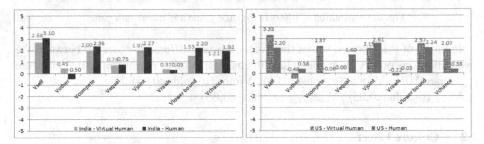

Fig. 4. Reported values in the dictator game

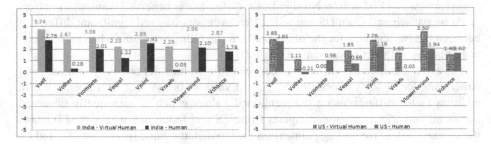

Fig. 5. Reported values in the ultimatum game

4.1   Game Effect

The average amount of offers made to the other party in the dictator game was 39.6 points whereas this amount was 47.6 points for the ultimatum game (see Figure 6 for the full distribution across all conditions). The offers made in the two games are significantly different from one another (p-value= 0.00).

The main difference between dictator game and ultimatum game is that proposers do not have to deal with the possibility of having their proposals rejected and that is most likely the reason why the average offer in ultimatum game is higher than the average offer in the dictator game.

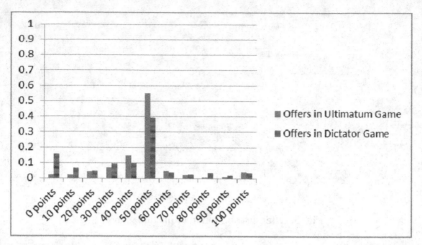

Fig. 6. Distribution of offers in dictator game and ultimatum game

In terms of the reported values there is significant difference observed between the two conditions on the following value dimensions: Vother (p value=0.00), Vcompete (p_value<0.01) , Vequal (p_value=0.00) , Vjoint (p_value<0.05) ,
V_{rawls} (p_value<0.05) , $V_{lower\ bound}$ (p_value<0.05)

4.2   Culture Effect

The average offer made by Indians was 43.85 whereas the average offer made by Americans was 43.02 points. No significant difference is observed between the offers made by participants from US and India. However we observed significant difference between the two cultures for the offers made in the ultimatum game when participants were playing with virtual humans (p value<0.05).

There is significance difference between the values reported by Indians and Americans for V_{self}(p value<0.01), $V_{compete}$ (p value=0.00), V_{chance} (p_value<0.05). In addition to the differences on the mentioned values which is consistently observed across all conditions, when participants from US and India play with virtual humans we also see difference on V_{other} dimension for the dictator game (p value=0.00) and on V_{lower} bound dimension when they are playing ultimatum game (p value<0.05). No such difference is observed when they are playing these games with another human.

4.3   Opponent Effect

Playing against a virtual human or a human does not bring about significant difference in the offers made in the games. The only condition under which significant difference among offers was observed was when Indians played the ultimatum game (p value<0.05).

However there were significant differences in the values reported V_{self} (p value= 0.00), V_{other} (p value=0.00), $V_{compete}$ (p_value<0.05), V_{rawls} (p_value=0.00), $V_{lower\ bound}$ (p_value=0.00) V_{chance} (p value<0.05).

5   Discussion

Our goal is to make culturally inspired negotiating virtual humans and in this work we set out to answer the following questions: Is it possible to use virtual humans as representative of humans? Do humans behave the same way towards virtual humans as they would with other humans in economic domains? Would the same marketing strategies hold with virtual humans? Can virtual humans be successfully applied in the e-commerce domains and online interactions?

Our result shows that people from US and India both treat virtual humans similar to how they would have treated another human. A general look over the results shows that the most prominent cause affecting the game behavior and the offer values is the type of the game being played. Our results are consistent with reported results in the literature [11]. Considering the simplicity of these games, it's not surprising that the effect of the culture or the opponent (Human/Virtual human) might not be captured in these two games. However our results showed a strong correlation between culture and the opponent in the games with the values reported by participants. These results show that the valuation functions used by people from the two countries are different and the reasons should be further investigated. We took a closer look to the application of Virtual Humans in economic domains and we conclude that virtual humans can be a reasonable substitute to humans in online economic interactions.

Our future work involves creating culture-specific decision-procedures for virtual humans based on the reported values for each culture. These models will be validated by comparing game play of virtual humans using these models to individuals from the cultures.

Acknowledgements. We would like to thank Simcoach team members Eric Forbell, Nicolai Kalisch, Kelly Christofferson, and Fabrizio Morbini for their generous help in authoring our virtual characters and completing our online experiments.

References

1. Amir, O., Rand, G.D., Kobi Gal, Y.: Economic Games on the Internet: The Effect of $1 Stakes (2012)
2. Buhrmester, M., Kwang, T., Gosling, S.: Amazons mechanical turk: a new source of inexpensive, yet high quality, data? Perspectives on Psychologcal Science 6, 3 (2011)
3. Camerer, C.F.: Behavioral game theory - Experiments in strategic interaction. Princeton University Press (2003)

4. Cameron, L.: Raising the stakes in the ultimatum game: Experimental evidence from indonesia. Economic Inquiry 37, 47–59 (1999)
5. Carpenter, J., Verhoogen, E., Burks, S.: The effect of stakes in distribution experiments. Economics Letters 86, 393–398 (2005)
6. Chesney, T., Chuah, S.-H., Hoffmann, R.: Virtual world experimentation: An exploratory study. Journal of Economic Behavior Organization 72(1), 618–635 (2009) ISSN 0167-2681, doi:10.1016/j.jebo.2009.05.026
7. de Melo, C.M., Carnevale, P., Gratch, J.: The effect of virtual agents' emotion displays and appraisals on people's decision making in negotiation. In: Nakano, Y., Neff, M., Paiva, A., Walker, M. (eds.) IVA 2012. LNCS, vol. 7502, pp. 53–66. Springer, Heidelberg (2012)
8. Forsythe, R., Horowitz, J., Savin, N., Sefton, M.: Fairness in simple bargaining experiments. Games and Economic Behavior 6, 347–369 (1994)
9. Guth, W., Schmittberger, R., Schwarze, B.: An experimental analysis of ultimatum bargaining. Journal of Economic Behavior & Organization 3(4), 367–388 (1982), http://www.sciencedirect.com/science/article/B6V8F45GSF2VH/2/a458fe2117c85c23081869d475210a09
10. Henrich, J., Boyd, R., Bowles, S., Camerer, C., Fehr, E., Gintis, H., McElreath, R., Alvard, M., Barr, A., Ensminger, J., Henrich, N.S., Hill, K., Gil-White, F., Gurven, M., Marlowe, F.W., Patton, J.Q., Tracer, D.: In cross-cultural perspective: Behavioral experiments in 15 small-scale societies. Behavioral and Brain Sciences 28(06), 795–815 (2005), http://dx.doi.org/10.1017/S0140525X05000142
11. Hoffman, E., McCabe, K., Smith, V.: On expectations and the monetary stakes in ultimatum games. International Journal of Game Theory 25, 289–301 (1996), http://dx.doi.org/10.1007/BF02425259
12. Horton, J., Rand, D., Zeckhauser, R.: The online laboratory: Conducting experiments in a real labor maker. Tehcnial report, National Bureau of Economic Research (2010)
13. Kiesler, S., Waters, K., Sproull, L.: A Prisoner's Dilemma Experiment on Cooperation with Human-Like Computers. J. Pers. Soc. Psychol. 70, 47–65 (1996)
14. Morbini, F., Forbell, E., DeVault, D., Sagae, K., Traum, D., Rizzo, A.: A Mixed-Initiative Conversational Dialogue System for Healthcare. In: Proceedings of the SIGDIAL 2012 Conference (2012)
15. Neumann, J.V., Morgenstern, O.: Theory of Games and Economic Behavior. Princeton University Press (1944)
16. Nouri, E., Traum, D.: A cultural decision-making model for virtual agents playing negotiation games. In: Proceedings of the International Workshop on Culturally Motivated Virtual Characters, Reykjavik, Iceland (2011)
17. Nouri, E., Gerogila, K., Traum, D.: A Cultural Decision-Making Model for Negotiation based on Inverse Reinforcement Learning. In: Cognitive Science 2012 (2012)
18. Rand, D.: The promise of mechanical turk: How online labor markets can help theorists run behavioral experiments. Journal of Theoretical Biology (2011)
19. Rawls, J.: Some reasons for the maximin criterion. The American Economic Review 64(2), 141–146 (1974), http://www.jstor.org/stable/1816033
20. Rigdon, M., Ishii, K., Watabe, M., Kitayama, S.: Minimal Social Cues in the Dictator Game. Journal of Economic Psychology (2009)

21. Rizzo, A., Lange, B., Buckwalter, J.G., Forbell, E., Kim, J., Sagae, K., Williams, J., Rothbaum, B., Difede, J., Reger, G., Parsons, T., Kenny, P.: An Intelligent Virtual Human System for Providing Healthcare Information and Support. Medicine Meets Virtual Reality 18, 503–509 (2011)
22. Swartout, W., Artstein, R., Forbell, E., Foutz, S., Lane, H., Lange, B., Morie, J., Noren, D., Rizzo, A., Traum, D.: Virtual Humans for Learning. AI Magazine (to appear, 2013)
23. Suri, S., Watts, D.: Cooperation and contagion in web based, networked public goods experiments. PLoS One 6, e16836 (2011)

Best Practices for Using Enterprise Gamification to Engage Employees and Customers

Marta Rauch

Oracle Communities, USA
marta.rauch@oracle.com

Abstract. Enterprise gamification is one of the major human-computer interface trends of the 21st century. Using techniques borrowed from software games, gamification can be used to drive behavior in situations outside of games. As defined by Michael Wu, gamification "uses game attributes to drive gamelike behavior in a non-game context."[1] When implemented successfully, gamification can give enterprises an edge by increasing user motivation and achievement of goals. Gamification can also help enterprises engage employees and customers, and meet business needs. Given these benefits, it is no surprise that the move to enterprise gamification is accelerating. Enterprises of all sizes and in many industries are ramping up on products, communities, and processes based on gamification principles, and enterprise gamification is growing at an impressive rate. This rapid rate of implementation brings opportunities for enterprises that can implement gamification effectively. To adapt to this trend, professionals in the field of human-computer interaction must understand best practices, and develop expertise and skills in enterprise gamification. To meet this need, this paper looks at why enterprises benefit from gamification; provides selected examples of enterprise gamification; and lists best practices for gamification projects.

1 Why Enterprises Benefit from Gamification

According to the market research firm Gartner, by 2014 over 70% of companies will have at least one gamified product, and by 2015 over 50% will gamify innovation.[2]

In addition, the market for gamification has enjoyed dramatic growth, surging from 155% in 2011 to 197% in 2012. The market research firm M2 expects the market to jump from $100M in 2011 to over $2.8B in 2016.[3] With 47% of implementations currently focused on user engagement, M2 finds that enterprise is the largest market segment, consisting of 25% of the gamification market. M2 also notes that the gamification vendors surveyed report that 47% of client implementations supported user engagement, with brand loyalty accounting for 22% and brand awareness for 15% of implementations.

By increasing employee and customer engagement and motivation, gamification can help enterprises achieve business needs such as:

M. Kurosu (Ed.): Human-Computer Interaction, Part II, HCII 2013, LNCS 8005, pp. 276–283, 2013.
© Springer-Verlag Berlin Heidelberg 2013

- Spurring innovation
- Motivating and retaining employees
- Engaging internal and external communities
- Increasing engagement, adoption, learning, and loyalty
- Increasing revenue from software trials
- Raising efficiency and quality of service
- Helping the enterprise stay competitive within the industry
- Meeting customer expectations
- Reducing time and costs
- Increasing return on investment (ROI)
- Driving profits

In addition, gamification is an effective way to engage and motivate "millennials," also known as "Gen Y." This cohort makes up 25% of the US workforce as of 2012, and their number is expected to increase to 36% in 2014 and to 46% in 2020[4]. As noted by Jane McGonigal, this generation has typically spent 10,000 hours in gaming by age 21, about the same amount of time they have spent in school[5].

This extensive experience in gaming qualifies millennials as experts, according to Malcolm Gladwell's "10,000-Hour Rule" described in *Outliers: The Story of Success*[6]. As a result of this expertise, millennials are most engaged when using game-like user interfaces. To motivate this workforce, employers must provide attractive enterprise gamification solutions for corporate innovation and internal processes[7].

2   Examples of Enterprise Gamification Best Practices

2.1   Oracle: Internal and External Gamification

The following examples highlight several enterprise gamification initiatives at Oracle. (Note: The statements and opinions expressed here are the author's own and do not necessarily represent those of Oracle Corporation.)

Gamified Forum
The Oracle Forum [https://forums.oracle.com] is a gamified community. Members are encouraged to answer questions posed on the forum, and are given points for providing helpful answers. Top contributors are recognized on a leaderboard, with achievements shown by points and badges. The result is that participants are effectively motivated to contribute to the community.

Games for Engagement
To encourage engagement with products, Oracle provides games such as Oracle Vanquisher, Oracle Storage Master, and Oracle x86 Grand Prix. Examples are shown in the following figures.

Fig. 1. Oracle Vanquisher
(https://www.facebook.com/OracleHardware/app_135555269925766)

Fig. 2. Oracle Storage Master
(https://www.facebook.com/OracleHardware/app_448435698548238)

Fig. 3. Oracle x86 Grand Prix
(https://www.facebook.com/OracleHardware/app_448435698548238?ref=ts)

Internal Gamification

To encourage understanding of gamification, the Oracle Applications User Experience team held an innovative worldwide design jam. At the Oracle Apps UX Gamification All-Hands Day, teams held a fun, gamified competition to create new types of gamified interfaces. Participants agreed that the event was a success. According to Ultan Ó Broin, it was "a great way to learn about gamification, build team spirit, and create an innovative, contemporary user experience in a very agile way."[8]

Information Sharing through Conferences and Social Networks

Oracle employees share their learning about gamification at conferences such as the Gamification Summit[9], Society for Technical Communication Summit, LavaCon, and Enterprise Gamification. To share information about gamification activities, employees use designated Twitter handles and a hashtag: @GamifyOracle and #GamifyOracle. Employees also post a gamification blog at https://blogs.oracle.com/gamification/.

Fig. 4. GamifyOracle Twitter Handle

2.2   Cisco: Gamified Curriculum

Cisco takes gamification to the next level by providing gamified training on a Games Arcade[10] available on the Cisco Learning Network. Network administrators can download learning games for a fun way to gain networking skills and prepare for professional certification.

Fig. 5. Cisco Arcade
(https://learningnetwork.cisco.com/community/connections/games)

2.3   Adobe Systems: Gamified Tutorial

LevelUp for Photoshop is a successful interactive tutorial game that engages customers with using Photoshop. It motivates new and existing users to learn about the product. Mira Dontcheva, Senior Research Scientist at Adobe Systems, summarizes the benefits of the gamified approach: "Our field deployment showed that LevelUp for Photoshop is beneficial to both novices and experts. The game made it easy for novices to get started with Photoshop, while advanced users learned more efficient workflows for familiar tasks." Petar Karafezov, Senior Manager, Digital Marketing, EMEA, at Adobe Systems, notes that "So far feedback from our customers has been positive - even people who are not entirely new to Photoshop can learn about a tool or two."[11]

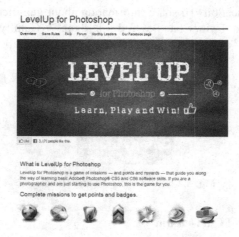

Fig. 6. Adobe LevelUp for PhotoShop
(http://success.adobe.com/microsites/levelup/index.html)

2.4   Autodesk: Gamified Tutorial

Autodesk provides a gamified tutorial within their AutoCAD product called Gami-CAD. At the ACM Symposium on User Interface Software and Technology, Wei Li, Tovi Grossman, and George Fitzmaurice of Autodesk Research reported on the effectiveness of this gamified approach. "We perform an empirical evaluation of Gami-CAD, comparing it to an equivalent inproduct tutorial system without the gamified components. In an evaluation, users using the gamified system reported higher subjective engagement levels and performed a set of testing tasks faster with a higher completion ratio."[12]

3   Best Practices for Gamification Projects

When planning gamification projects, it is critical to start by defining the business need. Throughout the project, ensure that the gamified system is designed to meet business needs.

Next, determine if associates have gamification design expertise. If inhouse gami-fication designers are not available, get input from knowledgeable experts or collabo-rate with consultants. Useful information on gamification vendors and resources is available at Gamification.co (http://www.gamification.co/). The Engagement Alliance (http://engagementalliance.org/) oversees industry certification for gamification designers.

After determining business requirements, gain an understanding of players and learn what motivates them. Designers can then plan target behaviors, and determine how gamification can be used to motivate those behaviors. Sample techniques:

- Game dynamics to motivate behavior. Examples include scenarios and rules.
- Game mechanics to help players achieve goals. Examples include teams, competi-tions, rewards, and feedback.
- Game components to track players' progress. Examples include quests, points, levels, badges, and collections.

The gamification plan should provide appropriate onboarding for novices, and then adapt to the player's journey as they gain expertise. Participants should be interested and motivated throughout all levels of the game, from beginner, to intermediate, to expert.

After the design is complete, appropriate tools can be selected, and then the system can be built. After prototypes are available, it is critical to schedule play testing, and plan for design iterations based on player feedback.

Useful guidelines for gamification design are provided in Kevin Werbach's six-step Gamification Design Framework. This framework was described in the Coursera Gamification course [13] in 2012 and in *For The Win: How Game Thinking Can Re-volutionize Your Business*.[14]

The "Six D's" of Kevin Werbach's Gamification Design Framework

1. **D**efine business objectives.
2. **D**escribe your players.
3. **D**elineate target behaviors.
4. **D**evise your activity loops.
5. **D**on't forget the fun.
6. **D**eploy the appropriate tools.

Accessibility[15] should also be addressed in enterprise gamification products. If a product is required to be accessible, ensure that gamified projects conform to the company's accessibility guidelines. Sample game accessibility considerations are shown at The AbleGamers Foundation's websites (see www.includification.com and www.ablegamers.org).

Another important consideration for enterprise gamification is localization[16]. Localizing games involves more than translation. Allow time for considerations of the target country and culture. Sample localization considerations:

- Rewards: The same reward does not appeal to all cultures
- Quests: Customize to the country and corporate culture
- Leaderboards: Being #1 is not desirable in all cultures

Because gamification is an emerging field, complete standards do not currently exist for all areas. As the industry matures, it is expected that standards and best practices will become better defined and adopted. In the meantime, best practices can be extrapolated both from gaming and from successful enterprise gamification projects.

4   Conclusion

Gamification brings exciting changes that promise to engage and motivate enterprise users. For example, Gartner predicts that, "by 2014, a gamified service for consumer goods marketing and customer retention will become as important as Facebook, eBay, or Amazon."[2]

To stay in the game, human-computer interaction specialists must prepare for 2014, when over 70% of companies will have at least one gamified product, and for 2015, when over 50% of companies will gamify innovation.[2] The leaders in this field will understand, develop, and deliver effective enterprise gamification systems that follow gamification best practices.

References

1. Wu, M.: What is Gamification, Really?, http://lithosphere.lithium.com/t5/science-of-social-blog/What-is-Gamification-Really/ba-p/30447
2. Gartner Press Release Ethan, UK (April 12, 2011), http://www.gartner.com/it/page.jsp?id=1629214
3. M2 Research Press Release, http://www.m2research.com/gamification.htm
4. UNC Kennan-Flagler Business School, Maximizing Millennials, http://www.kenan-flagler.unc.edu/news/2012/11/maximizingmillennials
5. McGonigal, J.: Reality is Broken: Why Games Make us Better and How they Can Change the World and TED talk on "Gaming" Can Make a Better World, http://blog.ted.com/2010/03/17/gaming_can_make/
6. Gladwell, M.: Outliers: The Story of Success. Little, Brown and Company (2008)
7. Rauch, M.: Gamification is Here: Build a Winning Plan, STC Intercom, Society for Technical Communication, pp. 7–12 (December 2012), http://intercom.stc.org/wp-content/uploads/2012/12/IntercomNovDec_WebForm.pdf and accompanying presentation: http://www.slideshare.net/MartaRauch/gamification-is-here-build-a-winning-plan
8. Oracle Apps Gamification Worldwide UX Design Jam, https://blogs.oracle.com/userassistance/entry/oracle_applications_gamification_worldwide_ux

9. Making Work Engaging at Oracle, http://www.gsummit.com/session/enterprise-user-experience-making-work-engaging-at-oracle/
10. Cisco Games Arcade, https://learningnetwork.cisco.com/community/connections/games
11. Karafezov, P.: Learning can be fun and rewarding – learn with LevelUp for Photoshop, http://www.karafezov.com/1/post/2011/11/learning-can-be-fun-and-rewarding-learn-with-levelup-for-photoshop.html
12. Li, W., Grossman, T., Fitzmaurice, G.: GamiCAD: A Gamified Tutorial System for First Time AutoCAD Users. In: UIST 2012 Conference Proceedings: ACM Symposium on User Interface Software & Technology, pp. 103–112 (2012)
13. Werbach, K.: "Gamification" course taught through Courser and the Wharton School in 2012, https://www.coursera.org/course/gamification
14. Werbach, K., Hunter, D.: For the Win: How Game Thinking Can Revolutionize Your Business, http://wdp.wharton.upenn.edu/books/for-the-win/
15. Accessibility, http://www.gameaccessibilityguidelines.com/guidelines/full-list/
16. Chandler, H.M.: Stephanie O'Malley Deming, The Game Localization Handbook. Jones & Bartlett Learning (June 5, 2011)

Gamifying Support

Anthony Chad Sampanes

Oracle Corp. USA, Redwood Shores, CA, USA
chad.sampanes@oracle.com

Abstract. When applied with care and consideration, gamification can have significant positive effects on support. Utilizing gamification elements, such an leaderboards, levels, badges, and rewards, within a community can help engage customers and encourage them to generate support content. This allows them to self-serve and more quickly resolve their issues. Internal support engineers can also be motivated when exposed to a point system with appropriate challenges, levels, and rewards. The result can increase overall job satisfaction, increase engineer positivity, and lead to better customer service.

Keywords: Gamification; Support; Enterprise; Ticketing systems; Customer help; Leaderboards; Badging; Rewards; Motivation; Self-Help; Self-service; Community.

1 Introduction

Talk of gamification seems everywhere and the numbers suggest that its popularity will only continue to flourish [1,2]. Many companies are experiencing great success as they implement gamification principles within their products [1]. Gartner has predicted [3] that "by 2015, more than 50 percent of organizations that manage innovation processes will gamify those processes" and "by 2014, a gamified service for consumer goods marketing and customer retention will become as important as Facebook, eBay or Amazon, and more than 70 percent of Global 2000 organizations will have at least one gamified application." Riding this wave of interest, and market and development movement, the present paper aims to discuss ways we can gamify enterprise support.

To understand concepts and terminology discussed later this paper, we must first define some items related to gamification. Gamification is the use of game elements design mechanics in non-game contexts [4,5]. Common aspects of gamification [4] are:

- Creating interest and fun
- Challenges, missions, and competitions
- Reputation
- Rewards
- Community and social connections

M. Kurosu (Ed.): Human-Computer Interaction, Part II, HCII 2013, LNCS 8005, pp. 284–291, 2013.

Common gamification terms:

- Points serve as encouragement and keep score. Points serve as feedback and track progression [4,6].
- Leaderboards allow people to track and visually monitor their progress relative to others [7].
- Levels are "rewarded increasing in value for the accumulation of points." Statuses are rank or level of an individual. [7]
- Badges are "visual representations of some achievement within the gamified process [4]."

2   Gamifying Customer Actions

Enterprise customers contacting support are commonly database administrators or system administrators in our industry. They are college educated and technical. In some circumstances customers know nearly as much (technically and in product knowledge) as support engineers. Furthermore, they collectively hold the knowledge about how their products are being used and any customization. Details about extensive customization are rarely communicated back to the support company. Customers with questions or issues could often learn from other customers (because they've experienced the same problem). The majority of issues within service requests have been logged previously by other customers.

How do you get customers to help each other in order to allow them to collaborate in a timely and effective manner without having to wait for "formal" help? It requires customers to do two things: 1) answer questions and offer advice to other customers experiencing difficulties. 2) author articles to help prevent other customers, so these answer can help other avoid creating formal request for service. Database administrators and system administrators are extremely busy and work in a demanding environment. They most commonly don't have the time and/or motivation to do these things. But they also don't like waiting for answers, especially, because of their expertise have that feeling that someone already knows the answer.

Communities are commonplace and becoming perhaps the most prevalent way companies attempt to facilitate customers helping customers. Communities allow customers to ask questions and have the customer community respond and help resolve their issues. This often leads to interesting discussions and examples. It may also spawn related questions and answers. With a quick sampling of the support space you can find communities that allow forums to be moderated by an expert customer and even some that allow customers to author articles on particular topics. But as you might expect, the quality can be of an "uncertain" nature.

Theoretically, this would be an easy way to engage with customers and to help offload service request handling. In practice, you will find some communities in a state of voyeuristic comatose. Customers often go to communities to read questions and responses to common issues or post their own question in hopes that somebody can help them out. Very few customers take the time to respond to questions raised by other customers. [8] Most do so with a brief response; participation drops dramatically if a response requires more. It's understandable given that customers don't work for the companies that host these support communities. It's not a core job requirement and there is nearly no incentive for them to spend time and effort helping others out. Interviews with intrinsically active community members (i.e., altruistic gurus) suggests that even these members often find responding time consuming and draining, deterring them from their job priorities. Given the voyeuristic nature of communities and job pressures and demands, how do we encourage customers to participate actively in communities?

Providing points to customers for each way they participate in the community (posting questions, responding to questions, moderating communities, authoring articles, rating other customer responses, verifying solutions, etc.) is a good place to start. These points should be weighted, such that simple tasks (like asking a question) get you fewer points than a more meaningful and effortful posting (such as posting a validated response to a question). [4] Companies need to be careful, otherwise they might encourage customers to post a bunch of uninteresting questions or rate a bunch of responses (without reading them thoroughly). Points may accumulate over time as the validity and effectiveness of the post is verified. For instance, if Customer A posts a question, they might get one point for posting the question, but if the rest of the community rates the question as a good and useful question, then Customer A gets five for the posting of the questions. Additional customers who mark this post as useful or "solved my problem" continue to accumulate points for the poster. The same principle should be carried through into responses as well; if a customer posts a response or solution they get some points, but not nearly as many points as they would get if the community rated the response or solution highly. The key is to give appropriate weighting for the behaviors your company wants to reinforce and make it proportional to effort and usefulness.

The points should be associated with levels. Those levels should be significantly challenging to get to. If the levels are too easy, it won't keep people engaged, but if they're too hard then people will get discouraged [4]. Typically gaming theory would have levels become more difficult to achieve as your investment in the game grows. The reinforcement of levels goes quickly early on (like reinforcing a new hire with praise), but starts to slows over time as one becomes a master. Challenges to get to the next level get harder, requiring more "value" to be provided, like uncovering new secrets. The same applies to technology challenges that a customer might overcome to provided sophisticated answers to complex problems. Sometimes you can get people engaged by making the first couple levels easy and then increasing the difficulty to make an equal incremental movement.[9] The individual's point total and associated status should be prominently displayed at all times. The community should also have a leader board displayed ubiquitously, which posts the top contributors of all time and top contributors for a smaller increment of time (e.g., daily, weekly, or monthly).[4] The hardest part is figuring out the point levels for each level. I suggest first piloting with a small group of customers or in a few verticals to test out your point system. It will likely need some adjustment prior to exposing to the whole customer base. It should be noted that this is not simply set up and go. Ongoing care and maintenance must be applied to monitor, tune, and validate the effective use of the system. Each level should be associated with a proper name and reward.[7] Sometimes the name is significantly rewarding enough. For example, to be called an Oracle Guru could carry some clout and therefore motivate people to participate in the community to get the title alone. For other people, a title won't be enough and you'll have to reward them with an additional element. Providing the ability for customer to badge external sites with their newfound "status" can enhance the value of the level. That is, provide an image or badge that can be added to Facebook, LinkedIn, or a résumé.

Rewards can be difficult. First, companies face monetary restrictions in compensating customers. Oracle, for example, can only give gifts to customers that have value of less than $10. This is hardly motivating to database administrators and system administrators making a professional salary. More importantly you need to know what actually motivates customers. If you don't know what motivates your customers, you won't be able to appropriately reward and reinforce desired behaviors. Our research with technical enterprise customers indicates that they want rewards that they can leverage to get further in their career and increase their salary. Customers indicated that they wanted something they could put on their resume, like a certification or special Oracle status. They also indicated that receiving free Oracle University classes or books would be motivating.

Gamification can have huge impact: generating support useful articles and documents, reducing service request creation, and reducing business costs. However, in order for this to happen, customers have to learn to trust the sources and be able to feed back results to further vet and verify the sources. If they don't use and value the content that other customers create, it all falls flat. It's important to note this because some customers have indicated that they won't accept just any solution or advice from another customer, particularly when issues involve complex problems. If they trusted and implemented an unvetted solution they might experience even more serious issues. These issues could end up costing their company millions of dollars. Customers want vetted solutions. They want a trusted Oracle support engineer to read through the suggestions and indicate which ones are Oracle recommended and which ones are not. If they had this validation from Oracle, then they could feel safe to trust the solution and implement a fix. If not, they might read it, but would rarely ever try it out (unless they were extremely desperate or in an extremely controlled and contained environment).

Simple knowledge games/quizzes might be used to educate customers and generate knowledge. For instance, a knowledge trivia game could be used to have customers type a short answer to generate knowledge material (like, "provide your best trick to increase performance"). An enterprise company could then collect this and generates support documents (like tips and tricks or FAQs). The game would tie correct responses, or responses seen by others in a forum and rated as valuable, to rewards (such as bonus points). It is tricky to balance points, interactivity, and customer value/effort.

It's easy to recognize how gamifying customer actions benefits a company offering support. It helps generate support material, it can help reduce service request creation, and it can help reduce costs to the business. However, it should also be recognized that the benefits extend to the company's customers as well. Customers can self-serve by quickly finding a greater number of solutions to their issues. Well regarded and rated solutions go the top of search results, like well rated products at a shopping site. Self-service offers the most expeditious and desirable means of resolving issues according to customers; many customers indicate that creating a service request is their "last resort". Furthermore, customers have greater access to customization information; customization spawns many customers' questions and issues and can be very difficult (for a company offering support) to acquire information about.

3   Gamifying Support Engineer Actions

Gamifying customer actions is important because many companies have large customer bases. Over the totality of the customer base, actions accumulate quickly for customers whose job it is to interact with a company for support on a regular basis. This is not typical of a consumer product, where you might never raise a support question for your phone, toaster, or speakers. But with sophisticated enterprise software working with a product vendor is standard practice. Gamification can also improve internal support processes even though the number of internal support engineers can be 100 to 1,000 times less than the number of customers. This is for two primary reasons: First, a single support engineer repeats actions more frequently over the course of the day than a customer. The frequency of these behaviors multiplied by the number of support engineers is often equitable to the frequency of customer behavior multiplied by the larger number of customers. Second, engineers are involved with more steps in the support process and at nearly every step have more control and influence over the process than customers do. Organizations with as few as 10 or as many as 10,000 representatives can benefit from gamification.

The first area to implement gamification principles into the internal support processes should be training. Just as you can use gaming principals and techniques to help educate customers, you can use those same methods to train support engineers (particularly technical support engineers, who require deeper understanding and experience than first level support engineers). Training of support engineers is often long, arduous, and most often a very isolating experience. They spend a lot of time familiarizing themselves with the product(s) and various types of environments, reading through collections of issues, and learning the support processes and methodologies. Simple games (such as the knowledge games mentioned above, games involving mock customer issues/scenarios, or training missions, quests, or challenges) along with testing and levels can help keep engineers engaged during training, help track their progress, and motivate them to do well. Training and testing engineers is not at the first start of a job, it can be continue through an engineer's tenure with a company; as new products and processes emerge.

The job of a support engineer is challenging. Issues tend to get repeated across different customers. The larger and more complex the products, the more likely engineers have specialties. Even unfamiliar issues have a ring of familiarity. Secondly, most support organizations have a specific process they want their engineers to follow, especially during the first steps in resolving a service request. They discourage and often reprimand engineers for deviation from that process. These support processes are followed with little variance on every service request. There are typically set steps that an engineer takes to clarify, validate, research, and resolve customer issues. The monotony of a support engineer's job often causes engineers to lose interest in their job and cut corners. Gamification can help to both reward complex tasks and encourage the following of rote processes that have little intrinsic reward for their completion.

Customers contact support because something isn't working properly. The very nature of that means support engineers deal with customer complaints. Some customers can be especially harsh and unkind when contacting support; support engineers take the brunt of that negativity. Furthermore, if the issue is critical, the support engineer must bear a certain level of stress as they attempt to resolve the issue quickly. Support organizations are always concerned about customer satisfaction; consequently, support engineers are instructed to remain calm and positive, regardless of the issue and/or how the customer treats them. The stress of dealing with customer complaints, while simultaneously being pressured to resolve as many service requests as possible, can lead to engineers burning out. How customers respond to survey's about the quality of their interaction, tied with the criticality of the issue (as a unbiased gauge of stress) could provide another source of points for the engineer. The feedback loop for them seeing the points accumulated from "tough" calls and how this is tracked and shared with the organization can help keep the engineer focused on the solution while working to keep their composure in stressful times. Other metrics, based on analytics within a call or support center can also drive points, badges, and esteem as we will discuss in a moment.

If done correctly, gamification can keep support engineers engaged in their work, increase job satisfaction, increase engineers' positivity (and consequently customer satisfaction), and improve their overall work experience. Having a point system, with goals and/or levels that the engineers work toward keeps them engaged and deters from the repetition and boredom in what they do. Working to overcome harder challenges and to attain higher levels brings novelty into their work environment (where there otherwise wasn't). These same point systems and levels/statuses attained by the support engineer also serve to reward them. As mentioned before, the nature of support makes it a complaint-based business. Customer can often be quite negative and irritated. Gamification can provide support engineers rewards and help them to feel positively about their job.

Support organizations track certain metrics very closely to evaluate how their support organization overall and their support personnel are performing. Time to resolve a service request, number of service requests closed, and customer satisfaction are key measures. During performance reviews how well a support engineer or support group is doing on these dimensions is commonly discussed. This sets up extremely well for gamifying support. Leaderboards placed in the internal support application(s) can help support personnel keep track of their numbers. These numbers can be shown over time, and in comparison to other engineers in their group or top-rated engineers. This can be very motivating, because individuals at the top work hard to stay there and individuals at the bottom work hard to get out of the basement. Where engineers rank on these scales can also be connected to levels, status, and badges. Individuals can take great pride in where their position on the scale. Furthermore, it's very easy to connect these ratings to rewards, such as bonuses, raises, promotions, PTO, and preferential choice in what they work on.

Much like we discussed earlier about customers creating support articles, it's even more critical that internal engineers create support documentation. Sometimes this gets deprioritized relative to service request handling, making it difficult for engineers to write new articles when they're dealing with high volumes of cases. If support organizations want to encourage the creation of more valuable support artifacts they can implement some gamification principles, like those we discussed above: points for useful articles generated, as measured by the customers' ratings of that particular document. More detail can be found above in the discussion of customers' participation in communities. It would work nearly identically for internal engineers, except that they would be generating more polished, detailed, and vetted documents.

4   Gamifying Support – Potential for Making It Worse

The bulk of this paper reviewed the opportunities to gamify support, gamification doesn't come without some risk to a support organization. Gamers quickly learn how to game the game.[4] Likewise, engineers will quickly learn what produces points and how to most efficiently collect them (particularly if they're motivated by the reward system). This means both customers and engineers will adapt their behaviors accordingly. These could be desired support behaviors or they could be undesired artifacts of how the gamification system was set up. Constant attention and tuning must be given to the system to ensure desired effects. It's critical that you don't reward people for pointless actions. It will decrease intrinsic motivation and increase meaningless behaviors.[10] Gamifying support could result in dehumanifying customers. Be careful that support engineers don't get so caught up in the "game" that they forget that customers are individuals whose feelings and thoughts must be considered throughout the process. Finally, don't let the games interfere with core business tasks. The job still needs to be every bit as efficient and effective as it ever was. Gamification is meant to enhance that, not get in its way.

5   Conclusion

When applied with care and consideration, gamification can have significant positive effects on support. Utilizing gamification elements, such as leaderboards, levels, badging, and rewards, within a community can help engage customers and encourage them to generate support content. This allows them to self-serve and more quickly resolve their issues. Internal support engineers can also be motivated when exposed to a point system with appropriate challenges, levels, and rewards. The result can increase overall job satisfaction, increase engineer positivity, and lead to better customer service.

References

1. Gamification Facts & Figures (October 2011),
   http://enterprise-gamification.com/index.php/en/facts
2. Meloni, W.: Gamification in 2012 Trends in Consumer and Enterprise Markets. Presented, Gamification Summit, San Francisco (2012)
3. Gartner Says By 2015, More Than 50 Percent of Organizations That Manage Innovation Processes Will Gamify Those Processes (2011),
   http://www.gartner.com/newsroom/id/1629214
4. Webach, K., Hunter, D.: For the Win: How Game Thinking Can Revolutionize Your Business. Wharton, Pennsylvania (2012)
5. Huotari, K., Hamari, J.: Defining Gamification – A Service Marketing Perspective. In: Proceedings of the 16th International Academic MindTrek Conference, Tampere, Finland (2012)
6. The Principles of Gamification (April 2012),
   http://playgen.com/the-principles-of-gamification/
7. Gamification Wiki (2012), http://www.gamification.org/
8. Noff, A.: Why People Participate in Online Communities (2008),
   http://thenextweb.com/2008/05/24/
   why-people-participate-in-online-communities/
9. Papayoanou, P.: Game Theory for Business; A Primer in Strategic Gaming. Probabilistic Publishing, Texas (2010)
10. Paharia, R.: Gamification Can Work – Just Don't Hire A Designer. Techcrunch (2013),
    http://techcrunch.com/2012/12/08/
    bad-gamification-design-leads-to-failure/

The Motivational GPS: Would a Rat Press a Lever to Get a Badge?

Kes Sampanthar

Cynergy, USA
kes.sampanthar@Cynergy.com

Abstract. Gamification is a new industry that has blossomed around technologies that incorporate Motivational Design. This is a game design method based on creating truly engaging software that incites player motivations. There has been a lot of new research into motivation over the last decade, but to understand what we have learned about motivation we need to come back to the question about the rat and the badge, which is drawn from Skinner's classic experiment. More recent research shows that 'Wanting' is at the heart of what is considered motivation and approach behavior, while 'Liking' is the feeling of euphoria that is experienced when a challenge is overcome. Based on this research, we describe an application of The Motivational GPS framework which uses the metaphor of maps and directions related to 'Wanting' and 'Liking' to help create design artifacts that can be used to create engaging software.

Keywords: Interaction design, Human Motivation, Gamification, Game Design.

1 Introduction

Would a rat press a lever to get a badge seems like a strange question, but the answer is at the heart of designing engaging or motivational software — Motivational Design. Game designers have been creating engaging experiences for decades by drawing from such diverse fields as psychology, economics and sociology. To create engagement in other applications (ecommerce, sales, training) software designers have been using some of the same techniques from games. A new industry has blossomed around these techniques called Gamification.

The first generation of Gamification takes the visible aspects of game design — badges, leader-boards and trophies — and adds them as scaffolding to business applications. Examples include adding leader-boards to sales software and using badges for a TV show's online community. Most of the time these motivational elements are loosely coupled to the actual experience, you could remove the badges without changing the experience. This is unlike games where the experience and motivational elements are intertwined and can't be removed without affecting each other.

To create truly engaging software we need to start where game designers do by understanding player motivations. There is obviously a lot more to human motivation

M. Kurosu (Ed.): Human-Computer Interaction, Part II, HCII 2013, LNCS 8005, pp. 292–298, 2013.

than just games. As varied as games are, they mostly tap into a handful of motivations. You just need to look at all the things people do that we don't need to or have to do: fishing, quilting circles, reading, exploring, stamp collecting, puzzles, etc. This is just scratching the surface of human activity, but you start to get a glimpse at the range of motivations that drive us.

There has been a lot of new research into motivation over the last decade expanding past the work in psychology and cognitive science and moving to some of the latest breakthroughs in neuroscience, evolutionary psychology, paleoanthropology and behavioral economics. To understand what we have learned about motivation we need to come back to the question about the rat and the badge.

2   Skinner's Rats

In the classic Skinner's experiment [1] when a rat is trained to press a lever to get food it's not really the food that is rewarding, it's the neurochemicals that are triggered in the brain that are rewarding. Food is considered a unconditioned stimulant (US) in the behavioral community, which basically means a rat's brain is innately primed (or hardwired) to trigger the release of a pleasurable neurochemical when it encounters it. The triggering of the pleasurable neurochemical has been called 'Liking' [2]in order to differentiate it from the other aspect of pleasure which is called 'Wanting'.

'Wanting' is at the heart of what is considered motivation and approach behavior or more specifically the desire to 'move towards' an object that is triggered when the brain anticipates a pleasurable experience. 'Wanting' is pleasurable, but in a slightly different way than the actual 'reward' or 'Liking' response. The difference between 'Liking' and 'Wanting' is best illustrated through games. 'Wanting' is best characterized by an intensity and focus when a player is in the middle of solving a complex challenge, i.e. fighting a boss in a typical first person shooter (FPS) game. 'Liking' is the feeling of euphoria that is experienced when the challenge is overcome, i.e. defeating the boss. 'Liking' and 'Wanting' stimulate the release of different neurochemicals that fire from different emotional circuits. It is important to understand how 'Liking' and 'Wanting' work together.

3   Anticipation

In some important experiments conducted by Wolfram Schultz and his team at the University of Cambridge, monkeys were trained to watch for some visual cues that preceded a squirt of sweet syrup [3][4],[5]. The activity in a key area of the brain - Ventral Tegmental Area (VTA) was being recorded while the experiment was being conducted. The VTA is considered to be the heart of the 'Wanting' circuit and driven by dopamine neurons. The dopamine that fires in the VTA causes the mild pleasurable feeling that is called 'engagement' which arises from solving a complex challenge in a game. In the diagram (figure 1) you can see the activity of the dopamine neurons in response to the visual cues and squirts of syrup.

The first time a 'green light' is flashed 2 seconds prior to a squirt of syrup (figure 1 - row 2). The dopamine neurons fire at the time the syrup is given. The trials are repeated — 'green light', 2 second delay and then the squirt of syrup. As you can see after the trials, the dopamine neurons spike when the green light flashes (figure 1 – row 3). This is why it is considered 'anticipation'. The dopamine neurons are firing in anticipation of a reward (the squirt of syrup).

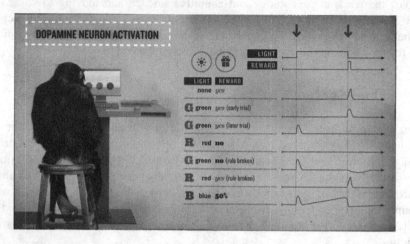

Fig. 1. Dopamine Neuron Activation: NOTE: Colored lights are denoted here, but the actual experiments were conducted using different visual patterns

You can also see in this diagram what happens when the 'Green Light - Syrup' rule is broken and no syrup is given. This time the dopamine neurons fire with the green light, but there is now a dip in dopamine at the point that the syrup was supposed to be delivered (after 2 seconds) (figure 1 - row 5). A drop in dopamine in the VTA is associated with an unpleasant feeling.

This mechanism is used to learn about our environments and the cues that lead to pleasurable outcomes. There are two main parts to this learning mechanism – the map and the compass.

3.1   Motivational Maps

When you stumble across a pleasurable experience the brain starts paying attention to any preceding cues. There could also be more than one cue in the sequence. For instance, in the previously described experiment involving monkeys a prior cue could be added to the procedure. For example, a bell could sound prior to the light and only then would the lever be enabled and the food delivered. In this chain of cues the dopamine would fire at the very first cue - the bell, then anticipation and the path to pleasure would begin. In a real life example of visiting your favorite restaurant, the initial cues could be the visual aesthetic of the building, the smell of cooking food as you walk in, the color and lighting of the dining room, and the sounds emanating from the kitchen. All these cues precede and line the path to the pleasure of eating your favorite foods.

For this mapping system to work there needs to be a way of updating the map based upon changing circumstances. In the aforementioned experiment, dopamine doesn't just fire with the light in anticipation of the syrup, but there is a checking mechanism that pays attention and corrects itself if the expectation isn't met (figure 1 - row 5). If the rule is broken, i.e. the syrup didn't come as expected then the drop in dopamine is used to adjust the rule. This is a fairly sophisticated learning mechanism. As long as the expectation is met the dopamine keeps anticipating the syrup (reward) by firing with the light, but if the prediction is no longer valid; something has changed in the world; then the system will course-correct.

This ability to map out pleasure has been compared to the children's game 'You're Getting Warmer' [6] In the game a toy is hidden in the room by an adult and a child is blind-folded and given clues to whether they are getting 'warmer' or 'colder' based upon the direction they are walking in. 'Warmer' if they move in the direction of the toy and 'colder' if they are moving away from it. Through a series of steps and feed-back from the adult (warmer, warmer, colder, cold, warmer), the child adjusts their direction to get closer to the toy. The warmer and colder feedback could be used to create a heat-map of the room to locate the toy. Our brain through a series of dopa-mine spikes and dips guides our path towards pleasure and away from pain similar to the 'You're Getting Warmer' game.

The brain uses motivational-maps created through past experiences to guide us through new experiences. Sometimes we are returning to a known source of pleasure such as our favorite restaurant and the dopamine feedback is directly related to the orig-inal cues. Other times the same 'map' is fired by a familiar cue, but this time for a new restaurant in a new location. In this case, your brain is reusing the map based upon some similar cues and starts anticipating pleasure even though you have never visited this restaurant before. This is where the true sophistication of the system plays out.

The real world is fairly complex and throughout our lives we have developed mul-tiple maps with multiple overlapping cues. Our brains are constantly juggling these competing maps and choosing the most appropriate maps for various situations. Since we don't live in a static world these maps are updated and remapped as we encounter new experiences. Some of these maps also get hard-wired over time and become ha-bits and are hard to change, while others are rewritten constantly due to ever-changing circumstances.

3.2   Motivational Compass

The creation of these motivational maps is triggered by a number of innate pleasures. We are all born with a set of core, innate motivations that our brains instinctively associate with unique pleasurable feelings.

There are a number of different theories surrounding these core motivations; the most famous being Maslow's 'Hierarchy of Needs' [1]. One of the most comprehen-sive and up-to-date theories in the social and biological sciences is called the 'Four Drive Theory' [7]. The four drives are described as:

— D1 - The Drive to Acquire — This is a socially competitive drive that is all about status.
— D2 - The Drive to Bond — This is the other side of our social motivations, the drive to bond.
— D3 - The Drive to Learn — This is our drive learn, master and understand our world.
— D4 - The Drive to Defend — This is the drive to survive, driven by fear and is probably one of the oldest.

Each of these drives has very unique neuro-chemical signatures with many overlapping physiological changes. These physiological changes have been categorized by emotion researchers.

Emotions elicit mapping in a manner that is similar to how food and the resulting pleasure response in our brains allow us to map the cues that precede it. More specifically, the four drives allow us to map the cues that consistently lead to the associated emotions. For instance, the cues that precede 'affection' map the path to pleasurable experiences triggered by the 'Drive to Bond'.

The way these motivational drives guide our behavior have been likened to a compass of pleasure [5]. We are all driven by slightly different motivations. Throughout our lives we have all stumbled upon different pleasurable experiences associated with the different motivational drives.

3.3 Motivational GPS

As rich as the world is there are many pleasurable experiences that are poorly mapped due to a lack of consistent and engaging cues. Throughout history we have designed and augmented many natural cues e.g. marketing. Similarly, digital technology allows us to make great strides in creating engaging experiences since it can generate unique, visceral and consistent cues that can be mapped to specific motivations for an individual. Through design we can move from the rudimentary compass and crude mental-maps we have to a more advanced 'Motivational GPS'. Cues can be designed to create turn-by-turn directions that speak directly to motivational systems.

3.4 The Motivational GPS Framework

The Motivational GPS framework uses the metaphor of the maps and directions to help create design artifacts that can be used to create engaging software.

- **Destinations:** These are the motivational goals that engage the software users. They are drawn from the Four-Drive Theory and are augmented through other motivational research: **Socially Cooperation** (Empathy, Reciprocation, Trust/ Reputation, Fairness), **Socially Competitive** (Competition, Status, Autonomy), **Learning** (Mastery, Curiosity, Exploration).

- **Directions:** These are the common cues that can be used to provide markers on the motivational maps. There are three main types of directions: **Action** Directions, **Feedback** Directions, **Progress** Directions.

4   Example – Retail Sales

In a recent project we designed an application for sales reps working in a retail store. The main focus of the application was to design an engaging system to provide feedback on how they were performing. The company used a number of different metrics to track how these reps were performing and the application needed to find a way of tapping into the rep's motivations to help improve these metrics.

As part of our research we investigated their motivational styles to determine the right motivations to focus on. We discovered that a high percentage of the sales reps were focused on customer satisfaction — matching the right product to the right customers 'Empathy'. The other key motivational factor was 'Mastery' and their drive for personal improvement.

We used the 'Motivational GPS Framework' to help us with the design of the 'Mastery' map.

5   Destination: Mastery

The main goal for 'Mastery' was a Monthly Key Performance Indicator (KPI) goal. We broke that goal into daily KPI goals and then we mapped the different cues (directions) to 'Mastery' destination (Figure 2). These Motivational Maps were used to guide the following design: on a daily basis, the sales reps could see how they were doing for that particular day; i.e. whether they had reached or exceeded their daily goal or how much more they needed to sell to reach their goal (Figure 3).

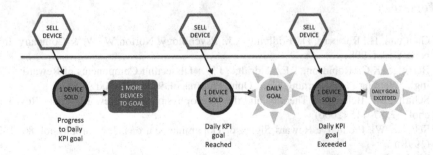

Fig. 2. Map showing the different cues (directions) to 'Mastery' destination

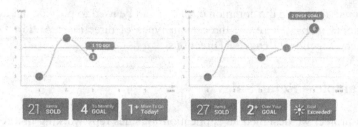

Fig. 3. Charts showing examples of how sales reps could see how much they were selling for that particular day

Similar to Schultz's monkeys we are providing cues that show how the sales reps are progressing on a daily basis to their ultimate goal which is mapped to one of their key motivations - Mastery. The Monthly KPI goal is a strong cue that will get translated in the brain to pleasure (Liking). Each of the daily breakdowns are intermediate cues that show how the sales rep is progressing. Furthermore, through this design we have developed strong visual cues that act as signposts along the way. Based on this design, the 'Wanting' circuit will fire dopamine giving the 'warmer', 'warmer' signal as they get closer to their Monthly KPI goals.

6   Motivational Design Summary

The next generation of 'Gamification' is going beyond using game mechanics as scaffolding to designing engagement and weaving this factor right into the experience and functionality of the software. The Motivational GPS Framework is one tool that allows us to understand the motivations of the users and map out unique engaging experiences while designing compelling applications.

References

1. Gleitman, H., Reisberg, D., Fridlund, A.J.: Psychology. Norton W. W. & Company, Inc., New York (1998)
2. Berridge, K.C., Robinson, T.E., Aldridge, J.W.: Dissecting Components of Reward: 'Liking', 'Wanting', and Learning. Curr. Opin. Pharmacol. 9, 65–73 (2009)
3. Schultz, W.: Behavioral Theories and the Neurophysiology of Reward. Annu. Rev. Psychol. 57, 87–115 (2006)
4. Schultz, W.: Predictive Reward Signal of Dopamine Neurons. J. Neurophysiol. 80, 1–27 (1998)
5. Linden, D.J.: The Compass of Pleasure: How Our Brains Make Fatty Foods, Orgasm, Exercise, Marijuana, Generosity, Vodka, Learning, and Gambling Feel So Good. Penguin Books, New York (2011)
6. Montague, R.: Why Choose This Book?: How We Make Decisions. Dutton Adult, New York (2006)
7. Lawrence, P.R., Nohria, N.: Driven: How Human Nature Shapes Our Choices. Jossey-Bass, New Jersey (2001)

Designing Serious Videogames through Concept Maps

Jaime Sánchez and Matías Espinoza

Department of Computer Science,
Center for Advanced Research in Education (CARE),
University of Chile, Blanco Encalada 2120, Santiago, Chile
{jsanchez,maespino}@dcc.uchile.cl

Abstract. The purpose of this study was to present and evaluate a new technique through the use of concept maps for the design of serious videogames using Ejemovil Editor. This was accomplished by using a method to easily transform concept maps into directed graphs, which are then used to generate the videogame sequence and the interdependencies between the various elements. With this tool teachers are able to define the storyline of the videogame, incorporating the concepts that they want to teach in a structured way. To these ends, an editor was created using this methodology that allows for the construction of mobile videogames. Teachers that currently use concept maps have evaluated the proposed methodology. Preliminary results show that the proposed methodology for the design and creation of serious videogames for education is appropriate, easy to use, generally accepted and understandable for the end users.

Keywords: Concept Maps, Serious Videogames, Videogames Editor, Videogames Design.

1 Introduction

In the last decades, two technologies have entered the classroom in support of learning. The first are concept maps, which were created by Novak in 1972 and which are used to support meaningful learning [5]. The second technology is the videogame industry, which paradoxically began with Pong in the same year, and which has evolved to become a billion dollar industry [10].

Currently, the development of educational, mobile videogames is limited to the category of trivia games [8]. Several experiences [8][9] have used such devices to take advantage of their potential for using specific messaging services. Mobile Author [15] is an application that aids teachers in creating and maintaining their educational resources on a virtual platform. Some experiences with this application have developed RPG videogame editors, such as RPGMaker [11], which is designed for amateur users. Although this editor provides a great deal of freedom regarding the ability to create videogames, it is not oriented towards the development of videogames in an educational context.

M. Kurosu (Ed.): Human-Computer Interaction, Part II, HCII 2013, LNCS 8005, pp. 299–308, 2013.

There are also several experiences based on the use of concept maps as pedagogical instruments that have demonstrated effective results in primary education [1][4][6]. A tool called Concept Gaming [0] can generate concept maps made by a teacher or a learner. Then the students can interact with the concept map in five different game modes by adding concepts or relationships. In this case the result is not a videogame, because the students are directly interacting with a concept map.

Wu et al. (2012) presented a teaching strategy that involved the use of concept maps for the design of videogames [16]. There are also methodologies based on concept maps that facilitate the creation of videogames [2][14]. Bellotti et al. (2013) proposed a serious game model related to cultural heritage, using an approach very similar to the mind-maps concept [2]. Treanor et al. (2012) presented a methodology involving a videogame authoring tool based on concept maps called Game-O-Matic, which generates games to represent ideas [14].

The purpose of this study was to present and evaluate a new technique through the use of concept maps that allows teachers to integrate concept mapping and mobile videogame technologies, enabling them to create serious videogames with content organized by using the Ejemovil videogame Editor [12]. In this case, the students interact with a mobile RPG videogame generated from a concept map.

2   Ejemovil Videogame Editor

Ejemovil Editor was previously developed [12] with the capacity to generate structures similar to concept maps, in order to design and create mobile serious videogames. The idea is to provide teachers with an easy-to-use tool that allows them to create videogames based on the concept mapping technique. Such games can then be provided to students of primary education, who can use them for learning.

The editor generates RPG style videogames, in which the player controls a character that interacts with other virtual players (see Figure 1). In these interactions, the player is presented with a series of questions that have three alternative answers, in which there is only one correct answer. In addition, the questions are progressively unlocked by other associated, dependent questions; in other words, the players must answer certain questions correctly before being able to unlock the questions associated with other virtual characters.

The questions are related to a specific topic, which in the videogame are represented by an icon and a bar that indicates the player's progressive score. Each videogame has a maximum of three topics upon which the questions are based. The maximum score per topic is 100. The maximum score per questions is equivalent to 100 divided by the number of questions associated with that particular topic. The maximum score is assigned when the player responds correctly to a question on the first try, without having made mistakes previously on the same question. When the player responds correctly on the second try, half of the maximum assigned for the question is awarded. Finally, when the player responds correctly after two or more tries, one quarter of the maximum score for that question is awarded.

Fig. 1. Videogame screenshot

2.1   Editor Sections

The editor has seven main sections for the creation of a videogame: Introduction, concept definition, diagnostic evaluation, selection of main characters, script definition, game over, and the export for download to the mobile device.

The Script Definition section is the main section of the editor (see Fig. 2). It allows the teacher to create a graph based on a concept map, and to provide each node with a position over the game map. It also allows the user to define the characters that will represent each of the concepts in the game, and to configure their particular properties and characteristics. This section includes the following main elements: (i) Start Node corresponds to the most inclusive concept on the concept map, which implies the most general concept. It is the starting point for the videogame. (ii) Node corresponds to any concept on the concept map, besides the most inclusive (start node). Teachers add nodes to the videogame, and these nodes have various associated properties (name, welcome text, question, answer choices, etc.). There can be two different kinds of nodes. A multiple-choice question node presents the player with a question and three possible answer choices. On the other hand, an item question node presents the player with a question that asks him to find one of three items that are dispersed throughout the map. (iii) End Node is the ending point of the game and does not correspond to any concept on the concept map.

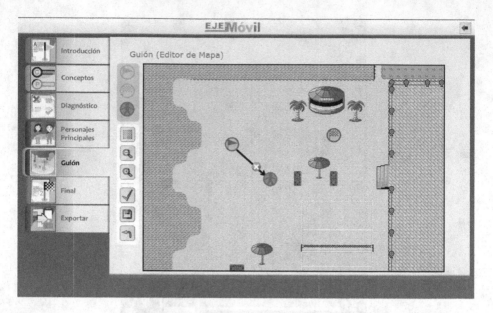

Fig. 2. The Script Definition section

2.2   Design Technique for Videogames

A concept map can be used as a road map to show some of the pathways that are available for connecting the meanings of concepts through the use of proposed concepts [7, 13]. The idea of using concept maps as a way to design serious videogames has emerged from this line of thinking.

A graph satisfies the properties of a concept map. Concept maps are hierarchical, with the more inclusive concepts located up high and the less inclusive concepts located below [7]. The absolute hierarchy of a node corresponds to the number of nodes that there are between the end node and the original node.

Another point to keep in mind is that graphs do not support edges composed of more than two nodes like the one shown in Figure 3.a. In order to deal with this problem, relationships on a concept map that link three or more concepts (N concepts) through one linking word need to be accommodated, as shown in Figure 3.b, linking the concepts through N – 1 linking words (Transformation 1).

Another characteristic from concept maps that is supported by the graph representation proposed is cross-links, which are relationships between concepts within different domains of a concept map. In order to represent the cross-links, an additional step is required (Transformation 2). For a cross-link from concept C1 to concept C2, a new concept needs to be added, concept C2'. Concept C2' has the same name as concept C2 and a link from C1 to C2' needs to be made. The original cross-link from concept C1 to C2 is then deleted. New links need to be made from concept C2' to each of the concepts to which concept C2 is linked (See Figure 4).

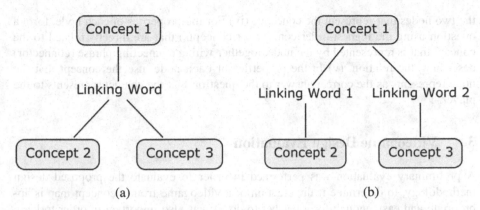

Fig. 3. (a) Relationship between three concepts on a Concept Map. (b) Transformation 1 required by the editor.

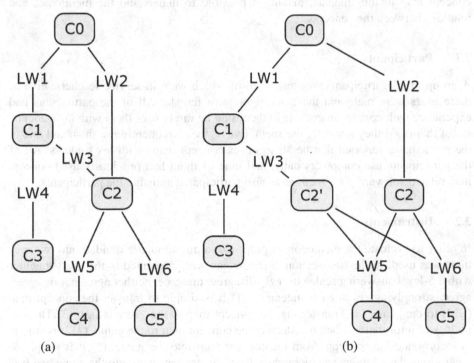

Fig. 4. (a) Cross-link between concept C1 and concept C2 on a Concept Map. (b) Transformation 2 required by the editor.

The proposed technique for videogame design consists of the following steps: (i) Checking whether the conditions necessary to perform transformations 1 and 2 have been met, and performing the desired transformations if possible. (ii) For each concept on the concept map, add a node (character) to represent it on the videogame screen map. (iii) For each relation that connects two concepts, add an arrow between the two nodes that represent the concepts. (iv) For the properties of each node, form a question using the highest-order concept (or concepts) that are directly related to the concept that is represented by the node, together with a connecting phrase (connector) describing the relation. (v) In the properties of each node, use the concept that the node represents as the correct answer to the question that the character presents to the player.

3   Videogame Design Evaluation

A preliminary evaluation was performed in order to evaluate the proposed design methodology, to determine if the creation of a videogame from a concept map is appropriate and easy enough for a teacher to do. It was also important in order to learn what the teachers thought of the methodology in pedagogical terms, or if they believed that the game is able to convey successfully the information contained in the concept map to the students, making it possible to understand the hierarchies and relations between the concepts.

3.1   Participants

A group of 13 participants was tested, all of which were in-service teachers. Five of these users were male and the other eight were female. All of the participants had experience with concept maps; one of them said he rarely uses them with his students, six of them said they normally use them, five of them frequently use them and one of the participants reported that he always uses concept maps with his students. All of the participants use computers daily, and nine of them had previously used concept map related software. Two facilitators also participated assisting the participants.

3.2   Instruments

In order to evaluate the methodology proposed, a questionnaire divided into two sections was used. In the first section, 9 statements were presented to the users together with a 5-level answering scale (strongly disagree, disagree, neither agree nor disagree, agree, strongly agree) to each statement: (1) It is simple to transfer the concept map (CM) to the game. (2) Transferring the concept map to the game is fast. (3) There is no loss of information when transferring the concept map to the game. (4) It is simple to incorporate the concepts from the concept map into the game. (5) It is simple to incorporate the relations and hierarchies from the concept map into the game. (6) It is simple to incorporate the proposals from the concept map into the game. (7) The end result coincides conceptually with the desired result. (8) I have successfully created a concept map-based game. (9) The proposals are well represented in the game through the dependencies defined in the editor.

In the second section, users were presented with 5 open-ended questions: "What did you like about this methodology?", "What did you not like about this methodology?", "What would you add to this methodology?", "What do you think you could use this methodology for?", and "What do you think about the result?" For these open-ended questions, the users were asked to write answers as long as they wanted. Also, an additional space was provided to allow the users to express any situation or opinion that they considered to be significant, and which they felt had been left out of the questionnaire.

3.3   Procedure

The first step was to explain the activity to the users. This was followed by an explanation of the methodology that would be used to create a concept map-based videogame, which was explained to each user individually. Afterwards, each user was provided with a pre-established concept map, based on the concept of the atom, and was asked to create a videogame based on this map using the editor. In order to standardize the evaluation, the users were not allowed to modify the structure of the pre-established concept map. The facilitators observed the entire process of the creation of the videogame, and took note of any relevant situations observed or that were mentioned by the user. In addition, a screen recorder was used to record the entire process. During the evaluation, the facilitators did not answer any questions asked by the participants regarding the creation of the videogame, in order to avoid contaminating the data collected. However, exceptions were made when the users were clearly stuck with something, and when the questions were related to the interface. Once the user had finished creating the videogame, they were given the evaluative questionnaire to fill out in order to capture their immediate impressions and opinions concerning the proposed methodology.

3.4   Results

The results are promising. Each statement obtained an average score of over 4.0 points out of a total of 5 possible points, which means that the users mostly agree with the statements (see Fig. 5). The most poorly evaluated statement is related to the speed with which the users were able to create a videogame from a concept map. The average result obtained for this statement was 4.08, which means that the users were barely in agreement with the statement (2). Despite this score, it is relevant to point out that 3 of the 13 users assigned a score of 2 to this statement (disagree), and 7 users assigned a score of 5 (strongly agree). The low result obtained, in comparison with the other statements, is not directly related to the methodology itself, but rather with the high number of properties that must be defined in the editor in order to create a videogame that is of interest to a player. The definition of the game includes 15 concepts, which mean the users had to fill in the properties of 15 different characters in the videogame.

The two most relevant statements regarding the methodology are: statement 1, and statement 3. These statements provide an idea of what can be achieved with the editor in pedagogical terms. The results obtained for each of these statements were 4.6 and 4.7, respectively, on a possible scale of 1 to 5. These scores are further corroborated by the users' comments that the videogame created conveys the information from the given concept maps satisfactorily. The users also stated that they believe that the students would be able to perceive the concepts and relations in the videogame's underlying concept map. The lowest score attributed to statement (1) was 4.0 (agree), while the lowest score assigned to statement (3) was 3.0 (neutral). However, only one user attributed this score, and all the rest either agreed or strongly agreed with this statement.

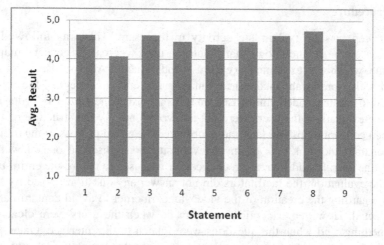

Fig. 5. Results from the methodology evaluation

The statements 4, 5, and 6 represent a disaggregate of statement 1. They are centered on each of the individual elements of a concept map independently. The results obtained from these statements strengthen the result obtained from statement 1. The result from statement 4 was an average score of 4.46, for statement 5 the average score was 4.38, and statement 6 presented an average score of 4.46.

One aspect that was commented on by most of the users is that they would have liked to see the videogame that they had recently created run on their mobile phones. However, this was not possible due to the fact that at the time of the evaluation only a very preliminary version of the videogame engine was used, which did not include appropriate graphics, and for which reason users could have felt somewhat disappointed with the result. They also mentioned that they would like for the students to create the videogames, based on a concept map, by using the editor.

4   Conclusions

In this study we present and evaluate a new technique through the use of concept maps for the design of serious videogames using Ejemovil Editor. The evaluation of the methodology is preliminary and a future full evaluation is needed that incorporates the students playing the videogame created by using the proposed methodology to determine the cognitive impact of the application. However, in the meanwhile it can be pointed out that the perception of the end users regarding the methodology was satisfactory.

All of the users agreed that the transfer from the concept map to the videogame is natural, the validity of which was corroborated by observing the results obtained from the questions regarding the same aspect, but differentiating between the varying elements of a concept map. This is a significant result, as it implies that the users had no problems understanding and applying the proposed methodology. As was previously mentioned, teachers are generally reluctant to incorporate new technologies into the classroom, for which reason having a methodology that is natural for them to use is an important advantage when developing a tool that is oriented towards use by teachers. All of the research subjects mentioned that the editor could be a useful tool for teaching. Some pointed out that it would be useful in order to introduce the subject of a new educational unit, while others mentioned that it would be more useful after a unit had been entirely taught, in order to help students to review the most important concepts and the relationships between them.

The evaluation provides initial data that indicate that the proposed methodology is accepted by end users and could be appropriate and easy to use in the design and creation of serious, educational videogames. This is mainly because it incorporates a conceptually organized and hierarchical way to present concepts, and because it is simple and natural to use. Finally, a wider-ranging evaluation regarding the design methodology presented is needed in order to verify and corroborate that it is understandable and easy for teachers to use. The following step is to design an evaluation that includes students playing the videogame created by teachers using the same methodology, in order to determine if they are able to make cognitive progress by playing the game.

Acknowledgments. This report was funded by the Chilean Fund to Promote Scientific and Technological Development, Fondef TIC-EDU #TE12I1002, the Chilean National Fund of Science and Technology, Fondecyt #1120330, and Project CIE-05 Program Center Education PBCT-Conicyt.

References

1. Aparecida, C., Pacifico, F.: Los mapas conceptuales progresivos: un estudio de los estudiantes de la escuela primaria. In: Cañas, A.J., Novak, J.D., Vanhear, J. (eds.) Proc. of the Fifth Int. CMC, Valletta, Malta (2012)
2. Bellotti, F., Berta, R., De Gloria, A., D'ursi, A., Fiore, V.: A serious game model for cultural heritage. J. Comput. Cult. Herit 5(4), Article 17, 27 (2013)
3. Eronen, P., Nuutinen, J., Rautama, E., Sutinen, E.: Concept Gaming. In: Proc. ICCE 2002, p. 997 (2002)
4. Hunter, J., Monroe-Ossi, H., Wehry, S., McLemore, B., Fountain, C.: Improving the odds: using concept mapping strategies and informational books to build children's and educators' background knowledge. In: Cañas, A.J., Novak, J.D., Vanhear, J. (eds.) Proc. of the Fifth Int. CMC, Valletta, Malta (2012)

5. Novak, J.D., Cañas, A.J.: The Theory Underlying Concept Maps and How to Construct and Use Them,
   http://cmap.ihmc.us/Publications/ResearchPapers/
   TheoryUnderlyingConceptMaps.pdf
6. Merrill, M.: The nature of third grade students' experiences with concept maps to support learning of science concepts. In: Cañas, A.J., Novak, J.D., Vanhear, J. (eds.) Proc. of the Fifth Int. Conference on Concept Mapping, Valletta, Malta (2012)
7. Novak, J.D., Gowin, D.B.: Learning how to learn. Cambridge University Press (1984)
8. Petrova, K.: Mobile learning as a mobile business application. International Journal of Innovation and Learning 4(1), 1–13 (2007)
9. Petrova, K.: Mobile Learning Using SMS: A mobile business application. In: Proc. NACCQ 2005, pp. 412–417 (2005)
10. Prensky, M.: Digital game-based learning. Comput. Entertain. 1(1), 21 (2003)
11. RPGMaker, http://www.rpgmakerweb.com (last accessed: September 15, 2010)
12. Sánchez, J., Espinoza, M.: Ejemovil: A Web-Based Tool to Create Mobile Learning Videogames. In: Proc. EUC 2011, pp. 205–212. IEEE Computer Society, Washington (2011)
13. Sánchez, J., Flores, H.: Concept Mapping for Virtual Rehabilitation and Training of the Blind. IEEE Transactions on Neural Systems and Rehabilitation Engineering 18(2), 210–219 (2010)
14. Treanor, M., Schweizer, B., Bogost, I., Mateas, M.: The micro-rhetorics of Game-o-Matic. In: Proc. of FDG 2012, pp. 18–25. ACM, New York (2012)
15. Virvou, M.: Mobile authoring and management of educational software applications: usefulness and usability for teachers. In: Proc. ED-MEDIA 2004, pp. 5212–5217 (2004)
16. Wu, C.-T., Chung, S.-M., Chang, S.-S.: Designing an interactive storytelling game. In: Göbel, S., Müller, W., Urban, B., Wiemeyer, J. (eds.) GameDays 2012 and Edutainment 2012. LNCS, vol. 7516, pp. 155–160. Springer, Heidelberg (2012)

The Business Love Triangle- Smartphones, Gamification, and Social Collaboration

Lynn Rampoldi-Hnilo[1] and Michele Snyder[2]

[1] Oracle Mobile Applications User Experience, Broomfield, US
lynn.rampoldi-hnilo@oracle.com
[2] Oracle Mobile Applications User Experience, Redwood Shores, US
michele.snyder@oracle.com

Abstract. Gamification is becoming popular in enterprise applications due to benefits such as motivating employees to work harder through team competition and rewards. Mobile workers are a perfect audience for gamified applications as they need to be connected to their teams and aware of important business goals. Smartphones have specific characteristics that make them an ideal medium for gamified applications. However, designing these types of applications correctly is critical in determining their success. This paper will discuss gamification in terms of mobile workers and their needs, smartphone characteristics, and five mobile gamification design principles that help mobile workers stay connected to the business goals at hand.

Keywords: Gamification, Mobile, Smartphones, Design, Social Networking.

1 Introduction

As the computer industry matured, designers and researchers started evaluating the role of play and fun in computer applications. For example, in the early 1980s, Malone created a set of heuristics for designing enjoyable user interfaces and Draper discussed when "fun" is an important component of software design. The field of user experience became more popular in the 1990s and 2000s and further investigation was done to understand what created an enjoyable computer interaction and enhanced user satisfaction. For example, Blythe, Overbeeke, Monk & Wright discussed how interfaces do not just need to be usable, they could be fun as well by using things such as graphics, sound, challenges, etc. to elicit positive emotions.[1]

Fast forwarding 30 years, a new approach to engaging users has emerged. The term "gamification" has become a buzzword across industries and software companies are quickly working to gamify their applications. Gamification goes beyond just making applications fun; it consists of using game design techniques and elements in non-game contexts.[2,3] "The overall goal of gamification is to engage with consumers and get them to participate, share, and interact in some activity or community. A particularly compelling, dynamic, and sustained gamification experience can be used to accomplish a variety of business goals."[4] This can be achieved by using the right

M. Kurosu (Ed.): Human-Computer Interaction, Part II, HCII 2013, LNCS 8005, pp. 309–315, 2013.

set of game mechanics, which are the tools or actions or behaviors that create the game infrastructure. Examples of these include points, levels, challenges, leaderboards, and virtual goods. Game mechanics work best when they naturally tap into a user's motivation or human desire such as reward, status, achievement, competition, and self-expression. [4,5]

The gamification market rose in 2012 by 150% compared to the prior year, and equals 242 million dollars. Of all the gamified applications, consumer applications account for 64% and the other 38% is comprised of enterprise applications. [6]

Gamification has become popular in the enterprise space because it has the potential to: increase user engagement, influence user behavior, motivate participation, increase user adoption and loyalty, meet customer expectations, and increase ROI. In addition, there are benefits to the workforce such as energizing employees, driving performance, identifying leaders, and motivating teams . [7]

Another reason for the popularity of gamification in the workplace was described by Arun Sundararajan, digital economics professor at NYU Stern School of Business. He told *Network World* that people want workplace technologies similar to home technologies. In addition, concepts similar in gamification have had a long history in the enterprise space. For example, sales contests are nothing new. [8]

In addition to desktop applications, enterprise companies are also considering mobile platforms. According to Carter Lusher, a research fellow and chief analyst at Ovum who speaks regularly at industry events, many companies start with mobility when gamifying applications. This is because employees can access these applications from anywhere. Also, these applications can extend to roles such as sales and other on-the-go employees that normally have limited access to desktop computers [8]

2   Mobile Workers

The division of what constitutes a worker on-the-go has blurred. The trend is now for companies to provide mobile devices to all of their workers, because all workers are on the move to some degree and the work day is no longer confined to 9 to 5. Being able to monitor progress, quickly know what is coming up next, giving updates on status, entering new information, and performing certain actions (e.g., approving a time card, assigning a task) are essential tasks all employees and managers appreciate being able to complete at all times of the day no matter where they are.

The Oracle Mobile User Experience team recently completed an international ethnographic study of the enterprise mobile workforce in 2012. They followed and observed 31 mobile workers in four locations: Stockholm, Sweden; Beijing, China; Chicago and the San Francisco Bay Area, U.S.A. Researchers spent between 5 and 6 hours observing each participant throughout their work day. Each participant also was interviewed at the start and end of the observation period. It has become crystal clear that the dedicated field worker has become a true mastermind of using smartphones and other mobile technologies as an extension of themselves. Since the last time the Mobile User Experience team conducted field research, we found that mobile users download and keep many more mobile applications than they did four years ago.

They can and do most of their work throughout the day using their mobile devices, only logging into their laptops and desktops at the end of the day to use applications that aren't available to them. Key mobile tasks across all mobile roles included: taking notes, researching information for a client or something they needed for work on the web, verifying and making appointments, emailing, messaging, tracking what they are doing, taking photos related to their work, and noting what they need to do. If they had a dedicated enterprise application for their work then they used it. Most users had dozens of other applications, including many utility and business oriented apps. For example, VPN access, banking, note taking, and applications for public transportation schedules.

Since mobile devices are used throughout the day in various locations, there are generally some gaps in a person's daily schedule where they are waiting for the next meeting, client, or activity to begin. Mobile devices are often used to fill these gaps and often non work related activities such as communicating with friends or family, surfing the web, and playing games offer just the right amount of distraction – a little, but not too much to interfere with the upcoming job. Of particular note, was the amounts of social networking mobile workers were engaged in. Social networking was important for those in the field to keep up with what is going on. We even discovered that in most of the locations we visited, the mobile workers who did play some games on their mobiles, preferred to play against other players they knew rather than strangers or against the computer. They tend to find it more social to play against someone they know and they find it more rewarding to win the game when knowing who they played against.

Sales is one area that many enterprise software companies, such as Salesforce, SAP, and Oracle, have looked to enrich the user experience through gamification. After conducting many research studies at Oracle it is known that one of the driving factors of sales representatives is to make money. This often is very important to the sales rep because their income is based solely on commission. Therefore, a traditional mobile sales application can be gamified easily by including a competition with other sales reps in the organization to make the most sales in a given timeframe. In order to play the game, sales reps would be required to track all their sales activities in the mobile application – which they are already expected to do. By making it competitive against other sales reps it will keep them motivated to play the game for three reasons. First, we know from past research that mobile workers prefer to play against each other. Second, they will stay informed of how they and their team are doing as a whole (information is important to them).Third, it would meet their own intrinsic needs of "winning" which translates to higher commissions. The outcome of the game would be a bonus or monetary reward for the sales reps that make the most sales.

The company who is providing the mobile application would also "win" in this situation for several reasons. Employees are driven to go above and beyond to make the most sales for the monetary reward and to beat their colleagues in the game. In addition, sales data would be entered in the system, which is often overlooked by sales representatives because they have other tasks they feel are more important to do.

3   Smartphone Characteristics – A Gamification Match

Smartphones have characteristics that make them an ideal medium for gamification. First, they are personal devices with people having an intimate connection with them which increases the likelihood of a higher impact. Second they are time sensitive devices, people always have their mobile device on them and they are always connected to the network. Therefore, time based mechanics can be used, such as the ability to define when an interaction should take place (e.g., something pop-ups up after meeting a client). Direct response is easier through mobile applications because they provide more simplified interactions than web-based applications. Third, they are optimized for rich graphical information, making them a natural medium for analytics, gamification, and visual content. Lastly, since applications are real time on a mobile device, interactions can be tracked resulting in more accurate measurement.[9]

Even with mobile devices being an ideal medium for gamification with benefits for both companies and their workforce, careful consideration needs to be made when designing these applications. According to Gartner, 80% of current gamified applications will not meet their intended business objectives due to bad design. The reason for this according to Brian Burke, research vice president at Gartner is "The focus is on the obvious game mechanics, such as points, badges and leader boards, rather than the more subtle and more important game design elements, such as balancing competition and collaboration, or defining a meaningful game economy." In other words, the target users are not having a meaningful experience with rewards that are beneficial to them. [10]

A properly designed game would result in mobile workers using their mobile enterprise solutions more to accomplish their daily tasks not only because they had to, but because they want to. In addition, companies greatly benefit from employees using these types of applications to get data entered into the enterprise system in a timely manner and to increase overall profits.

4   Mobile Gamification Design Principles

There are many general mobile design principles, including Oracle's Mobile Design Principles. [11] Based on our recent mobile research and enterprise design trends, we would like to focus on five principles that will make gamification mechanics more successful in your mobile application and leverage the strengths of the smartphone. At the heart of this discussion is the concept of "staying connected" – whether it is to the company, data, or people.

1. Pick ONE motivational factor. Determine only one motivational factor that you want to drive an increase in a specific behavior. Make sure it is specific to a business goal that can be translated to the individual user. Too many motivations or goals can overwhelm the user or cause them to ignore any of the additional objectives, as a user can't determine what is important to the business. Another

reason it is important to keep it to one motivational goal is that well designed mobile applications focus only on essential tasks required while a user is out in the field. Mobile workers are constantly on the move and distracted by their environment. Therefore, they only have a few seconds to a few minutes to accomplish a task. If there are many motivational factors trying to be accomplished, too many gaming mechanics will clutter the application and take the focus off the essential tasks at hand. Motivational areas that synch with typical mobile users are: complete more of a certain activity, do it more quickly, and include more information or details. Do you want the user to increase a certain behavior, for example, make more sales? Do you want the mobile worker to do their job faster: complete a service request more quickly? Do you want more information about what is happening in a timely fashion: log notes or details about a client meeting after it occurs? These are business goals that a simple gamification mechanic could provide the right amount of information to help a user know what they need to be doing and provide the incentive to motivate them to continue with the new behavior (e.g., I'm at the top of the sales chart, I shaved 3 hours off of my service requests this week, all of my client folders are at 100% complete).

2. Include analytics that complement the business goal that you are gamifying. Analytics have become an important element in smartphone design as they provide information that a user can act upon or help in the decision making process. Both of these are key to a mobile worker's core tasks. What do I need to do next? How am I doing right now in my job? Where is an area that I need to focus on or fix? Having a synthesized graphical view of information that communicates meaningful patterns in data that is relevant to the user and provides insights allows our users to make more meaningful decisions. Analytics should be considered in conjunction with any gaming mechanic used. These are not separate objectives and should be considered at the same time. Often it is these analytics that will be used to drive the user to want to compete in the game. Without this type of view there is often no way for a user to know how they are doing compared to others or compared their individual goals set by their manager or company.

3. Keep it simple. Smartphones have a limited amount of screen real estate. Keep gamification mechanics proportional to the task at hand. In other words, don't create large gaming mechanics that overwhelm the rest of the user interface and experience. Subtle is better. This is particularly important with the new design trend to simply user interfaces. For example do not just stick badges or colorful elements all over the screens. Consider other options such as having separate pages with the key gamification analytics that users can easily navigate to when they have the time to do so. Also, gamification elements can be hidden to the user but affect their overall score in the game, for example the action of entering in the appropriate information could raise their place in the game, which they then can be notified later by email, a notification in their application, or in some other unobtrusive way.

4. Incorporate collaboration and social elements. These elements are strong tools to consider when mapping out how to gamify a mobile application. Smartphones are a natural communication medium. Oracle's field research validates the importance

of mobile workers staying connected with both work and personal sources throughout the day. Workers are often in the field alone and finding ways to keep them connected to the rest of the company would be of benefit to all parties. Motivating users through playing on teams or understanding how they are doing with respect to the organization (e.g., sales leaderboards, etc.) can provide workers additional incentives to accomplish certain business goals. We would caution against too much competition, but if put forth in a positive way or keeping it more team based can re-energize a company toward a unified focus. It also gives users greater visibility into what is happening in a company and make them feel more integrated.

5. Leverage mobile device capabilities as part of the gamification strategy. Encouraging behaviors that meet the business goal while leveraging the fact that the person is using a mobile device takes your application beyond just being another tracking tool. For example, if you have mobile workers use their smartphone camera to post pictures of interest to others in the company (e.g., clients, company head quarters, environments, how your product is being used, etc.) then you bring value to those remote workers and useful information back into the company. It will make your employees feel valuable and give you added information to use in your business. This tightens the communication channels with your remote workers and makes everyone be a team. If you tie these behaviors with a business goal , such as updating an opportunity after meeting with a client (e.g., get extra points for posting notes, photos, something relevant to the location you are in) your company will be the winner with having robust and complete client records.

5   Conclusion

Recently there has been a trend for companies to include gamification in their enterprise applications. These types of applications are beneficial for employees because they often provide both intrinsic rewards such as motivation along with extrinsic rewards such money or prizes for winning the game. In addition companies win from implementing these applications because employee performance often increases as they try to succeed in the game.

Mobile technologies lend themselves perfectly for supporting gamification of mobile enterprise applications as they work well with visual content and anything that increases mobile workers connectivity to the company (e.g., team based incentives) is positive to the revenue line. However, just because they have inherent characteristics that make them a perfect technology to support gaming mechanics does not mean that the applications will automatically be successful. Companies cannot just simply include some badges and assume they have gamified their application in a way that employees will adopt it and look at it favorably.

When including gamification in your mobile enterprise applications consider using the five mobile design principles we have included to help guarantee the success of the product. These include narrowing it down to one motivational factor, incorporate analytics to complement the business goal you are gamifying, keep it simple, use social collaboration and social elements, and leverage mobile device capabilities. Smartphones, gamification, and social collaboration work well together as they increase workers ability to stay connected – to their company, to the information necessary for business, and to the important people in their lives.

References

1. Fitz-Walter, Z.: Games Everywhere: Making Games Using Everyday Interactions (2013), http://zefcan.com/2013/01/a-brief-history-of-gamification
2. Deterding, D., Dixon, D., Khaled, R., Nackev, L.: From Game Design Elements to Gamefulness: Defining Gamification. In: Proceedings of the 15th International Academic MindTrek Conference: Envisioning Future Media Environments, pp. 9–15. ACM, New York (2011)
3. Duggan, K.: Using 'Gamification' to Better Engage Customers Online (2012), Washingtonpost.com, http://www.washingtonpost.com/business/on-small-business/using-gamification-to-better-engage-customers-online/2012/02/14/gIQADVW6fR_story.html
4. Gamification 101: An Introduction to the Use of Game Dynamics to Influence Behavior (2010), Bunchball.com, http://www.bunchball.com/sites/default/files/downloads/gamification101.pdf
5. Game-mechanics and Game-dynamics of the Gamification Process (2010), alittleb.it.com, http://www.alittleb.it/gamification/gamify-your-business-game-mechanics-and-game-dynamics
6. Meloni, W.: Gamification in 2012 Trends in Consumer and Enterprise Markets. Presented, Gamification Summit, San Francisco (2012)
7. Rauch, M.: Tapping Enterprise Communities Through Gamification. Presented, STC Summit (2012)
8. Dubowski, S.: Gamification in the Enterprise: How to Win with Mobility (2013), Blog.allstream.com, http://blog.allstream.com/gamification-in-the-enterprise-how-to-win-with-mobility/
9. Krief, G.: How Gamification can Drive Levels of Consumer Engagement (2011), Mobilemarketer.com, http://www.mobilemarketer.com/cms/opinion/columns/10671.html
10. Gartner Says by 2014, 80 Perecent of Current Gamified Applications Will Fail to Meet Business Objectives Primarily Due to Poor Design (2012), Gartner.com, http://www.gartner.com/newsroom/id/2251015
11. White, B., Rampoldi-Hnilo, L.: Design for the Mobile Experience (2009), http://www.oracle.com/webfolder/ux/applications/successStories/071115_mobileExperience.html

Building Internal Enthusiasm for Gamification in Your Organization

Erika Noll Webb[1] and Andrea Cantú[2]

[1] Oracle Corporation, Broomfield CO
[2] Oracle Mexico, Zapopan, Jalisco, Mexico
{erika.webb,andrea.cantu}@oracle.com

Abstract. Gamification has become a hot topic in a variety of areas from consumer sites to enterprise software. While the concept of using game mechanics to attract and retain customers in the consumer space is now well accepted, the use of gamification in the enterprise space is still catching on. In this paper, the authors explore ways to build internal enthusiasm for gamification within an organization while maintaining good practices and processes.

Keywords: Gamification, Game Mechanics, Enterprise Software, User Experience, User-centered design, Employee Engagement.

1 Introduction

Gamification has become a hot topic in a variety of areas from consumer sites to enterprise software. While the concept of using game mechanics to attract and retain customers in the consumer space is now well accepted, the use of gamification in the enterprise space is still catching on. However, there are a number of reasons to believe that gamification will grow in the enterprise space. The most likely of these is that companies are increasingly concerned about the effect of employee engagement on productivity. Employee engagement is the degree or extent to which employees feel committed to their work and their organization. The idea is that if employees are engaged in their work, they will be more involved in things that make the company successful. Engaged employees could be reasonably expected to produce more than disengaged employees, and that idea has been born out by several studies. For example, the Hay Group [1] found that actively engaged office workers were 43% more productive. Towers Perrin [2] found that companies that have engaged workers have 6% higher net profit margins, and Kenexa's [3] research claims that companies with engaged workers have five times higher shareholder returns over five years. Lockwood [4] studied sales teams and found that there was a performance-related cost of low- versus high-engagement teams of more than 2 million dollars. Also, engaged employees are said to be less likely to switch jobs.

As a result, companies are concerned about the effects of employee engagement on their bottom lines. And these companies are trying to figure out how they can get their employees more engaged in their work.

M. Kurosu (Ed.): Human-Computer Interaction, Part II, HCII 2013, LNCS 8005, pp. 316–322, 2013.
© Springer-Verlag Berlin Heidelberg 2013

And that's where gamification may come in. Gamification in the enterprise has a specific focus on business goals of the company, and how to keep people engaged in their work. As the Pew Research Center's Internet & American Life Project and Elon University [5] concluded "Playing beats working. So, if the enjoyment and challenge of playing can be embedded in learning, work, and commerce then gamification will take off."

Let's consider a few areas where gamification in the enterprise has been successful. Call centers have been one of the first places to employ successful gamification. Call centers have a huge turnover rate. Turnover is expensive. The Society of Human Resource Management [6] states that the cost of replacing one $8 per hour employee can exceed $3,500, so companies have a strong financial incentive to hold onto employees, even those who are not highly paid. Live Ops, a call center outsourcing firm, added gamification to their training and for their employee work tasks, rewarding employees for things like time to complete a call and customer satisfaction. They showed a 23% improvement in call metrics over employees not using the system, 9% higher customer satisfaction and training time was reduced from 4 weeks to 14 hours [7]. Other studies have suggested that you can reduce the turnover rate at a call center from every 3 months to every 6 months. Numbers like that are very compelling.

Another compelling use case is in the sales aspects of Customer Relationship Management (CRM). Companies buy CRM tools in order to better track and understand the activities of their sales force. Companies would like to know who their sales team is talking to within a company, what they talk about and what works best to close a deal. However, sales people view entering information into CRM tools as time they aren't out selling. Companies want more insight into their sales team, but the sales team does not want to take the time to enter that information. Companies can use a carrot and stick to incent their sales folks to enter information but what if you could create a way that your sales team would want to use the system? More and more, companies are turning to gamification as a way to entice sales users to enter information into the CRM system. And those methods appear to have been successful.

Based on these studies, it would seem gamification would be a natural fit for many companies. Nonetheless, it is sometimes difficult to get organizations on board with gamification, and actually push the concepts into design and product. This case study examines ways that we have worked to get gamification adopted in our organization.

2   Building Support

At Oracle, we have met resistance to gamification on several levels, but now are managing to move our groups into a more receptive space. Over the last two years, we have developed a variety of techniques to convince an internal audience that gamification is a useful and could be effective in enterprise systems.

2.1 Socialization

The first solution we have taken is to socialize the message through presentations to user experience and development teams. Although some groups see the value of gamification, we have encountered resistance to the term gamification on the basis that it is not serious enough for enterprise users. There was concern about the idea of trying to make serious software into a game. However, through presentations and socializing the research in the field, that resistance has diminished.

Presentations to Product Teams

One of the first ways we introduced gamification to our organization was to present to the Applications User Experience (Apps UX) group at Oracle. This group of 130+ individuals are the primary usability design and research support for Oracle Applications and a direct connection to the enterprise application product teams. By presenting an introduction to gamification to this group, we were able to start the conversation with both the user experience groups as well as all of the product teams.

Following this introduction to gamification, we invited this group to discuss the topic with their product teams in all enterprise areas, including CRM, Financials, Human Capital Management and Supply Chain Management and we offered to present an introduction to each of these groups.

Blog and Social Networks

We wanted to make sure that groups within Oracle could find more information on gamification and our team, so we created a blog and used social networks to connect internal teams interested in the topic. We utilize a twitter account as well as our internal Oracle Social Network to create discussions on gamification and a location for file sharing, so that others could find information on the topic and discover the various ways gamification is being implemented in Oracle.

2.2 Design Jam

Once we had introduced the topic of gamification to the teams, we decided the best way to move this forward was to conduct a large gamification exercise so that all of the members of Apps UX would be involved in gamifying an actual product flow.

Step One: Executive Support

The first step to this Design Jam was to get executive support for an offsite All Hands meeting with the entire organization. However, this could also be conducted as individual group events at separate locations if your organization doesn't allow for travel. In our event, we brought together employees from different locations in the US, Canada, India, Australia and Mexico. In addition, we invited some outside guests to attend from other Oracle groups as well as Oracle advocates.

Step Two: Scenarios and Teams

We have run this several times with different scenarios, but for the initial event, we asked for 15 different product flows (e.g. creating an opportunity record in a CRM application) from the various Apps UX product teams. For each of these, we asked for a user profile or persona of the typical user and screenshots with an explanation of the possible business goals. Each team received a thumb drive with the user profile or persona as well as a PowerPoint with all of the screenshots, an explanation of the flow and a description of the possible business goals. We also found a guru for each group who could explain the flow and answer any questions about the business goal for each team.

In order to level the playing field, we arranged the teams so that no one worked on their own product area.   Everyone worked on a flow that would be novel to them.

Step Three: Gamifying the Day

To ensure that the day was fun and fit the spirit of gamification, we gamified the exercise in a number of ways. Each team had a game mascot from various video games (e.g. Mario, Arthus, Kirby, Laura Croft, etc). We began the day with a check in, in which each participant was given an envelope marked top secret. The envelope contained a pin with a picture of the game mascot for their teams and the product flow.

We started with an overview of game mechanics and how they could be used as well as an explanation of the goals of the day.   When this exercise was complete, everyone opened their envelopes and ran to their assigned team table.

Fig. 1. The team tables with application monitor in the foreground

For the purposes of the day, we also had developed an app to gamify the event it-self. This app allowed the event administrators to score the 15 teams on their use of game mechanics as well as to assign badges to teams. The event could be run without the app by scoring and tallying team scores. The app featured a leaderboard and an infoboard. The leaderboard showed the team with the highest number of points while the infoboard showed which badges the teams had earned. The majority of the badges were based on use of game mechanics while some of the badges were just for fun, such as the Coffee Addicts badge, granted to tables with more than 5 coffee cups.

Fig. 2. An example page from the app developed for the event, showing an individual team page

Teams were scored at 3 points during the event and the winning team at each round received a small prize. At the end of the day, each team put together a PowerPoint deck and presented their design concepts to the rest of the group. At the end of that, the participants all voted on the ultimate winner of event and that team won prizes for each of the individuals.

This event did convince even skeptical participants that gamification could be used in ways they had not considered. Following the event, a number of projects to gami-fy enterprise flows were developed, including one based on the work of one of the teams during the event.

2.3   Research

In addition to the gamification event, we conducted research within our organization about terminology and specific game mechanics, to determine acceptance and aware-ness of gamification, through surveys to the larger development organization in which Apps UX is housed. This both raised the visibility of the concept while helping de-fine which game mechanics were most useful and understandable to the organization.

A Gartner report in 2012 concluded that 80% of current gamified applications would fail to meet business objectives, primarily due to poor design [8]. Conscious of this possibility, once we started working with product teams to gamify some of our application flows, we have been careful to include research into our designs as part of our design cycle. For example, we took product designs to an Oracle User Group conference and tested them with people who met the description of a typical end user of the systems. Based on the testing, we then modified our designs prior to development. This research, in which we tested an ungamified flow against the same flow with gamification, is useful for convincing product teams that gamification would be a desirable addition to our product lines.

2.4   Individual Product Teams

And finally, we have made ourselves available to work with individual product teams to conduct specific brainstorming events to gamify a product. Working with those groups to help define the business objectives and possible methodologies has been useful both in promoting gamification as part of the user experience and for encouraging teams to consider how gamification could be used to achieve business objectives.

3   Conclusions

All of these methods are presented to help those who are also trying to build internal enthusiasm for gamification within their organization. We have found each of these efforts, coming from a user experience group, have helped to position gamification as a usability issue.

References

1. Engage Employees and Boost Performance. The Hay Group, http://www.haygroup.com/downloads/us/engaged_performance_120401.pdf (cited: December 12, 2012)
2. Case Study-The LV= Employee Engagement Survey. TowersWat-son.com. (November 2012), http://www.towerswatson.com/en/Insights/IC-Types/Case-Studies/2012/the-lv-employee-engagement-survey (cited: December 12, 2012)
3. Engagement Levels in Global Decline: Organizations Losing a Competitive Edge. HRE Online (2011), http://www.hreonline.com/pdfs/02012012Extra_KenexaReport.pdf (cited: December 6, 2012)
4. Lockwood, N.: Leveraging Employee Engagement for Competitive Advantage: HR's Strategic Role. Society for Human Resource Management, s.l. (2007)
5. Anderson, J., Rainie, L.: The Future of Gamification. Pew Internet (May 18, 2012), http://www.pewinternet.org/Reports/2012/Future-of-Gamification/Overview.aspx (cited: November 26, 2012)

6. Burns, M.: What Does It Cost To Replace An Employee? Abenity (April 8, 2011), http://www.abenity.com/celebrate/employee-engagement-cost-to-replace-an-employee/ (cited: No-vember 26, 2012)
7. Silverman, R.E.: Latest Game Theory: Mixing Work and Play. Wall Street Journal Online (October 10, 2011), http://online.wsj.com/article/SB10001424052970204294504576615371783795248.html (cited: November 26, 2012)
8. Burke, B.: Gartner Says by 2014, 80 Percent of Current Gamified Ap-plications Will Fail to Meet Business Objectives Primarily Due to Poor Design. Gartner.com (November 27, 2012), http://www.gartner.com/technology/research/gamification/ (cited: January 6, 2013)

Navigation Experiences – A Case Study of Riders Accessing an Orientation Game via Smartphones

Annika Worpenberg and Barbara Grüter

University of Applied Sciences Bremen, Flughafenallee 10, 28199 Bremen, Germany
{annika.worpenberg,barbara.grueter}@hs-bremen.de

Abstract. Usability and playability of a game are two dimensions merging into each other and affecting the experience. Within this paper we study the navigation experiences of a small rider group playing an orientation game by means of smartphones. The players are inexperienced in using smartphones and try to reach the first game station. Studying their navigation process we learned how the players adopted the game device, solved a navigation problem and entered the game world. The case study illustrates three development stages of navigational behavior of the rider group in the analyzed mobile game.

Keywords: Mobile Game, Location-based Game, Play Experience, Evaluating Mobile Games, Navigation.

1 Introduction

In consequence of the increasing distribution of smartphones with integrated GPS-sensors more mobile applications and games enter the market, offering experiences in mixed worlds. Using the geographical position and the physical movement of the player as one condition of the interaction mechanics these games combine the every-day world with virtual dimensions. Digital maps are often a core element of the visual interface, integrated to assist the user navigating in the game world. (e.g. GPS Mission, Mister X mobile, Shadow Cities, Ingress). A game is entered through the game controls [2]. This includes also the mastery of the game mechanics, seen as the interface between the player and the game world [9].

Orientation and navigation, finding and tracking a path, are conditions of moving in space. Navigation is an important element interacting with a mobile application. Bouwer et al. (2012) observed the navigational behavior of study participants on a fair. The researchers organized a test with predefined way finding tasks to determine how a mobile application can serve as an aid for orientation and navigation in a fair context and what problems in terms of way finding and usability may occur. The results show that it was difficult for many participants to associate their own view of the map with their perception of their immediate environment. [1] The orientation problems expressed the fact that the users were not able to situate themselves within the mixed world: the real space linked to the digital map.

M. Kurosu (Ed.): Human-Computer Interaction, Part II, HCII 2013, LNCS 8005, pp. 323–332, 2013.

Rukzio et al. (2009) conducted a similar study with pedestrians, comparing navigation behavior using various media, including paper maps and mobile devices. The participants were asked to find predetermined routes in the environment. Results show that many participants did not perceive their direct surroundings and even blind out traffic and other pedestrians. Furthermore they had difficulties establishing the relationship between the information provided by the map and the environment. [10]

The problem is a usability problem. The problem has to be solved to ensure the users access to the mixed world. Our question is, however, if focusing on the usability of a software supporting navigation in space really is enough. Most approaches of usability testing focus the user interface as the direct contact of the user with the system. They single out and test functional relations of particular interface elements and risk to miss the whole. To ensure meaningful measures the entire functional architecture of the system and the complex cognitive and emotional scale of the users might be taken into consideration. [5] Mobile games and applications are used in dynamic fragmented contexts and this might affect the behavior and the perception of the player. [4,6]

This paper applies a more holistic approach in studying the user experience as a moment of the activity process unfolding in time [7]. We analyze the navigation experiences of a group of riders performing an orientation ride. The process-oriented method allows us to analyze synchronized data-streams to reconstruct the user's activity in time and to develop an understanding of the user's experience. The study focuses the rider's navigation process in order to determine how a mobile application, in this case a mobile game running on a smartphone, can become a medium of navigation (and following a medium of game play) for riders who so far navigated by means of paper maps only.

2   The Game Event

The mobile game "Orientierungsritt Ziemendorf" has been developed by the BMBF[1]-research project Landmarks of Mobile Entertainment at the University of Applied Sciences in Bremen in cooperation with the "Vereinigung der Freizeitreiter und –fahrer"[2] Germany (VFD).

2.1   The Game

The game is an orientation ride in the surrounding area of the hotel "Pferde- und Freizeitparadies" in Ziemendorf, a tiny village in the sparsely populated former German border region. It is running on smartphones as a mobile application. An orientation ride is based on the game mechanics of a scavenger hunt [11]. A group of riders

---

[1] Federal Ministry of Education and Research.
[2] Association of Leisure Riders and Drivers Germany.

moves on a predefined route from station to station and solves tasks. Traditionally, performing an orientation ride needs many volunteers organizing the stations and the tasks during the ride. In this case, the smartphone organizes the play action. Sound and haptic signals alert the riders approaching a station. On arrival the rider receives a task. The fulfillment of the task and the performance is detected by the game system. The way to the next station gets visible, when the task is performed. Beyond that, the game provides a rough overview of the whole route for the players if wished.

The main design goal was to support the experience of riders in the surrounding nature, and to the strengthening the relationship between rider and horse and between the members of the rider group. This aim was accomplished by specific tasks and a system of sensory, auditory and tactile, signals.

2.2 The Play Test

The play test took place during a rider camp in Ziemendorf organized by the VFD. 35 players participated organized in 11 groups. For studying navigation experience in the way it happens we focus on one the groups. The group consists of three women, one of them, Kate, older (52) than the other two, Jane and Mary (14 and 16). The group has a leader, who handles the device and acts as communicator between game on smartphone and group. This role changes during the ride, but has been taken mainly by the 16 year old, Mary. To support the common game and the experience in nature, each group disposes one device.

3 Methods

The method of data collection aims to capture the (game) experience and game activities as a process that develops over time. The collected data include game activities in space and time in form of log files and communication of the players in form of audio files. The players know, that their use of the device, their movements and the total conversations are recorded. They take along a flyer, which explains functionality and interface of the game.

The method of data analysis is process-oriented. The activity of players is monitored, studied and explained with reference to time. The goal is to understand the play experience and its development in the game process. The tool used to analyze the data is ChronoViz[3]. The program allows us to analyze the data streams synchronously and in their temporal sequence. For example the riders are approaching a station; the synchronized data streams allow us to understand the particular event happening; it can be seen where they are, what they say or what task is presented. The temporal order of the data allows us to understand how an activity event started, how it happened, how it ended and what consequences it had for the next step.

---

[3] "ChronoViz is a tool to aid visualization and analysis of multimodal sets of time-coded information, with a focus on the analysis of video in combination with other data sources." [3]

4   Results

4.1   Overview on the Whole Ride

The following descriptions are results of the ongoing analysis. They are used as a framework for the specific results presented in this paper. The total ride lasts 4.5 hours and can be divided into four phases that are aligned to turning points in the game.

- The first phase marks the entry into the game world,
- The second phase is dominated by social dynamics within the group. The dynamics proceed over the entire course, but have particular influence in this section,
- The third phase is characterized by routine in the game procedure,
- The fourth phase describes the phase-out of the game world.

To provide a better understanding we introduce two visualizations formats of the ride, one in space and the other one in time. The Figure 1 presents the orientation ride of the three women in space. This allows the reader to allocate the observations in space. The Figure 2 introduces the same orientation ride of the group of women in time. The temporal visualization helps the reader to understand the empirical observations within the temporal order of the process.

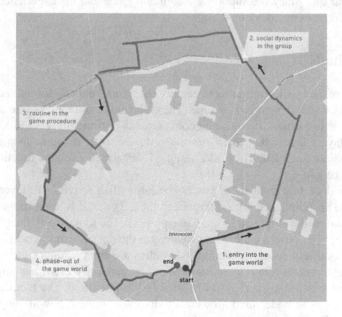

Fig. 1. The four phases of the ridden route in space displayed on Google Maps

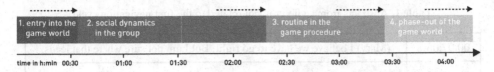

Fig. 2. The four phases of the orientation ride event in time

The following analysis focuses the first one of the presented phases. It covers the first half hour of the game, in which the group of players tries to enter the game and to understand its requirements. Defined in the games' core mechanics, the immediate objective of the players is to arrive at the first station. In the course of this activity a navigation problem arises.

Starting point - According to the data we characterize the situation of the players as follows: The players know the game mechanics of an orientation ride, they have minimal experience with the game device, a smartphone, and they have a rough idea about the environment; the older rider in the group has some experience in the region. This minimal knowledge is insufficient to solve the navigation problem directly.

Endpoint - At the end of the first phase they are on the right track, they are able to understand the relation between themselves and the mixed game world with its real and its virtual dimension and perform first play activities.

Main question: How do they solve the navigation problem? How do they develop competencies in handling the navigation device? How can a mobile application become a medium of navigation? In the following we present the data allowing us to mark generalizable characteristics of the developing navigation activity of the players.

- A basis navigation activity cycle becomes repeated and refined over time
- A change of the focus from the game goal to navigation and vice versa
- Three states, which can be distinguished in the development of the navigation.

4.2 Navigation Activity Cycles

The process unfolds as a succession of four navigation cycles. One navigation activity cycle, cf. [8], consists of the determination of the own geographical position, the determination of the target point, the determination of the path between these two points, the movement to the target point and the interpretation of the results. The cycles are presented referring to the empirical data of the analysis. The tables show abstracts from the audio protocol translated from German into English.

First Navigation Cycle. During the first cycle the group leader, Mary gives a direction and the group moves in this direction. Mary proves the position on the digital map and after recognizing that it is wrong, she corrected it.

Table 1. Abstracts from audio protocol related to the first navigation cycle

00:07:06-8	(Mary) I believe we have to go right. But I am not sure where that leads.
00:08:55-4	(Mary) No, I believe that is wrong.
00:08:57-5	(Mary) We have to go there.

Interpretation: This first cycle displays the first impression that the riders get from the game situation. They do not know what to do and act without a plan.

They are trying to locate themselves in space. This process belongs to the use of maps or mobile devices for navigation. In this special example the players are not used to mobile devices and do not know the environment. Furthermore familiar landmarks are too rare to be used for navigation. The presented example shows the generic process of localization in space using mobile devices.

Second Navigation Cycle. The second cycle indicates a selective experiment of localization. The group rides a particular distance and observes the change of their position on the digital map. They permanently observe the position displayed on the map. After this cycle they are still on the wrong way.

Table 2. Abstracts from audio protocol related to the second navigation cycle

00:10:30-9	(Kate) And if we, we ride straight ahead for a while and then we will see if we are wrong or not, aren't we?
00:11:31-4	(Mary) We are totally wrong.

Interpretation: The performance of the group is more controlled and the experiment gets to a higher level of navigation. The sensible observation of their movement on the digital map indicates, they recognized, that navigating with the device is different to the navigation with paper maps and that they have to learn first. In the first cycle they think, they are able to navigate, this second cycle shows that they try to learn the navigation by setting a sub goal. This includes the try to get their position on the route on the digital map (see change of focus).

At the end of this cycle the older rider (Kate) takes the leading role and gets the device.

Third Navigation Cycle. After some time of getting to know the handling with the device Kate makes a suggestion about the route. In this third cycle doubts about the right handling of the device come up and theories about the inaccuracy of GPS occur. During the process Mary gets back the device and recognizes that the group is on the right route.

Table 3. Abstracts from audio protocol related to the third navigation cycle

00:13:22-7	(Kate) Show me. I want to see it now.
00:13:44-1	(Jane) Has it started correctly?
00:14:13-7	(Kate) Over here…
00:14:17-7	(Kate) …and then to the left.
00:16:56-5	(Kate) What does the green dot, has it moved?
00:17:57-5	(Kate) We just go on and have a look in a moment again, to see what happens.
00:20:08-0	(Mary) We are riding the right way.

Interpretation: Again, the group makes use of a selective experiment of movement. The experiment is successful and they meet the sub goal. The position is shown on the route on the digital map.

Fourth Navigation Cycle. After a short time of certainty the group loses its way again.

Table 4. Abstracts from audio protocol related to the fourth navigation cycle

00:25:41-1	(Jane) Yes, we are totally; we have to go back again.
00:27:04-0	(Kate) Turn around; we don't care about the station now.
00:27:08-8	(Kate) Go on, we ride on the route and observe what happens. If nothing happens, that's it.
00:28:33-0	(Mary) We are not riding on the right way.
00:33:48-2	(Mary) Yes, we are right.

Interpretation: The fourth cycle is indicated by the search of the correct route again. At the end of this cycle they found the right way.

4.3 Change of Focus

The developing navigation activity is initiated, accompanied and finished by four changes of the focus of the players. The game goal is to reach the first station. The focus on this goal is replaced by the focus on the appropriation of the navigation device and the other way around. After difficulties of localization and using the device, the group sets a sub goal; the correct representation of their own position on the route on the digital map.

First Change of Focus. The first change of focus happens between the first and second cycle of activity. The focus changes from the game to the own position on the digital map.

Table 5. Abstracts from audio protocol related to the first change of focus

00:10:30-9	(Kate) And if we, we ride straight ahead for a while and then we will see if we are wrong or not, aren't we?
00:11:00-3	(Mary) We ride parallel to the route. I believe we have to ride along the street, not on the sandy way.

Second Change of Focus. After the third cycle they recognize that they are on the right route. The focus changes directly from the sub goal to the game goal and they are looking for the next station.

Table 6. Abstracts from audio protocol related to the second change of focus

00:21:39-2	(Mary) Indeed we are on the right way, but somehow the station is not displayed; the flag.
00:24:40-2	(Kate) What is displayed there, how far is the next station? That is displayed at the top or not?

Third Change of Focus. Another change of focus takes place before the fourth cycle of activity, when the group is on the wrong track again. The group decides to ignore the station until they are on the right way.

Table 7. Abstracts from audio protocol related to the third change of focus

00:26:43-5	(Kate) Ignore the stupid flag it doesn't matter. We are the test persons.
00:27:04-0	(Kate) Turn around; we are not interested in the station right now.
00:27:08-8	(Kate) Go on, we ride on the route and observe what happens. If nothing happens, that's that.

Fourth Change of Focus. After the fourth cycle the group is on the right way again and not far away from the next station; the focus changes to the game goal.

4.4   Three Development Stages

The transition from the navigation problem to the solution of the problem and the mastery of the device takes place as a process of iterative approaches.

Comparing the succession of navigation activity cycles three stages in the development of the navigation activity and the growing navigation competence can be distinguished: At first, the players try using trial and error to get on the right track. Then, they carry out targeted experiments. The systematic comparison of digital map and real world environment is one characteristic of the third stage in the development of the navigation activity.

To control the groups' position Mary, as the group leader, observes the map and tries to make suggestions about the environment. Kate controls these suggestions in relation to the real environment.

Table 8. Abstracts from audio protocol related to the comparison of map and real world

00:19:44-8	(Mary) Is here a route on the right?
00:19:49-6	(Kate) Here is a way on the right.
00:29:41-3	(Mary) …has the way a slight hiccup to the right?
00:29:44-0	(Kate) Yes, it goes slightly to the right.
00:31:57-8	(Mary) It goes straight ahead forever.
00:32:01-1	(Kate) Yes, this here is everlasting straight, too.

Their behavior changes from a relatively desultory strategy over targeted experiments to an ongoing systematic action until they have solved the navigation problem. During this development, the players learn to control the game device and are able to navigate at the end of the first phase.

5   Summary

The illustration of this process reconstructs the localization of the rider in the game world. The players go through a lengthy and progressive process of locating in space, not knowing their environment and the handling with the device. This locating process must be done by anyone who navigates using a mobile device. This process is influenced by context and personal experience. Detailed case studies provide a wealth of valuable information on navigation.

In the transition phase conditions for the game are build, but the game itself is not realized yet. The core mechanics of the game define finding and reaching stations. In the moment, the player start to search for a station, they successful entered the game world.

Acknowledgments. A special thanks goes to the riders of the play test, for participating and allowing us to evaluate the data. We want to give another thanks to our partner David Wewetzer from the TZI Bremen, who is also a member of the VFD. We thank to the members of the research project 'landmarks of mobile entertainment', especially Prof. Dr. Barbara Grüter and Prof. Dr. Heide-Rose Vatterrot.

References

1. Bouwer, A., Nack, F., Ali, A., El, A.: Lost in navigation: evaluating a mobile map app for a fair. In: Proceedings of the 14th ACM International Conference on Multimodal Interaction, pp. 173–180. ACM, New York (2012)
2. Brown, E., Cairns, P.: A Grounded Investigation of Game Immersion. Extended Abstracts on Human Factors in Computing Systems (CHI EA 2004), pp. 1297–1300. ACM, New York (2004)
3. ChronoViz Website, http://chronoviz.com/ (accessed on February 22, 2013)
4. De Sá, M., Carriço, L.: Designing and Evaluating Mobile Interaction: Challenges and Trends. Foundations and Trends in Human–Computer Interaction 4(3), 175–243 (2010)
5. Dix, A., Finlay, J., Abowd, G., Beale, R.: Human-Computer Interaction, 3rd edn., p. 237. Prentice-Hall (2003)
6. Dourish, P.: What We Talk About When We Talk About Context. Personal and Ubiquitous Computing 8(1), 19–30 (2004)
7. Grüter, B., Oks, M., Lochwitz, A.: System and Context – On a Discernable Source of Emergent Game Play and the Process-Oriented Method. In: Yang, H.S., Malaka, R., Hoshino, J., Han, J.H. (eds.) ICEC 2010. LNCS, vol. 6243, pp. 240–247. Springer, Heidelberg (2010)
8. Leontev, A.N.: Activity, Consciousness, and Personality. Prentice-Hall (1978)
9. Rigby, S., Ryan, R.: The Player Experience of Need Satisfaction, http://www.immersyve.com/downloads/research-and-white-papers/PENS_Sept07.pdf
10. Rukzio, E., Müller, M., Hardy, R.: Design, implementation and evaluation of a novel public display for pedestrian navigation: the rotating compass. In: Proceedings of the SIGCHI Conference on Human Factors in Computing Systems (CHI 2009), pp. 113–122. ACM, New York (2009)
11. Talton, J.O., Peterson, D.L., Kamin, S., Israel, D., Al-Muhtadi, J.: Scavenger Hunt: Computer Science Retention Through Orientation. In: Proceedings of the 37th SIGCSE Technical Symposium on Computer Science Education, pp. 443–447. ACM (2006)

Part III

HCI in Learning and Education

Evaluating Engagement Physiologically and Knowledge Retention Subjectively through Two Different Learning Techniques

Marvin Andujar[1], Josh I. Ekandem[1], Juan E. Gilbert[1], and Patricia Morreale[2]

[1] Human-Centered Computing Division, Clemson University, Clemson, SC
[2] Department of Computer Science, Kean University, Union, NJ
{manduja,jekande,juan}@clemson.edu,
pmorreal@kean.edu

Abstract. This paper describes the findings of a replication study conducted at a different location. This study measures the engagement level of participants objectively from two learning techniques: video game and handout (traditional way of learning). This paper may help other researchers design their own Brain-Computer Interface study to measure engagement. In addition, the results of this paper shows a correlation analysis between Engagement (measured physiologically) and knowledge measurement (subjective data). Further, this paper describes briefly the limitations of the Emotiv non-invasive EEG device, which may help researchers and developers understand the device more.

Keywords: Emotions in HCI, Brain-Computer Interface, Passive BCI.

1   Introduction

With the innovative and technological changes happening daily on a global stage, the consequences of having a poorly prepared work force could be staggering. In light of this conjecture, there has been a considerable amount of attention given to the American educational system. Discussions of international rankings [12], the effects of socioeconomic disparities [11] or preparation of teachers all serve as talking points in the effort to repair the current state of education. Frederick Hess, director of education policy studies at the American Enterprise Institute, a conservative policy think tank recently went on record stating that "We spend a lot of time debating pedagogies, a lot of time blaming teachers, a lot of time saying that there's a war on schools... I want to suggest that a lot of it actually misses what matters [16]." However this begs the question what does matter? In an age where information is far more attainable to the masses than ever before, how can our educational system be in such a crisis [3].

M. Kurosu (Ed.): Human-Computer Interaction, Part II, HCII 2013, LNCS 8005, pp. 335–342, 2013.
© Springer-Verlag Berlin Heidelberg 2013

USA Today columnist, Ruth Bettelheim has an answer. Bettelheim suggests more attention needs to be given to understanding how students learn. Furthermore, Bettelheim suggests that the educational failures can be mitigated by an overhaul of the traditional classroom based on the findings of cognitive neuroscience [4]. Likewise and following in the same order, researchers, professionals, and students all acknowledge the need for students to be engaged throughout the learning process [5]. It has been noted that students are bombarded with outside stimuli, causing a general lack of engagement towards the material. In response, educators and game designers have teamed up to provide more engaging experiences that have the advantage of maintaining attention by being entertaining. However, though these games may be entertaining, they cannot neglect instructional aspects that game is intended to serve [14]. As Nicholas Negroponte, the founder of MIT Media Lab points out "Many of the software products that are being developed for children today serve to narrow, rather than broaden, children's intellectual horizons [3]."

This has sparked interest in the evaluation of educational videogames and provides the background for this paper with the underlying question being: "Do educational video games really teach students, and if so how engaging are they? "[9,15]. Numerous works have measured engagement and information retention through assessments of educational video games and more traditional means such as textbooks. The growing amount of literature devoted to the use of games as educational tools serve as indicators of the popularity of this topic [8]. Research has repeatedly shown that in certain environments educational video games can be more attractive to students than traditional learning tools [6,10]. Moreover, studies have shown these educational video games do a better job at obtaining and maintaining student's attention [7]. However, there is no general consensus on which learning technique is more engaging, and which technique is best for knowledge retention. This paper discusses two studies that were conducted to investigate the overall student engagement and knowledge retention of an educational video game in comparison with a textbook that expressed the same information. The first study was conducted at a university in the Southeastern United States, where the results were reported [15]. Later, the replication of this study was conducted at a university in the Northeastern United States.

2   Experimental Design

2.1   Overall Design

The between-subjects design consisted of 32 participants (Male = 12, Female = 20). Participants randomly assigned to a group that received instruction via video game (15 participants) (figure 1) [17] or via handout (17 participants); a more traditional method of learning. Both groups received instruction about the Lewis and Clark Adventure. This combination allowed us to collect both subjective (traditional method to collect engagement) and objective data, in order to see if there was a correlation between both.

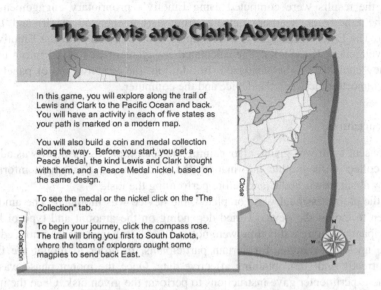

In this game, you will explore along the trail of Lewis and Clark to the Pacific Ocean and back. You will have an activity in each of five states as your path is marked on a modern map.

You will also build a coin and medal collection along the way. Before you start, you get a Peace Medal, the kind Lewis and Clark brought with them, and a Peace Medal nickel, based on the same design.

To see the medal or the nickel click on the "The Collection" tab.

To begin your journey, click the compass rose. The trail will bring you first to South Dakota, where the team of explorers caught some magpies to send back East.

Fig. 1. The Lewis and Clark Adventure Game

2.2   The Physiological Apparatus

The Emotiv EPOC (figure 2) is a wireless EEG data acquisition and processing device. This device consists of 14 electrodes (AF3, F7, F3, FC5, T7, P7, P8, O1, O2, T8, FC6, F4, F8, AF4) to obtain the EEG signal and these channels are based on the international 10-20 locations. The international 10-20 System is the standard naming and positioning for the EEG measurements of any EEG BCI device. This device connects wirelessly via bluetooth and a USB dongle to a computer. This device was chosen among others for its portability, which may provide the best user experience.

This device was used to measure engagement (objective data). It was measured by the EmoStateLogger which was modified to measure engagement for a period of 20

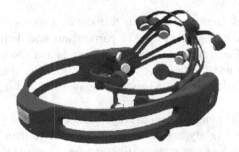

Fig. 2. Non-Invasive EEG Emotiv EPOC Device

minutes; the results were computed using Emotiv's proprietary engagement algo-rithm. The Emotiv engagement range is from 0 (not engaged at all) and 1 (very engaged). The EmoStateLogger is a C++ application bundled with the Emotiv Soft-ware Development Kit (SDK). The calculated engagement was saved into a text file where they could be further analyzed. In addition, the Emotiv control panel estab-lished a connection between the device and the computer.

2.3   Procedures

First a consent form was given, after gaining consent, a pre-assessment was adminis-tered to collect demographic information and to determine how much information they knew about Lewis and Clark before performing the task.

Once the pre-assessment was completed, the device was mounted. The amount of time taken to mount the device varied depending on the amount and type of hair of the participant. Although, this time were not recorded, it is important to noticed that it may take up to 15 minutes for certain participants, in order to mount the Emotiv device correctly and start obtaining affective data. Once the mount phase was com-pleted, the experimenter gave instructions to perform the given task. Once the instruc-tions were given, the participant started the task. As soon as the participant started the task, the experimenter started recording engagement with Emotiv. The task involved either playing the game or reading the handout. The same information was presented in both the game and in a handout. The participants performed the task for 20 mi-nutes. After 20 minutes the experimenter stopped recording engagement and dis-mounted the device from the participant's head. Following the dismounting of the device a 10-question quiz was given in order to measure the knowledge they have acquired. Both groups were given the same quiz. After this quiz was administered, an assessment was given to participants to obtain self-reported information on how much they felt they had learned (knowledge increment), how engaged they felt during the given task, and how interesting they thought the information was.

3   Quantitative Results

In trying to gauge how engagement affects test scores a regression analysis was per-formed on the average engagement level of participants and their test scores.   There was little correlation found between engagement levels and test scores. For the game condition $r^2 = 0.005$ and the handout was $r^2 = 0.002$. For this study, this finding suggests that there is little correlation between engagement and representation method and retention.

Table 1, represents the engagement average between the two groups. It shows that the game group had a slightly higher engagement average than the handout. In the previous report the handout group were slightly more engaged than the game group, unlike this second part of the study.

Table 1. Engagement Results

Group	Sample Size	Engagement	Engagement STD
Game	15	0.619	0.054
Handout	17	0.580	0.048

Table 2, shows the averages of the test scores and the anticipated test scores (ATS). It can be seen that the participants from the game group felt more confident on their performance than the handout group, but they performed worst than the handout. Interesting enough, the results reported on the first study conducted in the SouthEast, the handout group performend better in the test than the game group [15].

Table 2. Test Results

Group	Sample Size	Test Scores	Test Scores STD	ATS
Game	15	40.67	4.41	66.00
Handout	17	61.76	12.37	56.47

It is interesting to find some correlation in terms of test scores performance between two different set of population (Northeast and Southeast). In addition, the results were broken down into gender for further analysis.

3.1   Results by Gender

Table 3, demonstrates the engagement results by gender. It is seen that male were slightly more engaged than female in both groups. Comparing by same gender, both of them were more engaged in the game than in the handout. Although both genders were more engaged in the game, it can be seen from table 4 that the handout group got more information than the game group. Several assumptions can be made, but more studies are needed to clarify these assumptions.

- *First Assumption:* Male were more engaged than female in the game group because, male tend to like more video games.
- *Second Assumption:* Male were more engaged than female in both groups, because the contact between the Emotiv and the participant's scalp were more direct. Female tend to have more hair than male in many cases.
- *Third Assumption:* The participants from the handout group performed better in the test, because they were less distracted and just focused on the content, than playing the game itself.
- *Fourth Assumption:* The participants from the handout group performed better in the test, because they are used to the traditional way of learning, which is reading from physical paper (book, handouts, etc.) and they might not be used to learn from a video game.

Table 3. Engagement Results by Gender

Group	Male Avg.	Male STD	Female Avg.	Female STD.
Game	0.631	0.04	0.609	0.05
Handout	0.594	0.05	0.570	0.03

Table 4. Test Results by Gender

Group	Male Avg.	Male STD	Female Avg.	Female STD.
Game	45.0	20.73	37.7	14.81
Handout	57.14	12.53	65.0	11.78

4   Limitations

There are several limitations raised in this study that it is important to mention. The main limitation is the fact that the researchers did not know the details of the algorithm used to measure engagement. This proprietary algorithm is protected by the Emotiv Company and do not share any details with any researchers. Although, Emotiv is widely used, it is important to notice this issue, and correlate the physiological results with some subjective data or use an engagement formula, mentioned by Szafir, D., and Mutlu, B. [18]. The second limitation with Emotiv, it is the limitation with many non-invasive EEG BCI devices. People have different texture and length of hair, which interfere with the direct connectivity between the device and the scalp. Therefore, it is hard to obtain really good signal to obtain affective data. Also, reported by Ekandem et. al., it may require a long time to mount the device and establish an adequate connection, this varies per participant.

Further, some participants reported that after a while (specific time was not recorded), the device was hurting a little bit from the sides as something was grabbing their head. This may affect the performance of the user while trying to learn information, because they might feel some pain, which may lead to lack of concentration.

5   Conclusion

This paper provides a brief information on the misperception and the needs of finding an accurate learning technique. It also provides a study conducted in order to show as a basic guideline to other researchers of how BCI may be implemented towards their educational studies.

Further studies are needed to come up with conclusion in which method of learning is better or preferable by users: video games or the traditional way of learning. It is recommended from this paper to implement objective measurement to any educational studies, which may lead towards better understanding of the learners. The study presented in this paper may be applied to other studies and modified to the appropriateness of their methods. Lastly, this paper raises some research questions, which may be investigated in other studies.

— *First Question:* Physiologically speaking, while measuring engagement with an EEG non-invasive device such as Emotiv, do engagement results differ by the different texture and length of hairs?

— *Second Question:* While measuring engagement with an EEG non-invasive device such as Emotiv, do engagement results differ by the different sizes and shapes of human's head? How does it differ and what is the difference?

— *Third Question:* How does engagement differs objectively between different cultures or ethnicities while learning in different learning techniques? Can Passive Brain-Computer Interfaces help us understand better the behavior within a task by different cultures?

These questions were based on observations and comments made by the experimenters while the participants were performing the task. Therefore, further studies are recommended in order to understand and develop, concrete methodologies to implement EEG measurement of engagement in educational techniques.

Acknowledgement. This material is based in part upon work supported by the National Science Foundation under Grant Number DUE- 1060545. Any opinions, findings, and conclusions or recommendations expressed in this material are those of the author(s) and do not necessarily reflect the views of the National Science Foundation.

References

1. Ball, C.: Start Right: The Importance of Early Learning. Lesley James, Royal Society for the Encouragement of Arts, Manufactures and Commerce, London (1994)
2. Greenstone, M., Harris, M., Li, K., Looney, A., Patashnik, J.: A Dozen Economic Facts About K-12 Education. The Hamiliton Project (2012),
   http://www.hamiltonproject.org/files/downloads_and_links/
   THP_12EdFacts_2.pdf
3. Negroponte, N., Resnick, M., Cassell, J.: Creating a Learning Revolution. MIT Media Lab (1997)
4. Bettelheim, R.: Outdated teaching is failing our children. USA Today (2010),
   http://usatoday30.usatoday.com/news/opinion/forum/2010-11-
   10-column10_ST1_N.htm
5. Castell, S., Jenson, J.: Paying Attention to Attention: New Economies for Learning. Educational Theory, 381–397 (2004)
6. Gilbert, J.E., Arbuthnot, K., Hood, S., Grant, M.M., West, M.L., McMillian, Y., Cross, E.V., Williams, P., Eugene, W.: Teaching Algebra Using Culturally Relevant Virtual Instructors. The International Journal of Virtual Reality 7(1), 21–30 (2008)
7. McFarlane, A., Sparrowhawk, A., Heald, Y.: Report on the educational use of games: An exploration by TEEM of the contribution which games can make to the education process (2002), http://reservoir.cent.uji.es/canals/octeto/es/440
8. Oblinger, D.: The Next Generation of Educational Engagement. Journal of Interactive Media in Education (8) (2004)
9. Okan, Z.: Edutainment: is learning at risk? British Journal of Educational Technology 34(3), 255–264 (2003)

10. Rosas, R., Nussbaum, M., Cumsille, P., Marianov, V., Correa, M., Flores, P.: Beyond nintendo: Design and assessment of educational video games for first and second grade students. Computers and Education 40(1), 71–94 (2003)

11. Bowles, S., Gintis, H.: Schooling in capitalist America: Educational reform and the contradictions of economic life. Haymarket Books (2011)

12. Gao, H.: U.S. global education ranking is misleading, School of Education scholar argues. The Stanford Daily (2013),
http://www.stanforddaily.com/2013/01/24/stanford-scholar-reexamines-u-s-ranking/

13. Gibson, S.: Are our pre-service teachers prepared to teach in a digital age? In: Bastiaens, T., et al. (eds.) Proceedings of World Conference on E-Learning in Corporate, Government, Healthcare, and Higher Education, vol. 200, pp. 2609–2617 (2009)

14. Hubbard: Evaluating computer games for language learning. Simulation and Gaming (22), pp. 220–223 (1991)

15. Andujar, M., Ekandem, J., Alvarez, I., James, M., Gilbert, J.: Are Educational Video Games All They're Cracked Up To Be?: A physiological Approach for Measuring Engagement in Educational Video Games vs. Conventional Learning Techniques. In: Proceedings of World Conference on E-Learning in Corporate, Government, Healthcare, and Higher Education 2011, pp. 539–544. AA, Chesapeake (2011)

16. Shammas, B.: U.S. education model outdated says renowned researcher. Naples News (2013),
http://www.naplesnews.com/news/2013/jan/08/us-education-model-outdated-says-renowned/

17. Lewis and Clark Adventure Game. Class Brain Game,
http://www.classbraingames.com/2009/12/lewis-and-clark-adventure-game/

18. Szafir, D., Mutlu, B.: Pay Attention! Designing Adaptive Agents that Monitor and Improve User Engagement. In: Proceedings of the 2012 ACM Annual Conference on Human Factors in Computing Systems, CHI 2012, Austin, Texas, USA, New York, NY, May 5-10, pp. 11–20 (2012)

19. Ekandem, J., Alvarez, I., Davis, T., James, M., Gilbert, J.: An Epoc in Neuroscience: A Comparison of Commercial BCI Devices. Ergonomics 55(5), 592–598 (2012)

A New E-learning System Focusing on Emotional Aspect Using Biological Signals

Saromporn Charoenpit[1] and Michiko Ohkura[2]

[1] Graduate School of Engineering, Shibaura Institute of Technology, Japan
nb12103@shibaura-it.ac.jp
[2] College of Engineering, Shibaura Institute of Technology, Japan
ohkura@sic.shibaura-it.ac.jp

Abstract. E-learning is the computer and network-enabled transfer of skills and knowledge. It is widely accepted that new technologies can make a big difference in education. Although the advantages of e-learning over person to person teaching are still under debate, the latter is considered to be superior with respect to teaching effectiveness. One reasons for this advantage of human expert tutors is their ability to deal with the emotional aspects of the learner. In an e-learning system, emotions are important in the classroom. We thus proposed a new e-learning system that focuses on affective aspects. Our system equips sensors to measure biological signals and analyzes user emotions for the improvement of the e-learning system's effectiveness.

Keywords: E-learning, Emotions, Affective aspects, Biological signal.

1 Introduction

E-learning can mean a variety of different things to different people, but it is essentially the computer and network-enabled transfer of skills and knowledge. It can be self-paced or instructor -led and includes media in the form of text, image, animation, streaming video, and audio [1]. E-learning can have many benefits. In times of recession, the case for e-learning becomes much stronger. Key benefits include low cost, fast delivery, self-paced, less travel time, personalized and convenient scheduling, and lower environmental impact.

Thus, many universities have applied electronic communication for e-learning systems to enable people to learn anytime and anywhere, to deliver content and methods that build new knowledge and skills linked to individual learning goals, or to improve performance.

In e-learning systems, emotions are important in the classroom in two major ways. First, emotions have an impact on learning. They influence our ability to process information and to accurately interpret what we encounter. For these reasons, it is important for teachers to create a positive, emotionally safe classroom environment to provide for optimal learning. Second, learning how to manage feelings and relationships constitutes a kind of "emotional intelligence" that enables people to be successful [2].

M. Kurosu (Ed.): Human-Computer Interaction, Part II, HCII 2013, LNCS 8005, pp. 343–350, 2013.
© Springer-Verlag Berlin Heidelberg 2013

Learners are free to learn at their own pace and to define personal learning paths based on their individual needs and interests. E-learning providers do not have to schedule, manage, or track learners through a process. E-learning content is developed according to a set of learning objectives and is delivered using different media elements, such as text, graphics, audio, and video. It must provide as much learning support as possible (through explanations, examples, interactivity, feedback, glossaries, etc.) in order to make learners self-sufficient. However, some kind of support, such as e-mail-based technical support or e-tutoring, is normally offered to learners [3].

Biological signals are electrical or magnetic signals generated by some biological activity in the human body [4]. Biological signals have widely different sources, such as electrocardiography (ECG) originating from the heart, and electroencephalography (EEG) generated by the brain, making them very heterogeneous.

E-learning does not require a classroom, but it does require an understanding of how learning takes place. In this study, we focused on the emotional aspect of the e-learning system using biological signals. The purpose of this study is to design learning environments and tools that avoid inappropriate affective states, such as boredom, anxiety, or anger.

2   Literature Review

Daniel, the author of Emotional Intelligence, argues that the emotional quotient (EQ) is more important than the intelligence quotient (IQ) [5]. The issue is for e-learning to recommend ways in which to keep e-learning from being boring. We recognize that e-learning is different from face-to-face instruction lacking a trainer to address the emotional component and we provide some very sensible advice on how to keep e-learning relevant.

Khan developed a framework for e-learning that contained the following eight dimensions [4]:

- The pedagogical dimension of e-learning refers to teaching and learning. This dimension addresses issues concerning content analysis, audience analysis, goal analysis, media analysis, design approach, organization and methods, and strategies of e-learning environments.
- The technological dimension of the e-learning Framework examines issues of the technology infrastructure in e-learning environments. This includes infrastructure planning, hardware, and software.
- The interface design refers to the overall look and feel of e-learning programs. Interface design dimension encompasses page and site design, content design, navigation, and usability testing.
- The evaluation for e-learning includes both assessment of learners and evaluation of the instruction and learning environment.
- The management of e-learning refers to maintenance of the learning environment and distribution of information.

- The resource support dimension of the e-learning Framework examines the online support and resources required to foster meaningful learning environments.
- The ethical considerations of e-learning relate to social and political influence, cultural diversity, bias, geographical diversity, learner diversity, information accessibility, etiquette, and legal issues.
- The institutional dimension is concerned with issues of administrative affairs, academic affairs, and student services related to e-learning.

This framework provides a new e-learning system.

Kittanakere et al. summarized the main goals of e-learning systems, identified by different researchers, as below [6]:

- Focus on active learning.
- Accommodate various learning styles.
- Explicitly place the responsibility for learning on the students.
- Develop written and oral communication skills.
- Clarify the role of the teacher as facilitator and mentor.
- Provide better coverage of material.
- Develop a sense of self-confidence and independence in students.
- Include a teamwork experience
- Encourage peer review.
- Develop interpersonal communication skills when students are geographically apart.
- Support the entire educational process when students are apart both geographically and temporally.
- Learn to handle time management including the meeting of deadlines.

Many of the above goals reflect the advantages of e-learning systems over traditional learning approaches. Another advantage is that they are scalable. The number of learners that an e-learning system can handle with individual attention is much more than that can be accommodated in a classroom setting.

Kittanakere et al. introduced the design of an emotion sensitive e-learning system that gives emphasis to the complete learning process and is very cost effective. The system categorizes a learner's emotional state as follows: Happy, Neutral, and Sad. This motivates thinking about incorporating emotional aspects of teaching in e-learning systems to make them more intelligent. An intelligent e-learning system should be able to adapt to the knowledge, learning abilities, and needs of each learner. This would give them the feel of individual care, which would assist in the learning process.

Kaiser and Oertel also integrated an emotion recognition sensor system (EREC) into an e-learning system [7]. The system used EREC for emotion detection by the affective component, that EREC developed at the institute of genetics and development of rennes (IGD-R), consisting of a sensor glove, a chest belt, and a data collection unit. The affective component is based on Russell's circumplex model of emotion, a dimensional approach for classifying emotions.

Shen et al. also applied heart rate (HR), skin conductance (SC), blood volume pressure (BVP), and EEG brainwaves to detect learner emotions [8]. The results for emotion recognition from physiological signals achieved a best-case accuracy (86.3%) for four types of learning emotions. This affective e-learning system included only a subset of the factors that could be taken into account to assess a learner's emotional reactions in e-learning.

From the literature reviews, designing a system that focuses on user emotions using some biological signals is very promising. Therefore, we propose a new e-learning system design that avoids inappropriate affective states such as boredom, anxiety, or anger.

3   Design of E-learning System

Distance education and e-learning are becoming an increasingly important part of higher education. This type of education can take place over the Internet, through which the instruction and educational content are delivered [9].

We propose a new design of an e-learning system using biological signals that are affective to the learner and closer to actual classroom learning.

3.1   Overall System Design

In this section we discuss the overall design of the e-learning system (Fig. 1). This system uses an LMS (learning management system) for delivering, tracking, and managing education and a web server that provides the user with easy access via a web browser on a personal computer. While using our system, biological sensors measure user biological signals as EEG, ECG and eye tracking to detect user emotions.

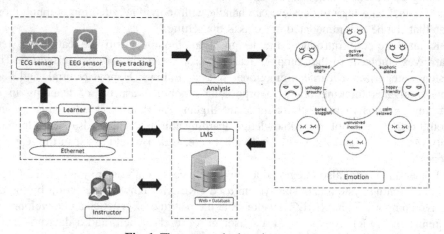

Fig. 1. The proposed e-learning system

3.2   Framework for E-learning

We used an e-learning framework [10] with eight dimensions (Fig. 2). These dimensions encompass various online learning issues, including pedagogical, technological, interface design, evaluation, management, resource support, ethical, and institutional. Various factors discussed in the eight dimensions of the framework can provide guidance in the design, development, delivery, and evaluation of flexible, open, and distance learning environments.

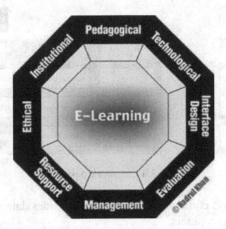

Fig. 2. Badrul Khan's e-learning Framework (Source: Khan, B. H., p.1)

3.3   Framework Design

The framework design of our e-learning system using biological signals consists of eight modules: I/O devices, learning management system (LMS), learner, instructor, server, and biological sensors. It analyzes learner emotions, as shown in Fig. 3. The details are described below:

I/O Devices. There are five I/O devices: speaker, monitor, touch screen, keyboard and mouse.

Learner. The learner is an individual who takes up e-learning by registering to the e-learning system. The learner can choose any of the courses provided by the system.

Instructor. The instructor is an important element of this system that creates and designs courses, content, tests, quizzes, and evaluations.

Server. The servers are the web server, LMS, and database that provide services to other computer application programs (and their users) in the same or other computers.

A web server is simply a computer program that dispenses web pages as they are requested. The machine the program runs on is usually also called a server and the two references are interchangeable in everyday conversation. Our design uses an internet information server as a web application server.

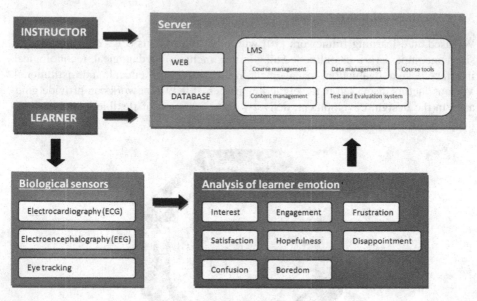

Fig. 3. Framework design

A database server is a computer program that provides database services to other computer programs or computers.

An LMS is a software application or Web-based technology used to plan, implement, and assess a specific learning process. Typically, an LMS provides an instructor with a way to create and deliver content, monitor student participation, and assess student performance. An LMS consists of the following five parts:

- Course management can help store, organize, and communicate the information for a course. It consists of three user groups, such as learner, instructor, and administrator, that can access the system anytime and anywhere.
- Content management includes tools for creating and helping the content.
- The test and evaluation system manages the exams, quizzes, and tests in the database system, such as directions and interactive quizzes, integrated tests, and quizzes to evaluate the learner.
- Course tools are used to help and guide each user.
- The data management system manages the files and folders of each user.

Biological Sensors. Learner emotions were measured with ECG, EEG, and eye tracking biological sensors. An EEG sensor measures voltage fluctuations from electric ions within the brain's neurons. An ECG sensor measures the heart's electrical activity over a period of time. ECG signals can be interpreted as heart rate in beats per minute (BMP). Eye tracking is a device for measuring eye positions and eye movement.

Analysis of Learner Emotion. We devised this design system to understand how learners' emotions evolve during the learning process, so as to develop learning systems that recognize and respond appropriately to students' emotional changes. We used Russell's 'circumplex model' to describe the user's emotion space [11], as shown in Fig. 4. The basic set includes the most important and frequently occurring emotions during learning, namely, interest, engagement, confusion, frustration, boredom, hopefulness, satisfaction, and disappointment.

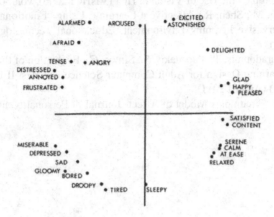

Fig. 4. Russell's 'circumplex model' (Source: Russell, J.A., p. 1168)

4   Conclusion

We have described our approach to designing a new e-learning system that focuses on emotional aspects. ECG, EEG, and eye tracking biological sensors were used for measuring learner emotion. The proposed e-learning system's aim is to avoid inappropriate and affective states such as boredom, anxiety, or anger.

In future work, we will perform experiments and improve our system. In addition, we will conduct further research on learner motivation and determine what is most effective for student learning.

References

1. The Learning Portfolio Ltd.,
   http://www.coursesforyou.com/overview/why-e-learning/
2. Linda, D.H., Jim, R., Kim, A., Suzanne, O., Daisy, M.: The Learning Classroom: Theory Into Practice, p. 90. Stanford University (2003)
3. Food and Agriculture Organization of the United Nations: E-learning Methodologies-A Guide for Designing and Developing E-learning Courses, Rome, p. 10 (2011)
4. The Biomedical Engineering,
   http://www.judex.dk/biomedical_engineering/about.html

5. Daniel, G.: Emotional Intelligence: Why It Can Matter More Than IQ. Bantam, New York (1995)
6. Khan, B.H.: A Framework for Web-based Learning. In: Khan, B.H. (ed.) Web-based Training. Educational Technology Publications, Englewood Cliffs (2011)
7. Kittanakere, L.N., Lakshmisri, L.N.R., Nirmal, K.S.: An Emotional System for Effective and Collaborative e-Learning. In: ACHI 2011 The Fourth International Conference on Advances in Computer-Human Interactions, pp. 260–266 (2011)
8. Kaiser, R., Oertel, K.: Emotions in HCI – An Affective E-Learning System. In: The HCSNet Workshop on the Use of Vision in HCI (VisHCI 2006), vol. 56 (2006)
9. Shen, L., Wang, M., Shen, R.: Affective e-Learning: Using "Emotional" Data to Improve Learning in Pervasive Learning Environment. Educational Technology & Society 12(2), 176–189 (2009)
10. Antonis, K., Daradoumis, T., Papadakis, S., Simos, C.: Evaluation of the Effectiveness of a Web-Based Learning Design for Adult Computer Science Courses. IEEE Transactions on Education 54(2) (August 2011)
11. Russell, J.A.: A Circumplex Model of Affect. Journal of Personality and Social Psychology 39, 1161–1178 (1980)

A Framework to Support Social-Collaborative Personalized e-Learning

Maria De Marsico[1], Andrea Sterbini[1], and Marco Temperini[2]

[1] Dept. of Computer Science, Sapienza University of Rome, Italy
[2] Dept. of Computer, Control, & Management Engineering, Sapienza University of Roma, Italy
{demarsico,sterbini}@di.uniroma1.it, marte@dis.uniroma1.it

Abstract. We propose a comprehensive framework to support the personalization and adaptivity of courses in e-learning environments where the traditional activity of individual study is augmented by social-collaborative and group based educational activities. The framework aims to get its pedagogical significance from the Vygotskij Theory; it points out a minimal set of requirements to meet, in order to allow its implementations based on modules possibly constituted by independent e-learning software systems, all collaborating under a common interface.

Keywords: Personalized e-learning, adaptive e-learning, social collaborative e-learning, zone of proximal development, reputation system.

1 Introduction and Motivations

This paper presents a framework for the dynamic configuration of paths of learning activities for both individual and group education. To define such a framework, one main issue is how to personalize the learning pathway according to the learning characteristics of, respectively, individual students and groups, and, going further along this line, how to make such pathways adaptive to the changing assessment of the above mentioned characteristics. The framework should then allow defining courses as learning paths – LP (i.e. sets of learning activities – la) and maintain a model of the student's characteristics relevant to learning. It should allow: to define a learning activity in such a way that collections of *la*s can be stored in repositories and appropriately selected to build a course; to discriminate the *la*s with respect to the learner's (or group's) learning characteristics, so to be able, once stated the aims to be met by a course, to select only what is needed and most appropriate to complete the course *LP*

This in turn requires: to model (represent) the learner's characteristics, such as the possessed knowledge and abilities, and/or the learning style; and to model the characteristics of a group of learners according to the individual ones, such as with the assessment of shared knowledge, or "sharable" knowledge that could determine the group dynamics; at the best of our knowledge, while a lot can be found in literature on how to set up effective group activities, very little is said about the formal relation

M. Kurosu (Ed.): Human-Computer Interaction, Part II, HCII 2013, LNCS 8005, pp. 351–360, 2013.
© Springer-Verlag Berlin Heidelberg 2013

between the kind of activities and the individual characteristics of group components, as well as about how to choose the components of an effective group.

Personalization and adaptivity are very relevant topics in e-learning research. Traditional investigations are on the accommodation of personal-individual study activity (see [1] for wider reference); the coordination of group study work is also a much frequent topic, also for its interconnections with aims different from direct education of students (cfr. [2,3] and see [4] for the use of e-learning technologies in professional group work). Moreover social-collaborative learning is coming to be more often studied, as a next step in motivating and augmenting study activity [5,6].

2   Framework Basics

According to the requirements identified above, the framework allows to map the core features of both the learner and the learning activity on a set of operational items which are exploited during content deployment and for its personalization. We list below the main elements that must be taken into account. Modeling the *Learner* (individual), requires to take into account and represent her/his personal characteristics such as: the skills (knowledge, abilities) achieved; the confidence we can assign to the above achievements, i.e. a measure of how a skill is more or less firmly possessed by the learner, to be compared with the requirements to be met to tackle a specific learning activity; the learning style; reputation gained during activities involving social/group collaborative e-learning It is worth noticing that we are defining here the backbone of the framework, and leaving aside the details about our implementation. For instance, we adopt the Felder-Silverman model (with the well-known *dimensions* active-reflective, sensing-intuitive, visual-verbal, and sequential-global [7-9]). In this way the high-level specification can accommodate different learning-style-qualified versions of the same content; during the delivery of a course, when a *la* is to be presented, the version corresponding to the current evaluation of the learner's learning style can be used. The definition of a model for the learner requires specifying the concept of *skill*. A skill is the representation of an ability/knowledge that can be possessed or pursued. A learning activity is deemed to let a learner acquire certain skills, and often, for the learning activity to be tackled, a set of prerequisite skills is needed. In our framework, a skill is defined as a predicate S() whose arguments state: a *main concept* (a conventional name for the ability or knowledge); an integer value (*level*)and a *keyword*, expressing the cognitive level to which the concept is possessed, according to Bloom's taxonomy [10]; an optional *matching concept* (possibly multiple), to which the achievement of the main one is related (for certain keywords in the Bloom's Taxonomy such matching concepts might be needed for further qualification of the cognitive level); a *context*, stating the disciplinary context in which the concept(s) is intended. In summary, we can speecify a skill as:

$$S(concept, k, keyword, matchingconcept(s), context)$$

The predicate expression of skills allows a (limited) set of inferences, such as

```
if S(c, 3, use,  c', ctxt) then S(c,2,describe,c',ctxt)
```

As for a *learning activity*, we adopt a general declination of the concept of learning object. It is an educational resource deemed to support either individual study (such as the case of a text page with images) or practical activities (such as the solution of an exercise with feedback by the teacher) or some more complex tasks, implying one (or more) group collaborative or social-collaborative learning activity. An activity is characterized as "individual" if its organization and design implies feedbacks, and possibly exchanges, only with the tutor/teacher. Group collaborative activities are based on the collaboration of a small group of learners (e.g. from the same class). Social collaborative activities are based on interaction and exchange among "peers" in a wider set of learners than the group (usually a set of groups, or the whole class, or even, in some advanced settings or during particular activities, participants external to the usual class context, such as users in a web-based Community of Practice – CoP [11,12]). Here the concept of reputation can get significantly into the framework [13,14], as a means to update the individual learner model according to her/his performance during learning activities in a social-collaborative environment.

In the proposed framework the components of a learning activity *la* are defined by the *la* designer (an expert in the learning domain) and are the following:

— *la.Content* – a collection of learning material, allowing the execution of an instructional process, possibly by the use of a supporting software platform: a web page containing the text to study, can be handled by a browser; an interactive exercise can be programmed and presented as a flash clip; a group activity can be performed via web through an accordingly programmed software system (Content Management System – CMS); a social collaborative learning activity can be performed in another dedicated web system, e.g. a CoP platform. In the la, for such material different versions should be comprised, according to different learning style to match for the students.

— *la.A* – Acquisition: a set of skills, whose achievement is expected after the *la* has been successfully tackled

— *la.P* – Prerequisites: a set of skills that are "needed" before being ready to fruitfully tackle the *la*.

— *la.Effort* – a quantification of the cognitive load associated to tackling the *la*.

Completing a *la* will take to the integration of *la.A* into the set of skills possessed by the student, with a *confidence* which depends on student's performance in, e.g., a final test, as we will see below. A repository of learning activities is a set of *la*s available to build courses on a given subject. We include in the repository those activities for which *la.A* is included in the power set of H, which is in turn the full set H of skills related to a certain subject:

$$R = \{la \mid la.A \in \wp(H) \}$$

Notice that *la.P* may intersect $\wp(H)$, but it may contain concepts from other subjects as well (for example physics theories require knowledge of mathematics). It is up to the course designer to include also related learning activities in the course.

We define a *learning path* as a set $LP = \{la_i\}_{i \in (1...n)}$. For a *LP* we can state the overall acquirements *LP.A*, and the overall requirements *LP.P* as

$$LP.A = \cup_{i \in \{1...n\}} la_i.A \qquad\qquad LP.P = \cup_{i \in \{1...n\}} la_i.P \setminus LP.A$$

and the overall effort imposed by LP on a learner as $LP.Effort = \sum_{i \in \{1...n\}} la_i.effort$

A course personalized for the learner l, is a learning path built basing on a student model of l. A *student model* represents the current evaluation of the individual learning characteristics, relevant for the learning process implemented by course tackling; the student model of l, SM(l), has to be continuously updated during course, to reflect the changes (evolution) of l's learning characteristics determined by the learning activities; such updates, in turn, are used to modify the course path and/or presentation themselves, having them adapting to the above mentioned evolution.

As already sketched above, a basic definition of SM(l) spans over

— l's learning style (that is the *current evaluation* of her/his learning style: $LS(l)$)
— l's state of skills, that is an informative representation of the set of skills that l is *currently possessing*, $SK(l)$, which is upgraded as the student tackles learning activities: $SM(l) = \langle LS(l), SK(l)\rangle$

Here, $SK(l)$ is more than just a list of skills: it represents both the skills possessed and the degree of trust (*certainty*) we can put on that. So it is a set of *qualified couples*
$$SK(l) = \{\langle s_1, c_1\rangle, ..., \langle s_{nl}, c_{nl}\rangle\}$$
where each c_i is the "certainty of possession", for the associated skill s_i.

The certainty of possession for a skill is a number $c \in [0...1]$: an higher certainty corresponds to greater confidence in the possession of the skill. The certainty is computed according to the assessment activities undertaken by the learner during the course: when (for example after having answered to multiple choice questions) the skill s is considered as acquired by the learner l, the couple $\langle s, C_{ENTRY}\rangle$ is added to $SK(l)$, where C_{ENTRY} is a suitable default confidence; after a further successful assessment for s, the certainty is updated to witness an increasing trust in the actual achievement of the skill; on the other hand, if a further assessment activity on s is unsuccessful, the certainty decreases. In this way, at any moment the state of skills for l shows the current evaluation of certainty for the achieved skills. Notice that iterating the assessment process beyond certain limits would not be sensible: when the certainty for s decreases below a level C_{DEMOTE} the couple $\langle s, c\rangle$ is extracted from $SK(l)$: the skill is not actually possessed and further study activity will be needed to acquire it back; on the contrary, when c in $\langle s, c\rangle$ climbs above a conventional value $C_{PROMOTE}$, the skill is to be considered firmly acquired, and further assessment for it will not be necessary anymore. We remind that for a student l to be considered able to access a certain activity, all skills in $la.P$ should be present in $SK(l)$. In the framework, $C_{ENTRY}, C_{DEMOTE}, C_{PROMOTE}$ have no predetermined value; as for our implementing system [8], we set some defaults for them (resp. 0.6, 0.35, 0.8), but allow the teacher to assign them differently, according to preferences related to the nature of the repository used, or even of the courses to build. *Course configuration* is the activity of construction of a learning path (a course) according to the student's state of skills and to her/his formative aims on the subject at hand. We define, for the set $SK(l) = \{\langle s_1, c_1\rangle, ..., \langle s_{nl}, c_{nl}\rangle\}$, its *s-projection* as the set of skills appearing in the qualified couples:
$$s\text{-}proj(SK(l)) = \{s_i, \text{ with } \langle s_i, c_i\rangle \in SK(l)\} = \{s_1, ..., s_{nl}\}$$

We also define

— the starting knowledge of l, with respect to the course to build, as the initial value of the state of skills $SK(l)_{INIT}$; this may result, for example, from a precourse assessment activity, stating that a certain set of skills is possessed with certainty at least C_{ENTRY}; in a similar way, $SK(l)_{FINAL}$ is the state of the student's skills at the end of a course

— the formative aims of l in tackling the course as the set of skills that l is expected to possess, with certainty at least $C_{PROMOTE}$, after taking the course (it may happen that certainty for certain skills continue to increase beyond CPROMOTE thanks to related activities, but in this context it is not deemed significant to continue measuring such increase)

$$T[l] = \{s_1, ..., s_{ml}\}$$

Then a course configuration for l, with starting knowledge $SK(l)_{INIT}$ and formative target $T[l]$ is a learning path $LP(l, T[l]) = \{la_1, ..., la_{tl}\}$ such that its learning activities, together with the initial state of skills can cover the formative needs:

$$\{<s_i, c_i> \mid s_i \in s\text{-}proj(SK(l)_{INIT}) \wedge c_i = C_{PROMOTE}\}$$

$$\cup$$

$$<s_j, c_j> \mid s_j \in LP(l, T[l]).A \wedge <s_j, c_j> \in (SK(l)_{FINAL}) \wedge c_j = C_{PROMOTE}\}$$

$$\supseteq$$

$$\{<s_p, c_p> \mid s_p \in T[l] \wedge c_p = C_{PROMOTE}\}$$

A course is considered successfully taken once

$$\forall s \in T[l], <s, c> \in SK(l)_{FINAL} \text{ with } c \geq C_{PROMOTE}.$$

In other words the course *can allow* to have $SK(l)$ eventually evolving to contain all the skills specified by $T[l]$, with *firm certainty* (at least $C_{PROMOTE}$). The definition of learning activity implicitly allow ro define a *Relation of derivation* (propedeuticy): Given two learning activities la, $\underline{la}$, if $la.A \cap \underline{la}.P \neq \varnothing$, some skills needed to take $\underline{la}$ are acquired through la and la precedes $\underline{la}$. This induces a relation of partial order in the repository R, that allows to depict it as a graph of learning activities.

Every course is a subset (subgraph) of R. When we want to present the learner with a sequence of learning activities   to tackle, the course built by configuration can be linearized in such a way to comply with the relation of derivation. Such linearization is usually not unique: there can be many equivalent sequences coming from the same LP. Moreover, assigning the learner with a LP where the order of *las* to take is too strictly predetermined, even when not necessary, may hinder learner's independence and motivation in attending the course. In addition, the framework aims to let the learner live and interact in a social–collaborative e-learning environment, and it is expectable for the "next learning activity" in the course to be selectable by the learner as freely as possible (according to her/his interest, motivations and opportunities). Of course, in order to avoid useless frustrations to the learner, such freedom should be bound by the "affordability" of the learning activity for her/him. This can effectively substitute a prior sequencing. In practice, the choice of the next learning activity should better be limited only by the actual possibility to tackle it, computed according to the current state of skills $SK(l)$. The Vygotskij theory [15] is a rich source of support for the student-system co-evolution pattern depicted above, and is well equipped to provide support to a truly social-collaborative approach to taking learning paths.

3   Enrichment of the Student Model

Given a learner l, working on the configured course $\underline{LP} = LP(l, T[l]) = \{la_1, \ldots, la_{tl}\}$, we can define some significant cognitive areas related to student's learning state as follows. The area of Autonomous Problem Solving (APS) is the area of firm knowledge in the present state of skills:

$APS(l) = \{s \mid <s, C_{PROMOTE}> \in SK(l)\}$. Where of course, $APS(l) \subseteq s\text{-}proj(SK(l))$.

Basing on $SK(l)$ and $APS(l)$, the Zone of Proximal Development (ZPD) for the learner can be computed at least as

$$ZPD(l) = s\text{-}proj(SK(l)) \setminus APS(l)$$

This is a zone where the learner has no firm achievements yet, but that can be explored with some help by the teacher or by peers. The area of Unreachable Problem Solving (UPS) can be defined as a consequence, and is the area of the course where it is not safe for the learner to enter, given the present level of skills.

$$UPS(l) = \underline{LP}.A \setminus (APS(l) \cup ZPD(l))$$

At any moment the student model can be determined as

$$SM(l) = <LS(l), SK(l), APS(l), ZPD(l)>$$

Actually, the ZPD can be defined in a more challenging way, which may better stimulate the student. The derivation of the new definition follows. Given a learning path $\underline{LP}$, its knowledge domain is $KD(\underline{LP}) = \underline{LP}.A \cup \underline{LP}.P$.

In particular, $KD(\underline{LP}) \setminus s\text{-}proj(SK(l))$ is the set of all skills in the course knowledge domain, that are not yet acquired in $SK(l)$. Such skills belong neither in $APS(l)$ nor in $ZPD(l)$ (as per the current definition of ZPD). Given one of such skills, s, we define the set of possible (sub)learning paths LP' in $\underline{LP}$, that can eventually allow to acquire s, and that are traversable starting with the current state of skills (without losing generality we assume that each subpath is a   propedeuticy-ordered set of learning activities):

$$Reach(s, SK(l), \underline{LP}) = $$
$$= \{G=\{la_i\}_{i \in \{1 \ldots nG\}} \subseteq \underline{LP} \mid s \in la_{nG}.A \wedge G.P \subseteq s\text{-}proj(SK(l)) \cup G.A\}$$

Notice that the last condition relating G.P to G.A expresses the possibility that the prerequisites of some $la_i \in G$ might be acquired through a previous $la_j \in G$.

The distance of s from the present $SK(l)$ is defined as $D(s, s\text{-}proj(SK(l)), \underline{LP}) = \underline{G}.Effort$, where $\underline{G}$ is an element of minimal overall effort in $Reach(s, SK(l), \underline{LP})$.

The set *Support*(s, SK(*l*), <u>LP</u>) = <u>G</u>.P∩ *s-proj*(SK(*l*)) denotes the skills already possessed by the learner that are necessary to reach *s* along a minimal-effort path in <u>LP</u>. We designate such a set as the *support set* to reach *s*. It is reasonable to think that the higher is the certainty associated to the skills in the support set, the better we could expect the learner to reach *s*. Likewise we may think that certainty in the support set can provide an estimate of how far from the SK(*l*) we can go trying to acquire new skills, with reasonable expectations. In other words, the level of certainty in the support set needed to reach *s*, can allow to assess how far in terms of D(), *s* could at most be, and yet still consider *s* in the ZPD(*l*). Actually, D() represents a measure of effort; however the concrete possibility for the student to achieve a certain skill does not only depend on the required effort, yet also on the certainty of the elements possibly supporting such achievement. In other words, supposing that D(s, *s-proj*(SK(*l*)), <u>LP</u>) ≥ D(s', *s-proj*(SK(*l*)), <u>LP</u>) while the overall certainty of the *Support(s, SK(l), LP)* is higher of *Support(s', SK(l), LP)*, we can assume that s might be reachable while s' might not, in spite of a closer distance. So, given the following definitions

$$A1 = AvgEffort(\underline{G}, Support(s, SK(l), \underline{LP})) = \sum_{la \in \underline{G}} la.effort \,/\, Card(\underline{G})$$
$$A2 = AvgCertainty(Support(s, SK(l), \underline{LP})) =$$
$$= (\sum_{<s,c> \in Support(s, SK(l), LP)} c) \,/\, Card(Support(s, SK(l), \underline{LP}))$$

the "daring threshold" is the distance from SK(*l*) below which to accept that *s* is in ZPD(*l*), and is defined as *DTreshold*(s, SK(*l*)) = (A2/A1) · *dF,* dF being the daring factor, an integer that is to be configured by the teacher, depending how far from the initial skills it is admissible to go (a multiplicative factor). Then

$$ZPD(l) = \{s \in KD(\underline{LP}) \setminus APS(l), \text{ such that}$$
$$D(s, s\text{-}proj(SK(l)), \underline{LP}) \le DTreshold(s, SK(l))\}$$

4   Group Activity

The main problem with group activities is selecting a LP suitable to let the group skills grow according to the individual characteristics of the group members.. This translates in the problem of consistently determining the overall group's state of skills (Group Knowledge - GK), and ZPD, basing on the individual ones. In principle, the group's ZPD should be the largest possible, so to maximize members' gain from the collaborative activities. On the other hand it may also include activities that are outside of some group member's ZPD provided they are not too far away. This is crucial to avoid leaving members behind. A first possible choice is to comprise the skills that are shared by all group members (the intersection of their SKs); this set would represent the minimal shared ZPD and would be bounded on the weakest members: the effect of (bottom) outliers on the group ZPD would be exalted, probably reducing motivation of the "smarter" participants. Moreover this choice would strongly limit the possibility of leveraging the support that could come from more experienced peers, which is a key feature in Vygotskij's model. On the other hand, the dual choice of building the group's GK as the union of all members' SKs, resulting in a maximal group ZPD, would obtain similar negative results as above: it would satisfy the brightest group members (top outliers), and leave the others behind. A mediated solution could satisfy both weaker and brighter students: we compute the group's GK as the union of the members' SK, where each skill has group-certainty equal to its average certainty in the members' SK, so to measure the confidence in the achievement of the skill by the group members. This model could better motivate brighter students to help their weaker peers; in addition it allows expanding the group ZPD, to encompass further, possibly more interesting, activities.

Let ST be a group of students, and LP its learning path. Let's start defining the APS for such group. An obvious choice would be to extend the definition of a student's personal APS, and say that the group-APS should represent the set of those skills that are firmly possessed by all the members of the group. Therefore:

$$APS(ST) = \cap_{l \in ST} APS(l)$$

However, this definition would ignore the possible group reciprocal support in a *group-autonomous* achievement. As for the APS of the group, we might consider a "pseudo-intersection" involving also the possession of knowledge in the individual SKs: skills that are not firmly possessed by *all* members are included in the *APS(ST)* iff they are in *APS(l')* for *some l' ∈ ST* and they are in *SK(l)* for all the other members *l∈ ST*. In this respect, we define a lower threshold τ_C for such certainty, which is:

$$\tau_C = C_{PROMOTE} - C_{ENTRY}/2$$

The *l* students above will support the *l' ones*; so they have to be sufficiently many to allow for the above calculated APS being reliable: suppose we state that there must be at least one of such group leaders for every g members in ST, where g is chosen by the teacher according to the activity, then we can say that *from a group viewpoint* the knowledge is "sufficiently firmly" possessed if in the set

$$APS(ST) = \{s \in \cup_{l \in ST} APS(l) \mid$$
$$\forall l \in ST(<s,c> \in SK(l) \wedge c \geq \tau_C) \wedge Card(\{l' \in ST \mid <s,c> \in SK(l') \wedge c=C_{PROMOTE}\}) \geq Card(ST)/g\}$$

The GK is defined basing on the members SKs as well: it comes out, reasonably, to be an expansion of APS(ST)

$$GK(ST) = \{<s,c> / \forall l \in ST (<s,c_l> \in SK(l) \wedge c=((\Sigma_{l \in ST, <s,cl> \in SK(l)} c_l) / Card(ST))\}$$

We use *GK(ST)* and *APS(ST)* to compute *ZPD(ST)*. Instead of direct construction we use a reverse strategy and define implicitly the group ZPD, through criteria of *admissibility* of activities. Two conditions are defined, by working on the *APS(l)*s the *ZPD(l)*s, and the SKs of the group members.

The first condition expresses requirements both on the group composition and on the selected activities; so it is divided in two parts. The group's member's (firm) starting points (APSs) must have some common intersection, and, in addition, the union of the starting points must allow the group to fulfill the activities prerequisites. So, given a group of students ST and a learning path LP, 1) *the group members must share a common portion of APS, and 2) each activity prerequisites is firmly possessed by at least one of the members:* $\cap_{l \in ST} APS(l) \neq \emptyset \wedge LP.P \subseteq \cup_{l \in ST} APS(l)$

The second condition states that students in a group ST must share some common proximal development, and that an activity $la \in LP$ is admissible for ST iff, though possibly being off the ZPDs of some members, it is *not too distant* from them, and it is comprised in the ZPD of at least a number of members sufficient to support the others - τ is a threshold to establish admissibility, for learner l, of an la not in ZPD(l):

$$\cap_{l \in ST} ZPD(l) \neq \varnothing \quad \wedge \quad \forall la \in LP \; \forall s \in la.A \; \forall l \in ST \quad D(s, ZPD(l), LP) < \tau$$
$$\wedge \quad \forall la \in LP \; Card(\{l \in ST \mid la.A \subseteq ZPD(l)\}) \geq Card(ST/g)$$

Where g, as above, represents the number of students which can be driven by a peer, and can be set by the teacher. Notice that if we used APS in place of ZPD, in the definition of the second condition, we would have some of the brighter members of the group left without anything new to learn in the admissible activities, which makes them useless for them besides, of course, dramatically decreasing their motivation.

Being τ a threshold controlling the span outside individual ZPDs, i.e. beyond the daring zone for the individual learner, one way to set it is to choose the minimum daring threshold for the skills in *la.A*.

Whatever is the chosen strategy, different groups may have different degrees of compatibility and suitability: compatibility among the members can affect the way the members interact and help each other, and in turn, get results out of such collaboration (results in terms of knowledge acquired, more or less firm). Compatibility could be considered with respect to several aspects: here we consider only the aspects related to the knowledge possessed by the students, i.e. the personal SK of the group members.

5   Conclusions

Personalized and adaptive e-learning is widely studied and show its applications in a variety of educational fields [16-19]. We have presented the definition of a framework devised to support the conjugation of learning activity based on individual study and group/collaborative activity in an environment of personalized and adaptive e-learning. Two main characteristics of this work are 1) in the fact that it is detached by any present implementation of actual systems for social-collaborative and traditional e-learning: we have in fact abstracted the framework from previous experiences that are based on existing systems; 2) that the framework is deemed to provide a ground layer for an interface based on the pedagogical principles of the theory of Vygotskij, by designing the formal bases for the implementation of concepts such as the Zone of Proximal Development in an e-learning setting.

References

1. Limongelli, C., Sciarrone, F., Temperini, M., Vaste, G.: Adaptive Learning with the LS-Plan System: a Field Evaluation. IEEE Transactions on Learning Technologies 2(3), 203–215 (2009), doi:10.1109/TLT.2009.25
2. De Marsico, M., Sterbini, A., Temperini, M.: The Definition of a Tunneling Strategy between Adaptive Learning and Reputation-based Group Activities. In: Proc. ICALT. IEEE Comp. Society (2011) ISBN 978-0-7695-4346-8

3. De Marsico, M., Sterbini, A., Temperini, M.: A strategy to join adaptive and reputation-based social-collaborative e-learning, through the Zone of Proximal Development. IJDET (2013), doi: 10.4018/IJDET

4. Nanni, U., Temperini, M.: eLearning for knowledge management in collaborative architectural design. Int. Journal of Design Sciences and Technology 19(2), 105–121 (2012) ISSN 1630 - 7267

5. Kreijns, K., Kirschner, P.A., Jochems, W.: Identifying the pitfalls for social interaction in computer supported collaborative learning environments: a review of the research. Computers in Human Behavior 19, 335–353 (2003)

6. Cheng, Y., Ku, H.: An investigation of the effects of reciprocal peer tutoring. Computers in Human Behavior 25 (2009)

7. Limongelli, C., Sciarrone, F., Temperini, M., Vaste, G.: The Lecomps5 Framework for Personalized Web-Based Learning: a Teacher's Satisfaction Perspective. Computers in Human Behavior 27(4) (2011) ISSN 0747-5632

8. Sterbini, A., Temperini, M.: Selection and sequencing constraints for personalized courses. In: Proc. 40th IEEE FIE (2010), doi:10.1109/FIE.2010.5673146

9. Felder, R.M., Silverman, L.K.: Learning and teaching styles in engineering education. Eng. Education 78(7), 674–681 (1988)

10. Bloom, B.S. (ed.): Taxonomy of Educational Objectives. David McKay Co. Inc., New York (1964)

11. Wenger, E.: Supporting communities of practice a survey of community-oriented technologies (2001), http://www.ewenger.com/tech

12. Limongelli, C., Sciarrone, F., Starace, P., Temperini, M.: An Ontology-driven OLAP System to Help Teachers in the Analysis of Web Learning Object Repositories. Information Systems Management 27(3), 198–206 (2010), doi:10.1080/10580530.2010.493810

13. Sterbini, A., Temperini, M.: SOCIALX: reputation based support to social collaborative learning through exercise sharing and project teamwork. Journal of Information Systems and Social Change 2(1) (2011), doi:10.4018/ijissc

14. Wei, W., Lee, J., King, I.: Measuring credibility of users in an e-learning environment. In: Proc. 16th Int. Conf. on World Wide Web, Banff, Alberta, Canada, May 8-12, pp. 1279–1280. ACM, New York (2007)

15. Vygotskij, L.S.: The development of higher forms of attention in childhood. In: Wertsch, J.V. (ed.) The Concept of Activity in Soviet Psychology. Sharpe, Armonk (1981)

16. Limongelli, C., Mosiello, G., Panzieri, S., Sciarrone, F.: Virtual industrial training: Joining innovative interfaces with plant modeling. In: Proc. ITHET 2012 (2012)

17. Limongelli, C., Sciarrone, F., Vaste, G.: Personalized e-learning in moodle: The moodle_LS system. Journal of E-Learning and Knowledge Society 7(1), 49–58 (2011)

18. Kreijns, K., Kirschner, P.A., Jochems, W.: Identifying the pitfalls for social interaction in comp. supported collaborative learning environments: a review of the research. Computers in Human Behavior 19, 335–353 (2003)

19. Gasparetti, F., Micarelli, A., Sciarrone, F.: A web-based training system for business letter writing. Knowledge-Based Systems 22(4), 287–291 (2009)

Challenges for Contextualizing Language Learning
Supporting Cultural Integration

Søren Eskildsen and Matthias Rehm

Department of Architecture, Design and Media Technology,
Aalborg University, Denmark
{se,matthias}@create.aau.dk

Abstract. To help facilitate language learning for immigrants or foreigners arriving to another culture and language, we propose a context-aware mobile application. To expand on the known elements like location, activity, time and identity, we investigate the challenges on including cultural awareness to ensure a better experience-based learning. We present methods used to collect information about everyday activities collected by immigrants or foreigners. This information will help structuring language learning assignments presented through the context-aware mobile application.

Keywords: context-aware, experience-based learning, cultural language learning, context logging, mobile application.

1 Introduction

The idea behind labeling a device 'smart' can be multifaceted, but one thing that is always expected is auto-completion of the many redundant and therefore trivial tasks. The truly smart applications on mobile phones will even know its users' schedule and the upcoming contexts in order to prepare the information. These applications requires knowing the right context all the time in order to function correctly thus making it the weakness, since providing wrong context scenarios would break the experience. Salber et al. (1999) was among the first to investigate and formalize how to aid developers in developing applications, which had the context-awareness as the driven parameter [1]. Dey (2001) discussed in [2] how we could understand and use context so applications could benefit from this, at that time unused, layer of information.

In this paper we will investigate and discuss the challenges in creating a context-aware language learning mobile application. A smart phone application gives the possibility to create an unrestricted and more contextualized learning platform for the individual. But getting the context automatically into the application based on a set of fixed elements like, location and activity is a challenge.

M. Kurosu (Ed.): Human-Computer Interaction, Part II, HCII 2013, LNCS 8005, pp. 361–369, 2013.
© Springer-Verlag Berlin Heidelberg 2013

The foundation for the application is based on that between 2007 and 2009 around 60.000 immigrants were arriving to Denmark each year [3]. The integration mainly consists of language courses, which is run by the local municipalities. This service is free of charge and the goal is to put the newcomers into a position, where they can participate in everyday Danish life. The course setup establishes a thorough theoretical understanding of the Danish language, but often lacks the possibility to motivate students and let them apply this knowledge in a real cultural setting and thus pro-actively participate in their host society.

To cope with this situation, we suggest an approach based on previous work done by Rehm et al. (2009) on intercultural communication that puts the cultural and language learning task in the context of its actual use by embracing training methods [4] –like situated and experience-based learning –that have shown to be more effective in terms of cultural integration [5]. This solution is aiming at working with the individual on a learning and cultural level.

Many approaches adapt to the individual by requiring a certain amount of user inputs to the system, which then based on a subjective input uses this data to determine what could be relevant for the user. The challenge consists of automating the experience and hereby eliminates any subjective inputs. Information have never been so accessibly as today and with the smart phone we are able to detect its user's location and physical activity through clever use of sensors, which are built into any phone that are being sold today. But if we add a deeper layer of integration between the application and the smart phone, we are able to read any user input like mails, SMS, calendars, installed applications etc. This opens for an ethical challenge with its use and handling of personal information. Also would we get permission to read these more private details in the phone? Before choosing methods how to get information from users it is important to understand what users see as a context. Due to the subjectivity regarding the issue it will have to be tested in smaller target groups. This will assure a better approach to record the experiences and construct a definition from that data, before introducing it to the larger user base.

2   Culture as Contextual Information for Mobile Language Learning

In the introduction we argue that situating the experience of learning a language into the actual context of its use will have a huge impact on learning gains and proficiency. But language learning is just one albeit very important aspect of the overall vision of a system that supports cultural integration by experience-based learning. On a theoretical level, the project aims at an integrated model of cultural interactions by taking the system and user perspective into account. This is based on our previous experience with culture aware interactive technology and mobile embodied interactions and will pave the way for learning activities that are integrated into the student's everyday activities. On a practical level, we develop a mobile solution for smart phones that proposes Danish multimedia exercises to the student based on an interpretation of the student's context at that time and taking the student's background in terms of language expertise, cultural integration and learning preferences into account.

To realize this vision, culture is a central notion that has an impact on several levels and presents an important contextual factor where it is more or less unclear how this can be capture and represented. On the one hand, aspects of the target culture are the main learning goal of the system. Thus, there is a need of capturing what are such relevant aspects of the target culture, where do they become apparent in the everyday situations, i.e. what is their context of use, and how can that be mapped to appropriate exercises for mobile learning. As the notion of culture is used by several disciplines (e.g. linguistics, social sciences, psychology, business, anthropology) attempting to provide a definition of the constituting elements (e.g. [6]; [7]; [8]) this is not a trivial task. Additionally, it has been shown in intercultural training that cultural groups can also be distinguished in terms of how they learn [7], and that people progress through a number of stages from ethnocentric to ethnorelative [9] when they make intercultural experiences, which also influence which aspects of a target might be relevant for the current stage and in what way this information should be presented. Ultimately, this means that extended user models will be necessary to capture these partly static, partly dynamic features involved in cultural integration.

3   Application Development Stages

We suggest that an approach to create experience-based learning with cultural preferences would be through mobile context-aware computing. In order to achieve that goal several challenges has to be addressed. We have divided our application development into 3 main stages as depicted on Fig.1, which all have a specific focus that needs to be solved in order to create a convincing context-aware language learning experience.

The stages are each an isolated investigation. This paper focuses on the first stage of the 3 stage development. As shown on Fig.1 our stage 1 box contains various topics. The focus is on identifying experience-based learning contexts together with the end user. This is primarily investigated as a field study and collected through an application created for the specific purpose. Each topic within stage 1 is discussed in individual sections hereafter.

3.1   Stage 1 – Definition of a Context

We use Dey's (2001) definition of a context, which is as follows:

> "Context is any information that can be used to characterise the situation of an entity. An entity is a person, place, or object that is considered relevant to the interaction between a user and an application, including the user and applications themselves." [2]

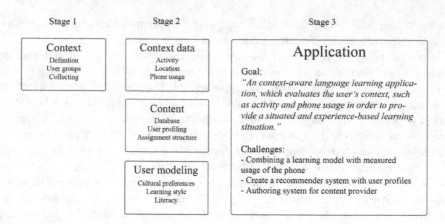

Fig. 1. Overview of the multiple stages in the development of a language learning application

We want to have incorporated several key elements in the chosen definition, which are important to our solution. The definition by Dey (2001) encompass the much used elements in context-aware computing, like location, identity, interaction (activity), but lacks the actual mention of time. We do believe that this is covered by including the interaction device as a measurable parameter. Dourish (2004) mention several studies and compare their definitions of a context and it is clear that the main foundation apparently regardless of case in which the context is used have location, identity and time as parameters [10]. Based on these three elements we can predict several situational contexts that will be useful information in a language learning application. The device holds another layer of context relevant information, such as physical actions or activities. These physical motions can be captures by sensors in the phone or sensor only devices, which are demonstrated by [11–14]. The definition by Dey (2001) also allows for collecting information based upon phone usage. This will involve SMS, calendar, mails, frequently used programs, RSS feeds, cloud services or social networks like Twitter and Facebook. By including personal profiling, it will open a discussion regarding privacy, which is not relevant in this paper and therefore will not be addressed.

3.2   Stage 1 – What Is a Language Learning Context?

The application is meant to invoke experience-based learning by using the assignments in the language class at a later time. Schmidt (2005) introduces Implicit Human Computer Interaction (iHCI) as the interaction conducted by the user with the environment or artifacts in order to accomplish a goal [15]. The implicit interaction or input is measured by the system depended on behaviors or actions of the user. We believe that the experiences may not all be measurable and will become implicit feedback to the context understanding for each user when using the application. This will provide a more situated experience for the user and thereby be essential learning of how a situation may work, since these can be very cultural depended.

Current language courses are still class room based, learners interact with other learners that have an equal level of mastery of the language. Thus, exercises done during the class have one severe shortcoming, even if they are motivating and well-designed, e.g. including role-plays or other experience-based elements. Learners interact with other non-native speakers, rendering it nearly impossible to experience "real" conversations in terms of what is discussed, how it is discussed down to phonetic accuracy for the language that is learned.

By complementing class work with situated learning in real situations, we aim providing the learners with opportunities to experience and practice in real situations following the idea of coaching in intercultural training [16]. Imagine e.g. a situation where the student stands in line at the train station in order to purchase a ticket. This can be seen as an ideal situation to trigger a learning session on buying a train ticket. The student has some time for this session as he is waiting for his turn, he is in the right context for the knowledge that is conveyed and he is able to apply the knowledge shortly afterwards in a real situation. These experiences can then feed back into the classroom, providing feedback to the teacher about the actual performance of the learners in the class and allowing them to structure the lessons more around real problems the learners are facing.

One of the challenges raised by this approach is the necessity to define which kinds of language learning contexts are likely to be relevant for situated learning. The example above shows that location might be relevant information. Other information could be the learners' calender. If there is e.g. a meeting scheduled with the boss in the afternoon, a useful learning exercise could focus on interactions with higher status individuals. Or if the learner has recently begun to browse real-estate websites, exercises centered around houses and the real-estate market might be very appropriate. As this is largely uncharted territory, we are proposing methods for capturing relevant language learning context in the next section.

3.3   Stage 1 – Approach to Context Identification

In this section we present and discuss how a diary study and a context logging applications can be used to collect knowledge about context relevant scenarios for our experience-based language learning application. These investigations are necessary due to the inclusion of the cultural layer. Foreigners and immigrants will not have the same cultural behavior and understanding as ethnic Danes of everyday instances. Thus the participants for the two studies are actual foreigners and immigrants attending language courses offered by the local municipality. The following sections will explain the purpose by conducting a diary and context logging study.

Diary Study. Situational information can be difficult to collect due to several issues; like ethics on when and where to log data or what is important data for this user and therefore should be logged. The solution, which is the straightest forward by, is a diary study. This allows notating current activity, location, date, time of day and comments. However this is relaying on participants willingness to actively do an effort and might require a more instructed survey. An instructed survey can alter the premises towards a more biased data gathering than originally envisioned. It's important that a schedule for the complete study is in place before starting, since major events might interfere with the actual normal activity level. An example could be measuring how often do you do sport related activities. This can be a very seasonable measurement, which will make a false impact on the study if only conducted during the winter or summer. Depending on what study that is being conducted different lengths can be discussed as the best measurement. If weekly routines are important then it's not enough to conduct the study below of one week, since the measurement might not be normalized from that period. A diary study can be anonymously conducted or with an identification possibility. What not so great about an anonymously approach is that if during the analysis an answer don't make sense or is very interesting, it's not possible to get the participant to elaborate on it. If participants are asked to leave their name or each diary is registered then it's possible to conduct interviews afterwards if needed, but on the potential cost of honesty.

What can you expect to get from a diary study?

- Structured study.
- Specified activities and day cycles of activities.
- Duration, labeled location and date.
- User comments.

What can you not expect to get from a diary study?

- Readable notes.
- Fast feedback
- Continuous results
- Corrections

Context Logging Application. The context logging application is installed on smart phones, which then are lend to end users for a time span of at least one week. Longer time spans have through preliminary trails shown a decrease in interest and would not provide any additionally results. It is therefore a better return on investment, with more participants contributing one week of activities each than fewer submitting after longer periods of use.

The participants are taught in how to use the phone and the actual context logging application. Fig.2 depicts a use case scenario, where the user is waiting for the bus to arrive, so he can take a photo of that specific scenario. The application is built as a 2 stage system. The main layout provides basic instruction on how to use the application and what the study is about. Beyond the instruction the

Fig. 2. Non-Danish speaking student using the context logging application at a bus stop

user can either start the logging or send the collected data to the database. By pressing the start button the application request the user to take a photo of the current context relevant scenario or situation, which is the first stage. During and including after the photo the application also records all audio, which is the second stage. Until the user determines that the scenario or situation is done and presses the stop button, it will remain active. In parallel with the active user involved logging the application collects passively GPS coordinates (if available), time and date on each started session. Location data is interesting, since it can relate the user to various defined topics like transport, leisure etc. depending on what can be found within a certain geographical vicinity of the user.

4   Discussion

The major, but interesting challenge is how should the collected data consisting of qualitative (user opinions) and quantitative data (location, activity, phone usage), be used to generate an experience that can be qualified as context relevant, with the inclusion of case specifics (culture)? Based on language learning models and experience-based learning a decision framework will sort the sensed information and propose assignments for the user. A database will allow external push options and that can be utilized with creating a web-based editor that is aimed towards educators for assignment creation. The editor can incorporate the necessary parameters required by the decision framework so created assignments easily can be pushed to the users. This will add an extra layer of control for the educators to reach the individual so any profiling regarding learning styles or cultural preferences on users can be added in this interface. Table1 shows the different key elements necessary to determine a specific context and what technologies or methods would be used to collect them.

Table 1. Context-aware technologies or methods available for a smart phone is placed according to traditional context types, with the addition of case specifics

Location	Identity	Activity	Time	Case specifics
GPS	Phone usage	Accelerometer	System clock & date	Users' culture
Patterns	Social media	Gyroscope	Duration of action	Target culture
Google places API	Cloud services	Location data	Events	Experience-based

For example, if the system only were given the location data it would not be sufficient to create an automatic experience-based learning application, due to central elements would be missing from our used context definition. To close this gap and add to the real experience-based part, user activities will be an important function, since this information will allow a combined decision based on a location and the current activity. User activities can be physical or mechanical movement like walking, riding the bus etc. Collecting activity data can be sensed anonymously through sensors in mobile phones. Time is able to use the location data to search for events in the phones calendar or over cloud and social services, which will further add to the dimension of context-awareness. Lastly we have a cultural understanding of the user, which will help structuring the presentation of a language learning assignment.

5   Future Work

Next stage in the development will encompass an analysis of collected data through diary studies and a context logging application with foreigners or immigrants whom arrives to Denmark and have the goal to learn the culture and language. Further work will likewise consists of creating a recognition system for activities and prior to that collect the data needed to classify them. The last stage of development will draw on the findings to propose a working prototype, with user profiles calculated from cultural preferences in order to provide experience-based language learning.

Acknowledgment. Special thanks goes out to foreign students at Aalborg University - Department of Architecture, Design and Media Technology for participation in preliminary studies and providing valuable feedback.

References

1. Salber, D., Dey, A.K., Abowd, G.D.: The context toolkit: aiding the development of context-enabled applications. In: Proceedings of the SIGCHI Conference on Human Factors in Computing Systems: the CHI is the Limit, pp. 434–441. ACM (1999)
2. Dey, A.K.: Understanding and Using Context, vol. 5, pp. 4–7 (February 2001)
3. Grunnet, H.: Statistical Overview Migration and Asylum 2009 (2010)
4. Rehm, M., Nakano, Y., André, E., Nishida, T., Bee, N., Endrass, B., Wissner, M., Lipi, A.A., Huang, H.H.: From observation to simulation: generating culture-specific behavior for interactive systems. AI & Society 24(3), 267–280 (2009)
5. Landis, D., Bennett, J., Bennett, M. (eds.): Handbook of intercultural training, 3rd edn. Sage Publications, Incorporated (2003)
6. Allwood, J.: Intercultural communication. In: Tvärkulturell Kommunikation (Papers in Anthropological Linguistics 12) (1985)
7. Hofstede, G.: Cultures Consequences: Comparing Values, Behaviors, Institutions, and Organizations Across Nations. Sage Publications, Thousand Oaks (2001)
8. Henrich, J., McElreath, R.: Dual inheritance theory: the evolution of human cultural capacities and cultural evolution. In: Dunbar, R., Barrett, L. (eds.) Oxford Handbook of Evolutionary Psychology. Oxford Univ. Press, Oxford (2007)
9. Bennett, M.J.: A developmental approach to training for intercultural sensitivity. International Journal for Intercultural Relations 10(2), 179–195 (1986)
10. Dourish, P.: What we talk about when we talk about context. Personal Ubiquitous Computing 8(1), 19–30 (2004)
11. Lane, N.D., Miluzzo, E., Lu, H., Peebles, D., Choudhury, T., Campbell, A.T.: A survey of mobile phone sensing. IEEE Communications Magazine 48(9), 140–150 (2010)
12. Kwapisz, J.R., Weiss, G.M., Moore, S.A.: Activity recognition using cell phone accelerometers. SIGKDD Explor. Newsl. 12(2), 74–82 (2011)
13. Saponas, T., Lester, J., Froehlich, J., Fogarty, J., Landay, J.: iLearn on the iphone: Real-time human activity classification on commodity mobile phones. University of Washington CSE Tech Report UW-CSE-08-04-02 (2008)
14. Choudhury, T., Consolvo, S., Harrison, B., Hightower, J., LaMarca, A., Legrand, L., Rahimi, A., Rea, A., Bordello, G., Hemingway, B., Klasnja, P., Koscher, K., Landay, J.A., Lester, J., Wyatt, D., Haehnel, D.: The Mobile Sensing Platform: An Embedded Activity Recognition System. IEEE Pervasive Computing 7(2), 32–41 (2008)
15. Schmidt, A.: Interactive context-aware systems interacting with ambient intelligence. Ambient Intelligence (Part 3), 159–178 (2005)
16. Fowler, S.M., Blohm, J.M.: An analysis of methods for intercultural training. In: Landis, D., Bennett, J.M., Bennett, M.J. (eds.) Handbook of Intercultural Training, 3rd edn., pp. 37–84. Sage Publications Inc. (2004)

Usability of a Social Network as a Collaborative Learning Platform Tool for Medical Students[*]

Leonardo Frajhof[1], Ana Cláudia Costa Arantes[1], Aline Teodosio dos Santos Cardozo[1],
Carlos José Pereira de Lucena[2], Carlos Alberto Pereira de Lucena[2],
and Claudia Renata Mont'Alvão[2]

[1] Hospital Universitário Gaffrée e Guinle, Núcleo de Telemedicina,
Universidade Federal do Estado do Rio de Janeiro, UNIRIO - Rio de Janeiro, Brasil
[2] Pontifícia Universidade Católica do Rio de Janeiro, PUC-Rio - Rio de Janeiro, Brasil
(leonardo.frajhof,anaccarantes)@gmail.com,
aline-tsc@hotmail.com, eto.lucena@affero.com.br,
cmontalvao@puc-rio.br, lucena@inf.puc-rio.br

Abstract. One of the fundamental characteristics of social networking platform is its versatility. Regarding to pre defined pedagogy premises it is possible to elaborate educational programs for any type of theme. Health is one of the areas that are being influenced by the possibilities offered by social networking platform. There are already many ongoing projects dedicated to the teaching of health practice and concepts of health. In this context, this paper focuses primarily on the development of a solution for teachers and students engaged on their 3rd year of undergraduate Medicine course, in the University Hospital. All the participants are enrolled in the Internal Medicine discipline, defining the student's entrance into the hospital routine. The model views for an open dialog that should allow an exchange of medical knowledge, in the sense of reaching a better solution for specific problems within each group.

Keywords: eHealth, collaboration, learning, usability.

1 Introduction

By definition, social network is a frame composed of individuals and/or organizations, with different types of relationships, connected directly or indirectly, to share knowledge, experiences and interests. It enables the development of horizontal relations and collaborative activities among its users [1].

Since social networks are widespread in different social contexts, such as entertainment, Facebook and Twitter, and professional, LinkedIn, it has been accepted as a learning management system in the process of teaching and learning. Teachers can act as a mentor in the process of teaching and learning, encouraging students to share and build knowledge together. Therefore, an active process of cooperation

---

[*] This study have received the financial resource from CNPq – National Council for Scientific and Technological Development.

M. Kurosu (Ed.): Human-Computer Interaction, Part II, HCII 2013, LNCS 8005, pp. 370–375, 2013.

between students and teachers replaces the traditional structure of passive learning, in which the students acquire the knowledge transferred by the teacher [2-3].

In this context, through the discipline of Internal Medicine, at the School of Medicine of the Federal University of the State of Rio de Janeiro (UNIRIO), held at the Gaffrée e Guinle University Hospital (HUGG), a case study was realized by using the social networking platform, named YouKnow, developed as a tool for collaborative learning for medical students. This study aimed to present a system that focuses on collaborative learning and interactive activities on multiple platforms (computers, tablets, smartphones). It also shall promote the exchange of experience between students and teachers, health institutions, teaching hospitals and other interest groups. Through the access to patient case studies, the groups involved in this process could share opinions and medical practices in a collaboratively manner.

2   Material and Methods

The tool used during the study was the **Youknow** software, SLMs - Social Learning Management System, developed by Affero, with the main purpose of promoting learning through a collaborative manner among participants. This software focuses on the interaction between the traditional model of teaching and processes based on the collaboration between people.

Fig. 1. Example of screenshot of the Youknow's homepage

The methodology to this study was the usage of the software Youknow, during weekly meetings, by a group of students of the third year of medical school at the Federal University of the State of Rio de Janeiro (UNIRIO), as a tool of learning during Internal Medicine's discipline. The result was a course that provided the students with a startup hospital's routine, based on clinical cases analysis at Gaffreé e Guinle University Hospital. The tool's usability consisted on a case study regarding medical record envolving a patient that was treated by the teacher/tutor. For this purpose, the teacher gradually provided patient's record information to students, in which students were able to consolidate analysis, associated with the theoretical and practical content learned during the Internal Medicine discipline.

Fig. 2. Image 2: Example of screenshot when the user logs on

Fig. 3. Example of screenshoot of the Internal Medicine community

At first, a Group of Interest was created and nominated as Internal Medicine. Furthermore, the students published the information from the medical records, regarding relevant questions, such as research materials and scientific literature, differential diagnoses, and the patient's diagnosis confirmed by teacher/tutor. This information was organized from items previously established in the Group of Interest such as *lectures, best practices, articles, forum, image gallery, videos, interviews and column.*

3   Results

In order to initiate content publishing, the students chose the methodology item *Lesson learned*. The choice was motivated by the fact that this item had already indexed questions that could precisely guide the case's content by students. After publishing the patient's anamnesis on this item, named CASE 1, which contain differential diagnoses and illustrations related to the topic, the teacher/tutor used the item *Best practices* to disclose the imaging that was used to diagnose the patient's disease: Computed Tomography and Magnetic Resonance Cholangiopancreatography. Related to this experience, students then published a scientific article in item *Article*, entitled "Diabetes mellitus and ductal carcinoma of the pancreas", once it was considered relevant and similar to the case studied.

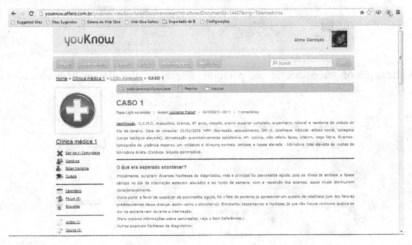

Fig. 4. Example of a screenshot showing the item *Lesson learned*, with the *CASO 1* published

During the process analysis of the case, the questions were published under the item *Forum*, with the purpose of being answered by the teacher or even by the students.

On weekly meetings, the teacher release by date the complementary exams performed by the patient into the item *Gallery* and two streaming videos from Endoscopy and Cholangiography into items *Videos*. In the item *Interview*, imaging and laboratory exams were posted. This item was also used to transcribe the patient's record. Gathering all of this information, released by the teacher, and browsed by the students, the latter were able to diagnose correctly the case. After the teacher/tutor's approval, confirming the diagnosis, the case study was published under item *Lesson Learned* as a summary. And at the item *Column*, a Power Point presentation was published based on patient pathology.

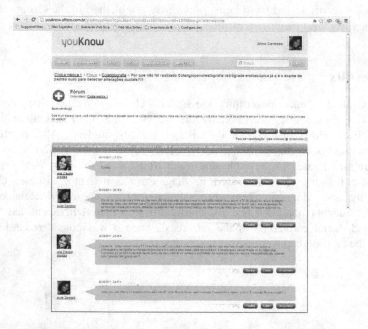

Fig. 5. Example of screenshot of the platform, displaying the *Forum* item created by the students

Fig. 6. Example of a screenshot of the collaborative learning platform displaying images related to the case in the item *Gallery*

At the end, the students gathered all the information posted through the items *THIS ITEM IS RELATED TO*, since all the information was related. The students used all the available learning tools, except for the item *Podcast*, since they lacked suitable material to perform audio recordings.

4   Conclusion

Students and teacher/tutor had a positive evaluation regarding the usage of Youknow, a collaborative learning platform in the process of teaching and learning. The usage of a collaborative learning platform stimulates students' participation, allowing them to express their opinions, and discuss with experienced professionals. Students have learned how to collect bibliographic data and to critically analyze it. Considering the complexity for searching the right diagnosis, a collaborative discussion allowed students to understand the relevance of browsing through different sources, and how an interactive discussion can save time in order to formulate the right diagnosis, which is not often reached during classes. Also, online tool enables content's access anytime/anyplace and shape their own learning's needs. One of main factors influencing positively the use of this platform was its easy access, which can be done through computers or mobile devices. The popularity of social networks as Facebook, Twitter, and Instagram contributed to the positive evaluation of Youknow, whereby students are familiar with its use and this tool allows a horizontal relation among users.

Finally, the social networking as a collaborative learning platform tool, in academic environment, can be useful because encourages students' autonomy, active participation and understanding of the complexity surrounding the studied cases. The interpersonal and intrapersonal relationships are also encouraged in this process, being important for the formation and maturation of an active individual in society.

References

1. Araújo, V.D.L.: O impacto das redes sociais no processo de ensino e aprendizagem. J. Anais Eletrônicos 3, 1–13 (2010)
2. O'Reilly, T.: What is Web 2.0: Design Patterns and Business Models for the Next Generation of Software. Communications & Strategies 1, 17 (2007)
3. Pimentel, M., Fuks, H.: Sistemas Colaborativos. Elsevier, Rio de Janeiro (2011)
4. Youknow (2012), http://www.eduweb.com.br/produtos-e-servicos/tecnologia/you-know
5. Cirilo, E., Nunes, I., Carvalho, D., Carvalho, G., Veiga, A., Lucena, C.: Engenharia de software em Telessaúde: aplicações e desafios. In: Gold Book, 50th Scientific Congress of HUPE, Rio de Janeiro, pp. 371–404 (2012)
6. Lucena, C.A.P., Mont'Alvão, C.R., Frajhof, L.: Collaborative learning platform in the field of telemedicine. In: IADIS International Journal on Computer Science and Information Systems, IADIS International Conference e-Health (2012)

Refining Rules Learning Using Evolutionary PD

Afdallyna Harun[1,2], Steve Benford[1], Claire O'Malley[1], and Nor Laila Md. Noor[2]

[1] University of Nottingham, UK
{psxafhh,steve.benford,claire.o'malley}@nottingham.ac.uk
[2] Universiti Teknologi MARA, Malaysia
norlaila@tmsk.uitm.my

Abstract. Using glyphs to associate digital media with physical materials has great potential to enhance learning. A key challenge, however, lies in enabling children to author their own glyphs that integrate well with their drawings. One possible solution lies in the d-touch system which uses a topological approach to structuring glyphs. Through a series of Participatory Design studies, we have explored how children can be supported in creating their own d-touch glyphs. Main highlights from our findings indicate that it is difficult for children to create glyphs following only written rules. A structured diagrammatic approach is then introduced in which colour-coded hierarchy diagrams support a mapping between their drawings and the underlying rules. We found this has significantly improved their drawing attempts. The paper then concludes with a potential to integrate the approach into more sophisticated learning experience.

Keywords: Drawing rules, visual diagrams, d-touch glyphs.

1 Introduction

Glyphs have emerged as a powerful and popular way of embedding digital media into physical materials. Current glyphs however are predesigned and do not always fit well aesthetically in terms of the content they project, the loci of their placement, or human preferences. This is because current systems operate on geometrical feature detection to localise the barcode placement and encode their unique identifiers. The challenge for us then is to enable children to author the glyphs for themselves in the same way that they can already draw pictures on a page.

Fortunately help is at hand due to a new approach to authoring personalised glyphs that is embodied in the d-touch system [1]. We feel that d-touch opens up an important opportunity for personalised glyphs to be used by children for learning in the classroom. However, while this technology is exciting, it also creates new issues, such as facilitating proper glyph making process. To do so, the needs of child users must be considered as they perceive differently and has different considerations and requirements from other user groups [2].

Our paper therefore reports an iterative exploration of working with children in schools to explore how they can be supported in authoring d-touch glyphs. We begin with an initial study of whether children can follow written rules for generating glyphs. The results of the study suggest that additional support is needed, leading us

M. Kurosu (Ed.): Human-Computer Interaction, Part II, HCII 2013, LNCS 8005, pp. 376–385, 2013.
© Springer-Verlag Berlin Heidelberg 2013

to introduce a more structured approach involving visual diagrams and supporting tools to guide the drawing process. Further studies suggests that children can work with this structured approach and that it has the potential to enable them to author d-touch glyphs that might be used as part of learning experiences.

2   The d-touch Glyph System

d-touch [1] is a glyph recognition system that allows users to create their own bar-codes. The novelty of d-touch lies in its topological recognition algorithm. With d-touch, glyphs can now carry direct visual cues that enable viewers to infer beforehand the information that they may hide.

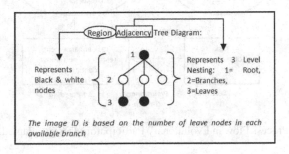

Fig. 1. d-touch Topological Glyph Recognition Algorithm

Glyphs are based on the form of a constrained binary tree as shown in Fig. 1. We say constrained because for a glyph to be valid, its associated tree must satisfy three key constraints: (i) there must be at least three levels of nesting (root, branch and leaf); (ii) there must be at least 3 branches present; and (iii) at least half of the branches must have at least one leaf each. These rules are intended to achieve a balance between flexibility of design and reliability of recognition as explained in [1].

However, it is not clear whether younger children would be able to apply the algorithm – which at first sight appear complex and technical sufficiently well to be able to create their own glyphs. Following this, we revised the drawing rules to assess how well this could facilitate glyph making process.

3   Evolutionary Participatory Design

In order to create valid glyphs, the algorithm properties of these glyphs need to be thoroughly understood. With that motivation, we have conducted several Participatory Design studies which we termed as Evolutionary Participatory Design (EPDs). The EPDs is inspired from the Seeding, Evolutionary Growth, Reseeding (SER) model [3], where results and observation from each study is fed to the consequent PD study by enhancing, restructuring, removing or continuing the task until the design goal is achieved. The process flow can be seen in Fig. 2.

There were four different PD sessions, each with different sets of children. In total we had 29 children (aged 10 to 11 years old) giving feedback to our rules learning process. The age group is selected as it is believed they could understand and follow rules and are able to express drawings well [Sawford, personal communication].

Recruiting different sets of children for each study allows the unbiased identification of design problems as none of the children would be influenced by prior experience.

Each PD set observes the session structure (one to one, group session, workshop), rules briefing (describing and presenting rules), artefacts (hand-outs, glyphs assessment tool) and task activities. Each component has its own distinguished characteristics which were designed to support and feed other components as a holistic rules learning process. These components were scrutinized as separate parts and formalized for the next PD session.

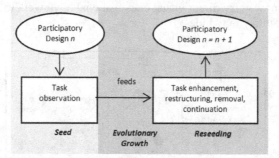

Fig. 2. Process Flow in Evolutionary Participatory Design adapted from [3]

4   Study 1: Following Written Drawing Rules

Study 1 was conducted as one-to-one where a facilitator sits next to a participant and briefs each of them on the study and rules. 7 children participated which lasts 45 minutes average for each session. The children were asked to draw their favourite animal by following our revised d-touch drawing rules. For each attempt, they are required to check the drawing validity using DTAnalyser (a drawing analysis tool that verifies how a drawing fits with the recognition algorithm [1]). A valid glyph is then used to trigger computer content which allows children to see how a glyph functions.

Table 1. Revised Drawing Instructions for Study 1

Previous d-touch Rules	Revised Drawing Instructions
A glyph must have at least and at most 3 levels of nesting – root, branch and leave	Using black marker pen, draw objects which can be considered as animal body parts (head, neck, body, etc). You should at least have 3 objects and all objects drawn must be joined together
A root is assumed as the black region which contains a minimum of 3 white regions	
At least half of the branch or white regions must contain black regions (leaves). The leaves should only connect to the branch and not the root	Using blue marker pen, draw lines or dots inside the black objects as animal features.
	The blue lines/dots should not touch the black object. If it does, overwrite it with black marker pen, or draw a new drawing but make sure the lines/dots appear smaller and no longer touch the black object.
	At least half of the object drawn should have some blue lines or dots inside it. Objects cannot appear inside objects.

4.1   Results and Findings

Table 2 summarises our observation of children's attempts in terms of the number of iterations required to create a valid glyph as well as common errors made, and also shows their final drawing. In general, we observed that children started off by drawing objects then adding lines/dots inside the objects. It was when adding the lines/dots that seemed to create most problems. As the drawing was analysed using DTAnalyser, lines/dots placed too close to the objects could be detected as being part of the objects. Additionally, incomplete pen strokes and gaps in large filled areas also modified the apparent topology. Such effects could easily lead to breaking d-touch rules such as: *"at least half of the objects drawn should have some blue lines or dots inside it"* and *"no objects are allowed inside objects"*. This caused confusion for the children who felt that they had followed the rules well. We also observed confusions over distinguishing objects and lines/dots and also the number of leaf and branch nodes required in an image.

Table 2. Summary of Children Output from Study 1

P1		P3		P5	
No. of iterations: 3		No. of iterations: 5		No. of iterations: 4	
Errors made: (i) Lines/dots touching objects, (ii) drew objects inside objects					
P2		P6		P7	
No. of iterations: 2		No. of iterations: 7		No. of iterations: 5	
Error made: Lines/dots touching objects					
P4		Error made: Drew objects inside objects Number of iterations: 4			

In short, it appeared to us that while the children could ultimately draw valid glyphs from the written instructions, that this was a frustrating process requiring multiple iterations while they struggled to comprehend both the rules and using DTAnalyser. We concluded they required greater support of some kind.

5   Study 2: Following Hierarchical Diagram

Study 2 was conducted as a group session where all 6 children sat in a group. A facilitator briefs them on the study and the rules. The study lasts 45 minutes. As we had learnt that children had difficulties in following textual instructions, we explored if rules presented using diagrams might be easier to understand. By doing so, we can reduce the amount of cognitive effort required in learning [4]. In response, and in-spired by the visual form of the d-touch rules in Fig. 1, we developed a form of hier-archical diagram (see Fig. 3) with the following characteristics:

1. Mimic the hierarchical topological structure of a d-touch glyph
2. Support rule inference though labelling in the diagram [5] and using colours

The intention behind using a diagram that mimics d-touch binary tree is to provide a starting point for user to think through the details that need to be present in a drawing so that it can act as a glyph, hopefully helping them bridge the gulf between the topo-logical structure required by d-touch and the visual detail that they, as an author, might want to include. The use of colours (e.g. blue for body parts, red for features) is intended to help with this and also enable easy referencing later on. We did not pro-ceed using black and blue as in previous study as these colours have similar hues making it difficult for children to tell them apart in a glance.

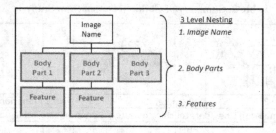

Fig. 3. Basic Hierarchical Diagram

The structures of these rules were presented using two slides; each slide containing hierarchical diagram and corresponding glyph. Children were described how red and blue blocks can be represented with drawings. They were explained that body parts (blue blocks) are represented with blue outline, while features (red blocks) are pre-sented with red filled patterns. No hand-outs were given as it was felt that the slide brief left on the projector screen was good enough as a reference point.

Children were asked to draw a glyph based on a given hierarchical diagram. They were encouraged to ask questions, discuss amongst themselves on how the valid glyph should look like. Due to the limited session time we had with the children, the children were only given two attempts regardless of the final results.

DTAnalyser was problematic in the previous study as it gave confusing feedback to the children which hindered productive learning process. We opted for a manual checking mechanism. This is simply facilitated with the use of colours and correct number of representation by cross-referencing between produced glyph to the given diagram.

5.1   Results and Findings

Table 3 summarises our observation of children's attempts in terms of errors made and also shows their final drawing. In general, we observed that children began by drawing body parts then adding in features. The use of contrasting hues has definitely helped in distinguishing body parts and features. The blocks in the diagram helps to visualize how features are calculated into the algorithm topology however the number of representation required in the glyph was still confusing to some.

Table 3. Output from Study 2

P1		P2		P6	
In terms of numbers, all of the body parts and features were correctly represented. However, the positioning (touches body parts) and patterns of all features were erroneous					
P3		P4		P5	
These three children didn't seem to grasp the concept of block's representation using shapes and patterns. Even the numbers of representation is wrong.					

A general conclusion that can be drawn from the children's drawing was they were keen in producing realistic drawing that did not fit technically to d-touch algorithm.

6   Study 3: Using Orderly Blocks and Templates

This session was conducted as a workshop setting with 8 children. The facilitator briefs them on the study and the rules and the study lasts 30 minutes.

We were able to observe from the previous study that the hierarchical diagram was helpful in visualizing algorithm rules to the children but they needed further support, particularly the form of drawings acceptable to the algorithm. Following this, we introduced the use of templates that suggests acceptable drawing types (See Fig. 4).

Following a suggestion from a teacher, we now called the hierarchical diagram orderly blocks (OB) as it involves putting the entire blocks label into an orderly fashion. Clearer definition were also devised; body parts were defined as *"distinctive parts of the image you can separate into big chunks"*, while features were *"tiny pieces that appear inside the body part"*. We also provided the following drawing guidelines: *"body parts drawn must be joined together"*, *"features must be drawn inside body parts it appears in and should not touch the outline of the body parts"* and *"features must appear in at least half of the body parts drawn"*.

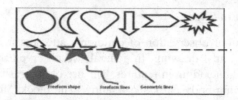

Fig. 4. Partial Template Guide for Body Parts (top) and Features (bottom)

Using Orderly Blocks. Compared to the previous studies, children relied on visual examples on how glyphs are structured. But in this study, we illustrated how OB can be constructed. We began by drawing a cat OB diagram, carefully choosing elements that best represent a cat and organizing them neatly. In addition to the placement of each block in its respective nesting level, the use of blue and red also makes it easy to identify which are body parts and features (see Fig. 5).

Making use of the templates, rules and definitions, a glyph is then produced through visual mapping process. Each of the blocks is represented using proper illustration from the templates, resulting into a glyph shown in Fig. 6. Again, the use of blue and red proves useful as one can easily cross reference between OB and the templates. The corresponding d-touch binary tree is also depicted in Fig. 6. Observing closely, one can see that the number of branch nodes and leaf nodes in the binary tree matches with the OB in Fig. 5. This indicates how we have made d-touch's recognition algorithm visible through OB.

Note as well, how the OB has a block labelled *'head + 2 ears'* (see green circled area in Fig. 5). These are not listed in three separate blocks (e.g. head, ear 1, ear 2) because, in the glyph, they have been drawn using one blue shape outline (see green circled area in Fig. 6). The use of the plus (+) sign implies that one outline represents a combination of two (or more) body parts. However, if the ears were drawn as shown in Fig. 7, then two additional blocks must be added to the OB as the ears are represented with two separate outlines (see green circled area in Fig. 7).

The hand-outs given to the children mimics the presentation briefing where it describes how glyphs can be produced using OB. It makes heavy use of diagrams where text serves as accompaniment to the diagrams.

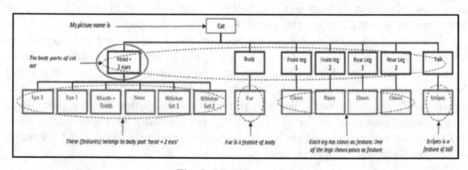

Fig. 5. OB of Image Cat

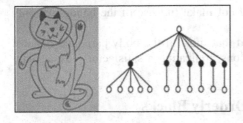 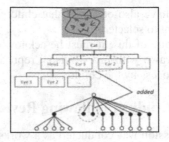

Fig. 6. Cat Glyph with Corresponding d-touch's Binary Tree

Fig. 7. An Alternative Glyph and Corresponding OB and d-touch's Binary Tree

Children were asked to draw a glyph based on a given OB. Even though children could manually check how their end glyph corresponds to the OB, we have prepared a d-touch glyph reader that plays a gif animation should the resulting drawing match the OB structure. This provides quicker evidence that something is not quite right with their attempt and would allow children to study their glyph and see what needs correcting.

6.1   Results and Findings

Table 4 shows glyphs produced by the children. Glyphs produced by P2 and P5 matches with OB. In contrast, the rest of the glyphs did not. Due to the limitations of d-touch's recognition system[1] embedded in the glyph reader, some drawing strokes and the room's lighting conditions could create drawing noise that unintentionally make additional outlines or patterns appear to be present in the drawing. When this happens, the reader scans the picture as matching the OB structure hence triggering the content. This has caused the children to miss the error made hence not able to learn from their mistakes. The scanning errors are highlighted with green circle and explained accordingly as missed errors.

Table 4. Output from Study 2

P2		P5		P3	
				Missed Errors: Objects more than required	
P1		P4		P6		P7	
Missed Errors: Lines drawn scanned as objects					

---

[1] An open-source application made available by d-touch author at www.d-touch.org

We have also observed that children did not make full use of the hand-outs, only referring to selected pages.

In spite of this, it must be acknowledged that most of the body parts and features were drawn with proper visual representations, indicating a satisfactory visual mapping process by the children.

7   Study 4: Following Revised Orderly Blocks

This session was conducted as a workshop setting where all 8 children sat in a group. The facilitator briefs them on the study and the rules. The study lasts 30 minutes.

Hand-outs are kept to minimal – only showing examples on cat OB and glyphs as well as templates. This kept their focus on the board and allows referencing to the hand-outs when in need of a clearer view of the rules description.

The same exercise and checking mechanism applied in Study 3 were observed in Study 4. However, we have learnt that children struggled when making representations for block labels with joined body part (i.e. 'head + antennae'). Therefore, children were further trained on this concept further through brainstorming exercises. To minimize recognition error by the d-touch reader, we emphasised the need for each blocks and drawing representation to be clearly and correctly presented. We indicated that computers are bound to errors so they need to design their glyphs clearly.

7.1   Results and Findings

Table 5 shows glyphs produced by the children. All of the children had no difficulty producing valid glyphs that correspond to the given OB within their first attempt. It is believed the brainstorming exercise conducted was useful in getting children to understand the concept of proper drawing representation that conforms with OB structure and labelling.

Table 5. Output from Study 4

8   Conclusion

Our studies reveal that authoring interesting and valid d-touch glyphs can be a challenging task for children. This is due to the relatively complex topological rules involved. Our studies also suggest that children may find it easier to understand the topological rule structure through the use of diagrams rather than only written instructions. Thus, the OB with the use of hierarchy, labelling, colours and supporting templates provide a foundation to bridge between the complex abstract topological rules and a particular concrete drawing.

When learning a new application, it is empirical that children are supported as much as possible. This comes in the form of facilitation, hand-outs, demonstration and checking mechanism. Children should also be trained as much as possible on rules application, particularly in the visual mapping process.

As the PD study progresses with each evolution phase, favourable response can be seen from participants indicating an improved learning structure. With this, we will conduct further studies to observe children author their own glyphs based on a learning theme. This not only further affirms our current observation but also allows the actual authoring itself without relying on pre-given data (i.e. OB). This reflects a further general finding from our studies – that authoring a glyph might best be thought of as a complex and iterative process rather than being a 'one off' process of making a drawing to some rules.

References

1. Costanza, E.: Designable Glyphs for Mobile Human-Computer Interaction. PhD thesis. Ecole Polytechnique Federale de Lausanne (2010)
2. Druin, A. (ed.): The Design of Children's Technology. Morgan Kaufmann, Burlington (1998)
3. Fischer, G., Ostwald, J.: Seeding, evolutionary growth, and reseeding: Enriching participatory design with informed participation. In: Binder, T., Gregory, J., Wagner, I. (eds.) Participatory Design Conference, pp. 135–143 (2002)
4. Larkin, J.H., Simon, H.A.: Why a Diagram is (Sometimes) Worth Ten Thousand Words. Cognitive Science 11, 65–99 (1987)
5. Nesbit, J.C., Adesope, O.O.: Learning with Concept and Knowledge Maps: A Meta-Analysis. Review of Educational Research 76(3), 413–448 (2006)

Sound to Sight: The Effects of Self-generated Visualization on Music Sight-Singing as an Alternate Learning Interface for Music Education within a Web-Based Environment

Yu Ting Huang[1] and Chi Nung Chu[2]

[1] Shih Chien University, Department of Music, No.70 Ta-Chih Street,
Chung-Shan District, Taipei, Taiwan, R.O.C.
yuting11@mail.usc.edu.tw
[2] China University of Technology, Department of Management of Information System, No. 56,
Sec. 3, Shinglung Rd., Wenshan Chiu, Taipei, Taiwan 116, R.O.C.
nung@cute.edu.tw

Abstract. This paper discusses the efficacy of self-generated visualization on pitch recognition for the music sight-singing learning from the Internet. The self-generated visualization on music sight-singing learning system incorporates pitch recognition engine and visualized pitch distinguishing curve with descriptions for each corresponding stave notation on the web page to bridge the gap between singing of pitch and music notation. This paper shows the conducted research results that this web-based sight-singing learning system could scaffold cognition about aural skills effectively for the learner through the Internet.

Keywords: pitch recognition, self-generated visualization, sight-singing, music education.

1 Introduction

Sight-singing skills tone up a music learner's ability to be more accurate when performing unread music[2,4]. Many constituent elements are involved in the process of sight-singing which includes an individual's perceptive competence, knowledge, and experiences. Multiple cognitive procedures are involved concurrently when learners read music by sight [1,6]. In traditional schooling, where students learn music from notations, sight-singing demonstrates a student's music literacy and music understanding. However the process of sight-singing involves the conversion of musical information from sight to sound [3]. It is hard for the learners to distinguish their sound of soundness by themselves. As the web environment is becoming an effective educational media [5], the goal of this study with pitch recognition design is to construct a facilitating sight-singing learning interface which adopts visualization strategy to transform the singing sound to a wave curve. By comparing with the standard wave curve of music notations, the learners would identify the correctness of their music sight-singing from the self-generated wave curve. Thus learners can build their own foundation of sight-singing skills by themselves from the Internet.

M. Kurosu (Ed.): Human-Computer Interaction, Part II, HCII 2013, LNCS 8005, pp. 386–390, 2013.
© Springer-Verlag Berlin Heidelberg 2013

2   Self-generated Visualization on Music Sight-Singing Design

The design of web-based learning system of self-generated visualization on pitch recognition (Fig. 1) is based on pitch recognition engine running on Windows platform. It integrates a voice recorder as a music sight-singing input producer. It also connects with the standard MIDI pitch producer from the music software Finale. The standard MIDI pitch producer could act like threshold for learners to distinguish their sight-singing status. Each pitch of music note sang by a user could be explicitly

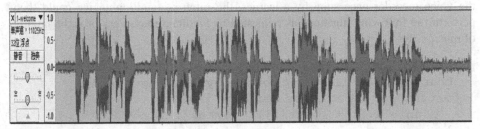

Fig. 1. Web-based learning system of self-generated visualization on pitch recognition

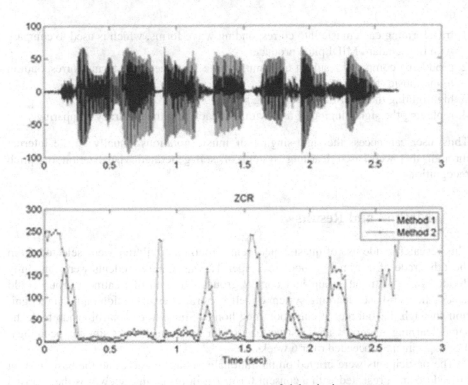

Fig. 2. Visual responding accuracy of sight-singing note

recognized by web-based learning system of self-generated visualization on pitch recognition and responded visually with the compared results of accuracy (Fig. 2). The integrated web-based learning system of self-generated visualization on pitch recognition software is installed at client side. This design not only reduces the overload of server computation, but also avoids redesigning of the existing web sites for the user's special hearing needs.

The design of web-based learning system of self-generated visualization on pitch recognition provides a useful visual mechanism of accessible learner sight-singing. The goal of this design is to construct automatic visual interfaces for sight-singing learning in web-based environment. For each the music notes would be sampled via the voice recorder once sung by a learner, the pitch recognition engine could then perform the following functions as requested to facilitate the access of sight-singing of music notes.

```
private static Double[] bytesToDoubles(byte[] bytes) {
  Double[] double = new Double[bytes.length / 2];
  for(int i=0; i < bytes.length; i+=2) {
    double[i/2] = bytes[i] | (bytes[i+1] << 8);
  }
  return double;
}
```

1. transforming each music into corresponding wave forms, which is used to compare with the standard MIDI pitch producer
2. producing compared result of each music note with the wave forms corresponding to the music staff
3. highlighting the error of sight-singing note
4. replaying the sight-singing of user with feedback of pitch accuracy comparing

Thus, user can access the sight-singing of music notations visually on the Internet through this web-based learning system of self-generated visualization on pitch recognition.

3   Method and Results

This research made use of quasi-experimental method. Children were selected from the 6th grade of a primary school in Taipei Taiwan. These students were randomly divided into treatment group and control group. Children of treatment group could access the web-based learning system of self-generated visualization on pitch recognition through the Internet at classroom and home. Students of control group took the same learning materials and instructions under traditional sight-singing pedagogy. The experiment proceeded over 6 weeks.

The participants were briefed on the rationale behind the test and the basic testing procedure and presented with a consent form. An informal interview was then carried out, to ascertain general information on the individual music backgrounds, their music and computer experience. Baseline measurement was taken while the participant of treatment completed the computer manipulation instructions. The participants of treatment then were encouraged to navigate learning materials in the Internet via using the web-based learning system of self-generated visualization on pitch recognition. This was used to create scaffolding mechanism for the treatment group in sight-singing learning. The questionnaire items were evaluated by computer and music education experts through Delphi approach and confirmed by experienced primary school teachers. The music performance test items were all evaluated and analyzed by music education experts to get the item's difficulty and discrimination coefficient. The students of the two groups received the pretest of music notation related performance after taking the first two weeks of traditional lessons and filled the attitude questionnaires. On completion, an informal interview was conducted to ascertain the state of the participant. The next phase of the experiment was conducted separately at the actually different learning environments. The participants were conducted with the experiment under normal schedule in primary school.

There were 40 children with evaluation of limited sight-singing skills conducted in this study. Participants were given pre and post-tests. The test included identifying pitch, intervals, and rhythm. And a System Usability Questionnaire proceeded after the post-test. In addition to overall satisfaction score, the responses can be divided into three sections: system usefulness, information quality, and interface quality.

The experiment data were gathered and analyzed using SPSS. Both performances of the two groups on pre-test and posttest have been given in Table 1. An independent t-test was inspected to examine if there was any significant difference between the two groups. The compared results of pretest and posttest for each group were presented in Table 2.

Table 1. Performances of the two groups on pre-test and posttest

Group	N	Pre-test		Post-test	
		Mean	SD	Mean	SD
Experiment	20	51.23	8.21	67.16	8,27
Control	20	51.20	7.80	59.80	10.85

Table 2. T-tests of pretest and posttest

	df	t	Sig.
Experiment Group Pretest/Posttest	19	6.76	.000[*]
Control Group Pretest/Posttest	19	3.16	.000[*]

The questionnaire data suggested satisfied in all three usability categories (system usefulness, information quality, and interface quality). System usefulness, which measures the users' perception of how the system can improve their sight-singing performance, improved the most with 93% scores.

4   Conclusion

The learning interface of self-generated visualization on music sight-singing could move learners beyond basic drill exercises to a competence that is tailored to the content of individual needs in the sight-singing training. And the recording and replay functionalities created from the web environment facilitate learners to master the skills. The remediation would be visualized by the exercise itself. Sight-singing skills development occurs when learners interact with the learning interface of self-generated visualization on music sight-singing in a continuous drill. Many singing sound faults could then be tuned up through the combination of practice and immediate visual feedback.

References

1. Grutzmacher, P.A.: The effect of tonal pattern training on the aural perception, reading recognition, and melodic sight-reading achievement of first-year instrumental music students. Journal of Research in Music Education 35(4), 171–181 (1987)
2. Lehmann, A.C., Ericsson, K.A.: Performance without preparation: Structure and acquisition of expert sight-reading and accompanying performance. Psychomusicology 15(1-2), 1–29 (1996)
3. Lehmann, A., McArthur, V.: Sight-reading. The science and psychology of music performance: Creative strategies for teaching and learning. Oxford University Press, New York (2002)
4. Sloboda, J.A.: Experimental studies of music reading: A review. Music Perception 2(2), 222–236 (1984)
5. Web-based Education Commission (WBEC). The power of the Internet for learning: Moving from promise to practice (Report), pp. 17–49. U.S. Department of Education, Washington, DC (2000)
6. Wolf, T.E.: A cognitive model of musical sight-reading. Journal of Psycholinguistic Research 5(2), 143–171 (1976)

Evaluation of Computer Algebra Systems
Using Fuzzy AHP at the Universities of Cyprus

Ilham N. Huseyinov[1] and Feride S. Tabak[2]

[1] Faculty of Management, University of Mediterranean Karpasia, Lefkosa, Cyprus
ihuseynov@yahoo.com
[2] Computer Engineering Department, European University of Lefke, Lefke, Cyprus
savaroglu@hotmail.com

Abstract. The paper proposes an evaluation model based on fuzzy AHP to help users select CAS that best matches their requirements. The subjectiveness and imprecision of the evaluation process are modeled using linguistic terms. The evaluation criteria framework based on the usability and problem solving capability of CAS is developed. Fuzzy AHP is employed to determine the relative importance weights of criteria and the preference order of alternatives. The applicability and effectiveness of the proposed methodology is illustrated.

Keywords: CAS, fuzzy AHP, usability, problem solving capability, linguistic evaluation.

1   Introduction

It has been appreciated that the goal of promoting mathematical exploration (through symbolic, numerical and graphical experimentation) is well served by computer algebra system (CAS) [1]. CAS(s) are computer based software packages for performing mathematical symbolic computations [2].

However, there are dozens of CAS available for users: Derive Maple, Mathematica, Maxima, and etc. Hence, users are faced with the challenge to select the most appropriate CAS that meets her/him requirements. From the human computer interaction perspective the usability dimension and from the functional perspective the problem solving capability dimension are the most wanted requirements for a software package [3, 4]. Thus, evaluation (or selection) of CAS can be viewed as a complex multi criteria decision making (MCDM) problem [5] since the student body in Cyprus is quite diverse, comprising of students from 50 countries. Recent research studies have demonstrated the applicability and flexibility of MCDM approach to evaluation of educational software [6, 7]. They employed the analytical hierarchy process (AHP) method of MCDM, which was developed by T.L.Saaty [8]. However, AHP does not give reliable results under fuzzy environment.

This paper proposes an evaluation model based on fuzzy AHP to help users select CAS that best matches their requirements. The subjectiveness and imprecision of the evaluation process are modeled using linguistic terms. The evaluation criteria framework based on the usability and problem solving capability of CAS is developed. Fuzzy AHP is employed to determine the relative importance weights of criteria and

M. Kurosu (Ed.): Human-Computer Interaction, Part II, HCII 2013, LNCS 8005, pp. 391–397, 2013.

the preference order of alternatives. The applicability and effectiveness of the proposed methodology is illustrated.

The paper is organized as follows. The description of fuzzy AHP and evaluation model is given in Section 2. A case study of evaluation of CAS is presented in Section 3. Finally, in Section 4 we present results and conclusion.

2   Description of Fuzzy AHP and Evaluation Algorithm

In this section, we present an overview of the literature on FAHP and describe the proposed evaluation algorithm. AHP is a powerful decision making tool of multi-criteria decision making methods. Its aim is to select the best alternative among different criteria. The main idea of AHP is to decompose a complex problem into several small problems by means of a systematic hierarchy structure [9]. A decision maker makes a reciprocal comparison for each element and layer of the structure using ratio scales. A reciprocal matrix is constructed. Then, using matrix algebra, the relevance weights of elements are calculated. However, AHP is not able to make decision under the environment of uncertain, vague, incomplete, fuzzy information. Hence, there is a need to modify AHP for fuzzy environment. It is presented in [10, 11], where fuzzy comparison ratios were introduced. The work [12] proposed an extent analysis method to handle fuzzy reciprocal matrix. Using this method we propose the following evaluation algorithm.

Step1. Identify the goal.

Step 2. Identify a set of alternatives: $A_j, (j = 1,2,...,n)$

Step 3. Identify a set of evaluation criteria (or sub criteria): $C_i, (i = 1,2,...,m)$ and construct a tree type hierarchy structure of criteria and sub-criteria.

Step 4. Get decision makers' evaluation judgments in the form of comparison scores a_{ij} in pairs of criteria $C_{ij}, (i, j = 1,2,...,m)$. Each comparison score should show how much important one criterion is than the other. The comparison scores form the matrix of pair-wise comparisons $A = [a_{ij}]$ that should satisfy the conditions: $a_{ij} = 1/a_{ji}$ and $a_{ii} = (1,1,1)$ for $i = 1,2,...,m$. The comparison scores a_{ij} represent linguistic terms [13] expressed by triangular fuzzy numbers $k = (k_1, k_2, k_3)$, where $-\infty < k_1 \le k_2 \le k_3 < \infty$, and described in Table 1.

Step 5. Calculate the relative importance weight w_i for each criterion $C_i, (i = 1,2,...,m)$ using the equation:

$$w_i = \sum_{j=1}^{m} a_{ij} \otimes \left[\sum_{i=1}^{m} \sum_{j=1}^{m} a_{ij} \right]^{-1} , \qquad (1)$$

Table 1. Linguistic scores for comparison and ratings

Linguistic scores	Fuzzy number
Just equal	(1,1,1)
Equally important (EqI)	(1,1,3)
Moderate important (MI)	(1,3,5)
Strong important (SI)	(3,5,7)
Very strong important (VSI)	(5,7,9)
Extremely important (ExI)	(7,9,9)

where addition, multiplication and division operations for two fuzzy triangular numbers $a = (a_1, a_2, a_3)$, and $b = (b_1, b_2, b_3)$ are defined as [14]:

$$a \oplus b = (a_1 + b_1, a_2 + b_2, a_3 + b_3), \ a \otimes b = (a_1 b_1, a_2 b_2, a_3 b_3), \quad \text{and}$$

$$a / b \cong (a_1 / b_3, a_2 / b_2, a_3 / b_1), \ [13], \text{ respectively.}$$

Step 6. Similar to Step4 we obtain decision maker's preferences, $d_{ij}, (i = 1,2,...,m, j = 1,2,...,n)$ about the performance of each alternative A_j within each criterion C_i using Table 1. These values form the decision matrix $D = |d_{ij}|$. Then, it is normalized as follows:

$$\left[\hat{d}_{ij}\right] = \frac{d_{ij}}{\sum\limits_{j=1}^{n} d_{ij}}, i = 1,2,...,m, j = 1,2,...,n. \tag{2}$$

Step 7. Calculate the fuzzy score of each alternative:

$$X_i = \hat{d}_{ij} \otimes w_j \tag{3}$$

Step 8. Calculate the ranking score of each alternative using the graded mean integration representation of the fuzzy number a [15] as follows:

$$R(a) = \frac{a_1 + 4a_2 + a_3}{6}, \tag{4}$$

where $a > (=, <) b \Leftrightarrow R(a) > (=, <) R(b)$.

Step 9. Choose the alternative whose ranking score is maximum as the best alternative.

3   Evaluation of CAS

In this section, we present an empirical study concerning the application of the proposed algorithm. It is carried out through a survey among students of University of

Mediterranean Karpasia and European University of Lefke. Three alternatives of CAS are identified: A1- Maple, A2- Mathematica, A3- Maxima. They are open source and easily available. Students are given a questionnaire about the user interface and problem solving capability of CAS. The user interface is closely related to the concept of usability that is central dimension in human computer interaction [3]. The usability is considered to be inherent in human computer interface, because it implies the interaction of users with the software product [16, 17]. The guidelines for the mathematical problem solving software design proposed in [4] are adopted in our case study. The results of the survey is analyzed and the following criteria set hierarchy is derived.

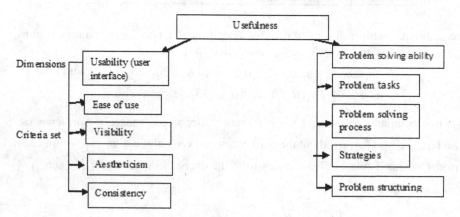

Fig. 1. Hierarchical structure of criteria set

We give a short description of each criterion [3, 4]. Ease of use - C_{11} - use of an interface with a minimum effort; Visibility- C_{12} - how interface looks indicates how it can be used; Aesthetics - C_{13} - the `look and feel` of the user interface intended to make the interface attractive and appealing; Consistency - C_{14} - makes the interface familiar and predictable by providing a sense of stability; Problem tasks – C_{21} - refers to a situation in which a person wants something and does not know immediately what sorts of action he/she can perform to get it; Problem solving process – C_{22} – means understanding , planning, solving, reviewing the problem and the solution; Strategies – C_{23} - refers to the ways to proceed that are planned and carried out; Problem structuring – C_{24} - enables students to recognize problems by their structure rather than their contextual setting. After obtaining criteria structure, we follow the algorithm described in section two.

Step 4. Matrices of pairwise comparisons obtained from the survey analysis are shown in Tables 2 and 3.

Table 2. The pairwise comparison matrix of the dimensions

Dimensions	C_1	C_2
C_1	(1,1,1)	(1,3,5)
C_2	1/(1,3,5)	(1,1,1)

Table 3. The pairwise comparison matrix of the usability criterions

	C_{11}	C_{12}	C_{13}	C_{14}
C_{11}	(1,1,1)	(1,3,5)	(1,3,5)	1/(1,3,5)
C_{12}	1/(1,3,5)	(1,1,1)	(1,1,3)	(1,1,3)
C_{13}	1/(1,3,5)	1/(1,1,3)	(1,1,1)	(1,1,3)
C_{14}	(1,3,5)	1/(1,1,3)	1/(1,1,3)	(1,1,1)

Step 5. Based on Eq. (1) the relative importance weights of dimensions and criteria are computed and presented in Table 4.

Table 4. Priority weights of dimensions and criteria in the AHP decision tree

Criteria	Weight between dimensions	Weight within the dimensions	Weight among the criterion
C_1	(0.25,0.76,1.86)		
C_{11}		(0.11,0.42,1.12)	(0.027,0.32,2.1)
C_{12}		(0.11,0.19,0.74)	(0.027,0.14,1.37)
C_{13}		(0.082,0.19,0.56)	(0.02,0.144,1.41)
C_{14}		(0.061,0.19,0.37)	(0.015,0.14,0.69)
C_2	(0.15,0.25,0.62)		
C_{21}		(0.13,0.35,1.04)	(0.02,0.086,0.64)
C_{22}		(0.11,0.19,0.7)	(0.016,0.047,0.43)
C_{23}		(0.077,0.23,0.52)	(0.01,0.57,0.32)
C_{24}		(0.07,0.23,0.35)	(0.01,0.57,028)

Step 6. Based on Eq. (2) the normalized decision matrix is computed and given in Table 5.

Table 5. Normalized decision matrix

	A1	A2	A3
C_{11}	(0.27,0.33,0.43)	(0.21,0.37,0.71)	(0.15,0.37,0.43)
C_{12}	(0.24,0.57,1.023)	(0.08,0.18,0.27)	(0.16,0.25,0.8)
C_{13}	(0.14,0.43,1)	(0.12,0.37,1)	(0.12,0.2,0.71)
C_{14}	(0.27,0.33,0.43)	(0.21,0.37,0.71)	(0.15,0.37,0.43)
C_{21}	(0.19,0.33,1.14)	(0.15,0.33,0.71)	(0.11,0.33,0.43)
C_{22}	(0.25,0.23,0.56)	(0.18,0.48,1.1)	(0.1,0.3,0.34)
C_{23}	(0.06,0.11,0.3)	(0.25,0.6,1.3)	(0.12,0.38,0.12)
C_{24}	(0.19,0.33,1.14)	(0.15,0.33,0.71)	(0.11,0.33,0.43)

Step 7. The scores and ranking of alternatives are computed using Eq. (3) and Eq. (4) and presented in Table 6.

Table 6. Scores and ranks of alternatives

	Scores X_j	graded mean integration R_j	Rank
A1	(0.028,0.59, 5.4)	1.3	2
A2	(0.021,0.83, 5.3)	1.44	1
A3	(0.017,0.77, 3.25)	1	3

The chart representation of Table 6 is shown in Fig. 2.

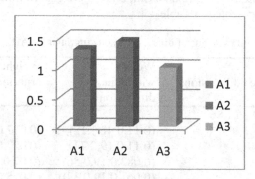

Fig. 2. Ranking of alternatives

4   Results and Conclusion

This study proposed a fuzzy AHP framework based on the combination of the extent analysis and the graded mean integration methods to effectively solve the problem of evaluation of CAS under fuzzy environment. Vague, incomplete, fuzzy preferences of decision makers are represented in linguistic terms by triangular fuzzy numbers. This enabled to have a more accurate, reliable and convincing evaluation process. As a result of evaluation of CAS alternatives, Mathematica is ranked first, Maple is ranked second and Maxima is ranked third. Of course, any evaluation process is context dependent. The proposed framework can be used for effective evaluation of any kind software product. The future work will be devoted to the research on integration of other MCDM into the proposed decision making methodology.

References

1. Vlachos, P., Kehagias, A.: A Computer Algebra System and a New Approach for Teaching Business Calculus. Int. Journal of Computer Algebra in Mathematics Education 7, 87–104 (2000)
2. Feride, S.T., Nilcan, C.: How to adapt CAS on the basis of Mathematical Background and Computer Background at EUL. Procedia – Social Behavioral Sciences (2012)
3. Dix, A., Finlay, J., Abowd, G., Beale, R.: Human Computer Interaction. Prentice Hall (2003)

4. Nolan, F.: CAI in Mathematical Problem Solving: Guidelines for Software Design and Purchase. Computers in the Schools 1(2), 71–80 (1984)
5. Hwang, C.L., Yoon, K.: Multiple Attribute Decision Making – Methods and Application. Springer, Heidelberg (1981)
6. Tanya, A., Borka, J.B.: Application of multi-attribute decision making approach to learning management systems evaluation. Journal of Computers 2(10), 28–37 (2007)
7. Daniel, Y.S., Yi-Shun, W.: Multi-criteria evaluation of the web-based e-learning system: A methodology based on learner satisfaction and its application. Computers and Education 50, 894–905 (2008)
8. Saaty, L.T.: The Analytical Hierarchy Process. McGraw Hill Company, New York (1980)
9. Huseyinov, I.N.: Fuzzy linguistic modelling cognitive / learning styles for adaptation through multi-level granulation. In: Jacko, J.A. (ed.) Human-Computer Interaction, Part IV, HCII 2011. LNCS, vol. 6764, pp. 39–47. Springer, Heidelberg (2011)
10. Laarhoven, P.M.J., Pedrycz, W.: A fuzzy extension of Saaty's priority theory. Fuzzy Sets and Systems 11, 229–241 (1983)
11. Chen, S.J., Hwang, C.L.: Fuzzy Multiple Attribute Decision Making Methods and Applications. Springer, Berlin (1992)
12. Chang, D.Y.: Applications of the extent analysis method on fuzzy AHP. European Journal of Operational Research 95(3), 649–655 (1996)
13. Zadeh, L.A.: Fuzzy sets. Information and Control 8(3), 338–353 (1965)
14. Zadeh, L.: The concept of a linguistic variable and its applications to approximate reasoning. Information Sciences 8(Pt. 1, 2, 3,), 199–249, 301–357, 43–80 (1975)
15. Chen, S.H., Hsieh, C.H.: Representation, ranking, distance, and similarity of L-R type fuzzy number and application. Australian Journal of Intelligent Processing System 6(4), 217–229 (2000)
16. Usability in Software Design, http://www.msdn.microsoft.com/en-us/library/ms997577.aspx
17. Nielsen, J.: Usability Engineering. Academic Press, Boston (1993)

Evaluation of an Information Delivery System for Hearing Impairments at a School for Deaf

Atsushi Ito[1], Takao Yabe[2,3], Koichi Tsunoda[3], Kazutaka Ueda[4],
Tohru Ifukube[4], Hikaru Tauchi[5], and Yuko Hiramatsu[6]

[1] KDDI Research and Development Laboratories, 3-10-10 Iidabashi,
Chiyoda-ku, Tokyo, 102-8460, Japan
at-itou@kddi.com
[2] Tokyo Metropolitan Hiroo Hospital, 2-34-10 Ebisu, Shibuya-ku,
Tokyo, 150-0013, Japan
[3] Tokyo Medical Center, 2-5-1 Higashigaoka, Meguro-ku, Tokyo, 152-0021, Japan
[4] University of Tokyo, 7-3-1 Hongo, Bunkyo-ku, Tokyo, 113-8656, Japan
[5] National Rehabilitation Center for Persons with Disabilities, 4-1 Namiki,
Tokorozawa, 359-8555, Japan
[6] KDDI Evolva Inc., 1-23-7 NIshi-Shinjyuku, Shinjyuku-ku, Tokyo, 160-0023, Japan

Abstract. We have been developing IDDD (Information Delivery System for Deaf People in a Major Disaster) system [7, 8] from 2007. In 2012, we have a chance to develop new IDDD system and test it at the school for the deaf in Miyagi. In this paper, we report the results the system performance test and the users evaluation of the new IDDD based on an experiment at the school for the deaf in Miyagi. As the result, the network performance was increased and application development cost might be half of that of the old IDDD. Also, Fast-Scroll is most legible for hearing impairments people.

1 Introduction

Based on research of the status of people with handicaps during the earthquake in Kobe and Tottori [1,2], we designed the Information Delivery System for Deaf People in a Major Disaster (IDDD), using mobile phone and ad hoc networking technology with an evaluation test conducted in many different locations since 2007. We found many of the deaf left without support during the disaster. Some of them were left in a house and could not go to shelter. In case of disaster, usually electric power supply is stopped, so that they could not receive information from TV. Half of the dead people of the earthquake in Kobe [1] were people who required support for evacuation, such as elderly people or disables people. So that, an information delivery method for hearing impairment people is strongly required. We developed information delivery system based on mobile phone network and without AC power and performed several trials [3, 4, 5, 6], and obtained good results for commercial release. This system was designed based on the following requirements [3,4].

M. Kurosu (Ed.): Human-Computer Interaction, Part II, HCII 2013, LNCS 8005, pp. 398–407, 2013.
© Springer-Verlag Berlin Heidelberg 2013

R1. Accurate information rapidly for deaf people
R2. Appropriate information according to individual situation
R3. Robust equipment to display information definitely
R4. Applicable for the use in daily life
R5. No complicated operation
R6. Work when blackout

To achieve these requirements, we designed IDDD as follows.

1. IDDD was designed to send disaster information at black out. The main components are mobile phone and LED display. Both can work with battery. Disaster information is sent through network or directly from a mobile phone.
2. IDDD displays disaster information on both mobile phones and displays.
3. A disaster message received by a mobile phone is directly transferred to a display via near field communication.
4. Display has function of ad hoc networking to transfer disaster information to rooms automatically. A large wall-mounted or rack-mounted LED display is used in an office or public space, and small box-type display is used in a residential living room.

We performed 19 trials of IDDD from 2007 to 2011, asked attendants to answer questioners, and received answers from 312 people. Fig. 1 is an example of a LED display of IDDD used for a trial in a hospital. In this case, the LED display shows the number of the person next in line, and we tested the display to show disaster information as part of the trial. The overall impression of 46 people was very good as described in Fig. 2. Details are described in [6]. Also, IDDD is used in three offices in Tokyo that employ people with hearing impairments. We confirmed that the size and color (Red for emergency messages and Green for normal messages) of characters are legible and recognizable.

During these trials, we received many different requirements at the different demo locations and from the different attendants. However, IDDD was expensive and not sufficiently flexible to meet every request. Also we received the cost down

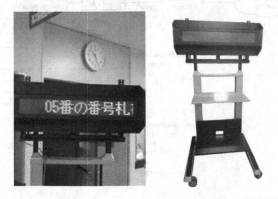

Fig. 1. An example of a LED display for testing IDDD in a hospital

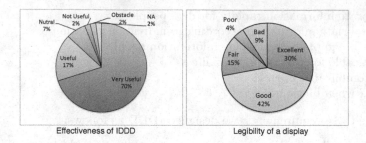

Effectiveness of IDDD   Legibility of a display

Fig. 2. Effectiveness of the system and legibility of the display of IDDD

of the LED display. So that, we re-designed new IDDD [7] and started a new project for the long-term evaluation of IDDD to check the usability at the school of deaf in Miyagi.

In this paper, we report the results the system performance test and the users evaluation of the new IDDD system [7] based on an experiment at the school for the deaf in Miyagi. In the section 2, we explain the outline of the new IDDD system, then the result of evaluation at the school of deaf in Miyagi is mentioned in section 3. At lat we conclude this paper in section 4.

2   Outline of the New IDDD System

Fig. 3 is an outline of the new IDDD system. A disaster message will be sent from Webserver to Android phone. Then the message is transferred to Display-1 and also transferred to Display-1 to Display-2 etc. using ad hoc networking function.

The difference between IDDD described in [3,4,5,6,7] and [8] is described in Table 1. To achieve flexibility, we changed the application platform for the LED

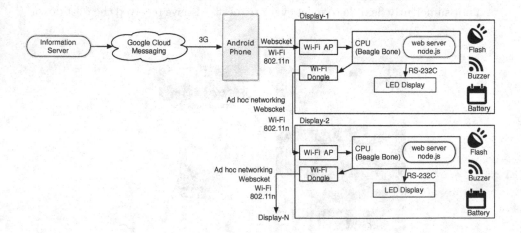

Fig. 3. Architecture of the new IDDD system

Table 1. Difference Between Previous System and New System

Items	Previous System	New System
OS	Linux	Linux
App	Native	Java Script
Display	LED 2 color	LED 3 color
WAN	SMS	IP (Google Cloud Messaging)
Local Communication	Bluetooth	WiFi

display to allow easy customization of APIs as described in [7,8], altered the communication method to increase flexibility, and reduced the development costs. We used Web technology to achieve these requirements. For communication between Android phone and LED display, also between LED displays, we used Websocket [9]. To execute application on LED display and communications among devices, node.js [10] is used as application engine.

This architecture is very effective. For example, we implemented ad hoc network, AODV [11] in one week on node.js using Java Script. As our experience, it may take two weeks to implement AODV by using C on Linux. So that this approach is useful to reduce development cost of application to meet various requirement from users to make IDDD better.

3   Evaluation and Result

We performed evaluation of the new IDDD from two aspects, one is network performance and another is legibility of the LED display of IDDD. In this section, we will explain the result of evaluation from these points.

3.1   Evaluation of Network Performance

First, we evaluated the performance of the system from the delay in sending messages from the information provider to the LED display. We measured the transmission delay in each section of the network described. The measured delay is described in Fig. 4.

We measured several aspects of this system by using the test configuration described in Fig. 4. We measured three delays to check the performance. One is

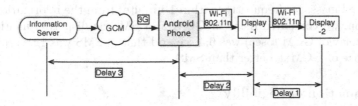

Fig. 4. Test setting to measure performance

delay between two LED displays, Display-1 and 2, (Delay 1 in Fig. 4) , the second is delay between Android phone and LED display (Delay 2 in Fig. 4) and the third is delay between information server and Android phone (Display 3 in Figure 5). Delay 1 is important to deliver information using ad hoc network function and Delay 2+3 is important to deliver urgent information as quickly as possible. We think that the following criterias are important to evaluate delay of information delivery. (C1) As fast as possible: Disaster information sometimes include urgent information such as tsunami alert and earthquake alert. So that, information should be delivered as soon as possible. (C2) Delay should be constant: Sometime the delay is short and sometime the delay is large, the system looks unstable and may give anxiety to people who use IDDD. So that the delay should be constant.

Delay between Two LED Displays (Delay1). As described in Fig. 3, we are using ad-hoc networking between two displays using Wi-Fi (802.11n). Fig. 5 (1) shows the delay between the two LED displays. There are two major delays, however almost under 200 msec. We are planning to set five LED displays in the school for the deaf in Miyagi, so that the maximum delay to display information on all LED display is one second. We think that this result satisfies criteria C2 and there is no problem for the delay in message transmission between two LED displays. In our previous system, we used Bluetooth for the message transfer between LED displays, and it usually took less than one second. We can conclude that Wi-Fi has the same performance as Bluetooth. Also, the range of Bluetooth is 10 m, but Wi-Fi is usually farther. Wi-Fi is useful for larger spaces or buildings like a school.

Delay between Android Phone and LED Display (Delay2). Our greatest concern was the delay in the GCM and mode change of 3G to Wi-Fi in Android phones. Firstly, we measured delay between Android phone and LED display. This delay means the delay of mode change of 3G to Wi-Fi in Android phones. For this test, we used IS17SH (Android 4.0) with DHCP to get IP address. As described in Fig. 5 (2), the delay was 5.69 sec and there was no significant difference among variation of sending message interval. We think that if we use fixed IP address, the delay might be reduced.

Delay between Information Server and Android Phone (Delay 3). Finally, we measured delay between information server and Android phone through GCM. We used the Galaxy Nexus with Android 4.0 for testing of the delay of GCM. If we would like to maintain a short, stable response time using GCM, we need to send messages frequently (within 1 minute) from the information server. In addition, we compared delay of GCM and SMS as displayed in Fig. 5 (3). Average delay of GCM (5sec) was 6.4 sec and that of SMS was 12.4 sec. So that performance of GCM is better than SMS.

3.2   Evaluation of Legibility

The second is the evaluation by the user. We plan to evaluate the system at the Miyagi School for the Deaf from October to December 2012. We plan to execute

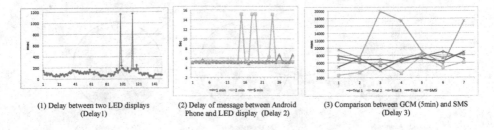

(1) Delay between two LED displays (Delay1)

(2) Delay of message between Android Phone and LED display (Delay 2)

(3) Comparison between GCM (5min) and SMS (Delay 3)

Fig. 5. Evaluation of Network Performance

two types of subjective evaluations: one is a test of awareness of the display and the other is a test of the legibility of the display. There evaluation items are decided based on the discussion with medical doctors and teachers of a school of deaf.

- The number of examinees was 66.
- The size of the tested LED display was as follows: 128 dots x 16 dots (eight characters), 768 mm x 96 mm.
- Scroll speed: "Fast" is 3.45 sec to display eight characters, "Medium" is 6.9 sec to display eight characters and "Slow" is 10.35 sec to display eight characters.
- Display mode: "Scroll" or "Not-Scroll"

Awareness of the Display: Firstly, we set up a LED display at the entrance of the school and displayed messages relating to the festival such as "Welcome to the festival" or "The next performance is "MOMOTARO" by 4th grade". We asked them whether they aware the display or not, and usefulness of them by using the following three questions.

Q1 Did you find and see the LED display?
Q2 Did you understand what was displayed on the LED display?
Q3 Do you think that this LED display is useful in showing various kinds of information?

77% of the examinees answered that they aware the Display as described in Fig. 6. 73% (Well Understand + Understand) of the examinees answered that they could understand the messages. 85% (Very Useful + Useful) of the examinees answered that this kind of display is useful. Awareness and understandability were lower than usefulness, so that we analyzed the effect of distance, speed of scrolling and color in the next subsection.

Legibility of the Display: To investigate the legibility, we tested the following parameters.

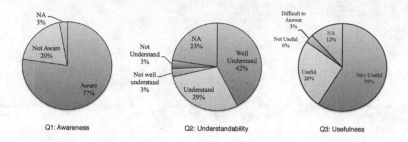

Fig. 6. Awareness and understandability of the Display

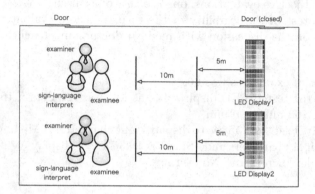

Fig. 7. Test setting to measure legibility

- Effect of color: Red, Green
- Effect of speed of scrolling: Slow and Fast
- Effect of scroll: Still or Scroll

For that purpose, we set up two LED displays in a class room as described in Fig. 7. We asked visitors of the festival to join the evaluation and brought them to the class room where the displays were set.

First, we explain the result from examinees who were hearing impairments.

- There was no effect by difference of color (Green or Red) for legibility of display (Table 2).
- Also, faster scrolling was better (Table 3) and they preferred scrolling rather than still (Table 4).
- Some examinees answered in the comments; if the sentence is correctly segmented, still display mode might be better.

For this experiment, we prepared message that contains ten characters. So that, if we use Not-Scroll mode, after changing displayed message, only two characters were displayed. This might be one reason that they preferred Scroll mode.

Table 2. Color of characters (Hearing Impairments): P-value 0.290

Condition	Easy to read	Difficult to read	Total
Green	37	7	44
Red	33	11	44
Total	79	18	176

Table 3. Speed of scroll (Hearing Impairments): P-value 3.761E-05

Condition	Easy to read	Difficult to read	Total
Slow	64	24	88
Fast	84	4	88
Total	148	28	176

Table 4. Usefulness of scroll (Hearing Impairments): P-value 4.082E-05

Condition	Easy to read	Difficult to read	Total
Scrolling	70	18	88
Not Scrolling	44	44	88
Total	114	62	176

Table 5. Color of characters (Normal): P-value 0.017

Condition	Easy to read	Difficult to read	Total
Green	38	24	82
Red	50	12	62
Total	88	36	124

Table 6. Speed of scroll (Normal): P-value 3.497E-07

Condition	Easy to read	Difficult to read	Total
Slow	73	51	124
Fast	111	13	124
Total	184	64	176

Table 7. Usefulness of scroll (Normal): P-value 2.696E-05

Condition	Easy to read	Difficult to read	Total
Scrolling	75	49	124
Not Scrolling	42	82	124
Total	117	131	248

Next, we explain the result form examinees who were not have hearing impairments. They preferred Red rather than Green (Table 5). For scrolling speed and display mode (Scroll or Not-Scroll), the answer was as same as examinees who are hearing impairments (Table 6,7).

We also checked the effect of combination of color, speed and distance. For the group of hearing impairments, the most legible combination was as follows.

- 5m, Green, Fast: 100%
- 5m, Red, Fast: 95%
- 10m, Green, Fast: 95%
- 10m, Red, Fast: 91%

We could conclude that Fast-Scroll is better. However, there is no clear result on the difference of color.

4   Conclusion

In this paper, we report the results the system performance test and the users evaluation of the new IDDD based on an experiment at the school for the deaf in Miyagi. As the result, the network performance was increased and application development cost might be half of that the old IDDD, and Fast-Scroll is most legible for hearing impairments people. However, we could not get the clear data of effect by color (Red and Green), so that this is one of the issue in 2013. Also, to add more LED displays in the school and test the IDDD system under the more realistic situation.

Acknowledgment. Part of this research was supported by the Ministry of Health, Labor and Welfare.

We thank to Mr.Ogure and Mr.Hatohara of the school of deaf in Miyagi to perform this research in the school. Also we also thank to volunteers who participated evaluation and developing this system.

References

1. Yabe, T., Haraguchi, Y., Tomoyasu, Y., Henmi, H., Ito, A.: Survey of individuals with auditory handicaps requiring support after the Great Hanshin-Awaji earthquake. Japanese Journal of Disease Medicine 14(1) (2009)
2. Yabe, T., Haraguchi, Y., Tomoyasu, Y., Henmi, H., Ito, A.: Survey of individuals with auditory handicaps requiring support after the Western Tottori earthquake. Japanese Journal of Disease Medicine 12(2) (2007)
3. Ito, A., Murakami, H., Watanabe, Y., Fujii, M., Yabe, T., Haraguchi, Y., Tomoyasu, Y., Kakuda, Y., Ohta, T., Hiramatsu, Y.: An Information Delivery and Display System for Deaf People in Times of Disaster. In: Proc. Telhealth 2007 (2007)
4. Fujii, M., Mandana, A.K., Takakai, T., Watanabe, Y., Kmata, K., Ito, A., Murakami, H., Yabe, T., Haraguchi, Y., Tomoyasu, Y., Kakuda, Y.: A study on deaf people supporting systems using cellular phones with Bluetooth in disasters. In: Proc. Exponwireless (2007)

5. Ito, A., Murakami, H., Watanabe, Y., Fujii, M., Yabe, T., Haraguchi, Y., Tomoyasu, Y., Kakuda, Y., Ohta, T., Hiramatsu, Y.: Universal Use of Information Delivery and Display System using Ad hoc Network for Deaf People in Times of Disaster. In: Proceedings of Broadbandcom 2008, pp. 486–491 (2008)
6. Ito, A., Murakami, H., Watanabe, Y., Fujii, M., Yabe, T., Hiramatsu, Y.: Information Delivery System for Deaf People at a Larger Disaster. In: Proceedings of Broadbandcom 2010 (2010)
7. Ito, A., Yabe, T., Watanabe, Y., Fujii, M., Kakuda, Y., Hiramatsu, Y.: A Study of Flexibility in Designing the Information Delivery System for Deaf People in a Major Disaster. In: Proceedings of SCIS-ISIS 2012 (2012)
8. Ito, A., Yabe, T., Tsunoda, K., Hiramatsu, Y., Watanabe, Y., Fujii, M., Kakuda, Y.: Performance Evaluation of Information Delivery System in a Major Disaster for Deaf People based on Embedded Web Systemr. In: Proceedings of AHSP 2013 (2013)
9. The WebSocket Protocol, http://tools.ietf.org/html/rfc6455
10. http://nodejs.org/
11. Ad hoc On-Demand Distance Vector (AODV) Routing, http://www.ietf.org/rfc/rfc3561.txt

Examining the Role of Contextual Exercises and Adaptive Expertise on CAD Model Creation Procedures

Michael D. Johnson[1], Elif Ozturk[1], Lauralee Valverde[1], Bugrahan Yalvac[1], and Xiaobo Peng[2]

[1] Texas A&M University, College Station, Texas, USA 77843
[2] Prairie View A&M University, Prairie View, TX, USA 77446
{mdjohnson,elifo,yalvac}@tamu.edu, lvalverde210@gmail.com,
xipeng@pvamu.edu

Abstract. As computer-aided design (CAD) tools become more integral in the product commercialization process, ensuring that students have efficient and innovative expertise necessary to adapt becomes more important. This work examines the role of adaptive expertise on CAD modeling behavior and the effect of contextual modeling exercises on the manifestation of behaviors associated with adaptive expertise in a population of student participants. A methodology comprising multiple data elicitation tools is used to examine these relationships; these tools include: survey data, model screen capture data analysis, and interviews. Results show that participants engaged in contextual exercises spent more of their modeling time engaged in actual modeling activities as opposed to planning when compared to a control group. Limited statistical support is provided for the role of contextual exercises leading to the manifestation of behaviors associated with adaptive expertise. The amount of time spent engaged in actual modeling is positively correlated with the adaptive expertise behaviors identified in the interviews.

Keywords: Adaptive Expertise, CAD, Evaluation Methods and Techniques, Modeling Processes.

1   Introduction

Students today will enter an industrial environment where computer-aided design (CAD) models are a nexus for the product commercialization process. These tools, when used along with product lifecycle management systems facilitate the efficient execution of complex development projects [1-4]. It is important that students are able to competently and efficiently use CAD tools; this is especially true given these tool's skill driven nature [5]. While students will likely gain CAD experience during their engineering education, the CAD tools they find in industry will probably not be the same ones used by their institution. Even if the CAD platform is the same, there are often numerous and significant updates associated with CAD platforms. An additional concern is the typical educational focus on declarative knowledge; these are the specific procedures required to carry out tasks in specific CAD platforms [6, 7]. This is in

M. Kurosu (Ed.): Human-Computer Interaction, Part II, HCII 2013, LNCS 8005, pp. 408–417, 2013.

contrast to strategic knowledge which is associated with general CAD expertise and has been shown to be transferable to other CAD platforms [8]. Namely, this expertise is adaptable. Adaptive expertise is defined as the ability to apply knowledge in new situations when key parts of that knowledge are missing [9]. Expertise can be categorized as either routine or adaptive in nature [10]. While routine experts are efficient in the domain of their expertise, adaptive experts are both efficient and innovative. Schwartz et al.,[11] propose that learning exercises be developed which promote both efficiency and innovation; these would promote adaptive expertise. It is thought that adaptive experts seek new learning opportunities, monitor their understanding and thinking, and view knowledge as more dynamic [11]. These characteristics are thought to make adaptive experts flexible, innovative, and creative particularly in novel situations [12].

Students are rarely provided with curricular activities that would promote the competencies associated with adaptive expertise [12]. The lack of opportunities for self-learning in engineering curricula has been noted [13]. Contextual exercises have a documented positive impact on students' cognitive and affective domains [14]. Students learn more effectively when they engage in activities that have personal meaning; with respect to CAD education, this may mean modeling objects connected to daily life or personal interest. This work seeks to examine two causal relationships: the effect of adaptive expertise on CAD modeling procedure and the effect of contextual exercises on the manifestation of behaviors associated with adaptive expertise. Multiple knowledge elicitation methods are used to examine these relationships and are described in the next section.

2   Methods

The data presented in this work are the result of a one semester examination of adaptive expertise and the role of contextual exercises in a combined product design and CAD course at Texas A&M University. A total of 32 students took part in some aspect of the exercise. Some student did not complete or consent to certain parts of the exercise; these cases are noted in the results section.

2.1   Adaptive Expertise Survey

One of the main goals of this work is to assess the relationship between adaptive expertise and CAD modeling. As such, the first step was to assess baseline adaptive expertise among the student population. As stated above, adaptive experts have characteristics that distinguish them from their routine counterparts. Fisher and Peterson [15] define four main constructs of adaptive expertise: multiple perspective, metacognition, goals and beliefs, and epistemology. Their work uses a 42 question, 6-point Likert-scale, instrument to assess the adaptive expertise of biomedical engineering students. This work has adopted their instrument to assess the adaptive expertise of the student population prior to the modeling exercise.

A subset of the 42 questions was used to determine dimensional scores using exploratory and confirmatory factor analysis. These analyses used a combination of almost 200 respondents to the survey and included both practicing engineers and students. The original four constructs of Fisher and Peterson [15] were maintained. The questions used for each construct were: multiple perspectives (5, 13, 34,36, 39); metacognition (2,6,10,14,26,30); goals and beliefs (3,7,23,27,38,41), and epistemology (12, 33). These questions were then averaged to determine a sub-score for each construct as well as an overall adaptive expertise score from the average of all 19 questions.

2.2   CAD Modeling Exercise

The purpose of the CAD modeling exercise was twofold: the first goal was to provide a modeling exercise with which to compare baseline adaptive expertise; the second was to evaluate the role of contextual exercises on both modeling behavior and the expression of behaviors associated with adaptive expertise. The modeling exercise took place after the adaptive expertise survey instrument had been administered. The students in the course were split into two groups based on their performance on a lab exercise (to ensure similar skill levels in each group): one group (control) was given a stylized exercise similar to one found in a CAD textbook [16]; the other group (contextual) was asked to bring in an object of moderate complexity they were familiar with to model. The contextual group students were given a ruler to determine dimensions from their object; all dimensions associated with the control object (a drawing) were given. Figure 1 shows the drawing and CAD model screenshot for the control group; Figure 2 shows the contextual object and a CAD model screenshot. Students were given one hour to complete the modeling exercise. During the exercise, the Camtasia screen capture software was used to record participant screens.

2.3   Interview

Both prior to and immediately following the CAD modeling exercise, pre- and post-interviews, respectively were conducted. The pre-interview questions included:

- What are the things you consider first when you are asked to model an object? Why?
- What are the challenges you often encounter in the modeling process?
  - How do you plan to overcome these challenges?
  - Which strategies do you anticipate using?
- Are you familiar with the object you are going to model today?
- How important it is to know about the object you are going to model?
  - If you are familiar with the object you are modeling or if you use it often in your daily life, is it easier for you to model it? Why, why not?

The post-interview questions included:

- The things you considered before you began modeling the object, were they helpful to you in the process? How and why?
- What challenges did you encounter during the modeling process?
  - How did you overcome the challenges you faced during the modeling process?
- Was knowing the object or being familiar with it, helpful to you in your modeling process? How and why?
- How confident are you in your model?

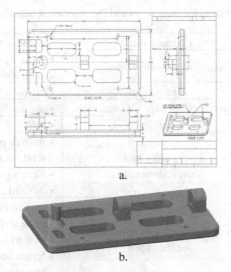

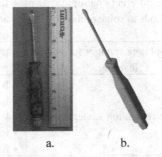

Fig. 1. Control item drawing (a.) and screen shot of control CAD model (b.)

Fig. 2. Contextual item (a.) and screen shot of example contextual CAD model (b.)

The interviews were audio recorded and transcribed verbatim. The constant comparative method was used to analyze the transcripts [17, 18]. First open and axial coding was used to analyze the interview responses. Next selective coding was used. The responses were coded along the four dimensions of adaptive expertise defined by Fisher and Peterson [15]. This coding was based on adaptive expertise characteristics; these codes, characteristics, and their associated dimensions are shown in Table 1. Pre- and post-interview instances for each dimensions were tabulated and used to determine an overall pre-, post-, and total interview adaptive expertise manifestation counts.

2.4   Model and Procedure Analysis

The modeling procedures of the student participants were examined in two ways. The first entailed the analysis of model and feature characteristics as detailed in Johnson

Table 1. Codes extracted from the interviews and the associated adaptive expertise dimensions

Dimension	Characteristics	Codes from Interviews.
Multiple Perspectives	Efficiency (consistency & accuracy)	• most efficient way to model • easiest way to model
	Innovation	• N/A
	Act flexibly to novel situation	• creating drawing of object
Metacognition	Confidence	• N/A
	Successfully monitor own understanding	• have to pay close attention while modeling • have a good starting point • in hand 3D part helps
	Recognize that own knowledge may be incomplete	• how to use the features • complexity of the object • how to model • forgot how to use some features
	Use different / multiple methods to solve problem	• creating drawing of object • look object from different angles • trying different methods
Goals & Believes	Seek out opportunities for new learning	• try to learn better (if you had problems)
	Self-regulation strategies	• have an approach • have a way to organize model • know what steps to take first • have a good starting point • have strategies to model
Epistemology	Pursue knowledge	• practice • reading more
	Others can provide information	• ask someone for help

and Diwakaran [19]. These included the number of features, amount of reference geometry used, incorrect feature terminations, the number of segments per feature (a proxy for feature complexity), and the number of weak dimensions. Interested readers are referred to Johnson and Diwakaran [19] for detailed definitions of these quantities.

The second way of examining modeling procedure consisted of using the Camtasia screen capture videos of the students modeling to assess how they used their time during the modeling process. The time was split into three main categories: thinking, searching, and doing. Thinking or planning time was deemed to be anytime that there was no cursor movement in the video. Searching time was that where students were looking for specific functions or tools; this was defined by the non-performance of any modeling action. Finally, doing time was defined by the participant engaging in a particular modeling procedure; time was coded as doing even if the participant later deleted or changed the original work. An additional waiting category is used for time that the system is processing data or model changes. The data elicited from these various methods was correlated with the original adaptive expertise survey data; an analysis of the data between the control and contextual groups was also performed.

3   Results

To examine the role of contextual exercises on modeling behavior and the manifestation of behaviors associated with adaptive expertise, results for the control and contextual groups were analyzed and compared using t-tests. Table 2 shows a summary of the data for the two groups; results that are significant at the $p \leq 0.10$ are bolded. Only participants that completed their modeling exercise are included in the data presented. Out of a total of 32 participants, 21 completed their modeling exercises (11 from the control group; 10 from the contextual group). As mentioned previously, student groups were formed based on their performance on a previous exercise. However, to provide a baseline comparison adaptive expertise survey data are shown for the two groups. An unexpected result is the statistically significantly higher score on the epistemology dimension for the control group. The survey results for the other dimensions were comparable.

Students assigned to the contextual exercise took a statistically significantly longer time to complete the exercise than their counterparts in the control group. One possible explanation for this could be that participants in the contextual group had to derive the dimensions for their component, while those in the control group had their dimensions provided on the drawing. This is not the case. The mean thinking time (which one would assume would contain dimensioning time) for the contextual group was 6.15 minutes (SD = 3.24) and that for the control group was 7.90 minutes (SD = 2.78). The number of features used in the control group was greater than that of the contextual group. The contextual group also used more reference geometry features; this was a statistically significant difference. However, given the variety of components used in the contextual group, these two result (features and reference geometry) are not meaningful. The feature density for the two groups was comparable. Higher feature density has been viewed as a proxy for modeling skill or expertise [6]. The contextual modeling group had less incorrect feature terminations, but produced models that had more weak dimensions. The contextual group spend a statistically significantly higher percentage of their modeling time doing actual modeling as compared to the control group. This relationship was reversed in the percent thinking category where the control group spent more time thinking.

The final comparison comprised pre and post interview data related to the manifestation of behaviors associated with adaptive expertise. The pre-exercise interview data related to multiple perspectives and goals and beliefs were higher for the contextual group than the control group; however, these differences were not statistically significant. The total pre-exercise data was also higher for the contextual group, but again this difference was not statistically significant. The post-exercise data related to metacognition and the overall post-exercise count of behaviors are both statistically significantly higher for the contextual group. The overall interview data related to the

Table 2. Comparison of variables for control and contextual modeling exercises

	Control	Contextual	t	p
Number of Students participating	16	16	-	-
Students Completing Exercise	11	10	-	-
Survey Data				
Epistemology	5.00	3.95	**2.60**	**0.012**
Goals and Beliefs	3.61	3.37	0.59	0.562
Multiple Perspectives	3.66	4.04	-1.31	0.204
Metacognition	4.62	4.42	0.70	0.490
Total Adaptive Expertise	4.09	3.94	0.62	0.542
Model and Procedure Data				
Completion Time	37.6	53.6	**-3.12**	**0.006**
Number of Features	19.64	14.30	1.39	0.181
Reference Geometry	0.45	2.00	**-1.78**	**0.090**
Incorrect Feature Terminations	4.27	1.60	1.70	0.106
Average Number of Segments	3.20	2.88	0.42	0.681
Total Number of Weak Dimensions	7.09	17.40	**-2.58**	**0.018**
Percent Doing	71.5%	83.9%	**-3.81**	**0.001**
Percent Searching	7.3%	4.6%	1.01	0.327
Percent Thinking	21.2%	11.3%	**3.66**	**0.002**
Percent Waiting	0.0%	0.3%	-1.64	0.118
Interview Data				
Pre- Multiple Perspectives	0.10	0.57	-1.72	0.105
Pre- Epistemology	0.30	0.29	0.05	0.963
Pre- Metacognition	1.10	1.00	0.22	0.830
Pre- Goals and Beliefs	0.50	0.86	-0.92	0.373
Pre- Total Adaptive Expertise	2.00	2.71	-1.27	0.222
Post- Epistemology	0.10	0.00	0.83	0.420
Post- Metacognition	0.10	0.71	**-2.32**	**0.035**
Post- Total Adaptive Expertise	0.20	0.71	**-1.80**	**0.092**
Interview Total Adaptive Expertise	2.20	3.43	-1.67	0.115

exercise was also higher for the contextual group; however, this difference was not statistically significant. This lends limited support to the role of contextual exercises increases the manifestation of behaviors associated with adaptive expertise.

To examine the role of adaptive expertise on modeling behavior, survey data correlations with model and procedure variables were examined. These correlations were examined for the contextual data, the control data, and the overall data set (combining both control and contextual). For participants in the contextual exercise, the epistemology dimension of the survey was negatively correlated the percent thinking time ($N = 10$, $r = -0.670$, $p = 0.034$). Contextual exercise participant data also showed a positive correlation between the multiple perspective dimension and the percent thinking time ($N = 10$, $r = 0.566$, $p = 0.088$). Neither of these correlations was statistically significant for either the control data or the overall data set. The episte-mology dimension of the survey was positively correlated with the number of features for both the control group (N = 11, r = 0.610, p = 0.046) and the overall data set (N = 21, r = 0.474, p = 0.030); the correlation for the contextual group was not statistically significant. There was a negative correlation between the goal and beliefs survey di-mension and the number of features for both the control group (N = 11, r = -0.722, p = 0.012) and overall population (N = 21, r = -0.422, p = 0.057); again the correlation for the contextual group was not statistically significant. The overall survey measure of adaptive expertise was negatively correlated with the number of features for the control group (N = 11, r = -0.541, p = 0.086). The multiple perspective measure was negatively correlated with the number of features used for the overall data set (N = 21, r = -0.373, p = 0.095). The lack of correlations between adaptive expertise meas-ures and features related to the contextual exercises is understandable given the wide variety of components that were modeled in the contextual exercise group. Next, in-stances of adaptive expertise data derived from interview data were compared to model attributes and modeling procedure data. It should be noted that not all partici-pants consented to interviews; this lowers the sample number. For the contextual ex-ercise group the following correlations were statistically significant: pre-interview metacognition and the number of weak dimensions (N = 7, r = -0.689, p = 0.087); pre-interview goals and beliefs and the number of reference geometry features (N = 7, r = 0.738, p = 0.058); post-interview metacognition and the number of incorrect feature terminations (N = 7, r = -0.679, p = 0.093); and the post-interview total and the num-ber of incorrect feature terminations (N = 7, r = 0.679, p = 0.093). For the control exercise group the following correlations were statistically significant: pre-interview metacognition and the number of features (N = 10, r = 0.754, p = 0.012); post-interview epistemology and the number of features (N = 10, r = 0.989, p < 0.001); post-interview epistemology and the number of segments per feature (N = 10, r = -0.608, p = 0.062); and the post interview total and the number of features (N = 10, r = 0.683, p = 0.029). Finally, for the entire data set, the following correlations were statistically significant: pre-interview goals and beliefs and the number reference geometry features (N = 17, r = 0.525, p = 0.030); post-interview epistemology and the number of features (N = 17, r = 0.909, p < 0.001); post-interview epistemology and the number of incorrect feature terminations (N = 17, r = 0.486, p = 0.048); post-interview metacognition and the number of reference geometry features (N = 17, r = 0.445, p = 0.074); and post-interview metacognition and the number of weak dimen-sions (N = 17, r = 0.501, p = 0.041). For the contextual exercise group, the statistically significant correlations between interview data and modeling procedure included: the total number of interview adaptive expertise manifestations and the percentage doing time (N = 7, r = 0.828, p = 0.021); and the total number of interview adaptive expertise manifestations and the percentage thinking time (N = 7, r = -0.874, p = 0.010). There were no statistically significant correlations of note for the control group. The overall data also had statistically significant correlations for the total number of interview adap-tive expertise manifestations and the percentage doing time (N = 17, r = 0.439, p = 0.078) and percentage thinking time (N = 17, r = -0.537, p = 0.026).

4   Conclusions

This work examined the role of adaptive expertise on CAD modeling procedure and the effect of contextual exercises on CAD modeling procedure and the manifestation of adaptive expertise. Prior to the modeling exercise, participants were administered a survey to assess their adaptive expertise on four dimensions: multiple perspective, metacognition, goals and beliefs, and epistemology [15]. A student population was divided into a control group, which received a stylized component drawing of moderate complexity and a contextual group, which modeled an item of intermediate complexity with which the participant had some familiarity. These models were analyzed to tabulate their attributes; screen capture software used and the resultant videos were analyzed to determine modeling procedure and time usage. Specifically, time usage was split into four categories: doing, thinking, searching, and waiting. Pre- and post- modeling interviews were also conducted and analyzed to determine if the exercises resulted in the manifestation of behaviors associated with adaptive expertise.

Analysis of the screen capture data showed that contextual exercises participants spent a greater percentage of the modeling time doing modeling activities than the control group. For the control group, a greater percentage of time was spent thinking. The analysis of interview data showed that the contextual group had more manifestations of behaviors associated with adaptive expertise. While not all categories were statistically significant, this provides partial evidence that contextual exercises promote adaptive expertise behaviors. Several statistically significant correlations were found between survey data and model attributes as well as modeling procedure. One of the more significant was the positive correlation between interview adaptive expertise related behaviors and the percentage of time spent modeling.

The above conclusions should be assessed in light of the limitations of the presented work. Namely, a small sample of students was used to collect these data. Future work will attempt to increase the number of participants and include practicing engineers.

Acknowledgements. This material is supported by the National Science Foundation under EEC Grant Numbers 1129403 and 1129411. Any opinions, findings, conclusions, or recommendations presented are those of the authors and do not necessarily reflect the views of the National Science Foundation.

References

1. Field, D.A.: Education and Training for CAD in the Auto Industry. Computer-Aided Design 36(14), 1431–1437 (2004)
2. Eppinger, S.D., Chitkara, A.R.: The New Practice of Global Product Development. MIT Sloan Management Review 47(4), 22–30 (2006)
3. Caldwell, B., Mocko, G.M.: Product Data Management in Undergraduate Education. In: ASME 2008 International Design Engineering Technical Conferences & Computers and Information in Engineering Conferences, Brooklyn, New York, Paper No. DETC-2008-50015 (2008)

4. Liu, D.T., Xu, X.W.: A Review of Web-based Product Data Management Systems. Computers in Industry 44(3), 251–262 (2001)
5. Adler, P.S.: The Skill Requirements of CAD/CAM: An Exploratory Study. International Journal of Technology Management 5(2), 201–216 (1990)
6. Hamade, R.F., Artail, H.A., Jaber, M.Y.: Evaluating the Learning Process of Mechanical CAD Students. Computers & Education 49(3), 640–661 (2007)
7. Chester, I.: Teaching for CAD Expertise. International Journal of Technology and Design Education 17(1), 23–35 (2007)
8. Lang, G.T., et al.: Extracting and Using Procedural Knowledge in a CAD Task. IEEE Transactions on Engineering Management 38(3), 257–268 (1991)
9. Wineburg, S.: Reading Abraham Lincoln: An Expert/Expert Study in the Interpretation of Historical Texts. Cognitive Science 22(3), 319–346 (1998)
10. Hatano, G., Inagaki, K.: Two Courses of Expertise. In: Stevenson, H.W., Azuma, H., Hakuta, K. (eds.) Child Development and Education in Japan, pp. 262–272. W.H. Freeman, New York (1986)
11. Schwartz, D.L., Bransford, J.D., Sears, D.: Efficiency and Innovation in Transfer. In: Mestre, J.P. (ed.) Transfer of Learning from a Modern Multidisciplinary Perspective. IAP, Greenwich (2005)
12. Hatano, G., Oura, Y.: Commentary: Reconceptualizing School Learning Using Insight From Expertise Research. Educational Researcher 32(8), 26–29 (2003)
13. Harris, M., Cullen, R.: A model for curricular revision: The case of engineering. Innovative Higher Education 34(1), 51–63 (2009)
14. Bransford, J., et al.: How people learn: brain, mind, experience, and school, xxiii, 319 p. National Academy Press, Washington, D.C. (1999)
15. Fisher, F.T., Peterson, P.L.: A tool to measure adaptive expertise in biomedical engineering students. In: 2001 ASEE Annual Conference and Exposition. ASEE, Albuquerque (2001)
16. Toogood, R.: Pro Engineer Wildfire 2.0 Tutorial and Multimedia CD. SDC Publications, Edmonton (2004)
17. Creswell, J.W.: Qualitative Inquiry and Research Design: Choosing Among Five Approaches. SAGE Publications, Thousand Oaks (2007)
18. Glaser, B.G., Strauss, A.L.: The Discovery of Grounded Theory: Strategies for Qualitative Research. Aldine de Gruyter (1967)
19. Johnson, M.D., Diwakaran, R.P.: An educational exercise examining the role of model attributes on the creation and alteration of CAD models. Computers & Education 57(2), 1749–1761 (2011)

Personality and Emotion as Determinants of the Learning Experience: How Affective Behavior Interacts with Various Components of the Learning Process

Zacharias Lekkas[1], Panagiotis Germanakos[2], Nikos Tsianos[1], Constantinos Mourlas[1], and George Samaras[2]

[1] Faculty of Communication and Media Studies,
National & Kapodistrian University of Athens, 5 Stadiou Str, GR 105-62, Athens, Hellas
zlekkas@gmail.com, {ntsianos,mourlas}@media.uoa.gr
[2] Computer Science Department, University of Cyprus, CY-1678 Nicosia, Cyprus
{pgerman,cssamara}@cs.ucy.ac.cy

Abstract. The aim of the present study is to develop a model that grasps the complexity of the concepts of personality and affect in a web-based learning environment. Furthermore, it presents the implications that these theoretical and empirical representations can have in an experimental setting. We are investigating the connection between personality factors, emotion regulation and cognitive processing tasks, decision making and problem solving styles. Decision-making and problem solving are cognitive processes where the outcome is a choice between alternatives. They are both an indirect way to make inferences to a person's learning pattern since learning includes continuous decision making and problem resolution. By implementing our model in the design of a web-based learning personalized setting, we provide evidence that behavior is altered by affective elements in decision making and problem solving routines as is performance in cognitive processing tasks.

Keywords: personality, affect, emotion, learning.

1 Introduction

Over the course of time, a combination of developments in statistical know-how and the evolution of thought within psychology enabled the refinement of measures, and subsequently the assessment of more specific factors in the field of individual differences like different kinds of ability, personality and emotion. The aforementioned concepts underpin psychology's attempt to identify the unique character of individuals. The terms describe properties of behavior which concern the individual's typical ways of coping with life events. Of particular interest is the field of learning and the processes that take place during the acquisition of knowledge. Many researchers used to believe that emotional processes were beyond the scope of a scientific study. Recent advances in cognitive science and psychology, however, suggest that there is nothing mystical about emotion. On the contrary, emotions and affect are a vital part of a continuous mental process. As such, learning procedure is influenced by our

M. Kurosu (Ed.): Human-Computer Interaction, Part II, HCII 2013, LNCS 8005, pp. 418–427, 2013.

emotional profile as well. Learning is acquiring new or modifying existing knowledge, behaviors, skills, values, or preferences and may involve synthesizing different types of information even emotional one.

An in-depth model that grasps the complexity of these underlying concepts is the first purpose of this paper. Instead of selecting one area of implementation, we are trying to combine various levels of analyses and form a typology that will help us circle effectively the affective mechanisms of the individual. The model of emotion mainly comprises the concepts of personality and emotion regulation. Personality is well established in psychological literature. We concentrated on a subset of personality attributes (extraversion, psychoticism and neuroticism) [1]. An effort to construct a model that predicts the role of specific emotions is beyond the scope of our research, due to the complexity and the numerous confounding variables that would make such an attempt rather impossible. We focus on emotion regulation as an emotional mechanism and not on a number of basic emotions because it can provide some indirect measurement of general emotional mechanisms since it manages a number of emotional factors. Emotion regulation is the way in which an individual perceives and controls his emotions. By combining the personality traits of the individual with his regulatory mechanism we can reach into a conclusion of how emotions influence his learning performance and his behavior.

We provide evidence that behavior is altered by affective elements in decision making and problem solving routines. At the same time our level of implementation after analyzing our findings in decision making and problem solving preferences, will concentrate directly on the user learning process.

2   The Model of Emotion Regulation

Theorists from a variety of orientations tend to agree in two emotional processing systems. There is considerable conceptual overlap in their formulations:

- A schematic, associative and implicit system that has connections with bodily response systems. This mode involves fast and automatic processes such as priming and spreading activation. It often involves large numbers of memories in parallel. It is not wholly dependent on verbal information – visual, kinaesthetic or other cues could provide the basis for priming or activating an emotional memory.
- An abstract propositional 'rational' system that is analytical, reflective, logical and relies on high level executive functions. It is primarily based on verbally accessible semantic information. Individuals can utilize these two systems to process information. The first system relies on experience and intuition. In particular, individuals consider issues intuitively and effortlessly. Rather than reflect upon the various considerations in sequence, individuals form a global impression of issues. In addition, rather than apply logical rules or symbolic codes, such as words or numbers, individuals consider vivid representations of objects or events. These representations are filled with the emotions, details, features, and sensations that correspond to the objects or events. Finally, learning is equated to ascertain associations from direct experiences.

The second system, in contrast, relies on logic and rationality. In particular, individuals analyze issues with effort, logic, and deliberation rather than rely on intuition. To decide upon issues, they rely on logical rules and symbolic codes. The context (details, features, and emotions) that correspond to objects or events are disregarded. To facilitate learning in this system, individuals learn the rules of reasoning that are promulgated in society.

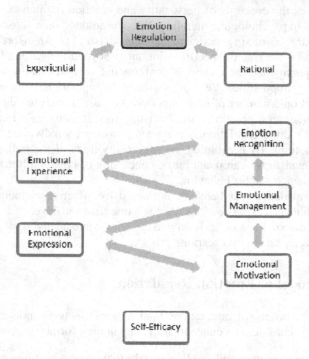

Fig. 1. The Emotion Regulation Mode

Recent neuroscientific findings are consistent with these multi-level conceptualizations. Le Doux [2] has reviewed evidence suggesting that emotion networks have direct anatomical connections to both the neocortex and the amygdala. Events that are highly emotional are likely to be registered at both subcortical and cortical levels. The subcortical route is shorter and rapid whereas the cortical route is longer and slower.

In the subcortical route sensory information goes from the thalamus directly to the amygdala. In the cortical route information is sent from the thalamus to both the cortex and hippocampus and is then projected to the amygdala. As noted by Samilov & Goldfried [3], these recent findings support a qualitative distinction between cortically based and subcortical levels of information processing. They imply that not all emotional responses are mediated cortically; rather, some may by initiated without any cognitive participation: "Emotional responses can occur without the involvement of the higher processing systems of the brain, systems believed to be involved in thinking, reasoning, and consciousness" (LeDoux, 1998, pp. 161)

Our Model of Emotion Regulation includes as well two levels of processing in relation to the aforementioned concept of processing but we consider that these two levels are connected closely with each other and that information is processed not only in a serial way but also concurrently. The experiential level includes the notions of emotional experience and emotional expression. Emotional experience is the covert emotional condition that a human is experiencing as a result of a stimulus or information of such kind. Emotional expression is the overt reaction of such a stimulus, the behavior that follows the experience. On the other hand, the rational level is comprised of the notions of emotion recognition, emotional management and emotional motivation. Emotion recognition is the ability to realize the true nature of an emotion as it is and to feel it in the appropriate degree. Emotional management is the ability to manipulate and to control an emotion while emotional motivation is the ability to transform an emotional experience into a motivational urge. A visual representation of our model can be seen in figure 1. We believe that these two systems can interact. If someone during the stage of emotion recognition realizes intuitively that the emotion that is about to be triggered will have a negative and unpleasant emotional experience as an outcome, then it will be implicitly transformed to a different emotion so that it will be easily manageable in the next stage. The human brain prioritizes based on the principles of self-regulation and not on the search of objectivity and truthfulness.

3   The Concepts of Emotional Experience and Emotional Expression

The study of emotional experience and emotional expression has a long history, which dates back to the 1870s with scientific investigations undergone by Charles Darwin [4]. Darwin's work emphasized the biological utility of emotional expression. Thus, it contributed to the development of an evolutionary-expressive approach to emotion, which suggests that emotion exists because it contributes to survival [5]. Emotional experience, emotional expression and emotional arousal have been conceptualized as three primary components of emotion [6] with emotional reflection as a secondary component, involving thoughts about the three primary components.

Our model of emotion regulation distinguishes mechanisms surrounding the experience of emotions, from those surrounding the expression of emotions. Whilst in practical terms this is probably a seamless process, we believe it is conceptually useful to distinguish experience from expression. We hypothesize that it is more fundamental and harmful to control emotional experience, than to control emotional expression. The expression of emotions is behavioral. Thus the mechanisms surrounding it, involve the real and imagined consequences of expression, cultural and family rules for acceptable expression. These mechanisms may be different from those involved in emotional experience, which is of course experiential, rather than overtly behavioral. Such emotional experience may involve feeling too much intensive emotion, feeling inappropriate emotion, or feeling numb. Also important, is how the initial negative stimulus is registered, whether emotions are experienced as a gestalt, rather than separate somatic constituents and understanding the causes and meaning of the emotional experience. In short, it could be said that emotional experience points more towards a stimulus event, and expression more towards the behavioral response.

In summary, emotion regulation is not so much concerned about whether emotional expression is right or wrong but more with what mechanisms underlie successful and unsuccessful processing. Failure to express emotions may be integrally related to failure to properly process an emotional event. However, this is only one important part within a more complex process, as emotion regulation is regarded as the overall concept within which, emotional expression simply constitutes the final stage.

4   Experimental Evaluation

In this experimental stage we wanted to investigate the implications behind the first level of emotion regulation and see how emotional experience and emotional expression interact with decision making and problem solving styles. Decision making and problem solving are two processes that circle almost every aspect of human activity. This way we can find some implications that connect emotion and its reactive responses with behavior in other areas that can be implemented in web design in various fields like elearning, e-assessment and e-commerce. We hypothesized that highly emotional human beings will have a tendency towards emotional styles and not rational ones. Respectively this information can be used in web design to personalize content and navigation to their likings. For example a user that as a decision maker is dependent (does not like to decide on his own, values the advice of others) will enjoy a more solid, concrete and "closed" navigational system and not a web interface with many links and freedom of navigation or will opt for help and guidance more often than someone who is not dependent and likes to decide always on his own.

4.1   Sampling and Procedure

The study was carried out within one week and the participants were all Greek citizens that live in Greece. All participants were of relatively young age studying or working at the time of administration. They could either participate in the experimental sessions that were held in the New Technologies laboratory in University of Athens or fill in the questionnaires that could also be found online at the web page designed specifically for that purpose. They were all given a battery of questionnaires. A total of 247 questionnaires were completed and returned. 55 of them were half completed or had double answers and were omitted from the sample. Our final sample included 192 participants giving a completion rate of almost 80%. Participants varied from the age of 18 to the age of 40, with a mean age of 27 and a standard deviation of 5. 73 respondents were male and 119 were female. Among other demographic characteristics that were examined were the profession and the computer experience level of each participant.

4.2   Questionnaires

The study used questionnaires to collect quantitative data. It included five measures, one each for personality, emotional arousal, emotion regulation, decision making styles and problem solving styles. Our first treatment involved the close examination of the experiential level of the emotion regulation questionnaire (emotional experience and emotional expression) and its correlation with decision making and problem solving styles. To evaluate Decision Making we used the General Decision-Making Style Inventory (DMSI) by Scott and Bruce [7] which includes 25 items and 5 scales (Spontaneous, Dependent, Rational, Avoidant, Intuitive) and for Problem Solving the Problem Solving Styles Questionnaire (PSSQ) by Parker with 20 items and four scales (Sensing, Intuitive, Feeling, Thinking).

4.3   Design

Internal consistency was assessed by computing Cronbach alphas for the three measures. Although there are no standard guidelines available on appropriate magnitude for the coefficient, in practice, an alpha greater than 0.60 is considered reasonable in psychological research [8]. After the inspection of the alpha coefficients, we performed descriptive statistics for the study sample as a whole and for the particular scales under investigation to examine the sample's suitability. Since our sample was normally distributed with variance of suitable proportions we continued our statistical analysis with the use of the statistical package SPSS. The statistical analysis used to perform this study was mainly one-way Analysis of Variance (ANOVA). Our research hypothesis stated that the experiential emotion regulation factors will have an effect on the participant's style of action. More specifically, participants that score high in emotional experience and emotional expression scales will have a tendency towards more emotional and less rational styles.

5   Results

For the purposes of the experiment, Analyses of Variance (ANOVA) were performed in order to indicate the relationships between the variables of the study. Table 1 presents the main findings between the scale of emotional experience and the scales of the DMSI and PSSQ. The analyses indicated that emotional experience correlated highly with the spontaneous, rational and avoidant styles of the decision making questionnaire and the feeling and thinking styles of the problem solving questionnaire.

Table 1. Statistical Significance between the Emotional Experience scale and Decision-Making and Problem-Solving Styles

Construct	F	Sig
DM-Spontaneous	18.160	.000**
DM-Rational	7.907	.005*
DM-Avoidant	10.116	.002*
DM-Intuitive	14.469	.000**
PS-Feeling	33.562	.000**
PS-Thinking	11.025	.001**

 * p<0.005
** p<0.001

Table 2. Statistical Significance between the Emotional Expression scale and Decision-Making and Problem-Solving Styles

Constuct	F	Sig.
DM-Spontaneous	18.033	.000**
DM-Rational	18.090	.000**
DM-Avoidant	12.155	.001**
DM-Intuitive	7.077	.008*
PS-Feeling	19.469	.000**
PS-Thinking	19.189	.000**

* p<0.005
** p<0.001

A person that experiences emotions vividly is typically afraid that he might feel anxious, tense and moody. He can get emotional easily and therefore is reasonable to react in a spontaneous and not thoughtful way in occasions or with an inhibition of action in others. His pattern of behavior is tense as his character and is subjective to strong feelings. On the other hand a less emotional individual is more rational and more methodical in his behavior.

The exact same pattern is repeated with the emotional expression scale as it can be seen in table 2. This is consistent with the idea that since expression is the consequence of experience it will follow the same set of rules that govern experience. In the general population a person that experiences an emotion of a specific magnitude will have a reaction of equivalent proportions.

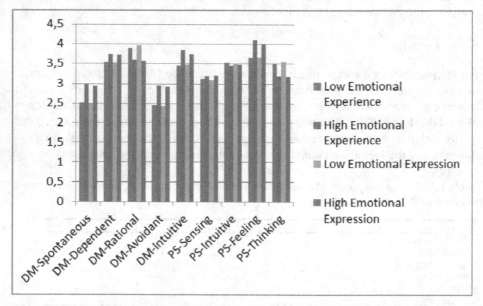

Fig. 2. Means of High and Low Participant Groups in Emotional Experience and Emotional Expression. Emotional participants have higher means in the more "emotional" styles of spontaneous, avoidant, intuitive and feeling while less emotional participants score higher in the "logical" ones such us rational and thinking.

In figure 2 we can see the means of both measures in all decision making and problem solving styles. The logical assumption is that the two notions of emotional experience and emotional expression will be highly correlated which indeed is the case. Pearson's r has shown a significance at the 0.01 level (two-tailed) of .626.

6   Discussion

It may come as no surprise that emotional factors are important in the decision and problem solving process. The emotion regulation factors comprise characteristics that people often exhibit in their decision making. Apart from the standard emotion regulation questionnaire we developed a theory and a corresponding battery of questionnaires for the concept of Affect [9]. The next step of our research is to combine these findings with the purely affective elements of our model. It has been argued that positive affect increases motivation, attention, pleasantness, participation and engagement, while negative affect is highly involved with boredom, fear, anger, displeasure and distraction. We have already developed a web system based on learning performance evaluation for the testing of the various instruments that we have incorporated in our model [10]. The cognitive elements are more straightforward since they are easier to measure and easier to quantify and we have already reached a level in which we can make inferences about how users with different cognitive abilities and preferences can be aided or guided through a personalized web interface [11].

The final step to complete the implementation of our model is to add the affective elements and to investigate the inner and deeper relations that exist between them. Personality type is also a fundamental construct since personality research is already established and developed to a great extent. Emotional and decision factors can be proven significant in defining user behavior in web applications and interfaces, taking into consideration psychometric challenges, as well as the complicated matter of quantifying and subsequently mapping emotions on a digital environment. Most theories of choice assume that decisions derive from an assessment of the future outcomes of various options and alternatives through some type of cost-benefit analyses.

The influence of emotions on decision-making is largely ignored. The studies of decision-making in neurological patients who can no longer process emotional information normally suggest that people make judgments not only by evaluating the consequences and their probability of occurring, but also and even sometimes primarily at a gut or emotional level [12]. We often have different preferences as to our approach, varying between thinking and feeling. When we use reason to make decisions, we seek to exclude emotions, using only rational methods, and perhaps even mathematical tools although emotions exist in the first stage of our decision making procedure and are followed by reasoning. The foundation of such decisions is the principle of utility, whereby the value of each option is assessed by assigning criteria (often weighted). Web systems until recently tried to integrate tools that aid user in a purely rational process (e-learning and decision-support systems). There is a whole range of decision-making that uses emotion, depending on the degree of reason that is included in the process. A totally emotional decision is typically very fast. This is because it takes time (at least 0.1 seconds) for the rational cortex to get going. This is the reactive (and largely subconscious) decision-making that you encounter in heated arguments or when faced with immediate danger. User Behavior is in its final analysis a decision making process.

The mediating role of technology can help the designers to understand the emotional mechanisms of the users and adjust more efficiently to their needs. One possible implementation of a Web-based system's interface that can appraise human emotion is through the use of a set of parameters that can adapt according to the emotional condition of the user and his preferred style of action. An emotionally tense or unstable individual will be able to adjust the contents of a webpage based to what he considers easier to control and manipulate. A certain emotional condition demands a personalization of equivalent proportions. The user will have the capability to respond emotionally either after being asked at a specific moment or after an initial profile construction. Such a system should be designed in a way that it can create a detailed profile for every user and can provide two basic services. One application-based that will have to do with the interface, the navigation and its usability and aesthetical appearance and one content-based that will have to do with the database, the allocation of content, the depth and the dissemination of information. Using these, the interface will take the form that the user wishes so that he can work there more efficiently and less anxiously. Research on decision making and problem solving is only the first step to map and model user patterns of behavior. The research results can be further used as more specific design guidelines.

Acknowledgements. The work is co-funded by the PersonaWeb project under the Cyprus Research Promotion Foundation (ΤΠΕ/ΠΛΗΡΟ/0311(ΒΙΕ)/10), and the EU projects Co-LIVING (60-61700-98-009) and SocialRobot (285870).

References

1. Lekkas, Z., Tsianos, N., Germanakos, P., Mourlas, C., Samaras, G.: The effects of personality type in user-centered appraisal systems. In: Jacko, J.A. (ed.) Human-Computer Interaction, Part I, HCII 2011. LNCS, vol. 6761, pp. 388–396. Springer, Heidelberg (2011)
2. LeDoux, J.: The emotional brain. Touchstone, New York (1998)
3. Samoilov, A., Goldfried, M.R.: Role of emotion in cognitive behaviour therapy. Clinical Psychology, Science (2000)
4. Darwin, C.: The Expression of the Emotions in Man and Animals. D. Appleton and Company, New York (1872)
5. Oatley, K.: Integrative action of narrative. In: Stein, D.J., Young, J.E. (eds.) Cognitive Science and Clinical Disorders. Academic Press, San Diego (1992)
6. Kennedy-Moore, E., Watson, J.C.: Expressing Emotion. Myths, Realities, and Therapeutic Strategies. The Guildford Press (1999)
7. Scott, S.G., Bruce, R.A.: Decision-making style: the development and assessment of a new measure. Educational and Psychological Measurement 55(5), 818–831 (1995)
8. Kline, P.: Handbook of Psychological Testing. Routledge, London (2000)

9. Lekkas, Z., Tsianos, N., Germanakos, P., Mourlas, C., Samaras, G.: Implementing Affect Parameters in Personalized Web-Based Design. In: Jacko, J.A. (ed.) HCI International 2009, Part III. LNCS, vol. 5612, pp. 320–329. Springer, Heidelberg (2009)
10. Germanakos, P., et al.: Capturing Essential Intrinsic User Behaviour Values for the Design of Comprehensive Web-based Personalized Environments. Computers in Human Behavior, Special Issue on Integration of Human Factors in Networked Computing (2007)
11. Tsianos, N., Lekkas, Z., Germanakos, P., Mourlas, C., Samaras, G.: User-Centric Profiling on the Basis of Cognitive and Emotional Characteristics: An Empirical Study. In: Nejdl, W., Kay, J., Pu, P., Herder, E. (eds.) AH 2008. LNCS, vol. 5149, pp. 214–223. Springer, Heidelberg (2008)
12. Damasio, A.R.: Descartes' error: Emotion, reason, and the human brain. Putnam Publishing Group, New York (1994)

Innovation in Learning – The Use of Avatar
for Sign Language

Tania Lima[1], Mario Sandro Rocha[1], Thebano Almeida Santos[1], Angelo Benetti[1],
Evandro Soares[1], and Helvecio Siqueira de Oliveira[2]

[1] Centro de Tecnologia da Informação Renato Archer – Ministério da Ciência e Tecnologia e
Inovação – MCT
Rodovia D. Pedro I km 146,3 CEP 13069 901 Campinas – São Paulo
tania.lima@cti.gov.br
[2] SENAI Ítalo Bologna
Av. Goiás, 139 CEP: 13301-360 - Itú – São Paulo
helvécio@sp.senai.br

Abstract. This paper presents the steps followed in developing an avatar-interpreter of the Brazilian sign language for deaf (LIBRAS), applied to an electro technical glossary. The research was done in collaboration between The Surface Interaction and Displays Division (DSID) and The National Service for Industrial Apprenticeship (SENAI "Ítalo Bologna"), a reference center in the attendance of people having physical or mental incapability. This work makes use of advanced techniques of motion capture, treatment of images and virtualization, to produce an avatar that mimics a teacher-interpreter of the specific electro technical signs of LIBRAS during the lesson.

The technology used in this work is a VICON system with 8 cameras that emit and capture infrared light, and the open source tools Blender and Make-Human.

1   Introduction

Sign Languages for deaf are everywhere in the world, but none of their forms is universal, because they differ greatly among different regions, except for some more obvious gestures [1, 2].

The Brazilian Sign Languages were developed   from the combination of the native gestures and the French Sign Language (FSL), at the time of the creation of the Imperial Institute for Young Deaf, in 1857 [1]. This combination gave rise to two Sign Languages: Kaapor and LIBRAS (Brazilian Sign Language) [1]. Kaapor is still used by the tribe of Brazilian Indians located in the state of Maranhão, where there are a high number of deaf people; and LIBRAS is in general used by the deaf Brazilian community, having many dialects, depending on the region.

Nowadays, several technologies are available to making avatar for sign languages, and a considerable amount of work has already been done in this direction. In the pioneer work of Kamata, K. et al, a method was developed for translating written language into a sequence of sign words of the Simultaneous Japanese Sign Language

M. Kurosu (Ed.): Human-Computer Interaction, Part II, HCII 2013, LNCS 8005, pp. 428–433, 2013.

(SJSL) [4]. After that, other animation systems of sign languages were created, such as HST (Hand Sign Language), VSigns, ViSiCast, etc.

Schneider, A. R. A. et al. developed an animation system for LIBRAS consisting of a virtual human modeler, a gesture generator and an animator, relatively close to the real gesture and easily understandable [5]. László Havasi and Helga M. Szabó described a low-cost hand-motion capture and data-processing system used to enable semi-automatic construction of the sign database [6].

Amaral, W. M. et al. proposed a transcription system to provide contents in LIBRAS through virtual models. The sign language elements with its respective attribute were conveniently represented by classes using the Object Oriented Unified Modeling Language (UML). The signs were described through minimal and distinctive units, and stored in a database of XML files.

The present work is part of a more general project whose objective is to build a large sign language database to be used in assistive software - i.e., interactive real-time Portuguese to Brazilian sign language translators. The primary target of the project was to establish a consistent and flexible workflow for the animation of 3D humanoid avatars by optical motion data captured from the body of a LIBRAS interpreter.

In this specific work, we aimed to develop a glossary with words and symbols in LIBRAS, using a virtual interpreter (avatar) as the communication interface. The idea is to replace the teacher-interpreter of LIBRAS by this avatar in electrotechnical apprenticeships.

The LIBRAS signs were captured for about 100 words taken from the electrotechnical vocabulary, by using a VICON system of motion capture.

2   Methodology

The equipment we have been using effectively in this line research is a VICON system with 8 infrared cameras, which are able to capture images in a resolution of 16 Megapixels, at 120 frames per second. The software used to making the avatar is the VICON software package, and the open source tools Blender and MakeHuman.

The steps followed in developing the avatar-interpreter of LIBRAS is illustrated in the workflow shown in Fig. 1.

The first step of this work was to identify the needs of the deaf students who participate in the vocational courses of the SENAI School. Thus, it was compiled into a book the representation and definition of the objects and tools currently used in the electro technical courses. The definitions are given both in Portuguese and in the LIBRAS grammatical structure, and the representations are given through illustrative photos and SignWriting. Photos of the interpreter performing the object representation in LIBRAS are also showed.

The development phase has basically three parts: the creation of a database with basic models of the avatar using the Makehuman software, optical data capture using the VICON system, and animation of the avatar using the Blender software.

Makehuman has the necessary features to set up and customize the character (3D avatar). The avatar is exported as a MHX rig, allowing fine control over the skeleton posing and facial expressions.

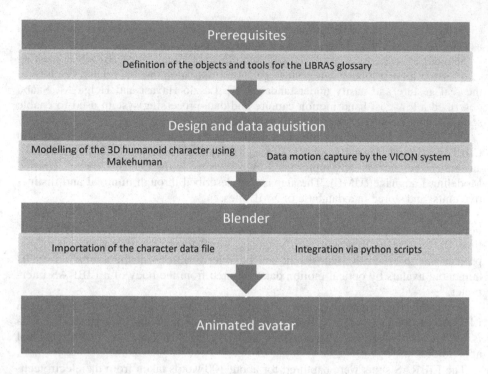

Fig. 1. Workflow for the development of the avatar-interpreter of LIBRAS

Before starting the data acquisition by the VICON system, we had to do some experiments to find the best configuration in number and positioning of the markers over the interpreter's body. After several tests, we set a number of 41 markers disposed over the upper body of the interpreter at strategic locations, as shown in Fig. 2. The model used in the motion capture was calibrated for each individual interpreter.

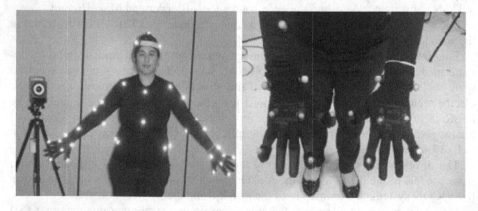

Fig. 2. Living interpreter with the markers for the motion capture by the VICON system

Every single electro technical term contained in the glossary was represented in LIBRAS by a professional interpreter, whose movements were captured in real time by an arrangement of 8 infrared cameras of the VICON system.

The cameras emit infrared light that is reflected by the markers attached to the interpreter's body at strategic locations on the superior members, trunk, face and head. The light is captured back by the cameras, and the movements can be viewed in real time (see Fig. 3), which helps correcting eventual fails in the capture, such as calibration errors of the cameras or bad adherence of the markers. In the beginning, this work is relatively complex, and must be followed by a specialist in the subject and by collaborators.

After the data is recorded, all signs are reconstructed in a virtual 3D space. The markers are labeled, and all trajectory gaps are filled by the program using interpolation methods. Finale, the captured LIBRAS sign is exported to c3d files.

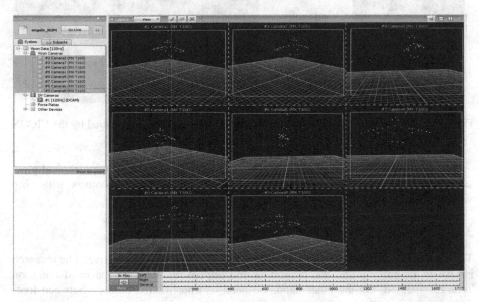

Fig. 3. Optical data, captured by the VICON system, from the body of the living interpreter

The selected model can be opened by Blender, an open source and cross platform suite of tools for 3D creation. The LIBRAS sign movements captured by the VICON system, and saved as .c3d files, are then imported by Blender.

In Blender, c3d and MHX files are imported and combined with a complex constraint setup that takes advantage of inverse kinematic to drive spine and arms. With this model, it is possible independently to manage data to control a specific hand and finger (thumb, index and pinky). Middle and ring fingers are constrained to be driven by the index or pinky finger, depending on the specific sign.

Head is driven by four vertices of a plane hooked to the head markers. Facial expressions are keyframed animations of shapekeys, but they are not present in the technical signs.

Post production is required in around 85% of the processed signs, for trajectory corrections and prevention against unnatural or impossible body movements. Once the movement is ready, the constraint set is baked to quaternions, generating actions ready to be concatenated in video or interactive (game engines) rendering.

Expressed concisely, the bones of the model are constrained by Blender to the moving markers, shown as dots on some of the Blender panels. And this is the main mechanism used to animate the model and make the avatar shown in Fig 4. This procedure has many steps and takes a considerable amount of time, and had been done by using only the mouse and keyboard. However, this problem was recently solved by putting almost all the commands used in the procedure in a python script that can be run from the Blender IDE.

Fig. 4. Final rendering of the 3D avatar animated by the motion data captured by the VICON system

This methodology developed in CTI was successfully applied to the technical glossary of LIBRAS, and will be fundamental for grater and ambitious projects, with a big volume of motion captures.

3   Conclusions

The techniques and methodology used in this work are quite innovative. The research is still in its early stage, but presents some improvements over the most common 'retarget' method. On the other hand, we need to improve the balance between freedom degree limitations and accuracy of motion capture data.

The results of this specific work show that our methodology is suitable for similar application in areas such as Engineering or Administration, where the availability of an avatar-interpreter of sign languages is helpful.

4   Next Steps

The VICON application software allows a straightforward animation of the models available in its environment. But its interface doesn't provide any mechanism for exporting these models (along with their bones constrained to the motion data) to third-party applications. Thus, we are now studying the viability of changing the source code of the script generated by the VICON application before exporting it to Blender, in order to improve the animation of the model made with MakeHuman.

This will be our first approach to refine the face and fingers movements of the avatar. The investment in complementary equipments that allow more precise capture of these types of movements is also possible.

On the other side, a database oriented on cheremes is an essential paradigm to eliminate data redundancy - a crucial prerequisite for the improvement of this project. In other words, the main elements in this database will be the position, orientation, configuration and trajectories of the hands, which will eliminate the need of recording the isolated words of the sign language.

One of the objectives of this collaborative work is to provide access to a comprehensive distribution. This will be accomplished by means of public licenses (ex: GPL, Creative Commons, etc), multiplatform solutions, and generalization of our LIBRAS glossary to other sign languages.

Another step in this research is to increase the number of partnerships with public teaching and research institutions, for instance, Federal University of Alagoas < http://www.ufal.edu.br/> - project FALIBRAS, and University of São Paulo <WWW.usp.br> - project POLIBRAS. Both institutions have complementary contributions to make to the development of the project.

Furthermore, our team is taking steps to increase the number of participants in the forum of debates and to create a nucleus of study on the subject. We hope that this initiative attracts the widest possible participation from among groups of different areas of knowledge, like Linguistic, Computer Science, Graphic Design, Sociology, Pedagogy and Physical Education.

References

1. Benarab, L., Oliveira, C.S.: História da Língua Brasileira dos Sinais e da Língua dos Sinais Fracesa e da influência do segundo Congresso Internacional de Milão na Educação dos surdos. In: Simpósio Internacional de Iniciação Científica (SUCUSP) – USP, 15, São Paulo (2007), Disponível em
   http://www.usp.br/siicusp/Resumos/15Siicusp/2185.pdf
2. Santos Jr., E.B., Oliveira, H.C., Oliveira, C.S.: Acessibilidade na TV Digital Aberta no Brasil para apoio a surdos
3. Falletto, A., Prinetto, P., Tiotto, G.: An Avatar-Based Italian Sign Language Visualization System. In: Weerasinghe, D. (ed.) eHealth 2008. LNICST, vol. 1, pp. 154–160. Springer, Heidelberg (2009)
4. Kamata, K., et al.: An approach to Japanese-sign language translation system. In: Proceedings of the Systems, Man and Cybernetics, vol. 3, pp. 1089–1090. s.n., S.l. (1989)
5. Schneider, A.R.A.: Virtual Human Animation Applied in Brazilian Sign Language. Master's thesis – Federal University of Rio Grande do Sul, Porto Alegre (2008)
6. Havasi, L., Szabó, H.M.: A Motion Capture System for Sign Language Synthesis: Overview and Related Issues. In: Bebis, G., Boyle, R., Koracin, D., Parvin, B. (eds.) ISVC 2005. LNCS, vol. 3804, pp. 636–641. Springer, Heidelberg (2005)
7. Amaral, W.M.: Sistema de transcrição da língua brasileira de sinais, voltado à produção de conteúdo sinalizado por avatares 3D. Doctor's thesis – Universidade Estadual de Campinas (UNICAMP). s.n., Campinas (2012)

A Teacher Model to Speed Up the Process of Building Courses

Carla Limongelli, Matteo Lombardi, Alessandro Marani, and Filippo Sciarrone

"Roma Tre" University,
Department of Computer Science and Automation,
AI-Lab,
Via della Vasca Navale, 79 - 00146 Rome, Italy
{limongel,sciarro,mat.lombardi,ale.marani}@dia.uniroma3.it

Abstract. Building a new course is a complex task for teachers: the entire process requires different steps, starting with the concept map building and ending with the delivery of the learning objects to students through a learning management system. Teachers have to spend a lot of time to build or to retrieve the right learning material from local databases or from specialized repositories on the web. Consequently, having a system supporting this phase is a very important challenge, considering that each teacher expresses her own pedagogy as well. Here we propose a novel Teacher Model that helps teachers to build new courses effectively. The model is based both on a didactic semantic network containing concepts and learning material and on Teaching Styles as proposed in the literature by Grasha. This framework gives teachers the possibility to share their teaching experience as well. A first experimentation of the system gives positive results.

1 Motivations and Goals

Quality of teaching is undoubtedly one of the most important ingredients for student learning and consequently for a course of success independently from the delivery platform. The process of preparing a new course is a very complex process where the teacher is involved in several tasks such as: i)building the concept map; ii)retrieving learning material from some didactic repositories or building a new one; iii) building a didactic storyboard; iv)delivering the course on a suitable didactic environment [10,9,5,14]. Our research addresses the course building process, in order to give teachers an instrument to speed up the overall process, decreasing their working load and increasing the quality of their didactic material. We propose a personalized approach to the course building process, where a model of the teacher, is based both on the Teaching Experience (TE) and on Teaching Styles (TS). The TS is based on the Grasha TS model [6], composed of five different dimensions while the TE is a dynamic framework which changes with the teacher's didactic choices, i.e., with her teaching experience and teaching styles. Such a semantic network is a directed graph composed by those concepts and by those learning materials used by teachers of a community to

M. Kurosu (Ed.): Human-Computer Interaction, Part II, HCII 2013, LNCS 8005, pp. 434–443, 2013.
© Springer-Verlag Berlin Heidelberg 2013

build courses. To each node of the network are linked all those learning materials used by the teacher to build a didactic concerning that particular concept. Furthermore, each link of the network has an associated weight which changes with time according to a dynamic temporal low based on the ant theory [4]. Starting from this framework, in this paper we address the following research question: can our teacher model help teachers to retrieve didactic material in order to build new courses faster and better? To test this research questions we built a framework, i.e., a 3-tier web application and by means of a sample of teachers we experimented their TM. In the literature there is few research on teacher's modeling, as the works of Grasha [6] and Felder and Silvermann [3] while the student modeling aspect has been more widely addressed (see for example [7,11,8]. We believe that a teacher centered research should be addressed as well, in order to give teachers a personalized support taking into account their own pedagogy, styles of teaching, and teaching experience. Our model takes into account all these components in a dynamic way. The paper is structured as follows. In Section 2 the proposed teacher model is shown. In Section 3 we propose the learning material retrieval mechanism. In Section 4 is shown the prototype system embedding the dynamic framework while in Section 5 the first experimentation of the model is performed. Finally in Section 6 conclusions are drawn.

2   The Teacher Model

To represent a teacher it is necessary to know at least both her way of teaching and her teaching experience. The teacher's teaching style and the information about concepts and materials chosen for the different courses taught, contribute to describe the Teacher Model. It has an *educational* component given by Teaching Styles, and an *ontological* one, given by all her own courses during her teaching activity: Teaching Experience (TE). In particular, the educational component builds a teacher profile regardless of the specific course taught. This component will be helpful to identify teachers who have similar teaching styles. The ontological component is the teaching experience, where courses are represented by ontologies. Summarizing, we have: $TM =$<Teaching Style, Teaching Experience>.

2.1   The Teaching Styles

As we said in the previous Section, Teaching Styles are devoted to detect pedagogical attitudes of the teacher. In our work we used the model of teaching styles proposed by Grasha [6], where they are represented by the following five categories: *Expert, Formal Authority, Personal Model, Facilitator and Delegator*. Each style is represented by a real number in the range $TS = [1.0, 7.0]$ and teachers can detect their own teaching styles at the Grasha-Riechmann Teaching Style Survey web site[1].

---

[1] http://longleaf.net/teachingstyle.html

2.2   Teaching Experience

Teaching Experience representation is more complex to manage being composed by information coming from all courses built by the teacher. A course is represented by an ontology, i.e., a direct graph, based on prerequisite relationships between nodes, i.e., the concepts used by a teacher in all her courses. Every concept is linked to all the didactic material retrieved and used to explain that concept. The union graph of all the ontologies related to a teacher represents her teaching experience and we call it Didactic Semantic Network (DSN).The DSN contains all the courses taught by the teacher over her teaching life.

Definition 1. *We define a course by the following triple:* $C_j = <L_j, T_j, O_j>$

where L_j represents the general level of the course (elementary, middle school, university level...), T_j indicates how many times the teacher thought that course and O_j is the ontology related to that course.

Definition 2. *A concept* c_k *is defined as:*

$$c_k = <name, L_k, \{RC_q\}, \{<LM_i, n_{k_i}, e_k>\}>$$

where *name* is the name associated to that concept, L_k is the level associated to that concept, RC_q is a prerequisite concept and LM are possible learning materials associated to that concept with some information about the use of that material from the rest of the community (n) and the teacher herself (e). The set of all concepts contained in teacher's courses constitutes the DSN of the Teacher Model.

Definition 3. *Given a teacher we define her* DSN *as follows:*

$$DSN = \bigcup_{j=1}^{n} O_j$$

where n is the number of courses taught by that teacher and O_j their ontologies. At the beginning a teacher has associated only her Teaching Styles, while her teaching experience is empty.

2.3   The Connection Concept – Learning Material

Each concept c in the DSN is associated to a list of Learning Materials and each association is labeled with a weight $\rho_{k,i}$ that depends on $n_{k,i}$, representing the *social* aspect, and e_k and the *personal* aspect of the teacher. The parameter $n_{k,i}$ represents how many times the i-th material has been chosen for the concept k-th by all the teachers belonging to the community, so tracing the popularity of this link. This component excludes, if used alone, the personal choices of the teacher: the parameter e_k represents the experience of the teacher in teaching the concept k-th. Therefore, is fair to give a higher weight to the link as the teacher acquires experience in teaching the concept k-th.

Definition 4. *We define the weight ρ as:*

$$\rho_{k,i} = n_{k,i}\lambda + e_k(1 - \lambda) \quad \text{with } \lambda \in [0,1] \tag{1}$$

The contribution of the individual components is balanced by the value assigned to the constant λ. A high value for λ shifts the weight on social aspect, on the contrary teacher experience is magnified. n and e are updated as follows:

$$n_{k,i}^{new} = \begin{cases} n_{k,i} + 1 & \text{if someone else has chosen that } LM_i \\ n_{k,i} & \text{else} \end{cases} \tag{2}$$

$$e_{k,i}^{new} = \begin{cases} e_{k,i} + 1 & \text{if the teacher has chosen that } LM_i \\ e_{k,i} & \text{else} \end{cases} \tag{3}$$

Another key feature is the dynamic computation of weights. What we want to look for is a strengthening of connections when the teacher selects a given LM, and a consequential weakening of all other connections between the concept and the LMs that are not chosen.

Weight Updating. In order to model the behavior of the connections with time, we observe that in the literature there are mainly two approaches to such problems of learning: the Logistic function that is usually employed for weights updating in Artificial Neural Networks [12,13], and the ANT System approach by pheromone updating [4]. Logistic function is defined in $[0, 1]$; in our case, since ρ is always a positive number, the interesting co-domain is restricted to $[0.5, 1]$. We might overcome this problem by letting ρ to assume also negative values, but it would raise a semantic problem, in fact ρ would lead to give too high advantage to the new materials associated. Indeed, the first choice of a material for a certain concept, $\rho_{k,i}$ would be equal to 1 since both $n_{k,i}$ and e_k are equal to 1, in fact the convex combination of two numbers equal to 1, (regardless of the value of λ) will always be equal to 1. Therefore it would happen that the logistic function would assign as first choice $\rho = 0.5$. To address this problem we can shift the x-axis by a positive constant, however, since such a function domain interval is $(-\infty, +\infty)$ is not easy to understand how to translate the logistic function without making it too expensive to climb to 1 and maintaining the fair semantic meaning. A better tailored approach for our purpose is the ANT System approach by pheromones updating [4] based both on evaporation rate and on the choice made by ants (teacher) to follow (choose) or not a given path (link between concept and LM). This function is inversely proportional to the length of the path followed by ants, and directly proportional to the number of ants that have chosen that path, since they leave a fixed amount of pheromones. In our case the system proposes to the teacher the choice of the LM with highest ρ and if the teacher chooses that material the weight becomes stronger, on the other way the weight decreases, basing on the following function:

$$\rho_{k,i}(t + 1) = (1 - \tau)\rho_{k,i}(t) + \Delta\rho_{k,i}(t) \tag{4}$$

where τ is the evaporation rate, and $\Delta\rho_{ij}(t)$ is defined as

$$\Delta\rho_{k,i}(t) = \begin{cases} n_{k,i}\lambda + e_k(1-\lambda) & \text{if } LM_i \text{ is chosen to explain } C_k \\ 0 & \text{else} \end{cases} \qquad (5)$$

where $n_{k,i}\lambda + e_k(1-\lambda)$ is the weight $\rho_{k,i}$ (see Eq.1).

3   Learning Material Retrieval

We implemented two algorithms for LM retrieving. First a *dummy search*, i.e., a simply search of all the learning materials associated with any concept that has the same name as the concept the teacher is looking for, without taking into account the teaching context, the ontology, the cluster membership etc. .... Secondly an *ontological search* algorithm was implemented, that selects the ontologies basing on a *distance relationship* among ontologies by which the LM associated to the closest ontology is suggested to the teacher. The algorithm for distance evaluation is briefly described from a qualitative point of view. It is based on the idea presented in [2] that defined an algorithm for stating concepts similarity w.r.t. the ontology that contains them. For our purpose we consider three kind of distances:

- The Hamming distance between the nodes common to both ontologies d_h
- The incidence of common nodes on the nodes common to both ontologies d_N
- The ratio of excess nodes (Nodes Exceeding Ratio, NER), defined as the ratio between the cardinality of ontology largest and the cardinality of the of common nodes (CN).

The distance d will be defined as follows:

$$d = d_h + d_N + NER$$

For this similarity measure d, symmetry and reflexive properties hold, but it is not a metric since triangle inequality does not hold. This is due to the fact that for graphs sometimes triangle inequality is too restrictive or incompatible with the considered problem domain [1].

4   The Prototype System

In this Section we briefly describe the framework implemented to experiment the LM selection by teachers whose model has been just proposed. The system is still a working progress, but the main functionality are already provided. In fact the system can:

- create a community of teachers;
- classify teachers into groups according to their Teaching Styles;
- record all actions taken by the teachers in the development of the courses;
- save the associations of Learning Material with the concepts taught in the courses;

– suggest teachers learning materials deemed most relevant for each concept;
– record selected LM, updating the SDN of the teacher who made the selection.

5   TM Evaluation

In this Section we propose a first evaluation of the TM as explained in Section 2. We evaluated the model and its added value to the retrieval of learning material from the local database. To this aim we used our prototype available on the web to allow remote teachers to participate to the experiment.

5.1   The Research Question

As stated in Section 1, the research question to test is if the proposed TM can help teachers in the course building process. In the first evaluation the teacher, after having used the system was asked to assess the ranking of didactic material as proposed by the system while in the second evaluation the teacher was asked to assess her model. According to the proposed TM, we evaluated the TE component of the model. In this first evaluation we set the parameter λ to 0.5 in order to balance in the same way the two TM components. The retrieval method was based on an ontology distance metric:first the nearest ontology was found in the didactic semantic network, and second the didactic material has been proposed.

5.2   The Evaluation Process

The experimental evaluation was divided into the following steps:

1. *The sample.* It was composed by 20 teachers, 10 from University and 10 from technical high school, randomly selected.
2. *Teaching Styles detection.* Here the teachers were required to take a self-evaluating method questionnaire from the internet at the Grasha-Riechmann Teaching Style Survey web site[2]. The Grasha-Reichmann Teaching Style Inventory is a web-based assessment, that asks for a Likert-type response to 40 of questions designed to objectively categorize teaching styles, according to the Grasha TS model. A teacher is asked to respond to statements such as *I set high standards for students in this class.* The teacher responds within a five-point range from *strongly disagree* to *strongly agree*. Teaching styles are then calculated via a numeric score and the results are presented in a table that presents whether the respondent is low, moderate or high, based on the numeric outcome, in a particular style. As output one has five real numbers representing her teaching styles. These numbers were used by the system to insert each teacher into the Grasha clusters to set the TS component. In Fig. 1 the TS distribution of the sample is shown.

---

[2] http://longleaf.net/teachingstyle.html

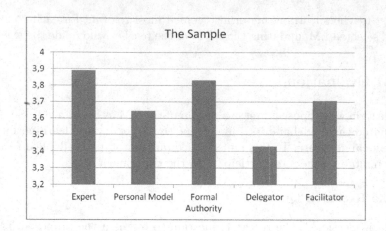

Fig. 1. The distribution of the Grasha Teaching Styles of the sample

3. *Local Repository Analysis.* Teachers were invited to analyze the learning material already stored in the local repository, with the possibility of adding new didactic objects.

4. *Concept map building.* In this phase teachers were required to build a new concept map to start a new course on java programming. In Fig. 2 we show a screen shot of the concept map setting: teachers could build the ontology starting from the concepts already stored in the local data base. The system allowed for concept prerequisite setting. In this way a didactic semantic network for each teacher was built.

5. *Learning material retrieval.* In this step teachers were asked to retrieve didactic material from the local repository. The system, in order to better evaluate the different components of the TM, proposed two modalities of retrieval: i)dummy retrieval,i.e., the learning material was retrieved and proposed without taking into account the TM; ii)TE retrieval: the learning materials are proposed to the teacher starting from the concepts shared among different ontologies, as explained in Section 2, i.e., by means of an ontology distance metric. In Tab. 1 an example of retrieval is shown. The user searched for some learning material from the local repository, to link to the *boolean* concept. The system retrieved three materials: boolean1, boolean2 and boolean3 and the user was required to assess the ranking of the retrieved learning material through a 7-points Likert scale(not at all, strongly disagree, disagree, neutral, agree, strongly agree, very strongly agree). Next the teacher was asked to select the learning material to link to the boolean concept. This procedure to be performed for each concept of the course to build.

6. *Model assessment.* Finally, once having completed the connections learning material-concept, teachers were required to assess their own model through a 7-points likert scale. In particular teachers assessed the ranking of the proposed material for each concept of their course to build.

Table 1. An example of learning material retrieval and ranking: the boolean concept

Material ID	Weight
boolean1	0.65
boolean2	0.48
boolean3	0.17

5.3 Experimental Results

The results are shown in Fig. 2 and Fig. 3. In Fig. 2 the evaluations on the retrieved material, ranked by the system according to the teacher model is shown. As we can see from Fig. 2, the dummy retrieval system, histograms with full color, have their distribution shifted towards low levels of the likert scale with respect to the ontological retrieval, represented by dashed histograms. Most users have appreciated the contribution of the user model. In Fig. 3 we show the last assessment, i.e., the teacher model assessment. Here also the 70% of users have appreciated their model, expressed as the way by means the system proposes a ranking of didactic material.

5.4 Research Conclusions

With respect to our research question, we can say that the first experimental results are encouraging. Certainly we did not perform a hypothesis test to inference from our sample to the entire universe of teachers, but this task is planned for the next future. Moreover here we tested one component only of the TM, i.e., the TE component.

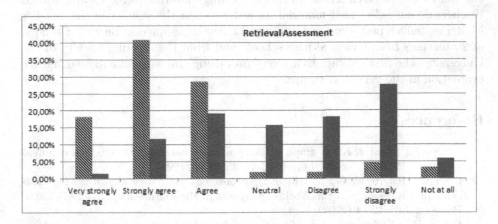

Fig. 2. Experimental results for the retrieval assessment: dummy retrieval (full color) Vs. ontology-based retrieval (dashed color)

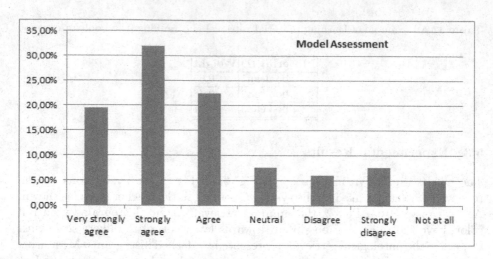

Fig. 3. Experimental results for the TM assessment

6   Conclusions

In this paper we presented a novel model of teacher in order to speed up the process of course building. The TM is composed by two mail components: the Teaching Styles, according to the Grasha model and the Teaching Experience, based on a didactic semantic network, i.e., a semantic network adapted to didactic goals. Teaching Styles are first detected by a questionnaire in the Grasha-Riechmann web site. The Teaching Experience is built in a dynamic way as teachers add learning materials to concepts. The connections concept-learning material is weighted during time by means of a ant-like pheromone mechanism: the connection between a concept and a learning material decreases with time if teachers do not select that material. In order to test the validity of the Teacher Model we built a prototype and conducted a first experimentation with a sample of 20 teachers from technical high schools and from Engineering Faculty of our University. The first indications are very promising and we plan a more extensive evaluation in the very next future.

References

1. Bunke, H., Shearer, K.: A graph distance metric based on the maximal common subgraph. Pattern Recogn. Lett. 19(3-4), 255–259 (1998)
2. Culmone, R., Rossi, G., Merelli, E.: An ontology similarity algorithm for bioagent. In: Proceedings of the Workshop Agents in Bioinformatics (NETTAB 2002), Bologna, July 12-14 (2002)
3. Felder, R.M., Silverman, L.K.: Learning and teaching styles in engineering education. Engineering Education 78(7), 674 (1988)
4. Dorigo, M., Di Caro, G., Gambardella, L.M.: Ant algorithms for discrete optimization. MIT Press Journals 5(2), 137–172 (1999)

5. Gasparetti, F., Micarelli, A., Sciarrone, F.: A web-based training system for business letter writing. Knowledge-Based Systems 22(4), 287–291 (2009)
6. Grasha, A.: Teaching with Style: A Practical Guide to Enhancing Learning by Understanding Teaching and Learning Styles. Alliance (1996)
7. Limongelli, C., Miola, A., Sciarrone, F., Temperini, M.: Supporting teachers to retrieve and select learning objects for personalized courses in the moodle-ls environment. In: Proceedings of the 12th IEEE International Conference on Advanced Learning Technologies, ICALT 2012, pp. 518–520 (2012)
8. Limongelli, C., Mosiello, G., Panzieri, S., Sciarrone, F.: Virtual industrial training: Joining innovative interfaces with plant modeling. In: International Conference on Information Technology Based Higher Education and Training, ITHET 2012 (2012)
9. Limongelli, C., Sciarrone, F., Starace, P., Temperini, M.: An ontology-driven olap system to help teachers in the analysis of web learning object repositories. Information Systems Management 27(3), 198–206 (2010)
10. Limongelli, C., Sciarrone, F., Temperini, M., Vaste, G.: The lecomps5 framework for personalized web-based learning: A teacher's satisfaction perspective. Computers in Human Behavior 27(4), 1310–1320 (2011)
11. Limongelli, C., Sciarrone, F., Temperini, M., Vaste, G.: Adaptive learning with the ls-plan system: A field evaluation. IEEE Transactions on Learning Technologies 2(3), 203–215 (2009)
12. Mitchell, T.: Machine Learning. McGraw-Hill, New York (1997)
13. Sciarrone, F.: An extension of the q diversity metric from single-label to multi-label and multi-ranking multiple classifier systems for pattern classification. In: Proceedings of the International Conference on Machine Learning and Cybernetics, ICML 2012, vol. 1, pp. 6–10 (2012)
14. Sterbini, A., Temperini, M.: Dealing with open-answer questions in a peer-assessment environment. In: Popescu, E., Li, Q., Klamma, R., Leung, H., Specht, M. (eds.) ICWL 2012. LNCS, vol. 7558, pp. 240–248. Springer, Heidelberg (2012)

Development of Push-Based English Words Learning System by Using E-Mail Service

Shimpei Matsumoto[1], Masanori Akiyoshi[1], and Tomoko Kashima[2]

[1] Faculty of Applied Information Science, Hiroshima Institute of Technology,
2-1-1 Miyake, Saeki-ku, Hiroshima 731-5193, Japan
[2] Faculty of Engineering, Kinki University,
1 Takaya Umenobe, Higashi-Hiroshima City, Hiroshima, 739-2116, Japan

Abstract. At present, common e-Learning systems have been designed for positive learners whose learning habits are already established to some degree. To assist students other than the positive learners, most of who has more difficulty in learning with the usual e-Learning systems, this paper focuses on a new type of e-Learning system called "push-based e-Learning". The push-based e-Learning is for learners who cannot establish study habits or take an active part in learning, and be an essential tool for supporting self-study continuity. This study realizes push service by e-mail technology of cell-phone. The system, used in conjunction with an interactive e-mail service through cell-phones, allows users to automatically receive up to some exercise e-mails a day. For our system, this paper implemented COCET 3300, a corpus of English words, and made a trial operation of our system with several university students for training English vocabulary. This paper firstly shows the detail of system configuration, and then evaluates our implementation of push-based e-Learning with the result of the trial operation. From the trial operation, the effectiveness of our system was shown by questionnaire while the result was on the students' subjective viewpoint.

1 Introduction

As e-Learning has been an extremely broad term, but most of e-Learning represents educational environment on the Web which are based on Content Management Systems (CMS). CMS mainly used for the purpose of educational support have been generally called as Learning Management Systems (LMS). In Japan, LMS has been already accepted as being indispensable in educational institutions around universities. With LMS, anytime lecture materials are available for students, and similarly advisers can easily and freely operate LMS as administrator by using open source software such as Moodle.

Of all the e-Learning operations, mobile learning which works via a personal digital assistant and most of which cooperates with web-based services is one of the most appealing educational topics at the moment. Today numerous examples introducing into real lectures have been reported [1]-[3]. If we make use of various functions in mobile communication tools like cell-phones and PDAs including

M. Kurosu (Ed.): Human-Computer Interaction, Part II, HCII 2013, LNCS 8005, pp. 444–453, 2013.
© Springer-Verlag Berlin Heidelberg 2013

smart phones, educational services will lead to a more efficient way of learning. Actually, under such conditions as this, the effectiveness of learning through the use of mobile devices has begun to be reported in many academic educational journals. To carry out a mobile blended learning, Internet accessible mobile devices are needed to be popular, and at the same time, students have to be used to dealing with Internet via mobile devices. According to a survey performed by Ministry of Internal Affairs and Communications, 2011, the overall rate of Internet access from mobile devices is quite high [4]. Besides, various surveys such as Nikkei BP consulting, NTT NaviSpace, and Google report similar result where penetration rate of smart phone is approximately 20% for the population of Japan, and also the penetration rate including future phone is approximately 90%. So introducing mobile devices for Internet blended learning is assumed to be no problem but effective.

Considering the above mentioned high diffusion rate of Internet accessible mobile devices, as the simplest Internet access method, the authors consider that e-mail based educational support is useful because the e-mail software is the most basic and most-used feature, but also low communication charge. Moreover e-mail software on mobile devices can realize push service, and this feature is unique technical advantage. Based on the background, the authors have developed a push-based e-Learning system with mobile e-mail technology [5,6]. With the system, students are not required to continually access the learning contents for themselves, different from other e-Learning systems. In addition, by accessing the system's website, a user can grasp his/her own learning conditions, for example how much he/she achieved of the goal. Since every answer a user send is stored in database, at any moment a user can utilize accumulated answer-data and can contribute to his/her own markings and understandings of the levels of achievements. Additionally, at the same time, the history data will help adviser understand each user's learning condition and understanding degree, and this will also contribute to design a lecture plan.

This paper firstly shows the concept of push-based e-Learning comparing with common LMS based e-Learning in Section 2, and especially this paper explains who is intended by the push-based e-Learning. Section 3 shows how this paper implements push-based learning service, and the detail of system structure. Section 4 shows the condition of trial operation; concretely speaking, this paper develops a push-based English words learning environment by implementing COCET 3300, a corpus of English words for students of science and technology in higher education. Learning history information was obtained through a test operation for 120 days, and as the result, the effectiveness was confirmed subjectively. Based on the result of trial operation, this paper discusses the possibility of our system, and also the future plan in Section 5.

2   Educational Support with Information Technology

Generally Moodle is assumed to be as a representative of LMS based e-Learning. With Moodle, a lecturer can easily publish learning materials, and can practice an education on social constructionist pedagogy [7] with Moodle's various functions called Wiki, chat, and forum. The effectiveness of LMS blended education has been actively reported by many educational journals.

In the informatization of education, supporting self-study is as important subject as improving real lectures. Generally speaking, a student actively using LMS based e-Learning is assumed to be one whose learning habits are already established to some degree, and who relies less on assistance than the student who has more difficulty in learning. As Sakai divided all human resources into 3 categories [9], and with Sakai's words, learners whose learning habits are already established were categorized as "Positive Learners", the learners who has more difficulty in learning were categorized as "Negative Learners", and the learners who hate to change their own habit were categorized as "Resisters to Learning". This paper understands that learners who can positively use common LMS based e-Learning are positive learners, on the other hand, learners who poorly use it are negative learnersDBy rights, those who should be supported are the students who cannot establish study habits or take an active part in learning, just they are negative learners. Because negative learners would like to avoid learning itself until they have to, so to support them, a new e-Learning system that has more functions than common LMS is needed.

This paper names usual LMS based e-Learning "pull based e-learning" because users of LMS should access learning contents from them, on the contrary, e-Learning which provides learning contents from the system is named as "push based e-Learning". Also this paper considers that the push based e-Learning may be effective for negative learners, which the conclusion was reached from the experience of the authors who have been teaching university students of science and technology. The authors expect that if a negative learner improves his/her scholastic ability, he/she has a better chance of a good result, and if a negative learner has an experience making a good result, he/she will be positive for learning. The authors also think that in the beginning, a lecturer should force students to provide learning opportunity as much as possible until they gain basic skills. To make a negative learner to a positive learner, the function of push-based e-Learning, actively-providing learning materials from service to users is assumed to be effective.

3   Details of the Proposed System

The proposed system automatically creates exercise mails, and each student can continually receive the questions based on his/her system configurations such as the delivery time and the number of questions. This system follows three procedures: (1) One or more questions are continuously delivered by an e-mail to a user automatically. (2) A user adds his/her answer to a received e-mail. (3) By replying the e-mail to the system, a user can obtain scoring result immediately.

All questions are given in the form of multiple-choice. After receiving an exercise e-mail, a student has to select the function "reply with received text as citation" on e-mail software and replies the e-mail with his/her best option at

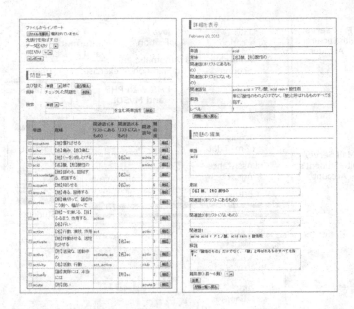

Fig. 1. An example of user interface of the developed system on the Web. This figure shows exercise management function. The left side of this figure shows the list of a part of words stored, and the right side shows edit function. All English words of COCET 3300 are managed.

designated section. After replying to the e-mail, the student's scoring result is instantaneously available. What's more, a user can grasp his/her own level of achievement, collective ranking, and weak points by accessing and checking the website of this system. The data of all users' history and answers is stored in a database. This communal information then contributes to the understanding of class trends and individual learning levels.

The developed system consists of two principal functions: LMS service and e-mail exchange service. The service of LMS works LAMP environment, which is constructed by Linux kernel 2.6.38, Apache 2.2.22, PHP 5.3.5, MySQL 5.1.54, and CakePHP 2.2.5 for user interface. With the service of LMS, various functions are available via Web browser. The types of service are different between learners and lecturers. On the learner side, there are following services: score inquiry, learning history inquiry, and some user settings such as exercise delivery time, the number of questions, and user information. On the lecturer side, there are following services: user management, exercise management, history management of e-mail exchange, dialogue function with a user, and analysis function of user's learning history data. Various kinds of data, such as the number of delivery of each English word and its accuracy rate, user's reply rate, user's accuracy rate, and user's experience point, are stored in database uniquely developed by this study, and they are always available.

This paper uses COCET 3300 as database of exercises. COCET3300 is an educational material to support English words for students of science and technology

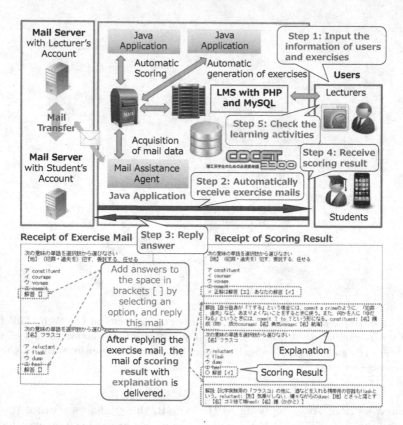

Fig. 2. This figure shows the utilization procedure of the developed system. At first a system administrator input some types of information. After inputting some data, a user can receive exercise e-mails automatically. By replying an e-mail with user's answer, scoring is also automatically operated. The data of learning condition is managed by database. Examples of an e-mail with questions and an e-mail of scoring result are shown at the bottom of this figure.

in higher education, and it has achieved satisfactory results at some educational institutions mainly national college of technology. As each English word in the corpus has Japanese meaning, related term, related phrase, and explanation, the proposed system uses these attributes to create each exercise e-mail. After replying an exercise e-mail, a scoring result of the e-mail is automatically delivered. Each word is divided into 7 levels depending on its difficulty. An example of exercise management screen is shown in Fig. 1.

This paper developed 3 server applications which work on java 1.6.31, and the one server application of them provides e-mail exchange (sending and receiving) we call as Mail Assistance Agent. An e-mail with questions is routinely delivered on a time that is set by a student registered to the developed system. The server application monitors e-mail exchange at 10 seconds interval by using "ScheduledExecutorService" in "concurrent" package. When it is time to deliver an exercise e-mail, the other server application to generate exercise statement is called. All questions are given in the form of multiple-choice: select the best English/Japanese word of same meaning as the Japanese/English word from the following options to each question, and describe the Japanese letter "a", "i", "u", or "e" to the place in brackets at e-mail text area. The words used by each question are randomly chosen from the database of COCET 3300. A question is generated by selecting one correct word and three wrong words. The three wrong words are randomly given, but the developed system selects these words similar with the correct word in some characteristics such as parts and initial letter with relatively high rate. Since the combination of words and these sequences varies every time and from individual to individual, the possibility to generate or to deliver same question for many learners is extremely low. Two questioning methods are randomly decided; the one is a question to answer proper Japanese meaning from English words, and the other is to answer proper English meaning from Japanese words. By the operations above mentioned, a question text is generated, and it is added to an e-mail text, and at the same time, a unique hash value is also added to the e-mail subject. The e-mail is set to waiting state to be transmitted, and is added to the sending table in database. The server application of e-mail exchange obtains e-mails of waiting state, and then they are sent to a SMTP server, and at the same time, their state is changed to transmission completion. After a user received the e-mail, the user replies the e-mail with his/her answer at designated point. All users should reply an e-mail with hash value at the subject, i.e., if the subject is "12126221801", then the subject should be "Re: 12126221801" or a similar form. After a POP server receives an e-mail from a user, the server application of e-mail exchange obtains the e-mail from the POP server, and it is added to the receiving table in database by setting waiting state to be scored. The other server application of automatic scoring which is working as other thread obtains all e-mails with waiting state to be scored, and they are scored. At the same time with scoring, some statistic information is updated. A scored e-mail is set to waiting state to be transmitted, and then it is added to the sending table. By the above processes, a user can receive scoring result with explanation immediately. Each word in COCET3300 is given the value of difficulty, so every time a user has the correct answer, the user obtains experience point depending on the value of difficulty. The utilization procedure of the developed system is shown in Fig. 2.

4   Experiment and Result

This paper used the developed system for a small group and evaluates its effectiveness. Specifically the developed system was applied for students in laboratory. 7 senior students joined in the experiment, and the period of experiment is 120 days. Learning condition of 7 students is shown in Table 1, and relation between the number of experimental days and each one's reply rate is shown in Fig. 3. Subject name represents as A - F, and experience point which is given each time a user has the correct answer is shown as "Obtained Score". Here each

Table 1. 7 subject's learning results. Subjects are described as A - F, and obtained experience point is shown as "Obtained Score"DThere is no relationship between reply rate and obtained score because two or more questions are often set for one e-mail.

Subjects	A	B	C	D	E	F	G
Obtained Score	342	501	207	1879	551	68	373
Total of Mails Sent	160	137	122	122	123	122	124
Number of Mails Replied	133	122	32	62	49	30	46
Reply Rate	83.1%	89.1%	26.2%	50.8%	39.8%	24.6%	37.1%

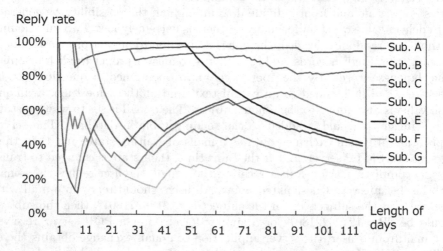

Fig. 3. Change of reply rate. The reply rates were fluctuating between 60-70% in earlier period, but declining overall toward the end of period.

subject's learning condition is discussed by considering reply rate. The obtained score of subject D is the highest. Subject D set two or more questions for one e-mail, but subject D did not reply consciously. Subject D hoped a function to temporarily pause delivery in response to one's schedule, but said that continuous push delivery was effective. The obtained score of subject E is the second highest and subject E is good at English. At first, subject E expressed a strong interest in the developed system, but subject E abandoned the learning in the middle of experimental period because of the loss of interest. Subject E hoped more words than the existing system, and would continue to use if there were a lot of words in database. Subject E is also said that delivery of questions from e-Learning system is effective. Subject A and B with high reply rate are students who regularly use cell-phone a lot. They are interested in English, but they do not learn English positively from themselves. Subject A and B said that delivery of questions with e-mail was convenient for learning. Subject C, F and G are not good at English, and in addition, they are negative learners who cannot positively use common LMS. Since some e-mails were replied from them in

Table 2. Frequency distribution until replying e-mail. Most of e-mail was replied within a day, but there were many e-mails over a day, which were replied together.

Interval (Days)	Sub. A	Sub. B	Sub. C	Sub. D	Sub. E	Sub. F	Sub. G
1	123	51	28	21	30	21	19
2	5	13	2	5	4	2	4
3	2	9	1	9	3	3	0
4	0	9	0	3	3	0	2
5	0	6	0	3	3	1	1
6	1	5	0	3	3	1	1
7	1	4	0	3	2	0	2
8	0	3	0	2	0	0	1
9	0	3	0	4	0	0	1
10	0	1	0	3	0	0	1
11	0	5	0	2	0	0	0
12	0	1	0	1	0	0	0
Over	0	11	0	3	0	2	14

spite of negative learners, this result was considered that using push delivery is more effective than using only usual LMS. Subject C, F and G hardly replied e-mails containing a question too difficult for them because they do not like English learning too much. They requested a delivery method to contain questions according to their understanding. Developing algorithmic improvement will be needed to provide a suitable question for user's understanding including by applying recommendation technique.

Secondly this paper investigated time interval from the delivery of an exercise e-mail to the reply of its answer. Table 2 shows the number of e-mails according to time intervals for each subject, and the value of time interval is based on day. From Table 2, each subject's learning style is shown, for example, there are roughly 3 groups: subject A and C, subject B, D and G, and subject E and F. Table 2 shows various learning styles which were invisible by only the analysis of reply rate. The time interval of most of e-mails was within a day, and the number of e-mails decreased monotonically according to the length of time interval. Most of e-mails replied after long time interval were sent together with two or more e-mails. Since the time interval might fully depend on each one's schedule, a delivery method of exercise e-mail considering each one's schedule is needed. Exercises are constantly delivered, so the authors expect that the developed system might make students aware of learning. However the effectiveness of the developed system was not evaluated by only some evaluation criterion such as reply rate and time interval, so the effect for making aware of learning should be quantitatively-analyzed.

5 Discussion

The proposed e-Learning environment has been examined for approximately 120 days, and there still exist some learner-oriented functionality problems. One is how to reflect a leaner motivation, for instance, suppose a learner continues making almost full score for the duration, he/she will be eager to try more exercise than ones so far. On the other hand, suppose a learner cannot make good scores, the system should send review-style exercises rather than brand-new exercises. It seems to be realizable by using some rules for controlling functionalities, however, the authors believe the system should infer a learner's motivation through the interaction to some extent and make flexible way of controlling functionality. To achieve this goal, psychological insights on motivations should be introduced to the system, but it may be extremely difficult work. So as a short term work, the authors will add some user configurations to improve a method of exercise delivery. Concretely, some methods considering user's understanding are now planned: a delivery method to overcome one's weak area, or a delivery method to improve one's strong area. Alternatively, the developed system should provide a function which can customize delivery schedule and learning target depending on user's learning style. The other problem is how to provide more practical exercises to test English words, this means that even if a learner memorizes English words, the final goal for a learner is to understand sentences that include such words in newspaper, books, magazines and so forth. Therefore we have to integrate two phases on test English words and related sentences. Some other problems are to train proper use of synonyms, correct listening of similar pronunciation and so forth. Based on the current learning environment, we will tackle the above-mentioned further improvement.

6   Conclusion

In this paper, the authors introduced a learning system which encourages continuous learning of students, and which can nurture the interest of students. When students consider "simplicity," "convenience," "easy continuation," and "portability" as significant factors in individual learning, it is transparent that using e-mail feature of cell-phones is very appealing. While various kinds of e-Learning methods have been produced up till now, any systems of e-Learning for the purpose of "establishment of learning habits," "developing the consciousness about everyday learning" such as in this paper, have not been developed. For those reasons, the proposed system, which takes into account the situation of each learner, is extremely original. The proposed system for self-study can give a quick answer and explanation to each response from the students, and should contribute to the raising of, not only the students' English ability, but also their motivation.

This paper ultimately has two goals; firstly, to let students learn through using mobile devices, and, secondly, to stimulate English learners in Japan (who are thought to be behind the rest of the world regarding second language acquisition). This study aims at, not only introducing a self-study system, but also at creating a more dynamic and vital English learning environment. With the effort of this study, the effectiveness was shown while the result was on the students' subjective viewpoint, and only a trial operation was performed. From the standpoint of enjoyable English learning, this system will promote more functions that will catch a learner's interest through adopting game-like properties and quiz-like procedures. By grasping the degree of achievement of learners exactly and completely in database, it will reveal the weak points of English learners and deliver them questions with which they can make more progress. Ultimately, this system aims to be flexible enough for learners to mix and match according to their learning-styles and levels. As a final point, the authors intend to assemble a database of questions corresponding to TOEIC content over the next few years for use with the proposed system.

Acknowledgments. This work was partly supported by the Grant-in-Aid for Young Scientists (B-23700998), The Ministry of Education, Culture, Sports, Science and Technology, Japan.

References

1. Ogata, H., Yano, Y.: A practice of u-Learning at the University of Tokushima. Journal of Multimedia Aided Education Research 1(2), 19–27 (2005) (in Japanese)
2. Kyuri, T.: An Experimental Operation of e-Learning Introducing Cell Phones on a University Lecture with Large Students. Journal of Multimedia Aided Education Research 1(2), 145–153 (2005) (in Japanese)
3. Kuroda, R., Tsuji, M.: Development Methodology of Service Oriented e-Learning - An Example of Development of Questionnaire Service for Cell Phones. Journal of Multimedia Aided Education Research 3(1), 109–115 (2006) (in Japanese)
4. Ministry of Internal Affairs and Communications, Information and Communications Statistics Databases (February 21, 2013) (in Japanese), http://www.soumu.go.jp/johotsusintokei/statistics/statistics05a.html
5. Ooki, M., Matsumoto, S.: How to Nurture Students' Study Habits Using a Handy E-Learning System with Cell Phones. J. of the Society for Teaching English through Media 12(1), 231–255 (2011)
6. Kashima, T., Matsumoto, S., Ihara, T.: Proposal of an e-Learning System with Skill-based Homework Assignments. In: Proc. of the International MultiConference of Engineers and Computer Scientists, pp. 1405–1410 (2011) (in Japanese)
7. Richardson, V.: Constructivist Pedagogy. Teachers College Record 105(9), 1623–1640 (2003)
8. Rice, W.: Moodle 2.0 E-Learning Course Development: A Complete Guide to Successful Learning Using Moodle. Packt Publishing (2011)
9. Sakai, J.: The text of the best campany developing human resources in Japan. Kobunsha (2010) (in Japanese)

E-learning: The Power Source of Transforming the Learning Experience in an ODL Landscape

Blessing Mbatha[1] and Mbali Mbatha[2]

[1] Department of Communication Science
[2] Centre for Professional Development,
University of South Africa, Pretoria, South Africa
{mbathbt,mbathmp}@unisa.ac.za

Abstract. This paper reports on e-learning as a transformational educational tool amongst Communication Science students at Unisa. The study targeted executive members of the Communication Science Association (COMSA) which consists of ten members and Unisa Radio employees which comprise 200 Communication Science students. A survey research design was used whereby questionnaires were administered to all COMSA executives and 50% of Unisa Radio student employees who were chosen using simple random sampling. Data was analysed through thematic categorisation and tabulation and the findings were presented descriptively. An examination of data indicates that students do not actively engage in e-learning. They use myUnisa for basic educational needs and not for the purpose that *myUnisa* was intended which is to bridge transactional distance in order to ensure increased engagement amongst all stakeholders. Unisa needs to examine its current e-learning policies against the backdrop of the society in which it operates.

Keywords: Open Distance Learning, e-learning, dialogue, transactional distance, ICTs in Higher Education, myUnisa.

1   Introduction and Aim of the Paper

The paper is set to map e-learning as a transformational educational tool amongst Communication Science students at Unisa. To achieve the stated aim, the paper set out to investigate students' use of Unisa's e-learning forum called myUnisa. myUnisa is the e-learning resource developed by the university to improve communication between lecturers and students as well as its services to students to ensure a seamless learning experience. This is especially critical in bridging the transactional distance in Unisa's Open Distance Learning (ODL) context. The term open distance learning refers to teaching that is conducted by someone removed in time and space from the students, referred to as 'transactional distance'. ODL further aims to include greater dimensions of openness and flexibility, in terms of access, curriculum including other elements of structure [1], [2], [3], [4]. myUnisa is a web-based system for academic collaboration and study related interaction. This system has been developed to supplement and enhance academic interaction and improve communication between

M. Kurosu (Ed.): Human-Computer Interaction, Part II, HCII 2013, LNCS 8005, pp. 454–463, 2013.

Unisa and its students, as well as provide opportunity for engagement amongst students. At Unisa, the learning process involves being part of the learning community where students can engage with their peers. In a typical distance learning environment, this opportunity for engagement is limited and therefore myUnisa was launched with the intention to help bridge this gap.

Unisa was founded in 1873 as a university college which offered courses to learners through correspondence. Subsequently, the university migrated through the various developmental stages of distance education and in January 2004 it was constituted as a comprehensive open distance learning university after amalgamation with two similar educational bodies. The 'new' Unisa effectively became the fifth largest mega Open Distance Learning education institution in the world, as it services approximately 300 000 learners. Students at Unisa come from both rural and urban areas. This geographical difference impacts on the service delivery of Unisa, which is exacerbated by the mandate given to Higher Education Institutions to enrol 'a large and diverse student body'. Hence, not only is the infrastructure in these areas vastly different, but also the level of exposure to, and availability of modern technology which impacts on the level of technical support that can be given by the learner support system [5].

In order to realise the objectives of this paper, information regarding students' access to computers and the internet were elicited as a starting point. Respondents were further required to provide information pertaining to their awareness and participation on myUnisa. They were also required to rate the effectiveness of myUnisa on their studies. Lastly, respondents were required to provide suggestions for improving the effective use of e-learning at Unisa. The paper is based on the assumption that e-learning facilitates and opens avenues for effective teaching as a result of its potential in bridging the transactional distance amongst all stakeholders at the institution.

The significance of this paper is the contribution that it will make towards encouraging and increasing the use of e-learning at Unisa's Department of Communication Science which may improve throughput and retention rates throughout the University.

The problem that was investigated in this paper pertains to students' inadequate access to e-learning facilities as well as their superficial interaction with the e-learning forum. Unisa's vision 'towards the African university in the service of humanity' addresses its enhanced learner support methodologies, processes and facilities, all of which are underpinned by a focus on a service-oriented culture within the university. This includes the use of Information and Communication Technologies (ICTs) in the learning process. Unisa is accessible to all students, specifically those on the African continent, and the marginalised, by way of a barrier-free environment, while responding to the needs of the global market. This is further emphasised by the university's acknowledgement in its 2015 Strategic Plan that it is vital to establish a leading-edge information and communication technology architecture in order to sustain a competitive edge in education [6].

E-learning at Unisa is conducted through the online forum called myUnisa which intends to change the way students access and synthesise information. Furthermore, myUnisa is also intended to align the university in the Open Distance Learning context where transactional distance is minimised, thereby effecting transformation at the institution by restructuring traditional models of distance learning in the areas of interaction with lecturers, courseware, associated resources and students. The introduction of myUnisa is not intended to replace printed material, but rather to enhance the learning process by creating a seamless learning experience for students.

2   Theoretical Framework

This study is informed by Paulo Freire's dialogic process of communication [7], which focuses on the premise that in order for communication to be effective, it has to be participatory, dialogical and reciprocal [8]. Freire's concept of conscientisation focuses on bringing the individual to critical reflection about his/her own living conditions whereby he/she actively participates in the communication process [9]. People thus become the subjects of their own development and not simply objects of technology or processes [8].

Rather than a "banking" model in which the teacher makes deposits which the students patiently receive, memorise, and reproduce – a form, he argued, that serves only to increase the recipients' dependence upon the teacher, and in this instance does not provide lifelong learning which is one of Unisa's primary goals – Freire suggested a model where education becomes a dialogue in which the teacher and student engage with one another. In this model, the student is enabled to acquire skills to equip him/her with knowledge to better his/her life, which Freire called conscientisation or consciousness raising [10]. Freire emphasised that the mere transfer of knowledge by an authority source to a passive receiver did nothing to help promote growth in the latter as a human being with an independent and critical conscience, capable of influencing and changing society. According to him, for learning to be effective, it has to be linked not only to the process of acquiring technical knowledge and skills, but also to awareness-raising. Freirean dialogue is relevant in this paper because of its reference to the concepts of dialogue, reciprocation as well as participation in the learning process. These elements are necessary in Unisa's ODL context, in order to effect a deep and meaningful learning experience, failing which will result in superficial interactions.

3   Methodology

A survey research design was used whereby questionnaires were administered to all COMSA executives and 50% of Unisa Radio student employees who were chosen using simple random sampling. The paper focused on COMSA executives and Unisa Radio employees because these groups were able to provide valuable data emanating from their active involvement at the Muckleneuk and Sunnyside campuses, where the hub of the university's activities originate. The instrument sought information pertaining to personal characteristics of the respondents, student access to e-learning facilities, the use of *myUnisa* as an e-learning resource and recommendations to improve the use of e-learning at the university. The data collected was analysed through thematic categorisation and tabulation, and the findings were presented descriptively.

4   Findings and Discussions

The findings are reported under the following headings: demographics of the respondents, computer access, internet access, awareness of myUnisa, participation in the discussion forums on *myUnisa*, submissions of assignments via *myUnisa*, and the effectiveness of *myUnisa* on students' studies.

4.1   Demographic Profile of the Respondents

The respondents were BA: Communication Science students from Unisa. There was a male dominance (75%), with most of the respondents under the age of 29 (94.2%).

4.2   Computer Access

The study sought to establish whether respondents had computer access. The respondents were provided with a list of four categories of computer access and were required to choose the relevant option/s.

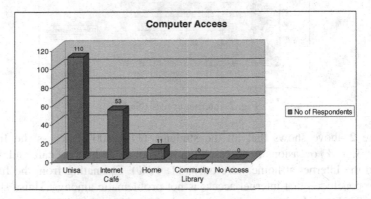

Fig. 1. Computer access (N=110)

An examination of data indicates that all students (110; 100%) have computer access at Unisa; while those who have computer access at the Internet café were (53; 48%); (11; 10%) had access at home; whilst none had access at community libraries. Interestingly, the results show that all the students had computer access which is encouraging because this indicates that active engagement between the students and lecturers through e-learning can be realised. This result could be attributed to the fact that most of the targeted students were based in urban areas and have physical access to Information and Communication Technologies (ICTs).

Many people around the globe have personal computers in their homes [11]. However, in Africa this is not the case since the availability of desktop computers in Africa is globally one of the lowest. Statistics provided by the International Telecommunications Union [12] indicate that in 2002 Africa had 1.23 desktop computers per 100 inhabitants. The theory informing this study suggests that in order for meaningful communication to occur, there should be a change in focus from information supply to meaning production. To view communication as a process of meaning production is to recognise revolutionary developments in communication technology. This is why access to ICTs at Unisa is critical in creating a conducive e-learning environment for active engagement.

4.3 Internet Access

Figure 2 below provides responses from the respondents on the question, *"Do you have internet access?"* Figure 2 below summarises the responses where respondents were provided with a list of six categories to choose from. Respondents could choose more than on e-option and were also given the opportunity to identify other sources that were not listed.

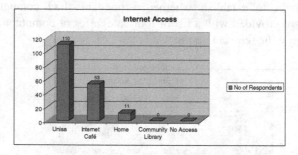

Fig. 2. Internet access (N=110)

Figure 2 above shows that all the students (110; 100%) access the Internet at Unisa; (53; 48%) occasionally accessed the Internet at the Internet café and those who accessed the Internet at home were only (11; 10%). Emanating from the findings, it could be concluded that internet access is not problematic amongst Unisa students in Pretoria. This may be because Unisa's head office is situated in Pretoria and this is where all activities originate. This is a positive reflection of the diffusion and adoption of e-learning resources which is one of the aims in ODL. The results further show that none of the students accessed the internet at their community libraries. It is evident that students do not access their local libraries despite being encouraged to do so, for reasons not discovered in this study.

Internet users in South Africa for year-end 2008, were estimated at 4,590,000 [13]. For year end 2007 the number of Internet users in South Africa were 4,070,000; for year end 2006 the number was 3,830,000; and for year-end 2005 total Internet users were 3,600,000 [13]. This use of communication technology is referred to by some as the use of cyberspace as a potential source of empowerment locally and globally [14].

Modern electronic communication technology has greatly increased the power and speed of interactive communication and easy access to information sources, information transmission, storage and processing, which is the technical source of empowerment in cyberspace. The theory used in this study encourages dialogue whereby e-learning enables students in cyberspace to quickly and efficiently interconnect themselves, enter into regular discussions and dialogues, and form virtual communities. According to the theory informing this study, the human interaction on networking is a potent source of democratic empowerment [8].

4.4   Awareness of *myUnisa*

One of the objectives of the study was focused on students' awareness of the university's online forum called *myUnisa*. In order to measure their responses a binary choice of 1=Yes and 2=No was used. The study established that all targeted students (110; 100%) were aware of *myUnisa* which is encouraging especially as the use of online resources is promoted by the university in an attempt to bridge the transactional distance in ODL. On close evaluation of Freire's theory, it is observed that he places great emphasis on the educator as initiator of the conscientisation and dialogue process [10]. In this study, the initiator of the learning process is Unisa, and more specifically, the lecturer. Should the lecturer not initiate dialogue with students, then the learning process becomes linear, whereby tasks are given to students without authentic transactional communication occurring. However, it should be noted that this conscientisation and learning process cannot be totally dependent on the lecturer because of the dangers that dependency may pose.

4.5   Participation in the Discussion Forum on *myUnisa*

The study sought to establish whether the students participate in the discussion forum on *myUnisa*. The discussion forum is a tool intended to provide a forum for engagement amongst students, as well as between students and lecturers. The respondents were provided with a list of three options as illustrated in the figure below.

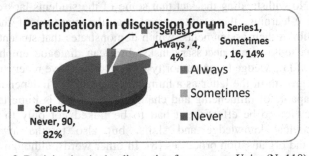

Fig. 3. Participation in the discussion forum on *myUnisa* (N=110)

The figure above shows that a significant number of respondents (90; 81%) have never participated in *myUnisa's* discussion forum; (16; 15%) indicated that they sometimes participate while the minority (4; 4%) indicated that they always participate on discussion forums. Overall, the findings reveal that the majority of the students do not participate on discussion forums, which could be attributed to the fact that students lack the necessary skills to partake in e-learning. This study uses the concept of dialogue as the common and grounding factor and the basis for participatory communication. The theory informing this study states that only in terms of mutuality and meeting can human life achieve meaning and fulfilment [8]. Dialogic communication in the theory further resonates with the importance of students' participation in discussion forums in this study and it may be further stated that it is the dialogic encounter which has the potential to create meaning in the learning process.

4.6   Submission of Assignments via *myUnisa*

Responses were required from the students on the question: "Have you ever submitted your assignments via *myUnisa*?" Respondents were provided with a list of possible methods to choose from as illustrated in Figure 4 below.

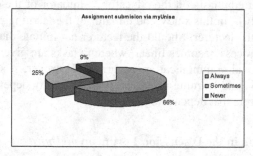

Fig. 4. Submission of assignments via *myUnisa* (N=110)

The figure above illustrates that a significant number of the students (66%) have indicated that they always submitted assignments using *myUnisa*, followed by those who indicated that they sometimes submit their assignments using *myUnisa* (25%). Only (9%) indicated that they never use the *myUnisa* resource to submit their assignments. Notwithstanding the fact that some of the students lack computer skills to partake in e-learning, the results reveal that the majority of the students use *myUnisa* to submit their assignments, which demonstrates that students use *myUnisa* to perform the tedious and necessary tasks. Freirean dialogue emphasises that the mere transfer of knowledge by an authority source to a passive receiver did nothing to help promote growth in the latter as a human being with an independent and critical conscience, capable of influencing and changing society. It is important to note that for communication to be effective, it had to be linked not only to the process of acquiring technical knowledge and skills, but also to the awareness-raising, politicisation and organisation processes [8]. In other words, although using *myUnisa* to submit assignments assisted with the tedious task of having to post the assignments, it does not equip the student with the requisite knowledge for empowerment and lifelong learning.

4.7   The Effectiveness of *myUnisa* on Students' Studies (N=110)

One of the objectives of the study was to establish the effectiveness of *myUnisa* on students' studies. The students were therefore provided with a list of possible options to choose from and asked to rate them accordingly on the Likert Scale of 1 (very effective) through to 3 (ineffective). The figure below summarises the responses.

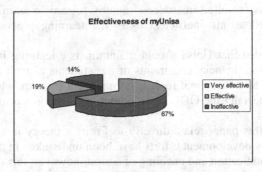

Fig. 5. The effectiveness of *myUnisa* (N=110)

When asked to comment on the effectiveness of *myUnisa* in their studies, the majority (74; 67%) indicated that it was very effective, while (21; 19%) indicated that it was effective. The minority (15; 14%) were those who felt that it was ineffective. It should be noted that *myUnisa* has been introduced by the university as a platform to assist students during their studies.

5   Conclusion

The paper set out to map e-learning as a transformational educational tool amongst Communication Science students at Unisa. It should be noted that these results are not transferable to the entire Unisa community because of the limitations of the chosen target population to generalise the findings. If Unisa is to continue to compete in a global higher education market, it must continue to embrace the technological advancements and use it as a strategic tool, capable of transforming its education delivery.

This relates to the underpinning theory of this paper which argues that for communication to be effective, it has to be participatory, dialogical and reciprocal, and this will only be possible once the issues of access to facilities and active participation are addressed by the initiators of the communication process, which correlates directly with Freirean dialogue.

Although technological growth and expansion are inevitable and necessary, there is a danger that technology could result in the widening of the knowledge gap. Rather than achieving widespread adoption, information now becomes power in the hands of a privileged few [8]. This resonates with the issue of access to computers and the internet. Although students have indicated that they have access to these facilities, it is limited to facilities on campus only. This limitation therefore impedes students' engagement in e-learning. Emanating from recommendations from the respondents, one of the objectives of ODL is to transcend transactional distance, therefore Unisa should take a closer look at the service offerings at regional offices.

The paper further argues that although majority of the respondents have access to e-learning, the results show that their interactions in the e-learning arena are not meaningful. Effective two-way communication is encouraged with the aim of enhancing dialogue amongst all stakeholders in the learning process. However, the results of the study show that there is insufficient meaningful interaction present. This lack of dialogue has resulted in students' apathy towards e-learning at Unisa which could further translate into inefficiencies in the learning process in Unisa's ODL context.

It is recommended that Unisa should maintain its e-learning initiatives, but must take into account the financial constraints of the students as well as the suitability of the technology as an educational tool. It is important to acknowledge that in higher education, and especially the ODL environment, e-learning is a means to an end and not the end in itself.

The results of this paper relate directly to Freire's theory in respect of authentic participation. Many development efforts have been undertaken in the past by focusing on effective communication and enabling of action; however, this narrow focus leaves such efforts vulnerable to eventual failure. They fail because people lack ownership and relevant in-depth knowledge to assume control of activities in the long term and, more importantly, because they lack the sense of a community [18]. It is therefore recommended that the Department of Communication Science form an advisory board to include students' input in the decision-making process on matters that affect them directly, including e-learning. This resonates with Freire's reference to the 'freeing' and emancipatory experience of dialogue.

Our advanced technological society is rapidly making objects of most of us and subtly programming us into conformity to the logic of its system [7]. To this degree that this happens, we are also becoming submerged in a new 'culture of silence'. The paradox is that the same technology which contributes to this culture of silence also stimulates a new sensitivity to our global environment.

6   Recommendations

Unisa should examine its current e-learning policies against the backdrop of the society in which we live. It is in this light that the paper recommends that a more in-depth study be conducted to ascertain core issues in respect of why students do not engage actively in what is meant to promote a deep learning experience.

This paper also recommends that a further investigation into each regional centre should be conducted to ascertain the issues of access in respect of facilities provided and support rendered. This study focused on the Pretoria region, which is the hub of Unisa's activities, as an initial study. It is therefore recommended that ongoing research is conducted at the regions to ensure maximum geographic reach. It is further recommended that a study be conducted into Unisa's collaboration with community libraries and community centres throughout the country. These collaborations are key in providing free internet facilities as well as other educational resources which are critical components in transcending the transactional distance.

References

1. Pachler, N., Daly, C.: Key Issues in e-Learning: Research and Practice. Continnum. International Publishing Group, London (2011)
2. Holmes, B., Gardner, J.: E-learning: Concepts and Practices. Sage, London (2006)
3. Mason, R., Rennie, F.: The key concepts. Routledge, New York (2006)
4. UNESCO, http://unesdoc.unesco.org/images/0012/0012/001284/128463e.pdf
5. Sonnekus, P., Louw, W., Wilson, H.: Emergent learner support at Unisa: An informal report. Progressio 28, 12–23 (2006)
6. Unisa 2015 Strategic Plan, http://staff.unisa.ac.za/cmsys/staff/docs/unisa_2015_strategicplan_nov_final.pdf
7. Freire, P.: Pedagogy of the Oppressed. In: Gumucio-Dragon, A., Tufte, T. (eds.) Communication for Social Change: Historical and Contemporary Readings, pp. 44–48. Communication for Social Change Consortium, South Orange (1970)
8. White, A.S., Nair, K.S., Ascroft, J.: Participatory communication: working for change and development. Sage, New Dehli (1994)
9. Servaes, J., Jacobson, T., White, S.: Participatory Communication for Social Change. Sage, New Delhi (1996)
10. Srampickal, J.: Development and Participatory Communication. Communication Research Trends 25, 3–30 (2006)
11. Van Brakel, P., Chisenga, J.: Impact of ICT-Based Distance Learning: the African Story. The Electronic Library Journal 21, 12–23 (2003)
12. International Telecommunication Union, http://www.ictregulationtoolkit.org/en/Publication.2288.html
13. Internet Services Provider Association, http://www.ispa.org.za
14. Servaes, J.: Advocacy Strategies for Development Communication. In: Servaes, J. (ed.) Walking on the Other Side of the Information Highway: Communication, Culture and Development Development in the 21st Century, pp. 103–118. Southbound, Penang (2000)
15. South African Yearbook, http://www.gcis.gov.za/docs/publications/yearbook/2008/chapter5.pdf
16. Wireless Federation, http://wirelessfederation.com/news/cell-c-subscribers-base-up-by-58southafrica/
17. Yoon, C.S.: Facilitating Participatory Group Processes: Reflections on the Participatory Development Communication Experiments (2006)

Mobile Inquiry-Based Learning

A Study of Collaborative Scaffolding and Performance

Jalal Nouri, Teresa Cerrato-Pargman, and Karwan Zetali

Department of Computer and Systems Sciences, Stockholm University, Sweden
{jalal,tessy,karw-zet}@dsv.su.se

Abstract. This paper presents a study on mobile learning that could be viewed as a manifestation of strong voices calling for learning in natural contexts. The study was based on a sequence of inquiry-based mobile learning activities within the domain of natural sciences and mathematics education. We questioned *the effects of collaborative scaffolding, and the effects scaffolding provided by technology have on learning and performance*. Based on a quantitative interaction analysis, findings suggest that low-achievement students benefit from inquiry-based mobile activities; that the use of mobile technologies bring multiple effects on students' learning, both positive and negative, and that the roles of teachers remains as crucial as before the introduction of learning technologies.

Keywords: mobile learning, scaffolding, across contexts, performance.

1 Introduction

Since the Industrial Age, and as a response to a need for mass-education, learning has, to a high extent, been considered to take place in traditional classroom environments of lectures and books. As a consequence of the mechanical spirit of the industrial era, learning traditions were developed describing knowledge not as something that can be constructed by learners in appropriate contexts, but rather as information that should be transferred from textbooks and teachers into the minds of learners [1].

As time has elapsed, many strong voices have emphasized the importance of natural contexts [2] [3]. In the beginning of the 20th century, one of the first authors warning about the de-contextualized nature of learning and challenging the assumption that the classroom is the optimal place for learning to occur was John Dewey (1916), advocating that meaningful learning should take place in the setting of real-world activities [2]. Since then, several theories on learning and cognition have been introduced, such as situated learning [3] and situated cognition [4], which emphasize authentic problems and natural contexts as powerful learning resources for learners' generalization process. Also, since the emergence of the mobile learning field, more and more research projects are investigating learning outside of the classroom, in the world and in authentic contexts. The step out of the classroom into more dynamical environments, combined with the increased mobility of the students and the utilization of technology, change radically conditions for providing scaffolding support.

M. Kurosu (Ed.): Human-Computer Interaction, Part II, HCII 2013, LNCS 8005, pp. 464–473, 2013.
© Springer-Verlag Berlin Heidelberg 2013

From our own experiences, we have observed that the design of mobile learning activities can dramatically restrict young students' opportunities to share knowledge and scaffold each other [5] [6].

Thus, in the empirical study reported on in this paper, we attempted to further question *the effects that collaborative scaffolding facilitated by technology have on students' learning and their performance.* In order to investigate these questions, a sequence of inquiry-based learning activities was designed within the domain of natural sciences and mathematics education.

2   Related Work

Little is still understood in terms of what scaffolding needs younger students have interacting with mobile technology in field activities where teachers are not as readily available. A large body of productive research work has been conducted on the notion and importance of scaffolding in educational settings, for instance as conceptualized within situated learning [3] [7] [8]. These approaches have nevertheless, either emphasized teachers scaffolding functions in face-to-face conventional classrooms with their physical and social constraints, or focused on computer-based environments where teachers are not present [9].

Scaffolding learning processes in outdoor mobile learning activities brings other challenges than learning in the classroom, as demonstrated by [5] [6]. While mobile technology can be utilized to provide scaffolding to some extent, for example as demonstrated by [10], it is nevertheless a design challenge to determine what scaffolds to incorporate given the dynamical needs of learners and the constrains of mobile phones [11]. Furthermore, from previous studies conducted by the authors of this paper, presented in [5] and [6], we learned that young students could have difficulties to collaboratively scaffold each other in field activities.

If we are to meaningfully realize situated, inquiry- and problem-based mobile learning approaches, the question of how the students are to be pedagogically supported remains crucial. Thus, in the empirical study reported on in this paper, we attempted to further investigate the following questions: i-how students scaffold each other in field activities where teachers are not readily available, ii-what scaffolding needs these situations create among students, and, iii- what effects collaborative scaffolding and scaffolding provided by mobile technology have on students' learning and performance.

3   Methodology

3.1   Study

mVisible was a research project where small groups of students use smartphones and pads outside the classroom, in the woods to explore characteristics of species of plants and trees and their biotopes in the north of the Stockholm area.

Design Process. Three areas have informed the design process conducted in the mVisible project: 1. A literature review summarizing previous research in the field of mobile learning, in particular findings presented in [5] and [6], 2. pedagogy and didactics (Inquiry-based learning theory through collaborative learning), and 3. Workshops with school children and teachers that were conducted from a perspective on participatory design). In other words, every step of the interaction design loop, here presented as tasks, has been considered from what we know is problematic in mobile learning design, together with the project's pedagogical and didactical perspectives.

Inquiry-Based Learning. We adopted the pedagogical framework of inquiry-based learning for the design of the present study. According to [12], the framework is grounded on the idea that science is essentially a question-driven, open-ended process and that students must have personal experience with scientific inquiry to understand this fundamental aspect of science. Inquiry-based learning thus advocates a teaching and learning of science in the way it is actually practice by scientists [12].

Inquiry-based learning, prototypically, involves learner-centered and non-structured investigations that are based on students' own choice of questions, hypothesis, observations of phenomena [12]. However, it is argued that more structured and guided inquiry activities are preferable if the indented students are young and lack experience of inquiry [12]. As this was the case of our study, we chose to apply a high degree of structure to guide the students' trough the inquiry-based learning activity.

The Sequence of Learning Activities. The study conducted consisted of three main activities, namely an indoor introduction to the sequence of activities, an outdoors field activity, and an indoors post-activity. The day began with an *introduction activity* which provided the students an opportunity to both familiarize themselves with the technology intended to be used in the outdoors activity, and to create a understanding of the tasks they were to perform – guided by the attended researchers and teachers.

The *field activity* started with a group of students arriving at one of four different areas in the forest behind the school. Each student had a smartphone, and there is one common device, a pad, belonging to each area.

The field activity was designed as a sequence of seven tasks playing out as follows; all three students in the group use their mobile devices to *scan the QR code for the nature square* they arrive at. The code initializes the mobile devices to show a list of what species are available in the current nature square. On the common device, the students read the *task instruction* to *identify each species*. The students used their mobile devices individually to scan QR codes attached to each species to identify them and to take photos of what they believed is characteristic for each species. For the next task, the three students reconvene at the common device, where they use a pie chart to *calculate the distribution of trees* in the area. Also on the common device, they get the task to *define what type of forest* they are in based on the distribution of trees.

The mobile device provided the students in-situ descriptions of species and their biotopes and allowed for multimodal data collection in form of pictures and video. The pad, on the other hand, constituted a common tool that scripted the collaboration between the students by forcing the students to provide individual codes each time a task instruction was needed from the pad. As such, the design of the common device indented to encourage the students to create a joint task understanding and be delivered equal task information in order to not empower the students asymmetrically [6]. Besides these functions, the common device also provided affordances to collaboratively create dynamical pie charts that were used to visualize the tree distribution.

The last part of the sequence of activities was the *indoors post-activity* in which the students analyzed the collected multimodal data from the outdoors activity, transformed it into conclusions and new representations collaboratively, ending up with multimodal presentations that were discussed together with the whole class. Two available teachers scaffolded the students' work during this post-activity.

Participants. Seven groups of three students, 21 in total, took part in the study. The students were from the same fifth grade class, participating in the study as part of their mathematics and natural sciences curriculum. Apart from which students were known to be able to work together and which students were not, the teachers used high heterogeneity as the basis for group formations. Six out of seven groups had both female and male students and the differences in background knowledge on the subject were as large as possible in all seven groups.

3.2   Data Collection and Analysis

As we were interested in the relation between scaffolding children's needs/interactions and their performance, the methodological approach taken directed particular interest towards investigating correlations between i-performance and ii-frequencies of different scaffolding interactions,. Accordingly, collected video data has been transcribed and analyzed using interaction analysis [13].

The primary data used for analysis was video from handheld video cameras following each group in the field. Seven hours of outdoor activity video data was collected, approximately one hour per group. Additional data was collected through the pre- and post-tests. These tests were constructed to examine three aspects, namely, students understanding of name and characteristics of the species, the characteristics of their biotopes, and the students skills to interpret pie charts.

Transcription and Coding. The video-data collected were transcribed using Transana software, a tool that is specifically designed for video analysis. As a total, three researchers transcribed the entire video data excluding only speech and interactions that were not task-related.

Further, a coding scheme was constructed based on the six scaffolding types described by [14] and [15], i.e. technological, affective, procedural, conceptual, strategic, and metacognitive scaffolding (see Table 1). The three researchers coded the transcribed data independently, deploying the coding scheme with the aim to capture the occurrence of: 1.) Scaffolding provided by the students within the groups, and 2.) Scaffolding provided by the mobile technology. An inter-rater reliability coefficient of 84 % was obtained. Upon the coded transcriptions, quantitative analyses of how frequently the various scaffolding interactions occurred were done along with an analysis of correlation with performance scores (presented in the next section).

Table 1. The deployed coding scheme

Collaborative Scaffolding	Definition
Technical	The students provide support with technical issues
Affective	The students provide emotional support.
Procedural	The students provide "how-to"-support.
Conceptual	The students provide support on a conceptual level.
Strategic	The students support each other in formulating strategies
Metacognitive	Students share strategies about how to learn something.
Technology Scaffolding	
Procedural	The students read task instructions from the mobile technology
Conceptual	The students read or use the (QR-) information loudly or silently.

4   Results

In the following sections the performance results of the pre- and post tests are presented (see Table 2) and correlated with collaborative and technology scaffolding.

4.1   Performance

Considering the overall results of the entire student sample, with a mean performance increase of 44 % we observed that learning indeed have occurred. Now this can certainly reflect a Hawthorne effect and does not say anything about the efficacy of learning activities of this kind in comparison to learning occurring in the frame of the classroom and of more traditional pedagogical models. With that said, there is no reason to conclude the inverse with certainty as there are other indications speaking in favour of the benefits of learning in natural contexts supported by mobile technology.

In this study, for instance, we have observed the occurrence of quite interesting context-related discussions amongst the students that indicated the presence of higher reflection on the subject matter, triggered by an intrinsic motivation and engagement with the task and the physical context. In the following excerpt a group of students are attempting to identify a pine tree and face some difficulties in doing that.

> *S1: I don't think that a pine tree can flourish here on the meadow ...   but rather on such soil, do you see? (points at pine trees outside of the square)*
> *S2: They flourish in shadows!?*
> *S1: A pine tree flourish in sunlight but casts shadows for other*
> *S2: I wonder if that is a pine three S1? (points at a tree)*
> *S1: No, it has too short needles. According to the information here (the mobile) pine trees should have long needles.*
> *S1: The pine tree is a big needle tree. You see them over there (points at pine trees outside the nature square)*
> *S2: It (the mobile phone) says that pine trees are tall and have a slim stem.*
> *S1: Consider that they can be and are very small in the beginning.*

Table 2. Individual and group performance increase. The mean group increase percentage is based on absolute scores for each group.

Individual	Group	Individual increase	$\bar{x}$ group increase	σ
S1	1	42%	69%	0,36
S2	1	67%		
S3	1	113%		
S4	2	42%	40%	0,20
S5	2	57%		
S6	2	17%		
S7	3	550%	56%	3,07
S8	3	30%		
S9	3	7%		
S10	4	29%	36%	0,17
S11	4	31%		
S12	4	60%		
S13	5	22%	33%	0,34
S14	5	113%		
S15	5	10%		
S16	6	22%	42%	0,24
S17	6	100%		
S18	6	20%		
S19	7	1000%	38%	5,6
S20	7	29%		
S21	7	29%		
		Mean increase: 44		**Tot**: 0,33

When trying to identify the pine tree, the environment surrounding the trees are analysed with aid from the information provided by the mobile technology, which highlights the critical features of the learning objects. As a result the students arrive in correct conclusions such as that pine trees flourish in certain biotopes with specific characteristics, and that pine trees have certain characteristics such as long needles. Simulating the richness and complexity of this particular learning context, which the students are utilizing freely, and guided by mobile technology, for inquiries and reflections can be difficult in the ordinary classroom. The situated, multimodal and embodied learning experience is likely to explain a portion of the performance results.

In this particular learning activity, mobile technology was also providing the students the possibility to capture their experiences through the use of the camera function. The representations created through the camera function was later brought inside the classroom for further transformation, analysis, reflection, and discussion, this time with a more available teacher supporting these processes.

4.2   Performance of Otherwise Low-Achievement Students

What may be the most noteworthy regarding the performance results is that four out of the five students with weakest pre-test results, namely students S7, S14, S17, and S19 (see Table 2), achieved the most performance increases in relation to the whole student sample. Certainly, different explanations could be provided for these results, amongst them, that these were high-achievement students that happened to have poor motivation during the pre-test. That explanation has however been put aside after consultation with the teachers who verified that these particular students belong to the poor-achievement set of the class. In fact, student S19 for instance is an immigrant student that struggles with both ADHD and poor language skills, while S17, also an immigrant student, is described as a student with concentration difficulties.

Consequently, what we believe explains these results are a combination of others factors such as motivation/engagement, structure/guidance, individual work, collaborative scaffolding, and situated and embodied learning. We understood from the post-interviews with the students that the learning activity was fun and engaging, i.e. the motivation/engagement factor. The students learning and inquiry was also guided by a distinct structure mainly provided by the mobile technology in terms of task instructions, hints, and information that highlighted the critical learning features of the tasks. As such, this structure facilitated the student's navigation towards the knowledge expected to be acquired [7]. Furthermore, the otherwise low-achievement students had the possibility to both explore individually within the provided structure, and if needed, operate in the Zone of Proximal development through the support of the more capable peers within the groups.

Table 3. The scaffolding types provided within the groups correlated with mean group performance increase (see Table 2 for performance increase). Correlation is significant at 0.05.

Group	Technical	Affective	Procedural	Conceptual	Strategic	Metacognitive
1	6	2	17	13	6	3
2	14	7	21	22	8	2
3	5	1	18	14	3	1
4	12	5	19	19	7	4
5	15	4	35	23	4	1
6	12	3	13	13	2	1
7	8	7	32	21	6	2
Total	72	29	155	125	36	14
p	0,04	0,09	0,23	0,04	0,79	0,83

4.3   Collaborative Scaffolding

In considering the performance of the students, and to come closer to an understanding of how we support them further in the future, we looked at how they scaffolded each other in the outdoor activity according to the six scaffolding types of [14] and [15]. Presented in Table 3 is an account of the collaborative scaffolding provided within the groups correlated with mean increase in performance.

In terms of salient correlations of scaffolding types such as technical, procedural, and conceptual, interesting conclusions arise from the results. For instance, the statistical significant negative correlation between performance and technical scaffolding may shed light on the sensitivity of introducing technology - and in particular new technology - in the curriculum. Clearly the technology, while supporting some students as shown in the next section, still obstructed the learning of others.

Another interesting finding regard students need for procedural and conceptual scaffolding and the correlation between these scaffolding types and performance. Noticeably, there is a negative correlation present; indicating that the students relative extensive scaffolding needs were not satisfied by collaboration, which in fact negatively influenced the performance scores. Primarily, a significant correlation exists between conceptual scaffolding and performance. We believe that the reason for this is poor quality of the scaffolding provided by the students, which to some extent is dependent on their young age and limited knowledge level, and the circumstance that the particular subject and the technology used was quite new to them.

In general our data generated negative correlation coefficients for all of the scaffolding types, which in a sense, is a counter intuitive result considering previous research on the positive effects of collaborative learning. Evidently, the scaffolding provided by the group members when called for did not satisfy the student's needs, which may indicate the necessity to have a teacher more available to the students, and further investigate how we can utilize technology to provide needed scaffolding to a higher extent. It should also be considered if its more appropriate to design mobile learning activities such that emphasis on learning on a conceptual level is put in the indoors activities where teachers are more available, and consider the outdoor activities as opportunities for students to gain situated/embodied experiences and for collection of data that is analysed more in depth in the classroom.

4.4   Scaffolding Provided by the Mobile Technology

The mobile technology in the present study was designed to provide two different scaffolding types, namely conceptual in terms of providing information about the species and biotopes through the QR-functionality, and procedural in terms of providing task-instructions. In Table 4, the students' utilization of scaffolding offered by the technology is presented.

Based on the data gathered, the obtaining and use of information trough the QR-functionality significantly correlates to the student's performance scores. These results are quite expected considering that the questions in the pre- and post-tests to a high extent were aligned with the information offered through the mobile technology; information that was believed to highlight critical features intended to be learnt. Although this could be considered as a positive finding emphasizing that mobile technology may enhance situated learning experiences by highlighting critical features and providing in-situ information, it also raises questions and challenges that need to be considered. Evidently, a considerable set of students did not read or take advantage of the information provided by the technology, which raises two questions, how do we design learning technologies to encourage and facilitate accessing information through these means? And from which pedagogic objective? After all, in rather complex and rich learning contexts of this kind, where teachers are not readily available, it is vital to consider how we support students to highlight critical learning features.

Table 4. QR-information use correlated with performance. Correlation is significant at 0.05.

Group	Conceptual (QR-info use)	Procedural (Task instructions)	Performance
1	10	13	0,69
2	8	7	0,39
3	9	12	0,56
4	8	8	0,36
5	4	9	0,33
6	6	12	0,42
7	5	9	0,38
p	0,04	0,03	

5   Conclusions

In regards to the potentials of mobile learning, the findings of the study indicate that some learning certainly occurred. For instance, a 44 % mean increase in performance is not inconsiderable, although it can be gradated with the Hawthorne effect. Obviously, one could also question what learning we assessed and how we did that in the first place, calling for richer assessments focus beyond performance scores. In terms of performances scores however, the most noteworthy finding is the impressive performance increase of otherwise low-achievement students. It seems that these students are particularly responsive to learning situations of this kind, characterized by structured activities that allowed and guided both individual and collaborative work, also providing concrete experiences of the learning material supported by the mobile technology that highlighted and captured critical features.

On the other hand, the findings also demonstrated that we, as researcher, designers, and teachers, should not rely on collaboration to unfold satisfactorily in a way that provides the students the required scaffolding. In fact, some of the findings indicate that collaborative scaffolding amongst young students can have negative impact on learning, especially if the students are not capable and knowledgeable enough to provide the required scaffolding. These findings emphasize two things; firstly, the still important role of teachers in these kinds of activities, and secondly, the importance of a thoughtful technology- and primarily - activity design. After all, our analysis suggests that the mobile technology used, with all its utilized positive affordances, also gave rise to problems among students managing the technology, and to scaffolding interactions that had significant negative influence on performance scores.

The analysis presented in this study also suggests that designers, whether its researchers or teachers, should thoughtfully consider how learning activities across contexts are planned for, taking account of the scaffolding needs that different tasks, learning processes, and learning contexts can give rise to. One should, for instance, not put to much focus on conceptual learning in outdoor contexts, where teachers are not as readily available, and the concerned students are believed to be incapable of providing required conceptual scaffolding to their fellow group members. Essentially, designers of mobile learning activities across contexts should thoughtfully ask which learning tasks are suitable for different contexts and how learning tasks can be distributed across contexts in order to provide students with the required scaffolding for meaningful learning to occur – for as many as possible.

References

1. Figueiredo, A.D., Afonso, A.P.: Context and Learning: A Philosophical Framework. In: Afonso, A.P. (ed.) Managing Learning in Virtual Settings: The Role of Context, pp. 1–22. Information Science Publishing, Hershey (2005)
2. Dewey, J.: Democracy and Education. The Free Press, New York (1916)
3. Lave, J., Wenger, E.: Situated learning: Legitimate peripheral participation. Cambridge University Press, New York (1991)
4. Brown, A.L., Collins, A., Duguid, P.: Situated cognition and the culture of learning. Educational Researcher 18, 32–42 (1989)
5. Nouri, J.: Eliciting the potentials of mobile learning trough scaffolding learning processes across contexts. International Journal of Mobile Learning and Organisation (2012)
6. Nouri, J., Cerratto Pargman, T., Eliasson, J., Ramberg, R.: Exploring the Challenges of Supporting Collaborative Mobile Learning. International Journal of Mobile and Blended Learning 3(4), 54–69 (2011)
7. Wood, D., Bruner, J.S., Ross, G.: The role of tutoring and problem solving. Journal of Child Psychology and Psychiatry 17, 89–100 (1976)
8. Vygotsky, L.S.: Thought and language. The MIT Press. Cambridge (1986)
9. McLoughlin, C.: Scaffolding: Applications to learning in technology supported environments. In: Collis, B., Oliver, R. (eds.) Proc. of World Conference on Educational Multimedia, Hypermedia and Telecommunications, pp. 1826–1831 (1999)
10. Chen, S., Kao, T., Sheu, J.: A mobile learning system for scaffolding bird watching learning. Journal of Computer Assisted Learning (19), 34 (2003)
11. Luchini, K., Quintana, C., Soloway, E.: Design Guidelines for Learner- Centered Handheld Tools. In: Computing Systems, pp. 135–142. ACM, Vienna (2004)
12. Edelson, D., Gordin, N., Pea, R.: Addressing the Challenges of Inquiry-Based Learning Through Technology and Curriculum Design. Journal of the Learning Sciences 8, 391–450 (1999)
13. Jordan, B., Henderson, A.: Interaction analysis: Foundations and practice. IRL Technical Report, Palo Alto, IRL (1994)
14. Hill, J., Hannafin, M.: Teaching and learning in digital environments: the resurgence of resource-based learning. Journal of Educational Technology Research and Development 49(3), 37–52 (2001)
15. Masters, J., Yelland, N.: Teacher scaffolding: an exploration of exemplary practice. Education and Information Technologies 7(4), 313–321 (2002)

A Comparative Evaluation of Podcasting-Based and Mobile-Based Material Distribution Systems in Foreign Language Teaching

Yuichi Ono[1], Manabu Ishihara[2], and Mitsuo Yamashiro[3]

[1] University of Tsukuba, Foreign Language Center, Ibaraki, Japan
`ono.yuichi.ga@u.tsukuba.ac.jp`
[2] Oyama National College of Technology, Electrical and Computer Engineering, Tochigi, Japan
`ishihara@oyama-ct.ac.jp`
[3] Ashikaga Institute of Technology, Electrical and Computer Engineering, Tochigi, Japan
`yamashiro@ashitech.ac.jp`

Abstract. This paper examines two independent multimedia distribution systems in terms of user's impression and the download time on the basis of the two experiments which were carried out in English teaching settings in Japan. The two are the podcasting system and the mobile-based system. The results of the two studies indicated that the students feel that mobiles are more friendly and easy to operate. Although it takes them longer time to download digital materials from the server, they do not feel so much frustrated or irritated for being delayed to a certain degree. These implications imply the future possibility for blended-instruction model of foreign language teaching in Japan.

Keywords: e-learning system, podcasting, mobile device, second language acquisition.

1 Introduction

The use of ICT provides learners with opportunities for linguistic input and output especially in a English-as-a-Foreign Language (EFL) environment such as Japan, since there is little chance to communicate with other people in that foreign language. In Japan the use of ICT is strongly recommended as a national policy in schools of both elementary and higher school administrations. On the other hand, how to incorporate ICT into curriculum is an urgent research topic that has be investigated.

This paper considers how the multimedia system for foreign language education should be carried out in Japan, and evaluates two multimedia distribution systems on user's impression which were actually carried out in a foreign language instruction in Japanese national college of technology. One of the traditional issues on foreign language teaching in Japan is how to guarantee a large amount of linguistic input in a foreign language classroom. As Web 2.0 advanced, several ICT-utilized systems to

M. Kurosu (Ed.): Human-Computer Interaction, Part II, HCII 2013, LNCS 8005, pp. 474–483, 2013.

distribute digital teaching materials like sound and movie, which we call Multimedia Distribution System (MDS), have been proposed to be incorporated naturally into foreign language classrooms. This study places much focus on the two of such systems that had an impact on the field of foreign language education: Podcasting and Mobile MDS.

Our earlier studies [1-2] reported the actual use of podcasting systems for TOEIC course and other studies [3-5] described the new type of blended-instruction model for reading course with the use of iPod Touch in the classroom and demonstrate the pedagogical effect and validity of incorporating this mobile tool into a non-wired traditional classroom.

The issues to be discussed in this paper include (i) construction of two multimedia tools and evaluation of the systems by learners, and (ii) effect of the length of download time on learner's frustration. It will be shown that the survey on Study (i) suggested that the factors such as "operability" of mobile devices were outstanding rather than that of podcasting, which implies the practicality for mobile-based blended instruction. Study (ii) suggested that the downloading time for the students to wait should be limited to less than 90 seconds. On the basis of these findings, this paper implies the future possibility of blending lecture and mobile-based e-Learning in classroom.

2 Outline of the Two System and Implementations

Our studies [1-2] describe the podcasting system outline adopted in the study. The schematic model of the system and the hardware and software adopted in our administration is given in Fig. 1 and Table 1 below.

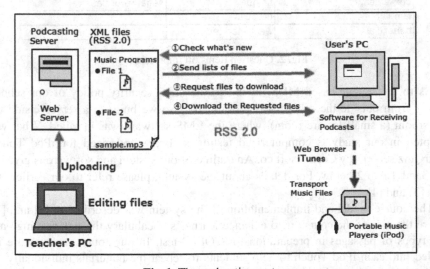

Fig. 1. The podcasting system

Table 1. Hardware and software (podcasting MDS)

CPU	Intel Pentium III 600MHz
RAM	768MB
HDD	20GB
OS	Fedora Core 5
HTTP Server	Apache 2.0.34
PHP	PHP 5.1.6
RDBMS	MySQL 5.0.18
Blog System	WordPress ME 2.0.9
WordPress Plugin	PodPress 3.8

After 15-week course was finished, the questionnaire was given to students. Participants answered all the items asking about the impression in using the system by scoring them on a 7-point Likert scale where 7 was very strongly affirmative and 1 was very strongly negative. The question items are adjectives describing impression in using the system. All the question items were written in Japanese and the translated list of adjectives is illustrated in Fig. 2 below:

feeling as if you were there	slow	desirable
easy to use	enjoyable	friendly
feeling united with others	not intelligent	constrained or uncomfortable
easy to listen to	feering free	dull
one-sided	relieved	feeling emptiness
good voice of speakers	common or ordinary	sociable
direct	causing willingness	dark
easy to understand	not interesting	strong
convenient	unique	negative or passive
familiar	difficult	
beneficial	warm-hearted	

Fig. 2. Question items on impression

As to the mobile-based MDS, owing to the strict security policy of our school, access from outside the school was prohibited. So we built up a server inside the classroom (a small lecture room), where the LMS software was installed. What was adopted in our study is computerized testing software optimized for iPod Touch, "starQuiz server" by Cosmicsoft co. An outline of our system and software is given in Fig.3 and Table 2 below. For details about the system, please refer to our earlier studies [3] and [4].

The course model and implementation of the system was described in [3] and [4], where the aim of the course is to enhance learner's vocabulary through reading various types of passages in preparation for TOEIC test. In our course, movies are installed into each iPod Touch to help students to repeat the materials individually for shadowing activities. After 6-week course, we carried out the questionnaire research asking the same questions on impression.

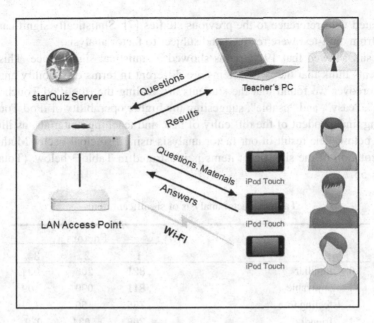

Fig. 3. Outline of mobile-based MDS

Table 2. Hardware and software (Mobile MDS)

CPU	Mac Mini Server	Intel Core 2 Duo 2.53GHz / 4GB Memory / 500GB ×2 HDD / Mac OS X Server Snow Leopard
Back-up HDD	Buffalo HD-CL1. OTU2	
Wireless LAN × 2	AirMac Extreme base station	IEEE 802.11n
Software	starQuiz Server	
USB Hub	ELECOM U2H-Z10SWH	10 port ×2
iPod	Touch iPod Touch 8G	

3   Study (1): Difference between Two Systems

79 forth-year students of national college of technology participated in this study. The aim of Study (1) is to find the difference of learner's impression on these two systems. The fourth-year student of college of technology is equivalent to first-year students in college or university. After completing the course, we carried out a survey on the basis of "Image Evaluation" method [6]. The 31 question items given in Fig. 2

were created with reference to the previous studies [7]. Statistically significant items resulted from out t-test were retained and subject to factor analysis.

The result showed that 19/31 items showed a statistical significance. This means that students think that the two systems are different in terms of usability and operability. Moreover we found that the students are feeling that the iPod Touch is more "friendly", "easy", and "usable", suggesting the higher operability of iPod Touch than podcasting, independent of the difficulty of task and teaching materials, as illustrated in Fig. 4 below. The result of our factor analysis using Principal Factor Method with Promax rotation of the significant items is illustrated in Table 3 below. (Total factor loading = 55.7 %)

Table 3. Factor analysis of significant items

		Factors		
		1	2	3
10	familiar	.821	.206	-.094
13	enjoyable	.811	.090	-.109
15	feeling free	.755	.156	-.129
24	friendly	.708	-.034	.079
2	easy to use	.644	.022	.030
9	convenient	.643	-.012	-.105
19	not interesting	.555	-.268	.132
23	desirable	.538	-.386	.128
11	beneficial	.484	-.181	.102
18	causing willingness	-.401	.157	.182
20	unique	.370	-.338	.066
27	feeling emptiness	.079	.842	.015
26	dull	.006	.738	.029
31	negative or passive	.063	.624	.244
29	dark	.113	.597	.281
4	easy to listen to	.212	-.446	.127
21	difficult	-.076	-.091	.917
25	constrained or uncomfortable	.027	.306	.524
17	common or ordinary	-.061	.142	.415

Table 3 indicated that four factors were abstracted. Factors 1, 2 and 3 were labeled as "Holistic impression toward the system", "Task" and "Materials" , respectively, on the basis of the items related. These results suggest that participants seem to recognize these three factors to be independent factors. Fig.4 further suggests that the operability of mobile devices seem to be highly evaluated, which has an implication for the

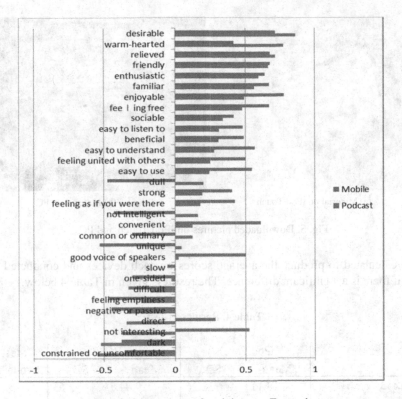

Fig. 4. Comparison of each item on Factor 1

possibility of introducing mobile MDS into a traditional classroom in foreign language teaching.

4   Study (2): Download Time and Frustration

As a pilot study, we made an attempt to deliver 10MB movie file on mobile-based system. As was expected, more than one-third of participants were not able to receive the digital materials within three minutes. This situation is really hard to manage in real classroom settings. Therefore, we gave up sending a digital movie file and decided to send only compressed digital picture files from the server instead (about 300KB) so that the time would be within about one minute. Each participant recorded the time taken to receive the file, and answered the questions about the impression and feelings about the time on a 5-point Likert scale. The pictures on both devices are given in Fig. 5 below.

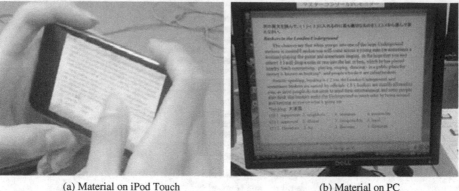

(a) Material on iPod Touch   (b) Material on PC

Fig. 5. Downloaded pictures on iPod Touch and PC

We calculated to produce the average scores on each devices and conducted t-test to see if there is a significant difference. The result is given in Table 4 below.

Table 4. Result of t-test

	iPod Touch		PC		t-test
	Mean	SD	Mean	SD	(two-tailed)
Download Time (sec)	53.11	38.26	9.44	2.63	**
took longer time	2.40	1.33	2.31	1.31	ns
comfortable	3.57	1.29	3.39	1.36	ns
frustrated	2.29	1.32	2.14	1.40	ns
found it easy	3.54	1.15	3.92	1.30	ns

(*:5% **:1%)

Although we can see a significant difference as to the time between the two devices, we find no significance about the impression or feeling toward the difference.

Next, we considered the relationship between items on feeling and the actual time. The correlation was listed in Table 5 below.

Table 5 suggests that there is a significant tendency on the correlation between the download time and frustration in the case of iPod Touch. The reason, it seems, comes from the fact that iPod Touch took longer time than PC. However, interestingly, there is a significance between the time and the feeling that it took longer time on the part of PC. Clearly PC took less time in downloading. It can be considered that students expect the PC-based system to be quicker in operation than iPod Touch.

Table 5. Correlation among items

Correlation(iPod Touch)

	Download Time	took longer time	comfortable	frustrated	found it easy
Download Time	1.0000	0.1562	-0.1769	0.2657	-0.2258
took longer time	0.1562	1.0000	-0.5691	0.4614	-0.2714
confortable	-0.1769	-0.5691	1.0000	-0.5670	0.5253
frustrated	0.2657	0.4614	-0.5670	1.0000	-0.3653
found it easy	-0.2258	-0.2714	0.5253	-0.3653	1.0000

p-value(*:5% **:1%)

	Download Time	took longer time	comfortable	frustrated	found it easy
Download Time	-	0.2503	0.1921	0.0478	0.0943
took longer time		-	0.0000	0.0003	0.0431
confortable		**	-	0.0000	0.0000
frustrated	*	**	**	-	0.0056
found it easy		*	**	**	-

Correlation(CALL PC)

	Download Time	took longer time	comfortable	frustrated	found it easy
Download Time	1.0000	0.4828	-0.2973	0.0992	-0.0893
took longer time	0.4828	1.0000	-0.5524	0.4931	-0.3562
confortable	-0.2973	-0.5524	1.0000	-0.5865	0.3437
frustrated	0.0992	0.4931	-0.5865	1.0000	-0.5617
found it easy	-0.0893	-0.3562	0.3437	-0.5617	1.0000

p-value(*:5% **:1%)

	Download Time	took longer time	comfortable	frustrated	found it easy
Download Time	-	0.0029	0.0783	0.5649	0.6045
took longer time	**	-	0.0005	0.0022	0.0330
confortable		**	-	0.0002	0.0401
frustrated		**	**	-	0.0004
found it easy		*	*	**	-

Lastly, we carried out the cluster analysis using Ward method with Euclidean distance on the basis of the data and how participants of each cluster recognized the situation. Four clusters were created for iPod Touch and three for PC. We calculated average scores on each cluster. The result was given in Table 6 below.

In this Table, we can observe that the cluster 1 of iPod Touch is the group for shortest downloaded time and that the cluster 2 has the most people, almost on the average. The clusters 3 and 4 are those who took longer downloaded time. Especially, people in cluster 4 spent more than 140 seconds. Looking at the "frustrated" row, we can find a clear difference in average scores between clusters 2 and 3. This means that here is a boundary on the scale of frustration; the estimated "comfortable" download time is less than 90 seconds. On the other hand, the cluster 3 of PC reveals that they were as frustrated even in 29 seconds. This is an interesting result again, and the students seem to expect PC will operate more quickly.

Table 6. Averages of each cluster

Cluster	Size	Download Time	took longer time	confortable	frustrated	found it easy
1	10	20.200	2.500	3.700	2.000	3.500
2	16	42.063	2.125	3.813	1.813	3.563
3	6	91.667	2.833	3.000	3.333	3.833
4	3	144.667	2.667	3.000	3.667	3.000

Class 1 (iPod Touch)

Cluster	Size	Download Time	took longer time	confortable	frustrated	found it easy
1	7	21.400	2.000	4.600	1.200	4.400
2	15	4.667	1.417	4.250	1.833	4.167
3	8	29.000	3.833	2.833	3.500	3.000

Class 2 (PC)

5   Concluding Remarks

This paper evaluated two multimedia distribution system actually carried out in a national college of technology in Japan in terms of usability and downloading time. The mobile-based MDS as proposed in our project showed that students feel friendly and easy to use, independent of the contents and difficulty of the materials, according to our factor analysis. This will provide an interesting implication that the in-class blended instruction, a combination of face-to-face lecture and the use of e-Learning, can be properly introduced in a foreign language teaching setting. This seems to be a very important point to be discussed. There are at least two major reasons for this. First, the cost for managing the Computer-Assisted Language Learning (CALL) System and such classrooms is surprisingly expensive. Secondly, it is a heavy burden for many foreign language teachers who are not familiar with computer use to conduct and manage the system. The use of friendly mobiles in a non-wired classroom can be a substitute for cheaper and more friendly post-CALL "one-to-one" learning environment. Although there are a lot of things to solve for implementation of the new system, this trend seems to be much worth pursuing in the future.

References

1. Ono, Y., Ishihara, M., Ideo, M.: A Design and a Practice of ELDP Project — LMS, Podcasting, and English Presentation Class. In: Proceedings of the 5th International CDIO Conference (2009) (CD publication)

2. Ono, Y., Ishihara, M.: Integration of the podcasting system and multimedia tools in second language teaching: practice, evaluation, and future implications in the theory of second language acquisition. In: Proceedings of Audio Language and Image Processing (IEEE/ICALIP), pp. 46–51 (2009)
3. Ono, Y., Ishihara, M.: Integrating mobile-based individual activities into the Japanese EFL classroom. International Journal of Mobile Learning and Organisation 6(2), 116–137 (2012)
4. Ono, Y., Ishihara, M.: The mobile-based training in an EFL classroom. In: Proceedings of the 19th International Conference on Computers in Education, pp. 422–424 (2011)
5. Ono, Y., Ishihara, M., Yamashiro, M.: Mobile–based shadowing materials in foreign language teaching. In: Proceedings of the 1st IEEE Global Conference on Consumer Electronics, pp. 90–93 (2012)
6. Maki, K.: What is 'image' engineering? – in order to analyze and utilize image properly. Maruzen Planets, 95–119 (2000)
7. Sakumoto, K., Ali, F.F., Sakurai, H., Sugimoto, M., Ishihara, M., Shikata, Y.: A comparison between voice-based and image-based WBT. The Educational Technology Research Journal 28, 249–252 (2004)

Recommendation of Collaborative Activities
in E-learning Environments

Pierpaolo Di Bitonto, Maria Laterza, Teresa Roselli, and Veronica Rossano

Department of Computer Science, University of Bari,
Via Orabona, 4 – 70125 Bari – Italy
dibitonto@di.uniba.it,
{teresa.roselli,veronica.rossano}@uniba.it

Abstract. In distance education environments, collaborative activities such as wikis, forums and chats play an important role in the e-learning experience because they promote communication among students and so allow cooperative learning settings to be implemented. Nevertheless, it could be difficult for learners to pick out the most interesting and appropriate collaborative activities to meet their learning needs. Recommender systems integrated in e-learning platforms are usually used mainly to help learners choose teaching resources, but they can also be useful to suggest the collaborative activities that best fit their learning objectives from a pedagogical point of view. In this context, the paper presents a recommendation approach able to suggest collaborative activities such as forums, chats, wikis and blogs, that combines dynamic clustering and prediction calculus on the basis of the learners' profiles and needs.

Keywords: Recommender system, collaborative learning, dynamic clustering.

1   Introduction

Collaborative activities, such as chats, forums, blogs, wikis, file sharing, are becoming increasingly popular in the field of Education because they are helpful tools that support both teaching and learning activities. In particular, they allow cooperative learning settings to be implemented in distance education, that foster deeper reflection and mutual growth processes in students. Although these activities promote communication among students, which is one of the basic requirements for a successful e-learning experience, it could be difficult for the learner to pick out the most interesting and appropriate activities for her/his learning needs. Ideally, e-learning platforms should be able to help students to address their information overload, suggesting the best collaborative activity to tackle next according to her/his preferred learning style, cognitive and metacognitive abilities, interests, and learning needs.

Recommender systems have taken on a leading role in many applications (such as in e-commerce, e-government, e-learning, etc.) where users have too many choices, too little time, and in which the information explosion makes the problem even more

M. Kurosu (Ed.): Human-Computer Interaction, Part II, HCII 2013, LNCS 8005, pp. 484–492, 2013.

difficult. A recommender system integrated in an e-learning platform could help learners not only to choose the best teaching resource, as usually happens, but also to suggest the best collaborative activity for her/his learning needs. Up to now great numbers of recommender systems in e-learning have been developed to suggest courses, learning materials [1], as well as relevant topics in a forum [2] but only few researches have combined clustering with recommendation techniques for suggesting collaborative activities to stimulate and support cooperative and collaborative learning [3].

The paper presents a recommendation approach integrated in an open source e-learning platform, designed to suggest collaborative activities such as forums, chats, wikis and blogs. The approach combines dynamic clustering of learners on the basis of their learning needs and prediction calculus of the most suitable new collaborative activities (in the sense that the specific user has not yet been involved in them) for the current learner on the basis of similar users' interests.

The paper is structured as follows: section 2 presents examples of recommendation systems in e-learning settings; section 3 provides a brief description of the proposed recommendation approach; section 4 illustrates an example of interaction on the Moodle platform; section 5 reports a preliminary evaluation of the recommendation approach's effectiveness and, finally, section 5 outlines some conclusions and future works.

2   Related Works

Nowadays, one of the most interesting challenges in the e-learning research field is to address the problem of information overload. Most of the existing recommender systems merely suggest educational resources such as: learning objects (LOs), simulations, demos, exercises and so forth. Altered Vista [13], for example, suggests web-based teaching resources to both students and teachers on the basis of a collaborative user-based method [14] and the multidimensional users' opinions. In particular, users can judge the usefulness of the resource, the accuracy of the information, the educational relevance for a specific learning objective and so on. Also the RACOFI system (Rule-Applying Collaborative Filtering system) [15], which suggests audio LOs via a collaborative technique, uses multidimensional ratings to evaluate LOs and to predict evaluations of the new resources that best fit the user queries.

In the Web 2.0 era, an e-learning experience cannot be limited to using the Net to convey learning materials, because it is also important to promote communication among students using collaborative activities such as chats, forums, blogs and wikis, which are one of the essential factors for a successful e-learning experience. Although they are becoming increasingly popular in Education, up to now only few researches have aimed to suggest collaborative learning resources. Among the examples of research in this direction there is the Personal Recommender System (PRS) [16], which suggests the most suitable learning activities to help the specific learner improve her/his learning path. In particular, the PRS employs a switching hybridization strategy in order to identify which is the most suitable prediction technique, between knowledge-based [17] and collaborative with demographic features. In other words, if only the student's interests are available, the system uses a knowledge-based technique; otherwise, if further information is available (motivation, time spent studying and so on) it uses the collaborative technique.

However, the use of merely recommender system methods, either pure or hybrid, is not sufficient to make effective suggestions. Usually, it is fruitful to combine the recommendation approach and web mining techniques. An example is Zaiane's research [18] that recommends, using the agents approach and web mining techniques, on-line learning activities or shortcuts in web-based learning on the basis of the user's access. The proposed e-learning recommender system, in fact, by using the association of rule mining, analyzes text messages sent during a specific discussion, identifies the context or theme of the discussion and offers the participants suggestions about exercises, previous users' posted messages on a conferencing system, on-line simulations, or simply a resource in the web. Another example is the recommender system described in Tang and McCalla [3], that suggests learning activities using clustering techniques. In particular, the proposed recommender approach firstly groups learners according to their learning interests and background knowledge using a clustering technique, then makes predictions based on the users' explicit ratings by a collaborative filtering technique.

Tang and McCalla stated that applying clustering before the prediction is made allows collaborative filtering to be guided towards obtaining more accurate recommendations. In accordance with this statement, our aim is to suggest collaborative activities to stimulate and support cooperative learning using clustering and collaborative recommendation techniques, but unlike the Tang and McCalla solution, the proposed approach combines dynamic clustering and collaborative filtering in order to predict the most suitable new collaborative activities (in the sense that the user has not yet been involved in them) for the current learner on the basis of similar users' interests.

3   The Recommendation Approach

Usually, a Recommender System is used to identify sets of items that are likely to be of interest to a certain user, exploiting a variety of information sources related to the user, the content items and perhaps also the recommendation context. The recommendation process starts with the specification of the initial set of data that is either explicitly provided by the user or is implicitly inferred by the system [9].

Over the past two decades many different pure or hybrid [10] algorithmic approaches have been proposed both to select and to rank the item set to be suggested. These algorithms can also be classified as *heuristic-* or *memory-based* and *model-based* according to the formulation of the function R [11].

The first two require all ratings, items, and user data to be stored in the memory and estimate the utility of each item for the current user using all the data collected, based on a certain heuristic assumption. For example, the assumption that two users who show similar preferences for already-seen items will have similar preferences for unseen items as well. The latter approach learns a predictive model offline (using statistical or machine learning methods) and uses this model to compute the function R for unseen items [12].

Collaborative recommendation algorithms are probably the most familiar and most widely implemented in many domains [10]. Beyond the data gathering and storing method, these algorithms aggregate ratings or recommendations of objects, recognize common features among users on the basis of their ratings, and generate new recommendations based on inter-user comparisons [10].

In particular, collaborative filtering is one of the most popular recommendation methods used in e-learning environments, because it estimates the utility of a teaching resource for a user on the basis of the ratings attributed to that particular resource by the community. In other words, a collaborative algorithm uses ratings on items already seen both by the active user and other system users to predict ratings for unseen items.

Despite the fact that the collaborative method has always been considered one of the best recommendation methods to use in e-learning, it has been proven that when it is combined with AI approaches the predictions can be more accurate and more effective recommendations are supplied to users. In particular, clustering techniques may be advantageous for group users (students or teachers) of an e-learning platform as a means of offering personalized learning contents, paths and activities. But study of the state of the art demonstrates that the use of clustering techniques is not yet widespread. This is probably due to the fact that the most popular clustering algorithms require the number of clusters in which the users will be divided to be known a priori, which is not the most efficient approach for use in an e-learning community where users and preferences evolve continuously.

The proposal presented here addresses this problem, achieving dynamic clustering of learners by combining the Silhouette index and K-means algorithm.

3.1   The Dynamic Clustering of Learners

The main aim of the proposed algorithmic approach is to suggest collaborative activities such as forums, chats, wikis and blogs in an e-learning environment. In particular, the defined approach combines *dynamic clustering*, that clusters the learner on the basis of her/his learning needs, with the prediction of the most suitable new collaborative activities to be proposed on the basis of the interests of similar users to the target one.

In general, the main goal of clustering is to group objects into clusters so that the objects in the same cluster are more similar to each other than to those in other clusters. One of the most commonly used clustering algorithms in recommender systems is the K-means [4], which classifies a given data set in a number of clusters specified in advance. In the e-learning context, where the learning dimensions (preferences, goal, background knowledge, etc.) have a high level of dynamism, the need to specify a priori the number of clusters is an important drawback of this clustering method. For this reason, the proposed solution uses dynamic clustering [6], which classifies learners on the basis of similar learning needs and interests, without requiring an initial indication of the number of clusters. In particular, the proposed approach uses the *Silhouette index* [5] to estimate the optimal number of clusters in which to group the data set and the *K-means algorithm* [4] to cluster the data set into the optimal, previously defined partition.

Let us consider a data set with n samples that has to be divided into k clusters, whereby the Silhouette index will be:

$$Sil(i) = \frac{b(i) - a(i)}{\max\{a(i), b(i)\}} \tag{1}$$

where $a(i)$ is the average dissimilarity of sample i to all other samples within the same cluster computed using a distance measure; $b(i)$ is the lowest average dissimilarity of i to any other cluster. In other words, the lower the values of both $a(i)$ and $b(i)$ the better the match. Function $Sil(i)$ ranges from -1 to 1; when it is close to 1 it means that the sample is appropriately clustered; if it is close to 0 it means that the sample is on the border of two natural clusters; otherwise if it is close to -1 it is misclassified.

In the e-learning context the sample is composed of learners, and each learner will be represented by a vector describing her/his learning needs inferred in several ways according to the available tracking data in the e-learning platform, such as the assessment test results, time spent by the learner on a teaching resource, and so on.

Using the formula (1), in an iterative procedure, it is possible to calculate several values of *Sil* corresponding to different clustering solutions. The optimal number of clusters corresponds to the largest value of the *Silouette index*. The number of clusters calculated is the input of the K-means algorithm, which aims to classify the sample of learners in the defined number of clusters [19].

When the clustering process is completed the data set is partitioned in several clusters of users, so that the learners in the same cluster have similar learning needs. In each cluster there is a center, named *centroid,* that is used during the prediction calculus in order to identify the neighbourhood of the target learner. The neighbourhood is defined by computing the similarity of two clusters, i.e. the similarity of their centroids. Those clusters that have the highest Pearson correlation coefficient from the centroid of the target learner cluster is the learner's neighbourhood. Thus, the prediction calculus step computes a score for all the collaborative activities in which the target learner has not yet been involved, on the basis of the interests showed by the users belonging to the learner's neighbourhood. In other words, the learner's favourite collaborative activities are inferred through the rate of interventions of pairs that have similar learning needs and interests in a collaborative tool (chat, forum, wiki or blog).

The proposed recommender approach can be easily implemented and integrated in any e-learning platform, in order to suggest the best collaborative learning activity for the learner. In particular, we have implemented a plug-in for one of the most commonly used open source e-learning platforms: Moodle

4   Example of Interaction in Moodle

In order to validate the proposed recommendation system a plug-in in Moodle has been implemented, which allows forums, chats, and wikis to be suggested. The plug-in architecture consists of three components (Fig.1):

— The *Data Gathering Component* (DGC) analyses and extracts the tracking data from the Moodle DB. As described above, each learner is described by using a vector in which learning needs and interests are coded. The learning needs are inferred using data about her/his participation in courses and test results. The learner's interests are inferred using her/his participation in forums, chats and wikis. In particular, as regards interest in a forum, it is calculated as the percentage of the user's posts, in the forums of a specific course, out of the total number of posts since her/his first intervention. For chat the measure of interest is the user's participation in different chats about a course, in other words the percentage is calculated on the number of chats in which the learner has taken part, out of the total number of chats in the course. The same process has been used for wikis, whereby the percentage is calculated as the number of actions in the shared documents out of the total number of actions;

— The *Clustering Component* (CC) clusters the users using the data collected by the DGC. Firstly, using the Silhouette index it defines the optimal number of clusters, then by using the K-means algorithm it classifies learners in the defined number of clusters. The output of this component is the definition of classes of users with similar learning needs;

— The *Prediction Component* (PC) computes a score for all the collaborative activities in which the user has not yet been involved. Firstly, the target learner neighbourhood is identified by computing the Pearson correlation coefficient [7] among this and all the other cluster centroids; then, using the data about the interest in forums, chats and wikis of neighbours, the prediction on the unseen collaborative activities is calculated.

Fig. 1. Recommender system components

5   Results and Discussions

There are already a large number of studies offering empirical evidence that users prefer a recommender system that provides more accurate predictions. In the e-learning domain, we assumed that a recommender is successful if it is able to provide accurate predictions and to promote a deeper level of learning. Thus, for the defined approach it is necessary to measure both the prediction accuracy. In our pilot study we measured the prediction accuracy only for the forums, because they were the collaborative activity used in the specific experimental context. In particular, the prediction accuracy has been evaluated using the popular precision and recall metrics [8], where the precision is the fraction of retrieved items that are relevant to the search, while recall is the fraction of relevant items that are retrieved by query. A forum was assumed to be relevant for the target user if after the recommendation the learner decided to participate in it.

In order to have a meaningful sample to measure the quality of the suggestions supplied, students and forums focusing on different courses at the Multimedial Advanced Educational Technology Laboratory of the Science Faculties at the University of Bari were enrolled. This Laboratory offers e-learning services to different degree courses of the Science Faculty. In particular, the recommendation system has been applied in two degree courses on Informatics and Digital Communication (located in Bari and Taranto). The sample considered consists of 234 students, 10 courses and 26 forums.

The recall points were fixed and the precision was calculated for each of them. Because precision values were lacking for some standard recall points (0%, 10%, 20%...,100%), interpolated precision values were computed. The average precision values were computed considering 50 recommendation requests corresponding to standard recall levels.

Finally, a precision-recall curve was drawn. It emphasizes the proportion of preferred items that were actually recommended (Fig.2).

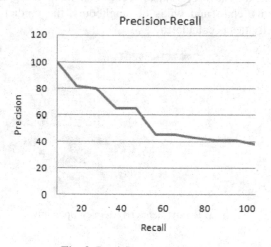

Fig. 2. Precision-recall curve

Results showed a high prediction accuracy mainly for low recall values (up to 30%). Average values of precision ranged between 20% and 50% of recall. Finally, the precision value is lower when recall is about 60% and remains constant up to 100%. Moreover, the curve is very distant from the origin of the axes. To summarize, the recommender system shows a good performance and supplies accurate predictions.

6   Conclusions and Future Works

Collaborative activities are very helpful tools in e-learning environments because they promote cooperative learning and deeper reflection. However, due to the great number of activities in which the learner could be involved in an e-learning platform, it may be difficult for her/him to choose the most appropriate activities for her/his learning needs and interests.

This problem can be solved by using recommendation systems integrated in e-learning platforms that suggest the best collaborative activities according to the user's preferred learning style, cognitive and metacognitive abilities, interests, and learning needs.

The paper illustrates the added value of combining dynamic clustering with collaborative filtering. The proposed solution, in fact, is a two step approach that combines the *dynamic clustering* of the learner on the basis of her/his learning needs and interests, and the *prediction calculus* of the most suitable collaborative activity (in which the user has not yet been involved) for the current user according to the favourite collaborative activities of users with similar learning needs and interests.

The defined recommender approach can be easily implemented and integrated in any e-learning platform, in order to suggest the collaborative learning activities best suited to each learner. In order to evaluate our approach, we have implemented it in a plug-in for one of the most commonly used open source e-learning platforms: Moodle. The approach was evaluated using data gathered from interactions of students on different courses in the Multimedial Advanced Educational Technology Laboratory of the Science Faculties at the University of Bari. Based on the results obtained, it is clear that the accuracy of the recommendation is very high. An evaluation aimed at comparing the recommendation accuracy of the proposed approach with traditional recommendation algorithms is currently being planned.

References

1. Wang, P.Y.: The Analysis and Design of Educational Recommender Systems. In: Carlsen, R., et al. (eds.) Proceedings of Society for Information Technology & Teacher Education International Conference 2007, pp. 2134–2140. AACE, Chesapeake (2007)
2. Castro-Herrera, C., Cleland-Huang, J., Mobasher, B.: A recommender system for dynamically evolving online forums. In: Proceedings of the Third ACM Conference on Recommender systems (RecSys 2009), pp. 213–216. ACM, New York (2009)
3. Tang, T., McCalla, G.: Smart recommendation for an evolving e-learning system. International Journal on E-Learning 4(1), 105–129 (2005)
4. Steinbach, M., Karypis, G., Kumar, V.: A comparison of document clustering techniques. In: KDD Workshop on Text Mining, vol. 400, pp. 525–526 (2000)
5. Jaafar, A., Sareni, B., Roboam, X.: Clustering analysis of railway driving missions with niching. COMPEL: The International Journal for Computation and Mathematics in Electrical and Electronic Engineering 31(3), 920–931 (2012)

6. Chiang, M.M.-T., Mirkin, B.: Experiments for the Number of Clusters in K-Means. In: Neves, J., Santos, M.F., Machado, J.M. (eds.) EPIA 2007. LNCS (LNAI), vol. 4874, pp. 395–405. Springer, Heidelberg (2007)

7. Ben Schafer, J., Frankowski, D., Herlocker, J., Sen, S.: Collaborative Filtering Recommender Systems. In: Brusilovsky, P., Kobsa, A., Nejdl, W. (eds.) Adaptive Web 2007. LNCS, vol. 4321, pp. 291–324. Springer, Heidelberg (2007)

8. Shani, G., Gunawardana, A.: Evaluating recommendation systems. In: Ricci, F., Rokach, L., Shapira, B. (eds.) Recommender Systems Handbook, pp. 257–298. Springer (2011)

9. Adomavicius, G., Kwon, Y.: New Recommendation Techniques for Multi-Criteria Rating Systems. IEEE Intelligent Systems 22, 48–55 (2007)

10. Burke, R.: Hybrid Recommender Systems: Survey and Experiments. User Modeling and User-Adapted Interaction 12(4), 331–370 (2002) ISSN: 0924-1868, doi:10.1023/A:1021240730564

11. Ricci, F., Rokach, L., Shapira, B., Kantor, P.B. (eds.): Recommender Systems Handbook. Springer Science + Business Media, New York (2011) ISBN/ISSN: 9780387858197 0387858199, doi: 10.1007/978-0-387-85820-3_2, LLC 201

12. Breese, J.S., Heckerman, D., Kadie, C.: Empirical analysis of predictive algorithms for collaborative filtering. In: Proceedings of the 14th Annual Conference on Uncertainty in Artificial Intelligence, pp. 43–52 (1998)

13. Walker, A., Recker, M., Lawless, K., Wiley, D.: Collaborative information filtering: A review and an educational application. International Journal of Artificial Intelligence and Education 14, 3–28 (2004)

14. Ben Schafer, J., Frankowski, D., Herlocker, J., Sen, S.: Collaborative filtering recommender systems. In: Brusilovsky, P., Kobsa, A., Nejdl, W. (eds.) Adaptive Web 2007. LNCS, vol. 4321, pp. 291–324. Springer, Heidelberg (2007)

15. Anderson, M., Ball, M., Boley, H., Greene, S., Howse, N., Lemire, D., McGrath, S.: RACOFI: a Rule-Applying Collaborative Filtering System. IEEE/WIC, Halifax (2003)

16. Drachsler, H., Hummel, H.G.K., Van den Berg, B., Eshuis, J., Berlanga, A.J., Nadolski, R.J., Waterink, W., Boers, N., Koper, R.: Recommendation strategies for e-learning: preliminary effects of a personal recommender system for lifelong learners, Maastricht (2007)

17. Burke, R.: Knowledge-based Recommender Systems. In: Kent, A. (ed.) Encyclopedia of Library and Information Systems, Marcel Dekker, New York (2000)

18. Zaiane, O.: Building a recommender agent for e-learning systems. In: ICCE, pp. 55–59 (2002)

19. Wang, K., Zhang, J., Li, D., Zhang, X., Guo, T.: Adaptive Affinity Propagation Clustering. Acta Automatica Sinica 33(12)

Nature Sound Ensemble Learning in Narrative-Episode Creation with Pictures

Kosuke Takano[1] and Shiori Sasaki[2]

[1] Department of Computer and Information Sciences, Kanagawa Institute of Technology, Japan
takano@ic.kanagawa-it.ac.jp
[2] Graduate School of Media and Governance, Keio University, Japan
sashiori@sfc.keio.ac.jp

Abstract. This paper presents a Web-based nature sound ensemble learning system that allows students to create a narrative-episode with "visual", "auditory", and "experimental" effects. Main component of our system is implemented in the Web environment and can be easily introduced to PCs in a classroom for nature sound ensemble lessons among remote learners, classes, and schools. In this study, we show the feasibility of our Web-based ensemble learning system, where several learners actually participate in the remote nature sound ensemble lessons using example "narrative-episode" with pictures and nature sounds.

Keywords: music, nature sound, collaborative learning, physical expression, sensor, Web-based system, sensibility expression, sensibility education.

1   Introduction

It has been important issues in computer-assisted music learning that the design and development of interactive learning materials for fostering learner's skills and abilities of performing musical instruments. In this paper, we focus our discussion on the ensemble lesson at school, where it is pointed out that not only the progress of playing technique is important, but also the development of each learner's abilities in collaboration and creativity in expression should be focused on. For example, the new textbook for elementary school teachers from the Japanese Ministry of Education, Culture, Sports, Science and Technology (MEXT) defines the objectives of music education for the next generation as "fostering not only basic ability of musical activities but also love, Kansei (Sensibility in Japanese) and sentiment for music by appreciation and expression focusing on musical elements and mood." [1]

On the contrary, as seen in consumer game products, there are advanced computer-based technologies that allow users to play instruments by simple combinations of physical gestures without a high playing technique for musical instrument. By applying such computer-based technologies, we have designed ensemble lessons focused on the development of the learner's sense of collaboration with tempo, rhythm and melody. In music education, it is an important issue to teach concepts of rhythm, structure, and musical expression using movement [2].

M. Kurosu (Ed.): Human-Computer Interaction, Part II, HCII 2013, LNCS 8005, pp. 493–502, 2013.
© Springer-Verlag Berlin Heidelberg 2013

Eurhythmics proposed by Émile Jaques-Dalcroze [10] and *Eurhythmy* promoted by Rudolf Steiner [11] are famous methodologies to cultivate learners' sense and interest for music and help learners to discover the way to compose music not only by teaching playing techniques, but also by physical awareness and experience of music in the pleasure. Several researches based on similar approaches have been studied and developed to realize interactive and physical music learning environment using computer-based technology and physical music devices as well as lesson curriculums. For instance, Antle and Bakker focus on the learning of music creation and suggest lesson curriculum by leveraging embodied metaphor learning methods [3, 4, 5]. In addition, many researches attempt to make a new music instrument for improving performance skill of music players or giving more opportunities to express a person's ideas using music [6, 7, 8, 9]. Gao et al. [6] propose an adaptive learning approach based on maximum a posteriori to adapt a player's foot-tapping to synchronize with music based on the knowledge perceived from the previous excerpt. Holland et al. [7] present a Haptic Drum Kit for teaching and refining drumming skills as well as fostering skills in recognizing, analyzing, and composing rhythms.

Based mainly on these music learning methodologies and concepts such as Eurhythmics, we present a prototype of Web-based music learning system that allows students to create a narrative-episode with "visual", "auditory", and "experimental" effects. Our system is designed for nature-sound ensemble lessons among remote learners, classes, and schools. We have implemented our prototype in the Web environment where ensemble information can be delivered broadcast/multicast. In addition, our system can obtain sensor data from acceleration sensor devices (Nintendo Wii controller) so that students can play nature sound according to their actual physical motions.

In our ensemble learning system, nature sounds caused by such objects as wind, river, leaf, animal and insect, can be assigned to each animated picture for narrative-episode creation. In the lesson, attendees/learners make "narrative music" by improvisation according to their feelings and imagination. To support their imagination process, other multimedia such as still-images (photos or pictures), motion pictures (films, animations, or video clips), audio (reading poetries, BGM, or narrations), or text data are provided as materials indicating a theme of the improvisation. For example, a nature-themed narrative music is created based on a sequential three images: (1) clear sky, (2) sudden rain, (3) rainbow. The participants/learners perform improvisation by playing natural sounds associated with the photos or pictures. By using these kinds of multimedia, the participants/learners can make collaboration based on the theme and their imagination even if they cannot read musical score.

In this paper, in addition to practical lesson scenarios using our prototype system, we present the feasibility of our Web-based ensemble learning system, where several learners actually participate in the remote ensemble lessen using narrative-episode with pictures and nature sounds. By using this prototype system, we conducted initial studies focusing on the capability of ensemble data transmission and ensure that nature sound ensemble and animation effects can be performed at proper timing in each remote PC client.

2   System Architecture and Implementation

Fig.1 shows the architecture of our system. Our system provides a remote ensemble learning system using nature sounds and pictures for narrative-episode creation by sharing ensemble information among remote clients on the Web environment.

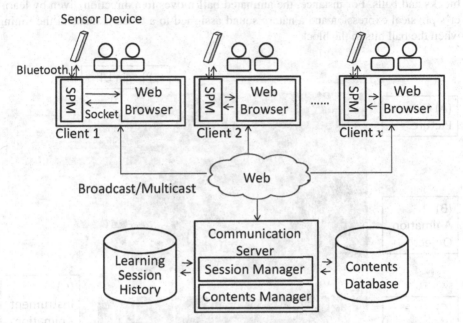

Fig. 1. Architecture of proposed system

Each client's component consists of a Web-based GUI, a sensor device, and a sensor processing module. The sensor processing module receives sensor values such as acceleration data from the sensor device via Bluetooth connection, and sends them to a main component of the ensemble system running on a web browser. Our ensemble learning system uses the sensor values for making nature sounds and changes a movement of animation object on the GUI.

2.1   GUI of Nature Sound Ensemble Learning System

The GUI of our system is provided on the Web browser, and consists of (A)(B) a current picture of episode with animation objects, (C) pictures for making an episode with time-line, and (D) CG instruments (Fig. 2).

As shown in Fig. 2, in the component of the "current picture of episode with animation objects", leaners shows animation objects that assorts well with pictures and episodes and add suitable motion representation to the animation objects. The motion representation of animation objects is changed according to sensor values received from sensor devices by learner's physical expression. Fig. 4 indicates basic motion of animation objects based on learner's physical expression that we defined in [2]. In the component of the "pictures for making an episode with time-line", user can sort pictures and photos by drag and drop them, and create an original episode on the timeline (Fig. 3).

In addition, the CG Instrument is a user interface for visualizing timing of making a sound by physical expression, and consists of images or simple shapes such as blocks and balls. For instance, the animated ball moves to a direction given by learner's physical expression and a nature sound assigned to a block is made at the timing when the ball hits to the block.

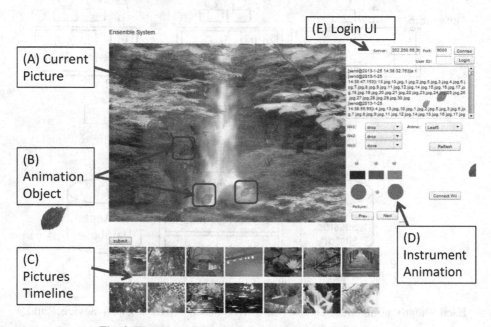

Fig. 2. Web-based GUI of our nature sound ensemble system

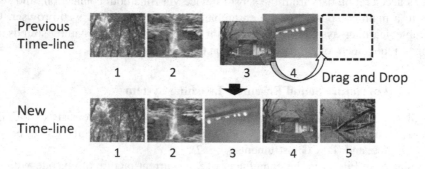

Fig. 3. Pictures for episode with time-line

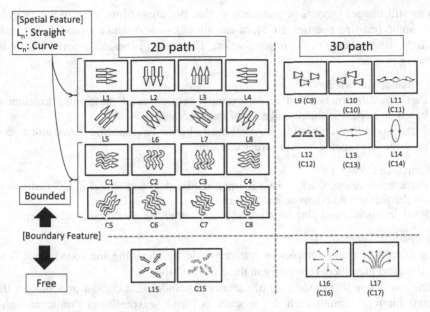

Fig. 4. Basic motion of animation object by physical expression

2.2   Network Communication Server

Network communication server is running on a single host. Clients communicate ensemble information each other via TCP/IP connection. The clients share an ensemble learning session by logon to the communication server. The ensemble information from each client is transmitted to the communication server using commands as shown in Table 1, and delivered to each client from the communication server by broadcast/multicast.

Table 1. Commands of transmitting/receiving ensemble information

	Command	Argument	Example
Sound	s	ID of sound	s:1
Picture	p	ID of picture	p:2
Animation objects	a	ID of animation object	a:1
Order of episode	i	Array of picture ID	i:1.jpg,2.jpg,...,n.jpg
Basic motion of animation objects	l	ID of basic motion	l:1
Additional motion of animation objects	m	8 direction	m:1

3   Lesson Scenario and Example Narrative-Episodes

In lesson scenario, attendees/learners make "narrative music" according to their feelings and imagination. To support attendees/learners imagination process, multimedia such as still-images (photos or pictures), motion pictures (films, animations, or video clips), audio (reading poetries, BGM, or narrations), or text data are provided as materials indicating a theme of the improvisation. The lesson is basically performed in the following steps:

[Performance Knowledge]
1. Participants/learners listen to the example sequences of performing instruments based on a specific theme and a set of multimedia.
2. Participants/learners play improvised music based on a specific theme and a set of multimedia prepared by an instructor/teacher.

[Performance Context]
3. Participants/learners select favorite multimedia data and sound in CG instrument, set the theme, and compose a story/narrative.
4. Participants/learners play improvised music under the condition fixed in step 3.

[Performance Adaptation]
   Participants/learners complete narrative music by changing the sounds in CG instruments and play them repeatedly in the collaboration.
   Here, we show three examples of narrative-episodes that consist of 4 images that selected for representing each theme such as "four seasons" and "walk through a mountain in early summer". The example episodes are as follows:

[Episode 1]

	Scene 1	Scene 2	Scene 3	Scene 4
A	Cherry blossom	Fire flake	Maple	Snowflake
L	C2	L15	C2	C2
S	bird	fire flower	wind bell	wind

A: animation objects, L: basic motion, S: sound

[Theme] Nature and seasonal tradition in four seasons
[Episode and performance instruction]

Scene 1: A bush warbler is idyllically singing in full cherry blossom.
   <Performance> Move to Scene 2 after second singing of the bush warbler

Scene 2: Fireworks are rising in the night sky.
   <Performance> Add suitable motions to "fire flake" at the timing of "fire flake" sound

Scene 3: Maple is beautifully in red leaf, and a wind bell is ringing in silence.
   <Performance> Move to scene 4 after third ringing of the wind bell

Scene 4: The weather is fine in a snow mountain, but cold wind is blowing.
<Performance> Add to right and left motions to "snowflake" at the timing of wind sounds.

[Episode 2]

	Scene 1	Scene 2	Scene 3	Scene 4
A	Clover	Leaf	Drop	Blink star
L	C2	C2	L2	C2
S	Frog, tiny bird	Walk on grass, buzz of a cicada	Water dropping	River

[Theme] Waking through a mountain in early summer
[Episode and performance instruction]

Scene 1: Red bridge is in our view and we can hear frogs and tiny birds sing.
   <Performance> Tiny birds begin to sing after singing of frogs, and move to Scene 3.

Scene 2: We walk through trees with young leaves.
   <Performance> Cicada starts to buzz after sound of walking. Then move to Scene 3.

Scene 3: When taking a break, we can see water is dripping from leaf of grass
   <Performance> Move to scene 4 after repetition of water-dripping sound

Scene 4: We can see river stream and hear its sound.
   <Performance> Add right and left motions to "blink star" at the timing of wind sounds

[Episode 3]

	Scene 1	Scene 2	Scene 3	Scene 4
A	Blink star	Drop	Rain	Blink star
L	C2	L2	L8	C2
S	Wind bell	Thunder, water dripping	Rain, wind	Cicada, wind bell

[Theme] Sudden rain
[Episode and performance instruction]

Scene 1: Wind bell is ringing in the brisk blue sky of summer.
   <Performance> Move to Scene 2 after second ringing of the wind bell.

Scene 2: The rain cloud begins to cover sky, and we can hear clap of thunder.
   <Performance> Rain drop starts to fall after the clap of thunder. After the sound of rain-dropping, move to Scene 3.

Scene 3: The rain is strongly falling.
   <Performance> Make a sound of strong rain at switching Scene 3. Make a sound of wind at a proper timing, and add left motion to "rain" with the sound of wind. Move to scene 4 after repetition of the wind sound

Scene 4: We can see rainbow in the sky after the heavy rain.
   <Performance> Cicadas start to buzz. Make sounds of wind bell in the last.

4   Experiment

In the experiment, we conducted a nature sound ensemble lesson using three example episodes and scenario as described in Section 3. Three learners participated in the lesson using their own client PCs. Learner 1 and 2 connected to the same university network where the communication server is located, and learner 3 used an external Internet connection provided by a commercial Internet provider. The rolls of each leaner are as follows:

Learner 1: Picture (p), order of episode (i)
Learner 2: Sound (s)
Learner 3: Animation objects (a), additional motion of animation objects (m)

In order to make a sound or add an animation motion, the learners 2 and 3 use Nintendo Wii controllers as acceleration sensor devices.

In the evaluation, we mainly focus on the capability of ensemble data transmission in order to test that nature sound ensemble and animation effects can be performed at proper timing in each remote PC clients. Table 2 shows the performance time of each episode in the lesson, and Tables 3, 4, 5, and 6 show the average time of data transmission in each command. All participants synchronize clock on their PCs using Internet Time Server in advance, but, we could not synchronize clocks in a milli-seconds unit. So, we checked the difference of time on each PC's clock in a milli-seconds unit, and correct the latency time in Tables 3, 4, 5, and 6.

From these results, we can confirm that the network latency of each command by multicast is within 200[ms], and it is deemed that this latency is not affected to perform nature sound ensemble among remote clients. Actually, all participants could feel that their ensemble of each example episode was performed smoothly without any stresses arisen from the network latency.

Table 2. Performance time of each episode

	Time
Episode 1	1 min.
Episode 2	1 min 40 sec
Episode 3	2 min 10 sec

Table 3. Average time of data transmission in episode 1

	Command	Frequency	Average time of data transmission [ms]
Sound	s	9	180.08
Picture	p	3	142.08
Animation objects	a	3	179.16
Order of episode	i	1	148.75
Additional motion of animation objects	m	39	192.70
		[Total] 55	[Average] 168.55

Table 4. Average time of data transmission in episode 2

	Command	Frequency	Average time of data transmission [ms]
Sound	s	7	158.46
Picture	p	3	96.08
Animation objects	a	3	171.50
Order of episode	i	1	131.75
Additional motion of animation objects	m	65	171.50
		[Total] 79	[Average] 147.92

Table 5. Average time of data transmission in episode 3

	Command	Frequency	Average time of data transmission [ms]
Sound	s	11	136.65
Picture	p	3	104.08
Animation objects	a	4	181.50
Order of episode	i	1	109.75
Additional motion of animation objects	m	68	160.60
		[Total] 87	[Average] 138.51

Table 6. Average time of data transmission (Average of episode 1 to 3)

	Command	Frequency	Average time of data transmission [ms]
Sound	s	27	158.40
Picture	p	9	114.08
Animation objects	a	10	177.38
Order of episode	i	3	130.08
Additional motion of animation objects	m	172	178.37
		[Total] 221	[Average] 151.66

5 Conclusion

In this paper, we have presented a prototype of Web-based nature sound ensemble learning system with "visual", "auditory", and "experimental" effects.

In the evaluation, we mainly focus on the capability of ensemble data transmission in order to test that nature sound ensemble and animation effects can be performed at proper timing in each remote PC clients. From the experimental results, we confirmed that the network latency of each command by multicast is within 200[ms]. We conclude that this latency is not affected to perform nature sound ensemble among remote client. Our Web-based ensemble learning system can be developed as a practical application where multiple learners actually participate in the real-time remote ensemble lessons for making narrative-episode creation with pictures and nature sounds.

As future work, we will perform demonstration experiments at an elementary school. Through the practical use in the class, we will validate the effectiveness of our proposed music system based on the feedback from teachers and learners, as well as improving our system and lesson curriculum.

Acknowledgments. We appreciate that Ms. Kaede Yamazaki and Mr. Ryo Hoshino at Kanagawa Institute of Technology participated in our experiments.

References

1. Sasaki, S., Watagoshi, K., Takano, K., Hirashima, K., Kiyoki, Y.: Impression-oriented music courseware and its application in elementary schools. Interactive Technology and Smart Education (ITSE) 7(2), 85–101 (2010)
2. Takano, K., Sasaki, S.: An Interactive Music Learning System in Ensemble Performance Class. In: The Proceedings of Sixth International Conference on Broadband and Wireless Computing, Communication and Applications (BWCCA 2011), pp. 65–74 (2011)
3. Antle, A.N., Droumeva, M., Corness, G.: Playing with the sound maker: do embodied metaphors help children learn? In: Proceedings of the 7th International Conference on Interaction Design and Children (IDC 2008), pp. 178–185 (2008)
4. Bakker, S., Antle, A.N., van den Hoven, E.: Identifying embodied metaphors in children's sound-action mappings. In: Proceedings of the 8th International Conference on Interaction Design and Children (IDC 2009), pp. 140–149 (2009)
5. Bakker, S., van den Hoven, E., Antle, A.N.: MoSo tangibles: evaluating embodied learning. In: Proceedings of the Fifth International Conference on Tangible, Embedded, and Embodied Interaction (TEI 2011), pp. 85–92 (2011)
6. Gao, S., Lee, C.-H.: An adaptive learning approach to music tempo and beat analysis. Proceedings of IEEE International Conference on Acoustics, Speech, and Signal Processing (ICASSP 2004) 4, 237–240 (2004)
7. Holland, S., Bouwer, A.J., Dalgelish, M., Hurtig, T.M.: Feeling the beat where it counts: fostering multi-limb rhythm skills with the haptic drum kit. In: Proceedings of the Fourth International Conference on Tangible, Embedded, and Embodied Interaction (TEI 2010), pp. 21–28 (2010)
8. Stanley, T.D., Calvo, D.: Rhythm learning with electronic simulation. In: Proceedings of the 10th ACM Conference on SIG-Information Technology Education (SIGITE 2009), pp. 24–28 (2009)
9. Tanaka, A., Tokui, N., Momeni, A.: Facilitating collective musical creativity. In: Proceedings of the 13th Annual ACM International Conference on Multimedia (MULTIMEDIA 2005), pp. 191–198 (2005)
10. Mead, V.H.: Dalcroze Eurhythmics in Today's Musi Classroom. Schott Musik Intl. (June 1996)
11. Karl Stockmeyer, E.A.: Rudolf Steiner's Curriculum for Waldorf Schools. Steiner Waldorf Schools Fellowship (1985), 4th Revised (April 1, 2001)

Private Cloud Cooperation Framework
for Reducing the Earthquake Damage
on e-Learning Environment

Satoshi Togawa[1] and Kazuhide Kanenishi[2]

[1] Faculty of Management and Information Science, Shikoku University, Japan
doors@shikoku-u.ac.jp
[2] Center for University Extention, The University of Tokushima, Japan
marukin@cue.tokushima-u.ac.jp

Abstract. In this research, we have built a framework of reducing earthquake and tsunami disaster for e-Learning environment. We build a prototype system based on IaaS architecture, and this prototype system is constructed by several private cloud fabrics. The distributed storage system builds on each private cloud fabric; that is handled almost like same block device such as one large file system. For LMS to work, we need to boot virtual machines. The virtual machines are booted from the virtual disk images that are stored into the distributed storage system. The distributed storage system will be able to keep running as one large file system when some private cloud fabric does not work by any troubles. We think that our inter-cloud framework can continue working for e-Learning environment under the post-disaster situation.

Keywords: e-Learning environment, inter-cloud framework, disaster reducing.

1 Introduction

On March 11, 2011, a major earthquake attacked to Eastern Japan. Especially, the east coast of Eastern Japan was severely damaged by the tsunami attacking. In Shikoku area including our universities in Tokushima prefecture, it is predicted that Nankai earthquake will happen in the near future. It is expected to have Nankai earthquake in the next 30 years, and its occurrence rate is between 70 percent and 80 percent. We have to prepare for the major earthquake. It will be like Eastern Japan Great Earthquake that the damage caused by earthquake and tsunami was heavy. It is very important disaster control, and it is same situation for information system's field.

On the other hand, the informatization of education environment on universities is rapidly progressed by evolutional information technology. Current education environment cannot be realized without education assistance system, such as LMS, learning ePortfolio, teaching ePortfolio and so on. The learning history of students is stored these education assistance system. The fact is that awareness of the importance of learning data such as learning histories and teaching histories. The assistance systems are important same as learning data. In addition, an integrated authentication

M. Kurosu (Ed.): Human-Computer Interaction, Part II, HCII 2013, LNCS 8005, pp. 503–510, 2013.

framework of inter-organization is used to share the course materials. For example, Shibboleth Federations is used to authenticate other organization's user for sharing the course materials within consortium of universities. Today's universities educational activity cannot continue smoothly without those learning data and assistance system. If the data and assistance systems lost by disasters, it is difficult to continue educational activity.

We can find applications for constructing information system infrastructure by the private cloud technology for universities. Generally, those application examples are based on a server machine virtualization technology such as IaaS (Infrastructure as a Service). For example, we can find Hokkaido University Academic Cloud [1]. One of the aims of this system is to provide a lot of Virtual Machines (VMs) which are kitted out with the processing ability of huge multiple requests by VMs administrator. The VMs administrator can get constructed VM with an administrator authority. It is server hosting service with adaptive configuration for VM's administrator. Other case is to provide huge resources for distributed data processing infrastructure such as Hadoop framework [2]. Their aims are to provide effective use of computer hardware resources, and providing a centralized control of computer hardware resources. It is different purpose for disaster prevention and the reduction of damage in earthquake situation.

Nishimura's study [3] provides a remote data backup technology for distributed data keeping on multiple organizations such as universities. This study is considered migration transparency of distributed backup data using a storage virtualization technology. This system guarantees a security of the backup data, and transparency by Secret Sharing Scheme. However, the main target of this architecture is the data backup and keeping its transparency. Therefore, it is not designed to continue users request handling with user data.

In this research, we have built a framework of reducing earthquake and tsunami disaster for e-Learning environment. We build private cloud computing environment based on IaaS technology. This private cloud environment is constructed from any private cloud fabric with the distributed storage system into several organizations. The Learning Management Systems such as Moodle build on several private cloud fabrics. Each VM has a LMS and the related data. General IaaS platform such as Kernel-based Virtual Machine (KVM) [4], Xen [5] and VMware vSphere [6] has a live-migration function with network shared storage. General network shared storage is constructed by iSCSI, NFS and usual network attached storage (NAS) system. Unfortunately, these network shared storage systems are bound to any physical storages on the each organizations. As a result, it is difficult to do the live-migration of VMs between inter-organizations such as universities.

Our prototype platform is built with distributed storage system and KVM based IaaS architecture on a lot of usual server hardware with network interfaces. It is able to handle many VMs including LMS and the data with enough redundancy. And, this prototype platform will operate on the inter-organizations. As a result, our prototype platform will be able to integrative operate each organization's private cloud fabric. If one organization's e-Learning environment is lost by some disaster, it will be able to keep running same environment on other organizations environment. When the rebuild an infrastructure on the damaged organization, lost environment will be able to reconstruct by other organizations environment. Therefore, we think that the damaged organization can keep running e-Learning systems, and does not lose data such as learning history.

In this paper, we propose the inter-cloud cooperation framework between private cloud fabrics on several organizations, and we show a configuration of the prototype system. Next, we show the results of experimental use and examine these results. Finally, we describe future study, and we show conclusions.

2   Assisting the Disaster Reduction for e-Learning Environment

In this section, we describe the inter-cloud cooperation framework of e-Learning environment. Especially, the purpose of this framework is a disaster reduction for LMS such as Moodle, and to keep running LMS and related data.

Fig.1 shows a framework of disaster reduction assistance for the e-Learning environment. Each organization such as university has a private cloud fabric, it is constructed a lot of server hardware and network connections between many server hardware. Each server hardware does not independent other server hardware on the private cloud fabric. They provide computing resources and data store resources via VMs, their resources are changed adaptively by the request from the administrators. Each VM which exists on the private cloud fabric is generated from the resources in the private cloud fabric, it is able to process any function such as authentication, and LMS function on the VM. In addition, Each VM can migrate between other private cloud fabrics, and it is able to continue to keep processing.

A live migration function needs a shared file system to do the VM's migration. The product of Sheepdog Project [7] is applied to our framework. Sheepdog is a distributed storage system optimized to QEMU and KVM hypervisor. Our proposed framework builds by KVM hypervisor, and Sheepdog distributed storage system provides highly available block level storage volumes. It can be attached to QEMU based VMs, it can be used to boot disk image for the VMs. Sheepdog cluster does not have controller or meta-data servers such as any SAN storage or GlusterFS [8]. The controller and meta-data servers could be a single point of failure under the disaster situation. We will lose all VM's image and all any history data when we lost meta-data servers. Therefore, we cannot take the distributed storage solution such as meta-data server model. The distributed storage system which is based on Sheepdog product does not have the single point of failure. Because, Sheepdog has a fully symmetric architecture, this architecture does not have central node such as a meta-data server. If some server hardware which compose Sheepdog cluster, it has small risk to lost the VM image file and history data. In addition, we think each VM image is able to find other organization's private cloud fabric. Because, Sheepdog based distributed storage system is constructed integrally on the several organization's private cloud fabrics. It can be able to reboot the VMs on other organization's private fabric under the disaster situation. Where possible, the VMs which are running on the several organizations move to riskless other private cloud fabric, and keep running the VMs.

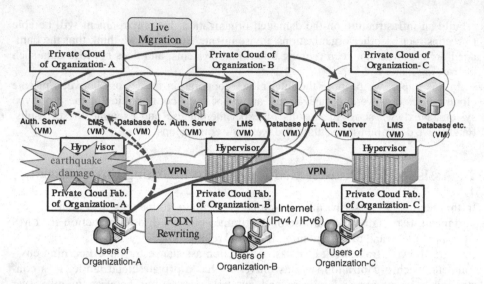

Fig. 1. Framework of disaster reduction assistance for the e-Learning environment

However, if VMs migrate between several private cloud fabrics in working condition, it is not true that each organization's users can use several services. The hostname which is used to access the services, it must be rewrite to the previous organization's FQDN (Fully Qualified Domain Name). Generally, the users of organization-A want to access own LMS, they use the FQDN of organization-A. When the VM of organization-A is under controlled by the private cloud fabric of organization-B, that VM's FQDN has to provide the hostname related to organization-A. This function must operate at the same time as the live migration function.

As a result, we think we can assist to provide this inter-cloud framework against the disasters for e-Learning environment.

3   System Configuration

We show the configuration of proposed system in Fig.2. This is a prototype configuration of proposed framework.

This system has three components and two internal networks. The first one of the components is the server hardware cluster. This is a core component of our prototype system. They are constructed by eight server hardware as shown by node1 to node8. This server hardware is based on Intel architecture and three network interfaces. Each server has the function of KVM hypervisor, virtualization API and Sheepdog distributed storage API. Each server can be used for the VM execution infrastructure, and it is also to use the composing element of Sheepdog distributed storage system. As a result, it is realized sharing the hardware to use VM executing infrastructure, and it is implemented a reliability and a scalability of the storage.

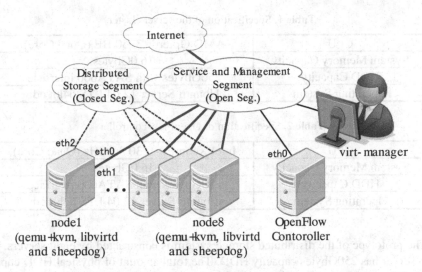

Fig. 2. System configuration of prototype system

The second one of the components is a Software Defined Network (SDN) controller based on OpenFlow [9] architecture. These servers which compose the VM execution infrastructure have the function of OpenFlow switch based on Open vSwitch [10]. This function is used for making optimum path, and it is also used for integrating several distributed storage.

The third one of the components is the Virtual Machine Manager [11]. This function is used for management several VMs by VM's administrator on this prototype system. In addition, any alert system of earthquake will control VMs live migration and saving the learning history via virt-manager interface on this prototype system.

On the other hands, our prototype system has two internal networks. The one of the internal network is provided to make closed segment, it is used to make a keep-alive communication, and making the storage data transfer between Sheepdog distributed storage clusters. The second of the internal network provides network reachability to the Internet, and it provides the connectivity between the users and LMS services. In addition, this network segment is used to make a connection for VM controls under the secure environment with optimized packet filtering.

4   Experimental Use and Results

This prototype system was tested to confirm its effectiveness. We made the virtual disk images and virtual machines configuration on our prototype system. And, several VMs was installed LMS such as Moodle. Each size of the virtual disk image is about 20GB on this experimental use.

Table 1 presents the server hardware specification for the distributed storage system's cluster, and the OpenFlow controller specification is presented in Table 2.

Table 1. Specification of the server cluster

CPU	AMD Opteron 3250 HE (Quad Core)
System Memory Capacity	16.0Gbytes
HDD Capacity	250Gbytes with SATA600 interface
Operating System	Ubuntu Server 12.04 LTS 64bit ed.

Table 2. Specification of OpenFlow controller

CPU	Intel Xeon E3-1230 3.2GHz (Quad Core)
System Memory Capacity	16.0Gbytes
HDD Capacity	250Gbytes with SATA600 interface
Operating System	Ubuntu Server 12.04 LTS 64bit ed.

The prototype of the distributed storage system is constructed by eight servers, and each server has 250Gbytes capacity HDD. The total amount of physical HDD capacity is about 2.0Tbytes. Each clustered server uses about 4Gbytes capacities for the hypervisor function with an operating system. We think this amount is ignorable small capacity. However, the distributed storage system has triple redundancy for this test. As a result, we can use about 700Mbytes storage capacity with enough redundancy. The total capacity of the distributed storage system can extend to add other node servers, exchange to larger HDDs, and taking both solutions. We can take enough scalability and redundancy by this distributed storage system.

We tried a live-migration the VMs from the node1 to node2. We show the screen capture in Fig.3 of the test. We used to operate VM's live-migration by the interface of Virtual Machine Manager. The time of live-migration is needed about 10 to 15 seconds on this test. We think it is enough live-migration time for a disaster reduction of provided VMs. And, we could get a complete successful result with active condition.

However, the live-migration of this experimental use is operated by my hands. Naturally, we think we have to make an operation of VMs live-migration automatically. The problem of this future work is how it can be make a trigger of this migration. We think we will use a vibratory sensor via serial communication interface or USB interface. But, we think this method have a lot of false detection situation. For example, when someone touches or moves the vibratory sensor, the false detection is kicked up by these faults. In addition, it is difficult to keep similar level of each organization's sensing capability. Each sensor device has definitely a variation of sensing capability.

We think we will use an emergency notification of the disaster from any mobile communication carrier such as NTT DoCoMo, KDDI and Softbank via their smart phones. The custom application program is installed to any smart phone such as Android platform and iPhone platform. If we can get the information of emergency notifications via smart phone with near field communication method such as USB interface, Bluetooth communication method and so on, we will be able to make a trigger of VMs live-migration with more precision.

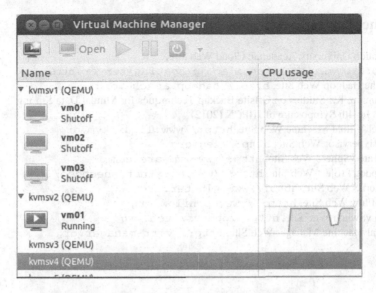

Fig. 3. Live-migration result by Virtual Machine Manager

The results of this experimental use are pretty good. The time requirement for VMs migrating was a short period. However, the results were getting under the initial conditions. The VMs which are installed Moodle system were quite new condition. Generally, when the VMs are operated to continue long period, each VM has large history data. Therefore, the time of live-migration will need more than initial condition. We think we have to make the experimental use under the actual conditions.

5 Conclusion

In this paper, we proposed a framework of disaster reduction for e-Learning environment. Especially, we described an assistance to use our proposed framework, and we show the importance of an against the earthquake and tsunami disaster for e-Learning environment. We built the prototype system based on our proposed framework, and we described a system configuration of the prototype system. And, we shown the results of experimental use and examine.

For the future, we have a plan to implement the function of getting earthquake notifications from any smart phone. And we will try to test the cloud computing orchestration framework such as OpenStack and CloudStack. And, we will try to experiment confirming its effectiveness under the inter-organization environment.

Acknowledgment. This work was supported by JSPS KAKENHI Grant Number 24501229.

References

1. Hokkaido University Academic Cloud Web Site,
   http://www.hucc.hokudai.ac.jp/hosting_server.html
2. Apache Hadoop Web Site, http://hadoop.apache.org
3. Nishimura, K.: Studies on Offsite Backup Techniques for Mutual Data Storing by Universities. In: 4th Symposium of JHPCN (2012)
4. Kernel Virtual Machine Web Site, http://www.linux-kvm.org
5. Xen Hypervisor Web Site, http://xen.org
6. VMware vSphere Web Site, http://www.vmware.com
7. Sheepdog Project Web Site, http://www.osrg.net/sheepdog/
8. GlusterFS Web Site, http://www.gluster.org
9. OpenFlow Web Site, http://www.openflow.org
10. Open vSwitch Web Site, http://openvswitch.org
11. Virtual Machine Manager Web Site, http://virt-manager.org

Design and Evaluation of Training System
for Numerical Calculation Using Questions in SPI2

Shin'ichi Tsumori[1] and Kazunori Nishino[2]

[1] Kyushu Junior College of Kinki University, Japan
tsumori@kjc.kindai.ac.jp
[2] Kyushu Institute of Technology, Japan
nishino@lai.kyutech.ac.jp

Abstract. We are developing the training system for numerical calculation aiming at improving calculation ability. There are two main purposes of realizing this system. One is to increase students' motivation to study mathematics by using the questions in SPI2 adopted by many companies as employment examinations. The other is to support a student's learning efficiently by giving the questions according to the student's ability. In order to give an adaptive question, our system has functions to estimate each student's ability and item difficulty in the test item database. This paper reports the basic concept, the features and the experiment conducted to verify the usefulness of the system and its result.

Keywords: Training System, Numerical Calculation, SPI2, Web-Based Learning.

1 Introduction

In recent years, in many universities or colleges, the students who lack calculation ability are increasing in number, and it interferes with some lectures premised on calculation ability. In addition, since many companies give calculation tests as a part of their employment examinations nowadays, it is difficult for students with low abilities to pass them. For these reasons, many universities/colleges give remedial mathematics course to the freshmen students. However, since the difference of the calculation ability between students is large, it is difficult to raise learning effectiveness with the same curriculum. In such a case, the individualized learning which has been adapted for each student's understanding is more effective than group lessons. However, since most of arts students do not like to study mathematics generally, it is difficult for them to maintain the motivation to study using the existing mathematics materials. Instead, their motivation to study for an employment examination is comparatively high. Therefore, it is expected that the teaching materials made for employment examinations will raise their motivation for learning.

We aim to realize the web-based training system for numerical calculation using the questions of SPI2 (Synthetic Personality Inventory 2) which is widely adopted as an employment examination in Japan. This system is supposed to be used especially

M. Kurosu (Ed.): Human-Computer Interaction, Part II, HCII 2013, LNCS 8005, pp. 511–520, 2013.

in the entrance into universities/colleges or the period when a student takes an employment examination in order to acquire calculation ability. Repeated calculating is the most important until a question comes to be solved in order to gain ability. However, since there are around twenty study units in SPI2, in order to raise a learning effect in a limited time, it is important to extract the study units adequately which the student should study because she/he does not understand it well.

The system characterized by giving the questions according to the student's ability has been considered for many years. Papers [1] and [2] are featured by choosing the question which is adapted for the student's ability from the question database. They are effective methods when the test item difficulties are set to all questions beforehand, but the problem is that a load is required of a teacher. Papers [3] to [7] show the methods of generating questions automatically. Although the advantage is that they can give many questions to the students, the problem is how the validity of the difficulty of the test item in question is guaranteed.

We are developing the training system for numerical calculation equipped with two functions, ability analysis and a calculation training[8]. One of the features of the system is to avoid generating questions that will be too easy/difficult, and showing the question according to academic ability by using Item Response Theory (IRT). However, since the questions in SPI2 are added and updated frequently, there is a problem regarding how the difficulty of the test item stored in the question database is maintained. We are examining how to estimate the test item difficulty using the number of the formulas contained in the process of a numerical calculation. By using this method together with the PROX method, we think that a system which can respond to the frequent change of the contents of the question database can be realized.

This paper reports the basic concept, the features and the experiment to verify the usefulness of the system and its result.

2   System Overview

2.1   What Is SPI2?

Before we start explanation of the system developed now, SPI2 is explained briefly.

SPI is one of the aptitude tests broadly used as the employment examination of the company. It has been developed by present Recruit Management Solutions Co.,Ltd. and adopted 9,050 companies in the 2011 fiscal year. In addition, "2" of "SPI2" expresses the version number[1]. SPI2 consists of an ability test and a personality test, and the numerical calculation explained in this paper is a part of ability test. Although the range of questions of SPI2 is not exhibited, it includes around 20 study units such as probability calculation, speed calculation, and concentration calculation. SPI2 test requires the calculation ability from an elementary school to a high school. It also requires a student to answer the 30 calculation questions within 40 minutes.

In addition, although an actual ability test in SPI2 consists of multiple-choice questions, the training system which we are developing is a system which a numerical value is inputted as an answer.

---

[1] The version number of SPI as of February, 2013 is "3".

2.2   System Configuration and Operation

The system configuration is shown in Fig. 1. This system is a web-based training system and has two functions, ability analysis and calculation training. The student chooses one of the functions to use after login. The outline of two functions is explained below.

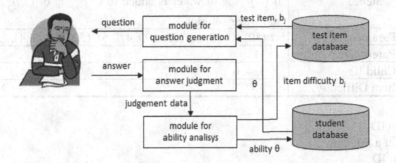

Fig. 1. Configuration of Training System for Numerical Calculation

1. Ability analysis
Ability analysis is the function to take the analysis test which consists of test items stored in the test item database. Since each of the abilities needs to become clear in advance in order to perform an adaptive training, all the students who want to use the function of calculation training must take this test. In addition, before performing ability analysis, all item difficulties in the test item database must be known. Chapter 3 explains the setting method of item difficulty.

The module for question generation gains some test items from the database, creates an ability analysis test, and gives a student the question. After a student's answer, the module for answer judgment transmits right-or-wrong information to the module for ability analysis, and the module for ability analysis estimates the student's ability θ.

We use Maximum Likelihood Estimation as the method to estimate the ability θ. It is the method of estimating θ from a viewpoint of the probability of a series of results in a test. By using the item difficulty b_j and the ability θ, the probability $P_j(\theta)$ for correct answer and the probability for incorrect answer can be calculated. Then, the probabilities that a series of student answers will take place are calculated, changing theta to various values. The largest value among the calculated values is an estimate of θ, and it is registered into the student database.

2. Calculation training
The calculation training is a function which extracts the test item suitable for the student's ability from the test item database and shows a student it. The test item has attributes and values as shown in Table.1. The contents of each attribute of a test item are as follows.

Table 1. Sample of Attributes and Values of Test Item

attribute	value
Item ID	7
Unit ID	6
Question Sentence	What percentage of salt water solution will be made if (p_1)g of water is added to (p_2)g of (p_3)% salt water solution?
Parameter set	(50, 100, 3, 2), (60, 100, 4, 2.5), (50, 200, 5, 4), …
Parent ID	11
Child ID	3, 4, 6
Item Difficulty	0.1

- Item ID
  ID of a test item
- Unit ID
  ID of a study unit
- Question sentence
  Question sentence given to a student. P_x (x=1,2,3,…) is a parameter which determines a value at the time of generating question.
- Parameter set
  Set of the numerical value given to a question sentence and the numerical value of a correct answer. There are some parameter sets in a test item, and one set is chosen at the time of generating the question. For example, when (50, 100, 3, 2) are chosen, p_1=50, p_2=100, and p_3=3 are set to a question sentence. The correct answer is 2.
- Parent ID
  IDs of test items containing the calculation process of this item
- Child ID
  IDs of test items used as the partial calculation process of this question
- Item Difficulty
  Value of test item difficulty

The module for question generation selects a test item and generates a question based on the teaching strategy. This paper does not discuss the details of a teaching strategy, but the following examples are shown as a teaching strategy.

- When a student answered a question correctly, the system gives a more difficult question using Parent ID.
- When a student answered a question incorrectly, the system gives an easier question one using Child ID.

3   Estimation of Item Difficulty

In this paper, we try to propose the method of giving a suitable question based on a student's probability of the questions stored in the test item database. We adopt the Rasch model (One-parameter logistic model) widely known for the field of IRT as a method of estimating the probability. According to Rasch model, when the item difficulty b_j and the student's ability θ is known, the probability $P_j(\theta)$ is calculated using following formula.

$$P_j(\theta) = \frac{1}{1 + e^{-(\theta - b_j)}}$$

Since $P_j(\theta)$ is a value for probability, following two points are guessed from a viewpoint of the difficulty of question.

- When $P_j(\theta)$ is close to 0, the problem is too difficult for a student.
- When $P_j(\theta)$ is close to 1, the problem is too easy for a student.

That is, the more the value of $P_j(\theta)$ approaches 0.5, the more the question will be suitable for a student. By using this view, an adaptive training system will be realized.

In order to perform ability analysis mentioned in 2.2, all item difficulties in the test item database must become clear in advance. We propose to use two methods together, the PROX method and the method of using the number of formulas contained in the calculation process in order to estimate the item difficulty b_j. These two methods are explained below.

3.1   Estimation Using PROX Method

The PROX method is one of the methods used in order to estimate student's ability θ and the item difficulty b_j required to apply Rasch model. Its feature is that the computational procedure for estimation is easier than other methods.

The example of a right-or-wrong situation where seven students answer the test, which consists of the six items, is shown in Table 2.

Table 2. Parameter estimation using the PROX method

Student ID	Question ID						θ
	1	2	3	4	5	6	
1	1	0	0	0	1	0	-0.940
2	1	1	1	0	1	0	0.940
3	0	0	1	0	0	0	-2.174
4	1	0	0	0	1	0	-0.940
5	1	0	0	0	0	1	-0.940
6	1	1	1	0	0	1	0.940
7	1	1	1	1	0	1	2.174
b_j	-2.525	0.256	-0.51	2.271	0.256	0.256	

Since a right-or-wrong situation is expressed with two values of 1 and 0, Table 2 means that the student 1 answered the question 1 and the question 5 correctly, and gave the wrong answer to other questions. The PROX method estimates θ and b_j using the logit scores calculated from Table 2 (as shown in shading). Explanation of the calculation process of the PROX method is omitted in this paper.

When θ and b_j are calculated like Table 2, the probability $P_j(\theta)$ that the student of $\theta=$ 0.5 answers the question 2 (b_j =0.256) correctly is calculated as follows.

$$P_j(\theta) = \frac{1}{1 + e^{-(0.5-0.256)}} = 0.56$$

If the difficulties of all the SPI2 items stored in the test item database are calculated in advance, when a student's ability θ becomes clear, the probability for all items will be calculated. Therefore, the system can extract the test item which is neither too easy nor too difficult for the student.

However, it is very difficult to actually set up all the item difficulties in the test item database in advance for the following two reasons.

(1) For the high updating frequency of test items in the database

The range of questions of the numerical calculation of SPI2 is wide, and also it is expanded every year. Moreover, since it is possible that various questions whose difficulties are low to high can be created, the frequency of the addition and update of the test item database becomes high. At actual schools, it is difficult to carry out frequent test for items whose difficulties are unknown.

(2) For a restriction of "assumption of local independence"

In order to apply IRT, assumption of local independence must be satisfied regarding each item of a test. Assumption of local independence means that the probability that an answer of certain item is correct does not affect the probability that answers of other items are correct. Fig. 2 shows the example of three items in the "concentration calculation" study unit. In this example, since the calculation process of item A contains the calculation process of item B, the student who cannot answer item B correctly cannot answer item A correctly. Therefore, item A and item B cannot be used for the test for ability analysis simultaneously because item A and item B are not in the relation of local independence (the relationship between item B and item C is the same). However, since it is necessary to create broadly from an easy question to a difficult one in order to give the problem according to student's ability, it is rather ordinary that items shown in Fig. 2 are simultaneously stored in the test item database. In this case, it is necessary to carry out two or more tests in order to set up the item difficulties because of assumption of local independence

3.2   Estimation Using the Number of Formulas in the Calculation Process

This section discusses how to estimate the item difficulty using the number of the formulas contained in the process of a numerical calculation.

Fig.2 shows the example of three items belonging to the "concentration calculation" and their calculation processes. In addition, all the formulas in this paper are expressed as dyadic operation.

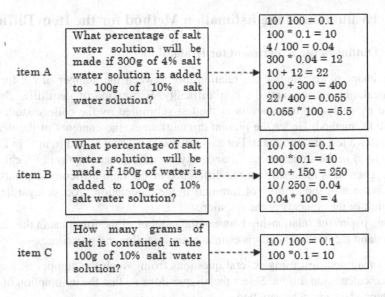

item A	What percentage of salt water solution will be made if 300g of 4% salt water solution is added to 100g of 10% salt water solution?	10 / 100 = 0.1 100 * 0.1 = 10 4 / 100 = 0.04 300 * 0.04 = 12 10 + 12 = 22 100 + 300 = 400 22 / 400 = 0.055 0.055 * 100 = 5.5
item B	What percentage of salt water solution will be made if 150g of water is added to 100g of 10% salt water solution?	10 / 100 = 0.1 100 * 0.1 = 10 100 + 150 = 250 10 / 250 = 0.04 0.04 * 100 = 4
item C	How many grams of salt is contained in the 100g of 10% salt water solution?	10 / 100 = 0.1 100 * 0.1 = 10

Fig. 2. Example of relationship between 3 items

As for the item C in Fig.2, the correct answer is calculated in the following process.

1. The percentage expression (concentration) is changed into the decimal expression.
2. The weight of salt is calculated by multiplying the weight and the concentration of the salt water.

As for the item B, its calculation process include one of the item C. Furthermore, some formulas are added to the item B. The calculation process of the item A include one of the item B as well. That is, the comparison of these three items guesses that the item difficulty becomes large at the order of item A, item B, and item C. For example, if the item difficulty of item B is known, the item difficulty of item A (or item C) will be estimated by getting the difference between the item difficulty of item A and item B (or item B and item C).

The number of formulas contained in the calculation process of each item of Fig. 2 are as follows.

item A: 8,   item B: 5,   item C: 2

Therefore, the difference between the number of formulas of item A and item B is 3. Then, we tried to make the relationship between the differences of the number of formulas and item difficulty experimentally clear. That is, we estimated the change of item difficulty corresponding to one formula in the calculation process by dividing the difference between the item difficulty of item A and item B by the difference of the numbers of their formulas of calculation processes.

The following chapter explains the experiment to perform the above-mentioned contents.

4   Evaluation of the Estimation Method for the Item Difficulty

4.1   Outline of the Experiment for Evaluation

In this chapter, we examine the relationship between the number of the formulas in the calculation process and the item difficulty. Estimation of item difficulty is performed by analyzing the answers of the test submitted by the college students using the PROX method. Under the present circumstances, the contents of the item which constitutes a test are important. For example, item A, item B and item C in Fig.2 cannot be used in the same test simultaneously because of assumption of local independence. Then, it is assumed that the difference of the item difficulty depends on only the difference of the number of formulas in the calculation process regardless of the study unit or the contents of the question.

In this paper, the relationship between the number of the formulas in the calculation process and the item difficulty is estimated in the following procedures.

1.   Constitute a test using several questions from which the number of formulas in the calculation differs. Select the all questions so that the assumption of local independence may be satisfied.
2.   Estimate the all item difficulties b_j of all the items in the test using the right-or-wrong situation of a student's answer.
3.   Get the expression of relation between the number of formulas in the calculation process and b_j.

4.2   Method of Experiment

The experiment was conducted on the following conditions.

- Contents of the test
  - 15 questions from 4 study units ("price computation", "dealing profit and loss", "speed calculation", and "concentration calculation") are used.
  - All the questions are the numerical calculations whose correct answers are numerical values.
- Subject
  80 first graders of Kyushu Junior College of Kinki University
- Answer method
  The student accessed the Web server which stored the test using the personal computers in the classroom and answered simultaneously.
- Answer time
  Although not specified in particular, all the students finished answering the questions in about 30 minutes.

4.3   Result and Consideration

The graph which plotted the number of formulas in the calculation process of an item and the item difficulty is shown in Fig. 3. In addition, for the questions which were solved by same number of formulas, the average value of those item difficulties are the representative value. The result is that there is a strong correlation between the number of formulas in the calculation process and the item difficulty because the Pearson product-moment correlation coefficient is 0.78. The regression coefficient was 0.47, and it means that one of the formulas corresponded with 0.47 of item difficulty. Therefore, if the item difficulty of item B will be estimated at 1.00 (for example) by the PROX method, item A and item C may be estimated as follows.

- Item difficulty of item A
Since item A has 3 more formulas in its calculation process more than item B,

$$1.00 + 0.47 \times 3 = 2.41$$

- Item difficulty of item C
Since item A has 3 fewer formulas in its calculation process more than item B,

$$1.00 - 0.47 \times 3 = -0.41$$

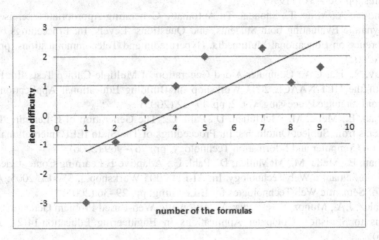

Fig. 3. Relationship between number of the formulas and item difficulty

As explained so far, it is possible that all the item difficulties can be estimated by two methods, PROX method and the method using the number of formulas contained in the calculation process. Therefore, the student's probability of each test item can be estimated with applying IRT.

5   Conclusion

We are now developing a system with the feature described so far. Moreover, we proposed the method of estimating the item difficulty using the number of formulas in the calculation process. The result of the experiment suggested the probability that the number of formulas in the calculation process may be used for estimating the item difficulty.

However, since the number of subject and the number of questions on the experiment test was not enough, we could not estimate parameters with precision. Moreover, another problem to be solved is that the rate of correct answers in an experiment test was quite lower than anticipated. Many more tests by many more students must be carried out in order to estimate item difficulty with more precision.

Acknowledgement. This work was supported by JSPS KAKENHI Grant Number 23501191. We thank to the students of Kyushu Junior College of Kinki University who cooperated in the experiment.

References

1. Huang, S.X.: A Content-Balanced Adaptive Testing Algorithm for Computer-Based Training Systems. In: Proceedings of the Third International Conference Intelligent Tutoring Systems, pp. 306–314 (1996)
2. Suganuma, A., Mine, T., Shoudai, T.: Automatic Generating Appropriate Exercises Based on Dynamic Evaluating both Students' and Questions' Levels. In: Proceedings of World Conference on Educational Multimedia, Hypermedia and Telecommunications, pp. 1898–1903 (2002)
3. Mitkov, R., Ha, L.A.: Computer-Aided Generation of Multiple-Choice Tests. In: Proceedings of the HLT-NAACL 2003 Workshop on Building Educational Applications Using Natural Language Processing, vol. 2, pp. 17–22 (2003)
4. Holohan, E., Melia, M., McMullen, D., Pahl, C.: The Generation of E-Learning Exercise Problems from Subject Ontologies. In: Proceedings of The Sixth IEEE International Conference on Computer and Information Technology, pp. 967–969 (2006)
5. Holohan, E., Melia, M., McMullen, D., Pahl, C.: Adaptive E-Learning Content Generation based on Semantic Web Technology. In: AI-ED 2005 Workshop 3, SW-EL 2005: Applications of Semantic Web Technologies for E-Learning, pp. 29–36 (2005)
6. Gonzalez, J.A., Munoz, P.: e-status: An Automatic Web-Based Problem Generator - Applications to Statistics. Computer Applications in Engineering Education 14(2), 151–159 (2006)
7. Lazcorreta, E., Botella, F., Fernandez-Caballero, A.: Auto-Adaptive Questions in E-Learning System. In: Proceedings of the Sixth International Conference on Advanced Learning Technologies, pp. 270–274 (2006)
8. Tsumori, S., Nishino, K.: Proposal of a Numerical Calculation Exercise System for SPI2 Test Based on Academic Ability Diagnosis. Intelligent Interactive Multimedia: Systems and Services 14, 489–498 (2012)
9. Linacre, J.M.: Rasch Model Estimation. Journal of Applied Measurement 5(1), 95–110 (2004)

Zoom Interface with Dynamic Thumbnails Providing Learners with Companionship through Videostreaming

Takumi Yamaguchi[1], Haruya Shiba[1], Masanobu Yoshida[1], Yusuke Nishiuchi[1],
Hironobu Satoh[1], and Takahiko Mendori[2]

[1] Kochi National College of Technology, 200-1 Monobe, Nankoku, Kochi 783-8508, Japan
yama@ee.kochi-ct.ac.jp
[2] Kochi University of Technology, 185 Miyanokuchi, Tosayamada, Kami-city,
Kochi 782-8502, Japan

Abstract. We have developed the TERAKOYA learning system, which helps students study actively anywhere on a local area network (LAN) linked to multipoint remote users. However, if many students frequently sent their questions to the teacher, it is very difficult to correspond to quickly answer that for the teacher. In addition, the teacher hardly clarifies how much each student understood because he cannot watch students' face and reaction. This paper discusses the graphical user interface (GUI) system that is used a little ingenuity to prioritize students' screens through variably changing the GUI interface on the teacher's PC. The aspect of window that was displayed as thumbnails of the students' PC screen was zoomed dynamically each thumbnail by their understanding level. By sorting out their priorities on the teacher's PC screen, the teacher can timely observe the students' work and support their thinking process.

Keywords: GUI, Interactive system, Advanced Educational Environment, Ubiquitous Learning, Distance Education.

1 Introduction

In today's environment of ubiquitous computers, promoting the use of computers in school is very important. E-learning and learning through web content, however, are passive methods, and it is difficult to cultivate comprehensive active learning, which has recently gained prominence. Because active learning requires learner participation, computers are expected to complement classroom lectures given by teachers to students. Systems for computer-based active learning enable in-class participation by transparently manipulating the input instruments of the students and the teacher. Several researchers have suggested that the challenge in an information-rich world is not only to make information available to people at any time, at any place, and in any form, but to specifically say the right thing at the right time in the right way [1]. In particular, the fundamental pedagogical concern is to provide learners with the right information at the right time and place in the right way instead of enabling them to

M. Kurosu (Ed.): Human-Computer Interaction, Part II, HCII 2013, LNCS 8005, pp. 521–528, 2013.

learn at any time and at any place [2]. More importantly, as Jones and Jo [3] pointed out what you, as educators, should aspire to combine the right time and right place learning with a transparent and calm method to allow students to access lessons flexibly, calmly, and seamlessly. Such an approach seems to be a calming technology for the ubiquitous computers, and it adapts itself to students' needs by supporting specific practices.

In the present study, we have developed the new collaborative TERAKOYA learning system [7] for remedial education, which helps students study actively anywhere on a LAN linked to multipoint remote users, as shown in Fig. 1. The TERAKOYA learning system provides both interactive lessons and a small private school environment similar to the 18th-century Japanese basic schools called terakoya. In particular, the system provides an interactive evening lesson that uses tablet PCs on a wireless LAN (WLAN) and custom-built applications that link students in the dormitory and at home with a teacher in the school or at home. In this new system, the students and the teacher cooperate and interact in real time, as in some existing systems, using a personal digital assistant (PDA) [4]. This system can be used to submit and store lecture notes or coursework using a tablet PC.

We define TERAKOYA as a new, evolving virtual private school realized on the network. This makes it slightly different from the 18th-century terakoya. Our TERAKOYA indicates a system for simultaneously achieving the following:

(1) Small group lessons for students, like those at a private school in which the teacher becomes the leader.
(2) Interactive lessons that can provide dialog with the teacher and allow students' work to be checked and their thinking processes supported by online collaboration.
(3) Lessons enhanced by mutual assistance that can clarify any misperceptions in the students' thinking processes and provide appropriate support for each student through giving other students' opinions and answers.

In other words, TERAKOYA is an educational support system that can correspond flexibly to the learning demands of many students today by applying a private school model for small group lessons. Therefore, the TERAKOYA system realizes personal learning support for students in a dormitory or at home from a teacher in the school or at home.

In the original terakoya environment, it was not easy to maintain the focus on learning, except for students with a high willingness to learn. On the other hand, our TERAKOYA is a more flexible learning system environment that allows teachers to freely switch between the conventional terakoya environment and the mutually supportive environment using teacher-centered learning or self-paced learning, as needed. Because of this flexibility, we consider that this system can reach a wide range of vulnerable-looking students and accommodate contemporary students' attitudes toward learning. In addition, this system is expected to allow teachers to provide additional learning assistance to students with less additional work for the teacher than supplementary lessons conducted in the classroom or in the dormitory.

We consider a realistic scenario of dynamically providing an interactive lesson for students in an active learning environment in their own living space. As a serious problem in the present system, if many students frequently sent their questions to the teacher, it is very difficult to correspond to quickly answer that for the teacher. In addition, the teacher hardly clarifies how much each student understood because he cannot watch students' face and reaction. Accordingly, the GUI of the system uses a little ingenuity to prioritize students' screens through variably changing the GUI interfaces on the teacher's PC. These are blinked, sorted and scaled the students' viewing, etc. In particular, the aspect of window that was displayed as thumbnails of the students' PC is zoomed dynamically each thumbnail by their understanding level. If the PC screens of students can be sorted out their priorities on the teacher's PC screen, the teacher can timely observe the students' work and support their thinking process as an effective teaching aid. The teacher could also clarify any misperceptions in their thinking processes, providing appropriate support for each student.

This paper presents a basic configuration of a system that provides dynamic delivery of full-motion video while following target users in ubiquitous learning environments. The delivery of full-motion video uses adaptive broadcasting. The system can continuously deliver streaming data, such as full-motion video, to the teacher's display as thumbnails of the students' PC screen. Because it maintains the information about the user's attitude in real time, it supports the user wherever he or she is, without requiring a conscious request to obtain their information. This paper describes a prototype implementation of this framework and a practical application.

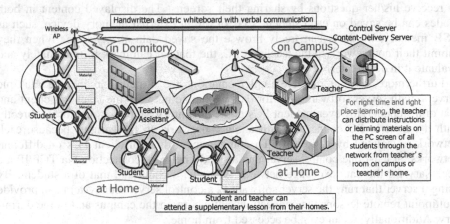

Fig. 1. TERAKOYA learning system

2   Basic Configuration

The system consists of tablet PCs, a server machine, and software to enable collaboration among the tablet PCs over a WLAN, which covers the campus, the dormitory, and their homes. The interactive system software consists of server software, authoring software for the teacher, and client software for the students. The authoring software synchronizes with the clients via the server software. The system works in two modes: collaboration mode and free mode. The authoring software is launched on the teacher's PC, which has a 12-inch XGA display. Its main functions are to distribute teaching material, select collaboration mode or free mode, give a specific student's PC the permission to write, view a student's PC screen, share files between a specific student's PC and another PC using the client software, and submit coursework using remote control from the teacher's PC. The main functions of the client software are browsing lecture notes, storing learning material, and submitting coursework. Using the authoring software, teachers can view students' PC screens as thumbnails. The thumbnail view can display 50 client PCs. When students submit coursework from their PCs, the filenames are displayed in the order of submission on the teacher's PC. Thus, the teacher can immediately confirm the submission status of a student's coursework.

In the collaboration mode, the display on the teacher's PC is shared by the PC screens of up to 50 students. Each student PC serves as a handwritten electronic board. All students in the class can view the activity of a selected student on their PC screens when that student is completing his/her coursework. Furthermore, students with write access can post discussions on the process of completing the coursework because the teacher can control the ability to write data to each of their PC screens. All students can browse through or view these discussions, resulting in a group discussion.

In the free mode, a student can freely write on the teaching material and coursework sent by the teacher on his/her PC screen. The teacher can watch all students' PC screens, although each student's writing is displayed only on his/her PC screen. If a student cannot complete the coursework, the teacher can provide hints to the student or receive his/her questions by sharing their screens. The displayed content in both modes can be saved on each student's PC or on an external memory device, such as USB memory. Students can freely browse the saved data at any time. When they submit their coursework to the teacher's PC, the teacher can mark it immediately and evaluate it in detail later.

Furthermore, as one possible implementation, the system can include multiple servers, with server software used for data exchange between the teacher's client and that of a student. However, student PCs in the dormitory cannot communicate directly with a teacher's PC connected with another network on the campus because each network is isolated by a firewall. To communicate through client PCs on different networks, at least one control server and a steady network connection via TCP/IP are necessary for the data exchange between a teacher's client and that of a student. By using a server that runs the server software as a control server, our system can provide multipoint remote lessons via connections anywhere on the campus and in the dormitory. Additionally, it can even be accessed from home.

Because interactive lessons are provided, each client must continuously maintain its connection to other computers. Thus, the traffic load between the server and clients grows when the number of connected users increases. Consequently, network hardware must provide adequate system performance for real-time information sharing. This system was optimized to work smoothly between one server PC and 50 client PCs, each with a 12-inch XGA display, for one lesson, and the network speed was maintained at 500 kbps or less for each connection. To limit the amount of data exchange between the client PCs, all teaching material and coursework were sent to the PC screens of all students when each interactive lesson began. After the lesson begins, this system sends only their own written data and the data controlled by the teacher to the students' PC screens.

Although we have already pointed out another problem of this system, if many students frequently sent their questions to the teacher, it is very difficult to correspond to quickly answer that for the teacher. In addition, the teacher hardly clarifies how much each student understood because he cannot watch students' face and reaction. By conducting a pre-survey of this system, as freely provided advice in the subjective evaluation, we received useful comments such as "It may take some time before a student's question gets a response from the teacher."

Accordingly, the advanced GUI of the system is configured to use a little ingenuity to prioritize students' screens through variably changing the GUI interfaces on the teacher's PC. These are blinked, sorted and scaled the students' viewing, etc. In particular, the aspect of window that was displayed as thumbnails of the students' PC is zoomed dynamically each thumbnail by their understanding level, as shown in Fig. 2. If the PC screens of students can be sorted out their priorities on the teacher's PC screen, the teacher can timely observe the students' work and support their thinking process as an effective teaching aid. The teacher could also clarify any misperceptions in their thinking processes, providing appropriate support for each student.

Fig. 2. Overview of GUI interfaces for viewing the students' PC screens as thumbnails on the teacher's PC zoomed dynamically by their understanding level

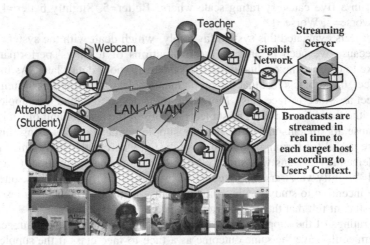

Fig. 3. Experiment of prototype system and its image that we see through five to twenty client hosts

3   Practice and Evaluation

To evaluate the current implementation of our system, we measured its performance in actuating a target host for a broadcast and then measured the response in delivering a streaming video to the whole target host. For this experiment, we used a delivery server and target hosts from five to twenty as shown in Fig. 3. The delivery server ran on a Core i7 (3.4 GHz) processor with Windows 7 Professional and the self-customized BigBlueButton 8) with Ubuntu; BigBlueButton is an open source web conferencing system developed primarily for distance education, and supports multiple audio and video sharing, presentations with extended whiteboard capabilities. Each target host ran on a Core i5 (2.53 GHz) Mobile processor with Windows 7 Professional and web browser as a BigBlueButton client. The system interconnects via a Gbit LAN from the server on our campus to an IEEE 802.11g/n WLAN for the target hosts. The streaming video for one target host is played in a 320×240-pixel (QVGA size) window with a webcam.

We verified the connection speed between the WLAN and the Gbit LAN for the server. When the twenty target hosts for students and the host for the teacher were used in the campus, as shown in Fig. 3, the minimum throughput speed between the server and a host was 12 megabit per second (Mbps). We also measured the time lag before a target host's actuation. The latency from capturing a webcam to passing a streaming server's IP address to a target host was less than 10 ms and the latency of the web browser's connection between a streaming server and a target host over a TCP connection set a minimum.

On the other hand, we carried out a questionnaire survey to investigate the subjective impression of the prototype system as a subjective evaluation. Test subjects are 10 students of the department of electrical engineering in their twenties. The subjects in their twenties are experienced in the PC operations in their daily life. We explained and demonstrated how to use the prototype system for the subjects before they filled out the questionnaire. After that, questionnaires on the subjective impression were evaluated in a five category rating scale where: Better=5, Slightly better=4, Fair=3, Slightly worse=2, Worse=1.

The subjects evaluated this system favorably, which dealt with the system's operability. Because we need to analyze the evaluations of teachers' performances, we would like to discuss the evaluation of the system in more detail later. As the educational effect, the subjects feel that the supplementary lessons using this system had the same effect as a face-to-face class. Moreover, their desire to attend the supplementary lessons in the future increased. The subjects' rating of the useful habit of studying was high because all students answered that the supplementary lessons using this system were more useful for forming the habit of studying, whereas the study time outside of the supplementary lessons was slightly low. Regarding the study time, two students answered "slightly yes," and one student answered "slightly no." Thus, one student had more incentive to study for the course because of the supplementary lessons, and the other student felt that the lessons were sufficient.

These ratings of the supplementary lessons provided by this system suggested that this system could have the same outcome as a face-to-face class if the supplementary lessons are provided as multipoint remote interactive lessons. Also, the evaluated value of the prototype system for these users might prove greater with more familiarity and experience with this system.

4   Related Work

Studies of interactive support systems used in class with a pen-based interface focus on the way in which the system helps the student answer questions and use the teaching material with an electronic board, a PDA, or information and communication technology (ICT) equipment. To compare our TERAKOYA system to related work, we weigh two technical areas: interactive systems [5] and active learning environments, both with pen-based computers [6].

Although each of these related systems is very interesting, ours has the following distinguishing features. First, our system can make it easier for students to ask the teacher questions the same as they could in face-to-face interactions. Second, it is very satisfying for the students that their queries are answered immediately anywhere on a LAN linked to multipoint remote users, which is achieved by directly connecting the teacher and the students. In addition, students may feel a sense of security and of being looked after because the psychological distance between the student and teacher is small. As a result, students can maintain their study concentration longer than in a normal remedial education class. Thus, the TERAKOYA system not only expands the accessibility of popular tablet PC support methods, but also accommodates a wide variety of learning styles by leveraging a transparent, calm learning environment.

5   Conclusions

This system helped students study actively anywhere on a LAN linking multipoint remote users and provides an interactive evening lesson using tablet PCs and custom-built applications both in the dormitory and at home, so students and teachers can stay in their own living spaces. As a prototype, the proposed learning system was implemented in a classroom with a teacher in the teacher's office on the campus. The implementation employed a handwritten electric whiteboard with verbal and non-verbal information. After this test was conducted, the effectiveness of the system in helping students study actively and willingly as an example of "right time, right place learning" was verified.

In addition, ours configured to help the teacher quickly answer students' questions for the teacher. Thus, the teacher can clarify how much each student understood through watching students' face and reaction via a LAN. The GUI system that is used a little ingenuity to prioritize students' screens through variably changing the GUI interface on the teacher's PC. The aspect of window that was displayed as thumbnails of the students' PC screen was zoomed dynamically each thumbnail by their understanding level. By sorting out their priorities on the teacher's PC screen, the teacher can timely observe the students' work and support their thinking process. Using this system, the teacher distributed instructions or learning materials on all the students' PC screens via the network. On receiving this material on their PCs, the students could note their views and answer the questions in the learning material on their PC screens using the pens attached to their tablet PCs. They could also submit their answers as an image to the teacher. Because the PC screens of students were viewable on the teacher's PC screen, the teacher could check the students' work and support their thinking processes by online collaboration. The teacher could also clarify any misperceptions by providing appropriate support for each student.

More specific and effective education programs are required. We would like to further evaluate the effect of this system on the understanding and learning motivation of the students when the system is used as an effective teaching aid. We would also like to study the configuration of the new interactive system under active learning conditions. We also would like to further study the configuration of a new interaction system by adding entities. This system is an ambient human interface system, which becomes friendly advisers and gives users naturally awareness, through making real images via a network to follow users. We would like to expect to realize ambient human interface system of a user-oriented ubiquitous computing through implementing this system.

Acknowledgments. We thank Ryuichi Watanabe for his helpful experiments and cooperation. This study was partially supported by a Grant-in-Aid for Scientific Research (C, Area #1602, Project No. 24501236).

References

1. Fischer, G.: User Modeling in Human-Computer Interaction. Journal of User Modeling and User-Adapted Interaction (UMUAI) 11(1-2), 65–86 (2001)
2. Ogata, H., El-Bishouty, M.M., Yano, Y.: Knowledge Awareness Map in Mobile Language-Learning. In: Proceedings of the Sixth IEEE International Conference on Advanced Learning Technologies (ICALT), pp. 1180–1181 (2006)
3. Jones, V., Jo, J.H.: Ubiquitous learning environment: An adaptive teaching system using ubiquitous technology. In: Proceedings of the 21st ASCILITE Conference, pp. 468–474 (2004)
4. Roschelle, J.: Unlocking the learning value of wireless mobile devices. Journal of Computer Assisted Learning 19(3), 260–272 (2003)
5. Miura, M., Kunifuji, S., Sakamoto, Y.: Practical Environment for Realizing Augmented Classroom with Wireless Digital Pens. In: Apolloni, B., Howlett, R.J., Jain, L. (eds.) KES 2007, Part III. LNCS (LNAI), vol. 4694, pp. 777–785. Springer, Heidelberg (2007)
6. Hurford, A., Hamilton, E.: Effects of tablet computers and collaborative classroom software on student engagement and learning. In: Proceedings of Frontiers in Education Conference, FIE 2008, pp. S3J-15–S3J-20 (2008)
7. Nishiuchi, Y., Matsuuchi, N., Shiba, H., Fujiwara, K., Yamaguchi, T., Mendori, T.: Evaluation of TERAKOYA Learning System Linking Multi-point Remote Users as Supplementary Lessons. In: Proceedings of the 18th International Conference on Computers in Education, ICCE 2010, pp. 486–488 (2010)
8. BigBlueButton, http://www.bigbluebutton.org/

Part IV

In-Vehicle Interaction

WheelSense: Enabling Tangible Gestures on the Steering Wheel for In-Car Natural Interaction

Leonardo Angelini[1], Maurizio Caon[1], Francesco Carrino[1], Stefano Carrino[1], Denis Lalanne[2], Omar Abou Khaled[1], and Elena Mugellini[1]

[1] University of Applied Sciences of Western Switzerland, Fribourg
{Leonardo.Angelini,Maurizio.Caon,Francesco.Carrino,
Stefano.Carrino,Omar.AbouKhaled,Elena.Mugellini}@Hefr.ch
[2] University of Fribourg
Denis.Lalanne@unifr.ch

Abstract. This paper presents WheelSense, a system for non-distracting and natural interaction with the In-Vehicle Information and communication System (IVIS). WheelSense embeds pressure sensors in the steering wheel in order to detect tangible gestures that the driver can perform on its surface. In this application, the driver can interact by means of four gestures that have been designed to allow the execution of secondary tasks without leaving the hands from the steering wheel. Thus, the proposed interface aims at minimizing the distraction of the driver from the primary task. Eight users tested the proposed system in an evaluation composed of three phases: gesture recognition test, gesture recognition test while driving in a simulated environment and usability questionnaire. The results show that the accuracy rate is 87% and 82% while driving. The system usability scale scored 84 points out of 100.

Keywords: Tangible gestures, smart steering wheel, in-vehicle user interface, in-car natural interaction.

1 Introduction

Every year more and more people spend a considerable part of their life in cars. Recent statistics demonstrated that the average Swiss resident drove 23.8 km per day in 2010 [1]; in U.K., the average motorist spent 10 hours per week in his car [2]. For this reason, car makers are trying to make this "in-vehicle life" more enjoying, by equipping the car with various In-Vehicle Infotainment Systems (IVISs). All these systems need to be controlled by the car inhabitants and the common approach is to position most of these controls in the central dash board, in order to make them accessible also to the passenger. Typical approaches make use of knobs and buttons, but over the years many car makers have replaced these primordial systems with touchscreens, or advanced haptic controls like the BMW i-Drive [3]. When control systems are placed in the central dashboard, the driver has to leave one hand from the steering wheel and the eye gaze from the road. According to Bach et al. [4], most cases of general withdrawal of attention are caused by the loss of visual perception, often because of

M. Kurosu (Ed.): Human-Computer Interaction, Part II, HCII 2013, LNCS 8005, pp. 531–540, 2013.

eyes-off-the-road distraction. Indeed, moving the controls on the steering wheel allows the driver to avoid a consistent source of distraction. This is already a common practice for car makers, which offer, since several years, levers and buttons on the steering wheel to control the infotainment system and other electronic appliances in the car. However, the exponential growth of controls in the car cannot be supported only by buttons and knobs placed over or next to the steering wheel. In fact, these forms of interaction often cannot be adapted to dynamic content shown on digital screens [5]. Moreover, the arrangement of physical buttons is fixed and the space for mechanical input is limited [6]. In order to improve the car-living experience, many researchers are investigating interaction modalities that could be more natural and engaging, e.g., gestural interaction [7]. While free-hand gestures could be troublesome for the driver, gestures performed on the steering wheel appear as a safer natural interaction approach [8].

While most researchers focused on performing gestures on a touchscreen integrated in the center of the wheel [9], we explore gestures performed on the external ring as first theorized by Wolf et al. in [10]. This exploration takes into account modern theories on tangible gesture interaction which brings advantages from both tangible and gestural interaction [11]. The WheelSense system provides a novel interface based on tangible gestures performed on the steering wheel allowing the user to safely and naturally interact with the IVIS while driving.

In this paper, we analyze related work in Section 2. Then, we discuss the interaction and the gestures proposed for the control of the IVIS in Section 3. Section 4 depicts the architecture of the system, while the tests performed on eight users are presented in Section 5. In Section, 6 we make a brief discussion about our findings and we conclude the paper in Section 7 presenting also the future work.

2   Related Work

In the last years, several researchers have explored gestural interaction in the car as an alternative and more natural interface to control IVIS. Recently, Riener has affirmed that "in-vehicle gestural interfaces are easy to use and increase safety by reducing visual demand on the driver" [8]. So far, different approaches have been proposed. Although free-hand gestures could seem unsafe, Rahman et al. developed a system to control multimedia devices through free-hand gestures recognized by a 3D camera [12]. A safer approach was proposed by Endres et al.: instead of gesturing in the air with the whole hand, the user can move just a finger, with the hand still on the steering wheel [13]. In this case, finger gestures were recognized through electric field sensing. A similar system was exploited by Riener and Wintersberger near the gearshift to control a mouse cursor on an in-car screen [5]. In order to assess if gestures could improve and make safer the interaction with the IVIS, Bach et al. compared touch gestures on a touch screen to a classic tactile system and a touch Graphical User Interface [14]. Even if they did not noticed improvement on driving task errors, the study evidenced that touch gestures were able to lower the visual demand. These results suggest that gestural interaction could be safer than other approaches if interaction designers manage to reduce the cognitive load with appropriate feedbacks, and proposing gestures that are easy to remember. Bach et al.'s test was performed on a touchscreen integrated in the dashboard. Several researchers investigated a different position for a touch screen, i.e., integrated in the steering wheel. Pfleging et al. [9] integrated a standard tablet in the steering wheel combining touch gestures with speech commands. Döring et al. used a rear mounted projector to display information inside a steering wheel with a Plexiglas core and a camera to detect gestures performed with the thumbs on its surface [6]. While the SpeeT system [9] required detaching the hand from the steering wheel, Döring et al.'s system grants the possibility to make gestures while still grasping the external ring, which is required by the primary task.

The importance of keeping "eyes on the road and hands on the wheel" was stressed also by Gonzalez et al., [15] who proposed a text input method based on small thumb gestures on a small touchpad mounted on the wheel external ring. As an alternative approach for text input, Murer et al. explored the use of buttons on the rear of the steering wheel [16].

The analysis of the related work showed that many researchers aimed at displacing the interaction from the central dashboard to the steering wheel, granting as much as possible hand contact with the steering wheel. The design of gestures to be performed while grasping an object has been analyzed in depth by Wolf et al. [10], who described a large set of microgestures associated to a cylindrical grasp, i.e., the typical grasp for the steering wheel.

3   Design of Tangible Gesture Interaction on the Steering Wheel

Tangible gesture interaction has been recently defined by Hoven and Mazalek as "the use of physical devices for facilitating, supporting, enhancing, or tracking gestures people make for digital interaction purposes" [11]. Tangible gesture interaction still belongs to the broader field of tangible interaction, conjugating its most important property, i.e., physicality, and the communicative role of gestures. In this project, the physicality is brought by the steering wheel, which can be seen as a tangible interface not only for the driver's primary task [17], benefiting of the direct manipulation of the car behavior and of the haptic feedback from the road, but also for secondary tasks. In this section, we analyze the design of gestures performed on the steering wheel for the interaction with the IVIS discussing both their physics and semantics.

Wolf et al. analyzed from an ergonomic point of view the possibility to use microgestures on the steering wheel to perform secondary tasks while driving [10]. In particular, they identified some gestures that are particularly easy to perform while the driver holds the steering wheel. Following Wolf et al.'s analysis for the palm grasp, we chose three gestures: tapping with the index and dragging fingers around the wheel (in both directions). A fourth gesture, squeezing, has been chosen even if it was not considered in the Wolf et al.'s analysis. In fact, this latter gesture requires minimal effort and cognitive load for the user as well as the other three gestures. Several systems used squeezing as interaction modality with objects; Fishkin et al. showed in

[18] some advantages of the squeeze gesture, for example the possibility to perform a squeeze without moving the hand from the object, which indeed is very useful while driving.

In order to facilitate remembering the four chosen gestures, embodied metaphors [19] have been used to associate their corresponding functions for controlling the infotainment system. The driver can start performing the tap gesture on the steering wheel in order to make some music: indeed, a single tap with the index is interpreted by the system as turning on the music. Dragging up and down the fingers on the steering wheel allows browsing up and down in the playlist. Squeeze is used to turn off the music, which intuitively binds closing the hand to closing the music player. The four gestures are shown in Fig. 1.

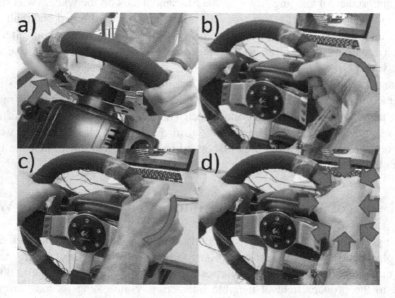

Fig. 1. Representation of the four gestures: a) tap, b) dragging up, c) dragging down, d) squeeze

The design of a gestural interface requires a proper feedback in order to acknowledge the user on the result of the command. Tangible gesture interaction on the steering wheel involves doing an intensive use of haptic senses for the driver. Gestures are designed to be as intuitive as possible, without need of visual attention on the interface. Thus, it could be given as an opportune practice to convey the feedback to the user on the same haptic channel, using vibration motors or tactile displays [20]. However, as stressed from Bach et al. [4], there is a risk of increased distraction if the secondary task competes on the perceptual resources required by the primary task. Indeed, haptic feedback coming from the road and perceived through the steering wheel has an important role in the driving task. As suggested by Wickens and Hollands [21], the perceptual resources needed for the secondary task can be distributed over other senses. Moreover, we avoided tactile cues that could help the driver to detect sensors positions for two main reasons: first, we would like to maintain the surface of the steering wheel as smooth as possible, in order to avoid pain for the user during the test session; secondly, we would like to let users forget about the underlying technology, making the interaction as intuitive as possible.

In our application, we exploit the auditory feedback generated by the media player: tap and squeeze can be easily detected respectively by the presence or absence of the music. Dragging gestures can be identified with a change of the song: in the case of a playlist, the dragging up gesture is acknowledged by the music of a new song (next track), while the dragging down gesture corresponds to a song already listened (previous track). Obviously, the purpose of the application, i.e. listening to music, ensures that the auditory channel is not disturbed, thus the feedback is effective. In case of doubt, or for further information about the song, the user can still look at the screen on the central dashboard.

4   System Architecture

The sensing system implemented in the first prototype is based on five Tekscan FlexiForce sensors with a range of 0-1 lb [22]. They are connected to an Arduino Duemilanove board that converts signals to the digital domain and sends measured data to a PC for further elaboration through a wired serial connection. Data are acquired with a rate of 50 Hz. We augmented a Logitech G27 Racing Wheel with four sensors for the right hand and one sensor for the left hand. The sensors placement on the steering wheel is depicted in Fig. 2. Sensor 1 is placed to recognize the tap gesture with the index finger. In a relaxed position, the hand generally covers the three other sensors. The wrist flexion and the wrist extension performed for the dragging up and down gestures uncover respectively Sensors 3 and Sensor 4. Sensor 5 is used to segment gestures with the left hand in order to minimize false positives during the execution of the primary task: the driver squeezes the left hand while gestures are performed with the right hand. We placed the 5 pressure sensors in the specific regions of the external ring to be compliant with the hands position suggested by the Swiss driving school manual [23].

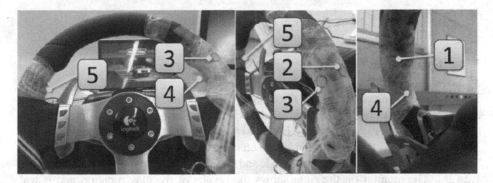

Fig. 2. The five FlexiForce sensors placement

The raw data are elaborated using the ARAMIS Framework [24], which allows a fast implementation of a recognition system through chainable services. First, gestures of the right hand are segmented setting a threshold on the left hand sensor. Afterwards, the segmented data are used as input for a Hidden Markov Model (HMM) classifier. The HMM classifier was configured with 4 hidden states with forward topology and implementing the Baum-Welch algorithm to find the unknown parameters. The data supplied to the HMM classifier are modeled as temporal signals (as depicted in Fig. 3). The whole architecture of the WheelSense system is reported in Fig. 4.

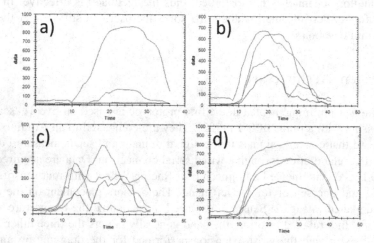

Fig. 3. Representation of the temporal signal associated to the four gestures: a) is tap, b) is dragging up, c) is dragging down and d) is squeeze

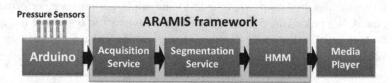

Fig. 4. Block diagram of the WheelSense system architecture

5   Evaluation

The evaluation was composed of three phases: the gesture recognition accuracy test, the gesture recognition accuracy calculated while the user was driving using a simulator and the usability questionnaire. Eight users (six males and two females, aged 25 - 31) participated to this evaluation. The setup, depicted in Fig. 5, is composed by a laptop that executes the recognition task and the City Car Driving Simulator version 1.2 [25]. The monitor on the right shows the results of the classification and it was used by the experiment supervisor.

Fig. 5. A user participating at the evaluation

5.1   Gesture Recognition Accuracy

During the first part of the evaluation process, the users were asked to perform 40 times each gesture while the PC was recording for a total of 160 gestures. The order of the gesture to be performed was chosen randomly and the user was guided by a graphical interface. The user was requested to rest at half of the recording phase. We applied the 10-fold cross-validation test on the recorded data. The resulting average accuracy is 87% and standard deviation was 17%.

5.2   Gesture Recognition Accuracy While Driving

Using the data recorded during the first phase, we trained the HMM classifier. Then, we asked to every user to drive using the City Car Driving simulator and to interact with the IVIS through the gestural interface. In this case, the gestures were used to control a music player with the gesture-function association explained in Section 3. We requested the gestures that the user had to perform; he/she had to remain focused on the driving task and to perform the gesture only when he/she was feeling confident, that means when the user evaluated the maneuver as not dangerous. The total number of gestures that each user had to perform during the driving simulation was 40 (10 per type of gesture). The average accuracy was 82% and the standard deviation among users was 16%. In fact, during the experience, we noticed a high variability between the users. The confusion matrix is reported in Table 1.

Table 1. Confusion matrix of the second phase of the evaluation: gesture recognition accuracy while driving

	Up	Down	Squeeze	Tap
Up	**64**	9	3	4
Down	4	**69**	1	6
Squeeze	9	4	**64**	2
Tap	7	4	4	**65**

5.3   Usability

After the second phase, we asked to the users to fill a System Usability Scale questionnaire (SUS) [26]. We calculated three factors from the SUS: the overall usability, perceived usability and the learnability. The overall usability (calculated following the standard procedure) scored 84 points out of 100 (standard deviation: 13); the perceived usability scored 82 points out of 100 (standard deviation: 12); the learnability scored 91 points out of 100 (standard deviation: 17). We calculated the last two factors as suggested by Lewis and Sauro in [27].

6   Discussion

The two performance evaluations showed a high variability among users, which affected also the results of the usability evaluation. This high variability could be explained with the different hands position of the users during the interaction. In some cases, the left hand was not always positioned over the pressure sensors, which decreased consistently the quality and the strength of the acquired signals. Variations could also occur over time: for example, in one case, the system confused several times a squeeze with a dragging up gesture, because the user was not pressing anymore on Sensor 1 (see Fig. 1). This suggests that a robust system should be difficult to achieve without taking into account the changes in the behavior of user's gestures. An adaptive learning approach could be implemented in order to avoid this issue.

7   Conclusion and Future Work

This paper presented WheelSense: a novel interface based on tangible gestures performed on the steering wheel. The proposed interaction modality allows the user to safely and naturally manage the IVIS while driving. We presented also the design of four tangible gestures: tap, dragging up, dragging down and squeeze. Gestures are used to control the media player, thus the auditory feedback is generally sufficient to avoid eye-off-the-road distraction. The evaluation of the WheelSense system assessed the accuracy being equal to 87%. We performed the evaluation of the same configuration during a simulated driving experience and WheelSense scored 82% of recognition accuracy. The system usability scale assessed the system score as 84 points.

As future work, we plan to integrate automatic segmentation and we will conduct some evaluation tests in order to compare the performances between the two different approaches: automatic segmentation versus manual segmentation. Moreover, we will implement an adaptive machine learning approach for the classifier.

Acknowledgements. This work has been supported by Hasler Foundation in the framework of "Living in Smart Environments" project.

References

1. Swiss average utilization of transport means in 2010. Swiss Federation (March 2013), http://www.bfs.admin.ch/bfs/portal/fr/index/themen/11/07/01/01/unterwegszeiten/01.html
2. Britons spend more time driving than socialising. The Telegraph (March 2013), http://www.telegraph.co.uk/motoring/news/8287098/Britons-spend-more-time-driving-than-socialising.html
3. Niedermaier, B., Durach, S., Eckstein, L., Keinath, A.: The new BMW iDrive – applied processes and methods to assure high usability. In: Duffy, V.G. (ed.) ICDHM 2009. LNCS, vol. 5620, pp. 443–452. Springer, Heidelberg (2009)
4. Bach, K.M., Jæger, M.G., Skov, M.B., Thomassen, N.G.: Interacting with in-vehicle systems: understanding, measuring, and evaluating attention. In: Proc. of BCS-HCI 2009, pp. 453–462 (2009)
5. Riener, A., Wintersberger, P.: Natural, intuitive finger based input as substitution for traditional vehicle control. In: Proceedings of AutomotiveUI 2011, pp. 33–34 (2011)
6. Döring, T., Kern, D., Marshall, P., Pfeiffer, M., Schöning, J., Gruhn, V., Schmidt, A.: Gestural interaction on the steering wheel: reducing the visual demand. In: Proceedings of the 2011 Annual Conference on Human Factors in Computing Systems, pp. 483–492 (2011)
7. Riener, A.: Gestural Interaction in Vehicular Applications. Computer, 42–47 (2012)
8. Carrino, F., Carrino, S., Caon, M., Angelini, L., Khaled, O.A., Mugellini, E.: In-Vehicle Natural Interaction Based on Electromyography. In: Proc. of AutomotiveUI 2012, pp. 1–3 (2012)
9. Pfleging, B., Schneegass, S., Schmidt, A.: Multimodal Interaction in the Car - Combining Speech and Gestures on the Steering Wheel. In: Proc. of AutomotiveUI 2011, pp. 155–162 (2011)
10. Wolf, K., Naumann, A., Rohs, M., Müller, J.: A taxonomy of microinteractions: Defining microgestures based on ergonomic and scenario-dependent requirements. In: Campos, P., Graham, N., Jorge, J., Nunes, N., Palanque, P., Winckler, M. (eds.) INTERACT 2011, Part I. LNCS, vol. 6946, pp. 559–575. Springer, Heidelberg (2011)
11. van den Hoven, E., Mazalek, A.: Grasping gestures: Gesturing with physical artifacts. Artificial Intelligence for Engineering Design, Analysis and Manufacturing 25(03), 255–271 (2011)
12. Rahman, A., Saboune, J., El Saddik, A.: Motion-path based in car gesture control of the multimedia devices. In: Proc. of DIVANet 2011, pp. 69–76 (2011)
13. Endres, C., Schwartz, T., Christian, M.: Geremin: 2D Microgestures for Drivers Based on Electric Field Sensing". In: Proc. of IUI 2011, pp. 327–330 (2011)
14. Bach, K.M., Jaeger, M.G., Skov, M.B., Thomassen, N.G.: You can touch, but you can't look: interacting with in-vehicle systems. In: Proceeding of the 26th Annual SIGCHI Conference on Human Factors in Computing Systems, pp. 1139–1148 (2008)

15. González, I.E., Wobbrock, J.O., Chau, D.H., Faulring, A., Myers, B.A.: Eyes on the road, hands on the wheel: thumb-based interaction techniques for input on steering wheels. In: Proceedings of Graphics Interface 2007, pp. 95–102 (2007)

16. Murer, M., Wilfinger, D., Meschtscherjakov, A., Osswald, S., Tscheligi, M.: Exploring the Back of the Steering Wheel: Text Input with Hands on the Wheel and Eyes on the Road. In: Proc. of AutomotiveUI 2012, pp. 117–120 (2012)

17. Fishkin, K.P., Moran, T.P., Harrison, B.L.: Embodied User Interfaces: Towards Invisible User Interfaces. In: Proc. of the IFIP Seventh Working Conference on Engineering for Human-Computer Interaction, pp. 1–18 (1999)

18. Fishkin, K.P., Gujar, A., Mochon, C., Want, R.: Squeeze Me, Hold Me, Tilt Me! An Exploration of Manipulative User Interfaces. In: Proc. CHI 1998, pp. 17–24 (1998)

19. Bakker, S., Antle, A.N., Van Den Hoven, E.: Embodied metaphors in tangible interaction design. In: Personal and Ubiquitous Computing (2011)

20. Kyung, K.U., Park, J.S.: Ubi-Pen: Development of a Compact Tactile Display Module and Its Application to a Haptic Stylus. In: Proc. of the Second Joint EuroHaptics Conference and Symposium on Haptic Interfaces for Virtual Environment and Teleoperator Systems, pp. 109–114 (2007)

21. Wickens, C.D., Hollands, J.G.: Engineering Psychology and Human. Prentice Hall (2000)

22. Tekscan FlexiForce (March 2013), http://www.tekscan.com/flexible-force-sensors

23. Teaching manual for the formation and examination of driving instructors, Manuel d'enseignement pour la formation et l'examen des moniteurs de conduite, Département fédéral de justice et police (March 2013),
http://www.asa.ch/media/archive1/Shop/Ausbildungsunterla-gen/gratis/Leitfaden_Fahrlehrer_Fachgruppe_7_f.pdf

24. Carrino, S., Péclat, A., Mugellini, E., Abou Khaled, O., Ingold, R.: Humans and smart environments. In: Proceedings of the 13th International Conference on Multimodal Interfaces, ICMI 2011, p. 105 (2011)

25. Multisoft, City Car Driving Simulator (March 2013),
http://citycardriving.com/

26. Brooke, J.: SUS: A Quick and Dirty Usability Scale. In: Usability Evaluation in Industry, pp. 189–194 (1996)

27. Lewis, J.R., Sauro, J.: The factor structure of the system usability scale. In: Kurosu, M. (ed.) HCD 2009. LNCS, vol. 5619, pp. 94–103. Springer, Heidelberg (2009)

Reducing Speeding Behavior in Young Drivers Using a Persuasive Mobile Application

Anne Bergmans[1] and Suleman Shahid[2]

[1] Department of Communication and Information Sciences,
Tilburg University, The Netherlands
acmbergmans@gmail.com
[2] Tilburg Center for Cognition and Communication, Department of Communication
and Information Sciences, Tilburg University, The Netherlands
s.shahid@uvt.nl

Abstract. This paper presents a solution to the problem of speeding in male young drivers. This paper outlines the design of a persuasive mobile application that aims at reducing speeding behavior by providing various incentives. The application targets both weak and strong habit drivers between the age of 18 and 26. Early results show an overall acceptance of the application, mainly due to its unique rewarding mechanism, and its ability to demonstrate the actual speeding behavior with major impact on safety, fuel costs, environment, and possible fine costs. Results further indicate a behavior change for weak habit drivers and attitude change for strong habit drivers.

Keywords: Speeding behavior, persuasive technology, mobile application, speeding behavior model, usability test, driving behavior.

1 Introduction

Unsafe driving can lead to accidents, serious injuries, and sometimes even death. There are several types of behavior that causes accidents, for example distraction, negative emotions, and speeding. To elaborate on the latter, speeding is responsible for one out of three fatal accidents [1]. When a road and associated traffic situation becomes more complex as a result of speeding and environmental factors (e.g. country road), the driver is forced to process more information in a shorter time span. Furthermore, it is likely that the driver is forced to make more decisions, which significantly increases the chances for an accident.

Studies have been performed in which drivers were rewarded for complying with the speed limit. The majority found that rewarding is an effective measure for changing speeding behavior [2]. However, these studies focused on all types of driving behavior rather than solely speeding. In addition, participants only complied with the speed limit when they received a reward. Solely giving out rewards does not confront drivers with the badness of their behavior, and results in a reversion to same old state. City engineers in Garden Grove, California undertook a different approach with neither punishment nor reward [3]. They put up Dynamic Speed Monitoring

M. Kurosu (Ed.): Human-Computer Interaction, Part II, HCII 2013, LNCS 8005, pp. 541–550, 2013.

Displays (DSMD) (also known as *driver feedback signs*). Interestingly these signs simply show drivers what they already know (namely their speed) and are not followed by punishment. Nevertheless, the average speed decreased with 14 percent due to the increased awareness of the current speed. According to SWOV [4], especially men between the age of 18 and 24 have a higher chance of involvement in serious car accidents (six times more the than drivers between the age of 30 to 59) in the Netherlands.

This paper focuses on reducing speeding behavior of male young drivers (age 18 to 24) by using *persuasive technology,* which is defined as technology designed to change attitudes or behaviors of users through persuasion and social influence, rather than through coercion [5]. The main purpose of this paper is to propose the design of a new mobile interface for reducing speeding behavior. The design of the application which is the main contribution of this paper is based on a longitudinal user study and literature review. This paper also presents the results of an early evaluation of this interface.

2   Theoretical Framework

2.1   Previous Work

Currently there are several mobile applications to stimulate save driving behavior. However, all applications force drivers to change their behavior and do not make them aware of their current bad driving practices. Previous scientific research focused on extensive programs such as *Graduated Driver Licensing* [6] or influencing the *driving locus of control* [7]. Results of these programs showed that young drivers understand that they should not drive unsafe and know how to deal with unsafe situations. However, such programs are a time consuming activity for young drivers and these drivers usually find it hard to finish them. Another interesting system, named as *Intelligente Snelheidsassistentie (ISA)* (*Advanced Driver Assistance Systems*), was developed by the SWOV. It is an advanced support system for drivers [8]. The ISA-systems determine the general position of the car, compares the current speed to the speed limit, and subsequently gives feedback to the driver or manually reduces the car speed. Results of using an ISA-system show that speeding decreases with two to seven kilometers per hour, depending on the type of ISA-system.

Other than few examples, most of the existing systems or methods are mostly focused on punishment and do not lead to a deliberate behavior change. Helping drivers in willingly changing their behavior, by making them aware of their bad habits and by offering them right incentives, is the main purpose of this study.

2.2   Persuasive Technology

Fogg defines persuasion as an attempt to change attitudes, behaviors, or both [5]. *Captology* states that a computer can be the source of persuasion (e.g. it can encourage, provide incentives, negotiate) [9]. Fogg and Hreha present the *Behavior Wizard* [10], which is a method for matching target behavior with solutions for achieving those behaviors. The basis for the Behavior Wizard is formed by the

Behavior Grid, which consists of fifteen types of behavior change. This Wizard is relevant for studies regarding persuasive technology as it provides a simple overview of the desired behavior change (e.g. permanent) and how to achieve that behavior (e.g. immediately stop). According to Fogg [5], timing and context are critically important to influence attitudes and behaviors of people. Mobile devices are pre-eminently the right instrument for this, as they can influence people at an optimal time and place.

2.3   Speeding Behavior Model and Theory of Planned Behavior

De Pelsmacker and Janssens [11] developed the reduced *Speeding behavior model*, which shows that *norms* influence the *attitude towards speeding*. The latter subsequently influences the *intention to speed*, which in turn influences the *actual behavior*. The model further stresses the importance of *habit formation, cognitive* and *affective attitude towards speeding* components. *Habit formation* is equally important as *intention to speed*, because habits are able to directly influence the *actual behavior*. However, habits can also indirectly effect behavior through *intention to speed*. That is, people intend to speed simply because they are used to do so. Therefore the researchers argue that breaking bad habits is crucially important to reduce speeding behavior. The Speeding behavior model functioned as primary theoretical model in the current study as it specifically focuses on speeding behavior. Furthermore, it provides a detailed overview of all components and is therefore useful for identifying what a persuasive application should influence to reduce speeding behavior.

The *Theory of Planned Behavior (TPB)* [12] has also often been used in studies regarding speeding behavior. Ajzen argues that when human behavior is goal-directed, people perform actions to achieve that goal. This is relevant to persuasive technology as goals can be used to motivate behavior change. To extent the TPB, Greaves and Ellison [13] focused specifically on driving behavior and found that aversion to risk reduces speeding. Furthermore, Jager [14] states that routine behaviors are performed with a minimum of thinking, and are therefore defined as habits. To induce behavior change by changing the habit, one must provide direct and timely feedback. The TPB and extensions functioned as addition to the Speeding behavior model, as it provides insight into how behavior can be changed in a more specific way.

3   User Research and Results

An extensive user research phase was conducted to determine the rationales for speeding in male young drivers. One questionnaire, two rounds of interviews, and a diary study were used to study users' practices and requirements. The questionnaire was administered to gain participants from a large group of university students in a relatively quick and easy manner. Semi-structured interviews were conducted to gain insight into rationales for speeding and to evaluate the diary. A diary study was conducted in-between two interviews for comparing statements and for the recording of actual behavior. All male drivers were between the age of 18 and 26, with a mean age of 24 were selected for this study. Elements from the *Speeding behavior model* [11], namely *attitude towards speeding*, *norms*, *habit*, *self-standard*, *intention*, and *actual behavior* were used as measurements. Few other measurements were *sensation seeking*, smartphone use, and persuasion.

3.1   Results

Results from the first interview show that the rationales for speeding differ. Most participants speed because the road is familiar to them, from which they subsequently and gradually started speeding. Participants additionally set boundaries for themselves so they do not speed excessively. These boundaries range from speeding with 10 km per hour to a maximum of 30 km per hour. Many participants have family members who feel that they should not speed, although these family members do not try to persuade them. The family members state their opinion both outside as inside the car. The majority of the participants reported a weak habit of speeding. Participants stated they would regret their speeding if there were vulnerable road users present (e.g. cyclists or children) or if they would get a fine, although the latter is not persuasive enough to reduce speeding. Most of the participants showed concerns about the possible negative consequences of speeding but also stated that while speeding these negative consequences go in the back of mind. They further do not judge themselves as being bad when they exceed the speed limit. The majority does not experience speeding as risky, but they do acknowledge that it is more risky in critical situations (e.g. when something unexpected happens and they have no control). All participants believe that when all drivers would comply with the speed limit, it will reduce the number of accidents but they do not see how would it happen. They believe that currently many accidents occur as a result of differences in speed, and because speeding causes unsafe situations in general. However almost all drivers felt that they think they have a good control over car while speeding. Finally, participants state that they could be persuaded not to speed by providing them with a reward (e.g. discount on road taxes).

Results from the diary study show that the majority of the statements match the results from the diary, mostly regarding the rationales for speeding. Almost all drivers over speeded everyday especially on familiar roads. A few participants claimed that they did not gain more awareness of their speeding behavior by keeping the diary because they either did not think much about what they wrote down (in terms of what it meant) or because they were already aware of the speed they drove. Majority of them reported to notice their actual speeding behavior, which indicates they were not completely aware of their speeding behavior before.

4   Early Prototyping and Final Design

In the first phase, design alternatives were developed based on a brainstorming session and design requirements. These design requirements included all major triggers for behavior change that the application must hold. For example, the application must persuade drivers to obtain goals and make drivers aware of their speeding behavior. The design alternatives were divided into two parts: application functions that can be used while driving, and functions that can be used outside the car. Aspects from nearly all design alternatives were used in a paper prototype. The paper prototype was tested with end user for improving the contents and structure of the application.

Previously interviewed participants were selected to participate in the paper prototype test. It was made sure that participants with different behaviors, habits, and opinions were selected for the paper prototype test. Six tasks were defined that covered the complete interface. Although the test succeeded without many problems, several improvements needed to be made in the design. The whole process resulted in the final working design, which is shown in Figure 1 and 2.

Fig. 1. Main screen of the application with links to the in-car live screen, traffic game, profile, help-section, and overview of goal achievement. The screen presents the progress and goal requirement per key goal.

The final application was developed for iPhone, and all native interface design guidelines and standards were used for this design. The final design consists of a main screen that shows four key goals to be achieved in order to obtain a reward (Fig. 1). The behavior triggers behind different design elements and goals are discussed in the next section. The four key goals are *CO2 emissions*, *overview of fine costs*, *fuel costs*, and *chance for an accident*. Furthermore, this screen contains navigation to several sections. Firstly, the profile in which friends can be invited and possible competitions can be started between friends. Secondly, an overview section was added in which users can view their overall goal progress and previously obtained rewards. Thirdly, a traffic game section was added as a fun-factor so drivers would still be reminded of less speeding even while not driving. Fourthly, a help section was added with basic information regarding the purpose and functions. However, the most important aspect is the in-car live screen. The in-car live screen (Fig. 3) shows real-time goal progress while driving, possible fine cost at the current speed, damage at the current speed represented by a dented car, and possibility to personalize the car. This in-car live screen is the most important aspect of this design. It tracks actual speeding behavior and presents it to users who can immediately change their behavior if necessary. The design of the application therefore requires drivers to take the smartphone with them in the car to track their speeding behavior.

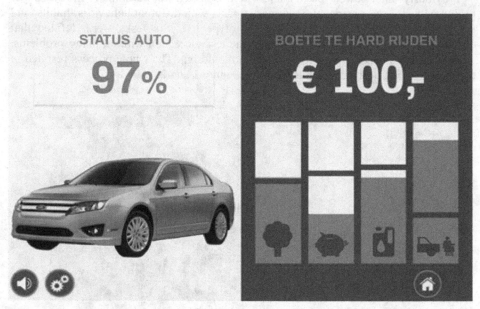

Fig. 2. In-car live screens in which users can adjust the appearance of the car, see the health status of the car and the possible fine costs at the current speed, and overview of the goal achievement. This screen is shown while driving.

4.1 Behavior Triggers

The Behavior Wizard of Fogg and Hreha [10] served as basis for determining the target behavior (i.e. reduce/eliminate speeding), and matching solutions (i.e. persuasive application with various sections) for achieving that behavior. The application holds several triggers that stimulate the use of the application. Ideally, the application changes the current bad habit of speeding into the good habit of complying with the speed limit.

The overall trigger to use the application is the chance of obtaining a desirable reward. In order to receive that reward, users must achieve goals by not (or less) speeding. This trigger is the most important one, since it should directly influence drivers to immediately reduce or eliminate their speeding behavior when they speed. A warning border indicates which goals are critically low, and is therefore also considered a trigger because users can adjust their speeding behavior accordingly. Another trigger is viewing the progress from friends, which can lead to a competition. In order to win or remain in first place, users must continuously use the application in their car. The traffic game is a similar activity, in which users can earn points and rise in the overall game ranking. A trigger for outside the car is the overview of statistics per goal on the home page and in the "Progress" section. These elements confront users with their speeding behavior, negative consequences such as increased petrol costs, and the consequences on obtaining their reward. This is a major trigger, because when users see they are doing bad they will most likely start using the application in the car. In case users stopped using the application and subsequently witnessed a decrease in progress, they will most likely start using the application again. This is a back-up trigger for a scenario when users are solely using the application outside the car. A final minor trigger is the possibility to change the settings of the car, as users might prefer to manually choose and/or personalize the car to be displayed (e.g. similar to their own car) which will improve the overall acceptance of the application.

5   Evaluation

In this section, we present the early evaluation of the application. The goal of evaluation was to improve the usability of the application and to verify if young drivers accept it as a possible mean of persuasive intervention. These participants were routine derivers with bad driving habits and performed real tasks while driving. The experimenter observed and recorded all actions.

In the first round, the usability of the application was evaluated. This part of evaluation specifically focused on the *perceived ease of use* and *perceived usefulness* of the application [15]. Following the usability test, an observational study together with post interviews was conducted to measure the overall acceptance and persuasion of the application. The tasks were, to a large extent, identical to the tasks used in the paper prototype test, except for some minor changes to increase efficiency of the task executions (e.g. different formulation of a sentence).

5.1   Results

Results of the all three phases of evaluation show that the application holds more advantages than disadvantages, and a user can relate to at least one of the goals. Participants realized the added value of the application for themselves and for others. They said that they would recommend it to other drivers in their social circle because they appreciated the learning-factor (i.e. confrontation with actual speeding behavior), the social factor (competition with friends and scoring), and the fun-factor (i.e. traffic game). All participants mentioned that the application uses an unusual and positive approach (i.e. reward and insight in the four goals of speeding behavior) for improving driving habits. They mentioned that they would keep an eye on the achievement of goals while driving the car and the possible reward or incentive gained after achieving a goal would be the major persuasive factor. One participant said, "The app warns when you are speeding and what the consequences are. This makes it easier to adjust speeding behavior because it is a constant (positive) reminder while driving the car".

In all phases of evaluation, all participants liked the idea of 'four key goals' on the main screen and they mentioned that the 'dented car' picture and the impact of bad driving on the 'wallet' were quite persuasive. The impact of bad driving on environment was also appreciated, but majority said that it would never work as a primary factor. All participants rated the application as easy to use because of the clear structure of the goals, flexibility, responsive interaction style and intuitive navigation. One participant said, "The design is very basic and it is very easy to use even when you are driving. You can quickly scan the interface for knowing the current status and therefore it does not threaten your and others' lives on road". Furthermore, the learning curve was extremely low. Participants were able to learn the application without any tutorial and they were able to use all major features fairly quickly. During the test, not even a single participant asked for any assistance.

Several participants mentioned that it becomes socially unacceptable to speed when friends score higher. This kind of a social influence is much stronger than the one when your friends or family members warn you about the speeding in a more general way. Only three participants did not realize the persuasive power of scoring. Participant also appreciated the offline part of the app. The possibility of reviewing their current journey and statistics of previous journeys made them aware of their habits. Most of the participants believed that this app has the potential to change their speeding behavior in the long run. They mentioned that if all works as proposed in this version of app, the application would decrease their speeding behavior in the long run. Finally the results show that the application seems to work for both weak and strong habit drivers; the weak habit drivers were effected and persuaded much more quickly and strongly than strong habit drivers.

In summary, majority of the participants claim that the application alters the (affective) attitude towards speeding through the four goals, encourages them to achieve goals by offering a reward, confronts them with their actual speeding behavior, shows anticipated regret, communicates risk aversion, and create a social atmosphere where their friends can influence each others behavior. They think that it is a positive step towards to a long-term behavior change.

6   Discussion and Future Work

The aim of this study was to design a new mobile persuasive application, which could assist young drivers in changing their speeding behavior in a more eagerly and voluntarily manner. The design of the application was based on a longitudinal user study and detailed literature review. The final application, developed for an iPhone, was appreciated by the drivers for its design, usability and utility. The results of the first evaluation show that the application has the potential to positively effect the speeding behavior of male young drivers. The results also show that the level of persuasiveness is determined by the type of habit. Weak habit drivers indicate an immediate reduction in speeding behavior, whereas strong habit drivers indicate a change in attitude and at later stage reduction in speeding behavior. This result is inline with the results of [16], who also showed that weak habit users can easily be influenced as compared to strong habit users and that is why weak habit users should be the first target for a persuasive intervention.

The reward mechanism and confrontation with actual behavior using timely and relevant feedback are the major reasons for the possible behavior change. Other aspects such as competition with friends (social influence), continuous warning about possible fines (anticipated regret and risk aversion), and the offline reviewing of journeys (personal reflection) also contribute to the overall utility of the application. These results again confirm the results of early studies. For example, a study by Mazureck, et. al. [17] showed that giving rewards on good driving behavior can improve speeding behavior. Another study showed that the use of direct and timely feedback about the appropriateness or inappropriateness of certain behavior positively influences the behavior [14].

Finally, all drivers realized the added value of our application, because all drivers were able to find at least one feature or function, which was influential, relevant for their needs and suitable for their personality. Based on the early results, we think that the application was able to accommodate a diverse user group due its flexible design. Overall the application was rated very positive by all drivers because it employs a positive approach with regard to reducing speeding behavior and none of the participants had experienced this kind of approach before.

This study has a number of limitations. One of the major limitations of this study is the evaluation phase. The evaluation presented in this paper is very short and was done in the early phase of the design. The final design was once again improved after this evaluation. In the next round, the application should be extended by a longitudinal study to accurately measure if the speeding behavior changes in the long run. Based on the early results, we can say that this application has the potential to influence the behavior but we will have to verify it in the next round of evaluation. The current results should only be taken as trends.

In future research, it is not only important to test the application in long run but also test it multiple times after certain intervals to see if the speeding pattern reemerges once people stop using this application.

References

1. Organization for Economic Co-operation and Development & European Conference of Ministers of Transport: Speed Management. Organization for Economic Co-operation and Development OECD/European Conference of Ministers of Transport, Paris (2006)
2. SWOV-factsheet Beloningen voor verkeersveilig gedrag (2011), http://www.swov.nl/rapport/Factsheets/NL/Factsheet_Belonen.pdf
3. Goetz, T.: Harnessing the power of feedback loops (2011), http://www.wired.com/magazine/2011/06/ff_feedbackloop
4. SWOV-factsheet (Stichting Wetenschappelijk Onderzoek Verkeersveiligheid) Jonge beginnende automobilisten (2010a), http://www.swov.nl/rapport/Factsheets/NL/Factsheet_Jonge_automobilisten.pdf
5. Fogg, B.J.: Persuasive technology: Using computers to change what we think and do. Morgan Kaufmann Publishers, San Francisco (2003)

6. McKnight, A.J., Peck, R.C.: Graduated driver licensing and safer driving. Journal of Safety Research 34, 85–89 (2003)
7. Huang, J.L., Ford, J.K.: Driving locus of control and driving behaviors: Inducing change through driver training. Transportation Research Part F: Traffic Psychology and Behaviour 15, 358–368 (2012)
8. SWOV-factsheet Intelligente Snelheidsassistentie, ISA (2010b), http://www.swov.nl/rapport/Factsheets/NL/Factsheet_ISA.pdf
9. Fogg, B.J.: Captology: The study of computers as persuasive technologies. In: Edwards, A., Pemberton, S. (eds.) Extended Abstracts on Human Factors in Computing Systems Looking to the Future. ACM, New York (1997)
10. Fogg, B.J., Hreha, J.: Behavior wizard: A method for matching target behaviors with solutions. In: Ploug, T., Hasle, P., Oinas-Kukkonen, H. (eds.) PERSUASIVE 2010. LNCS, vol. 6137, pp. 117–131. Springer, Heidelberg (2010)
11. De Pelsmacker, P., Janssens, W.: The effect of norms, attitudes and habits on speeding behavior: Scale development and model building and estimation. Accident Analysis and Prevention 39(1), 6–15 (2007), doi:10.1016/j.aap.2006.05.011
12. Ajzen, I.: From intentions to actions: A theory of planned behavior. Action Control from Cognition to Behavior 2(1), 11–39 (1985)
13. Greaves, S.P., Ellison, A.B.: Personality, risk aversion and speeding: An empirical investigation. Accident Analysis and Prevention 43(5), 1828–1836 (2011)
14. Jager, W.: Breaking bad habits: A dynamical perspective on habit formation and change. In: Hendrick Wander, L., Steg, L. (eds.) Human Decision Making and Environmental Perception: Understanding and Assisting Human Decision-Making in Real Life Settings, Libor Amicorum for Charles Vlek Groningen, Netherlands (2003)
15. Davis, F.D., Venkatesh, V.: Toward preprototype user acceptance testing of new information systems: implications for software project management. IEEE Transactions on Engineering Management 51(1), 31–46 (2004)
16. Verplanken, B., Aarts, H.: Habit, attitude, and planned behaviour: Is habit an empty construct or an interesting case of goal-directed automaticity? European Review of Social Psychology 10, 101–134 (1999)
17. Mazureck, U., van Hattem, J.: Rewards for safe driving behavior: Influence on following distance and speed. In: Transportation Research Record: Journal of the Transportation Research Board, Washington, DC, pp. 31–38 (2006)

Auditory and Head-Up Displays in Vehicles

Christina Dicke[1], Grega Jakus[2], and Jaka Sodnik[2]

[1] Quality and Usability Lab, Telekom Innovation Laboratories, TU Berlin, Germany
christina.dicke@tu-berlin.de
[2] University of Ljubljana, Faculty of Electrical Engineering, Slovenia
{grega.jakus,jaka.sodnik}@fe.uni-lj.si

Abstract. The aim of the user study presented in this paper was to investigate the efficiency of single and multimodal user interfaces for in-vehicle control and information systems and their impact on driving safety. A windshield projection (HUD) of a hierarchical list-based visual menu was compared to an auditory representation of the same menu and to a combination of both representations. In the user study 30 participants were observed while operating a driving simulator and simultaneously solving tasks of different complexity with the three interfaces. The variables measured in the user study were task completion times, driving performance and the perceived workload. Our study shows that the single modality auditory interface is the least efficient representation of the menu; the multimodal audio-visual interface, however, shows a strong tendency to be superior to both the auditory and visual single modality interfaces with regards to driver distraction and efficiency.

Keywords: Human-computer interaction, auditory interface, head-up display, car simulator, driving performance.

1 Introduction

Head-up displays (HUDs) are the current state-of-the-art solution intended to reduce driver errors originating in distractive interfaces, such as onboard entertainment displays or navigation systems. HUDs reduce the frequency and duration of glances at Head-down displays (HDDs) by presenting information directly on the windshield in the driver's field of vision.

HUDs, when compared to HDDs, have been shown to reduce the response times to unanticipated road events [1], reduce navigational errors [2], and lead to smaller variances in lateral acceleration and steering wheel angle [3]. Charissis et al. [4] found that HUDs dramatically reduce the number of collisions and improve the maintenance of following distance in low visibility situations.

On the other hand, HUDs have also been shown to increase mental workload as indicated by longer response times in high workload situations [5, 6]. The so-called cognitive capture, i.e. when the drivers' attention is unconsciously shifted away from the road and is mainly focused on processing the information presented by the HUD [7, 8], has been identified as one of the disadvantages of HUDs. The resulting

M. Kurosu (Ed.): Human-Computer Interaction, Part II, HCII 2013, LNCS 8005, pp. 551–560, 2013.
© Springer-Verlag Berlin Heidelberg 2013

perceptual tunneling may lead to a delayed reaction or a complete absence of response to situational changes in the driving task [9, 10].

The results of our previous study [11] give grounds for the assumption that by presenting information non-visually, negative influences such as visual distraction and cognitive capture can be reduced. The results also suggest that auditory information presentation can reduce the perceived workload and lead to fewer driving errors when compared to visual interfaces presented on a HDD. These findings are supported by the results of a recent study by Weinberg et al. [12], who established that navigating through aurally presented lists had a lower impact on mental workload when compared to HDDs and HUDs.

These findings support the assumption that a combination of auditory, especially speech-based information presentation and text-based information presentation through a HUD may in fact present the "best of both worlds": the attention and safety benefits of an eyes-free approach with the higher information processing rate of visual information presentation. By offering drivers a multimodal interface, they can choose to either listen to or read the required information depending on their situational cognitive capacities and/or their personal preferences.

The study presented in the following chapters was conducted to evaluate this assumption and to gain further insight into the subjectively and objectively measured impacts of using a single modality or a multimodal in-car information display while driving.

2   User Study

The aim of our user study was to evaluate the potential benefits of a multimodal user interface compared to two single modality interfaces for an in-vehicle information system through a series of representative tasks. The study used a within-subjects design (repeated measures) and compared a spoken auditory representation of a hierarchical menu structure to a visual representation (in the form of a HUD) of the same structure and a combined, multimodal representation. To imitate a realistic environment, the study was conducted in the driving simulator shown in Fig. 1, left.

The simulated on-board computer was operated through a custom-made interaction device attached to the steering wheel (see Fig. 1, right) enabling various tasks related to navigation, communication, and various on-board control systems. The primary interest of this study was to evaluate the efficiency of the interfaces and their impact on driving performance.

The efficiency was assessed by measuring the time required to complete a given set of tasks and the self-reported mental effort. The individual driving performance was analyzed by noting and rating anomalies and unsafe driving - such as swerving, sudden and unnecessary speed reductions, disobeying the traffic rules or even causing an accident - which occurred while performing the tasks.

2.1   Interaction with the Menu

Participants were asked to perform a set of tasks with the simulated on-board information system. The system imitated various navigational, communicational and other functionalities, while the interaction was based on a structured set of menu options. The top-most level of the structure was labeled the "Main menu". It consisted of five sub-menus that were further structured into sub-sub-menus.

The menu was operated through a custom made device located at the backside of the steering wheel (Fig. 1, right). The device's scrolling wheel and its two buttons supported the following three interactions: descending into a sub-menu, confirming an option and exiting a sub-menu or returning to the next higher level.

2.2   Conditions

Three experimental conditions were compared:

1. a visual representation of the menu (V),
2. an auditory representation of the menu (A), and
3. an audio-visual representation of the menu (AV).

Visual Interface (V). The visual interface was a HUD displaying the available items of the menu structure. The menu was projected to the right-central part of the windshield (Fig. 1, left). The approximate size of the projection was 20 x 20 cm. The text was displayed on transparent background in high contrast colors:

- the title of the active menu was displayed in green on the top of the HUD,
- the available but unselected items were displayed in yellow,
- the selected item was highlighted in red and a slightly bigger font size .

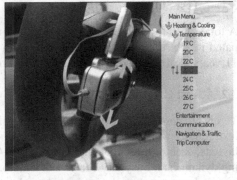

Fig. 1. The visual interface implemented as a HUD (left) and the interaction device (right). By clicking the lower mouse button (yellow highlight), the participants selected an item or descended in the hierarchy; the scrolling wheel (red highlight) was used to select an item; the upper mouse button (yellow highlight) was used for ascending in the hierarchy.

The HUD was implemented as a "sliding window" displaying at most five of the available items of the active menu. When available, the remaining items became accessable by scrolling up or down the menu.

Auditory Interface (A). In the auditory interface condition, pre-recorded readings of menu items were played through two computer speakers placed at the sides of the simulator imitating the in-vehicle speakers mounted in the side doors. The title of each sub-menu was announced upon entering the menu and menu items were read each time the virtual cursor's position/selection was changed. When participants reached the last (first) item of the menu, the end (beginning) of the list was indicated to them by a repeated reading of the item.

Audio-Visual Interface (AV). In the audio-visual condition, the visual and auditory interfaces described in the previous sections were presented simultaneously.

2.3   Tasks

Within each of the three experimental conditions, each participant was given three simple ("conventional") tasks followed by two difficult ("complex") tasks. All tasks in the conventional and all tasks in the complex group had the same minimum number of interactions (clicks, turns of the scrolling wheel) required for completion. The tasks in each group were chosen to be comparable in cognitive workload (e.g. scanning through text, listening to messages, considering options). A sample of a conventional task is: "Set the temperature to 24 degrees." A sample of a complex task is: "You are waiting for an e-mail from Denny Crane with the name of the restaurant where he would like to meet you. Please check your e-mail inbox and tell the name of the restaurant mentioned in the e-mail to the experimenter."

3   Methods

3.1   Test Subjects

A total of 30 test subjects (9 female and 21 male) with a valid driving license participated in the study. The participants were in average 29 years old and had in average 11 years of driving experience. They all reported to have normal sight and hearing.

3.2   Test Groups

To ensure comparable driving conditions, all participants were given loose navigation instructions while driving. To eliminate the influence of traffic density and street layouts, each of the three conditions (A, V, AV) was repeated with two different driving dynamics: a busy city center and a motorway. To avoid learning effects, six experimental groups were formed, each with a different combination of conditions and routes. For example, the participants from the group "A" started with the auditory interface on the "high speed motorway" route, then proceeded with the visual interface on the same route, and concluded with the AV interface on the "low speed city" route.

In the "high speed" scenario, participants drove on a motorway with a low traffic density with an average speed of 72 km/h (45 mph). In the "low speed" scenario, participants drove through a busy city center with an average speed of 33 km/h (21 mph).

In order to obtain a measure of the overall driving performance without the interference of a secondary task, a virtual control group was formed. The data of this control group was obtained by evaluating the driving performance of all drivers in the intervals between tasks.

3.3   Experiment Procedure

Before the experiment participants were informed about the nature and structure of the study. Participants were then asked to complete a pre-study questionnaire (age, gender, hearing and sight disabilities, driving experience, prior experience with simulators, and proneness to sea or simulator sickness). The participants were then thoroughly introduced to the driving simulator, the interaction device, the structure and content of the menu, and the three interfaces. Finally, they were given 20 minutes to familiarize themselves with the simulator while driving on a test route.

Participants then proceeded with a series of tasks.. Each task was read to participants loudly and clearly. Participants were asked to perform the given tasks as quickly as possible, but to also obey traffic rules and drive the car safely.

Task completion times, interaction activity and driving behavior were recorded automatically for each task. The measurements started when participants started to solve tasks and were stopped when the task was completed successfully. For the purpose of post-evaluation of the driving performance, the entire user study was recorded with a digital video camera.

After finishing each of the experimental conditions, participants were given an electronic version of the NASA TLX questionnaire [13] to evaluate their perceived workload for each particular interface.

After all three conditions were completed, participants were asked to fill in a short post-study questionnaire on their overall perception of the interfaces, their design, the design and realism of the driving simulator, and the complexity of given tasks.

3.4   Technical Setup

The experimental environment consisted of three basic elements: the driving simulator, the user interface application (UI) and the management and logging software (ML) suite.

The UI application controlled the interaction device and the output interfaces (A, V, AV). The application reported events associated with the interaction device (button clicks, scrolling wheel turns) to the ML software suite. The setup of the experimental environment was described in more detail in [14].

4   Results and Interpretations

4.1   Efficiency of Interfaces

The efficiency of the interfaces was measured through task completion times. The averaged results (of all participants in the study) are presented separately for each condition.

The average task completion times are presented in Fig. 2, left. Due to non-homogeneity of variances between data groups, the Kruskal-Wallis test was chosen to confirm the significance of differences between experimental conditions: $H = 40.279$, 2 d.f., $p < .001$. A post-hoc Games-Howell test with a .05 limit on family-wise error rate confirmed significant differences ($p < .001$) between the auditory interface (A) and other two interfaces (V and AV). The difference between the V and AV interfaces was not found to be significant.

The results confirm one part of our initial hypothesis: the auditory interface proved to be the least efficient among the three tested interfaces, as it was found to be the slowest and it required the most (physical) effort to complete tasks. However, a superiority of the multimodal interface over the visual interface could not be confirmed.

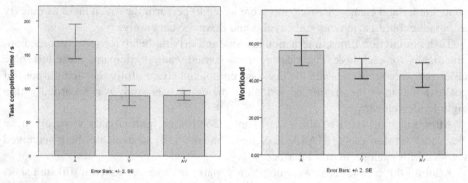

Fig. 2. Average task completion times (left) and subjectively perceived workload (unweighted) for all thee interfaces (right)

4.2   Workload

Participants' perceived workload was measured using the NASA-TLX assessment tool [13]. The procedure derives an overall workload score from the ratings on the following six subscales: mental demand, physical demand, temporal demand, performance, effort and frustration.

Fig. 2, right shows the overall workload for all three interface conditions. The results of the ANOVA show a significant difference between the three conditions: $F(2.87) = 4.035$; $p = .021$. The post-hoc Bonferroni test with a .05 limit on a family-wise error rate revealed that the reported workload in the audio condition (A) was significantly higher ($p = .019$) when compared to the workload in the AV condition.

The differences between the visual (V) and other two conditions (A and AV) were not found to be significant.

No significant difference between the visual and the multimodal interface was found, but again a trend towards a lower impact of the multimodal interface on the overall perceived workload is indicated.

4.3   Driving Performance

The driving performance was evaluated on the basis of the logged data in the simulator and then revised by a retrospective analysis of the video recordings. Four aspects were assessed: (a) lateral instability (swerving), (b) anomalies in driving speed (sudden and unnecessary speed reductions, inappropriate speed for a certain situation), (c) obeying common driving rules and signs (d) and causing accidents.

For each aspect, the performance of the participants was rated using the following system:

- 0 points – no anomalies were observed
- 1 point – one or very few anomalies were observed
- 2 points – anomalies were repeated several times
- 3 points – anomalies were repeated constantly resulting in very unsafe driving.

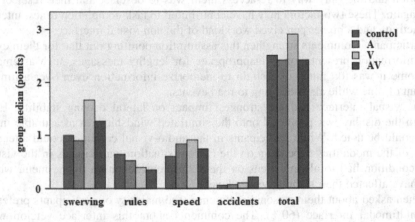

Fig. 3. Penalty points for driving errors per error category and total for all three interfaces and the control group

The scores of the individual aspects were then combined into an overall driving performance assessment. For the purpose of comparability, the performance of the control group was determined by measuring the performance of participants while driving without any distraction from secondary tasks. The results are shown in Fig. 3.

The results showed no significant differences between the four groups regarding the overall driving performance. However, significant differences were established for lateral control (H = 9.294, 3 d.f., p = .026.). A post-hoc Games-Howell test revealed a significantly lower number of errors for the control group when compared to the visual condition (p = .016) and for the auditory condition when compared to the visual condition (p = .047). This result corresponds with the findings of our initial study [11], in which the auditory interface caused the least lateral instability.

The results show no significant difference in the overall safety (total) of the individual interfaces. As expected, the analysis indicates that the driving simulator itself acts as a confounding variable, as it has a major influence on the overall driving performance. This influence is somewhat inevitable as the simulator allows for a semi-realistic scenario yet without causing any threats to safety. However, special care has been taken to create a high degree of realism of both the driving experience and the tasks.

5   Discussion

The analysis of task completion times shows a significant difference between the auditory interface and the other two interfaces. The auditory interface required more time and interaction activity from the participants to complete the given set of tasks. We assume this result is a consequence of the sequential nature (and hence lower information density) of sound, making a quick "scanning" of a menu for an item impossible. The transience of sound also implies that, in order to understand the meaning of the spoken words, one has to focus on the playback. In the other two conditions information was continuously projected on the windscreen until participant decided to make changes to the display. Information was presented just once in the auditory condition and the only way to re-access them was to deselect and then reselect the item again. These two factors may have contributed to task completion times, interaction activity and a higher perceived workload of the non-visual interface.

Participants' comments strengthen this assumption pointing out that for them eyes-free information presentation is inappropriate for lengthy messages, such as emails. For some it was too much of a strain to memorize information even over a limited amount of time while also attending to road events.

The visual interface had the strongest impact on lateral driving stability. Even though the display was projected onto the simulated windshield, a measurable influence could be noted. While participants in the audio-visual condition could attend to either of the modalities depending on the current situation, participants in the visual-only condition had to always focus on the visual representation of the menu which may have affected their stability within lanes.

When asked about their personal preference, the majority of participants preferred the multimodal interface (60%). The comments about this interface version were mostly positive. Only 16.7% preferred the visual interface and even fewer participants preferred the auditory interface (23.3%). Besides the benefits of the AV already mentioned, we assume that while the A and V interfaces are especially efficient with "auditory" or "visual" types of people, the multimodal AV interface, allows participants to exploit the part of the interface that best suits his or her preferences and needs.

Our data suggests that for an average, randomly selected user, the multimodal interface may not perform significantly better than a single modality interface, but it is likely to have the least disadvantages. In most aspects of the evaluation, the multimodal interface proves to have a slight (although not always significant) advantage, but it never has the strong disadvantages of the auditory interface (high task completion times) and of the visual interface (worse lateral control).

6   Conclusion

Visual interfaces based on HUDs proved to be very efficient and easy to learn. HUDs already represent a safer alternative to HDDs in many modern high-end vehicles. However, the majority of existing HUDs is used for displaying only a limited amount of information, such as navigation directions and speed or RPM. We believe their functionality could be extended to also enable advanced interaction with, for example, entertainment and communication systems.

The non-visual auditory interface proved to be safe but significantly less efficient than the HUD. Despite this fact, we see its great potential particularly in a combination with a HUD. Such a combined interface would take advantage of two non-competing human senses and enable the driver to rely on just one of them depending on the driving and traffic conditions. Although our experiment did not confirm any significant benefits of such a combination of interfaces, the majority of users responded positively to them.

The aim of our future research is to find new, efficient, safe, and enjoyable combinations of visual and auditory displays. We believe audio and visual output could be used simultaneously or interchangeably, depending on the driving conditions. We also believe that new and better alternative or supplement haptic interfaces to input devices attached to the steering wheel could be explored. Eye-gaze systems offer a big potential and could enable the on-board system to be aware of the user's current focus and eye activity. Similarly, tangible tracking has the potential to expand the driver's interaction beyond the limitations of physical buttons and knobs.

References

1. Sojourmer, R.J., Antin, J.F.: The effects of a simulated head-up display speedometer on perceptual task performance. Human Factors 32(3), 329–339 (1990)
2. Burnett, G.E.: A Road-Based Evaluation of a Head-Up Display for Presenting Navigation Information. In: Proc. of the Tenth International Conference on Human-Computer Interaction, pp. 180–184. Lawrence Erlbaum Associates (2003)
3. Yung-Ching, L.: Effects of using head-up display in automobile context on attention demand and driving performance. Displays 24(4-5), 157–165 (2003)
4. Charissis, V., Papanastasiou, S., Vlachos, G.: Comparative Study of Prototype Automotive HUD vs. HDD: Collision Avoidance Simulation and Results. In: Proc. of the Society of Automotive Engineers World Congress 2008, Detroit, Michigan, USA (2008)
5. Fisher, E., Haines, R.F., Price, T.A.: Cognitive issues in head-up displays. NASA Technical Paper 1711, NASA Ames Research Center (1980)
6. Wickens, C.D., Martin-Emerson, R., Larish, I.: Attentional tunnelling and the head-up display. In: Jensen, R.S. (ed.) Proc. of the Seventh International Symposium on Aviation Psychology, pp. 865–870. Ohio State University, Columbus (1993)
7. Tufano, D.: Automotive HUDs: The overlooked safety issues. Human Factors 39(2), 303–311 (1997)
8. Prinzel, L.J., Risser, M.: Head-up displays and attention capture. Tech. Rep. NASA/TM-2004-213000. NASA – Langley Research Center, Hampton, VA (2004)
9. Haines, R.F.: A breakdown in simultaneous information processing. In: Obrecht, G., Stark, L. (eds.) Presbyopia Research, pp. 171–175. Plenum, New York (1991)

10. Thomas, L.C., Wickens, C.D.: Visual Displays and Cognitive Tunneling: Frames of Reference Effects on Spatial Judgments and Change Detection. In: Proc. of the Human Factors and Ergonomics Society 45th Annual Meeting, pp. 336–340 (2001)
11. Sodnik, J., Dicke, C., Tomazic, S., Billinghurst, M.: A user study of auditory versus visual interfaces for use while driving. Int. J. Human-Computer Studies 66(5), 318–332 (2008)
12. Weinberg, G., Harsham, B., Medenica, Z.: Evaluating the Usability of a Head-Up Display for Selection from Choice Lists in Cars. In: Proc. of the International Conference on Automotive User Interfaces and Interactive Vehicular Applications (AutomotiveUI 2011), Salzburg, Germany (2011)
13. Hart, S.G., Wickens, C.: Workload assessment and prediction. In: Booher, H.R. (ed.) MANPRINT, an Approach to Systems Integration, pp. 257–296. Van Nostrand-Reinhold, New York (1990)
14. Dicke, C., Jakus, G., Tomazic, S., Sodnik, J.: On the Evaluation of Auditory and Head-up Displays While Driving. In: Proc. of the Fifth International Conference on Advances in Computer-Human Interactions (ACHI), Valencia, Spain, pp. 200–203 (2012)

Anti-Bump: A Bump/Pothole Monitoring and Broadcasting System for Driver Awareness

Mohamed Fekry, Aya Hamdy, and Ayman Atia

HCI Lab, Faculty of Computer Science and Information Systems
Helwan University, Cairo, Egypt
{m.ramadan,Aya.hamdy}@fcih.net,
ayman@fci.helwan.edu.eg

Abstract. This paper presents a system for bump detection and alarming system for drivers. We have presented an architecture that adopts context awareness and Bump location broadcasting to detect and save bumps locations. This system uses motion sensor to get the readings of the bump then we classify it using Dynamic Time Wrapping, Hidden Markov Model and Neural Network. We keep records for the bump location through tracking its geographic position. We developed a system that alarms the driver within appropriate profiled distance for bump occurrence. We conducted two experiments for testing the system in a street modeled architect with different kinds of bumps and potholes. The other experiment was on real street bumps. The results show that the system can detect bumps and potholes with reasonably accepted accuracy.

Keywords: Context awareness, Location awareness, Pattern Recognition.

1 Introduction

Nowadays, a lot of vehicles are released to the public and there are a huge number of cars all over the world. The vast number of vehicles leads to a new challenging problem for traffic control systems. The most popular one is traffic accidents because of high speed vehicles. People moved to change the structure of roads in order to decrease the number of accidents by constructing bumps in the streets to force drivers slow their vehicle's speed.

Moving many times on these bumps or potholes with inappropriate speed affects negatively the vehicles and sometimes these bumps cause many accidents, According to Portland government report that shows the effect of Speed Bumps on Traffic Crashes [1].

Traffic accidents are one of the main reasons for death of many people in Egypt. Bumps have been used a long time ago to decrease the speed of fast vehicles. According to "Ahram newspaper" issue 14th August 2012. Egypt is suffering from the massive increase of bumps. They give an example of chaos in building bump such that at a distance of 50 kilometers, 94 bumps can be found. Moreover, driver behavior on the road in certain locations could highly increase the possibility of having accidents.

M. Kurosu (Ed.): Human-Computer Interaction, Part II, HCII 2013, LNCS 8005, pp. 561–570, 2013.
© Springer-Verlag Berlin Heidelberg 2013

Most streets in Egypt almost devoid from one or more between industrial bumps set up by the province and bumps that have been constructed by the citizens, which led to force the drivers going far away from these bumps to avoid harming their vehicles.

Repairing the streets needs a lot of money, time and planning, so we have implemented a system which has the ability to warn the driver about the bump before moving on it to reduce their speed to avoid harming their vehicles. Recently most of the smart pads and phones have embedded motion sensing devices and location aware services. Hence we developed a system that aims to use the PDA and smart phones to automatically detect and warn the drivers about an incoming bump.

Ramjee et al. [2] Discussed Rich Monitoring of Road and Traffic Conditions using Mobile Smart phones and Jakob Eriksson et al. [3] Discussed The Pothole Patrol: Using a Mobile Sensor Network for Road Surface Monitoring and capturing potholes and bumps locations. However, their system lacks the accuracy of detection and there was no alarming system.

Related work is discussed in section 2, Section 3 determines the system overview, the description of experiments and its results has been determined in section 4, and finally, section 5 summarizes our conclusion and future work.

2   Related Work

Accelerometers are used in many fields and have solved a lot of challenges, James F. Knight et al. [25] discussed uses of an accelerometer which can be used for a lot of purposes like teaching, context aware computing systems, coaching sporting activities and in physical education. A. Krause et al. [4] Presents Toward community sensing where we can exact information from a population of privately-held sensors helping us creating useful application that may be used as distributed networks of velocity sensors for traffic monitoring which helps making data sharing acceptable, like GPS devices and embedded cell phones.

Accelerometer sensor is used for automotive safety applications such as detecting crashes and notify emergency services automatic. W. D. Jones [5] presents a work that predicts what the traffic would be like after some hours to avoid crowding and save more time.

Furthermore, in healthcare the accelerometer was used in human activity recognition where Jennifer R. Kwapisz et al. [6] Described and evaluated a system that uses phone-based accelerometers to detect the human activities in order to improve human healthcare, Lee et al. [7] Presents a work that recognizes the Physical activities using tri-axial accelerometer. N. Ravi et al. [26] presents a work on multi-level and meta-level of the classification algorithm for human activity recognition, it uses a device which has an accelerometer, Bluetooth transmitter and iPad mobile phone for uploading data. M. Zhang et al. [27] presents a view of a framework for detecting human activities based on Sensor data. It previews multi-stage of classification which provided better accuracy for detecting human activities. It uses nearest neighbor classifiers which evaluate the different k- neighbors for detecting activity.

In road surface monitoring for collecting data of the vehicle's motion, Yang and J. [8] Presented a work of motion recognition which was so helpful to detect motion using simple accelerometer features with mobile phones. Ramjee et al. [2] Discussed Rich Monitoring of Road and Traffic Conditions using Mobile Smart phones which focuses on using sensing technology embedded in smart phones to detect honking, bearking and bumps/potholes. J. Eriksson et al. [3] Presents P2 system " Pothole Patrol system " which describes an application using mobile sensing to detect bumps and potholes on road surfaces, the application depends on collecting data from the accelerometer and GPS sensors to be processed.

Mikko Pertunen et al. [9], presents a system that improves the traffic process using smart phones mobiles to detect bumps in order to decrease the amount of accidents, the system Performs a spectral analysis of tri-axial acceleration signals in order to get a reliable road surface anomalies label. Gonzlez et al. [10] Presents the Vehicle system dynamics, which collects data from an accelerometer fixed in some specific vehicle to estimate the road surface conditions and how to describe the road's profile with more accuracy.

GPS receiver listed as one of the sensing types that used to get the location of something. Bernhard B. et al. [11] presents a system design and implementation to integrate wireless data acquisition in order to get high accuracy position applications. J. Yoon et al. [12] presents a method that describes a traffic conditions using data collected from GPS location training files which helps getting updates of road conditions in order to increase its accuracy.

B. Hull et al. [13] installed Cartel system to monitor the vehicle's movement using GPS and report it back using Blue tooth.

3   System Overview

The system stores and synchronizes a shared repository for bump locations. Whenever a driver approaches to the bump with predefined distance. The system warns the driver for the location of the bump and remaining distance to pass through.

Figure 1 shows the system overview a) A car number 1 capturing and broadcasting the bump location. A car number 2 warned for bump location before passing through it. In car number 3, GPS saves the bump location into the database. b) A screenshot of the developed prototype.

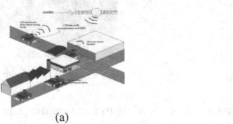 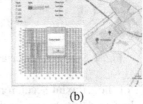

(a)   (b)

Fig. 1. System Overview

When the vehicle moves on some bump or pothole for the first time the accelerometer detects the pattern of the bump/pothole then the GPS saves this bump/pothole's location in its local database. When the system is connected to the internet the saved locations in the local database broadcasted to the shared database to be shared to all users who are using the system. When any vehicle moves to the saved location the system alarms the driver about incoming bump or pothole in order to slow the vehicle's speed.

3.1   System Architecture

Detecting bumps using accelerometer and GPS have been done in some steps determined as follows:

1. The accelerometer starts recording readings of accelerations when the speed of the car being less than 30 km/h and this has been gotten from GPS, will be discussed in the next section, and when the vehicle's speed being more than 30 km/h the accelerometer closes recording accelerations. We have collected data for three bumps and two potholes by 20 samples for every bump and pothole.
2. The acceleration data that have been recorded is filtered to get the accelerations on the bump only using threshold filters.
3. The filtered data entered as input to the classifier to test if this acceleration data is really bump or not, the classifier that we used in our work is Hidden Markov Model which will be discussed later.
4. If the classifier detected a bump or a pothole, the GPS save the location of it to warn the driver in next time he will move on it.

Figure 2 shows the system architecture.

Motion Sensing. The accelerometer is a device that measures all accelerations X, Y and Z axes depending on the earth's gravity, we use the tri-axial accelerometer which helps in a lot of fields like: engineering, industry, biology and HCI. Figure 3 shows the Wii-remote that is used to measure all accelerations.

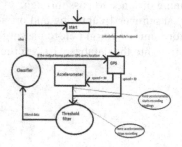

Fig. 2. System Architecture   **Fig. 3.** Wii-Remote

The role of the tri-axial accelerometer in our work is to measure the change of X, Y and Z values to detect bumps in the streets. The design part of the accelerometer is discussed in how the accelerometer will be positioned in the vehicles to get the required pattern of bumps. So, assuming the orientations of the accelerometer are x-axis for moving forward or backward, y-axis for moving right or left and z-axis for moving up or down a case of bumps / potholes. There are two ways to position our accelerometer: Well-oriented and Disoriented.

These ways for orientations of the accelerometers were discussed in Nericell System [2]. In this work, we used well-oriented way of positioning our sensor to be oriented as the vehicle's orientation in order to make the vehicle's orientation, which represented by the orthogonal X, Y , and Z axes, with X points directly to the front, Y to the right, and Z into the ground, being oriented with accelerometer orientation.

Using disoriented way needs to calculate tilt angle to get the right accelerations of the accelerometer according to the vehicle's orientation as discussed in Nericell System [2].

Detection Algorithms

Hidden Markov Model. Hidden Markov Model algorithm is a probabilistic model representing a process with states and only the output of the model is visible and states are hidden. Hidden Markov Models used in many applications such as speech recognition, sign language recognition [14], handwriting recognition [15] and biometric gait recognition [16]. For building and training Hidden Markov Models, we used Hidden Markov Model Toolkit htk [17]. It has helped in the training and testing of Hidden Markov Models. A 4-state HMM was used and data represented by matrix of three columns x, y and z acceleration values.

Dynamic Time Warping. Dynamic time warping [18] is an algorithm used to measure similarity between two different two sequences in time or speed. It has been used in video, audio and graphics or any data, which can be turned into a linear representation such as speech recognition [19]. Dynamic time warping matches a sample against the template of bump and pothole. Every bump and pothole represented by a sequence of feature vectors. Assume that S is a sample and T is a template, where S= {s1, si} and T= {t1, tj} and each feature vector consists of the x, y, z-axis acceleration values. We want to compute the matching cost by DTW (S, T). The first step constructed distance matrix D by computing the distance between each vector in S and T using formulation 1 for each S (x, y, z) and T (x, y, z).

$$d(si,tj)=(\ si - tj \ )2 \tag{1}$$

After that we compute the matching cost: DTW (S, T) using this formulation 2, Sample is then recognized as the bump or pothole corresponding to the template with the lowest matching cost.

$$D(i, j) = d(si,tj) + \min\{D(i-1, j), D(i-1, j-1), D(i, j-1)\} \tag{2}$$

Artificial Neural Networks. An artificial neural network is an algorithm based on simulation of the brain [20]. Artificial neural networks have been applied to problems ranging such as speech recognition, predictions of time series, classification of cancers and gene prediction. ANNs has implemented using Encog 2.5 for C# [21]. Neural network required a fixed length feature vector; the data need to be resampled and normalized between 0 and 1 for Sigmoid Activation Function [22]. Data normalized using Encogs normalization class [23]. Data resample using an algorithm described in [24] was implemented and data were resampled to 100 points. With 100 points each for the three x, y and z, feature vector of 300 was used as input to the neural network. We used back propagation neural network and desired error 0.001.

Bump Location Awareness. We used GPS Data Logger device to know the location of the bumps and to calculate the speed of the vehicle. The roles of the GPS device in our work are as follows:

— During driving the vehicle, the GPS device always recording readings to all its features so, when the GPS records that the vehicle's velocity being less than 30 km/h then comes the role of the accelerometer to record accelerations.
— When the GPS device that records the vehicle's velocity being more than 30 km/h the accelerometer closes recording acceleration to go ahead to filtration and classification steps.
— So, if the classifier detects some bump, then here is the second role of the GPS device, and it is to save the bump's longitude, latitude and altitude in its database.
— During driving, the GPS device continues recording the vehicle's velocity and comparing the current location of the vehicle with which in its database using the altitude, longitude and latitude.

The location that the GPS saves in its database is the location of the bumps to warn the driver about before moving on it.

4   Bump/Pothole Recognition

We used the Wii remote as the accelerometer to get the required acceleration readings and the GPS device to get the current location of the vehicle. Our experiments were about two types of environments:

— Lab Street Modeled Architect: Taking training files from an RC "remote controlled" car connected to the Wii-remote to record acceleration data then filter the data to import it to the classifier.
— Road Experiment Evaluation: The second one was taking training files from existent bumps from the street by putting Wii-remote in the car and recording the data to be filtered then classified. This one is a real bump detection experiment.

We used three algorithms for our recognition process:

— Hidden Markov Model.
— Artificial Neural Network.
— Dynamic time wrapping.

4.1   Lab Street Modeled Architect

In this section, we discussed the implementation and evaluation of street modeled architect by determining the design and results of it.

We have recorded the training data form RC car connected to the accelerometer as in figures 4.

Fig. 4. Remote Control car connected to the Wii remote

We tested the system on three different types of bumps and two potholes as shown in figure 5.

Fig. 5. Street Modeled Architect

We tested each bump/pothole by recording 15 training reading files and tested each one by five readings for each algorithm, and the results showed that HMM and DTW are good algorithms for detecting street modeled architect's potholes, and ANN is good for detecting its bumps. Table 1 shows the results.

Table 1. Street modeled results

	Bumps	potholes
HMM	73.3%	100%
ANN	86.6%	60%
DTW	53.3%	100%

By implementing HMM and DTW on modeled architect the result determined that they have detected all potholes with accuracy 100% and ANN is better in detecting bumps on modeled architect with accuracy 86.6% and the rest has been detected as potholes.

4.2   Road Experiment Evaluation

We have recorded our data set of Real bumps/potholes. We tested the system on different types of bumps in east and west of Cairo.

We tested each bump/pothole by recording 15 training reading files and tested each one by five readings for each algorithm, and the results showed that HMM is a good algorithm for detecting real bumps but DTW and ANN are good algorithms for detecting real potholes and Table 2 shows the results of real bumps and pothole's detection using the three algorithms.

Table 2. Real bump results

	Bumps	Potholes
HMM	100%	80%
ANN	73%	100%
DTW	73%	100%

We have recorded the data sets in many places in east and west of Cairo in Egypt.

Applying HMM Algorithm. The system database contains of three bumps and two potholes. We use 15 samples for training for every bump and pothole and five samples for testing. Results show that HMM detection accuracy for bumps was 100% and 80% for potholes. We construct a confusion matrix between bumps and potholes, and the result is shown in Table 3.

Table 3. HMM results

	Bumps	Pothole
Bumps	15	2
Pothole	0	8

Applying ANN Algorithm. We used back propagation neural network and 15 samples for training and 5 for testing. The ANNs architecture has 300 input layers, one hidden layer, number of hidden neurons and output layers five output layers. Results show that ANNs detection accuracy was 73% for bumps and 100% for potholes. We constructed confusion matrix shown in table 4.

Table 4. ANN results

	Bumps	Pothole
Bumps	11	0
Pothole	4	10

Applying the DTW Algorithm. We used one template matching for every bump and pothole and five samples for testing. Results show that DTW detection accuracy 73% for bumps and 100% for potholes. We constructed confusion matrix and the result is shown in table 5.

Table 5. DTW results

	Bumps	Pothole
Bumps	11	0
Pothole	4	10

By implementing ANN and DTW on real bumps and potholes the results determined that they have detected all potholes with accuracy 100% and HMM has detected all bumps with accuracy 100%.

5   Conclusion and Future Work

We have implemented a system that can detect bumps and potholes with the highest accuracy using tri-axial accelerometer and GPS receiver; the role of the accelerometer is to detect bumps and potholes by identifying the change of accelerations using the classifiers, and the role of GPS is to locate the vehicle and calculate its velocity. The experiment's results showed that the hidden Markov model can detect the bumps with 100% accuracy, and the artificial neural network can detect potholes with 100% accuracy. In future work, many filtered samples will be extracted to cover more patterns for more types of bumps or potholes. The system has a good potential to be deployed as a mobile application.

References

1. http://www.portlandoregon.gov/transportation/35934?a=85425 (last visited on February 27, 2013)
2. Ramjee, R., Mohan, P., Padmanabhan, V.N.: Nericell: Rich Monitoring of Road and Traffic Conditions using Mobile Smartphones. In: SenSys (2008)
3. Hull, B., Newton, R., Madden, S., Eriksson, J., Girod, L., Balakrishnan, H.: 'The Pothole Patrol: Using a Mobile Sensor Network for Road Surface Monitoring. In: MobiSys (2008)
4. Kansal, A., Krause, A., Horvitz, E., Zhao, F.: Toward Community Sensing. In: ACM/IEEE International Conference on Information Processing in Sensor Networks, IPSN (2008)
5. Jones, W.D.: Forecasting Traffic Flow. IEEE Spectrum (2001)
6. Gary, M., Jennifer, W., Kwapisz, R., Moore, S.A.: Activity Recognition Using Cell Phone Accelerometers. SIGKDD Explorations (2008)
7. Kim, J., Lee, K., Jee, I., Lee, S.H., And Yoo, M.: Physical Activity Recognition Using a Single Tri- axis Accelerometer. In: Proceedings of the World Congress on Engineering and Computer Science (2009)
8. Yang, J.: Toward physical activity diary: Motion Recognition Using Simple Accelerometer Features with Mobile Phones. In: First International Workshop on Interactive Multimedia for Consumer Electronics at ACM Multimedia (2009)

9. Cong, F., Kauppila, M., Leppanen, T., Kantola, J., Collin, J., Pirttikangas, S., Haverinen, J., Ristaniemi, T., Pertunen, M., Mazhelis, O., Riekki, J.: Distributed Road Surface Condition Monitoring Using Mobile Phones. At UIC (2011)

10. O'brien, E.J., Li, Y.Y., Cashell, K.: Gonzlez and A. "The use of vehicle acceleration measurements to estimate road roughness. Vehicle System Dynamic". In: Vehicle Mechanics and Mobility (2008)

11. Buchli, B., Sutton, F., Beutel, J.: GPS-equipped wireless sensor network node for high-accuracy positioning applications. In: Picco, G.P., Heinzelman, W. (eds.) EWSN 2012. LNCS, vol. 7158, pp. 179–195. Springer, Heidelberg (2012)

12. Noble, B., Yoon, J., Liu, M.: Surface Street Traffic Estimation. In: MobiSys (2007)

13. Chen, K., Goraczko, M., Miu, A., Shih, E., Zhang, Y., Balakrishnan, H., Hull, B., Bychkovsky, V., Madden, S.: The CarTel Mobile Sensor Computing System. In: SenSys (2006)

14. Starner, T.E., Pentland, A.: Visual recognition of American sign language using hidden Markov models. Masters thesis, Massachusetts Institute of Technology (1995)

15. Schlapbach, A., Bunke, H.: Using hmm based recognizers for writer identification and verification. In: IWFHR 2004: Proceedings of the Ninth International Workshop on Frontiers in Handwriting Recognition, p. 167172 (2004)

16. Busch, C., Nickel, C., Mbius, M.: Using Hidden Markov Models for Accelerometer-Based Biometric Gait Recognition. In: IEEE 7th International Colloquium on Signal Processing and its Applications (CSPA), pp. 58–63 (2011)

17. Gales, M.J.F., Hain, T., Kershaw, D., Moore, G., Odell, J., Ollason, D., Povey, D., Valtchev, V., Young, S.J., Evermann, G., Woodland, P.C.: The HTK Book, version 3.4. Cambridge University Engineering Department, Cambridge (2006)

18. Ratanamahatana, C.A., Keogh, E.: Exact Indexing of Dynamic Time Warping. In: VLDB 2002: Proceedings of the 28th International Conference on Very Large Data Bases, pp. 406–417 (2002)

19. Sakoe, H., Chiba, S.: Dynamic programming algorithm optimization for spoken word recognition. IEEE Transactions on Acoustics, Speech and Signal Processing 26 (1978)

20. http://en.wikipedia.org/wiki/artificial_neural_network

21. http://www.heatonresearch.com/encog

22. http://www.heatonresearch.com/wiki/sigmoid_activation_function

23. http://www.heatonresearch.com/wiki/range_normalization

24. Wilson, A.D., Wobbrock, J.O., Li, Y.: Gestures without libraries, toolkits or training: A $1 recognizer for user interface prototypes. In: UIST 2007: Proceedings of the 20th Annual ACM Symposium on User Interface Software and Technology (2007)

25. Knight, J.F., Bristow, H.W.: Uses of accelerometer data collected from a wearable system (2006)

26. N. Ravi, N. Dandekar, P. Mysore, M.L. Littman: Activity Recognition from Accelerometer Data. Department of Computer Science Rutgers University Piscataway, NJ 08854, nravi,nikhild,preetham,mlittman@cs.rutgers.edu

27. Zhang, M., Sawchuk, A.A.: Manifold learning and recognition of human activity using body area sensors. In: IEEE International Conference on Machine Learning and Applications (ICMLA), Honolulu, Hawaii, USA, 713 p. (December 2011)

Emotion and Emotion Regulation Considerations
for Speech-Based In-Vehicle Interfaces

Helen Harris

Stanford University, Stanford, CA., USA
helenh@alumni.stanford.edu

Abstract. Speech and dialogue systems have been used in a variety of domains, from acting as human operators, to assisting those who have difficulties using other modalities, and more recently facilitating smartphone input. Speech has been more readily adopted by in-vehicle speech systems as the safest way to both communicate to the driver and to have the driver provide input to the system. Much of the work on speech dialogue systems has focused on the cognitive aspects of speech interfaces by evaluating different information architectures, e.g. [1], or comparing mixed modality interfaces, e.g., [2]. This paper argues that advanced speech-based interfaces will have the need and opportunity to be emotionally responsive.

Keywords: emotion, emotion regulation, speech dialogue systems, in-car interfaces.

1   Emotion in the Car

Perhaps one of the most important contexts for monitoring and modifying temporary emotional states is driving. When it comes to driving, three distinct groups of emotional states have emerged as states of interest. The first state is defined by a slightly positive valence and a moderate level of arousal, closely associated with the emotional state of happy. An optimal state, thought of as a flow state [3], involves a moderate level of arousal, allowing for attention, focus, and productivity. While a state of high arousal or extreme positive valence may potentially lead to distraction, states of a positive affect have also been shown to improve performance in non-driving contexts [4], [5], [6]. The second state characterized by very low arousal and sometimes accompanied by a slight negative valance; when broadly defined, this state encompasses both sadness and drowsiness. A sad or negative state degrades task performance, and within the car this state is manifested as inattention. Similarly, a subdued state nearly to the degree of drowsiness is quite dangerous. Drowsy driving and falling asleep at the wheel are often responsible for fatal collisions and off-road accidents [7].

The last state of interest is characterized by an extreme level negative valence and high arousal, usually classified as anger. Frustration is distinguished from anger by the degree of negativity and arousal. Often, frustration is referred to as a gateway

M. Kurosu (Ed.): Human-Computer Interaction, Part II, HCII 2013, LNCS 8005, pp. 571–577, 2013.

emotion that leads to anger, and ultimately to aggression and road rage [8]. There have been numerous attempts to classify aggression on the roadway [9], [10], [11], with all definitions holding the common belief that aggressive driving behaviors include tailgating, weaving through traffic, not cooperating with other drivers, driving at excessive speeds, and running stop signs and lights [12]. The perception of aggressive driving as a safety issue is widespread [11], [13]. In 2008 survey, seventy-eight percent of respondents rated aggressive drivers as a serious traffic problem, and nearly half of the same sample reported driving at excessive speeds [14]. Furthermore, the behaviors associated with aggressive driving are significant contributing factors to vehicle accidents and fatalities [15], [16]. Excessive speed is a factor in nearly one-third of fatal accidents and about fifty percent of vehicular fatalities involve at least one aggressive driving behavior [17]. Given these implications of driving under the influence of particular emotional states, it is unquestionably important to be able to identify and respond to such states in drivers.

2   Appropriate Responses to Driver Emotion

The underlying assumption that this work holds is that understanding the user's emotional state will create more effective interfaces. Affect is a fundamental cue in human-to-human communication, so much so that emotion in the voice can be understood by children before they can understand speech. People also carry expectations that interactive media will behave in a human-like manner [18], so it is crucial that speech-based interfaces feature some degree of emotional responsiveness.

Recognizing and classifying emotion are necessary first steps for interactive technologies. These attempts to capture affect fall into three major categories---facial expressions, voice characteristics, and physiological markers. While there visual and physiological methods of predicting affect, speech-based assessments prove to be the most promising. Visual methods of analysis struggle with individual differences in the expression of affect, environmental factors such as low light, or contextual factors like corrective eye glasses or a turned head. Physiological methods have difficulty determining much more than user arousal and are commonly physical intrusive. The advantage of speech-based in-vehicle systems is not only that speech allows drivers to keep their hands on the steering wheel and eyes on the road, but also that the speech input is a rich signal of the driver state. Speech characteristics can be assessed to classify the user state with variables such as pitch range [19], [20]. The results are systems that can vary their response depending on the affective state of the user.

The power of interpreting the affective state of the driver is the potential to react appropriately to it. Emotional aspects of an interface can be used to gain trust [21] have positive effects on user stress levels [22], and generally improve the perception of the interface [23]. Much work has discussed the importance of have an affective component in interfaces, e.g., [24], [25], but most of this work has relied on facial expressions [26] and gesturing [27] to express an affective state. While textual or visual representations of agent affect may be effective in computer-based and non-cognitively demanding contexts, the best way is to express emotion for an in-vehicle system in through speech. In one study, voice characteristics were manipulated by trained voice actors [28] and effects on drivers illustrated the attitudinal and behavioral importance of having a speech-based interface match the emotion state of its user.

This previous research has experimentally tested social responses to driver emotion. Nass and colleagues used a 2 (induced emotion) x 2 (voice interface emotion) between-subject factorial design [28]. Without the benefit of a naturalistic setting and real-time assessment of driver emotion, researchers relied on the method of using emotionally-charged clips to induce emotion [29], [30]. Two five minute videos, one inducing the state of *happy*, and the other for *sad/subdued* were created from a pre-tested image database. Half of the participants in the study were induced to be *happy*, and the other half were *sad/subdued;* the effectiveness of the inducement method was verified by self-report data from the Differential Emotional Scale (DES) [31].

In keeping with the factorial design, half of the participants from each inducement group drove through a simulated driving course while engaged in conversation with a *happy* voice interface; the other half interacted with the *sad/subdued* voice. The voice interface was actually a series of brief questions and comments, played at exactly the same time in the simulator for every participant. The same female voice talent recorded both the *happy* and *sad/subdued* versions of the script; there was no difference in content between the two versions, only a distinction in intonation and expression.

Contrary to common beliefs that *happy* is always best, results from the study showed that matching the voice emotion to the driver emotion proved more beneficial to emotion than simply presenting all drivers with a *happy* voice. This surprising result reveals the importance of designing socially appropriate in-car voice interfaces. Drivers who were induced to be *sad/subdued* expected their conversation partner to be aware of their state and respond accordingly, in a more subdued manner. Thus, the ability to detect driver emotion is not only helpful in predicting driver behavior, but necessary for designing smart, adaptive, and beneficial driver interfaces.

In order to implement socially appropriate interfaces [18], [28], several hurdles must be overcome before the technology and knowledge can be integrated in vehicles. Some first steps have been made, but the studies that have been completed only begin to touch upon the range of human emotional states. The field of psychology, among others, provides a significant body of work to aid in addressing negative emotions and promoting healthier states.

3   A New Strategy for Emotion Regulation

Although properly designed affective interfaces could aid drivers, precisely understanding the driver state and responding appropriately is a tricky proposition. For example, Breazeal [32] developed synthesized speech with angry, calm, distressed, fearful, happy, sad, or surprised affect, but participants sometimes confused discrete emotions across valence or arousal (but neither both). A new line of research suggests that neither knowledge of the user emotion nor interface expression of emotion is necessary to positively influence driver affect and behavior [33]. By constructing a dialog system that is intelligent enough to understand the driving context and to produce output to regulate driver emotion by using cognitive reappraisal prompts, speech can have a far greater impact than any other modality.

The study by Harris and Nass [33] experimentally tested the use of cognitive reappraisal prompts in response to frustrating driving contexts. The work targeted potentially negative states of lower activation that may lead to aggression [8], [34], [35], [36]. The frustration-aggression hypothesis [35] highlights the danger of negative states by offering a model in which thwarting progress towards a goal results in aggression. Berkowitz offers a clarification of the frustration-aggression hypothesis by defining frustration as an "external instigating condition" rather than "an organism's reaction to this event" [34]. When drivers encounter frustrations such as traffic slowdowns, these frustrations can trigger negative states that lead to aggression [8]. Given that aggressive driving behaviors are a primary cause of many accidents and driving fatalities [17] it could be important to react to these external conditions rather than the driver state.

The authors in the above-mentioned work [33] leveraged the process model of emotion regulation [37], [38], [39] which fit regulation strategies around the "modal model" of emotion [40]. The modal model of emotion is a generalization of appraisal theories, e.g., [41], [42], that assume people automatically and implicitly appraise everything. When the cognitive evaluation of events occurs, this forms an essential part of the experience of emotion. The model contains four timing-dependent components related to the experience of an emotion. The first component is the situation; the individual exists in a psychologically relevant situation. The second is attention. An individual must attend to aspects of the situation. Based on the situation and the attention given to it, the individual appraises the situation. Finally, based on the appraisal, the individual internally and externally responds.

The related model of emotion regulation [37], [38], [39], posits that emotions may be regulated at one of five points: selection of the situation; modification of the situation; deployment of attention; change of cognitions; and modulation of the response. Previous research indicates that a change of cognitions may be the most effective strategy, e.g., [43]. Broadly speaking, a change of cognitions means that an event is cognitively reprocessed. Under the assumption that emotions are consequences of cognitions about events and stimuli, there is an opportunity to change the experience of the stimuli (e.g., the emotional state) by changing the cognitions about the event. Individuals can up-regulate their emotions to increase their emotional response to an event, or down-regulate emotions to interpret an event in a less unemotional way.

Applying this theory to the driving context, Harris and Nass [33] used a 1 X 3 (regulation type: no regulation, down-regulation, and up-regulation) between-subjects design to see if a speech-based intervention could leverage the idea of cognitive reappraisal. The speech-based interface was actually a series of 10 prompts played at exactly the same time for every participant during a 15 minute driving simulation. The prompts were placed precisely after potentially frustrating events (e.g., being cut off) and suggested ways to interpret the event such as *The driver must not have seen you, otherwise, he would not have chosen to change lanes* (down-regulation condition) or *The driver must have chosen to change lanes despite the danger of running into your car* (up-regulation condition). The same female voice talent recorded both the down-reappraisal and up-reappraisal versions of the script; there was no difference in expression between the two versions, only a distinction in the words spoken.

The down-regulation resulted in better driving performance and a better self-reported emotional state than drivers with the up-regulation interface or no interface at all. This shows that in-car voice interfaces do not have to be aware of the driver state or express emotion to positively influence the driver. Despite cognitive issues of fatigue [44] and workload [45] inherent in the driving task, using the speech-based interface to present drivers with reappraisals benefitted their emotional states and performance. The speech-based interface designer's work may be made easier by only relying on traffic, weather, and other environmental information.

4   Conclusions

Driver emotion is strongly linked to behavior on the roadway. Whether the affective state is established outside of the vehicle or influenced by events while driving, it is crucial for future in-car speech-based systems to appropriately address the driver state. Future research should aim to understand how advanced speech systems will incorporate emotionally appropriate features as a fundamental component of complex infotainment and personalized interfaces.

References

1. Tashev, I., Seltzer, M., Ju, Y.-C., Wang, Y.-Y., Acero, A.: Commute UX: Voice enabled in-car infotainment system. In: Mobile HCI, vol. 9, (2009)
2. Müller, C., Friedland, G.: Multimodal interfaces for automotive applications (MIAA). In: Proceedings of the 14th International Conference on Intelligent User Interfaces, pp. 493–494. ACM (2009)
3. Csikszentmihalyi, M.: Flow: The psychology of optimal experience. Harper & Row Publishers, New York (1991)
4. Groeger, J.A.: Understanding Driving: Applying Cognitive Psychology to a complex everyday task. Psychology Press, Hove (2000)
5. Hirt, E.R., Melton, R.J., McDonald, H.E., Harackiewicz, J.M.: Processing goals, task interest, and the mood-performance relationship: A mediational analysis. Journal of Personality and Social Psychology 71, 245–261 (1996)
6. Isen, A.M.: Positive affect and decision making. In: Lewis, M., Haviland-Jones, J.M. (eds.) Handbook of Emotions, Guildford, pp. 417–435 (2000)
7. Dement, W.C.: The perils of drowsy driving. The New England Journal of Medicine 337, 783 (1997)
8. Galovski, T.E., Blanchard, E.B.: Road Rage: A domain for psychological intervention? Aggression and Violent Behavior 9, 105–127 (2004)
9. Goehring, J.B.: Aggressive driving: background and overview report (2000)
10. Hauber, A.R.: The social psychology of driving behaviour and the traffic environment: Research on aggressive behaviour in traffic. Applied Psychology 29, 461–474 (1980)
11. Mizell, L., Joint, M., Connell, D.: Aggressive driving: Three studies. Retrieved from American Automobile Association Foundation for Traffic Safety 1, 2002 (1997)
12. Tasca, L.: A review of the literature on aggressive driving research (2000)

13. Beirness, D.J., Simpson, H.M., Mayhew, D.R., Pak, A.: Aggressive Driving. The Road Safety Monitor Traffic Injury Research Foundation, Canada (2002)
14. AAA: 2008 Traffic Safety Culture Index. AAA Foundation for Traffic Safety, Washington, D.C. (2008)
15. Dula, C.S., Ballard, M.E.: Development and Evaluation of a Measure of Dangerous, Aggressive, Negative Emotional, and Risky Driving. Journal of Applied Social Psychology 33, 263–282 (2003)
16. King, Y., Parker, D.: Driving violations, aggression and perceived consensus. Revue Européenne de Psychologie Appliquée/European Review of Applied Psychology 58, 43–49 (2008)
17. AAA: Aggressive Driving Research Update. AAA Foundatation for Traffic Safety, Washington, D.C. (2009)
18. Reeves, B., Nass, C.I.: The media equation: How people treat computers, television, and new media like real people and places. Center for the Study of Language and Information, Cambridge University Press, Chicago, New York (1996)
19. Jones, C.M., Jonsson, I.-M.: Detecting emotions in conversations between driver and in-car information systems. In: Tao, J., Tan, T., Picard, R.W. (eds.) ACII 2005. LNCS, vol. 3784, pp. 780–787. Springer, Heidelberg (2005)
20. Grimm, M., Kroschel, K., Harris, H., Nass, C., Schuller, B., Rigoll, G., Moosmayr, T.: On the Necessity and Feasibility of Detecting a Driver's Emotional State While Driving. In: Paiva, A.C.R., Prada, R., Picard, R.W. (eds.) ACII 2007. LNCS, vol. 4738, pp. 126–138. Springer, Heidelberg (2007)
21. Weizenbaum, J.: ELIZA—a computer program for the study of natural language communication between man and machine. Communications of the ACM 9(1), 36–45 (1966)
22. Prendinger, H., Ishizuka, M.: The empathic companion: A character-based interface that addresses users' affective states. Applied Artificial Intelligence 19(3-4), 267–285 (2005)
23. Maldonado, H., Lee, J.E.R., Brave, S., Nass, C., Nakajima, H., Yamada, R., Morishima, Y.: We learn better together: enhancing elearning with emotional characters. In: Proceedings of the 2005 Conference on Computer Support for Collaborative Learning: Learning 2005: The Next 10 Years! International Society of the Learning Sciences, pp. 408–417 (2005)
24. Picard, R.W., Vyzas, E., Healey, J.: Toward machine emotional intelligence: Analysis of affective physiological state. IEEE Transactions on Pattern Analysis and Machine Intelligence 23(10), 1175–1191 (2001)
25. Picard, R.W.: Affective computing: challenges. International Journal of Human-Computer Studies 59(1), 55–64 (2003)
26. Elliott, C., Rickel, J., Lester, J.: Lifelike pedagogical agents and affective computing: An exploratory synthesis. In: Veloso, M.M., Wooldridge, M.J. (eds.) Artificial Intelligence Today. LNCS (LNAI), vol. 1600, pp. 195–211. Springer, Heidelberg (1999)
27. Kapur, A., Kapur, A., Virji-Babul, N., Tzanetakis, G., Driessen, P.F.: Gesture-based affective computing on motion capture data. In: Tao, J., Tan, T., Picard, R.W. (eds.) ACII 2005. LNCS, vol. 3784, pp. 1–7. Springer, Heidelberg (2005)
28. Nass, C., Jonsson, I.-M., Harris, H., Reaves, B., Endo, J., Brave, S., Takayama, L.: Improving Automotive Safety by Pairing Driver Emotion and Car Voice Emotion. In: Proceedings of CHI 2005, Portland, Oregon (2005)
29. Gross, J.J., Levenson, R.W.: Emotion elicitation using films. Cognition & Emotion 9(1), 87–108 (1995)

30. Detenber, B.H., Reeves, B.: A bio-informational theory of emotion: Motion and image size effects on viewers. Journal of Communication 46(3), 66–84 (1996)
31. Izard, C.E.: Patterns of Emotions: A New Analysis of Anxiety and Depression. Academic Press (1972)
32. Breazeal, C.: Emotive qualities in robot speech. In: Proceedings of the 2001 IEEE/RSJ International Conference on Intelligent Robots and Systems, pp. 1388–1394. IEEE (2001)
33. Harris, H., Nass, C.: Emotion Regulation for Frustrating Driving Contexts. In: Proc. CHI 2011. ACM Press, Vancouver (2011)
34. Berkowitz, L.: Frustration-Aggression Hypothesis: Examination and Reformulation. Psychological Bulletin 106(1), 59–73 (1939)
35. Dollard, J., Miller, N.E., Doob, L.W., Mowrer, O.H., Sears, R.R.: Frustration and aggression (1939)
36. Shinar, D.: Aggressive driving: the contribution of the drivers and the situation. Transportation Research Part F: Traffic Psychology and Behaviour 1(2), 137–160 (1998)
37. Gross, J.J., Thompson, R.A.: Emotion regulation: Conceptual foundations. In: Gross, J.J. (ed.) Handbook of Emotion Regulation, Guilford Press, New York (1997)
38. Gross, J.J.: The emerging field of emotion regulation: An integrative review. Review of General Psychology 2(3), 271 (1998)
39. Gross, J.J.: Antecedent-and response-focused emotion regulation: Divergent consequences for experience, expression, and physiology. Journal of Personality and Social Psychology 74(1), 224 (1998)
40. Scherer, K.R.: Toward a concept of modal emotions. The nature of emotion: Fundamental questions, 25–31 (1994)
41. Frijda, N.: The laws of emotion. American Psychologist 43, 349–358 (1988)
42. Scherer, K.R., Schorr, A., Johnstone, T.: Appraisal processes in emotion: Theory, methods, research. Oxford University Press, USA (2001)
43. Gross, J.J.: Emotion regulation: Affective, cognitive, and social consequences. Psychophysiology 39(03), 281–291 (2002)
44. Baumeister, R.F., Heatherton, T.F., Tice, D.M.: Losing control: How and why people fail at self-regulation. Academic Press (1994)
45. Wegner, D.M.: Ironic processes of mental control. Psychological Review 101(1), 34–52 (1994)

Adaptations in Driving Efficiency with Electric Vehicles

Magnus Helmbrecht[1], Klaus Bengler[1], and Roman Vilimek[2]

[1] Technische Universität München, Institute of Ergonomics, Garching, Germany
{helmbrecht,bengler}@lfe.mw.tum.de
[2] BMW Group, Concept Quality, Munich, Germany
roman.vilimek@bmw.de

Abstract. The results of previous MINI E field trials provided initial indications that driving electric vehicles (EV) leads to adaptations in driving behavior and might increase driving efficiency. This paper presents the methodologies to measure changes in driver characteristics by logging velocity, acceleration, and cruising range, on smartphones. In this experiment, 25 MINI E were provided as electric test vehicles for a diversified spectrum of subjects consisting of private and corporate customers. The field trial included both longitudinal and transverse components in order to assess long-term and situation specific changes. Participants operated both combustive and electric vehicles. Driving dynamics data from these vehicles was collected over a six month period time. Additionally, these same participants were required to perform a 2 hour drive, which served as a comparison drive, three times over the period of EV usage. The frequency of intermittent usage of combustion vehicles was captured by logbooks.

Keywords: Electric Vehicle, Driving Behavior, Field Trial, MINI E.

1 Introduction

Bringing electric vehicles into the market is necessary in order to direct future mobility in a way that is independent from fossil fuels. In order to ensure an acceptable cost and performance range for these electric vehicles, completely new vehicle models need to be designed. The first MINI E field trials in Germany reported by [1], [7], and [11] showed that using electric vehicles instead of conventional vehicles with combustion engines does not limit mobility in urban and suburban areas. However, in-depth results describing characteristic parameters of EV-typical driving behavior are still rare until now. Especially adaptations in driving strategies and subsequent changes in driving efficiency are substantial characteristics to be known as conceptual basis for coming generations of electric vehicles.

2 Theoretical Background

The next chapter will give a short overview over the subject of strategies for efficient driving, specifics of electric driving and learning procedures in the context of electric mobility.

M. Kurosu (Ed.): Human-Computer Interaction, Part II, HCII 2013, LNCS 8005, pp. 578–585, 2013.

2.1   Strategies for Efficient Driving

Efficiency is a very important aspect in electric driving. The fact is that the battery of electric vehicles cannot be recharged as easily as the fuel tank of a combustion vehicle can be refilled. Additionally, certain destinations are only reachable either by making long recharging stops or by a adopting a conservative driving behavior. In contrast to combustive driving, saving battery is not only motivated by economical or ecological aspects.

The driver's influence on driving efficiency, in conventional vehicles, has been proved by several analyses and studies (e.g. [3], [12]). If adequate strategies are applied, such as anticipatory driving, a significant reduction of the combustion vehicle's fuel consumption is possible.

Due to the different power characteristics of e-machines, these results cannot be directly transferred to electric driving. Even though regenerative braking (recuperation) operates with loss due to a technical limited efficiency factor, the driver of an electric vehicle may similarly increase the cruising range by using the battery energy responsibly. In fact, [15] proved that the drive efficiencies of electric vehicles vary significantly by driver. According to interviews in previous MINI E field trials, users discovered anticipatory driving with constant speed and the avoidance of unnecessary accelerating as the most successful strategy for efficient locomotion with electric vehicles.

2.2   Specifics of Electric Driving

The comparatively small operating range resulting from the limited battery capacity, the long loading/charging times, and the availability of energy, are currently primary disadvantages of electric mobility. According to previous studies (e.g. [11]) there is not much difference in common mobility behavior between electric vehicles and combustion vehicles for urban use cases. Further work by [14] confirmed that the usage of electric vehicles, in these cases, lead to very similar daily driven distances and a similar coverage of mobility needs. Also, the average parking times of the used electric vehicles were mainly comparable to those of conventional cars.

As a result of the technical perspective, cars with combustion engines can be replaced by state-of-the-art electric vehicles for the majority of everyday trips in urban areas. Compared to driving with conventional cars, there are not only psychological aspects, such as the fear of insufficient range (e.g. [9]), which may affect the typical electric driving behavior. The fact that the driving dynamics characteristics of electric vehicles are very different to those of combustion vehicles is quite important here. The e-motor's/engine's maximum torque is delivered at any speed and without the need to shift; meaning that an electric vehicle accelerates the moment the driver pushes the accelerator down, whereas conventional vehicles need some time to find the right gear and increase the torque. This acceleration behavior and the deceleration of regenerative breaking, create a very specific driving performance which is different to that of combustion vehicles.

2.3   Learning Procedures

Previous field trials with MINI E showed that successfully dealing with the barriers of electric mobility is a result of adapting to electrical powered driving. According to [14], electric vehicle drivers deal with the limitations of electric mobility better over time. With advanced e-driving experience, drivers become used to specific circumstances, such as the cruising range and the recharging process. This is additionally reflected in an increasing satisfaction with the vehicle used. Over the usage period, an appropriate estimation of operating distance becomes perceivable by fewer but longer charging stops [8]. Amongst others, [5] has discovered that driving experience with electric vehicles does not only lead to an optimized driving behavior with such cars, but might also affect the non-electric driving habits towards a more efficiency based way of driving conventional cars.

A more detailed analysis by [13] shows three typical phases of EV-initiated learning procedures, namely: discovery, translation, and application. Discovery includes learning about the unique attributes of the vehicle, such as its drive feel, regenerative braking, cruising range, and recharging. The evaluation and appreciation of newly discovered facts takes place in the translation stage. Finally – in application – the drivers incorporate translated discoveries into their everyday driving habits and consolidate the adapted behavioral patterns. Using the example of limited range the three phase learning procedure is the following. Initially the driver perceives that driving fast reduces range. In the next step, the driver decides that driving slower to get more range is worth it. Finally the driver changes the permanent driving behavior for the benefit of a slower but more efficient motion.

As previous MINI E field trials showed, trends towards novel behavioral patterns with the objective of compensating disadvantages of electric mobility are detectable in characteristics concerning everyday use, charging and range [14].

2.4   Generic Data Collection Procedure in Previous MINI E Field Trials

None of the previous MINI E field trials were set up with the goal of measuring changes in driving behavior. The main objectives were concentrated on acceptance, general using behavior and the substitutability of conventional cars. Therefore, mainly subjective data was collected; [1], [2] and [10] described these methods in detail. The users' motivation and attitude were evaluated by telephone interviews and face-to-face-interviews before receiving the MINI E. Further interviews and supplement online questionnaires were conducted halfway through and at the end of the usage period. Using behavior parameters such as the frequency of use and the suitability for certain types of trips were captured by travel diaries which were administered three times for one week [14]. Charging diaries (two times for one week) provided information about charging habits.

Only few of the test vehicles were equipped with onboard data loggers for collecting trip-length, speed, and acceleration. This makes the existing vehicle related database insufficient for investigations with a focus on behavioral changes. Therefore, another field trial with the main objective of detecting and understanding EV-effected changes in driving behavior has become necessary.

2.5   Research Questions

According to the assumptions of [8] and [14] e-drivers are running through a certain learning process to handle the challenges of electric mobility successfully. It is supposed that with increasing time the driver adapts his driving behavior to the electric vehicle. Though [13] already offers a model describing the learning procedure, the knowledge of preliminary studies is mainly based on subjective data acquisition by interviews and travel diaries. The whole experimental design of previous field trials was developed with objectives other than analyzing changes in driving characteristics. Detailed driving dynamics data which is essential for the parameterization of adaptation and learning procedures has not been provided until now. The basic question is whether driving experience with electric vehicles causes a measurable variation of driving strategies. Furthermore, it is very important to understand how driving strategies might be modified. Trying to reach destinations at the limits of range by highly efficient driving is not the only possible driving patterns adaptation. It is also conceivable that gained confidence in terms of range estimation may lead to a more sporty driving behavior by using the cars performance potential. Hence, it needs to be known whether the altered driving behavior results in higher efficiency and increased range. The influence of periodical interruptions in the adaptation process by simultaneous usage of conventional combustion vehicles is also relevant. Progress in developing an e-optimized driving behavior may be annihilated by re-habituation to combustive driving. Another question is how far the success of the adaptation process is depending on intermittent usage of combustion vehicles. Finally, specific driving patterns adapted during a longer usage period of an electric vehicle probably also affect combustive driving. This leads to the question whether an efficient EV-adapted driving behavior is sustainably transferred to the usage of conventional cars.

3   Methodology

In order to parameterize adaptations in driving efficiency with electric vehicles, 25 MINI E were provided as electric test vehicles. Participants were either considered as private (EV for private use) or corporate (EV for official purposes). The field trial was composed of two complementary data collections. One was the long-term data collection in combustive and electric vehicles over several months. Another three comparison drives, 2 hours each, on a reference route completed the long-term analysis with situation specific reference data.

3.1   MINI E as Vehicle for the Electric Field Test

The electric vehicle used for the purposes of this study was a MINI E. It is a MINI Cooper which has been converted to an electric vehicle. The installed e-machine offers 150 kW. With about 1500 kg of weight, this car is able to keep up even with well motorized combustion vehicles in terms of driving performance. The speed of the MINI E is electronically limited at 95 mph and its battery capacity lasts for cruises as far as 100 miles. Complete recharging at 230 V and 32 A takes up to 4 hours (or up to 10 hours with 12 A). Concerning these characteristics, the 2009 built MINI E is still representative for today's electric vehicles. The substantial contrast to conventional combustion vehicles is the very strong regenerative brake, which allows decelerations of up to 0.24 g [4]. The regenerative brake is controlled through releasing the accelerator pedal. It is, therefore, possible for the driver to operate this electric vehicle through the use of only the accelerator pedal, except in emergency circumstances, where a higher deceleration is necessary.

3.2   Data Collection by Smartphones

In order to trace learning procedures with electric vehicles, the driving dynamics data was collected with a smartphone (Apple iPhone 4) in each car. Using the smartphones' sensor technology, acceleration was recorded at a frequency of 25 Hz, position and velocity out of the GPS signal at a frequency of 1 Hz. Gathered data packets were sent to a webserver by an application especially designed for this purpose. This flexible logging method makes it possible to collect driving dynamics data both in electric and in combustion vehicles comparably with the same platform. Furthermore, a pre-analysis of collected data allows first insight into the field trial's progress during the running operation. In order to measure the relevant longitudinal accelerations, the smartphones were positioned into the test vehicles with one of their coordinate axes exactly parallel to the longitudinal axis of the vehicle. An appropriate fastening mechanism prevented the measuring devices from uncontrolled movement.

3.3   Test Area around Munich

[14] showed that the majority of daily trips in suburban areas is possible with currently existing limits of range. Also, the test vehicle MINI E provides the required everyday suitability for usage cases in and near the city. The urban and suburban areas of Munich were selected as test environment for the long-term data collection. Furthermore, this region is one of the typical application areas of electric vehicles. This ensures that the results of this field trial are representative for the majority of electric vehicle usage cases.

Additional two-hour comparison drives which were conducted every two and a half month allow the measurement of situation-specific influence on the adaptations of electric driving. Therefore, a 20 mile long course north of Munich was selected as a reference route. Passing through towns and continuing along country roads and motorways, this track contains a variety of common driving situations according to [6]. These range from simple road intersections or short motorway trips to multi-lane traffic light junctions. Amongst others, the numerous accelerating and decelerating operations at speed limits and traffic lights are particularly important for analyzing and parameterizing EV-specific driving patterns.

3.4   Two Groups of Subjects

The influence of intermittent usage of conventional vehicles on the success of adaptation procedures was determined by two different groups of subjects. Fifteen MINI E were allocated to private individuals. Another ten were provided to FMG (Munich Airport) and SWM (Stadtwerke München, Munich City Utilities). The vehicles were used as part of the corporate car pool and were used by a larger number of drivers. Among these, 15 drivers took part in the current study. While each of the 15 private users had access to his MINI E at all times, the 15 corporate participants could use the electric vehicle only as an additional car pool vehicle for official purposes and had to switch back to their own combustion vehicles for personal use; corporate users had to change between cars with electric engine and those with combustion engine more frequently (some changed every day) than the private participants, who mainly drove electric. Apart from this different using condition all subjects of both groups were running through the same test procedure. Therefore, all measurable learning effects can be described as a result of intermittent usage of conventional vehicles.

3.5   Test Procedure

Short and long-term changes in driving behavior were examined during a five-month collection of driving dynamics data from MINI E test vehicles in daily use. The variation of measured values with time describes the progress of learning procedures. Therefore it is possible to parameterize EV-specific driving behavior and the adaptation process leading to this. Furthermore the success of EV-adapted driving patterns (e.g. a variation of range) is measureable by the analysis of the participants' everyday using behavior. The frequency of EV usage which indicates the degree of intermittent usage was captured by logbooks.

To identify before-and-after effects, data logging smartphones were installed into the subjects' combustion vehicles the three weeks before and the three weeks after the EV usage period. During the pre-electric-measuring, the initial driving behavior, which served as the driving baseline in conventional cars, was recorded. The post-electric-measuring subsequent to the five-month usage of MINI E allows analyzing the transferability of adopted driving behavior back to conventional driving. Likewise, the sustainability of e-optimized driving patterns was evaluated.

In terms of special test trials, the subjects were driving the reference route once with a conventional vehicle and once with a MINI E (with changed order between the subjects). In this way, it is possible to compare the determining variables of driving behavior in specified situations. There were two standardized comparison drives used in this field study. The one at the beginning provided situation specific baseline data of different driving behavior with conventional cars and electric vehicles. Finally, situation dependent variations of driving patterns become measurable by using the data of the second comparison drive at the end of the EV using period.

Additionally, by another comparison drive, where the reference route was driven two times with the electric vehicle, the potential of successful energy saving strategies is quantifiable. Therefore, in one of the two test runs the subjects were instructed to drive according to their common driving habitation while the other one had to be done by driving in the possibly most efficient way.

4   First Results

A first impression of changes in driving behavior is obtained from a statistic pre-analysis of the first two month of MINI E usage. A trend analysis of the means of all subjects, showed no significant general variation in any variable which was measured to specify driving strategies for the whole group. This effect seems plausible as learning processes have to be analyzed on an individual level. Only by a closer look at the recorded data it becomes obvious that the driving behavior of single participants changes – but with contrary trends. One reason for this might be the influence of different using conditions in private and corporate use. Another assumption is that there are generally various types of drivers who adapt to electric driving in their specific way.

Further results, describing the influence of intermittent usage and assessing the adopted efficiency driving, will only be possible as soon as the field trial has been completed.

5   Conclusions

Changes in driving behavior with electric vehicles can be measured and analyzed with the methodologies presented here. Long-term effects as well as the influence of intermittent combustion driving have become measurable by different phases of data collection. A pre-analysis of the data has already shown that the usage of electric vehicles may lead to opposed changes in measurable parameters of driving habitation. For this reason, further analysis of the collected data has to be done in consideration of different types of drivers.

Acknowledgements. The authors would like to thank the Bavarian Ministry of Economic Affairs, Infrastructure, Transport and Technology and the BMW Group for making this research possible.

References

1. Bühler, F., Neumann, I., Cocron, P., Franke, T., Krems, J.F.: Usage patterns of electric vehicles: A reliable indicator of acceptance? Findings from a German field study. In: Proceedings of the 90th Annual Meeting of Transportation Research Board (2011)
2. Cocron, P., Bühler, F., Neumann, I., Franke, T., Krems, J.F., Schwalm, M., Keinath, A.: Methods of evaluating electric vehicles from a user's perspective – the MINI E field trial in Berlin. IET Intelligent Transport Systems 5, 127–133 (2011)
3. Dorrer, C.: Effizienzbestimmung von Fahrweisen und Fahrerassistenz zur Reduzierung des Kraftstoffverbrauchs unter Nutzung telematischer Informationen. Dissertation. Universität Stuttgart (2003)
4. Eberl, T., Sharma, R., Stroph, R., Schumann, J., Pruckner, A.: Evaluation of interaction concepts for the longitudinal dynamics of electric vehicles – Results of study focused on driving experience (2012)
5. Everett, A., Walsh, C., Smith, K., Burgess, M., Harris, M.: Ultra Low Carbon Vehicle Demonstrator Programme. In: EVS 25. Proceedings of the 25th World Battery, Hybrid and Fuel Cell Electric Vehicles Symposium & Exhibition, Shenzen, China (2010)
6. Fastenmeier, W.: Autofahrer und Verkehrssituationen – Neue Wege zur Bewertung von Sicherheit und Zuverlässigkeit moderner Straßenverkehrssysteme. Verlag TÜV Rheinland, Köln (1995)
7. Franke, T., Neumann, I., Bühler, F., Cocron, P., Krems, J.F.: Experiencing range in an electric vehicle: understanding psychological barriers. Applied Psychology (2011), doi: 10.1111/j.1464-0597.2011.00474.x

8. Franke, T., Cocron, P., Bühler, F., Neuman, I., Krems, J.F.: Adapting to the range of an electric vehicle – the relation of experience to subjectively available mobility resources (2012),
http://www.tu-chemnitz.de/hsw/psychologie/
professuren/allpsy1/pdf/Franke_et_al._2012_AdRange.pdf
(retrieved)
9. Hajesch, M.: Abschlussbericht BMW. Klimaentlastung durch den Einsatz erneuerbarer Energien im Zusammenwirken mit emissionsfreien Elektrofahrzeugen – MINI E 1.0 (2012), http://www.pt-elektromobilitaet.de/projekte/
foerderprojekte-aus-de-konjunkturpaket-ii-2009-2011/
pkw-feldversuche/abschlussberichte/
abschlussbericht-mini-e-1.0_bmw.pdf (retrieved)
10. Krems, J.F., Franke, T., Neumann, I., Cocron, P.: Research methods to assess the acceptance of EVs – experiences from EV user study. In: Gessner, T. (ed.) Smart Systems Integration: Proceedings of the 4th European Conference & Exhibition on Integration Issues of Miniaturized Systems, VDE Verlag, Como Italy (2010)
11. Neumann, I., Cocron, P., Franke, T., Krems, J.F.: Electric vehicles as a solution for green driving in the future? Afield study examining the user acceptance of electric vehicles. In: Krems, J.F., Petzold, T., Henning, M. (eds.) Proceedings of the European Conference on Human Interface Design for ITS, Berlin, Germany (2010)
12. Rommerskirchen, C., Müller, T., Bengler, K.: Validation of fuel consumption calculated by a driving simulator. In: Proceedings of the Driving Simulator Conference Europe, Paris (2012)
13. Turrentine, T., Garas, D., Lentz, A., Woodjack, J.: The UC Davis MINI E Consumer Study. University of California, Davis (2011)
14. Vilimek, R., Keinath, A., Schwalm, M.: The MINI E Field Study - Similarities and Differences in International Everyday EV Driving. In: Stanton, N.A. (ed.) Advances in Human Aspects of Road and Rail Transport, pp. 363–372. CRC Press, Boca Raton (2012)
15. Walsh, C., Carroll, S., Eastlake, A.: UK Electric Vehicle Range Testing and Efficiency Maps (2011)

In-Car Information Systems: Matching and Mismatching Personality of Driver with Personality of Car Voice

Ing-Marie Jonsson[1] and Nils Dahlbäck[2]

[1] Ansima Inc, Los Gatos, CA 95033, USA
ingmarie@ansima.com
[2] Department of Computer and Information Science, Linköping University, SE-581 83
Linköping, Sweden
nils.dahlback@liu.se

Abstract. Personality has a huge effect on how we communicate and interact with others. This study investigates how dominant/submissive personality match and mismatch between driver and voice of the in-vehicle system affects performance and attitude. The study was conducted with a total of 40 participants at Oxford Brookes University in the UK. Data show that drivers accurately discern the personality of the car voice, and that car voice personality affects drivers' performance. The dominant car voice results in drivers following instructions better regardless of driver personality. The matched conditions showed 2 -3 times better driving performance than the mismatched conditions. Drivers with the submissive voice in the car felt significantly less at-ease and content after driving than drivers with the dominant voice. Design implications of in-vehicle systems are discussed.

Keywords: In-car System, Driving Simulator, Driving Performance, Speech system, Attitude, Personality, Dominant and Submissive, Similarity Attraction.

1 Introduction

Humans are tuned to detect characteristics in a voice and use that skill when communicating with both humans and speech-based computer systems [1]. The linguistic and para-linguistic properties of a voice can influence people's attention and affect performance, judgment, and risk-taking [2, 3]. Previous studies show that voices used by in-car systems can influence driving performance in the same manner [4, 5, 6]. Characteristics of the voice affects listeners perception of liking and credibility of what is said, regardless of if the speaker is human or computer-based system [3]. The psychological literature suggests that consistency is important. People expect consistency and prefer consistency to inconsistency. When inconsistency is encountered, people enter a state where they are motivated to adapt their perceptions in order to resolve inconsistency [7]. This process increases their cognitive load. The need for consistency is well understood in traditional media, but is less clear for human-computer interaction. In the context of in-car information systems, Nass et al. [8] show a clear positive effect of matching the emotional characteristics of the in-car voice to the emotional state of the driver.

M. Kurosu (Ed.): Human-Computer Interaction, Part II, HCII 2013, LNCS 8005, pp. 586–595, 2013.
© Springer-Verlag Berlin Heidelberg 2013

Communication is also more effective [9] when source and receiver share common meanings, belief, and mutual understanding. Lazarsfeld and Merton [10] showed that most successful human communication will occur between a source and a receiver who are alike, i.e., homophilous, and have a common frame of reference. People prefer people with personalities and accents similar to themselves. Communicating with entities that are markedly different requires more effort to reach common ground.

In general terms, theories of similarity-attraction and consistency-attraction [11] would suggest that personality has a huge effect on how we communicate and interact with others. Previous studies [12] show that matching personality when communicating with a computer systems matters and Dahlbäck, Swamy et al. [13] show that even matching accents matters. A system is always rated higher, and the user's perception of the systems performance better in matched cases.

The study reported here was designed to investigate if the voice of an in-car system would be subject to similarity-attraction and consistency-attraction. In particular, the personality of the voice, and how that would affect attitude and driving performance.

2   Study Design and Apparatus

To investigate the effect of matching and mismatching personality of voice with driver personality, a study with 100 participants was designed. The study was conducted at Oxford Brookes University in the UK and a replicated study was done at Stanford University in the USA. Reported here are the results from the UK study.

2.1   Study Design and Participants

The design was a 2 (Personality of driver: dominant, submissive) x 2 (Personality of car voice: dominant, submissive) between subject and gender balanced study.

There were 40 participants in the study (20 dominant and 20 submissive) Participants were screened based on the Interpersonal Adjective Scale [14] where questions were selected to assess participants along the dominant-submissive dimension. This is a standard commercial questionnaire, where the dominant-submissive dimension represents the degree to which an individual is assertive and willing to exercise control over others.

All participants were students at Oxford Brookes University and they were awarded 10GBP for their participation.

2.2   Apparatus

Driving Simulator. The studies were done using a driving simulator, and hence the results provide an indication rather than a determination of behavior in real cars and real traffic.

The main factor that motivates the use of driving simulators for initial testing is the controlled environment. Despite the dangers involved in driving, the average driver will have very few accidents in their lifetime. Due to the rarity of incidents, it would be extremely time consuming to set-up an experiment with the characteristics of real driving within the defined parameters of the study, and wait for a significant number of events to occur. The best way to examine new driving related systems and practices is to challenge people using a driving simulator. The experience is immersive; the degree of immersion varies with the fidelity of the simulator, but the effect is there even for very low fidelity simulators [15].

Fig. 1. STISIM Drive - Driving simulator

A commercial driving simulator, STISIM Drive model 100 with a 45-degree driver field-of-view, from Systems Technology Inc. was used in the studies. Participants sat in a real car seat and "drove" using a Microsoft Sidewinder steering wheel and pedals (accelerator and brake). The simulated journey was projected on a wall in front of participants.

Fig. 2. STISIM Drive – Driving scenario with a small village, an intersection and pedestrians

Driving scenarios in STISIM Drive consist of a road and objects placed along that road. It is important to note that a driving scenario in STISIM Drive is static, drivers can turn left or right at any intersection, but are nevertheless driving on the same road as if they had continued straight ahead. This ensures consistent driving environment from start to finish for all participants regardless of turns.

Fig. 3. STISIM Drive – Driving scenario with roadwork and road signs. Note the rear-view mirror located in the top right corner of the picture. Traffic can either be programmed to follow traffic regulations or drive without adherence to traffic regulations.

The driving scenario was 52 000 feet (15.85 kilometers) long. It was especially designed to take the drivers through rural areas, villages and intersections in a varied and realistic road scenario. All properties of the simulator, vehicle dynamics, weather conditions and traffic were set to be the same for all participants in the study. The exception of course, being the voices used by the navigation system.

In-Car System. A navigation system was designed to take the driver to five locations by interacting with drivers at certain locations along the driving scenario.

The navigation system consisted of 38 utterances. 32 of the utterances were directions or suggestions, and six utterances were facts about the immediate surroundings. Directions and suggestions were designed to guide the drivers to the pre-programmed destinations. The facts were added to investigate how much attention drivers were paying to the system.

There were two versions of the navigation system. One version used a dominant male voice, and the other version used a submissive male voice. A panel of researchers using the same IAS scale used to screen participants assessed and selected the voices for the in-car systems. Even though the information was the same in both versions, the utterances varied in choice of words and voice characteristics. The main linguistic features used to distinguish between a dominant and a submissive voice, were choice of words, pitch range and speed of speaking.

The dominant voice used words such as "will", "must" and "definitely, and the submissive voice used words such as "might", "could" and "perhaps". When the dominant navigation system used assertive language "You should definitely turn right" the submissive system was more timid, "Perhaps you should turn right". For choices the dominant voice would, for instance say, "Continuing straight is shorter but may have more traffic. Turning right will definitely be faster" and the submissive voice would say, "Continuing straight is shorter but may have more traffic. Turning right will probably be faster". The dominant voice was furthermore given a higher overall frequency, a larger range of pitch during speech, and greater speed than the submissive voice [12].

3   Procedure and Measures

3.1   Procedure

All participants were informed that the experiment would take one hour and started the experimental session by signing a consent form. After this, participants drove a five-minute test run of the simulator to familiarize themselves with the simulator and the controls. This enabled participants to experience feedback from the steering wheel, the effects of the accelerator and brake pedals, a crash, and for us to screen for participants with simulator sickness [16]. Two of the signed up participants felt nauseous or discomfort during the training course and did not conclude the study. The remaining 40 participants filled in the first questionnaire consisting of general information such as gender and age in addition to driving experience.

Participants where then randomly divided into two gender-balanced groups of 20 in the UK. The dominant and submissive participants were matched and mismatched with the personality of in-car voice.

All participants drove the driving simulator with the driving scenario scripted to take the driver to five destinations, and all participants were subjected to the factual information inserted at six locations along the road.

After the driving session, participants filled in post driving questionnaires. One of the questionnaires asked participants to assess the personality of the navigation systems, and how similar the navigation system voice was to them. A second questionnaire asked participants to recall information volunteered by the navigation system during the drive.

3.2   Measures and Dependent Variables

Personality. Participants were screened based on the Interpersonal Adjective Scale [14] where questions were selected to assess participants along the dominant-submissive dimension. This is a standard commercial questionnaire, where the dominant-submissive dimension represents the degree to which an individual is assertive and willing to exercise control over others.

Similarity. An important aspect of how voices influence attitude and perception of spoken messages is *similarity-attraction*. Similarity-attraction predicts that people will be more attracted to people matching themselves than to those who mismatch. Similarity-attraction is a robust finding in both human-human and human-computer interaction [12, 17] human-computer interactions, the theory predicts that users will be more comfortable with computer-based personas that exhibit properties that are similar to their own. Attraction leads to a desire for interaction and increased attention in human-computer interaction [18, 19]. A standard questionnaire on homophily [20] was used to identify measures of similarity. An index for similarity was constructed as a combination of attitudinal similarity and behavioral similarity. Participants were asked to rate the statements based on the questions "On the scales below, please indicate your feelings about the person speaking?" Contrasting statements were paired on opposite sides of a 10-point scale such that, 'similar to me' and 'different from me' would appear at different ends.

Driving Performance. This is a collection of measures that consists of accidents and adherence to traffic regulations. The driving simulator automatically collected the data for these measures. *Bad driving* is comprised off-road accidents, collisions, speeding and running red lights. Because it is much more difficult to drive in a simulator than to drive a real car in real traffic, the number of incidents are much higher than in real traffic, which makes this a useful measure of driving performance.

Navigation System. This is a collection of measures related to the voice used by the navigation system and how drivers reacted to it. The measure *Instructions followed* simply counts how many of the driving instructions drivers followed. *Time to destination* measures drivers' time to complete the driving scenario to the last destination. *Facts remembered* measures how many of the driving scenario facts that drivers remembered after the driving session ended. The measure *Voice competence* was based on a 30-term instrument, where participants were asked to assess the voice using a 10-point Likert scale. *Feeling calm or annoyed* after driving was measured using a 17-term DES [21] instrument where participants assessed their emotional state using a 10-point Likert scale.

4   Results

The effects of the matching and mismatching the car voice personality of a navigation system with driver personality were measured by a two (Personality of of Navigation System voice) by two (Personality of Driver) between-participants ANOVA.

4.1   Prior Driving Experience

To ensure that there was no bias based on drivers' prior driving experience, data from the two most recent years of driving was collected. The data, that included number of accidents and tickets, was averaged for each group of drivers. No significant differences were found across conditions.

4.2   Manipulation Check

The manipulation check showed that drivers perceived the voices to be dominant and submissive. All drivers rated the dominant voice as dominant (Mean=43.3, SD=5.7) and the submissive voice as submissive (Mean=30.8, SD=6.5), $F(1, 36) = 42.8$, $p < 0.001$. There were no effect of driver personality, and no interactions effects.

4.3   Similarity – Homophily

Data from the similarity assessment show an interaction effect. Dominant drivers felt similar to the person behind the dominant voice (Mean=6, SD=0.6), and dissimilar to the person behind the submissive voice (Mean=4, SD=0.3). Submissive drivers, however, felt equally similar to both the person behind the dominant voice (Mean=5, SD=0.3) and the person behind the submissive voice (Mean=5.3, SD=0.7), $F(1, 36)= 45.2$, $p < 0.001$.

4.4   Driving Performance

Bad Driving. There were no main effects of driver personality or voice personality on bad driving. There was however an interaction effect such that mismatched conditions showed significantly worse driving performance than matched conditions. Dominant drivers drove significantly better with a dominant voice (Mean=6.5, SD=2.3) than with a submissive voice (Mean=20.4, SD=2.3). Similarly, submissive drivers drove significantly better with a submissive voice (Mean=7.7, SD=2.3) than with a submissive voice (Mean=15.5, SD=2.3), $F(1, 36) = 22.7$, $p < 0.001$.

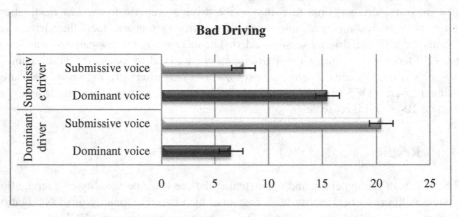

Fig. 4. Bad driving- accidents, speeding and running red lights

4.5   Navigation System

Voice Competence. Participants were asked to rate the competence of the navigation system voice. Data show no main effect of driver personality or voice personality. There is however an interaction effect so that dominant drivers rated the dominant voice more competent (Mean=70.0, SD=11) than the submissive voice (Mean=58, SD=11), and submissive drivers rated the submissive voice more competent (Mean=69.3, SD=10) than the dominant voice (Mean=62, SD=9), $F(1, 36) = 8.1$, $p < 0.007$.

Instructions Followed. The data show that voice matching matters when following instructions. There was an interaction effect so that dominant drivers followed instructions significantly better when given by the dominant voice (Mean=18.4, SD=2) than when given by the submissive voice (Mean=15, SD=3). For submissive drivers, the data show that the voice makes no difference for following instructions. Mean=16.6. SD=3 for the dominant voice and Mean=16.7, SD=1.7 for the submissive voice, $F(1, 36)=4.2$, $p < 0.05$.

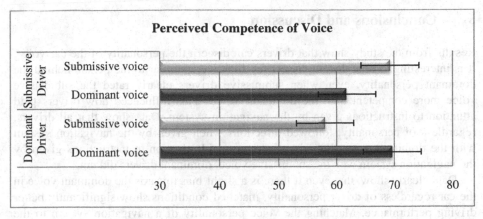

Fig. 5. Perceived competence of voice

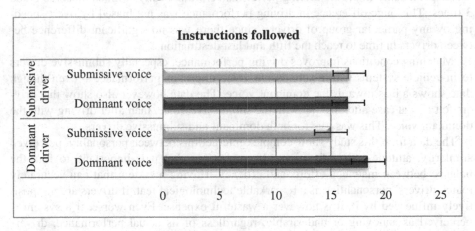

Fig. 6. Instructions followed

Facts Remembered. The data show that voice matching matters, with a main effect of voice. Drivers remembered facts told by the submissive voice (Mean=2.65, SD=0.3) significantly more often than when facts are told by the dominant voice (Mean=1.1, SD=0.3), F(1, 36)=9.4, p <0.005.

Time to Destination. The driving simulator automatically collected the time it took for drivers to reach their fifth destination. There were no main effects or interaction effects for time to reach the fifth and last destination.

Feeling Calm or Annoyed. The data show a main effect of voice personality. Drivers that drove with the submissive voice (Mean=4.8, SD=1.4) felt more annoyed and less at-ease after driving than drivers with the dominant voice (Mean=3.6, SD=1.2), F(1, 36)=8.4, p < 0.006.

5   Conclusions and Discussion

Results from the study show that drivers can discern the personality of the car voice. It is interesting to note that all drivers felt they were similar to the person behind the dominant personality, even when submissive drivers clearly rated the submissive voice more competent than the dominant voice. This influenced how drivers paid attention to instructions given by the navigation system. Data show that all drivers, regardless of personality, followed directions when given by the navigation system with the dominant voice. Submissive drivers paid attention to instructions given by the navigation system with the submissive voice, dominant drivers did not.

Data clearly show, that even if there is a slight bias towards the dominant voice in the car regardless of driver personality, matched conditions show significantly better driving performance. Matching the voice personality of a navigation system to the driver personality improves driving performance dramatically, with as much as 2 and 3 times. This huge difference in driving performance was not biased by overt speeding by any particular group of drivers, since there was no significant difference between drivers in time to reach the fifth and last destination.

Matching conditions improves driving performance, especially submissive drivers to in-vehicle systems with a submissive voice improves performance – even though data shows a bias towards the dominant voice. The data however also show that drivers felt less at ease after driving with the submissive voice, than after driving with the dominant voice. This was true for both dominant and submissive drivers.

The data from this study show complex interactions between personality, perceived similarity, attitude and performance. It emphasizes that it is important, to find the balance between matching-efforts and efficacy. Having a system that can accurately match drivers' personalities, is a remarkable technological feat, if drivers are not positively influenced by it, it is however a wasteful expense. Even worse, if a system is perceived as annoying or undesirable, regardless of its actual performance, drivers will be dissatisfied with both the system and the car. The bottom line is that even the technologically-best system may not satisfy or help all drivers: While in-vehicle information systems represent exciting technological advances, their deployment should be guided by significant caution.

Acknowledgments. This research was conducted in collaboration with Dr Mary Zajicek at Oxford Brookes University. We are grateful to Dr Zajicek's for her contributions and support of this study.

References

1. Banse, R., Scherer, K.R.: Acoustic profiles in vocal emotion expression. Journal of Personality and Social Psychology 70, 614–636 (1996)
2. Jonsson, I.-M., Nass, C., Endo, J., Reaves, B., Harris, H., Le Ta, J., Chan, N., Knapp, S.: Don't blame me I am only the Driver: Impact of Blame Attribution on Attitudes and Attention to Driving Task. In: SIGCHI, pp. 1219–1222. ACM Press (2004)

3. Nass, C., Brave, S.: Wired for speech how voice activates and advances the human-computer relationship. MIT Press, Cambridge (2005)
4. Zajicek, M., Jonsson, I.-M.: A Complex Relationship, Older People and In-Car Message System Evaluation. Journal of Gerontology 6, 66–78 (2007)
5. Jonsson, I.-M.: Conversational Interfaces and Driving: Impact on Behaviour and Attitude. In: IASTED Human-Computer Interaction, pp. 224–229 (2008)
6. Jonsson, I.-M., Dahlbäck, N.: The effects of different voices for speech-based in-vehicle interfaces: Impact of young and old voices on driving performance and attitude. In: Proceedings of the 10th Annual Conference of the International Speech Communication Association, INTERSPEECH 2009, pp. 2795–2798 (2009)
7. Fiske, S., Taylor, S.: Social Cognition. McGraw-Hill Inc., New York (1991)
8. Nass, C., Jonsson, I.-M., Harris, H., Reaves, B., Endo, J., Brave, S., Takayama, L.: Improving Automotive Safety by Pairing Driver Emotion and Car Voice Emotion. In: SIGCHI, pp. 1973–1976. ACM Press (2005)
9. Rogers, E., Bhowmik, D.: Homophily-Heterophily: Relational Concepts for Communication Research. Public Opinion Quarterly 34, 523 (1970)
10. Lazarsfeld, P., Merton, R.: Mass Communication, Popular Taste, and Organized Social Action. The Communication of Ideas, 95–188 (1948)
11. Byrne, D.: The Attraction Paradigm. Academic Press, New York (1971)
12. Nass, C., Lee, K.M.: Does computer-generated speech manifest personality? An experimental test of similarity-attraction. In: SIGCHI, pp. 329–336. ACM Press (2000)
13. Dahlbäck, N., Swamy, S., Nass, C., Arvidsson, F., Skågeby, J.: Spoken Interaction with Computers in a Native or Non-native Language - Same or Different? In: Proceedings of INTERACT, pp. 294–301 (2001)
14. Wiggins, J.S.: Interpersonal Adjective Scales: Professional Manual. Psychological Assessment Resources, Lutz, FL (1995)
15. de Winter, J., van Leuween, P., Happee, P.: Advantages and Disadvantages of Driving Simulators: A Discussion. In: Proceedings of Measuring Behavior, pp. 47–50 (2012)
16. Brooks, J., Goodenough, R., Crisler, M., Klein, N., Alley, R.: Simulator sickness during driving simulation studies. Accident Analysis and Prevention 42, 788–796 (2010)
17. Byrne, D.: The Attraction Paradigm. Academic Press, New York (1971)
18. Dahlbäck, N., Wang, Q., Nass, C., Alwin, J.: Similarity is More Important than Expertise: Accent Effects in Speech Interfaces. In: SIGCHI, pp. 1553–1556. ACM Press (2007)
19. Nass, C., Lee, K.: Does Computer synthesized speech manifest personality? Experimental tests of recognition, similarity attraction and consistency attraction. Journal of Experimental Psychology: Applied 7, 171–181 (2001)
20. Rubin, R., Palmgreen, P., Sypher, H.: Communication Research Measures: A Sourcebook. Guilford Press, New York (1994)
21. Izard, C.: Human Emotions. Plenum Press, New York (1977)

Subjective Ratings in an Ergonomic Engineering Process Using the Example of an In-Vehicle Information System

Michael Krause and Klaus Bengler

Technische Universität München, Institute of Ergonomics, Boltzmannstraße 15,
85747 Garching, Germany
{krause,bengler}@lfe.mw.tum.de

Abstract. The engineering process for a traffic light assistant system on a smartphone for use while driving as an In-Vehicle Information System (IVIS) was accompanied by assessment of subjective usability ratings using questionnaires, such as the System Usability Scale (SUS), AttrakDiff2 and NASA-TLX. The results during the development process are presented and discussed.

The SUS was an easy to apply and fast instrument for the project. Nevertheless, caution should be taken when a high percentage of users are repeatedly involved in examining the same system, as this will likely increase the SUS score.

Keywords: IVIS, usability, engineering, questionnaires, SUS, AttrakDiff.

1   Introduction

With the goal of traffic flow and traffic light optimization, the Institute of Ergonomics at the Technische Universität München created and tested a prototypical traffic light assistant on a smartphone [1, 2].

The assistant system works on a normal smartphone and can provide the driver with information about the state of an upcoming traffic light, so that he or she can adjust their driving behavior when approaching the next traffic light.

Because this application is to be used while driving, special care must be taken to minimize distraction effects. So, the main aim of most human factors experiments within the project was to assess driver distraction issues. Nevertheless, we were very interested in subjective usability and user experience ratings and repeatedly included questionnaires in the different experiments. The most often used was the System Usability Scale (SUS) [3] followed by the AttrakDiff2 [4].

This paper will show subjective ratings during the project, with special focus on the SUS.

1.1   Related Work – System Usability Scale (SUS)

The SUS was published by Brooke in 1996 [3]. Some historic background information can be found in [5]. The SUS variation used here is documented in the

M. Kurosu (Ed.): Human-Computer Interaction, Part II, HCII 2013, LNCS 8005, pp. 596–605, 2013.

method section 3.1. The SUS was originally intended as a "quick and dirty tool" to achieve a one dimensional "overall usability" [3]. Newer research proposes that the SUS results can be split into two sub-dimensions when needed: "Learnability", which includes item 4 and 10 and "Usability" which incorporates the rest [6,7].

[8] compared five questionnaires in a website usability study. SUS provided a fast discrimination in a simulation when a reduced number of subjects would participate. [9,10] reported some problems with the word "cumbersome" and was replaced with "awkward". [10] replaced the term "system" with "product". In [7] there is an Italian version.

In [10,11] an adjective scale is added to the SUS scores and scores are provided, which help to assess own data. Further data for a raw relative judgment of own SUS scores can also be found in [6].

[10] provides the evolvement of SUS scores along the engineering process, which inspired the work presented here and the application of SUS within the project presented here.

1.2   AttrakDiff2

The AttrakDiff2 questionnaire can be found in [4]. It consists of four sub-dimensions (PQ, HQ-S-HQ-I, ATT), each with seven semantic differentials (adjective pairs) on a seven step Likert-scale, thus a total of 28 items. The underlying model can be found in [12], for example. The creators of the questionnaire propose that a product can have pragmatic quality (PQ) and hedonic quality (HQ). The hedonic quality is further divided into stimulation (HQ-S) and identification (HQ-I). Consequently PQ and HQ contribute to the attractiveness (ATT) of a product.

2   Method – Experiments

In Table 1 different human factor subject tests within the KOLIBRI project and their main aims are described.

The abbreviation TDT stands for Tactile Detection Task. It is a detection response task (DRT). DRTs are currently in a standardization process by ISO TC22 SC13 WG.8. DRTs have shown to be sensitive to cognitive workload.

The percentage of repeated participation indicates the number of test subjects in a study had previous experience with the traffic light assistant from a former experiment.

Table 1. Studies conducted up to present

	SURVEY	K1 (HMI)	K2 (Customizing)	K3 (Comparison)	K4 (TDT, real)	K5 (Eye tracking, real)
KOLIBRI questionnaire	X					
AttrakDiff2		X	X		X	
SUS		X	X		X	X
NASA-TLX				X	X	X
TDT			X		X	
Video Recordings					X	X
GPS data				X	X	X
Eye tracking		X	X			X
Drv.sim.data		X	X	X		
%-repeated participation			19%	40%	35%	80%
Subjects (N)	694	20	22	20	23	22
Setting and main goal	Paper based and online survey, system described by words Goal: Do users want a traffic light assistant? How smartphones are currently used in relation to car/traffic issues.	Driving simulator. Goal: Find an appropriate HMI. Check feasibility and some behavior. Published in [1,2]	Driving simulator. Goal: (1) Users could customize the system to their needs (2) Acquire some tactile detection task (TDT) mental demand values	Driving simulator and real road. Same persons (within design) drive some settings in real and some in simulated driving. Goal: Compare behavior in real and simulated driving	Real road. Goal: Obtain a mental demand rating (TDT) of traffic light assistant system on the real road	Real road. Goal: Assess glance behavior with traffic light assistant system in real traffic while varying the display size (2.5", 3.5" and 6.5") and testing an additional acoustic notification sound
Study	SURVEY	K1 (HMI)	K2 (Customizing)	K3 (Comparison)	K4 (TDT, real)	K5 (Eye tracking, real)

3   Method – Questionnaires

3.1   System Usability Scale (SUS)

Figure 1 and Table 2 show the format and wording of SUS used in the experiments. In absence of an official translation, the instruction and items were presented bilingual. The instruction was taken from [11].

Bitte bewerten Sie die gerade genutzte Anzeigevariante mit den nachfolgenden Aussagen.

Please check the box that reflects your immediate response to each statement. Don't think too long about each statement. Make sure you respond to every statement. If you don't know how to respond, simply check box "3."

Bitte markieren Sie das Kästchen, das Ihnen als Antwort auf die Aussage spontan am geeignetsten erscheint. Beant-worten Sie jede Aussage und denken Sie nicht zu lange über eine einzelne Aussage nach. Falls Sie nicht wissen, wie Sie antworten könnten, wählen Sie Kästchen „3".

		Strongly disagree Stimme gar nicht zu				Strongly agree Stimme voll zu

1.   **I think that I would like to use this system frequently**
Ich denke, ich würde dieses System gerne regelmäßig benutzen.

     1   2   3   4   5

Fig. 1. Instructions and one item from the SUS questionnaire used

Table 2. SUS items from [3] with the translation used here

Item	Original	Translation used
1	I think that I would like to use this system frequently	Ich denke, ich würde dieses System gerne regelmäßig benutzen.
2	I found the system unnecessarily complex	Ich fand das System unnötig komplex.
3	I thought the system was easy to use	Ich fand, das System ist einfach zu nutzen.
4	I think that I would need the support of a technical person to be able to use this system	Ich denke, ich würde die Unterstützung einer technisch erfahrenen Person benötigen, um das System nutzen zu können.
5	I found the various functions in this system were well integrated	Ich fand, die verschiedenen Funktionen in diesem System sind gut integriert.
6	I thought there was too much inconsistency in this system	Ich denke, es gibt zu viele Inkonsistenzen in diesem System.
7	I would imagine that most people would learn to use this system very quickly	Ich könnte mir vorstellen, dass die meisten Leute sehr schnell lernen mit diesem System umzugehen.
8	I found the system very cumbersome to use	Ich fand das System im Gebrauch sehr umständlich.
9	I felt very confident using the system	Ich fühlte mich sehr sicher bei der Benutzung des Systems.
10	I needed to learn a lot of things before I could get going with this system	Ich musste eine Menge lernen, bevor ich mit diesem System zurechtkam.

3.2　AttrakDiff2

For the AttrakDiff2 the items and instructions from [4] were used in the different experiments (see section 2). Figure 2 shows one formatted item with a seven point Likert scale.

Bitte bewerten Sie die gerade genutzte Anzeigevariante mit den nachfolgenden Wortpaaren.

Denken Sie nicht lange über die Wortpaare nach, sondern geben Sie bitte die Einschätzung ab, die Ihnen spontan in den Sinn kommt. Vielleicht passen einige Wortpaare nicht so gut auf das Produkt, kreuzen Sie aber trotzdem bitte immer eine Antwort an. Denken Sie daran, dass es keine "richtigen" oder "falschen" Antworten gibt - nur Ihre persönliche Meinung zählt!

| technisch | ☐ ☐ ☐ ☐ ☐ ☐ ☐ | menschlich |

Fig. 2. Instructions and one item of the AttrakDiff2 questionnaire used

3.3　NASA-TLX

For the experiments which used the NASA-TLX [13], a German translation from [14] was used.

4　Results

4.1　Comparison of SUS Scores

The different SUS scores during the project are shown in Fig. 3. Five different HMI variants were tested in experiment K1. Two HMIs received low SUS values and three earned higher scores. Due to different considerations explained in [1], such as e.g. glance durations and portability, the HMI with the highest score (HMI2) was not the "winner", rather HMI3 was used for further experiments. In experiment K2 the participants drove with a preconfigured (complex) HMI and could customize it using different configuration parameters. Surprisingly, the self-configured HMI did not get much higher scores. As a conclusion, the configuration options of a final app will be reduced to a minimum. In K4 the HMI was tested on the real road. And in the (to the present) latest experiment K5, the HMI was displayed in different sizes on a tablet. The HMI_M (medium), which was the same size as the former display on a 3.5-inch smart phone, received the highest score. The HMI variant with an additional acoustic click (HMI_M_C) received the lowest score.

In regards to the desirable feature of retest reliability, it is a good sign that the dashed line is nearly horizontal between K1 and K2. The HMI got some minor tweaking between K2 and K4, e.g. to the display colors. In K2 the system was used in an artificial environment (static driving simulator), whereas K4 was carried out on the real road. Thus these are plausible reasons that a slightly better rating was achieved. What was not easily explicable to us was the shift from K4 to K5 of 78.7 to 86.4 (about 10%). A one sided t-test would also be significant: $t(38) = -1.866$; $p = 0.035$.

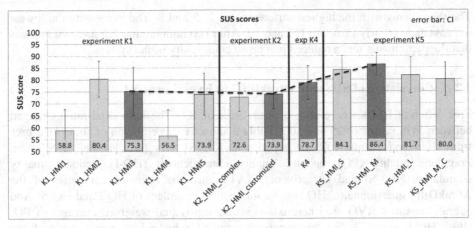

Fig. 3. SUS scores during the project

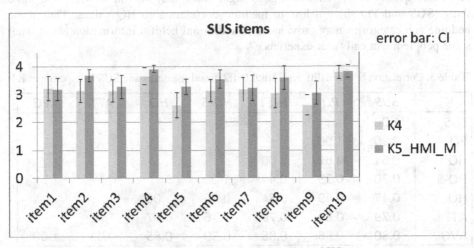

Fig. 4. Results of SUS items in K4 and K5

The main differences, to the best of our knowledge, should be the presentation on a smartphone (K4) and on a tablet (K5), the use of a tactile detection task (K4) and an eye tracking system (K5) and the proportion of test subjects that participated repeatedly: 35% in K4 and 82% in K5. Combinations of measurement tools, such as tactile detection task and an eye tracking system, were also used in K1 and K2 previously and appear not to influence SUS scores. As can be seen within the results of K5, presentation in different screen sizes can have a slight influence. Thus the presentation on different devices (tablet or smart phone) perhaps has an influence and should be checked in future experiments. The increasing proportion of repeatedly participating test subjects seems to be an easy explanation. With findings from [15] that experienced users score a system higher in SUS by about 11%, it would be a tempting conclusion. For a closer look at what causes the difference, **Fig. 4** shows the individual items. All items (positive/negative) are converted to a uniform range from 0 to 4.

The three items with the highest difference are 2, 5 and 8. The items with the lowest improvement (nearly zero) are 1, 7 and 10. After rereading items 2, 5 and 8, it appears that the participants feel a reduced perceived complexity of the system.

4.2   Correlation of SUS and AttrakDiff2 in Experiment K1

Five different HMIs where judged in experiment K1. The individual ratings ranged between SUS scores of 25 and 100. **Table 3** shows the correlation of some measures from SUS and AttrakDiff2 for experiment K1. SUS is the classical SUS score. Pragmatic quality (PQ), hedonic quality identification (HQ-I), hedonic quality stimulation (HQ-S) and attractiveness (ATT) are the four sub-categories of the AttrakDiff2 questionnaire. HQ is the combination (average) of HQ-I and HQ-S. And overall construct AVG used here is a combination (equal weighted average) of PQ, HQ-I, HQ-S and ATT. For this experiment, the SUS had a high correlation with the pragmatic quality (PQ). That is a good sign, since they should measure the same thing. SUS and PQ show a low to medium correlation to HQ values. Thus these hedonic sub-categories may provide some additional helpful information about what some people might call "user experience".

Table 3. Correlation between different AttrakDiff2 based measures and SUS in experiment K1

	SUS	PQ	HQ-I	HQ-S	HQ	ATT	AVG
SUS	1.00						
PQ	0.90	1.00					
HQ-I	0.61	0.62	1.00				
HQ-S	0.20	0.23	0.44	1.00			
HQ	0.47	0.49	0.84	0.86	1.00		
ATT	0.79	0.84	0.79	0.36	0.67	1.00	
AVG	0.80	0.86	0.86	0.59	0.85	0.93	1.00

4.3   Correlation of SUS and NASA-TLX

SUS and NASA-TLX were used in experiment K4 to assess one interface. The calculated correlation coefficient is $r = -0.37$.

In experiment K5, four interfaces were examined with SUS and NASA-TLX, with a correlation coefficient of $r = -0.28$. These results indicate a weak negative correlation between perceived demands (NASA-TLX) and overall usability (SUS). This modest correlation would be in line with findings from [16], which reported that a hard task could lower the SUS by 8%.

4.4   Maximum Price

In the SURVEY and in the experiment K4 subjects were asked what maximum price they would be willing to pay for a traffic light assistance app. In the survey the function of the app was described in words, while in the experiment the subjects could experience the app on the real road. In the paper-based and online survey the answers was most often "0 euro". This changed in experiment K4, in which the system could be used. The median increased fivefold from 2 euros to 10 euros (**Fig. 5**).We interpret the associated price as an indicator for the perceived system qualities of usefulness and satisfaction. Thus it can be stated that the opinion of subjects improved after they experienced the system. This is interesting, since [17] found the contrary effect with their system: The subjects judged the system more useful and satisfying before they experienced it in a simulator. Their system is similar to the interface K1_HMI4, which has been discarded for this project in an early stage (see SUS score of experiment K1 in **Fig. 3**)

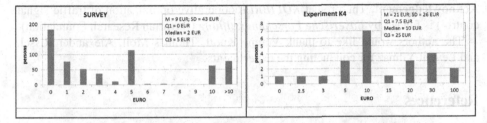

Fig. 5. Maximum price subjects will pay for a traffic light assistance application

5   Conclusion

The users show a high willingness to use the application and rate the current human-machine interface with high SUS scores. The 'willingness-to-use' and experience of such an assistance system will most probably be the key point of its success or failure.

The perceived demand (NASA-TLX) of the different interfaces in different experiments shows only a slight negative correlation with SUS scores; the hedonic subcategories of the AttrakDiff2 feature a small to medium correlation with the SUS scores. So the combination of SUS, NASA-TLX and AttrakDiff2 could examine a lot of nicely separated information. From the standpoint of efficient test planning and conduction, the six questions of NASA-TLX and the ten items of SUS are superior to the 28 items of the AttrakDiff2. Some participants even find it hard to fill in the AttrakDiff2.In our opinion, the SUS is an easy to apply questionnaire, which is also well accepted by participants.

For the SUS we will keep a special lookout for whether subjects participate several times.

We would welcome an official German translation, instead of the bilingual form used here. An improvement of the translation used here and proposed, would possibly be to replace "sicher" in item 9 (Table 2) with "selbstsicher". When not applied bilingually, and in a context to assess a car assistance system, "sicher" could have a slight unintended connotation in the direction of "safe" instead of "confident".

6   Outlook

In the real test the traffic lights acted on predetermined coordinated switching times (green wave). In the final project stage the traffic lights are switched back to a traffic flow adaptive scheme and report their current state to a central server. The central server, using this information, attempts to predict the future behavior of the traffic lights and sends estimated switching intervals to a new programmed app on smartphones. It will be interesting to examine whether this setup, with probabilistic information, is capable of providing a similar user experience as the configuration used up to now. The pilot project is set up to check the technical feasibility and assess human factors, such as driver distraction issues.

Acknowledgement. The project *KOLIBRI* (cooperative optimization of traffic signal control) is funded by *Bayerische Forschungsstiftung* (Bavarian Research Foundation).

The authors would like to thank Verena Knott, Thomas Moll, Alexander Rissel, and Levent Yilmaz for conducting the experiments.

References

1. Krause, M., Bengler, K.: Traffic Light Assistant Evaluation of Information Presentation. In: Salvendy, G., Karwowski, W. (eds.) Advances in Human Factors and Ergonomics 2012. Proceedings of the 4th Ahfe Conference 2012, pp. 6786–6795. CRC Press (2012)
2. Krause, M., Bengler, K.: Traffic Light Assistant - Driven in a Simulator. In: Toledo-Moreo, R., Bergasa, L.M., Sotelo, M. (eds.) Proceedings of the 2012 International IEEE Intelligent Vehicles Symposium Workshops (2012)
3. Brooke, J.: SUS: A quick and dirty usability scale. In: Jordan, P.W., Weerdmeester, B., Thomas, A., Mclelland, I.L. (eds.) Usability Evaluation in Industry, pp. 189–194. Taylor and Francis, London (1996)
4. User Interface Design GmbH: AttrakDiff a service of User Interface Design GmbH, http://www.attrakdiff.de/en/Home/ (last checked January 22, 2013)
5. Kirakowski, J.: The Use of Questionnaire Methods for Usability Assessment, http://sumi.ucc.ie/sumipapp.html (last check: January 3, 2013)
6. Lewis, J.R., Sauro, J.: The Factor Structure of the System Usability Scale. Human Centered Design 1, 94–103 (2009)
7. Borsci, S., Federici, S., Lauriola, M.: On the dimensionality of the System Usability Scale: a test of alternative measurement models. Cognitive Processing 10(3), 193–197 (2009)
8. Tullis, T.S., Stetson, J.N.: A comparison of questionnaires for assessing website usability. In: Proceedings of the Usability Professionals Association (UPA) 2004 Conference, pp. 7–11 (2004)
9. Finstad, K.: The System Usability Scale and Non-Native English Speakers. Journal of Usability studies 1(4), 185–188 (2006)
10. Bangor, A., Kortum, P.T., Miller, J.T.: An Empirical Evaluation of the System Usability Scale. International Journal of Human-Computer Interaction 24(6), 574–594 (2008)
11. Bangor, A., Staff, T., Kortum, P., Miller, J.: Determining What Individual SUS Scores Mean: Adding an Adjective Rating Scale. Journal of Usability Studies 4(3), 114–123 (2009)

12. Hassenzahl, M.: The thing and I: understanding the relationship between user and product. In: Blythe, M., Overbeeke, C., Monk, A.F., Wright, P.C. (eds.) Funology: From Usability to Enjoyment, pp. 31–42. Kluwer Academic Publishers, Dordrecht (2003)

13. Hart, S.G., Staveland, L.E.: Development of NASA-TLX (Task Load Index): Results of Empirical and Theoretical Research. In: Hancock, P.A., Meshkati, N. (Hrsg.) Human Mental Workload. North Holland Press, Elsevier Science Pub. Co., Amsterdam (1988)

14. Seifert, K.: Evaluation multimodaler Computersysteme in frühen Entwicklungsphasen: Ein empirischer Ansatz zur Ableitung von Gestaltungshinweisen für multimodale Computer-Systeme. Dissertation, Technische Universität Berlin (2002)

15. Sauro, J.: Does prior experience affect perceptions of usability? (January 19, 2011), http://www.measuringusability.com/blog/prior-exposure.php (last checked January 22, 2013)

16. Sauro, J.: How much does the usability test affect perceptions of usability? (May 17, 2011), http://www.measuringusability.com/task-effect.php (last checked January 22, 2013)

17. Pauwelussen, J., Hoedemaeker, M., Duivenvoorden, K.: CVIS Cooperative Vehicle-Infrastructure Systems: Deliverable D.DEPN.4.1b Assess user acceptance by small scale driving simulator research (2008)

Ergonomics Design on Expert Convenience of Voice-Based Interface for Vehicle's AV Systems

Pei-Ying Ku[1], Sheue-Ling Hwang[1]
Hsin-Chang Chang[2,*], Jian-Yung Hung[2], and Chih-Chung Kuo[2]

[1] National Tsing Hua University, Hsinchu, Taiwan 300
a60029@yahoo.com.tw
[2] Industrial Technology Research Institute, Hsinchu, Taiwan 310
piosn@itri.org.tw

Abstract. This research aimed to investigate and explore expert user interface design principle in adaptive user interface of in-vehicle full voiced-based interface. In this study, 3 stages of driving simulation experiments were established. The voice-based interface called Talking Car novice interface has been designed before. Through driving simulation experiments, subjects' behavior and response data when using voice-based interface were collected and analyzed. According to the result, the length of speech by Talking Car novice interface would be adjusted to fulfill expert users' requirements, and then switched to Talking Car expert interface. After that, a driving simulation experiment is conducted to verify the usability of the adapted interface as well as the implications on operation efficiency and traffic safety.

Keywords: in-vehicle full voice-based interface, Talking Car, driving simulation, expert user interface.

1 Introduction

1.1 Background and Motivation

Ministry of Transportation and Communications in Taiwan has amended 89th and 90th road safety traffic rules, indicating that drivers have to turn off all entertaining monitors within their eyesight, but not included the display of driving aided function. (Ministry of Transportation and Communications in Taiwan, 2011)

As we know, there is noticeable importance on developing an in-vehicle user interface by full voiced control. In other words, the drivers only depend on their auditory memory to use the interface, and thus it might be more difficult to teach novice users how to use the in-vehicle full voiced-based interface. On the other hand, the interface with convenience for expert users is also required. Therefore, in order to make the in-vehicle full voiced-based interface to be provided with novice elicitation and expert convenience, it's necessary to design an adaptive user interface.

---

* Corresponding author.

M. Kurosu (Ed.): Human-Computer Interaction, Part II, HCII 2013, LNCS 8005, pp. 606–611, 2013.

Regarding adaptive user interface in Human–Machine Interface, there are abundance of previous literatures on visual interface; however, there is little specific guidance on in-vehicle full voice-based interface. According to Jason (2010), novice users are generally concerned with how to do things instead of how fast they can do it. For this reason, novice user interface design must have complete aided functions to help novice user operating the interface step by step. Meanwhile, expert users are goal orientated and when using a user interface, they quickly deduce goals and actions to achieve those goals. They want a highly efficient interface and would thus like the number of interactions to be reduced. Hence, expert user interface design should reduce guides, and let users use the interface at their own choice to improve users' operation efficiency and traffic safety.

1.2   Objectives

In-Vehicle Speech Systems have been developed, and there is one (LUXGEN Think+) in-vehicle control systems in Taiwan. As a matter of fact, drivers need to use hands and eyes to complete the tasks to control systems in a vehicle. Distraction is easily brought up when drivers have to operate the control system while driving.

However, as things go, there has not been an in-vehicle speech control system with adaptive user interface. This study aimed to find the length of sentence the expert could tolerate in Talking Car, and then an In-Vehicle Speech Expert Interface with convenience was designed according to the experiment results. Furthermore, a follow up experiment was to ensure sufficient users' operation efficiency and a safe response to take care the road situations when controlling the AV System in-vehicle.

2   Research Method

2.1   Experimental Design

The Voice-based interaction interface with expert convenience was developed step by step through three stages of driving simulate experiments. This research chose music and radio functions which are commonly used by users to design the experimental tasks. The experiments include two independent variables - Talking Car users' familiarity and Talking Car's mode with novice, advanced-novice and expert. In driving simulated experiments, a camera was set to capture the subject's operations; we measure reaction time of the brakes when "STOP!!" message showed on the display, system speech times and words used by subjects using interrupt control button and the task completion time while carrying out the driving task. After the experiment finished, subjects would be asked to complete three questionnaires, included NASA-TLX, subjective and impatient-degree questionnaire to evaluation subjects' workload, satisfaction and the degree of impatient.

2.2   Experimental Procedure

Sixteen participants, including 9 males and 7 females, are students from National Tsing Hua University in different majors, and ages range from 22 to 30. Subjects have to hold the driving license for at least 1 year and have a habit of listening to radio or music while driving. None of them has experience of using In-vehicle speech interaction system. The following sub-section describes the testing process.

1. The process of experiment took around 1 hour in the first stage, 30 minutes in the second and the third ones.
2. Learning time took 10 minutes to introduce the system and practice to drive on the simulator.
3. Complete tasks took 15 to 20 minutes in the first stage, 5 to 10 minutes in the second and the third stages.
4. All tasks will be executed 2 times.

3   Experimental Results

3.1   Suitable Sentence Length for Expert Users Analysis

Among 15 types of sentences in Talking Car, 4 types of sentences were used more often. Therefore, the following were analyses for the 4 sentences (sentence 2, sentence 3, sentence 5 and sentence 13). To find out the sentence length that expert users could tolerate, we recorded the number of characters (Chinese characters) used in each sentence before subjects interrupted, and then calculated the accumulated percentage of interrupted times. We then identified whether the accumulated percentage of interrupted times was within 60% or there was a huge gap between the percentage, and used the number of characters in each sentence as an indicator for the next stage of experiment. The limitation of words in each sentence length is shown in Table 1. According to the result, the speech sentence was designed to fulfill Talking Car expert interface users.

Table 1. Result of limitation of sentence length from experiments. (number of characters)

	Sentence 2	Sentence 3	Sentence 5	Sentence 13
First Stage	16	13	17	19
Second Stage	7	5	5	5
Third Stage	7	5	5	5

3.2   The Suitable Timing of Interface Switch Moment

This section would analyse the suitable timing of changing the interface from novice to expert by system automatic switch. Base on Table 1, the limitation of sentence length could be known. In addition, we calculated the average of number of characters in each sentence used by subjects in every interrupt times; the result was shown in Table 2 and Table 3. Accordingly, we defined that novice interface (used in the first stage of experiment) could be changed into advanced-novice interface (used in the second stage of experiment) when novice users interrupted the sentence for 6 times, and advanced-novice interface could be changed into expert interface (used in the third stage of experiment) when advanced-novice interface users interrupted the sentence for 5 times. Especially, the interface was changed sentence by sentence rather than changed all the sentences once. In this manner, it could avoid the confusing situation that users listening the expert sentences without guidance.

Table 2. Average of interrupt moment in the first stage of experiment (number of characters)

Interrupt Times	1	2	3	4	5	6
Sentence 2	19.63	17.38	**15.56**	14.00	11.38	12.06
Sentence 3	16.44	15.44	17.00	14.38	13.31	**12.44**
Sentence 5	30.19	26.69	19.94	20.44	22.50	**14.81**
Sentence 13	24.88	21.75	20.56	17.69	20.25	**16.44**

Table 3. Average of interrupt moment in the second stage of experiment (number of characters)

Interrupt Times	1	2	3	4	5
Sentence 2	7.44	6.81	6.25	**6.63**	
Sentence 3	8.94	8.25	7.25	8.19	**6.6**
Sentence 5	7.69	6.31	5.5	6.44	**6.56**
Sentence 13	6.88	6.75	7.56	7.5	**5.56**

3.3 Impatient Degree of Speech Sentence

In these experiments, we would like to know whether the length or content of speech sentence made users irritable. Thus the subjects required to rate the degree of impatient on 15 speech sentences, including speech length and content. The rating scale was from 1 to 5, and the degree of 5 meant that the subject felt the most impatient on the sentence. According to Table 4 and Table 5, the degree of impatient on sentence length between novice and advanced-novice interface ($p>0.05$) was not significantly difference, and the same result on impatient degree of sentence content. Between advanced-novice and expert interface, there are significant difference both on the impatient degree of sentence length and content. Moreover, we could conclude that the speech sentence on Talking Car expert interface resulted in users the lowest impatient significantly.

Table 4. Paired t-test results of impatient degree of speech sentence length

	First Stage	Second Stage	Second Stage	Third Stage
Mean	2.659	2.583	2.583	1.876
P-Value	0.490		0.005*	

*$p<0.05$

Table 5. Paired t-test results of impatient degree of speech sentence content

	First Stage	Second Stage	Second Stage	Third Stage
Mean	2.546	2.563	2.563	1.771
P-Value	0.850		0.001**	

**$p<0.01$

3.4   Task Completion Time

The completion time of radio and music task was analyzed by Paired t-test. As shown in Tables 6 and 7, there were significant differences on all the tasks completion time. Moreover, the average operation time of Talking Car expert interface (third stage) was the shortest one in all interfaces due to the shortest speech sentence. It implies that expert interface has comparative convenience among these interfaces.

Table 6. Paired t-test results of task completion time on radio task

	First Stage	Second Stage	Second Stage	Third Stage
Mean(Sec)	359.84	127.78	127.78	102.75
P-Value	$< 0.001^{***}$		$< 0.001^{***}$	

Table 7. Paired t-test results of task completion time on music task

	First Stage	Second Stage	Second Stage	Third Stage
Mean(Sec)	187.13	95.22	95.22	79.44
P-Value	0.000^{***}		$< 0.001^{***}$	

$^{***}p<0.001$

3.5   Reaction Time

Subjects' reaction time is recorded by simulated software. The calculation method of reaction time is started from the "STOP!!!" message showing on the display till subject stepping the brake to stop counting. Analyzing the average reaction time with radio and music task and without task, the result showed that there was no significant difference between "talking" task and without "talking" task in the first stage, but was significant in the second stage ($p<0.001$). Furthermore, the result also showed that the reaction times of radio and music task between the second and the third stage was not significantly different.

3.6   NASA-TLX

After the simulation experiment, subjects required to answer a NASA-TLX questionnaire. As shown in Table 8, the Talking Car expert interface has the lowest mental workload. The results of Paired t-test indicated that mental workload of advanced-novice interface was significantly lower than that of novice interface ($p<0.01$), but there was no significant difference between mental workload of advanced-novice and that of expert interface. It implies that Talking Car expert interface provides a more efficient user interface to the driver so that the driver can operate the Talking Car System with less mental workload.

Table 8. Average weighted score of NASA-TLX

	NASA-TLX weighted score						
Items	Mental Demands	Physical Demands	Temporal Demands	Own Performance	Effort	Frustration	Total
First Stage	16.77	6.38	7.63	8.56	16.90	5.81	62.05
Second Stage	14.14	6.14	4.29	3.83	11.79	3.29	43.48
Third Stage	10.65	5.10	3.98	3.67	5.77	3.44	32.61

4   Conclusion

After three stage experiments, the results suggested the suitable sentence length of each interface as shown in Table 1. According to the experiment result, we could also define that novice interface sentence would be changed into advanced speech sentence when it has been interrupted for 6 times, and advanced-novice interface would be changed into expert interface sentence when it has been interrupted for 5 times. In addition, the sentence of expert interface resulted in lowest degree of impatient, and required less operation time and mental workload than that of other interfaces. Therefore, drivers not only feel more convenience but also have a safer driving condition.

Acknowledgements. This research was sponsored by the Ministry of Economic Affairs, Taiwan, R.O.C. through project No. C352SN3100 conducted by ITRI.

References

1. Ministry of Transportation and Communications in Taiwan, 89th and 90th Road Safety Traffic Rules, http://motclaw.motc.gov.tw/ Law_ShowAll.aspx?LawID=E0055087&Mode=0&PageTitle=%E6%A2%9D%E 6%96%87%E5%85%A7%E5%AE%B9 (accessed December 13, 2011)
2. Jason, B., Calitz, A., Greyling, J.: From the Evaluation of an Adaptive User Interface Model. In: SAICSIT 2010 Proceedings of the 2010 Annual Research Conference of the South African Institute of Computer Scientists and Information Technologists (2010)
3. Global Road Safety Partnership, Speed management: a road safety manual for decision-makers and practitioners, p. 6 (2008)
4. Transportation Engineering Online Lab Manual. Brake Reaction Time, http://www.webs1.uidaho.edu/niatt_labmanual/Chapters/ geometricdesign/theoryandconcepts/BrakeReactionTime.htm (data accessed December 2, 2012)

The Timeframe of Adaptation to Electric Vehicle Range

Stefan Pichelmann, Thomas Franke, and Josef F. Krems

Chemnitz University of Technology, Cognitive & Engineering Psychology, Germany
stefan.pichelmann@s2009.tu-chemnitz.de,
{thomas.franke,josef.krems}@psychologie.tu-chemnitz.de

Abstract. We explored how people learn to cope with the limited range of electric vehicles (EVs), and examined the relationship between personality traits and the amount of practice needed to achieve a maximum available range. Data from 56 participants who leased an EV in a 6-month field study were analyzed. The amount of practice needed until a participant achieved his maximum available range was assessed with four variables computed from data logger recordings: the amount of time, days, and distance the user drove the EV and the amount of days the user owned the EV. All four variables correlated strongly with each other ($r \geq .75$). The results showed that an average person needs approximately three months to complete adaptation to EV range and that speedy driving style, low need for cognition, high impulsivity, and high internal control beliefs are related to a longer adaptation timeframe.

Keywords: adaptation, electric vehicle, range, practice, need for cognition, driving style, impulsivity, control beliefs.

1 Introduction

Electric vehicles (EVs) are a promising form of sustainable transportation. However, limited range is a potential barrier for market acceptance. Recent research has focused on the interaction between the EV [1-2] and the user, with the goal of identifying approaches that could improve utilization of existing range resources. As a next step in this research, we analyze the *timeframe* in which users learn to cope with EV range and the factors that can account for variance in this timeframe. This analysis is based upon EV field study data.

2 Theoretical Background

When people use an EV, they adapt to the limited range over time [2-3]. In this paper, we define adaptation to EV range as the conscious or unconscious change in car drivers behavior that occurs after switching to an electric vehicle and influences the vehicles available range based on the definitions of adaptation in [4-5]. One facet of adaptation to EV range is the process of learning to better utilize the available battery power resources. In other words, users are expected to increase their competent range over time [1]. Adaptation can be considered complete when there is no further increase in attained available range over time (i.e., the maximum obtained range has been reached).

M. Kurosu (Ed.): Human-Computer Interaction, Part II, HCII 2013, LNCS 8005, pp. 612–620, 2013.
© Springer-Verlag Berlin Heidelberg 2013

The amount of practice (i.e., total learning time, number of trials) has always been considered fundamental to learning and skill acquisition [6]. However, learning can also be achieved by observation (i.e., being a co-driver) [7] and periods between practice trials have also been repeatedly pointed out as important for learning performance [8-9]. Thus, coping with EV range might benefit from both, (a) time engaged in the task and (b) the idle time in between practice trials.

2.1 Contributing Factors to the Amount of Practice Needed

An overview of possible factors (e.g., internal control beliefs, subjective competence, daily practice) that are related to more successful adaptation to EV range has been presented in [1]. We assume that the following variables presented in [1] also account for variance in the length of the adaptation timeframe (i.e., the amount of practice needed to attain a maximum available range): internal control beliefs, need for cognition, ambiguity tolerance, speedy driving style, impulsivity.

Need for cognition, which can be defined as a desire to understand complex systems [10], has been shown to positively influence complex task performance [11] through higher motivation [12]. Hence, a high need for cognition might be negatively correlated with the adaptation timeframe length (i.e., EV users with a high need for cognition need less practice to improve).

High *internal control beliefs* refers to a person's perception "that the event is contingent upon his own behavior or his own relatively permanent characteristics" [13, p.1] and often demonstrates higher motivation and performance [14]. Thus, it also might be negatively correlated with the amount of practice needed.

Ambiguity tolerance can be defined as a person's perception of "ambiguous situations/stimuli as desirable, challenging, and interesting" [15, p. 179] and has often been emphasized as important for learning [16]. Thus, this characteristic might be associated with a reduced amount of practice needed to adapt to EV range.

High *impulsivity* has been shown to be negatively related to learning outcomes [17]. It might be possible that people with high impulsivity need more time to show the same performance as people with low impulsivity.

Driving speed has been considered one of the most important determinants of driving task difficulty [18]. Hence, a *speedy driving style* might interfere with a systematic investigation of the underlying processes that influence the available range, as it requires more cognitive resources. Thus, persons with a speedy driving style might need more practice (i.e., a longer timeframe) to learn how to cope with the range of an EV.

2.2 Research Objective, Goals, and Hypotheses

The objective of the present study was to better understand the timeframe of adaptation to EV range. First, we aimed to assess the amount of practice required to complete adaptation. Second, our goal was to test the expected relationships between contributing factors and the amount of practice needed for a complete adaptation to EV range. We expected the required amount of practice to be negatively correlated with (1) high internal control beliefs, (2) high need for cognition, (3) high ambiguity tolerance and positively correlated with (4) high impulsivity, and (5) a speedy driving style.

3   Method

3.1   Field Study Setup

The present research was part of an EV field trial in Berlin, Germany. The trial was set up by BMW Group and Vattenfall Europe and funded by the German Federal Ministry for the Environment, Nature Conservation and Nuclear Safety. The trial consisted of two 6-month user studies (S1, S2) with 40 private users each. It was part of an international EV field trial [19]. The EV had a maximum range of around 250 km under ideal conditions and around 170 km under daily conditions. Subjective data were collected by interviews and questionnaires. Objective data were recorded by the BMW Group with car-based data loggers which recorded variables such as speed, trip length, range, and state of charge. Further methodological details can be found in [20-22].

3.2   Participants

Potential participants applied to lease an electric vehicle for a 6-month period via a public online application form. From this pool of potential early adopters of EVs, participants were selected who met several inclusion criteria (e.g., possibility to install charging infrastructure) and increased heterogeneity of basic sociodemographic and mobility-related variables. Participants were only included in the analyses if objective data could be safely allocated to subjective data, had sufficient logger data, and had completed the necessary questionnaires. The final sample consisted of 56 participants with a mean age of 48.23 years ($SD = 9.72$), including 9 women.

3.3   Criterion for the End of the Adaptation Timeframe

We operationalized completion of adaptation to range as the time at which users achieved their maximum available range. This score was calculated based on pre-processed logger data provided by the BMW group. The available range was assessed as the displayed remaining range for every data point of each participant. Each data point represented a driven distance of one kilometer. Values that referred to situations with the battery not fully charged were extrapolated to full charge range. As we expected a high measuring error for remaining range for low states of charge, all data points were excluded with a state of charge $\leq 5\%$. Because of the influence of temperature on range [23], data points with temperatures outside the interval of 0 to 30 °C were excluded. Finally, each estimated available range was divided by the mean available range for its temperature and multiplied by the mean estimated available range for 15°C (the middle of our temperature range) to further minimize the influence of temperature. Hence, for each user the data point with the maximum temperature-adjusted estimated available range was considered the end point of his/her adaptation.

3.4   Measures of the Amount of Practice Needed

Four variables were computed to measure the amount of practice the user needed to complete the adaptation to EV range: (1) the total distance driven by the participant until the criterion (see 3.3) was met, (2) the total time driven by the participant until the criterion was met, (3) the number of days the user owned the EV, and (4) the number of days on which the participant used the EV. While the first two variables are very precise measures that can differ because of standing times and speed profiles (e.g., traffic lights, jams), the last two variables also account for the idle time between practice (see 2.2). A factor analysis was conducted to combine all four variables into a general factor measuring the amount of practice needed to adapt to EV range, referred to as *practice needed* throughout the remainder of this paper. The principal component analysis identified a single factor solution according to the Kaiser-criterion (first factor eigenvalue = 3.57, second = 0.29, factor loadings for every variable > .85). The z-standardized four variables yielded a Cronbach's alpha of .96.

3.5   Measures of Contributing Factors

Internal control beliefs, ambiguity tolerance, and speedy driving style were assessed in S1 and S2; whereas, need for cognition and impulsivity were only assessed in S2. We used the 8-item *Internal Control Beliefs in Dealing with Technology Scale* [24] (n = 54), the 8-item *Ambiguity Tolerance Scale* [25] (n = 55), the speed scale of the *Driving Style Questionnaire* [26] (n = 55), and the *Need for Cognition Scale* [27] with 16 items (n = 30). For impulsivity, we used a single-item measurement from the German socio-economic panel [28] (n = 32). Cronbach's alpha was > .74 for all multi-item measures.

4   Results

4.1   Timeframe of Adaptation

Data obtained from each measure of the amount of practice needed and the criterion for the end of the adaptation timeframe were screened for outliers according to [29]. The Kolmogorov-Smirnov test was conducted to investigate if the variables deviated significantly from a normal distribution. All variables were normally distributed and only one outlier for the end of the adaptation timeframe criterion was detected. Nevertheless, this value was retained in analyses, as it was apparently not due to an error in data recording and also subjective data from the user supported a very high range value.

The mean of the maximum estimated available range was 192.63 km (SD = 26.82). All four variables measuring the timeframe of adaptation that were computed from the data logger recordings were strongly correlated ($r \geq .75$) with each other. The average participant needed 2397.80 driven kilometers (SD = 1708.74), 72.88 driven hours (SD = 47.81), 97.39 days of ownership (SD = 45.66 days), and 62.32 days to drive the car (SD = 35.25 days) before reaching the maximum estimated available range. Figure 1 shows the box plots for all four measures of the amount of practice needed.

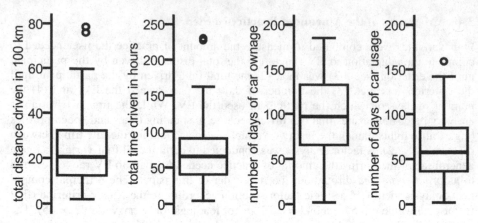

Fig. 1. Box plots of participants' amount of kilometers driven, amount of days driven, number of days of car ownership, and the number of days on which they drove the car until the end of their adaptation timeframe to EV range.

4.2 Contributing Factors to the Amount of Practice Needed

To screen for distortion of correlations between the practice needed and contributing factors caused by highly influential values, scatter plots were inspected. They did not show any disproportionately influential values. One-tailed correlation tests were conducted, because we had directional hypotheses. Correlations were interpreted in accordance with Cohen [30] as weak ($|r| = .10$), moderate ($|r| = 0.3$), and strong ($|r| = 0.5$).

In order to interpret our results regarding factors contributing to the timeframe of adaptation to EV range, we only used the magnitude of the correlation coefficients. The significance level was not used to determine whether the findings supported our hypotheses, because of the small sample size.

Hypothesis 1, which predicted a negative correlation between high internal control beliefs and the amount of practice needed, was not supported by our results. Instead, a weak positive correlation ($r = .27, p = .025, n = 54$) was observed, indicating that high internal control beliefs are related to a higher amount of practice needed. Future research should examine this result further.

Hypothesis 2, which predicted a negative correlation between high need for cognition and the amount of practice needed, was supported by our results, as we found a weak negative correlation ($r = -.26, p = .080, n = 30$).

Hypothesis 3, which predicted a negative correlation between high ambiguity tolerance and amount of practice needed, was not supported by our results, as the correlation coefficient was close to zero ($r = .03, p = .409, n = 55$). As the concept of ambiguity tolerance in relation to learning was mostly researched in the context of academic learning, it might be possible that it is less relevant for adaptation to EV range.

Hypothesis 4, which predicted a positive correlation between impulsivity and amount of practice needed, was supported by our results, as we found a weak positive correlation ($r = .25, p = .082, n = 32$).

Hypothesis 5, which predicted a positive correlation between speedy driving style and amount of practice needed, was supported by our results, as the correlation was weak and positive ($r = .22$, $p = .054$, $n = 55$).

5   Discussion

The specific aims of the present study were to (1) quantify the amount of practice needed (i.e., the timeframe) until adaptation to EV range can be assumed to be completed, and (2) to identify factors contributing to the amount of practice needed. We were able to identify a timeframe of roughly 3 months of car ownership corresponding to 2400 driven kilometers, 73 driven hours and 63 days on which the car was driven. Furthermore, we found some indication for a relationship of practice needed with internal control beliefs, need for cognition, impulsivity, and speedy driving style.

5.1   Critical Examination of the Methodology

Each study lasted for six months. Hence, it cannot be determined whether a higher available range might be achieved after six months (e.g., after a year of driving). Therefore, the real timeframe of adaptation (i.e., practice needed) might be much longer. Although this possibility cannot be ruled out, there is some evidence against it. The average participant achieved his or her estimated maximum available range after 97.39 days of car ownership. If the adaptation timeframe were longer than six months, the average should be much closer to 180 days.

The criterion for the end of the adaptation timeframe (maximum estimated available range) varied on an individual basis. Hence, the findings presented might have been different if a fixed reference value (e.g., an available range of 180 km) was used for all participants as a criterion. This was not possible to test, however, as participants' achieved available ranges varied considerably. A high value might not have been achieved by some participants and a low value might have resulted in an underestimation of the length of the adaptation timeframe for persons achieving a much higher available range.

As noted previously, we consider our estimates for the timeframe of adaptation to EV range to be rather conservative, as our criterion is the absolute maximum available range. Another study, which investigated adaptation to EV range based on changes in charging behavior, identified a critical timeframe of two weeks for adaptation [19]. There are two possible explanations for this difference. First, the researched facets of adaptation to EV range differ (attained available range vs. charging behavior) across the two studies. Second, our study tried to identify the absolute end of the adaptation period; whereas, the other study analyzed when major changes in the adaptation process where concluded. Hence, different aspects of adaptation to EV range might require different timeframes for completion.

5.2   Implications for Theory, Practice and Future Research

The present study showed that field research on everyday interaction with EV range should be conducted over several months, in order to validly assess the user experience and behavior of adapted EV drivers. The absolute minimum seems to be three months, corresponding to the average necessary number of days of car ownership, but more time is recommended. Under conditions in which the EV is driven over greater daily distances than the present study (on average around 37 km), shorter study periods may be possible.

The findings concerning factors contributing to the amount of practice needed suggest a relationship between practice needed and need for cognition. Hence, in order to help people adapt as quickly as possible to their EV, they should be encouraged to concern themselves with the influences on their available range as much as possible. Furthermore, for EV novices, a steady, non-impulsive driving style appears to promote faster achievement of the maximum available range. As internal control beliefs seem to be linked to high available ranges, but high amounts of practice as well, an implication for practice cannot be determined now.

All of our findings require further research, especially with regard to the causal nature of the relationships between contributing factors and necessary practice. Hence, we highly recommend further cross-lagged analyses, as experimental investigation is difficult in the field of personality traits. Also, the interaction between necessary practice, contributing factors, and achieved available range should be explored in more detail.

In the present study, we have focused on a specific facet of adaptation to EV range. Charging behavior, as examined by [19], also appears to be a promising approach to understanding adaptation to EV range. In fact, we believe there are several facets of adaptation to EV range which are worth further investigation: increase of trip length over time, personal range buffer changes over time, amount of trips until recharging, EV usage in comparison with other possibilities of transportation (e.g., other cars of the household, public transportation), but also indicators like experience of stress, or range anxiety. Therefore, future research should aim to develop a more comprehensive picture of adaptation to EV range.

Acknowledgments. This research was funded by the German Federal Ministry for the Environment, Nature Conservation and Nuclear Safety. We are grateful for the support of our consortium partners, BMW Group (G. Schmidt, Dr. Julian Weber, Dr. A. Keinath and Dr. R. Vilimek) and Vattenfall Europe AG (A. Weber and F. Schuth) who made our research possible. We gratefully thank Katja Gabler, Florian Fritzsche, and their colleagues at BMW Group for performing data pre-processing of the logger data.

References

1. Franke, T., Krems, J.F.: Interacting with limited mobility resources: Psychological range levels in electric vehicle use. Transportation Research Part A: Policy and Practic 48, 109–122 (2013)
2. Franke, T., Neumann, I., Bühler, F., Cocron, P., Krems, J.F.: Experiencing Range in an Electric Vehicle: Understanding Psychological Barriers. Applied Psychology: An International Review 61, 368–391 (2012)

3. Franke, T., Cocron, P., Bühler, F., Neumann, I., Krems, J.F.: Adapting to the range of an electric vehicle – the relation of experience to subjectively available mobility resources. In: Valero Mora, P., Pace, J.F., Mendoza, L. (eds.) Proceedings of the European Conference on Human Centred Design for Intelligent Transport Systems, pp. 95–103. Humanist Publications, Lyon (2012)
4. Lints, T.: The essentials of defining adaptation. In: 4th Annual IEEE Systems Conference, pp. 113–116. IEEE Press, New York (2010)
5. OECD ScientificExpert Group: Behavioural adaptations to changes in the road transport system. OECD, Paris (1990)
6. Newell, A., Rosenbloom, P.: Mechanisms of skill acquisitionand the law of practice. In: Anderson, J.R. (ed.) Learning and Cognition, pp. 1–55. Lawrence Erlbaum, Hillsdale (1981)
7. Bandura, A.: Self-efficacy: Toward a unifying theory of behavioral change. Psychological Review 84(2), 191–215 (1977)
8. Eysenck, H.J.: A three-factor theory of reminiscence. British Journal of Psychology 56(2-3), 163–182 (1965)
9. Stickgold, R., Walker, M.P.: Memory consolidation and reconsolidation: what is the role of sleep? Trends in Neurosciences 28(8), 408–415 (2005)
10. Cacioppo, J.T., Petty, R.E.: The Need for cognition. Journal of Personality and Social Psychology 42(1), 116–131 (1982)
11. Coutinho, S., Wiemer-Hastings, K., Skowronski, J.J., Britt, M.A.: Metacognition, need for cognition and use of explanations during ongoing learning and problem solving. Learning and Individual Differences 15(4), 321–337 (2005)
12. Steinhart, Y., Wyver Jr., R.S.: Motivational correlates of need for cognition. European Journal of Social Psychology 39(4), 608–621 (2009)
13. Rotter, J.B.: Generalized expectancies for internal versus external control of reinforcement. Psychological Monographs: General And Applied 80(1), 1–28 (1966)
14. Broedling, L.A.: Relationship of internal-external control to work motivation and performance in an expectancy model. Journal of Applied Psycholog 60(1), 65–70 (1975)
15. Furnham, A., Ribchester, T.: Tolerance of ambiguity: A review of the concept, its measurement and applications. Current Psychology 14(3), 179–199 (1995)
16. Chapelle, C., Roberts, C.: Ambiguity tolerance and field independence as predictors of proficiency in English as a second language. Language Learning 36(1), 27–45 (1986)
17. Gregory, D.A.: Impulsivity control and self-regulated learning. Pro Quest, Cambridge (2007)
18. Fuller, R.: The task-capability interface model of the driving process. Recherche Transports Sécurité 66, 45–57 (2000)
19. Vilimek, R., Keinath, A., Schwalm, M.: The MINI E field study – similarities and differences in international everyday driving. In: Stanton, N.A. (ed.) Advances in Human Aspects of Road and Rail Transportation, pp. 363–372. CRC Press, Southampton (2012)
20. Franke, T., Bühler, F., Cocron, P., Neumann, I., Krems, J.F.: Enhancing sustainability of electric vehicles: A field study approach to understanding user acceptance and behavior. In: Sullman, M., Dorn, L. (eds.) Advances in Traffic Psychology, pp. 295–306. Ashgate, Farnham (2012)
21. Cocron, P., Bühler, F., Neumann, I., Franke, T., Krems, J.F., Schwalm, M., Keinath, A.: Methods of evaluating electric vehicles from a user's perspective- the MINI E field trial in Berlin. IET Intelligent Transport System 5(2), 127–133 (2012)

22. Krems, J.F., Weinmann, O., Weber, J., Westermann, D., Albayrak, S. (eds.): Elektromobilität in Metropolregionen: Die Feldstudie MINI E Berlin powered by Vattenfall. Fortschritt-Berichte VDI/ Reihe 12 Nr. 766. VDI Verlag, Düsseldorf (2013)
23. Larminie, J., Lowry, J.: Electric vehicle technology explained. Wiley & Sons, New York (2012)
24. Beier, G.: Kontrollüberzeugungen im Umgang mit Technik. Report Psychologie 9, 684–693 (1999)
25. Dalbert, C.: Die Ungewissheitstoleranzskala: Skaleneigenschaften und Validierungsbefunde. Hallesche Berichte zur Pädagogischen Psychologie 1. Martin-Luther-Universität, Halle-Wittenberg,
   http://psydok.sulb.uni-saarland.de/volltexte/2004/393/pdf/bericht01.pdf
26. French, D.J., West, R.J., Elander, J., Wilding, J.M.: Decision-making style, driving style, and self-reported involvement in road traffic accidents. Ergonomics 36(6), 627–644 (1993)
27. Bless, H., Wänke, M., Bohner, G., Fellhauer, R.F., Schwarz, N.: Need for Cognition: Eine Skala zur Erfassung von Engagement und Freude bei Denkaufgaben. Zeitschrift für Sozialpsychologie 25, 147–154 (1994)
28. Siedler, T., Schupp, J., Spiess, C.K., Wagner, G.G.: RatSWD working paper no. 48. The German Socio-Economic Panel as reference data set (2008)
   http://ssrn.com/abstract=1445341
29. Grubbs, F.E.: Sample criteria for testing outlying observations. Annals of Mathematical Statistic 21, 27–58 (1950)
30. Cohen, J.: Statistical power analysis for the behavioral sciences. Routledge, London (1988)

Exploring Electric Driving Pleasure –
The BMW EV Pilot Projects

Jens Ramsbrock[1], Roman Vilimek[2], and Julian Weber[1]

[1] BMW Group, Innovation Projects E-Mobility, Munich, Germany
[2] BMW Group, Concept Quality, Munich, Germany
{jens.ramsbrock,roman.vilimek,julian.weber}@bmw.de

Abstract. An electric vehicle (EV) is more than just a car with an electric engine. It implies a major shift in everyday experience. Charging the vehicle at home, thinking about where this energy comes from, dealing with limited range or driving a silent vehicle without engine noise are only some aspects of a completely new ecosystem for an electric vehicle owner. Of course, EVs will only succeed in the mass market if they meet customers' expectations. With the decision to step into this unknown terrain, the BMW Group gathered data in field trials with pilot customers of the MINI E and BMW ActiveE. The field trials discovered that everyday driving does not differ significantly from conventional vehicles in the same segment. About 90% of intended trips can be realized, showing the gap that needs to be closed is manageable. In order to close it, BMW will offer innovative mobility services and charging solutions.

Keywords: Electric Vehicle, MINI E, BMW ActiveE, field trial, user study.

1 The Road towards Series-Produced Electric Vehicles

Global developments like climate change, decreasing availability of natural resources and increasing urbanization call for new solutions in many facets of everyday life. This demand implies also the need for changes in mobility patterns. Within the BMW Group, the sub-brand BMW i was created to respond to this situation. The goal is to design purpose-built electric vehicles and mobility services to support sustainable individual mobility. For the BMW i3, BMW Group's first series-produced EV, the life cycle global warming potential (CO_{2e}) is at least a third lower than for a state-of-the-art highly efficient combustion-engine vehicle in the same segment[1]. If the vehicle is charged with renewable energy, this can be increased up to well over 50 per cent. Recycled materials in the vehicle interior and exterior play a major role, as well as weight savings by extensively using innovative materials like CFRP (carbon fibre-reinforced plastic).

The focus on sustainability is not restricted to the operation of the vehicle itself but widened over the complete value chain. The BMW i3 will lead to a massive increase

---

[1] Estimated for an i3 concept car under the assumption of the European electricity mix (EU25).

M. Kurosu (Ed.): Human-Computer Interaction, Part II, HCII 2013, LNCS 8005, pp. 621–630, 2013.
© Springer-Verlag Berlin Heidelberg 2013

in the already high standards of BMW's sustainable production system. Recycling of materials used during the production process will be carried out wherever possible. These high standards are also laid upon the supply chain.

As the mobility needs of people will change when switching to electric vehicles with limited driving range, mobility services will also be offered as a part of the BMW i solution portfolio. On-demand vehicle solutions like DriveNow, a joint venture between the BMW Group and Sixt AG, and innovative functions within the vehicle itself and/or as Apps on smartphones target the requirements of urban personal mobility.

These offers lay a solid foundation to establish electric vehicles as a means of sustainable individual mobility. Of course customers will only accept them if they meet their needs and expectations. BMW launched a project in 2007 to perform thinking outside of the box and explore sustainable mobility solutions, called the *project i*. Analyzing EV customers with a conventional market research approach was not possible in the early phases, which was *project i*'s main intention to make this feasible. Hardly any EV customers were on the road and the interdependencies between the infrastructure and the car itself have not even been touched by large-scale research.

Therefore field trials with conversion electric vehicles were set up in cooperation with expert partners from universities and research institutions for scientific monitoring and with partners from the infrastructure sector as well as the energy sector. The trials were conducted in several countries in close collaboration and exchange with the local public authorities in order to assess long-term developments in policy towards e-mobility. These field trials are unparalleled worldwide in their scope. Starting with the first step in 2009 in the United States and in Germany, private and corporate pilot customers rented EVs from a fleet of over 600 MINI E cars. The MINI E is a conversion of the MINI Cooper developed to assess the general feasibility and acceptance of an EV as a megacity vehicle. Between 2009 and 2012, data from more than 16 million kilometers (10 million miles) driven by customers in the United States, Germany, the United Kingdom, France, Japan and China were gathered. More than 15,000 people applied to rent a MINI E, 430 private households took part in extensive mostly face-to-face interviews and 14 fleet user companies actively participated in the study. At the end of 2011 the second step of the learning projects for BMW i began. A fleet of over 1,000 BMW ActiveE vehicles, conversions of the BMW 1 Series Coupe, set for launch in several countries. This part of the field trials focuses more directly on technological innovations for EVs. For instance, the study will deliver customer feedback on using remote functions via smartphone apps, pioneering driver assistance systems and switching between comfort-oriented and efficiency-oriented driving with the so-called ECO PRO mode. In contrast to the MINI E field trial that analyzed fundamental aspects of everyday life with electric vehicles, the BMW ActiveE studies have their goals analog to usability tests: Identify specific optimization potential of certain (pre-production) functions. In both field trials an accompanying social media analysis was carried out. While the comments of pilot customers in blogs, newsgroups or social networks were used mainly to inform our research partners about issues from a direct customer's perspective in order to guide the design of quantitative methods, regular social media reports were additionally used during the BMW ActiveE field trials to assess the reaction of customers on newly introduced features. The transfer from sometimes even singular reactions in social media to a decision process in the development of vehicles is detailed in [1].

In the following, firstly the key results of the MINI E field trials are summarized first in a very condensed form. Secondly, already available data from the ActiveE study in Germany and the US are discussed. As the data reported here stems from field trials which are stretched massively over time (2009-2013) and which witnessed considerable changes during this time, the results should be regarded as tendencies. Only descriptive statistics are provided. If not otherwise state, numerical values (% agreement) refer to answers on a Likert scale from 1 (do not agree at all) to 6 (fully agree) and are dichotomized to top three ("agree) and bottom three ("disagree") judgments.

2   The MINI E Study

The MINI E is a two-seat development of the MINI hatch featuring a 204 hp (150 kW) electric motor that develops a torque of 220 Nm. The air-cooled 35 kWh Litihium-Ion battery consumes most of the luggage department as well as the space of the back seats. The range in real terms is up to 130-160 km (80-100 miles). Charging with 32 ampere takes about 4 hours or 10 hours with 12 ampere respectively.

In terms of user interface, the dashboard was adapted rather minimally to display EV specific functions as shown in Figure 1. The battery level indicator is mounted behind the steering wheel replacing the traditional rev counter. It shows in percentage figures how much charge is still available in the battery. The small display below the indicator allows to switch between a small set of additional items like battery temperature, consumption or charging voltage. The central gauge in the middle of the dashboard displays the current velocity. It also includes an LED display, the converted fuel gauge, indicating power consumption or regeneration. The display and control options of the MINI E are sufficient for the basic interaction with EV functions. However, the customers strongly demanded more detailed information on consumption and EV specifics as well as more options to control advanced EV functions like being able to set charging times or to remotely monitor the charging progress. These requests were fed into the development process and resulting solutions in the BMW ActiveE are again subject to customer test in field trials.

The MINI E field trial served to address key questions on everyday usage patterns, expectations, reactions to special and typical electric vehicle characteristics and additional aspects like the perception of the importance of ecological added value of EV driving to customers. Several universities and research institutions were involved in the field trial. Research partners were the Chemnitz University of Technology (Germany), the University of California at Davis (USA), Oxford Brookes University (UK), the Institute of Science and Technology for Transport, Development and Networks (IFSTTAR, France), the Waseda University and the marketing research company IID (Japan) and the Chinese Automotive Technology and Research Center as well as the market research company INS (China). The study was designed to maximize the participation on customer's everyday life with the EV. Travel and charging diaries were administered repetitively as well as a several interviews during the usage period [2-3].

Fig. 1. MINI E dashboard (Fotocredit: BMW Group): Battery level indicator (left) and central gauge (right)

Potential customers interested in driving the MINI E applied via an online application tool. Besides providing socio-demographic information and giving feedback on their motives and interests in electric driving, applicants needed to fulfill different selection criteria (e.g., be willing to take part in interviews, drive the vehicle on a regular basis, be willing to pay a monthly leasing fee). Background information on the large number of applicants, about 500-3500 per country for each 6-12 months usage period, allowed to form a study sample that was representative for the early adopter generation of EV customers. Details on rationale and procedure are described in [3].

The most important finding from the MINI E field trial was that electric vehicles are suitable for everyday life for a large customer segment. Onboard data logger information was read out from the MINI E cars and compared to conventional vehicles within the same segment (BMW 116i and MINI Cooper). Control group customers with combustion engine vehicles used their cars on average for 43.4 km (27.0 miles, MINI Cooper) and 42.0 km (26.1 miles, BMW 116i) per day. The average daily distances for MINI E vehicles range from 38.6 km (24.0 miles) in Germany over 44.2 km (27.5 miles) in France to 47.8 km (29.7 miles) in the UK to 49.0 km (30.4 miles) in the US and in China.

Customers were able to satisfy about 80% of their daily mobility needs with the MINI E. Based on the MINI E drivers' subjective estimation and travel diary data, they would have been able to use the vehicle for approximately 90% of the intended trips if the MINI E had more than two seats and standard storage space. Due to the limitations of the conversion vehicle concept, the MINI E had an extremely small luggage compartment. However, it should be noted that the range of the MINI E was not always available. As air cooling was the only thermal management of the batteries, the MINI E was not able to deliver the full range during cold temperatures in winter. This was regarded as major drawback by customers.

The MINI E study also showed that customers get used to charging procedure and range quickly. After less than one month of usage, customers charge only once every two or three days. If customers used a wallbox that allows to charge in less than 4 hours, average charging events per week stabilized at 1.9 (Germany) to 2.9 (UK). Only if charging takes longer (about 9-10 hours with a standard wall socket), customers needed to charge almost daily as data from the France field trial shows.

Regenerative braking is an advanced function for electric vehicles. It refers to using the electric motor as a generator when decelerating by lifting the foot from the accelerator pedal. The deceleration is quite strong with -2.25 m/s² in the MINI E and allows driving the car in most situations with one pedal only after some driving practice is gained. From an efficiency point of view, regenerative braking can be a powerful tool to save energy. To assess customer acceptance, a long-term evaluation was implemented. The customer feedback was overwhelming. After at least three months of usage, between 92% (China, Japan) and almost 100% (Germany, UK, US, France) customers unanimously said that they would not want to miss this feature in an EV.

In short, the international MINI E trials demonstrated that an electric vehicle with slightly larger and more stable range as well as more space for passengers and cargo will meet the mobility needs for urban use to a very large extent. A more comprehensive overview over the MINI results is provided in [4].

3   The BMW ActiveE Study

Like the MINI E, the BMW ActiveE is a conversion vehicle. It integrates all electric drive components in the vehicle body of a 1 Series Coupe while keeping the comfort of four full-fledged seats and a 200-litre luggage compartment. The electric motor develops a torque of 250 Nm with a 170 hp (125 kW) engine. The range in real terms is up to 160 km (100 miles), depending on the driving style. As the battery is liquid cooled and able to be tempered, fluctuations due to high or low temperatures are expected to be reduced significantly. Charging times are comparable to the MINI E. Battery and drive train of the BMW ActiveE are pre-series versions of the BMW i3. In addition to standard laboratory and test track development procedures, these components are tested during the field trials in everyday customer environments. The customers did not participate as professional test drivers in this setting. When the vehicle is handed over to them, all safety and standard tests are fulfilled. By giving the car additionally to pilot customers it will be possible to make sure that scenarios and usage circumstances currently not known to test engineers will also be covered.

A test fleet of over 1,000 BMW ActiveE vehicles was sent out to provide this vital knowledge. Field trials with user research are conducted in Germany, the United States and China starting with the first pilot project involving 15 private and 15 fleet customers in Berlin in December 2011. Additional vehicles are used in Germany as part of governmentally funded research programs. Approximately 190 BMW ActiveE vehicles contribute to projects in Germany. The majority of the BMW ActiveE fleet is on the road in the United States since January 2012. About 700 vehicles are part of a project that has been created to gather not only customer experience but also market experience. Sales and handling processes are evaluated, options for add on services assessed and requirements on service infrastructure for large EV fleets examined. In early 2013 user research projects in China begin, involving roughly 100 BMW ActiveE cars. Additional vehicles are in the hands of private and corporate customers in France, the United Kingdom, the Netherlands, Italy, Switzerland, South Korea and Japan.

As the user research focus is clearly directed to a usability / user experience design approach, the HMI components of the BMW ActiveE play a much more central role than in the MINI E. Figure 2 gives an impression of the interior design. The instrument cluster and the iDrive control system and display functions were adapted for the first time in a BMW vehicle for electric vehicle specifics. The instrument on the right side of the cluster shows the amount of energy regenerated while slowing down the vehicle or the energy being consumed from the battery while accelerating. It also informs the driver that the vehicle is ready to drive as there is no engine noise normally connected to a driving-ready electric engine. The battery charging level and onboard computer information such as the remaining range are also displayed.

Fig. 2. BMW ActiveE interior (Fotocredit: BMW Group): Location of the ECO PRO button (left), instrument cluster and central display with vehicle energy information. Smartphone display of vehicle energy functions (right)

Further EV related functions are available via the Central Information Display. Schematic representations of the vehicle energy flows are designed to make electric mobility better perceptible and comprehensible. Specific sections inform about energy consumption of in-vehicle systems, range details and charging details like percentage available and time required for a full charge. Special charging functions are also implemented. The charge control function allows to start and finish the charging process and to program the charge timer. Preconditioning is a new function first introduced in the BMW ActiveE. It offers the possibility to cool or heat both the batteries and the vehicle interior. By bringing these components to the ideal operating temperature the highest performance of the energy storage is ensured and energy consumption during the trip is drastically reduced as the interior is already adjusted to a pleasant temperature without consuming energy from the battery. The ECO PRO mode is a new driving mode that allows to increase range by activating a switch in the center console. Efficient driving is then optimized by an adapted accelerator pedal characteristic delivering less power than in normal driving mode at identical pedal travels. Air conditioning, heating and ventilation systems are also reduced in energy consumption. In

ECO PRO mode, the driver is additionally provided with tips on how to reduce energy consumption for best possible efficient driving.

In addition to onboard systems, several functions are available via BMW ConnectedDrive using direct internet connection, e.g. a charging station finder. With the "My BMW Remote" app, users are enabled to access functions remotely via smartphone. Besides standard functions like locating or locking the car, new remote functions for battery charge control and vehicle preconditioning as described above have been integrated.

Like in the MINI E, regenerative braking is initiated by taking the foot off the accelerator pedal. The strength of regenerative braking, -1.8 m/s², was somewhat reduced compared to the MINI E. Using a distinctive intermediate position of the accelerator pedal, the driver is able to set the BMW ActiveE in a "glide" mode. The vehicle then acts like when in neutral / no gear mode and coasts freely with its gained momentum.

In the following, results from the BMW ActiveE field trials in Germany and the United States are described. Due to the ongoing development process of the series vehicle and due to the page restriction here, only a small subset can be presented.

3.1   BMW ActiveE Field Trial Germany

From December 2011 to March 2012 the first BMW ActiveE user study involving 15 private customers was undertaken. On average the customers' age was 46 (14 male, 1 female), ten of these customers were former MINI E drivers.

The study was planned and carried out in cooperation with the Institute of Cognitive and Engineering Psychology at the Chemnitz University of Technology and the market research agency Spiegel Institut Mannheim. It was designed to maximally share the customers' user experience with a three-phased research procedure. Customers were first contacted – besides initial interviews during application – after roughly 4 weeks in an open telephone interview stating their impressions in general as well as likes and dislikes. The drivers' experiences were directly fed into the planning of focus group sessions which were held after 8 weeks. Each customer participated in one of two focus groups mainly concentrating in one group on EV winter usage and preconditioning or in the other group on general system usability (esp. display and interaction concept) and efficient EV driving (including assistance functions). Besides this qualitative input, users gave additional feedback by taking part in an online survey at the end of the trial. The online survey incorporated questions from relevant development and strategy departments as well as those aspects that customers brought up during the focus groups which needed further clarification.

One of the most intriguing findings was that the ECO PRO driving mode was accepted very differently. Usage varied from 5%-95% share on total distance driven with the vehicle. Customers stated in the focus groups that some of them used it rather permanently while others only wanted a kind of take-me-home "emergency" mode in case of low battery capacity or large distances. Especially in the later case the drivers expect a more drastic effect on driving dynamics and comfort functions. Because of the large variability in usage patterns it was decided to seek support for this finding with the larger sample of US customers.

The BMW ActiveE Berlin field trial took place completely during winter. Especially those customers with MINI E experience rated it very positively that even despite freezing temperatures electric driving was still possible. Although it took some time to get accustomed to using the preconditioning feature, it was welcomed after experiencing that it leads to range increase. However, several customers criticized that auxiliary systems like heating still reduced range considerably.

The option to monitor and control the charging process remotely was regarded to be an essential function for premium EV user experience. This holds especially for the preconditioning feature. Customers clearly showed a preference to use their smartphone to set the relevant parameters compared to carrying out the input operations in the vehicle.

When asking the ten former MINI E customers for a direct comparison, the BMW ActiveE was uniformly rated to be the more mature car which has a much higher potential to be used as the only car in the household. Several comparison dimensions are depicted in Figure 3. Although technologically less advanced it is interesting to see that the MINI E still was regarded as a potential candidate for the next vehicle purchase by three customers if the car was available on the market.

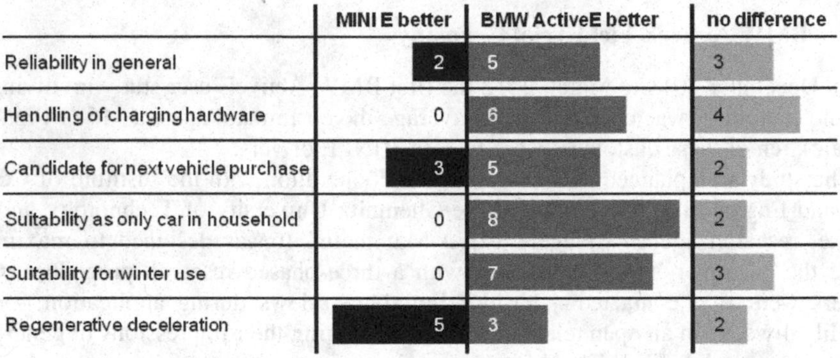

	MINI E better	BMW ActiveE better	no difference
Reliability in general	2	5	3
Handling of charging hardware	0	6	4
Candidate for next vehicle purchase	3	5	2
Suitability as only car in household	0	8	2
Suitability for winter use	0	7	3
Regenerative deceleration	5	3	2

Fig. 3. Direct comparison between the MINI E and the BMW ActiveE by 10 customers of the Berlin field trial with at least three months of usage experience with both vehicles

Regenerative braking was again a feature very much liked by the BMW ActiveE customers. As the MINI E field trials already revealed that individual preferences exist in the preferred level of the magnitude of deceleration when stepping off the accelerator pedal it is not surprising to see that several customers liked the MINI E deceleration characteristic better. Very important for future developments was that customers were able to use both, coasting and regenerative braking – depending on different use cases in deceleration and driving speed – as means of efficient driving.

3.2   BMW ActiveE Field Trial USA

The online survey from the Berlin field trial was extended with questions that either stemmed from development, sales or strategy departments or that were initiated by feedback in social media. Since the survey was still online during the creation of this document, preliminary findings based on N=79 customers are presented that shed more light on the results presented above.

The results on the strength of regenerative braking are put on a broader basis. Did the comparison to the MINI E mean that regenerative deceleration definitely needs to be stronger? The majority of customers in the US rate the design of the BMW ActiveE's regenerative braking quite positively: While the majority was satisfied or even very satisfied (27% and 67%, respectively), only 5% were not satisfied (with 1% having no opinion).

Usage patterns of the ECO PRO mode are verified with a larger sample. As shown in Figure 4 the results of the focus group discussion are replicated. Again, a significant group of customers uses the ECO PRO mode as default while driving. On the other end, a large group of customers never uses the ECO PRO mode. Qualitative comments in the survey again point out, that a distinction between a "standard" energy saving mode and an "emergency use only" energy saving mode would make sense.

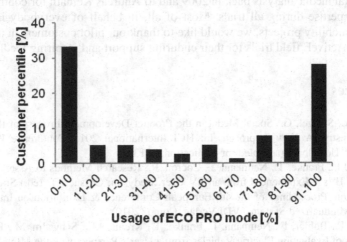

Fig. 4. Customers using ECO PRO mode as percentage of daily driving

Preconditioning was regarded to be a vital feature for future EVs. 82% of the drivers used this feature. The smartphone app did not work in all cases during the field trial which lead to customer complaints, providing further evidence for the importance of this option. The vast majority (84%) required the availability via smartphone for the series vehicle.

4   Conclusions and Future Developments

The field trials provided ample evidence that EVs are suitable for everyday use. Based on customer feedback important functions were introduced or refined for the BMW i3. For instance, one-pedal driving with regenerative braking was identified as a key characteristic for positive user experience in e-mobility. The BMW i3 will feature different modes for energy saving, ECO PRO and the additional ECO PRO + mode which further reduces energy consumption to add crucial miles to the driving range if necessary in unforeseen circumstances.

The field trials also demonstrated the necessity for functions that allow to better exploit the range available. The series vehicles will therefore come with advanced navigation functions that assist the driver by taking energy consumption based on driving characteristics into account as well as integrating geographical characteristics of route alternatives. Additional intermodal route planning options and so-called "last mile navigation" that continues to navigate the driver after already having parked the vehicle by sending instructions to the smartphone will make it easier to reach the final destination while charging the vehicle in a suitable location. Finally, in order to close any remaining mobility gap, BMW i will continue to develop fast charging technologies and mobility services targeting those use cases.

Acknowledgments. The authors would like to acknowledge the project i team at BMW for making the studies possible, especially Peter Krams with the project team involved in the Berlin field trial as well as Peter Dempster and Andreas Klein for their most valuable input in the US online survey. Thanks also to Juliane Schäfer for introducing social media analysis back in 2009 and to Andreas Keinath for contributing his research expertise during all trials. Most of all, in behalf of everybody involved in BMW's e-mobility projects, we would like to thank our pilot customers in the MINI E and BMW ActiveE field trials for their enduring support and inspiring feedback.

References

1. Klein, A., Spiegel, G.: Social Media in the Product Development Process of the Automotive Industry: A New Approach. In: HCI International 2013 Conference Proceedings. Springer, Heidelberg (accepted for publication, 2013)
2. Krems, J.F., Franke, T., Neumann, I., Cocron, P.: Research Methods to Assess the Acceptance of EVs – Experiences from an EV User Study. In: Gessner, T. (ed.) Smart Systems Integration. Proceedings of the 4th European Conference & Exhibition on Integration Issues of Minituarized Systems. VDI Verlag, Como (2010)
3. Cocron, P., Bühler, F., Neumann, I., Franke, T., Krems, J.F., Schwalm, M., Keinath, A.: Methods of Evaluating Electric Vehicles from a User's Perspective – the MINI E Field Trial in Berlin. IET Intelligent Transport Systems 5, 127–133 (2011)
4. Vilimek, R., Keinath, A., Schwalm, M.: The MINI E Field Study - Similarities and Differences in International Everyday EV Driving. In: Stanton, N.A. (ed.) Advances in Human Aspects of Road and Rail Transport, pp. 363–372. CRC Press, Boca Raton (2012)

Single-Handed Driving System with Kinect

Jae Pyo Son and Arcot Sowmya

School of Computer Science and Engineering,
University of New South Wales, Sydney, Australia
{json,sowmya}@cse.unsw.edu.au

Abstract. This paper proposes a Kinect-based system that can help people who
have difficulties with moving one of their arms, to drive and control the
vehicles with only one hand. The advantage of the system is that only the user's
hands need to be visible, so that users can use the system while seated.
Experiments to measure system performance have shown reasonable accuracy.
This system can be broadly applied to any wheeled electronic vehicles such as
an electronic wheelchair, robot or car in future.

Keywords: Assistive Technology, Kinect, Human-Computer Interaction, Hand
Tracking, Driving.

1   Introduction

With advances in technology, we are constantly looking for more efficient and
smarter ways to improve our daily lives. Human-Computer Interaction (HCI) is
applied to our daily lives very broadly and there may be more applications in the
future. The main objective of this paper is to create another successful example of
HCI with hand gestures that may be applied to driving wheeled vehicles by replacing
the steering wheels or a remote controller. This paper presents a system that can help
people with disabilities in their arms or legs to drive vehicles with just one hand.

2   Related Works

2.1   Assistive Technology

Past applications on assistive driving technologies for disabled persons include
Tongue Drive System [1] that enables disabled persons to drive vehicles with their
tongue and Adaptive Driving [2] that allows disabled persons to drive their car,
thereby allowing both disabled and able drivers to drive equally well. Assistive
driving technologies are not limited to people with hand or leg disabilities. There is a
Driver Assistive System that shows the surrounding environment to people with low
visibility through a Head Up Display (HUD) [3]. Olsheski et al. [4] presented In-
Vehicle Assistive Technology (IVAT) for drivers who have survived a traumatic
brain injury. The system takes the driver's individual cognitive abilities and
limitations into account to increase driver safety.

M. Kurosu (Ed.): Human-Computer Interaction, Part II, HCII 2013, LNCS 8005, pp. 631–639, 2013.
© Springer-Verlag Berlin Heidelberg 2013

2.2   Hand Tracking

Chai et al.   [5] presented a robust hand gesture analysis method using 3D depth data. This paper focused on accurate hand segmentation by removing the negative effect of the forearm part. The coarse hand region was detected with the depth data captured by 3D camera. The geometric circle feature was extracted to represent the palm region to determine the part in the coarse region that belongs to a hand. After the palm was located in the coarse hand region, the forearm cutting was implemented by determining whether the cutting direction was horizontal or vertical and using the spatial relationship between centre of the hand and centre of the palm.

Bao et al. [6] implemented a real-time hand tracking module using a new robust algorithm called Tower method to obtain hand region and used skin color for hand segmentation. The skin segmentation was based on YCbCr color space to use the system in unrestricted environment and morphological operations were used to smooth the image and remove the noise while extracting the hand with Tower tracking method. Tower tracking is a method that determines the features of the object and approximates the value of the distance between "towers". Then it generates the coarse towers with the distance reasonably and scans the signal in all coarse towers. With each signal, a boundary spreading algorithm is executed and refines the set of points found in the algorithm. The results showed that the proposed algorithm was reasonably robust.

Wang et al. [7] developed an entertainment robot which plays the rock, scissors and paper game. Image pre-processing was done to capture the hand image of a person by skin color-extraction to distinguish between hand and the background and dilation and erosion operations to obtain a clean gray image of a hand leaving the background black. Hand gesture recognition is performed by removing the hand image without fingers from the hand image with fingers, which leave the fingers only; then the number of fingers are counted to determine whether the gesture is rock, scissors or paper. The study indicates that image processing can be applied in human-robot interaction for a simple entertainment purposes. The strength of this research is that simple image-processing technique was used, but the limitations are that the scope and the techniques used are relatively low, and this explains why the result has relatively low success rate. The idea is good but another approach with newer techniques on this idea would make it better.

Raheja et al. [8] presented a new approach for controlling a robotic hand or an individual robot by showing hand gestures in front of a camera. The system captures a frame containing some gestures and extracts the hand gesture area from captured the frame. The hand gesture area was obtained by cropping the hand region after global thresholding. The result showed 90% accuracy in proper light arrangement and the accuracy got affected with poor lighting arrangement. Using a color transform such as YCrCb or HSV for segmentation would have solved that problem.

Yu et. al [9] presented a feature extraction method for hand gestures based on multi-layer perception. The hand was detected by skin segmentation using YCbCr color space. The hand silhouette and features were accurately extracted by means of binarizing the hand image and enhancing the contrast. Median and smoothing filters were integrated in order to remove the noise. The results showed 97.4% recognition rate which shows that the hand detection was robust enough.

3   Proposed System

The proposed system in this paper uses Kinect, OpenNI and OpenCV in order to perform hand segmentation and fingertip detection. Steering angle of the hand is measured by tracking the center of the segmented hand in real-time. Also other essential features such as acceleration, brake and gears are achieved using depth value of the hand and number of fingertips detected. More details on how the system works are explained in Section 5.

3.1   Kinect

Kinect [10] is a Microsoft product that was originally made for entertainment purposes (to work with the Xbox360 console) but due to its ability to obtain depth information and capture user motion, it has been widely used by programmers for both academic and entertainment purposes. There are many applications of Kinect already released, mostly by individuals or companies. One of the advantages of using Kinect is that it is inexpensive compared to a stereo or ToF (Time-of-Flight) camera while it can perform as well or even better, except for the depth range which is known to be approximately 0.7-6m. The Kinect and its in-built devices are illustrated in Figure 1.

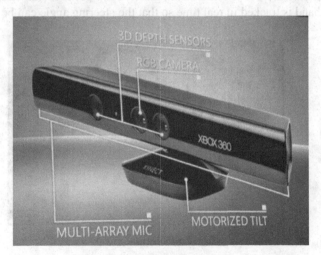

Fig. 1. Microsoft Kinect. [10]

3.2   OpenNI

OpenNI or *Open Natural Interaction* is an industry-led, open source framework focused on certifying the compatibility and improving interoperability of Natural Interaction (NI) devices such as Kinect, applications and middleware [11]. Even though Kinect with OpenNI can detect humans and return their body joints, it does not perform pointing direction estimation and pointing gesture recognition, which are major goals of this work.

3.3   OpenCV

OpenCV (*Open Source Computer Vision Library*) is a library of programming functions mainly aimed at real time computer vision, developed by Intel and now supported by Willow Garage. It is free for use under the open source BSD license. The library is cross-platform and focuses mainly on real-time image processing. [12]

4   Methodology

4.1   Hand Segmentation

Depth-segmentation was chosen for detecting hand. The reason is that when the system is applied to actual vehicle such as a car or wheelchair in the future, the environment would be light-dependent due to the sunlight. Also, Kinect can generate a 3D disparity map, as shown in Figure 2, that returns depth values of each pixel in the frame. Under the assumption that the user's hand will be always in the front, the hand was segmented by finding the smallest depth value after scanning the whole frame, then thresholding the frame based on that value with a constant (average hand thickness) added. The centre of the segmented hand was found by enclosing the hand with a minimum sized circle and obtaining the centre point of that circle. This center point of the hand is tracked in real time so that the steering angle can be measured.

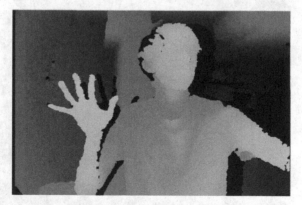

Fig. 2. 3D disparity map

4.2   Fingertip Detection

Fingertips were detected using OpenCV functions. Once the hand is segmented, a hand contour was drawn and convex hull found based on the points lying on the hand contour stored in a matrix. Then the inner angle of each hull corner was calculated within the upper region only, since the fingers are always in the upper region of the hand assuming that the hand is always upright.   The hull corners with the inner angle lower than a predefined threshold were marked as fingertips and drawn in the frame as shown in the Figure 3 below.

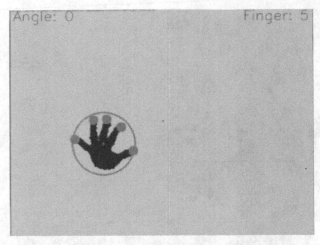

Fig. 3. Centre of the hand and fingertips detected

5   System Description

The system supports both steering types, namely nonholonomic steering and differential steering. Nonholonomic steering is for vehicles that have four wheels and change directions by rotating forward wheels like a car. Differential steering is for two-wheeled vehicles such as a wheelchair or robot. The vehicles with differential steering change direction by applying a different velocity on each wheel, so that one wheel moves faster than the other, which makes vehicles to turn.

Table 1. Comparison between two steering types

	Nonholonomic Steering	Differential Steering
Vehicles	Cars	Robot and electronic wheelchair
Acceleration/Brake	Depth information of the hand	Number of fingertips
Gear Shift	Number of fingertips	na
Change modes/functions	na	Number of fingertips

As shown in the Table 1, depth information of the hand and number of fingertips are used to switch between acceleration, brake and gears. Because the vehicles with nonholonomic and differential steering have different characteristics, depth information of the hand and number of fingertips are used differently for each steering type, as shown in Figures 4 and 5 below.

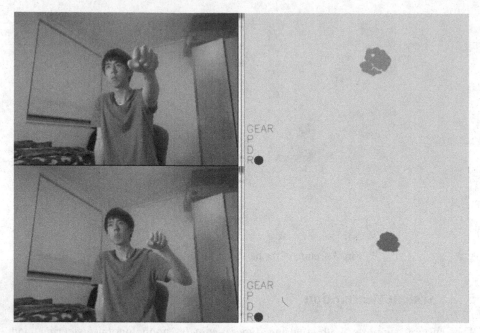

Fig. 4. Distinction between acceleration (green) and brake (red) using depth thresholding

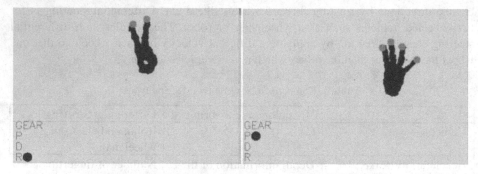

Fig. 5. Switching gears using different number of fingertips

5.1   Nonholonomic Steering

The steering angle for nonholonomic steering is measured similar to a real car steering. In the real world, the driver steers a car by grabbing the steering wheel first, then rotating it with the hands holding the steering wheel. In this work, since only one hand is used for steering and the steering angle can be measured by tracking the movement of the hand while it is holding the "virtual" steering wheel and measuring the angle of rotation, with the center of the frame as the center of rotation. In order to distinguish between a steering state (hand holding the steering wheel) and non-steering state (hand not holding the steering wheel), the status (open/closed) of the hand is used. The open hand and closed hand are distinguished by the number of fingertips detected. Five fingertips represent an open hand and zero fingertips represent closed hand.

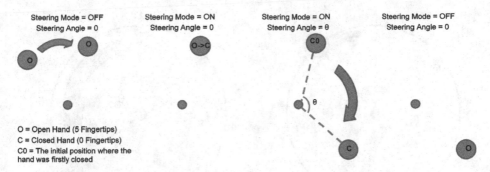

Fig. 6. Four different steps for nonholonomic steering algorithm

As shown in Figure 6, there are four different steps for steering. The first step shows that the user is moving the hand while it is open so that the steering mode is not activated. The second step shows that the user just closed the hand to begin steering. The steering mode is activated and records the coordinates of the initially closed hand C0. The steering angle is still zero since the hand is just closed and did not move after that. However, now the system is ready for measuring the steering angle. The third step shows that the user is moving the hand while it is closed. During this state, the steering angle is measured by measuring the angle difference between the initial position of the closed hand and the current position of the closed hand with the center of the frame as the center of rotation. The steering angle measuring algorithm divides the frame into quadrants. The steering angle within the same quadrant is measured using simple trigonometry. The previous position of the center of the hand is stored in a buffer so that when the centre of the hand moves to another quadrant, the system checks the quadrant that the hand came from, then the angle of rotation from the previous quadrant is added or subtracted depending on the direction of rotation. Because the system counts the number of quadrants that the hand has crossed (incrementing for clockwise direction, decrementing for anti-clockwise direction) in real time, there is no limit on the number of cycles for steering.

5.2 Differential Steering

Differential steering is simpler than nonholonomic steering, as two-wheeled vehicles move in a simpler way. As previously mentioned, differential steering is achieved by applying a different velocity on each wheel and this difference in velocity controls the rate of rotation. Since the desired output is the rate of rotation, the system is designed to generate the rate of rotation by measuring the angle of rotation (θ) of the hand in the same way as for nonholonomic steering except that the initial position for the closed hand is replaced with y-axis in the centre of the screen as shown in Figure 7.

The main difference is that the differential steering mode uses the number of fingertips to switch between forward, backward and neutral (idle) modes, while nonholonomic steering mode uses depth information of the hand to switch between acceleration, brake and neutral (no acceleration and no brake) modes.

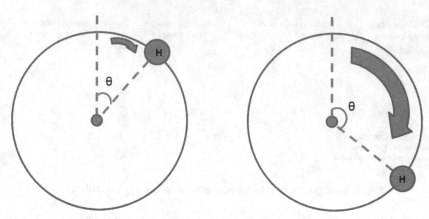

Fig. 7. How differential steering works

6   Experimental Results

For both steering modes, the accuracy for steering and the, success rates for switching between gears, acceleration, neutral and brake were measured to test the general system performance. While the user is performing steering using the system, accuracy for steering is measured by calculating the difference between the expected steering angle by the user and the actual steering angle computed by the system. This is repeated 50 times with different steering angles and starting point where the hand is initially closed. The success rates for the gear shift using fingertips and switching between acceleration, neutral and brake using depth values were measured for 50 trials as well. The results are shown as below in Table 2.

Table 2. Experimental Results

	With Visual Feedback	Without Visual Feedback
Steering Angle	92.8%	89.2%
Parking (4 Fingers)	98%	94%
Drive (3 Fingers)	96%	94%
Reverse (2 Fingers)	98%	92%
Acceleration	98%	80%
Neutral	98%	82%
Brake	96%	86%

The experimental results showed that the system generally works better when users have visual feedback while using the system. However, the difference is insignificant for steering angle and fingertip detection because the users can still see their hands and fingers without watching the screen. For switching between acceleration, neutral and brake, the difference was relatively huge and the reason could be that the screen displays how far the hand is from the Kinect by using a different colour for each depth range. For inexperienced users, it would be difficult for them to estimate how far their hands are from Kinect, but this can be solved if they try the system several times so that they would eventually know the depth range for acceleration, neutral and brake. In the real world, a car is more complicated since it includes other features such as indicator, window wiper, lights and others which are essential for driving. However, the experimental results show that this system can drive vehicles that only require those features or fewer such as a robot or electronic wheelchair.

7   Conclusion

A single hand driving system for disabled persons was presented in this paper. The significance is that the proposed system uses a single hand, unlike most of the other past works on vision-based driving systems, while achieving steering that works in a similar way to an actual steering wheel and allows switching between different modes. Also, the proposed system facilitates a new HCI application to drive vehicles for disabled persons and also explores the potential for applying HCI using Kinect to assistive technologies.

References

1. Tongue Drive Assistive Technology, Internet,
   http://users.ece.gatech.edu/mghovan/index_files/
   TongueDrive.htm
2. Vehicle Hand Controls and Adaptive Products for Driving,
   http://www.disabled-world.com/assistivedevices/automotive/
3. Driver Assistive System - Assistance in Low Visibility Conditions,
   http://www.license.umn.edu/Products/
   Driver-Assistive-System—Assistance-in-Low-Visibility-
   Conditions__Z00053.aspx
4. Olsheski, J., Walker, B., McCloud, J.: In-vehicle assistive technology (IVAT) for drivers who have survived a traumatic brain injury. In: The Proceedings of the 13th International ACM SIGACCESS Conference on Computers and Accessibility, Dundee, Scotland, UK (2011)
5. Chai, X., Fang, Y., Wang, K.: Robust hand gesture analysis and application in gallery browsing. In: IEEE International Conference on Multimedia and Expo, pp. 938–941 (2009)
6. Bao, P., Binh, N., Khoa, T.: A New Approach to Hand Tracking and Gesture Recognition by a New Feature Type and HMM. In: Sixth International Conference on Fuzzy Systems and Knowledge Discovery, FSKD 2009, vol. 4, pp. 3–6 (2009)
7. Wang, K., Wang, L., Li, R., Zhao, L.: Real-Time Hand Gesture Recognition for Service Robot. In: International Conference on Intelligent Computation Technology and Automation (ICICTA), vol. 2, pp. 946–979 (2010)
8. Raheja, J.L., Shyam, R., Kumar, U., Prasad, P.B.: Real-Time Robotic Hand Control Using Hand Gestures. In: Second International Conference on Machine Learning and Computing (ICMLC), pp. 12–16 (2010)
9. Yu, C., Wang, X., Huang, H., Shen, J., Wu, K.: Vision-Based Hand Gesture Recognition Using Combinational Features. In: Sixth International Conference on Intelligent Information Hiding and Multimedia Signal Processing (IIH-MSP), pp. 543–546 (2010)
10. Terdiman, D.: Microsoft looks to Kinect as game-changer, http://reviews.cnet.com/8301-21539_7-20007681-10391702.html
11. OpenNI, http://www.openni.org/
12. OpenCV, http://opencv.willowgarage.com/wiki/

Mobile App Support for Electric Vehicle Drivers: A Review of Today's Marketplace and Future Directions

Tai Stillwater, Justin Woodjack, and Michael Nicholas

UC Davis PH&EV Center, 1590 Tilia Street, UC Davis West Village,
Davis CA 95616, United States
tstillwater@ucdavis.edu

Abstract. Mobile device applications (apps) are becoming an important source of information, control, and motivation for EV drivers. Here we review the current ecosystem of mobile applications that are available for EV drivers and consumers and find that apps are available in six basic categories: purchase decisions, vehicle dashboards, charging availability and payment, smart grid interaction, route planning, and driver competitions. The current range of the EV-specific mobile marketplace extends from pre-sale consumer information, charging information and control, and EV specific navigation features among other services. However, the market is highly fragmented, with applications providing niche information, and using various methodologies. In addition, we find that the barriers to more useful apps are a lack of vehicle and charger APIs (application programming interfaces), lack of data availability, reliability, format and types, and proprietary payment and billing methods. We conclude that mobile applications for EVs are a growing market that provide important direct benefits as well as ancillary services to EV owners, although the lack of uniformity and standards between both vehicle and charger systems is a serious barrier to the broader use of mobile applications for EVs.

Keywords: Electric Vehicles, Mobile Apps, Energy Feedback.

1 Introduction

Smartphones are becoming more and more common among consumers, making up 54% of the US mobile subscriber market [1]. This growing ubiquity of connected devices in our population is greatly changing the way consumers both consume and generate information. These mobile devices have near constant internet connection, are usually always with an individual and have many sensors onboard including GPS, accelerometers, cameras, and magnetometers. As governments attempt to increase the adoption of electric vehicles, manufacturer and driver integration of mobile apps will become an increasingly important source of information, control, and motivation. This is because EVs have very different characteristics than conventional vehicles, including most notably their fuel source (electricity compared to gasoline), new units of energy and power (kilowatt-hours and kilowatts instead of gallons of gasoline and horsepower), shorter driving range (typically 50-150 miles), longer refueling times,

M. Kurosu (Ed.): Human-Computer Interaction, Part II, HCII 2013, LNCS 8005, pp. 640–646, 2013.

and new refueling locations (home, work, and parking lots). A recent study by the Plug-in Hybrid & Electric Vehicle (PH&EV) Research Center found that EV drivers go through a lifestyle learning process to explore and adapt to these vehicle differences over time [2]. The study concluded that consumers' perceptions and use of electric vehicles could be shaped by mobile information technology as it accelerates the lifestyle learning process. This paper attempts to further investigate the current ecosystem of mobile apps tailored for new car buyers and EV drivers and presents some preliminary hypotheses of the possible effects these apps might have on consumer perceptions and behavior.

2 Current EV Mobile Ecosystem

The current range of the EV-specific mobile apps extends from pre-vehicle-sale consumer information, charging information and control, EV specific navigation features, and EV-network specific energy efficiency competitions among other services. EV drivers are particularly well suited for mobile apps due to the high adoption rate of smartphones [3]. Figure 1 shows the difference in smartphone adoption between Californian EV drivers and the U.S. general population. As shown in the figure, the most noticeable variation is in the percentage of smartphone adoption rate among EV drivers (84% compared to 54%) and the major difference between iPhone and Android operating systems among those smartphone adopters.

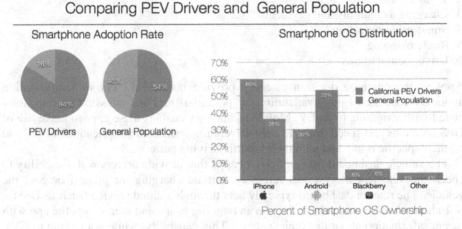

Fig. 1. PH&EV Research Center survey results comparing California EV drivers with U.S. general population in smartphone adoption rate and the corresponding smartphone operating systems

Clearly there is a high potential for the use of mobile apps to engage, encourage, and even create new EV drivers (by influencing purchase decisions). However, developers face a number of challenges that have limited the capability of mobile apps for EV drivers, including:

- Lack of vehicle and charger APIs (application programming interfaces)
- Lack of data availability, reliability, format and types
- Proprietary payment and billing methods

Some of these barriers are due to varying levels of manufacturer-specific agreements with software makers and telematics companies. For instance some charging stations have their own RFID (radio-frequency identification) cards that work only within their network, making it more difficult for EV drivers to easily refuel their vehicles in public. Another issue can arise from unknown data quality in apps, such as crowd-sourced charging station location and information, potentially reducing the reliability of the information.

Some other problems include the high marginal cost of starting mobile data services. For example, a time-of-use (TOU) charging control app can provide benefits to drivers by leveraging TOU rate tiers to reduce the cost of charging. However, a TOU app that requires a subscription telematics service may not be sensible from a financial perspective.

3   Mobile App Review

A search of mobile apps that serve the EV marketplace showed that there are six distinct use cases that have been approached by app developers:

1. Purchase decisions
2. Vehicle dashboards
3. Charging availability and payment
4. Smart grid interaction
5. Route planning
6. Driver competitions

Apps in the purchase decision category provide non-EV drivers with information about EV range, charging availability, or (potential) fuel and emission savings associated with switching to an EV. Mobile technology enables these apps to make use of GPS locations and speed traces to help drivers understand the implications of EV use on their specific route, and with their specific driving patterns.

The vehicle dashboard category covers apps that provide drivers with the ability to check the vehicle battery status remotely, initiate charging, or preheat or cool the vehicle. The remote dashboard typically acts through a cloud service (such as OnStar or Entune) that collects vehicle data on an ongoing basis, and then serves the app with recent information about the vehicle status. This capability, while not unique to EVs, is particularly important for EVs since battery state of charge and charging status can determine if and when a driver can initiate a trip.

The charging availability and payment category is the most active category for developers. These apps provide drivers with maps of charging locations, and may supplement the mapping data with specialty information such as community based comments, photos of chargers, etc. The breadth of choices in this category is due to both the availability of data on charging locations (provided by National Renewable Energy Lab and others), as well as a crowd-sourcing philosophy; created by the early EV driver social networks. Charging payment, however, is currently only served by a provider of charging locations. Although this makes intuitive sense, it is clear that integration of a charger reservation or payment system would make many of the other apps much more useful and convenient, and we therefore hope to see developer access to a payment API for privately owned charger networks.

The smart grid integration category is one that is still taking shape as vehicle manufacturers and electric utilities explore the smart grid implications of connected EVs. Very little smart grid interaction is currently possible, so the apps presented in this category are mostly prototypes or demonstrations. The primary use of these apps is to time EV charging to match lower rate tiers or lower environmental impact. Direct smart grid interaction is generally not yet possible because utilities do not release rate, load, or environmental information in a real-time fashion. It is interesting to note that even without demand response infrastructure, utilities could encourage smart grid interaction by simply making rate, load, and carbon intensity data available to developers through an API. This would allow developers to optimize charging schemes based on such utility data.

Route planning is an important aspect of EV driving that is also a complex issue. Currently there are only rudimentary tools available in this category. The route planning category, which we expect to grow in the future as the EV market expands, will cover apps that generate optimal routes, charge points, or charging schemes based on user requested destinations.

Driver competitions are another emerging use of EV connected apps. These tools provide drivers with two primary feedback mechanisms: additional information about driving efficiency and a comparison to peers driving the same model vehicle. These tools can help drivers increase their overall efficiency, and can help automakers engage their customers in a new way. In the future we expect to see competition and efficiency information apps that can allow drivers to compete against affinity groups, cooperate to save fuel, or view savings in comparison to drivers of other vehicles.

Below are the apps identified as of February 2013 for this review.

3.1   Purchase Decision Apps

- BMW Evolve: tracks driving patterns to show how much battery power, emissions, and charging cost a drive would consume in a BMW EV
- UC Davis EV Explorer web-app: Allows potential PEV customers to input their travel destinations and frequencies as well as charging infrastructure to find how well PEV technologies can meet their travel needs.
- iEV 2: tracks user trips statistics to help drivers determine if an EV can fulfill a driver's needs, and compares different vehicles
- eMotionApp (Swiss): version of iEV2.

3.2   Vehicle Dashboard

- HondaLink EV: an interactive vehicle charging remote control displaying charging status and vehicle range from the mobile app.
- Onstar RemoteLink: mobile app letting you start charging, change charge modes, lock/unlock doors, start volt remotely, search for destinations and send directions to vehicle. Additionally it allows for the viewing of real-time electric range, set

charge alerts, check current state of charge, view real-time tire pressure information, view latest fuel efficiency figures.

- GreenCharge: app that connects to Nissan Leaf, Plug-in Prius, and Chevy Volt that allows for viewing and sharing of charging history, carbon offset, and historical data to monitor driving habits and average costs to charge.
- Nissan Carwings: app that lets users check state of battery charge, start charging, check when battery charge will complete, see estimated driving range, and remotely turn on or off the climate control system.
- MyFord Mobile: app allows Ford Focus Electric drivers to find chargers and plan trips around charging stations using mapquest. It additional shows the vehicle's state of charge. Additionally it can lock/unlock, remote start of vehicle, precondition the vehicle cabin temperature by setting 'Go Times'.
- Volvo C30 Electric: app for monitoring vehicle including vehicle location, vehicle trip statistics, and owner's manual.
- Better Place Oscar:
- Toyota Entune: an app that houses 'mini-apps' including a fuel economy app, movie and restaurant bookings, sports and stocks information, charge management, remote climate control, vehicle locator, and internet radio.

3.3   Charging Availability and Charging Payment

- ChargePoint: app showing the location, real-time status and reservations of chargers within the chargepoint network.   It also shows the location of chargers outside its network.
- Blink: allows for finding public Blink chargers and receive charging status updates.
- Recargo:finds public charger from multiple charging networks and crowdsourced locations. Includes social features such as photo sharing and route planning.
- PlugShare: allows drivers to use each-others charge points (home or garage plugs)
- Plugsurfing (europe only): combines public and private charging into one map. Allows plug owners to share their plug on the network.
- CarStations: global database of charging locations. User updated database.
- TipCharge: charger map with fast filtering and routes.
- Chargelocator: includes pay versions with authenticated charger information.
- ChargeYourCar (UK only): is a charge network aggregator and mapping/payment service.
- Onstar: Park-Tap-Charge Prototype app tap phone against charger to select payment options.

3.4   Smart Grid Interaction

- MyFord Mobile: enables home charging based on local utility electric rates.
- IBM/EKZ project in Switzerland enables remote charging control and utility-rate dependent charging rules including selection of fossil or renewable energy based on charge timing.
- TENDRIL mobile app: with user selectable charging optimization schemes (fastest, cleanest, cheapest charge).

3.5   Route Planning

- Onstar: Spark EV Waypoint Tab - determines if a waypoint can be reached on a single charge.

3.6   Driver Competitions

- Onstar: Volt Driver Challenge App "It will log a Volt's daily and cumulative percentage of electric miles driven, its daily and cumulative miles per gallon, the total gallons of fuel saved, and let drivers compare their numbers to comparable data from other Volt drivers."
- Nissan Carwings: competition mode allows drivers to be ranked based on their driving efficiency, with 4 categories of platinum, gold, silver, bronze 'medals'.
- Toyota Entune: EV ecodriving ranking allows drivers to monitor their ECO status, ECO challenge, and Ranking for reduction of the vehicles carbon footprint.

4   Discussion and Conclusions

Mobile apps are transforming the way in which EV drivers interact with their vehicle and the electricity that powers it. Whereas interaction with a gasoline vehicle is much simpler (or at least well known) in terms of the relationship between refueling and driving, the interaction of time, range, and availability of electric "fuel" is both complex and novel. Mobile apps provide information across these categories helping the driver use his or her car in a greater variety of situations and using electricity as fuel more effectively.

This ability to use electricity more effectively has societal implications as well. Being easily able to find a charger in an unfamiliar area reduces the overall requirement to place chargers everywhere. One charger can serve the function of several if they are easy to find and reserve when needed. This reduces overall number of charger installations necessary and lowers the infrastructure barrier needed to encourage wider adoption. Using electricity as a fuel is also beneficial in terms of air quality and greenhouse gas emissions and mobile applications help increase the use of electricity for transportation and adoption of electric vehicles. On average, electricity is less polluting on both metrics.

There are barriers to using these mobile apps and some opportunities for improvement. As presented earlier, mobile apps are at a very early stage of development. There are many single purpose apps, and there is a significant opportunity to integrate functions. Currently there are situations where a user must switch between apps to get all the information he or she needs. For example, charging and vehicle monitoring can be controlled from proprietary apps from auto companies, but there are still other apps such as a charger location app that a user might switch to in order to find the nearest charger. A typical long distance trip may involve locating a charger with one app such as Recargo and finding its network affiliation such as Chargepoint or Blink. Then the user must switch to the app of the network provider to find its availability. Finally while charging, an app from a specific OEM must be used to control charging and check state of charge. If vehicle or charger data were available in some secure way, this app switching could be reduced, improving the consumer experience. This presents challenges with data security, but these could be overcome with cooperation between parties.

The same basic data sharing issues prevent EVs from optimizing their charging times based on grid-optimal or price-optimal signals. Currently, utilities do not make such data public or accessible through an API, making it difficult or impossible for 3rd party developers to generate apps that can help optimize charging cost, grid load, or environmental impact.

Mobile applications for EVs are prime for a surge of growth, both as the market penetration of EV grows as well as the integration of currently siloed and fragmented information becomes connected. This mobile app ecosystem could provide important direct benefits as well as ancillary services to EV owners, although the lack of uniformity and standards between both vehicle and charger systems is a serious barrier to the broader use of mobile applications for EVs.

References

1. ComScore Reports. U.S. Smartphone Subscriber Market Share. comScore, Inc. (December 2012), http://www.comscore.com/Insights/Press_Releases/2013/2/comScore_Reports_December_2012_U.S._Smartphone_Subscriber_Market_Share
2. Woodjack, J., Garas, D., Lentz, A., Turrentine, T.S., Tal, G., Nicholas, M.A.: Consumer Perceptions and Use of Driving Distance of Electric Vehicles: Changes over Time Through Lifestyle Learning Process. Transportation Research Record: Journal of the Transportation Research Board 2287, 1–8 (2012)
3. Tal, G., Nicholas, M., Woodjack, J., Scrivano, D.: Who is Buying Electric Cars in California? Exploring Household and Vehicle Fleet Characteristics of New Plug-in Vehicle Owners 16, UCD-ITS-RR-13-02 (2013)

Proposal for Driver Distraction Indexes Using Biological Signals Including Eye Tracking

Nobumichi Takahashi[1], Satoshi Inoue[1], Hironori Seki[1], Shuhei Ushio[1], Yukou Saito[2], Koyo Hasegawa[2], and Michiko Ohkura[1]

[1] Shibaura Institute of Technology, 3-7-5, Toyosu, Koto-ku, Tokyo,135-8548, Japan
{ma12066,109011,109057,109013,ohkura}@shibaura-it.ac.jp
[2] Alpine Electronics Inc, 1-7, yukigayaotsuka-machi, Ota-ku, Tokyo, 145-8501, Japan
{yukou-saito,k-hasegawa}@apn.alpine.co.jp

Abstract. According to the AAA Foundation for Traffic Safety, driver inattention is a major contributor to highway crashes. Above all, driver distraction is an important factor. As a result, many studies have been performed on it. We also performed experiments on candidates for biological indexes. In this paper, we employed new biological signals (eye tracking). Then, we performed an experiment to find new candidates for biological indexes. We obtained new knowledge from the result of that experiment.

Keywords: Driver distraction, Biological signal.

1 Introduction

According to the AAA Foundation for Traffic Safety [1], driver inattention is a major contributor to highway crashes. The National Highway Traffic Safety Administration estimates that approximately 25% of police-reported crashes involve some form of driver inattention, where the driver is distracted, asleep, fatigued, or "lost in thought" [2]. Estimates from other sources are as high as 35-50%.

Against these backgrounds, much research has been performed on driver distraction [3]. We also performed experiments to discover candidates for biological indexes of driver distraction, shown in Table 1, and found some useful ones.

Table 1. Candidates for biological indexes

Biosignals	Biological Indexes
ECG (Electrocardiogram)	RRI, heart rate, LF/HF
EEG (Electroencephalogram)	Power spectrum of alpha, beta, delta waves, ratio of each wave,
SPA (Galvanic Skin Potential)	SPR, SPL

M. Kurosu (Ed.): Human-Computer Interaction, Part II, HCII 2013, LNCS 8005, pp. 647–653, 2013.
© Springer-Verlag Berlin Heidelberg 2013

Then, we performed a new experiment employing eye-tracking data to find new candidates for biological indexes as the next step.

This article describes the experiment, its results, and the proposal of useful biological indexes for driver distraction.

2   Experimental System Including Driving Simulator

An outline of our experimental system is shown in Fig 1. The system consists of a driving simulator (DS) and measurement systems for biological signals. The driving simulator consists of the following components:

— Display(s)
— Speakers
— Wheel
— Pedals
— Sheet
— Radio channel tuning system(s)
— PC(s) to control simulator operation.

The measurement system consists of the following components:

— Sensors (or electrodes) and instruments to measure ECG, SPA and eye tracking
— PCs to control the measurement of these biological signals

To measure SPA, the palmar surface of the finger is commonly used. However, since palms are involved in holding steering wheels, we instead employed the bottom of the foot. Figure 2 shows a diagram of the eye-tracking system.

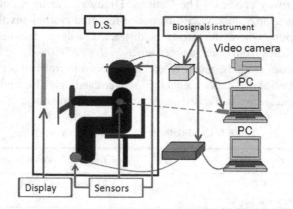

Fig. 1. Outline of experimental system

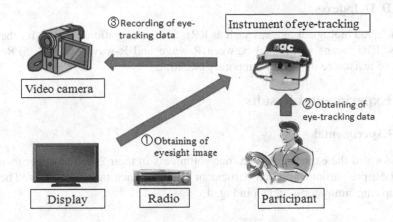

Fig. 2. Diagram of eye-tracking system

3   Experimental Method

3.1   Experimental Purpose

The purposes of this experiment are as follows:

- · to find some candidates of indexes for eye-tracking data.
- · to obtaining new indexes from combinations of biological indexes.

3.2   Test Course

The test course was a straight line with three lanes and flags set randomly to show the lanes for lane changes (Fig. 3). It takes three minutes to drive this course at 100 km/h.

Fig. 3. Test course with flags

3.3   Experimental Task

The main task was the driving task with lane change. The secondary task was radio channel selection. An ordinary car radio was employed, and the frequencies to be set were orally given by the experimenter.

The kinds of experimental tasks are as follows:

1. Driving (main task only)
2. Interval A (main task + secondary task with an interval of 2 seconds)
3. Interval B (main task + secondary task with changing lanes through flags 2 times)
4. Interval C (main task + secondary task with changing lanes through flags 3 times)

3.4   D. D. Indexes

We employed biological indexes such as RRI, SPR, and stationary point for the D. D. indexes. RRI means an interval between R-wave and R-wave of ECG. SPR means change of resistance of skin by temporary sweating.

4   Experimental Results

4.1   Experimental

We performed the experiment with four volunteers in their 20s. The experiment took about 1.5h per participant. Each participant repeated each task four times. The setup of the driving simulator is shown in Fig. 4.

Fig. 4. Appearance of driving simulator

4.2   Experimental Results of Eye Tracking

We considered indexes of eye tracking for candidates as follows:

— -stationary point
— -steady gaze at the radio
— -gaze-movement speed
— -gaze-movement amount
— -distance of gaze
— -pupil diameter

We will describe especially useful candidates.

— Gaze-movement speed

Figure 5 shows the average gaze-movement speed. We performed a two-factor analysis of variance and multiple comparison between each task. Both main effects of tasks and participants were effective at 1% and 5% levels. The results of multiple comparison are as follows:

$$\text{Driving} < \text{Interval A, B, C } (p<0.01)$$
$$\text{Interval B, C} < \text{Interval A } (p<0.01)$$

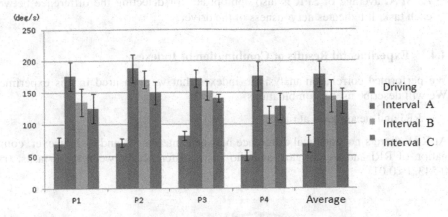

Fig. 5. Averaged gaze-movement speed

— Pupil diameter

Figure 6 shows average pupil diameter of subjects' left eyes. We performed a two-factor analysis of variance and multiple comparison between each task. Both main effects of participants and tasks were effective at 1% and 5% levels. The results of multiple comparison are as follows:

Driving < Interval A (p<0.01)

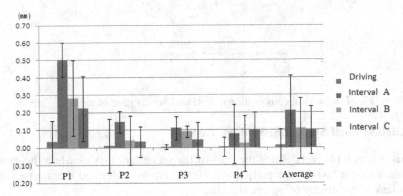

Fig. 6. Average pupil diameter of left eye

4.3   Experimental Results of ECG and SPA

Result of ECG and SPA indicates a similar tendency to previous research as follows [3].

— At ECG, RRI is very appropriate for detecting the difference between each task. It indicates mental work-load.

— At SPA, average of SPR is also appropriate for detecting the difference between each task. It indicates nervousness of the driver.

4.4   Experimental Results of Combination of Indexes

We performed correlation analysis to indexes that we measured in this experiment. We will describe useful combinations.

- RRI and steady gaze at radio

At RRI, there's no statistical difference between Intervals B and C. However, combination of RRI and steady gaze at radio has a difference between these tasks. (r= - 0.543, P<0.01)

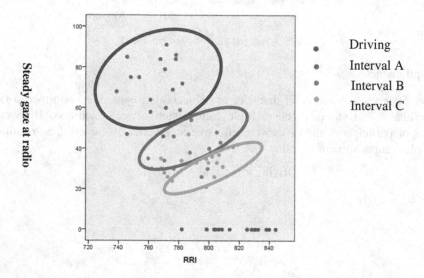

Fig. 7. Results of combination of RRI and Steady gaze of radio

4.5   Redefinition of Start of Secondary Task

In previous research [4], we defined the start of the secondary task as when the experimenter showed the task to the participant. However, we redefined the start of the secondary task more strictly using eye tracking.

5   Discussion

RRI and SPA showed a similar tendency to previous research. This means those are reliable indexes for measuring D.D. At some indexes for eye tracking, there's a statistical difference between tasks. This indicates those indexes could be indexes for D.D. However, we need further experiments to confirm the reliability of those indexes.

6   Conclusions

We performed an experiment and obtained the following conclusions.

- RRI and SPA are reliable indexes for D. D.
- Gaze-movement speed and pupil diameter may become indexes of D. D.
- From the result of combination of indexes, RRI and steady gaze at radio shows new possibility.

We must perform further experiments to confirm these new indexes.

References

1. Stutts, J., et al.: The Role of Driver Distraction in Traffic Crashes. In: AAA Foundation for Traffic Safety, Washington DC (2001)
2. Ranney, T., Garrott, W., Goodman, M.: NHTSA Driver Distraction Research: Past, Present, and Future. In: NHTSA, Washington DC (2000)
3. Young, K., Lee, J., Regan, M.: Driver Distraction: Theory, Effects, and Mitigation. CRC Press, New York (2008)
4. Ohkura, M., et al.: Proposal for driver distraction indexes using biological signals. In: ASME International Design Engineering Technical Conference & Computers and Information in Engineering Conference, Chicago (2012)

Ergonomics Design with Novice Elicitation on an Auditory-Only In-Vehicle Speech System

Ming-Hsuan Wei[1], Sheue-Ling Hwang[1],
Hsin-Chang Chang[2], Jian-Yung Hung[2], and Chih-Chung Kuo[2]

[1] National Tsing Hua University, Hsinchu, Taiwan 300
ericwei770910@gmail.com
[2] Industrial Technology Research Institute, Hsinchu, Taiwan 310
piosn@itri.org.tw

Abstract. This research is aimed to design an auditory-only in-vehicle speech system, named as Talking Car Novice Mode, and provide with elicitation that even a novice can easily handle. In this study, 19 participants were asked to use radio and music functions in two kinds of in-vehicle speech systems, the original Talking Car and Talking Car Novice Mode, while driving through a virtual world. Data of secondary task performance, the amount of time spent on tasks and the times of calling help function were recorded by a camera. The annoyed score of sentences, NASA-TLX questionnaire and subjective questionnaire were completed after the test. The result indicated that there was no significant difference between driving with and without tasks on either the reaction time of slamming the brake or the times user call for help. Besides, the learning curve of Talking Car Novice Mode is steep and ensures that Talking Car Novice Mode provides enough elicitation to novices. Hence, the Talking Car Novice Mode is expected to be friendlier and safer than original Talking Car in-vehicle speech system for a novice user.

Keywords: ergonomics design, Talking Car Novice Mode, elicited design, voice user interface.

1 Introduction

1.1 Background and Motivation

According to the investigation in 2010 by National Highway Traffic Safety Administration of America, distraction internal the vehicle was a critical reason of car accidents. These distracting tasks affect drivers in different ways, and can be categorized into three types: visual distraction, manual distraction and cognitive distraction (NHTSA, 2010). Both of visual and manual distraction happened all the time such as adjusting the radio channel or making a phone call while driving.

Wickens (1992) elaborated the general concepts of the multiple processing resources proposed by Kantowitz & Knight (1976) and Novan & Gopher (1979). He indicated that we can sometimes divide attention between the eyes and ears better than between two auditory channels or two visual channels. Base on this principle,

M. Kurosu (Ed.): Human-Computer Interaction, Part II, HCII 2013, LNCS 8005, pp. 654–660, 2013.
© Springer-Verlag Berlin Heidelberg 2013

many car manufacturers have developed In-Vehicle Speech Systems by which drivers can use speech/buttons to control the multimedia devices. Since lots of car accidents caused by distracted driving, government in Taiwan has legislated to forbid multimedia devices' display function to be used while driving (Ministry of Transportation and Communications in Taiwan, 2011). However, most of the current In-Vehicle Speech Systems still rely on a screen to transmit the commands or information to drivers.

1.2   Objectives

In the previous research, we proved that Talking Car System is better than the current In-Vehicle Speech System in Taiwan (Leong, 2012). However, similar to other speech systems, it cannot be used without a screen. Thus, Talking Car System may still cause visual distractions. Therefore, this research aimed to design an auditory-only In-Vehicle Speech System with enough elicitation that even a novice user can handle easily, and we named it "Talking Car Novice Mode".

2   Literature Review

The methodologies and design principles for auditory interface overlap substantially with those used for other types of user interface. However, there are a number of characteristics of voice user interfaces that pose unique design challenges and opportunities (Cohen et al, 2004). After the literature review, we sum up some principles that should be noticed before interface design.

Principle 1: Different kind of errors will be recovered in different ways

Errors are unpreventable because neither technology nor human are perfect. There were two kinds of errors occurred in the vehicle speech system. The first one is "reject" (no good match was found) which was due to the lower recognition, and could be solved by improving the technique. Another one is "no-speech timeout" which means no command received by the system. This error often occurred when novice users who don't know what to say, and increase more elicitation into the system is a way to solve this problem.

Principle 2: Consistency design helps users to be familiar with the system quickly

To reduce users' cognitive load, system should be designed as more learnable as possible. Consistency is an idea to let the user do similar thing in similar ways, and it efficiently and effectively helps user being familiar with the system and decrease the learning time.

Principle 3: Memory load need to be rethought in auditory interface

The 7±2 limitation of working memory (Miller, 1956) is important for system design, but may not be appropriate for the auditory interface. Gardner-Bonneau (1992) and Schwarz (1995) indicated that people can remember only about three items in average. And a reasonable guideline is to keep menus to three or four items.

Recency is a simple way to reduce users' memory load. It works by placing the keyword or command at the end of sentences, let the item users need to remember is the last thing they hear. For example, "if you need a command list, say, 'help'" is better than, "say, 'help' if you need a command list".

3   Research Method

3.1   Experimental Design

In this research, music and radio functions that most commonly used by drivers were chosen as the experimental tasks. There were nineteen subjects, including 11 males and 8 females. All subjects, 20 to 30 years old students from different majors in National Tsing Hua University, need to hold driver's licenses for more than one year and very often listen to music or radio while driving. To ensure all subjects are novice users, none of them has operated any kind of speech system.

There was one variable in this experiment, subjects' familiarity with Talking Car Novice Mode; and the degree of familiarity was decided by the experience that subjects had operated Talking Car Novice Mode twice or none. The goal was to observe the performance and reactions between the two groups, novices and advanced users. To ensure the safety of subjects, all experiment would be executed through a driving simulator called "SimuRide (Home Edition)" which is a simplified version of the full professional driving simulation Software used in driving schools in North America. In driving simulated experiments, a camera was set to capture the subjects' operations. To measure the distractions of users, we recorded the reaction time that users slammed on the brakes while a "STOP!!" message suddenly showed on the display. The number of the help function used by subjects and the task completion time would also be recorded. After the driving simulated experiments finished, subjects needed to complete three questionnaires, including NASA-TLX, subjective and impatient-degree questionnaire to evaluation subjects' workload, satisfaction and the degree of impatient.

3.2   Procedure

Talking Car Novice Mode was developed after three stages of driving simulated experiments. In the first stage of experiment, we asked three novice users to operate a simplified Talking Car system, which has no elicited sentences so that we could find out the need of the users by observing their behaviors and errors. The rest of two stages of experiments were used to compare the task performance with two kinds of user familiarity, novices and advanced users.

To balance the learning effect, we separate 16 subjects into two groups and 8 subjects each group. Group 1 would start the music function tasks first, and then the radio function tasks; group 2 would be opposite. Besides, the entire tasks would be executed in two rounds. The whole process of the experiment took around 40 to 60 minutes, including 10 minutes for tutorial and practicing the driving on the simulator, 20 to 40 minutes for driving simulated experiment with tasks, and 10 minutes for questionnaires.

4   Results

4.1   Behavior Analysis

In the first stage of experiment, we observed some behavior and errors while subjects were operating the in-vehicle system without elicitation nor visual display. We summarized the observed behavior below and would take these behavior into consideration while we designed the Talking Car Novice Mode. The results were as follows.

1) Subjects had no idea what commands could say.
2) Subjects did not know that they could switch or confirm the search result by buttons on the wheel.
3) Some sentences or commands made users confused.

4.2   Tasks Completion Time

The tasks completion time is an important index which reflects the degree of subjects' familiarity. We used Paired t-test to compare the two rounds in second stage of experiments, system operated by novices, and the last two stages of experiments. As the result showed in Table 1 and Table 2, the degree of subjects' familiarity significantly affected the tasks completion time. Novices spent more time at the first round of the novice experiment, and the tasks completion time which operated by novices was longer than that by the advanced users.

Table 1. Paired t-test results of tasks completion time in 2nd stage of experiments

	N	Mean (sec.)	StDev	SE Mean
1st round	16	353.7	82.7	20.7
2nd round	16	209.5	76.0 s	19.0
T-Test of mean difference = 0 (vs not = 0): T-Value =5.39 P-Value < 0.001				

Table 2. Paired t-test results of tasks completion time

Stage of experiments	N	Mean (sec.)	StDev	SE Mean
2nd stage	16	276.3	56.3	14.1
3rd stage	16	111.4	12.6	3.2
T-Test of mean difference = 0 (vs not = 0): T-Value =12.67 P-Value < 0.001				

4.3   Times of Assistance

Talking Car Novice Mode provided a command to assist users while they were not sure what to do or say next. This index, times of assistance, reflected the confusion of the users, in other words, it could measure the degree of familiarity more accurately than tasks completion time. In Fig. 1, we could find out that in the first round of the secondary experiment, subjects called for help 62 times, 30 times for music function and 32 times for radio function. In the second round of the experiment, these numbers

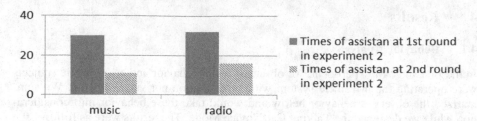

Fig. 1. Bar chart of times of assistance

rush down almost 60 percent, just 11 times for music and 16 times for radio function; and decreased to 0 at the next stage of experiment.

4.4   NASA-TLX

After the simulation experiment, subjects required to answer a NASA-TLX questionnaire; it's a questionnaire for measuring the mental workload. The result could help us to evaluate the degree of mind free, one of the conditions for safety driving indicated by NHTSA, in our system. In Table 3 and Table 4, the average weighted scores of NASA-TLX have significant differences. Advanced users gave lower scores than novices did. It means as the increase of the familiar in Talking Car Novice Mode, the mental workload of users would decrease quickly.

Table 3. Average weighted scores of NASA-TLX

Stage of experiments	Mental Demands	Physical Demands	Temporal Demands	Own Performance	Effort	Frustration
2nd stage	16.77	6.38	7.63	8.56	16.90	5.81
3rd stage	14.14	6.14	4.29	3.83	11.79	3.29

Table 4. Paired t-test results of average weighted scores

Stage of experiments	N	Mean (sec.)	StDev	SE Mean
2nd stage	6	10.34	5.12	2.09
3rd stage	6	7.25	4.59	1.87
T-Test of mean difference = 0 (vs not = 0): T-Value =4.31 P-Value=0.008				

4.5   Reaction Time

Subjects' reaction time is recorded by simulated software. The reaction time was from a "STOP!!!" message suddenly showing on the display till subjects stepping the brake to stop counting. A Paired t-test was conducted to compare the difference of average reaction time between driving with tasks or not in the last two stages of experiments. In Table 5, the result showed no significant difference on the reaction time with/without tasks in the second stage of experiments. However, Table 6 showed that for the advanced-users, the reaction time between driving with and without tasks was significantly different. Subjects performed better if they didn't need to operate tasks while driving.

Although the reaction time which needs to operate tasks increased significantly in the third stage of experiments, the time was still under 1 to 3.5 seconds, which meet the acceptable average reaction time of slamming on the brakes (AECPortico, 2003; McGee, 1983). Therefore, the Talking Car Novice Mode may not cause drivers distractions.

Table 5. Paired t-test results of reaction time in 2nd stage of experiments

	N	Mean (sec.)	StDev	SE Mean
No tasks	16	0.867	0.131	0.033
With tasks	16	0.887	0.131	0.038
T-Test of mean difference = 0 (vs not = 0): T-Value =-0.36 P-Value = 0.721				

Table 6. Paired t-test results of reaction time in 3rd stage of experiments

	N	Mean (sec.)	StDev	SE Mean
No tasks	16	0.757	0.085	0.021
With tasks	16	0.809	0.102	0.026
T-Test of mean difference = 0 (vs not = 0): T-Value =-4.18 P-Value = 0.001				

5   Conclusions

This research is aimed to design an auditory-only in-vehicle speech system with elicitation and to meet the goal of hands free, eyes free and mind free, as close as possible. From the results of tasks completion time and times of assistance, it's known that the learning curve of Talking Car Novice Mode is steep and ensure that Talking Car Novice Mode provides enough elicitation to novices, and made users to be familiar with the system easily. The results of NASA-TLX and reaction time showed that this system would not cause too much mental workload nor distractions. Therefore, drivers may focus on their driving while using the Talking Car Novice Mode, a safe, convenient and friendly in-vehicle speech system.

Acknowledgements. This work was sponsored by the Ministry of Economic Affairs, Taiwan, R.O.C. through project No. C352SN3100 conducted by Industrial Technology Research Institute (ITRI). The authors like to express their appreciation to all of the members involved in this project.

References

1. AECPortico, Transportation Engineering Online Lab Manual,
   http://www.webpages.uidaho.edu/niatt_labmanual/Chapters/
   geometricdesign/theoryandconcepts/BrakeReactionTime.htm
   (retrieved) (data accessed February 25, 2012)

2. Gardner-Bonneau, D.J.: Human factors in interactive voice response applications: "Common sense" is an uncommon commodity. Journal of the American Voice I/O Society 12, 1–12 (1992)
3. Leong, I.-C.: Human-Machine Interface Design of In-vehicle Speech Interaction System: Talking Car System. National Tsing-Hua University (2012)
4. Leong, I.-C., Hwang, S.-L., Wei, M.-H., et al.: Safety Oriented Voice- based interface for Vehicle's AV Systems: Talking Car System. Talking Car System. In: AHFE Conference, pp. 1422–1429 (2012)
5. Liu, Y., Wickens, C.D.: Visual scanning with or without spatial uncertainty and divided and selective attention. Acta Psychologica 79(2), 131–153 (1992)
6. McGee, H.W., Hooper, K.G.: Highway Design and Operation Standards Affected by Driver Characteristics. Final Technical Report, vol. II. PBellomo-McGee, Inc., Vienna, Virginia, Report No. FHWA-RD-83-015 (1983)
7. Miller, G.: The magical number seven, plus or minus two: Some limits on our capacity for processing information. Psychological Review 63, 81–97 (1956)
8. Ministry of Transportation and Communications in Taiwan, Regulation of Road Transportation Safety Rules 89-90,
   http://www.motc.gov.tw/ch/home.jsp?id=5&parentpath=0
   (retrieved) (data accessed March 15, 2012)
9. National Highway Traffic Safety Administration of America: Driver Distraction Program, pp. 7–11 (2010)
10. Schumacher Jr., R.M., Hardzinski, M.L., Schwarz, A.L.: Increasing the usability of interactive voice response systems: Research and guidelines for phone-based interfaces. Human Factors 37(2), 251–264 (1995)

Author Index